SILENCE AND POWER

A Reevaluation of Djuna Barnes

Edited by
Mary Lynn Broe

With an Afterword by
Catharine Stimpson

Southern Illinois University Press
Carbondale and Edwardsville

94 93 92 91   4 3 2 1

Library of Congress Cataloging-in-Publication Data

Silence and power: a reevaluation of Djuna Barnes / edited by Mary
    Lynn Broe.
        p.   cm.
        Includes bibliographical references.
        1. Barnes, Djuna—Criticism and interpretation.   I. Broe, Mary
    Lynn.
    PS3503.A614Z94   1991
    818'.5209—dc20   89-26358
    ISBN 0-8093-1250-6   CIP
    ISBN 0-8093-1255-7 (pbk.)

Frontispiece: Djuna Barnes; self-portrait in pencil; date unknown. Courtesy Special Collections, University of Maryland at College Park Libraries.

Permission to use text and photographs of Djuna Barnes materials has been granted by The Authors League Fund, New York, and The Historic Churches Preservation Trust, London, literary executors of the Estate of Djuna Barnes.

For Wilhelmina Amelia
and Patrick Dennis Broe

Contents

Plates

Djuna Barnes; self-portrait in pencil *frontispiece*

Acknowledgments

On behalf of all the contributors I wish to thank Herbert Mitgang, President of The Authors League Fund, New York, and administrator for the Fund and for The Historic Churches Preservation Trust, London. Both agencies are copyright holders under the will of Djuna Barnes. Herb Mitgang and his board have been exceedingly fair in granting us permission to use Barnes materials in this collection.

Special thanks to Saxon and Eleanor Barnes for use of the photograph of the splendid (anonymous) oil painting of Djuna at Pratt Institute *circa* 1912 which appears on the cover of the paperbook edition of this volume.

Thanks, too, to Kenney Withers, Director of the Southern Illinois University Press, whose supportive patience and continuing enthusiasm about the book saw us through to the finish.

I am particularly grateful to the various contributors, whose high spirits, patience, and generosity have been met, in the interim, with a growing climate of interest in Barnes and an increased market demand for a mature and sophisticated criticism of her work. In the years since 1984, many of the scholars represented in this volume have done research in the Barnes papers at the University of Maryland–College Park. They were assisted by Dr. Donald Farren, Associate Director of Libraries for Special Collections, and Dr. Blanche Ebeling-Koning, Curator for Rare Books and Literary Manuscripts. Together with the contributors, I wish to thank Dr. Farren and Dr. Ebeling-Koning for their expertise with resource materials and for the cordial help that they extended to all who visited the McKeldin Library. Tim Murray, Associate Librarian for Special Collections, and Alice Schreyer, Assistant Director of Libraries for Special Collections, University of Delaware-Newark have most generously made available recently acquired materials from the Emily Holmes Coleman papers; staff member Anita Wellner has been most helpful in mapping my way through these recent acquisitions. Additional thanks to Joseph Geraci, executor for Emily Holmes Coleman; to the Harry Ransom Humanities Research Center Library at the University of Texas–Austin and to the Bibliotheque Litteraire Jacques Doucet, Paris, for use of photographs.

Warm thanks to editors Dan Gunter and Sally Master, Southern Illinois University Press; to Roberto and Gianna Celli who fueled "la Bambina's" imagination with the fires of the Frati Chapel, Villa Serbelloni, during a cold March several years ago; to Kevin Engel for his invaluable research skills; to Lauren Brown, Jessie Hinkle, Roberta Atwell, Angie Johnson, Karen Groves, and JoAnn Lauritzen, who at various times and in various ways have helped with the completion of this volume.

Over the past several years, conversations with Saxon and Eleanor Barnes, the closest family members to Djuna, have proved lively and illuminating. I am grateful for their generosity, their extraordinary wit and high spirits, and particularly for their insights into Djuna's achievements. Duane Barnes' reminiscences about his childhood have also figured significantly in my understanding of Djuna. (Duane Barnes died 5 June 1990 as this book was in production.) And although he never met Djuna, Kerron Barnes has been a helpful and skilled conservator of his family's papers. Meridel LeSueur's vivid words late into the night transported me to the days of Djuna in Greenwich Village among the Provincetown Players. Esther Jamison's scholarly interest in *The Antiphon* and *Nightwood* opened a lively correspondence. William Burroughs, the late Virgil Thomson, and Charles Henri Ford have all suggested new, sometimes controversial, dimensions of Djuna. For their willingness to talk and to share with me anecdotes and impressions, I am grateful.

I could write no book without special thanks to Myron Jonathon Hack. For almost two decades, I have been privileged with his wit, his camraderie, his imagination, and his occasionally strained patience with the folly of academics.

Last of all, this book is the result of multiple voices, the enabling conversations, cooperation, and creative imaginations of its numerous contributors. I am particularly grateful to Marie Ponsot, Fran and David McCullough, Jane Marcus, Joan Retallack, Susan Lanser, Louise DeSalvo, Douglas Messerli, Nancy Levine, and Catharine Stimpson for their passionate discussions about Djuna Barnes as this volume was prepared for press. My discovery of Ponsot's moving 1959 review of *The Antiphon* ("Careful sorrow and observed compline") first prompted me to begin serious work on this collection. Our Special Session at the 1982 Modern Language Association, "Djuna Barnes: A Renaissance," introduced a new era of Barnes criticism, although by convention time at year's end our "renaissance" had become a memorial celebration of seventy years of Barnes' writing: Djuna Barnes died on June 18, 1982. Although we had hoped to see this book in print several seasons before the present one, I can only remind the gentle reader of the hazardous nature of assembling large collections and call his/her attention to one of the last entries in Djuna Barnes' notebooks at the Barnes Collection, University of Maryland–College Park: "Blaspheme not God. For we are only what we've thought we are." The final "are" is crossed out and in her famous green pen Barnes has scrawled "were."

Abbreviations

Unless otherwise indicated, all quotations from the works of Djuna Barnes derive from the following editions:

A   *The Antiphon.* 1958. Reprint in *Selected Works,* 79–224.

AB   *A Book.* New York: Boni and Liveright, 1923.

BRW   *The Book of Repulsive Women: Eight Rhythms and Five Drawings.* Bruno Chap Books 2, no. 6. New York: Bruno, 1915.

LA   *Ladies Almanack, showing their Signs and their tides; their moons and their Changes; the Seasons as it is with them; their Eclipses and Equinoxes; as well as a full Record of diurnal and nocturnal Distempers.* Written and illustrated by a Lady of Fashion. 1928. Reprint. New York: Harper & Row, 1972.

N   *Nightwood,* 1936. Reprint. New York: New Directions, 1961, 1977.

R   *Ryder,* 1923. Reprint. New York: St. Martin's Press, 1956, 1979.

SW   *Selected Works of Djuna Barnes: Spillway, The Antiphon, Nightwood.* New York: Farrar, Straus and Cudahy, 1962.

Introduction

Mary Lynn Broe

> *There was a gay lady named Djuna*
> *Who resembled in spirit a tuna*
> *When she wanted a man*
> *She demanded her fan*
> *And asked why it wasn't there sooner.*
> — *John Ferrar Holms, Hayford Hall*

From the rue St. Romaine to Patchin Place, the caped and cloched Djuna Barnes cut a striking figure in Paris and Greenwich Village of the 1920s and 1930s. Contemporary writers and artists praised her style, feared her tongue; she was a beauty, but a talented, acerbic, and powerfully intelligent one. "A very haughty lady," Robert McAlmon described her, "quick on the uptake, with a wise-cracking tongue . . . so Russian and so Synge-Irish." A British friend, Peter Hoare, claimed that she spoke "Stone Age wisdom in New York slang." Discussing her fondness for weak men, those who had "the courage of their cowardice," she admitted to Emily Coleman, "I want to be the boss covered with treacle."[1]

Who was this "famous unknown" whose cultural portrait is so legendary, yet whose place in literature has been until recent years a long ellipsis? Born on 12 June 1892 in Cornwall-on-Hudson, New York, the second of five children, Djuna Barnes grew up in a polygamist's household, a tarnished Eden. Both women and children of her father's two families mirrored each other, subverting traditional notions of kinship and dissolving usual boundaries of power, age, and intimacy while they encoded complex modes of eroticism for which we as yet have little theory.[2] The family was a nominal matriarchy—the son, Wald Barnes, and his children took the maiden name of the grandmother, Zadel Barnes Budington Gustafson—but it was the father's transgressions of bodily and spiritual taboos

3

that left their violent imprint on his two families. Most of Barnes' major writings—the short stories in *Spillway*, the novel *Ryder*, but particularly the heavily excised twenty-nine drafts of *The Antiphon*—encode the sexual violations and erotic entanglements in the patriarchal family. In a 1935 letter to Emily Holmes Coleman, Barnes wrote of the complex but empowering legacy from her grandmother, with whom she had an extraordinary cross-generational bond: "I always thought I was my grandmother," she claimed in a few scraps of memoir discovered recently. "My grandmother Zadel was my first mother and father. I did not accept my mother and father until later in life."[3]

Most of her education was reading—that is, whatever part was not devoted to listening to the journalistic travels of her grandmother Zadel or to reading from Zadel's brilliant feminist critical books on Maria Gowen Brooks (Maria del Occidente) and actress Genevieve Ward, or from her novel *Can the Old Love?* or her poems collected in *Meg, a Pastoral*.[4] The world of her childhood was enlarged by her father's musical talents, his operas, short stories, drawings, and inventions, and was tempered by the stern parenting of Franz Liszt, Lord Kitchener, or Jack London, who regularly "visited" the family at the Long Island farm through Zadel, a medium.[5] Except for the few months when she studied art at Pratt Institute in 1912, Djuna Barnes never went to school at all—a matter of some pride and also enormous anxiety; she all but memorized the dictionary.

At seventeen, Djuna Barnes was married in a home ceremony to Percy Faulkner, the brother of her father's second wife and a man three times her age. She left immediately for Bridgeport, Connecticut, surfacing again in 1912, enrolled as a art student at Pratt Institute. (The years 1909–12 are among the curious gaps or omissions in the Barnes chronology.) About this time she began as a cub reporter with the Brooklyn *Daily Eagle*, freelancing for a number of other New York newspapers. Both the publication of *The Book of Repulsive Women* and the exhibit of her antiwar drawings at Guido Bruno's atelier occurred before she left for Europe in 1920 on assignment for *McCall's*. In the late 1910s she lived in the Village (Clemenceau Cottage) with Courtenay Lemon, a script reader for the Dramatist's Guild. In 1916 the first of her eighteen plays was published, and in 1919–20 three of her plays were staged as part of the Provincetown Players' "Season of Youth" under the direction of Helen Westley.[6] Like Kay Boyle, Natalie Barney, and so many other bright women of her generation, Barnes chose to privilege marginality, to live ex patria ("like the dust of old Europe," she said to Emily Coleman) in Paris, Berlin, Tangiers, London, and later the Devon countryside.

For most of the 1920s Barnes lived in Paris with Thelma Wood, a silverpoint artist. During the 1930s she was a frequent resident at Peggy Guggenheim's English manors for writers—Hayford Hall, Warblington, and Yew Tree Cottage—but by 1940 she had returned to the United States, chronically sick and alcoholic. Barnes' problem, Antonia White wrote to

Emily Coleman, was "her hopeless unadaptability, her insistence on trying to live the same life she lived twenty years ago." Except for a single brief trip to Europe, Barnes remained in the United States until her death in 1982, living in Greenwich Village's Patchin Place, supported by a number of small grants, bequests, and the sale of her papers.

> Djuna Barnes: An elegant head lifted on a slender neck and long aristocratic body. Peach-blonde hair with ripples in it. Sharply tilted, scornful nose. Light eyes in shadowy hollows with a firm, bare gaze like a Siamese cat. Mouth forms an immobile ellipse, a trifle Hapsburg. Gives the effect of a solitary wading-bird, indifferent, poised and insulated, arrested in a long pause.
> —Peggy Bacon, *Off with Their Heads*

The litany of anecdotes and legends that trailed Djuna Barnes through her ninety years fill the memoir books today, as they echoed through the little Paris *boits*—Boeuf sur le Toit or the Six Bells pub—more than sixty years ago. The portraits create a figure as rich and controversial, and perhaps as little understood, as any of the modernists. Djuna Barnes was reclusive, but a performer; she would haunt peoples' memories as she has destabilized the margins of establishment discourses and disciplines in modernist writing.

Like the interstitial commentary from contemporaries and friends in this book, some quick glimpses of Djuna Barnes highlight her remarkable range of personality, from her brilliant, Rabelaisian vein of humor to her scathing misanthropism—even to her vulnerable old age, when she was desperately ill and seen only by her closest intimates. Dan Mahoney (Dr. O'Connor of *Nightwood*) gave her his "Concrete Waffle" award. Ezra Pound announced that she "weren't too cuddly." Walter Winchell bragged—mistakenly, yet appropriately—that she could hit a cuspidor twenty feet away. Peggy Guggenheim claimed she lived in a world of "romantic lies." And Antonia White compared her friendship with Barnes to a particular form of self-torture: "one has to endure the spectacle of self-laceration." In her black broadcloth suit, white ruffled shirtwaist, black hat, and long shepherd's crook, Barnes seemed to Burton Rascoe a "Watteau figure in a *fête galante*." For Barnes it was easy, drinking tea and absinthe at the Aldon, to hold up a fork to ogle an "old dame" who had just lorgnetted her. Or to threaten to cane John Hayward with her iron cherub's-head walking stick. Or to mime Sir Francis Rose in her purple and green makeup in the Tangier town square. Or, during the depression, to sit rouged in an expensive black lace negligee, waiting for her brother to give her nickels for carfare. Fiercely proud, she claimed that she was a doormat only once in her life—to Thelma Wood—and then she was "a damned good doormat." Complex in her privacy, refusing to be controlled by an audience or pinioned to a single representation, she once told Henry Raymont of the New York *Times*, "I used to be invited by people who said, 'Get Djuna for dinner, she's amusing.' So I stopped it."

Djuna Barnes could be tender, acerbic, nostalgic, offish, maudlin, pedantic, stubborn. Friends spoke of her "heavy animal mind," her refusal of self-analysis as a deliberate sort of vanity. What we learn of her passionate sensibility emerges in oblique and curiously indirect ways. Letters to friends and contemporaries portray her as a malcontent crone in a world fast going to the dogs.[7] To thwart intimacy, she used the armor of etymology in her letters, hectoring publishers and editors who were less learned than she:

Now in Italian there must be an equivalent for the word 'cast.' [The translation was "rectangolo."] The meaning in English is, in this case, taken from the idea of the worm's cast, or *the ring of earth cast up on the earth made by the worm when it comes up out of the ground . . .* the coffin is a ruinous mistake and spoils the image. Will you point this out to the person in charge? If I who know not a word of the Italian tongue found out that much, God knows what sort of a mess the manuscript may be in.[8]

One didn't argue with her firm tastes:

The New Directions edition of *Nightwood* is abominably laid out. The jacket is a horror among other things, but quite inexcusable is the repetition of errors I have corrected for Mr. Laughlin of New Directions at least twice, and fully. The omission of numbered chapter heads, and the absence of an index is quite beyond me. Please draw the publishers attention to this in case we all come to the decision that the translation can be printed. About which I am not at all sure.[9]

The persona revealed by archival materials remains a strong one, rich and complex, full of Barnes' voice. Over Emily Holmes Coleman's exuberant tract on *Nightwood*, Barnes scrawled "Emily's Sticky Apology" and responded with a thirty-two-point lecture on the novel. On the front of Bruno Chap Book's edition of her early poems, *The Book of Repulsive Women* (1915), she wrote a final comment on the aging graphomaniac Guido Bruno: "Balls!" In "Life among the Bohemians" she sketched Bruno sitting over vichy and milk, writing his entire last work on a paper napkin. And in the margins of her play *The Antiphon*, a drama of a daughter's violation, she wrote, "Justice, not revenge," indicating in the margins that for her the matter of the daughter's betrayal was "not dead."

Although she wrote for over seventy years, with the exception of the brief best-seller status of *Ryder* Barnes never received the publicity and accolades commensurate with her achievement. In her journalism, poetry (*The Book of Repulsive Women*, 1915), and short stories (*A Book*, 1923; *A Night among Horses*, 1929), and in the celebratory feminist myths of *Ryder* (1928), *Ladies Almanack* (1928), *Nightwood* (1936), and *The Antiphon* (1958), Barnes examines not only the failures of representational reality, but also the asymmetries of age and power and the contradictions inherent in gender definitions that undercut social and familial intimacies.

But such critical focus is new, often as recent as many of the essays in this volume. Until Jane Marcus' Marxist-feminist discussion of *Nightwood*'s "political unconscious" and her compelling argument that *Nightwood* "makes a modernism of marginality," this novel had been canonized as the emblematic male modernist text, whether in its celebration of "inverted love,"[10] or in its inscription of the decline of western civilization, its characters representing the decay.[11] For Joseph Frank the novel's greatness lay in its modernist enterprise of "transmitting the time world of history into the timeless world of myth."[12] As the great art novel of the twentieth century—a kind of epistemological romp on the figural plane—*Nightwood* invites theory construction[13] as it has encouraged critics over the past five decades to ransack the literary canon for analogies; at various times, *Nightwood* has been called surrealistic, Eliotic, Dantesque, elegiac, fugal, Elizabethan, baroque, even Gothic.

Even in those early reviews of the novel, so generously excerpted by Jane Marcus in "Mousemeat," critics showed the same uneasiness with positioning the novel in the literary canon. Scholars seemed unable to agree whether *Nightwood*'s canonical echoes derived from Christina Stead's Marpurgo, the mad speeches in Webster and Tourneur, von Hofmannsthal's Andreas, Baudelaire, Proust, Celine, the fin de siècle writers or Nathanael West. Yet as Jane Marcus points out, such comments do not entirely capture the spirit of the long, lush early reviews, many by famous writers of the left who provided Barnes with "the kind of press coverage which only cookbooks get today." Serious issues were dealt with seriously in the now buried but voluminous reviews: Barnes' exploration of perversion; the peculiar method of action relived in dialogue; the incomprehensive ending; the morality of the novel quite apart from T.S. Eliot's religious appropriation in the preface; the heavy demands placed on a reader's tolerance: "The test of a book's obscenity is said to be its power of corrupting those who are open to corruption; and, had I a daughter whose passions for mistresses and older girls were beginning to cause scandal and alarm, I should certainly insist that she read *Night Wood*."

Although there has been recent interest in reevaluating the dramatic and journalistic writing before *Nightwood*,[14] much contemporary criticism still privileges Barnes' production of writing over her radical sociopolitical views. Her search for a theory of fiction and her manipulation of reader and text has replaced, in the words of one critic, "thanantographical readings," or T.S. Eliot's substitution of "mimesis for diegesis" in his analysis of the novel.[15] Other critics are beginning to explore the relation between gender and literary form. Several use deconstructionist methods informed by French feminisms to offer playful readings of the inscriptions of gender and sexuality in the text. They underscore Barnes' actual subversiveness, as they discuss her lively strategies for changing our conception of what is marginal.[16]

Through belabored revisions (the actual text of *Nightwood* constitutes only a third of the original manuscript), excisions, threats to friends, and the burning of letters, Barnes developed a ritual of self-silencing, suggesting her refusal to privilege a single "authentic" voice and her uneasiness with canonical forms. Such silencing is also a textual response, perhaps, to the father's attempt to violate his daughter, then barter her in ritual exchange. Typical of the suppression or interruption in the sexual/ textual order is T.S. Eliot's "text bashing" of the twenty-nine drafts of *The Antiphon*. Eliot slashed his way through Miranda's reenactment of a painful and violent childhood episode (act 2, the hayhook scene). In this scene, a father attempts to violate his daughter, then, failing, barters her for a goat. Eliot advised Barnes to excise and displace parts of this story of a daughter's betrayal so that narrative coherence is all but missing in the final text. (See the essays by Curry and DeSalvo in this volume.)

For more than fifty years since the appearance of *Nightwood*, personal legends coupled with an impoverished critical representation have fixed an obsolete image of Djuna Barnes, praising her for a limited but influential role in modern letters. Early notoriety, forty years as a recluse, a scrappy publication history, and reduction to either stylistics or canonical echoes by the literary world—all this brings a new cultural and political challenge to her disclaimer, in a review of Synge, "I am not a critic; to me criticism is so often nothing more than the eye garrulously denouncing the shape of the peephole that gives access to hidden treasure."

This collection of essays attempts to recover the full range of Barnes' writings, the sexual, ideological, and textual dimensions. Here we see her reconstituting the cultural categories of "masculine" and "feminine," interrogating conventional gender dichotomies as she inscribes feminine desire. From the earliest poems of *The Book of Repulsive Women* through *The Antiphon*, the critics here formulate problems centered on shifting interpretations of "difference"—and feminine "difference within"—and the function of the political unconscious. Barnes' questions are no less intricate than her textual strategies; both aim to recover the story of the absent, the violated, or the underprivileged—something evident everywhere in her writings. She both privileges and critiques the lesbian body as she rewrites the female body (Robin), the outcast body (Nikka), and the body politic (the family). Likewise, Barnes flouts every possible taboo—sexual, textual, and excretory—making, as Jane Marcus reminds us in her essay, "the forbidden erotic a political cry for freedom." Her textual methods celebrate a multiplicity of voices, heterodox forms, and genres, transgressing those tenets of modernism that privilege the "high art" of a single, unified, textual identity or a discrete discourse. Generations of critics have drastically underestimated Barnes' abilities, so well described by Marcus, to "inscribe the political unconscious of a text in a profoundly humanistic way." This volume aims to redress that wrong.

From the time she began as a cub reporter with the Brooklyn *Daily Eagle* in 1912 until her contract ran out with *Theatre Guild* magazine in 1931, Barnes published thirty-nine poems, more than eighteen one-act plays, and more than 110 newspapers and magazine essays for *Vanity Fair*, *Charm*, *McCall's*, the *New Yorker*, and New York's *World*, *Press*, and *Morning Telegraph*. Most of these journalistic essays display an experimental variety and range that challenge a masculine economy of letters, even as they interrogate the boundaries between word and space. Barnes was known to dismiss her early work as "commercial," particularly the essays written for magazines and tabloids. Like her contemporaries Emily Coleman and Antonia White, she spoke of that voluminous body of early writing dismissively, as her "artistic apprenticeship," a compromised commercial venture that enabled the later "high art" of *Nightwood*.

The early work included interviews with famous artists and writers of her time—Stieglitz, Joyce, Harris—as well as popular figures such as evangelist Billy Sunday. If huckster Wilson Mizner called journalism "a sort of paper corpse of reportorial parts of intellectuals," Djuna's fascination with vaudeville, her irreverent love of theatrical personalities, her singular illustrations that transgressed the margins of the page, and her savaging of the commercial stage all provided a not-so-deadly revision of the tabloid journalism of the 1910s. Her topics were as heterodox as her pseudonyms: at times she was the arch "Lydia Steptoe," lady of fashion (1922–28); at other times she called herself "Gunga Duhl, the Pen Performer"; sometimes she simply remained anonymous.

In much of this early journalism Barnes was a brilliant, if savage, culture critic, sketching marginal street types, local color around Brooklyn, even the pseudodemocracy of the Village's Liberal Club or Webster Hall ("pompous beetles in the web of an old desire"). She mocked the gentrified pastime of "going slumming" in "How the Villagers Amuse Themselves" and lamented the loss of communal ideals and passions in her beloved Provincetown theatre that was "always about to be given back to the horses." A number of essays describe the clash between reform and privilege in Village life—between the grocer who tells French jokes and "wraps the prunes with subtleties" and the one who listens to the baker's daughter talk about the possibilities of reform in New York. She railed against the privileges of those with "mink-trimmed minds and seal-edged morals." Repeatedly, Barnes saw "real things that are beautiful . . . mixed in with that which is a sham . . . a wonderful terrible hash on the table of life."

At times brilliantly witty and political, particularly in its tension between the discursive and the figural, this early writing radically challenges conventional genres and ideologies and betrays some anxiety about gender and creativity. In one journalistic venture, Barnes reenacted as a media "rape" the force-feeding of imprisoned IWW agitator Becky Edelson and hundreds of militant British suffragists. Bound like a corpse with arms at her side, nostrils swabbed with anesthetic, she either had to swallow or choke on the pea soup poured down her throat through a red tube in her nose. What she reenacted was the violation not only of the personal body, but of the body politic. Her blistering critique named the misuse of power at the base of political injustice and personal violation: "I saw in my hysteria a vision of a hundred women in grim hospitals, bound and shrouded in the rough grip of callous warders. . . . I could hear the doctor walking ahead of me, stepping as all doctors step, with that little confiding gait that horses must have returning from funerals" (see plate 1). Literary history has called this a "stunt," but as Nancy Levine and Ann Larabee discuss in their essays, we can see here a strong political edge to the participatory aspect of Barnes' early writing.[17]

For Barnes, the interview format was flawed. The asymmetrical power distribution emphasized all that was predatory and distortive. As with the well-made play and the short-story genres, Barnes set about subverting the interview format, exposing the interviewer's power, as she shaped the whole exchange into a highly evaluative art. "We are going to take something from Gaby Delys," she writes:

Not her patience, for that has been taken and regained too often to count; not her right to a normal supply of clothes, for that, too, has been taken from her; nor her reputation, for long ago that was taken to make a column on.

I am going to take something away from Gaby that will be a new loss. No more can she be a picturesque little vagabond nor a shallow water siren, for I am going to take away her reputation for reckless deviltry. . . .

Barnes' "art" in the interview consists in playing deadpan to Donald Ogden Stewart's cliché-tossing tributes to luck. She displays less her art than his privilege—the economics of his clubmanship, his selling out to the North Shore elite: "'What's the matter,' he said. 'In need of money?' We laughed in that hollow way common to the little nonchalant match girl when she realizes that she has left her Dunhill at home."

Claiming that Barnes had a taste for "the bawdy, cheap cuts from the beast life" (N, 11), Levine examines Barnes' early journalism not so much on its own merits, but as the "seedbed for her greatest novel, *Nightwood*." Barnes was drawn to grotesques and oddities, according to Levine—the Wild Aguglia with monkeys in her dressing room, Twingeless Twitchell, snake dancers, seal trainers, all sorts of spectacles. It was when she covered the "Coney Island Burlesque" from 1913–17 that Barnes shifted from objective to subjective journalism: "her response to the sideshow . . . tilted from outside to inside, from the position of the observer to that of the observed." Cheryl Plumb has also observed, "Barnes was reporter to a culture, but also an outsider to the culture she observed . . . biting the hand that fed her."[18]

As Levine reminds us, Barnes "learned how to communicate the incommunicable good inherent in such people by studying the workers and actors she found on the margins of social 'acceptability.'" She sketched out-of-work laborers, talked to chorus girls, visited the IWW headquarters: "All revolt," she wrote, "has a color: the revolt of the mind is the same tint as the revolt of the body and the revolt of the soul. The color is red. Where one comes upon this color, one finds the hub of despair." With a dash of Pascal and a pinch of street hawker, her "Plain Mary Jones" announces: "I was born of the struggle and the torment and the pain. A child of the wheel, a brat of the cogs, a woman of the dust. For even iron has its dust, and when a laborer sweats his sweat of blood and weeps his tears of blood a remedy is thrust upon the world. I am remedy."

If Barnes set about criticizing the contemporary newspaper world, noting particularly her own social and economic differences from those she interviewed, she also introduced radical sexual ideologies into her plays. In "The Early Attic Stage of Djuna Barnes," Ann Larabee examines Barnes' Provincetown plays, dramas that question not only the notions of play and spectacle but also the "implicit voyeurism" of her audience. Barnes' one-acts stood out starkly in the context of the Provincetown Players' small-time husband-and-wife acts, psychodramas that were really just middle-class preservations of monogamy in theatrical drag, written by Neith Boyce, Floyd Dell, Hutchins Hapgood, and "American theatre's dark and darling boy," Eugene O'Neill.[19]

Three of Barnes' best plays—*Three from the Earth, Kurzy of the Sea,* and *To the Dogs*—appeared at Provincetown in the 1919–20 season, produced and directed by Helen Westley while Victorian father George Cram Cook was on sabbatical. Larabee makes a lively case for Barnes' psychological anarchy in these early plays. With her perverse stage families, unromantic sexual relations, and refusal of tragic conclusion or redemption of her characters, Barnes appears more radical, more undomesticated, and more innovative than Rita Wellman or Alice Rostetter, other women dramatists of Provincetown. Barnes' excessive textualizing challenges the production process, providing a poetics of resistance in these early plays. Repeatedly in the early one-acts, we find Barnes sabotaging public and participatory aspects of the form with her meticulously detailed directions.

In contrast to Larabee, Joan Retallack finds Barnes far short of triumphant in these one-acts, calling Barnes' attempts with drama "a misalliance" in which "the logic of description" clearly wins out over "the logic of the theater." Despite a keen and close attention to language, Barnes' plays still exhibit a woman modernist's "formal ambivalence" between the

vitality of the playwright's language and the stale, static dialogue spoken by
the characters: "Her characters hold each other and time itself at bay with
stalemates and diversionary epigrams — not quite non sequiturs, but close —
which neither advance the action nor contribute to their understanding of
one another: 'I — I don't know you'; 'You are either quite an idiot, or a saint';
'You are strange things.'" Helena Hucksteppe's elliptical one-liners in *To the
Dogs* suggest Barnes' difficulties in these early plays: "The problem is that
there is no cumulative power in the language, no increasingly charged field
in the encounter between this Woman and this Man (the entire 'action' of the
play)."[20] Retallack's excellent analysis of Barnes' women characters (Kate
Morley, Helena Hucksteppe, and the Dove) invites us to speculate about the
chilly climate of the modernist stage, its theatrical values and techniques
that are so ill-suited to the woman playwright.

Turning from the drama to the poetry of Barnes' early, prolific years,
Carolyn Burke challenges the legendary isolation of both Mina Loy and
Djuna Barnes. Opening, not concluding, interpretation of both women's
elusive texts, Burke interweaves three stages in the artistic life of these
women friends. In their first published poems, both Loy and Barnes developed artistic critiques of gender in order to reappropriate their subjectivity
from the fin de siècle attitudes toward the female artist. Barnes had to "kill
off the old images of women" of the pre-Raphaelite and Symbolist "art
school" aesthetics that Burke claims were visible in her early journalism. She
did this by publishing the sardonic *Book of Repulsive Women*, a collection
of "eight rhythms and five drawings." But Barnes carried her "American
Beardsley" routine to the death, so that it became impossible to separate her
fascination with "the dissolute and the decadent from her implicit critique
of the very attitudes she would satirize."

Burke creates for the reader an elegantly antihierarchical experience
of two coextensive lives and careers, inscribing the infamous "eccentricity"
of Barnes and Loy with that difference in discourse, art, and language
represented by "ex-centricity." Fascinating here is the intersubjective look
at Barnes and Loy in Paris of the 1920s.[21] Each responds to James Joyce; each
confirms her own modernist aesthetics, illustrating the plight of the exiled
artistic sensibility — Barnes in *Ryder* and *Ladies Almanack*, Loy in the 1923
collection *Lunar Baedeker*. A decade later, while both Barnes and Loy
explored the multiple relations between words and images in their respective
work, Loy began to write in a "deliberately unmarked or asexual poetic
voice," while Barnes sought expansive visual complements to the verbal
inventiveness of both *Almanack* and *Ryder*.

Ryder, Barnes' half-century family chronicle, has long puzzled readers with its layers of literary styles, parodies, and imitations, from the
King James Bible, Sterne, Fielding, and Chaucer to nineteenth-century
sentimental novelists. The "high panache of English on a rampage," the
large cast of characters, and the multiple voices and points of view seem to

overwhelm any notion of unified plot, creating a hugely transgressive modernist text. The celebration of Wendell Ryder, polygamist and picaro, sexual profligate and outlaw, rebel against restrictive moralities, has virtually excluded what Marie Ponsot claims is the powerful infraplot of the daughter, Julie, around whom circle motifs of birth and death, and particularly of childbed.

Ponsot adopts the subject position of Julie in her essay, enabling the daughter's suppressed voice to be heard—and the world of her experience to be seen—as she demonstrates Barnes' strategy of hiding what she shows. Like *The Antiphon* thirty years later, *Ryder* encodes family violence, family eroticism—all the contradictions inherent in gender definitions that undercut family intimacy. Ponsot offers a sensitive reading of the four Julie stories: Amelia, her mother's, painful childbed; Julie's nightmare; her waking with Sophia and Wendell standing over her; the fight with Wendell through Kate. No reader will be unmoved by this powerful portrait of the artist as a young girl, nor by Ponsot's retrieval of Barnes' tribute to Stephen Dedalus' "Silence, exile and cunning."

Ponsot knows better than do most readers that the "antics of the text" subject the unwitting to false readings. In a ritual attack on men, *Ryder*'s mixed structures defy coherence and consequentiality. With all their wit and contrivance, the literary antics are often ignored in favor of their effect on the plot or on the novel's "big motifs of birth and death." By focusing on Julie's perceptions, on images of life and death, and on the fear of childbed, Ponsot finds the "knife that cuts across the onion layers" of *Ryder*.

Focused more on recent theoretical concerns, Sheryl Stevenson explores how *Ryder* both exemplifies and extends Mikhail Bakhtin's notion of the carnivalesque. Stevenson sees Barnes offering a feminist challenge to this tradition, reworking, in her "extravaganza of literary styles," Bakhtin's carnivalesque strategies and motifs. *Ryder* also incorporates many female countertexts or myths that spoof the pious girls and voluptuous virgins of pulp fiction and parody such representations as Dante Gabriel Rossetti's "Blessed Damozel." The image of Wendell Ryder is also manipulated to confuse categories of gender: swaddler of his dying child ("Wendell Dresses His Child"), he is wrapped in masculine styles of writing.

Stevenson questions whether the "female laughter and abuse" that undermine male authority throughout *Ryder* are sufficiently powerful to override the negative aspects of sexuality and childbearing. Can the carnivalesque overcome the collective portrait of decay, pain, debasement, and death in store for the female? Feminist critics may still choose to view *Ryder* as Frances Doughty does—a male procreation text rather than a text in which male authority is undermined by constant female mockery.

If *Ryder* can be read as celebratory and defiant feminist myth, Barnes' artwork seems much less pathbreaking to Doughty. Barnes turned to the past for her literary and visual sources, according to Doughty, "us[ing] them to disguise experience rather than to create forms whose experiential referent was the creative process itself." Barnes' drawings, she claims, convey an obsessive struggle with her material, illustrating perpetual indecision and embracing neither heterosexual nor lesbian aesthetics.

I recall with delight my first glimpse of Barnes' art in *A Book*: stunning, realistic sketches, a tribute to her Pratt Institute training, but without the referentiality to text or personal identity that would restore a realistic context to the drawings. This uneasy rejection of verisimilitude figures as well in the imitation woodblock illustrations for *The Book of Repulsive Women*. Transgressing genres, Barnes' drawings that accompany the *Morning Telegraph* essays physically divide and dominate the text on the page, challenging boundaries between word and space, threatening to exile the printed word to the edges of the tabloid universe. Drawn with meticulous skill, these macabre illustrations at once underscore and are at variance with the interview form she deconstructs and the manners of the celebrities she debunks.

Nevertheless, none of the early illustrations prepared me for Barnes' oil painting of Emily Coleman, reminiscent of fifteenth-century Umbrian art with its bruised purples and greens. The Coleman oil is wholly unlike the 1949 realistic painting of an equestrienne commissioned by Cordelia Coker Pearson, one of Barnes' patrons. Nor is it similar either to that elusive painting of Peggy Guggenheim (whose "mean" mouth but "kind eyes," in a telling psychological twist, Barnes just couldn't get right) or to the unpublished sketches for *Ryder*. The Coleman portrait suggests a more troublesome relation between creativity and intimacy for the woman artist. At least in her oil painting, Doughty argues, the more emotionally involved Barnes was with her subject, the more likely she was to represent that person "in the idiom of her own inner world."

Barnes constructs a scholar's paper chase by hiding bits of autobiography in the profusion of styles and genres in *Ryder*. "Decoding" the illustrations depends upon the knowledge of readers—readers who know the original sources, the nineteenth-century engraver's books as well as the sexual habits and practices of the family individuals represented. For Barnes it was certainly true, as Doughty notes, that a "literal rendition that the reader finds unbelievable is as good a disguise as fiction." For the unwitting, her drawing passes for mere illustration of text.

Recounting the pleasures (male) and dangers (female) of sex in *Ryder* leads Doughty to conclude that Barnes lacks congruence between her sexual humor and freedom of sexual language, leaving doubt about her sexual allegiances. In both *Ladies Almanack* and *Ryder* we find the visual equivalent of sexually free writing, and in *Ladies Almanack* the world of women who love women; the exception is Patience Scalpel, the lone heterosexual voice. Convinced that Barnes "disowned the world of women," Doughty writes, "The issue is not whether Barnes was a lesbian or a heterosexual, but that she was neither." As researchers reveal new details about Barnes' complex family and her early erotic experiences, readers might consider carefully Doughty's suggestion that Barnes was less afraid of the social stigma in the lesbian network than she was of suffocation.

If Radclyffe Hall pleaded for "tolerance" toward lesbian life in 1928 with *The Well of Loneliness*, Barnes in the same year delighted the circle of Natalie Clifford Barney with a "mock epic of proselytizing that brings women into the lesbian fold," according to Susan Sniader Lanser in "Speaking in Tongues." While Barnes enlarged for all readers the borders of the sexually/textually possible, *Ladies Almanack* has not always been read—as Lanser reads it—as a "bawdy *discours à clef* that eludes classification and inscribes a world in which the lesbian is normative." Nor has it been read as a "slight satiric wigging" on Natalie Barney's world of women, "the glories and limitations of Mytilene in Paris." Quite the contrary: in line with previous critics, James Scott wrote in 1976 that "the book satirizes the absurdity of modern promiscuity among women, and it protests the absence of the decent restraints of privacy."

Lanser is of another mind about *Ladies Almanack*. Arguing against the relevance of any biographical information on lesbian experience—for example, Barnes' relation to Natalie Barney's Academie des Femmes—she cites three interwoven modes of discourse in the work: the narrative, the philosophic, and the mythic. These discourses, which permit the text to become "at once more radical and more covert," are not sequential and discrete, but are instead a mélange of modes and media that explores lesbian life from multiple points of view. Thus Barnes rewrites Radclyffe Hall, Proust, and other modernists. Together these modes create in Dame Musset a figure with an intertextual identity ("a text that speaks in tongues"). *Ladies Almanack* retrieves the notion of lesbian femininity from the negative throes of *The Well of Loneliness* and the fate of Stephen Gordon: "For Evangeline [Musset], then, the phallic Lack is as much the signifier of superiority as it is the site of feminist tragedy." One effect of coupling a narrative voice that is "evasive, devious, playfully indirect" with a "dense and highly allusive prose" is that the lines between "woman" and "lesbian," the poles of archlesbian or archheterosexual, blur and converge. As Lanser demonstrates, Barnes' prose heals the rift between the two.

Undoing Freudian notions of phallic supremacy, Barnes creates in *Almanack* a myth of the all-female birth—a fable of "angelic parthenogenesis" that unravels and parodies the *Summa Theologiae* of St. Thomas Aquinas and its account of woman's creation. As Lanser suggests, *Almanack*'s description of Evangeline Musset's funeral rituals is a textually memorable refusal of phallocentrism, a convergence of "woman" and "lesbian" into what Adrienne Rich calls a "lesbian continuum."

By contrast, Frann Michel places Barnes' inscriptions of gender and sexuality (what she calls her "feminine" writing) in *Almanack* within the context of the French feminist assertion that woman "cannot be placed, even to be displaced." Women and relations between women remain inevitably and mysteriously undefined, indeterminate amidst all the parodic styles and structures of *Almanack*. Thus, any affirmative reading of *Almanack*—even one such as Lanser's—depends upon what Michel calls the "unstable irony that also invokes the masculine: the text is always potentially compromised by that which it subverts."

In "The Outsider among the Expatriates: Djuna Barnes' Satire on the Ladies of the *Almanack*," Karla Jay offers a reading of *Almanack* even less affirmative than Michel's. Jay proceeds by recontextualizing *Almanack*, looking at it in the specific circumstances of its composition. Unlike Gertrude Stein, Peggy Guggenheim, or Natalie Barney—the presiding spirit of *Almanack*—Barnes was far from economically secure, dependent upon her skills as a writer and illustrator. When she turned from journalism to fiction, her earnings plummeted, leaving her "at the economic mercy of other women."[22] Her dependency rankled Barnes, and when she came to write her insider's view of Barney's circle, "she bit the very hands that brought *Ladies Almanack* into existence." In Jay's reading, Barney/Musset's apparent beatification is harshly ironic: ignoring Barney's intellectual accomplishments, Barnes presents her instead as a "conscienceless nymphomaniac," reduced at last to her flaming, flickering tongue in the Temple of Love. Other persons satirized in this roman à clef—for instance, Radclyffe Hall and Una Troubridge—are also etched with an acid pen, suggesting the extent to which Barnes considered herself an outsider.

But Barnes' attitude toward the other women of the Barney circle is indicated most incisively not by a presence, but by an absence—specifically, the absence of Barnes herself, who does not appear in the work. Thus Barnes "underscores her economic and sexual isolation from the rest of the circle," and her portrait of that circle becomes even more problematic.

"I'm not a lesbian. I just loved Thelma." Barnes' vehement denial of lesbian relationships is not what interests Carolyn Allen in the writer's seduction stories. As she makes clear, every denial carries evidence of its opposite. (In a letter of 12 October 1936 to Ottoline Morrell, Barnes wrote: "Please do not think of it—I was not offended in the least to be thought lesbian—it's simply that I'm very reticent about my personal life.") Allen prefers to look to the "textual shadows rather than to the surfaces" in her study of three "little girl" stories. "Cassation," "The Grande Malade," and "Dusie" belong to the "lesbian imaginative tradition," as do *Almanack* and *Nightwood*. All three interrogate gender identity and homosexuality by rejecting the binary categories of male and female: "By refusing to take maleness and the phallus as the norm, by questioning the construction of gender and the nature of sexuality, they rupture the surface of convention and illuminate the world of night."

Allen offers lucid summaries of the shifting value placed on "difference" and of the complexities of the mother-daughter dynamics in the lesbianism of *Almanack* and *Nightwood*. Even with Allen's explanation, the suggestion of "difference in the context of resemblance"—an idea central to Luce Irigaray's two companion essays, "Quand nos lèvres se parlent" and "Et l'une ne bouge pas sans l'autre"—is a complex one with which Frann Michel would not, I think, agree in her critical remarks on *Almanack*. Irigaray's two essays "rupture" the Lacanian model of woman's sexual difference as Other or Lack. Together with Nancy Chodorow's theory of how female sexuality is structured, they provide the theoretical platform for Allen's analysis.

While the three Barnes stories share common traits, perhaps the most startling is the power asymmetry of the characters: the little girl tells stories to "a lady." The stories are themselves "a fictional seduction of the older 'Madame' by the younger narrator." In the sudden midway shifts in power within the structure of each story, it is the "little girl" who comes to control the action. Language is charged with sexual meaning, and the narrative usually carries a strong and transgressive sexual subtext. If we read "Cassation" in the context of *Nightwood*'s "Go Down Matthew," as Allen suggests, but also in the context of such plays as *The Dove* or *She Tells Her Daughter*, the configuration both of difference in likeness and of mother-child dynamics between women intimates makes us radically question the role of mothering, while "Grande Malade" subverts any notion of heterosexuality with the "difference" of father-daughter couples.

In "The Sweetest Lie," Judith Lee argues that *Nightwood*'s excesses constitute a "strategy of disguise." The ambivalence between disguise and revelation is the problematic center of *Nightwood*, a novel that explores our beliefs concerning love and gender: "*Nightwood* is distinctively modern not only in its subject and form, but in its consideration of what our concepts of masculine and feminine imply." Lee deconstructs the false opposition between these terms, which she claims do not "define the most fundamental experience of difference: the difference between the identity one imagines (the self as Subject) and the identity one experiences in relationship with someone else (the self as Other)." Rather, it is the opposition between mother and child—and the figuration of that split in Kristeva's maternal body—that holds new possibilities for figuring female identity.

Barnes names the insufficiency of our cultural myths in three ways in *Nightwood*: in the relation between Nora and Robin, in the parodic tale of Hedvig and Guido; and in the ironic implications of the prince-princess primer story as a tale of narcissistic love. In these insufficiencies she reveals the psychology of "the sweetest lie": sexual oppositions. Heaped in dissociated fragments of the past, Robin and Felix continue to develop Barnes' parody of conventional notions of masculine and feminine: Felix bows before the fraudulent Grand Duke of Russia, "his head in his confusion making a complete half-swing, as an animal will turn its head away from a human, as if in mortal shame" (N, 123). It is this last image of Felix that prefigures our last image of Robin.

Lee reads Robin as an example of Kristeva's "monumental time," a parody of the values embedded in the feminine. Nora and Robin's coupling follows the pattern of fairy-tale romances, but with a difference specific to female experience, the mother-child dialectic replacing the masculine/feminine opposition and overturning illusory values mythologized in the masculine. Nora "experiences a split within herself that allows her double identity of both mother and child." The two dream sequences of the novel work dialectically to inscribe her shift from external cultural difference between masculine and feminine to the "internal difference" between self as subject and self as object.

Central to Lee's essay is her exploration of the textual construction of speech and silence. Robin and Matthew are two centers around which *Nightwood* turns, each promising redemption from sexual difference. Lee's is a bleak assessment, however. In his speech, Matthew "suppress[es] his feminine nature and the desire it represents, just as Robin's silence is a way of rejecting the experience of her own difference." The end of the essay revises the redemptive promise in Matthew's drunken speech, rejecting the possibility of making meaning through language. Finally, Lee notes that in Robin's final sacrifice in the chapel, Barnes denies "the signifying value of her own deconstruction."

In contrast to Lee's work with the structures of language and cultural mythology, Jane Marcus describes *Nightwood* as "the representative modern text, a prose poem of abjection, tracing the political unconscious of the rise of fascism, as lesbians, blacks, circus people, Jews, and transvestites— outsiders all—*bow down* before Hitler's truly perverted Levitical prescriptions for racial purity." From its interpretation as a moralistic biography of the infamous Paris nightworld, to its transgressive catalogues of genre, style, and even time itself, *Nightwood* has been valorized as "high modernist decadence." Such interpretations merely confuse the real sources of this novel, which takes all culture—high and low—as its signifying practice, refusing, as Marcus makes clear, to police the picket fence of canonicity. Bakhtin's Rabelais is a "model methodology" for making a radical new modernism out of the upside-down, topsy-turvy world that refuses domination. From Marlena Dietrich's "Blue Angel" to *Die Fledermaus*; from the Paris pissoirs to Talmudic texts; from E.T.A. Hoffmann's "The Sand-Man" to Victor Hugo, Eugène Sue, and Lacan's "privileged signifier," Barnes "mothers the Other" in *Nightwood*, a book of "communal resistances of underworld outsiders to domination."

Marcus' essay disrupts the old authority of Barnes' criticism; she has carnivalized literary history, which can never again partake of a Wordsworthian innocence. Marcus begins by interrogating Leviticus (19:27–28) with Kristeva's essay on abjection. Both the Levitical taboo against writing on the body (the patriarchal body is permitted only the one mark, the ritual cut of circumcision) and the prohibition against mixing things (seeds should not be mingled, nor linen and wool used in the same garment) are transgressed throughout *Nightwood*. Marcus uses Kristeva's concept of "abjection" (the ritual or symbolic cut replacing the natural cut of the umbilical cord) not as a pathology, but as a political case, a "kind of anarchist-feminist call for freedom from fascism." The body of the other—lesbian, Jew, transvestite—is the text in the novel. Writing on the body breaks this powerful patriarchal taboo: "A tatoo, then, is not only taboo; it is also the birthmark of the born-again—the self-created person who denies his or her birth-identity." *Nightwood* is a dangerous novel because it shows the social order turned upside down as in carnival or circus; boundaries are willfully transgressed, taboos ritually violated. If we read the body of Nikka (the black bear-wrestler from the Cirque de Paris) as inscribed with the sacred and profane, deliberately thwarting referential meaning, we read a text of "western culture's historical projections and myths about race."

By systematically presenting the world turned upside-down—as in the language of the latrine, the twin pissoir passages, the argot of the underworld—and by accepting death and decay as renewal and part of life, Marcus challenges any residual notion of *Nightwood* as a lesbian cult novel or as a text of high (male) modernism. Instead, she reads it as a powerfully antifascist text, a text whose political unconscious is at work on all levels—prophesying the Holocaust, attacking doctors, politicians, and psychoanalysts who set up the persistently dichotomous and exclusive world view: us and them. Barnes' dangerous novel, Marcus tells us, makes a "modernism of marginality. Its 'danger' is that the excluded object of its rage, the white Christian male, might read it."

In "Woman, Remember You: Djuna Barnes and History," Julie Abraham suggests that for Barnes "history" always had a double meaning, comprising both the official record of the powerful and the stories of the marginalized or completely excluded. Barnes could not be consistent in her definitions of history precisely because her textual and imaginative enterprise—the creation of multiplicity and overlapping social divisions between genders, classes, races, and sexual persuasions—challenged the very idea of a limited "history proper." According to Abraham, from the early stories to the late drama the question of history is both framework and central concern in Barnes' texts. Any question of a record is the question of "a record in *whose* gaze," indicating that "remembering" must include both "the desire and the record." "Barnes equates the gaze, 'looking at her,' with memory, memory with love, and love and memory with writing, being remembered with being both loved and recorded." As the "fundamental mode of her texts themselves," memory is also an action taken by characters within the text. If memory bears the weight of writing (history as record) in *The Antiphon*, memory is also a sexual act in *Almanack*, a disruption of the official record of history through lesbian sexual energy. In *The Antiphon*, history is enacted within the family:

The lesson at the center of history becomes the first lesson the daughter learns, and it is a sexual lesson, that of her father's favored access to her mother and of her own female inferiority. . . . The mother will never be for her. Unlike the Freudian daughter, this girl-child does not agree to transfer her desire from her mother to her father. . . . History begins with the heterosexual "facts of life."

Abraham's is by no means an essay to be read quickly. Nor does her examination of Barnes' uses of history leave the reader encouraged about the fate of women within the history of the official record, at least not as she describes it in the Augusta-Miranda tangle from *The Antiphon*. Nevertheless, Barnes' often complex and dense references to history meet a formidable critic in Abraham, who makes the case for Barnes' interrelation of the kinds and protocols of history throughout her writing.

To read *The Antiphon* is to interpret a study in textual politics—or "text bashing"—that reduced *Nightwood* to a third of its original size. As Lynda Curry dramatically shows, T.S. Eliot recommended "drastic cutting" of the play. He spoke in quantitative terms ("I feel sure there are pages in the middle which can be disposed of") to a woman who had labored more than eight years to break silence, yet to disguise her tale of a daughter's sexual violation and betrayal. Of those powerful original drafts of act 2, Eliot could only say, "It is undesirable far to overstep the limits of the essential." He spoke of the horrible intimacies of the excised sections as merely "what one feels to be good lines."

Andrew Field, in *Djuna: The Formidable Miss Barnes*, was among the first to retrieve *The Antiphon* from the status of "closet drama," a play "too busily static" with overdetermined language and no immediacy of character. Field disclosed the rape of the daughter in the play, "the story behind the story in Barnes' writing, either removed, or disguised, or only obliquely told." Field's reading, however, did not focus on the published play, but was instead derived from the intertext of the excised draft variants. Moreover, Field's was not an original discovery. Buried in the "Bibliography and Sources" (there are no footnotes in *Djuna*) is a tribute to Lynda Curry, whose 1978 dissertation meticulously examined the five major "draft" variants of *The Antiphon*. Curry's essay in this volume returns some of the most important cuts removed in the fifth—and last—revision of *The Antiphon*. Barnes slashed more than three hundred lines at Eliot's urging, leaving the final text with little family history and less comedy, pun, and play. The emotional context of the character of Miranda was excised. Miranda's silence increases, no doubt to protect what the cut drafts refer to as "the general precepts of her scruples." In the last draft, Jeremy remains disguised and is suspected of knowing too much about the past. Words seem to give way to suspicions; revelation yields to disguise and its protection. Masking, enactment, disguise, silence, and ambiguity are all brought to a level of textual self-consciousness, a prominent part of the Hobbs family history.

As Curry notes, Barnes "rewrote and substantially shortened the first two-thirds of the second act of *The Antiphon,* leaving only the masked attack scene and the dollhouse scene uncut." But Eliot's gain in "size" was a generation of readers' loss in understanding. With the disappearance of the hayhook scene from act 2 (the father's "first virginal sacrifice" of his own daughter) and Dudley's concise defense of Miranda, the whole passage has become distorted. The degree of the mother's complicity with the father, the painful intimacy of Augusta and Miranda, and the general exchanges of an entire family are removed. Curry retrieves for literary history Jack's "crystal speech" in the dollhouse scene, together with the omitted daughter's rape. It is revealing to note that both character motivation and plot clarification—the two "weaknesses" that have sunk this play critically—are restored in full by a glimpse at the original drafts.

In "'No Audience at All'?" Meryl Altman notes that *The Antiphon* is informed "by questions of speech and silence." Claiming that the play has been unfairly slighted as either pathologically interesting or as compelling only for its verbal "tricks," Altman explores *Antiphon* in the context of Barnes' knowledge of dramatic forms and her experiences in twentieth-century theater. By examining textual adaptations of theatrical metaphor, the plays within plays, and Barnes' ideas of performance and staging, she demonstrates that Barnes' inclusion of the spectator within the play "is crucial to *The Antiphon*'s self-referentiality, for this is a piece *about* theater as well as a piece *of* theater." One end to which Barnes uses this information, Altman writes, is to explore the dangerous effects of female role playing and female roles.

In this volume the essays on *The Antiphon* proceed from Altman's analysis of self-referentiality in the play through Curry's draft analysis to Louise DeSalvo's explorations of incest discourse. DeSalvo reads *The Antiphon* not only through contemporary incest discourse, but also through Shakespeare's *The Tempest,* focusing the extreme—and previously unexplored—violence of the language of the text. Barnes' language shows the mother privileging her sons over her daughter (she has internalized her husband's hatred of her own gender) and reveals Miranda's "lyric coprolalia" and the brother's sexual double entendres ("want," "gap," "rip," "tear"), which construct a network of assaultive and violent textuality.

DeSalvo's case for reading *Antiphon*'s incest discourse is convincing. Like the incest survivors whose case histories inform recent sociological and psychological research, Miranda is a threat to the very family structure itself because she is able to bear witness to the family atrocities. The other members of the family fear that Miranda will tell—or write—her tale, which makes her so threatening that they want to eliminate her. A whole network of family violence is perpetuated in the Hobbs household, revealing a massive breakdown of sexual taboos detailed in the deadly serious discussion of childhood sexuality in the "game" of animal masks played by the brothers; in the mother's complicity in the daughter's "prostitution" at the hands of the offending father; in Miranda's painfully ambiguous "privileged" status in the family. Polygamy, incest, and brutalization of children all transpire within the Hobbs household, "covered" by Titus' religious practice and by Augusta's language of deference and economic victimization that forestall her taking any radical action—or any action at all—on behalf of her daughter.

Future Barnes scholars will be guided by DeSalvo's reading of the dollhouse scene, particularly of the "Titus-doll" with its inversion of the father's former absolute power and authority. The textual details about the daughter's fate suggest startling implications, even more graphically depicted in the exchange between Miranda and Augusta in act 3. The psychology of betrayal that informs the incest survivor also shapes Miranda's perceptions. DeSalvo analyzes the rhetoric of this vicious (il)logic, a logic in which "in addition to suffering the torment of being victimized, Miranda is expected to pardon those who have degraded her." The mother-daughter nexus also requires a vicious collusion, one that protects, if not absolves, the father. Unmistakable in *The Antiphon* is the link between Hitler's behavior (the play is set in 1939) and Titus' household devastation. Like Marcus' study of *Nightwood*, DeSalvo's interpretation suggests the strong political unconscious of the text, which has been ignored by Barnes scholars. Also overlooked has been Barnes' challenge to the myths of motherhood, romanticized notions of women as nurturers, even the conciliatory possibilities for mothers and daughters under patriarchy.

In developing the dialectic between Miranda in *The Antiphon* and Miranda in *The Tempest*, DeSalvo examines the incestuous subtext of both plays and the absence of maternal protection. Both Hobbs' Ark and Prospero's island are described here as the "fantasy kingdom of every incestuous father: a world without adult women who might intervene." Parallels between Caliban's attempted violation of Miranda (an event that Prospero could have foreseen) and Titus' bartering of his daughter to a man three times her age (a scene cut from act 2) are remarkably similar. The barbarism, voyeurism, defilement, and father's imprint inherent in each of these acts is unmistakable: "Barnes' allusions to *The Tempest* (and to a score of other tragedies) serve to redefine the function of tragedy in a patriarchy, and she claims that form for women dramatists."

Djuna Barnes was legendary for her codedness, for her dense and historical textuality, for her scorn of confessional intimacy. It befits this remarkable woman writer that we should end our collection of essays with

DeSalvo's eloquent examination of the intertextuality of *The Antiphon*, the Elizabethan past, and the feminist future. Perhaps the best tribute to Djuna Barnes is to return feminist readers to her work, making us antiphonal respondents to her seventy years of writing. Surely *The Antiphon* is Barnes' own poignant antiphon to *The Tempest*; its tragedy, a response to Elizabethan comedy; and DeSalvo's interpretation (on behalf of all feminist critics), an antiphon to a half century of Barnes' scholarship.

¶ [Reginald] Marsh didn't do any caricatures for me; he did two- and three-column cartoon panels in charcoal of scenes of literary life. Djuna Barnes, who was as subtle and as individualistic in her caricatures as she was in her short stories and pseudo-Elizabethan stories of bawdry, was one of the handsomest women I have ever seen and one of the most amusing. I never saw her wear anything except a tailored black broadcloth suit with a white ruffled shirtwaist, a tight-fitting black hat, and high-heeled black shoes; and I rarely saw her without a long shepherd's crook which she carried like a Watteau figure in a fête galante. Her story of the "Odyssey of the King of the Ostermoors," in which she, Jane Heap, Margaret Anderson, and Georgette LeBlanc, Maeterlinck's first wife, figured hilariously, as Djuna told it, is one of the classical anecdotes of New York literary life which, unfortunately, I am not privileged to relate.

—Burton Rascoe,
"American Coming of Age"
in *We Were Interrupted*

¶ . . . one sees the Baroness [Elsa von Freytag Loringhoven] leap lightly from one of those new white taxis, with seventy black and purple anklets clanking about her secular feet. A foreign postage stamp—cancelled—perched upon her cheek; a wig of purple and gold caught roguishly up with strands from a cable once used to moor importations from far Cathay; red trousers—and catch the subtle dusty perfume blown back from her—an ancient human notebook on which has been written all the follies of a past generation.

—Djuna Barnes,
"How the Villagers Amuse Themselves,"
Morning Telegraph, 26 November 1916

¶ Djuna Barnes said that she was getting used to the dirt of Paris, it was a relief after *The Little Review*, anyway. "You know they always used to wash the soap before they used it." . . . "My husband was a scholar, he really had a fine mind. . . . He works on the *American* to earn a living—and uses his money to buy books. . . . He's writing a book on the philosophy of criticism—but it'll never be finished. He's been working on it seven years. . . . He had me absolutely stunned so that I didn't know whether I was coming or going . . . Oh, you couldn't pry me away from him . . . The amount that man knew was appalling: he knew about all sorts of different editions and things . . . But he thought earrings were very foolish; he couldn't understand why I should want to wear earrings . . . But I couldn't stand it any longer."

—Edmund Wilson,
The Twenties (1975)

1

"Bringing Milkshakes to Bulldogs": The Early Journalism of Djuna Barnes

Nancy J. Levine

Judging by her early career as a journalist, one could say that Djuna Barnes had a taste for "the bawdy, cheap cuts from the beast life," not unlike her character Felix Volkbein of *Nightwood*, who haunts the dressing rooms of Europe's actresses, acrobats, and sword swallowers (*N*, 11). Barnes combined the public demands of a career with a private fascination for the strange and bizarre. The assignments she drew as a "newspaperman" (her term) during the eight years before she left for Europe in 1920 led her inevitably to the grotesque. Barnes' tabloid journalism is elegant, witty, and surprisingly undated. Because her career as a journalist was the seedbed of her greatest novel, *Nightwood*, her early essays, interviews, and works of fiction are worth considering, setting aside questions of merit. The motif of the sideshow freak emerged from this early work and found its way into *Nightwood*.

In 1913 Djuna Barnes began working as a reporter and illustrator for the Brooklyn *Daily Eagle*. She free-lanced for the *Press*, the *World*, and the *Morning Telegraph* between 1914 and 1917, eventually writing for most of the other major New York papers. In addition to straightforward news reports, such as her page-one story for the *Daily Eagle*, "State Opens Case in New Delfer Trial" (1913), Barnes wrote interviews and feature articles on a startling variety of subjects. Tango dancers, chorus girls, Greenwich Village bohemians, and British suffragettes engaged her sharp-eyed, amused attention. She talked to out-of-work servant girls and to Lillian Russell in her opulent retirement. David Belasco the playwright, Diamond Jim Brady the financier, and Billy Sunday the evangelist responded to her questions with surprising openness and eloquence. Her early newspaper career kept her in touch with the popular entertainments of the 1910s—the circus, the vaudeville, the boxing ring, and the movies. Scattered among the big names she interviewed are these oddities: an Italian actress billed as "the Wild Aguglia," who kept monkeys in her dressing room; an "Indian" snake dancer named "Roshanara" (actually an English girl with a busy imagination); and a painless dentist, "Twingeless Twitchell," whose office was any Brooklyn street corner.

By 1917 Djuna Barnes was earning five thousand dollars a year as a free-lance feature writer. Fifteen dollars for an article was considered good payment in the 1910s; Barnes could, and often did, write several a day. By the time she left for Europe in 1920, she had published more than a hundred articles and over twenty-five short plays and fictions. The New York *Tribune* employed her as a stringer during her early years in Paris, Berlin, and the south of France. *McCall's, Vanity Fair, Charm,* and the *New Yorker* commissioned articles and interviews that featured personages famous, rich, or royal. *McCall's* editor, Harry Payne Burton, for example, sent Barnes a $500 check to a Barcelona address in 1925 for an article on international marriage among the elite.[1] During the 1920s, Barnes' popular journalism was an uncertain source of income, allowing her to publish her serious fiction and poetry in literary journals with small budgets. The *Little Review,* the *Dial,* and *transition* gladly took her work in return for the glory of the thing; occasional financial assistance from friends helped keep her afloat between checks.[2] From January 1929 to September 1931 she wrote articles and a gossipy monthly column, "Playgoer's Almanac" (retitled "The Wanton Playgoer"), for *Theatre Guild Magazine.* The big assignments became scarcer in the 1930s, however, and finally stopped altogether. But in the 1920s Barnes was known as a brilliant figure in literary and social circles on both continents. In May 1924 a young upstart named Ernest Hemingway warned the readers of the Paris-based *Transatlantic Review* that Djuna Barnes, "that legendary personality that has dominated the intellectual night-life of Europe for a century, is in town." It may well have been her reputation as a literary legend that finally ended her career as a popular journalist. By the late 1930s she had too much stature to write about what the crowned heads of Europe liked for dinner.

At the beginning of her career, however, there were few things Barnes would not do for the sake of a story, from risking the loss of "all dignity out of our lives as far back as our great grand uncles" on the slides, chutes, and whirling disks of Luna Park Steeple Chase to allowing herself to be lowered at the end of a rope from the top of a building for an article on firemen's rescues. Barnes' range in the 1910s was remarkably wide, but in almost every one of her light and engaging feature articles and interviews the real subject is the unexpected presence of the bizarre embedded in the everyday.

Sometimes the bizarre was not buried very deeply. For example, Barnes found Twingeless Twitchell, the dentist who pulled teeth for free, on a street corner in Brooklyn. The banner that headed her interview with Twitchell was the alliterative exuberance of a Coney Island "talker's" spiel:

"Digital Dexterity of the Dental Demonstrator Holds Audience in Awe."[3] The point of the article is that Twingeless Twitchell's act, however odd, is not tucked away in a freak show. One could encounter him or others like him on any municipal highway. One of Barnes' first assignments for the *Daily Eagle* was to explore the streets for "Types Found in Odd Corners Round about Brooklyn" (1913), as the heading for a series of her drawings proclaimed. Sometimes her searching eye picked out the unusual only to deflate it; in an interview with Ruth Royce, the comedienne, Barnes called her "the greatest 'nut' in vaudeville, eccentric beyond the limits of belief unless you have seen her."[4] But more frequently her goal was to make the reader aware of the strange and contradictory nature of the quotidian world. If one could "live each day apart," she wrote in "Found in the Bowery" (1917), "then and only then should we see something at once beautiful and real and perhaps not beautiful at all."[5]

In these early pieces Barnes is flexing muscles she will use when she creates the characters of *Nightwood*. In a voice that recalls Dr. Matthew O'Connor's verbal dexterity, Dr. Twitchell declaims to his audience, "I'm the man that put the 'dent' in dentist and the 'ees' in teeth." O'Connor himself gives a good imitation of a medicine show spieler when he tells the café crowd, "I was standing listening to a quack hanky-panky of a medicine man saying: 'Now, ladies and gentlemen, before I behead the small boy, I will endeavour to entertain you with a few parlour tricks'" (*N*, 163). Barnes was particularly drawn to high-talking charlatans. When it came time to write the doctor's monologues, she had more than one prototype on whose mode of speech she could have drawn.[6] The evangelist Billy Sunday may have suggested the doctor's favorite rhetorical device, attack by analogy. Side-stepping the question "Is war good or bad for religion?" Billy Sunday responds aphoristically: "Through ammunition one attains immunity: through battle one locates the knees. The eyes do not necessarily have to be acquainted with the Bible; the knees must be acquainted with the floor."[7] The balanced repetition of the preacher's language ("through ammunition . . . through battle") is echoed in the doctor's speech: "we all go down in battle, but we all go home" (*N*, 129). To a certain extent, Barnes invented *all* the people about whom she wrote. Since she seldom took notes, she may have had to depend on the cadenced language of her Methodist background to recreate the ecclesiastical rhythms of Billy Sunday's oratory. Her memory was copious; as she told the actress Helen Westley during an interview, she could always "make a paragraph out of a note automatically." No doubt Barnes drew on her past for the interviews, as later she drew on the interviews for *Nightwood*.

Djuna Barnes also wrote about: a seal trainer in Brooklyn; the above-mentioned snake dancer, "Roshanara, the Reincarnation of the Ancient East"; and a baby gorilla at the Bronx Zoo named Dinah, whom she "interviewed."[8] In words that Barnes, acting as "translator," put in Dinah's mouth, the "bush-girl" expresses a wish to try chewing gum so that she can find out "what it is that keeps so many people rotatory beneath their hats."

Most of Barnes' interviewees are in Dinah's position, at least some of the time, of having words—witty, alternately racy and orotund, but unmistakably Barnes' own—placed in their mouths. The Broadway producer Arthur Voegtlin, whom Barnes interviewed for the *Press*, sounds curiously like Billy Sunday, for example, and both men recall Dr. O'Connor. She even made a spokesperson out of Roshanara, whose verbal talents are rather unexpected coming from a snake dancer; "skill," Barnes remarks in *Nightwood*, "is never so amazing as when it seems inappropriate" (*N*, 11). Addressing a stumbling American public, enamored of such violent, mechanical dances as the turkey trot and the bunny hug, Roshanara says: "Incidentally, you don't know anything about dancing. That's why my act is a risk; it is moonlight to madness, and it is dream steps to the death charge. It is a hazy, calm, peaceful interpretation of a calm, peaceful race. Well, it's like bringing a milkshake to a bulldog."

In these early essays Djuna Barnes is always trying to bring milkshakes to bulldogs. The attempt to confound her readers' blunted expectations by mixing modes and forcing incongruous juxtapositions is an essential part of her style, both as a writer and as an artist. The drawings that accompanied most of her articles and interviews are an improbable but successful combination of the daily funnies and Aubrey Beardsley (see plates 2 and 3). One of Barnes' specialties was the vamp, a type that had its vogue in the 1910s. The pages of popular magazines were filled with drawings of slant-eyed women, dressed in sinuous wraps and wearing the bland, standardized expressions of fashion models. Barnes eschewed anodyne effects; her females are anything but bland. A fashionably dressed woman in a typical Barnes sketch of this period goes for a walk with her pet, but the animal at the end of the leash is a cubistic chicken. Barnes' first published graphic work owes a debt to the whiplash linearity of art nouveau. The prose style she employed in her feature articles for the *Daily Eagle* and the *Press* is harder to categorize. The term "euphuistic" hardly does justice to the deliberate campiness of her description of an ice cream soda as "cheerful chemicals in chiffon." There is an element of Coney Island burlesque in such a contradictory construction that makes the usual critical terminology seem stuffy.

Coney Island, not unexpectedly, was another Barnes specialty. From 1913 to 1917 she wrote four articles about her visits to that garish, red-painted amusement park. Built in 1904, Coney Island was the inspiration of two alert showmen, Elmer S. Dundy and Frederick Thompson, who also built the Hippodrome, thereby making themselves sleek fortunes. Barnes was more interested in the people who visited and worked in Coney Island than she was in the park itself. The following passage is from a piece she wrote for the *Press* in 1914:

I heard emanating from one of the sideshows a noise that was half-way between a melody and a regret; there were also inside some torrid war cries and a glimpse of some turbans. . . . [The performers] had a lot of sheeting wound around them and a good many spears, which they occasionally threw at one another or at the crowd, or sometimes at a target which, in spite of the fact that they never do anything else, they never hit in the right place. They showed us how they cleaned their teeth, how they nursed their babies, and how they chewed gum.

The last exhibit was rather the best.⁹

In an essay that appeared in the *Press* three years later, Barnes' impressions are still as sharply focused, but her response to the sideshow has tilted from outside to inside, from the position of the observer to that of the observed:

A sideshow attracts attention. Great posters of the "Fattest Fat Lady," of the "Ossified Man," of the "Snake Charmer," and of that unfortunate fellow who has legs like whips and who is advertised as the "Cigarette Fiend." You look down upon these people as from the top of an abyss, they are the bottom of despair and of life. The demonstrator comes forward, cane in hand, he touches the nearest freak on the shoulder and begins turning him around as if this turning were all that the unfortunate had been born for. He begins to enumerate this man's misfortunes as though they were a row of precious beads.

An explosion in the mines, a falling of stones and coal, a man pitching forward in the darkness, a stumbling foot, a prayer to God, and then a pick through the body—"You see," he gives the young man another turn, tapping him upon the stomach, "here is where the pick thrust its head out." He smiles, rubbing his hands. The young man turns again, a fixed look upon his face, neither pleasant or otherwise, a cool self-possessed stare, a little uncertain, perhaps, whether to be proud or sorry for the accident that has made him of interest to the gaping throng.¹⁰

These two passages could be read as evidence that between 1914 and 1917 a development, a deepening of the character of their author, took place. Such things happen in fiction, if not in the fiction that Barnes happens to have written. Actually, these two passages illustrate two perspectives she had mastered from the start: an objective and a subjective approach to reporting.

Barnes, who began her career writing front-page news items, always retained the ability to record the facts of a story with detachment and economy. Sent to the Bowery in 1917 by the *Telegraph* to dig out hidden pockets of grand opera, she noticed the poisonous colors of the cakes in an Italian bakery and wondered about their effect on the digestion—without losing sight of her reporter's obligation to tell how, when, and where the public could attend a performance of *Salome*.

Her best journalism is subjective, however. She had what Louis Kannenstine called "a gift for uncommon observation."¹¹ The facts that mattered to her were the marginal, concealed, but vital details that allowed her to respond to the atmosphere of an assignment, to what one might call its psychological environment. Her essay on the playwright John Millington Synge is "an atmospheric article on an atmosphere."[12] The introduction contains an important demurral: "I am not a critic; to me criticism is so often nothing more than the eye garrulously denouncing the shape of the peephole that gives access to hidden treasure." After this graceful hesitation, we are offered a selection of homely vignettes: the Irish playwright cooking a frugal meal of tea and eggs on a small stove, wandering alone in the windy dusk, playing the penny whistle for a few friends. Perhaps these are made-up "facts"—in any case, details no "critic" would find important. But they create the illusion of a presence, palpable and intense, that owed little of its effect to the historical facts, arranged in chronological order, around which her essay is discreetly constructed. Barnes has evoked an atmosphere of loneliness, detachment, and mystery. Most of the feature articles she wrote between 1913 and 1919 have a similar subjectivity.

Barnes' Synge is sad and a bit rumpled; in spite of his celluloid collar and his lyric genius, he resembles the tramps, barflies, and laid-off workers she sketched in the "Types Found in Odd Corners" series she did for the Brooklyn *Daily Eagle* in 1913. Above the high-flown caption "Because the Road He Took Was Wrong," a man in a rough cap and jacket sits in a chair with his face hidden in the crook of his arm (plate 4). Barnes gave the same posture of weary suffering to a young prostitute whom Nora encounters after she and Robin are separated (N, 157). Such outcasts of society are valuable, we are told, although "their good is incommunicable, outwitted, being the rudiment of a life that has developed, as in man's body are found evidences of lost needs" (N, 52). *Nightwood* is a gathering of the distressed, people she terms "*détraqués*"—O'Connor's "Tuppeny Upright," the boys and girls who hang around public toilets at night, the freak Mademoiselle Basquette, "built like a medieval abuse," and, above all, Dr. O'Connor himself. As a journalist, Barnes learned how to communicate the incommunicable good inherent in such people by studying the workers and actors she found on the margins of social "acceptability."

If much of Djuna Barnes' early newspaper work is "subjective journalism" rather than straight reportage, it was mainly because there was a demand for that work at which she, above others, excelled. She had, however, a reputation for reportorial energy and toughness, as well. "Djuna Barnes, the femme writer," Walter Winchell wrote in the late 1920s, "can hit a cuspidor twenty feet away." That particular talent belonged to someone else, but Barnes had earned the reputation. "Baby Face" Nelson and his girl friend gave her an interview at her Waverly Place apartment while nervous bodyguards patrolled the doors and windows. Once she climbed into an upstairs window to photograph the body of a murdered girl. She snapped the picture but failed to get an interview with the distraught father, who threw her out the first time she tried to enter the house. "This was the kind of thing that made me get out of the newspaper business," Barnes told a friend more than sixty years later. Between 1916 and 1918 her flow of articles diminished considerably. What ended her career as a news reporter (but not as a journalist) was her refusal to divulge to her editor the facts about a rape case she had investigated. He fired her on the spot.[13]

Barnes also earned her living by describing to a sedentary public how it felt to be a carefree young vamp, a comic or satiric persona she donned in the 1920s when she signed the pseudonym "Lydia Steptoe" to articles she wrote for *Vanity Fair, Charm,* and *Shadowland.* For a few years she gave it her all, until the role must have sickened her. Coming briefly out of deep seclusion in 1971 to give Henry Raymont of the New York *Times* an interview, she said: "Years ago I used to see people. I had to, I was a newspaperman, among other things. And I used to be rather the life of the party."[14] It is tempting to imagine a moment when, her bravado faltering, Barnes felt like the young man with the perforated stomach, "a little uncertain perhaps whether to be proud or sorry for the accident" that made her of interest to the throngs. But this is impertinent speculation. Her own terse words to Raymont will have to suffice: "I used to be invited by people who said, 'Get Djuna for dinner, she's amusing.' So I stopped it."

Barnes discovered fairly early that "subjective journalism" could be made to serve the needs of a personal and artistic, as well as a professional, integrity. The account of her experiment with force-feeding, which she wrote for the *World Magazine* in 1914, is graphically detailed, but it is not coolly detached (see plate 1). Her goal is to inspire the readers of the Sunday supplement with a sense of outrage on behalf of English suffragettes on a hunger strike. She writes: "If I, play-acting, felt my being burning with revolt at this brutal usurpation of my bodily functions, how they who actually suffered the ordeal in its acutest horror must have flamed at the violation of the sanctuaries of their spirit?"[15] "Empathy" has rarely been taken further by any writer.

For the average reader, the man who earned his living by displaying his perforated stomach in a sideshow would have seemed no more of a freak than the suffragette willing to risk having a tube forced into hers. What Barnes is looking for in her early pieces is a way to narrow the distance between the freakish unfortunates she encountered in "odd corners" of the city and the audience who "look[s] down upon these people as from the top of an abyss." One way is to enter the abyss herself. Thus she allowed the prison doctors and nurses to strap her to the infirmary table: "This," she thought quizzically as she looked up into their faces, "is one picture that will never go into the family album." Another way is to produce snapshots of the event that turned a human being, like ourselves, into a freak: "a stumbling foot, a prayer to God, and then a pick through the body." The world she introduces by these means is alien and threatening, but full of fascination. Unable to turn away, one experiences direct contact with the grotesque.

During the years she wrote for the daily papers, Barnes developed an eye for the diamond embedded in slug's meat. James Joyce, whom she met in Paris, told her, "A writer should never write about the extraordinary; that is for the journalist."[16] Fortunately, she was not that kind of journalist. Her extraordinary fact was almost always buried in the heart of the everyday, whether she was writing about the strange people she met in Greenwich Village and the Bowery, the circus acts at the Hippodrome, or the freak shows at Coney Island.

Nightwood is proof that Barnes absorbed, retained, and used what she had seen as a newspaper writer. The most obvious echo from her past is that collection of circus performers with suggestive names—the trapeze artist Frau Mann, for example, known onstage as "the Duchess of Broad-back"—whose presence on the novel's periphery caused some early re-viewers to label the book "a sideshow of freaks," to T.S. Eliot's dismay. Barnes would not have tried to duck the phrase. Frau Mann, after all, is "eccentric beyond the limits of belief unless you have seen her."

The word "freaks" appears nowhere in *Nightwood*. That Barnes would refrain from using the term marks a change in her attitude towards the use to which subjective journalism might be put. In some of her early work, she clearly itches to force the complacent to acknowledge their affinity with anomalous, marginal people. By the time she wrote *Night-wood*, the teacher had become an author without ceasing to be a humanist. Barnes herself would "never use the derogatory in the usual sense" (a "great virtue" she shared with Dr. O'Connor [N, 116–17]): she seems, rather, to have decided to trust her audience to summon up similar powers of discrimi-nation. "Freaks," to be sure, is a word that recoils upon the reader who would use it for the nonheterosexual characters in *Nightwood*. If some still do, that fact only proves that Barnes continues to bring milkshakes to bulldogs, even though the "milkshake" has turned to headier stuff.

¶ Dearest Courtenay:

Mary [Pyne] has been given up by 2 nurses, 2 doctors and a score of others at least 10 days back, but she still breathes. . . . I might be left alone with her in the last hours. . . . She is delirious but knows it is delirium while she is going through it, and she suffers a great deal — Yesterday she about killed me by trying to put her arms around me saying "You see the way it is with me" — and then "Can't you help me?" Of course the most terrible is that she has lived beyond her own death.

—Djuna Barnes,
letter to Courtenay Lemon,
on the stationery of the Hotel St. Regis,
Saranac Lake, New York (no date)

¶ . . . Djuna always felt some fundamental distrust of our life — of our talk. Her intense maternity covered the resentment for the first year or so.

You two poor things, she would say in her warm laughing voice. You're both crazy of course, God help you. I suppose I can stand it if you can, but someone ought to look out for you.

She looked out for us by bringing in the first strawberries of spring, the last oysters of winter, but to the more important luxuries of the soul she turned an unhearing ear. Djuna would never talk, she would never allow herself to be talked to. She said it was because she was reserved about herself. She wasn't, in fact, reserved — she was unenlightened. This led her into the construction of self-myths which she has never taken the pains to revise. Only this year she said to me in Paris:

Well, I like my inside much better than my outside, don't you?

Certainly not, I think your outside is often stunning and I think you don't know anything about your inside.

I may know nothing about it but it's very nice.

How can you know it's nice when you don't know what it's like?

There you go again. There's no talking with you.

For her there was always no talking with you. For us there was
no way of establishing a communication with her. It embarrassed her to
approach impersonal talk about the personal element. It embarrassed us
to accept a relationship with anyone who was not on speaking terms with
her own psyche. Her mind has no abstract facets. She is impatient of such
facets, suspicious of them.

—Margaret Anderson,
My Thirty Years' War (1930)

The Early Attic Stage of Djuna Barnes

Ann Larabee

The anarchistic Djuna Barnes, who for a time wrote for the Provincetown Playhouse, went beyond any of her contemporaries in her interrogation of theatrical form, finally questioning the whole notion of display and spectacle and her audience's implicit voyeurism. Barnes purposely presented "repulsive" women who resisted cultural indoctrination into heterosexual relationships and projected a dark wave of sensual violence. She thus disrupted the domestic drama, replacing the rebellious Noras with Theda Bara–like vampires — theatrical tricksters whose style was rebellion and self-parody.

Barnes' theatrical works preceding *The Antiphon*, written during her association with the Provincetown (1916–21), are uneven, but when she was good, she was very, very good, producing brilliantly subversive one-acts which foreshadowed her Rabelaisian epic novel, *Nightwood*. Her distinctly comic and anarchistic voice emerged in plays like *Three from the Earth*, *The Dove*, and *To the Dogs*, which were seemingly remote from anything written by her contemporaries. The Provincetown audiences found her works wonderfully bizarre, but could never understand what she was "driving at."[1]

The Provincetown Playhouse — which produced several important women writers and artists, including Susan Glaspell, Djuna Barnes, Edna St. Vincent Millay, and Marguerite Zorach, existed in an atmosphere of "sex antagonism" from its very inception in 1917. The tensions between progressive middle-class men and women, who were struggling with the boundaries which defined their separate spheres, surfaced everywhere in the writing of both sexes at the Provincetown, becoming the central conflict in their plays. These productions provided a "metacommentary" on the social drama which resulted from the defection of middle-class women from the domestic sphere and their demand for self-representation. While Provincetown playwright Eugene O'Neill retreated into a Melvillean world of men asea on the psychosexual voyages of the S.S. *Glencairn*, the Provincetown women explored ways of making the female voice a transgressive agent against even liberal, progressive definitions of gender. But monogamy and heterosexuality remained firm, if slightly renegotiated, behavioral standards.

Barnes did not share the Provincetown Players' overall fascination with restoring besieged monogamous heterosexual relationships by hardening them into dramatic form. If anything, she found "sex antagonism" amusing and worth preserving. She delighted in creating women who refused advances from men or who were involved in strange and extraordinary sexual relationships. In *An Irish Triangle*, Barnes' second play performed at the Provincetown Playhouse, Kathleen O'Rune allows her "good and generous" husband, John, to have an affair with the lady of the "Manor House" so that she herself can be educated in great literature and learn refined manners. Her conservative, disapproving friend Sheela asks, "Where would the like of the glory of Ireland and its women be, if they were all as strange as yourself?"[2] Kathleen replies: "Well, I'll be telling you where you'd be. You'd be sitting among the hedges like the elves or the Queen, and knowing so much that you would be afraid to open your mouth for fear of confounding the priests themselves, who do be knowing a word or two of Greek and Latin."[3] This access to knowledge, Kathleen suggests, will allow women to "outstrip" the men, and she herself will be "climbing the hill," for she has something to learn from the master of the manor which John cannot supply. Barnes thus undermines the philosophy of progressive Provincetown men, who believed that a "civilized," liberated woman made a good, monogamous sexual partner. The restriction of sexual relationships, Barnes suggests, is a way of controlling access to knowledge, language, and mobility.

In *Kurzy of the Sea*, Barnes further defines this new freedom and access to power with one of her first tricksters, an alleged mermaid hauled up in a net by an Irishman who wishes to marry her. The "mermaid" tricks the man into letting her go, then swims off laughing, revealing that she is human.[4] Carroll Smith-Rosenberg defines Barnes' trickster as a traditional literary character who "specifically embodies the disorder and the creative power we associate with liminality, a creature who exists to break taboos, violate categories, and defy structure."[5] Barnes' tricksters specifically disrupt gender rules and heterosexual relationships: in *The Dove*, three women, lesbians and virgins, psychologically and physically explore one another; a bastard son plants an incestuous kiss on his unwary mother in *Three from the Earth*; a woman prefers herself to her very masculine neighbor in *To the Dogs*. These characters mimic and mime romantic conventions, proving that socially defined roles have no real power over them. Unlike other Provincetown playwrights, Barnes does not make her odd characters tragic. They are not in need of therapy; they do not have a dramatic change of heart; no "cure" is suggested for their antisocial behavior. Barnes' characters are anarchistic, compelled by their own dramatic visions.

Barnes' creative response to the lively debate over anarchism among the liberal thinkers of her day echoed that of her friend Margaret Anderson, who wrote in 1916 that "art and anarchism are in the world for the same reason."[6] Anderson saw love, privileged by the artist, as the aspect of human behavior most threatening and subject to government control:

In love you will act just like a cave man or an Athenian or an early Christian or an Elizabethan or a modern, like a satyr or a traveling salesman or an artist—it depends on your type. Governments may come and go, may change or cease to be; and nothing remains except "your type." . . . But it's just here that your government has its functions. . . . If you think that love and freedom go together, the government can put you in prison.[7]

Djuna Barnes' "types," opaque and inviolable, are filled with a violent and resistant love that deconstructs civilization and its artifacts, including that instance of civilization, the theater. They are not altered by, but rather alter their prison, the stage, engaging the uncomfortable audience in a voyeuristic relationship.

The characters do not engage in expected courtship rituals, the social "cure" for difference. Rather, they expose the Freudian family romance, for, as Barnes wrote, she was writing "out of a certitude that I was my father's daughter."[8] Much of Barnes' drama is peopled with bloody, dead fathers, charade Madonnas, and child survivors of incest, especially in her plays written under the pseudonym Lydia Steptoe. In *She Tells Her Daughter*, published in 1923, Madame Deerfont relates tales of her past to her daughter, Ellen Louise Theresa. It is never quite clear whether Madame Deerfont is talking of her father or her lover, and her feelings for both of them are full of violence: "One night while I was lying in the hay, he came in. I could hear him breathing among the horses. I remember his breathing because it was so hurried among that big, slow breathing all about, and I sat up holding the knife so hard that the handle cut into my flesh."[9]

For an audience expecting the confirmation of their own value systems, which included preservation of monogamy and the family, such drama seemed unintelligible and mystifying. One reviewer wrote that *Three from the Earth*, which also contains a dead father and a bizarre discussion of family, "floats in a nebula of its own connotations, into which the audience tries to force a baffled entrance."[10] Barnes intentionally puts her audience at a great distance, just as her characters resist violation and control by others.

In *To the Dogs*, the fear of public control over private fantasy emerges in an exchange between Helena Hucksteppe and her frustrated suitor, Gheid Storm:

STORM: I've lain awake thinking of you—many nights.
HELENA: That is too bad.
STORM: What is too bad?

HELENA: That you have had—fancies.
STORM: Why?
HELENA: Theft of much, makes much to return—
STORM: The world allows a man his own thoughts.
HELENA: Oh, no.
STORM: At least my thoughts are my own.
HELENA: Not one, so far.
STORM: What does that mean?
HELENA: You'll know when you try to think them again. (*AB*, 54)

Gheid attempts to enact his fantasies (reduced to fancies by Helena) and rise to the "great moment of human contact" when Helena will divulge her secrets. But he represents not only a personal lust, but also a communal curiosity, for he has come to see if the town tales about the mythic Helena are true. But the unassailably stoic Helena, through her terse and guarded pronouncements, submits neither to the well-trimmed "man of property," Gheid Storm, nor to her equally prosperous audience. Although Helena represents the legendary Greek Helen, she resists both literary interpretation and Freudian psychological analysis based on myth interpretation. The face that launched a thousand ships remains as opaque and shallow as a statue's; Helena resists the attempts of her ardent Pygmalion to make her human. Storm resorts to romantic theatrical clichés ("No matter what you've been—done—I love you") but still gets no response. Helena, who strikes the same pose at both the beginning and end of the play—"back view to the audience, one arm lying on the mantel"—remains unrevealed; she is radically unchangeable.

Barnes once wrote that her plays were made "as a chalk line on the floor of a magician's home makes terror and expectation,—atmosphere and a dead line over which the general public could not go."[11] Behind that dead line, Barnes creates women's rooms decorated in colliding theatrical styles, decentering each other, a combination of the drawing room à la Pinero and cubist-inspired stylizations. Barnes spends a great deal of time textualizing her sets. In *Three from the Earth*, produced at the Provincetown in 1919, Kate Morley's boudour is a standard dramatic set pushed to extremes with many blue lacquered screens. This arrangement is further subverted when the curtain rises on three identical clowns, with wild ties, russet shoes, and purple asters in their buttonholes. *She Tells Her Daughter* takes place in Madame Deerfont's drawing room, which is also a funhouse of mirrors that reflect the set's many angles, just as a cubist painting attempts to render every surface of the subject. The women's apartment in *The Dove* is filled with weapons, disordering their "luxuriously sensual" red living space. These sets, overstatements of the social deviant's idiosyncratic world, are psychological projections run wild, freed from guilt and restraint.

The excesses of women's space begin to strain at theatrical limits when Barnes introduces dogs onto her sets. A dog lies across the threshold of the too perfectly domestic set of *To the Dogs*, and it must raise its head at a crucial moment in a gesture of maternal menace, warning Gheid not to advance. On the set of *Little Drops of Rain*, a "small, clipped spaniel runs around and around" in a clipped and passionless garden, just as the dialogue of two women moves in controlled circles.[12] To manage these animals on the stage, the director has few options. She might hire a trainer with a Pavlovian dog, which would take offstage commands. Or she might dress an actress as a dog, or use a puppet, or a wind-up toy dog. Or she might write the dog out altogether. In any case, Barnes introduces the dog as a symbol of her character's exiled dogginess, of an understanding which lies beyond language. The theatrical problems inherent in using animals theatrically become philosophically important: there is no such thing as true dogginess onstage, beyond the control of some master. The textualized or dramatized dog is no dog; the only true dog is an offstage dog, like Robin Vote in *Nightwood*. The uncontrollable longings of Barnes' performers to go to the dogs are continually frustrated by the theatrical apparatus.

Barnes began staging herself when she was one of the legions of dashing, devil-may-care girl reporters in New York City. In 1914, for instance, she engineered her own force-feeding for a story, establishing an anguished, physical connection with the suffragists. In the telling, the story became something more: the "impressionistic artist" was implicitly raped for a crowd of spectator doctors and readers: "Clamped in a sheet, the subject is held steady on the table while a physician examines her nose and throat with a speculum and electric lamp."[13] Before the stage lights of her examiners, Barnes had red tubing shoved down her numbed nostrils, swabbed with disinfectant and cocaine (see plate 1). "There was no progress on this pilgrimage," she wrote. "It was the futile defiance of nightmare."[14] A month later she staged another encounter between females when she entered the cage of Dinah the gorilla, a "wierd little forty-five-pound bunch of femininity."[15] The communication between these two strange beings, New Woman and gorilla—who clearly understood one another—takes place before a crowd who, Barnes writes, might as well have been a "row of cabbages." The red tubing of phallic menace is transformed into Dinah's "garden-hose" arms, hugging Djuna. The zoo keeper, Engeholme, "searching in vain for something that would symbolize Dinah's soul and personality," is ineffectual male authority. He is "Germany gaining on Africa with difficulty" in a slapstick race for possession of the girl and the gorilla. The two females empower one another, even in captivity, ignoring the crowd and eluding the keeper. Barnes' reaction to the spectacle of brutal rape was to create an environment in which she could laugh at her rapist, and this involved the establishment of a particularly female space.

The shift from news reports to drama was slight for Barnes, who had already begun her theatrical experiment. On the stage she continued to present not a sanctioned voice, but the bodies of the strange, the vision of

odd women who have rubber tubing thrust down their throats, their
consciousnesses invaded by a male eye. Within the idiosyncratic trappings of
the stage, china-doll women are broken to pieces, surprised to find in the
fragments their essential selves; charading Madonnas trade in their costumes; mothers peel back the layers of an invented past and are bared to the
bone: "VERA: Have you ever felt that your bones were utterly sophisticated
but that your flesh was keeping them from expressing themselves" (*AB*,
153). Some characters perform psychological stripteases, revealing all of the
dark secrets of their pasts in a violent world of knives, blunderbusses, sharp-
ended parasols, belt leather and boot straps. The only relationships possible
in such a world seem, at least from the outside, sadomasochistic, as when the
young and virginal Dove sinks her teeth into the flesh of Amelia, an old
maid.

But much of the violence in Barnes' plays is directed at fathers. In
Three from the Earth, the Corson brothers are discovered in the home of
Kate Morley, their father's mistress and perhaps their mother. A vaudevillian
comic thread slips through the action and dialogue. The oily brothers have
hair that stands straight up; Kate asks, "Ah yes, your father—he was a
barber, wasn't he?" They answer, "No, a chemist." To these three brothers,
who pose like the speak-no-evil, hear-no-evil, see-no-evil monkeys, Kate
addresses an absurd question, "Social?" They answer, "You might call it
that" (*AB*, 18). Between Kate and her bastard sons pass the father's letters,
bound in red ribbon. Their meeting hinges on his words, the sacred text of
his letters, but his authority and the emotional tyranny of his suicide are
shriveled with a dog's bark and a laugh. The powerful father has been
"played out," leaving nothing but his three sons, "three columns of flesh,"
as a stupifying monument to his memory.

The urge to kill the incestuous, bigamous father, to slip the blade into
the lover, is celebrated and explicit in Barnes' plays. Helena says, "I do not
enjoy the spectacle of men ascending." But the father is never a ponderous,
heavy ghost; he is included to satisfy some outrageous aesthetic sense with
his crumpled body. In *She Tells Her Daughter*, Madame Deerfont relates her
story of patricide to her daughter, Ellen Louise Theresa, in order to establish
a "bond of fundamentals":

MADAME DEERFONT: I want you to know me, not as I appear to the audience or
        those who accept the hospitality of my home, but as I am, dark, obscure,
        terrible—
ELLEN LOUISE THERESA: Mother, do behave! What is so dreadful in the fact that you
        are an actress and smoke cigarettes?[16]

Although Madame Deerfont's tale is a horrifying one, filled with dreamlike
scenes of sex and violence in which she acts out her feelings about men, it is
ultimately received as light entertainment to while away an aristocratic

ennui. Ellen Louise Theresa never gets the point: "Well, you see, I did know all about it, all but a few details; Brooklyn, and all that sort of thing."[17]

With the death of the father and his textual control comes freedom, for the women of Barnes' plays are thus no longer owned and are able to project themselves creatively:

AMELIA: I'm in an excellent humour—I could talk for hours, all about myself—to myself, for myself. God! I'd like to tear out all the wires in the house! Destroy all the tunnels in the city, leave nothing underground or hidden or useful, oh, God, God! (*She has danced until she comes directly in front of* THE DOVE. *She drops on her knees and lays her arm on either side of* THE DOVE.) I hate the chimneys on the houses, I hate the doorways, I hate you, I hate Vera, but most of all I hate my red heels. (*AB*, 162)

In the hysterical Amelia of *The Dove*, creativity, rage, and freedom are distilled into vital expression. She is the most animated player, and hate is her celebratory driving force. She dances like a Kali, bringing down the house and projecting a destructive energy into the world. The bourgeois house—the Gothic estate built on secrecy and suppression—is gutted, replaced with a personal, statuesque form of two women touching.

This play, about three women in love, is concerned with the rejection of prior models of female being, and the wild and expectant dance of continual self-creation is characterized by anguish. Vera and Amelia, two spinsters, have constructed themselves out of dirty French jokes, pictures of bathing girls and whores, chiffon and lace, Italian street songs, and an arsenal of weapons. They live with the young Dove, as "delicate as china with almost dangerously transparent skin" (*AB*, 148). The Dove is the most violent, vampirishly sinking her teeth into Amelia's neck and putting a bullet through Amelia's picture of Venetian courtesans.

The apartment in *The Dove* is decorated with an assortment of firearms, swords, and pistols, like the women's bohemian apartment in Rachel Crother's feminist play *A Man's World* (1909), which is adorned with "curious daggers, foils, Indian weapons, etc."[18] Crothers, whom Barnes once interviewed, creates an undercurrent of violence with this set imagery, enhanced by a child, Kiddie, who keeps opening and closing a pocketknife. But this violence is hidden beneath the mannered dialogue and careful plot of the play. In *The Dove*, Barnes exposes and celebrates the violence of latent feminism in a way unimagined by anyone else, as her women freely project themselves through the agency of violence:

VERA: Yes, yes, once I dreamed. A dream in the day, with my eyes wide open. I dreamt I was a Dresden doll and that I had been blown by the wind and that I broke all to pieces—but that I was surprised to find that my china skirt had become flexible, as if it were made of chiffon and lace. (*AB*, 153)

The destruction of artifacts, including the carefully created artifact of the public self, is a liberating drama of disintegration, providing a new ground for self-creation.

¶ . . . as it [*A Hasty Bunch*] was finished a flock of "expatriates" descended upon the Rue Jacob, Sts. Peres, St. Germain section. They were Kate Buss, critic for some Boston paper, Djuna Barnes, the *Broom* outfit—Alfred Kreymborg, Harold Loeb, Frances Midner, late of the Washington Square Bookshop, and Kreymborg's wife, Dorothy. They all stayed in the same hotel, and Vicki Baum's *Grand Hotel* couldn't touch the drama and intrigue which occurred in that hotel. . . . Djuna was a very haughty lady, quick on the uptake, and with a wisecracking tongue that I was far too discreet to try and rival. It seemed, however, that once I had written a letter to the *Little Review*, asking how came it that Miss Barnes was both so Russian and so Synge-Irish. Some comment in the letter Jane Heap apparently used frequently to cow Djuna, and Jane kept assuring her that McAlmon was not taken in by her cape-throwing gesture but understood her for the sentimentalist which she was. In the end Djuna had gathered the idea that I disliked her, and that I was a very sarcastic individual. She was wrong about the first idea at least, for Djuna is far too good-looking and witty not to command fondness and admiration from me, even when she is rather overdoing the grande dame manner and talking soul and ideals. In conversation she is often great with her comedy, but in writing she appears to believe she must inject metaphysics, mysticism, and her own strange version of a "literary" quality into her work. In her *Nightwood* she has a well-known character floundering in the torments of soul-probing and fake philosophies, and he just shouldn't. The actual person doubtlessly suffers enough without having added to his character this unbelievable dipping into the deeper meanings. Drawn as a wildly ribald and often broadly funny comic he would emerge more impressively.

—Robert McAlmon and Kay Boyle,
Being Genuises Together, 1920–1930 (1968)

One Acts:
Early Plays of Djuna Barnes

Joan Retallack

One acts, or more often one restrains oneself, according to inner stirrings and cautions not entirely understood. The strain shows in the best-known photograph of the young "authoress" as she turns with wounded equine pride at a ninety-degree angle from the overly inquisitive camera (see plate 35). There has already been a long struggle with premature bitterness, legacy of one of those impossible family situations which ejects children ill-prepared for anything beyond the taut circumference of its consuming melodrama. What energy is left after the insatiable needs and pretensions of the parents have been catered to is contaminated by rage.

The young Djuna Barnes displays a cool exterior to the world, a closed surface lacquered to a finish alarmingly hard for one still in her twenties. In the one-act plays written during this period (roughly 1917–23) rage is quite often transmuted into scorn, presuming and maintaining unbridgeable distances—scorn mainly for men, on the part of women as impenetrably sophisticated as the brittle author must have wanted to be, and as vulnerable as she must in fact have been. One such character, Helena Hucksteppe in *To the Dogs* says to Gheid Storm, the beleaguered suitor who admits he's been searching in vain for a point of contact, a weak spot: "—Spot? . . . *All* of me is vulnerable" (*AB*, 54).

Helena is a disappointing construction, a silhouette—as are all of Barnes' "characters"—flat black with sharp edges. One might see Helena as Miss Julie in search of Hedda Gabler, an angry woman who craves mastery. But we know nothing really of her cravings or her obsessions. We know only her evasive, pseudoprofound speech which is delivered in the form of throwaway one-liners: "Any man may accomplish anything he's capable of (*AB*, 48); "I began beyond bitterness" (*AB*, 48); "I limit no man, feel what you can" (*AB*, 51); "A magnet does not attract shavings" (*AB*, 52); "Only those who have helped to make such death as mine may go a little way toward the ardours of that decay" (*AB*, 55–56). That her character does not develop is not problematic in the world of the modern theater. The problem is that there is no cumulative power in the language, no increasingly charged field in the encounter between this Woman and this Man (the entire "action" of the play)—both candidates for an index of types at central casting.

Nothing really happens between Helena Hucksteppe and Gheid Storm. Her vulnerability is too great to permit variation in distance or level of control. His innocence leaves him chronically abashed and open to her unmitigated scorn. The reader's perspective is not altered as it is in, say, a Beckett piece in which "nothing happens." The play seems to be symbolically guarded from development by Helena's sentinel posture at the opening curtain when she is found "stand[ing] almost back view to the audience, one arm lying along the mantel" (*AB*, 45); and at the end when she "takes her old position, her back almost square to the audience" (*AB*, 58). Not even the "almosts" change; there is not the variation of Spanish exclamation marks. Yes, one actually longs for her to stand on her head at one end or the other; to relieve the grim brackets of a stasis in which playwright and characters are trapped—a dreadful limbo between obsessively polished surfaces and violent interiors. We know (from sources other than the play itself) that behavior such as Helena's is masking a terrible fury.

The static surface orientation is so consistent in all these early plays that their endings signal not resolution or denouement but the lacquer having lost its luster. ("STORM: You look tired. HELENA: Yes, I am tired" [*AB*, 58].) Tired, or crazed, or cracked—a repugnant fissure opens, from which we must avert our eyes. The "familiar" step of a long-awaited son turns out to be that of a donkey in *At the Roots of the Stars*. The sophisticate Kate Morley in *Three from the Earth* may be the mother of the strangely sensitive "bumpkins" who comes to visit. The *haute bourgeois* Madame Deerfont in *She Tells Her Daughter* is neither so *haute* nor so *bourgeois* as she at first appears; she may have murdered a lover (with whom she enjoyed smelling carriage varnishes) when she was eighteen. We are generally not taken beyond "may be" or "may have."

Barnes is condemned to surfaces, and that's where her brilliance lies—in description. Beyond description there is a mine field. Narrative must go somewhere, must advance into a future which, in her view, is doomed. The fatalism is too great to trust the sweep of events through time, so they become the narrow forced march of mechanical repartee. The past, as we learn in *Nightwood*, is all that is benign because it is finished. Things can't get any worse. Felix wants a child who will safeguard the past, but the futurity of birth destroys the plan. The child is doomed from the moment of its conception in Felix's mind. Similarly, drama involves a very real gestation—at the very least a passage through the elapsed time of the play. This minimal time frame is the only one Barnes permits herself, and it seems close to insupportable. Her characters hold each other and time itself at bay with

stalemates and diversionary epigrams—not quite non sequiturs, but close—
that neither advance the action nor contribute to their understanding of one
another: "I—I don't know you" (*AB*, 56); "You are either quite an idiot, or a
saint" (*AB*, 157); "You are strange things" (*AB*, 26).

The plays begin and end with the characters locked and isolated in
little mysteries that fail to fascinate us. This is because they are, like the past,
"finished" before the drama begins. Vera, one of three women in *The Dove*,
wonders aloud to the character called "The Dove," "why don't you do
something?" The Dove replies, "A person who is capable of anything needs
no practice" (*AB*, 155). The protective covering is one of omnipotence and
absolute self-sufficiency. There is no need for growth or for the exchange
with the outside world which leads to transformation. This is true of all of
Barnes' heroines. Their action, like God's, is at worst, superfluous; at best,
gratuitous. They are simply revealing or concealing what they already are.

In *Three from the Earth* we discover things not immediately apparent
about the "bumpkins" who come to ask Kate Morley for love letters their
father had sent her years before, but the encounter has a pro forma air about
it. Kate hands the letters over; she changes her mind and requests their
return within less than ten minutes without the hint of a struggle. This is
what the lines say she is to do. She is under orders from her superior, the
playwright. Somehow Barnes never manages that charged fusion of language and circumstance and motivation, however obscure, that seems to
emanate from the characters themselves. She is reluctant to surrender the
locus of control, perhaps in fear of what forces might be released.

The intimacy required by sustained dialogue without intervention of a
mediating author is frightening. It is usually avoided. A good deal of the
"dialogue" in these plays is more accurately monologue in the presence of
another. Direct confrontation has undercurrents of brutality (it seems the
"family romance" won't stop) which in *The Dove* erupts in a surprising way:

AMELIA: I'm in an excellent humour—I could talk for hours, all about myself—to
    myself, for myself. God! I'd like to tear out all the wires in the house!
    Destroy all the tunnels in the city, leave nothing underground or hidden or
    useful, oh, God, God! (*She has danced until she comes directly in front of*
    THE DOVE. *She drops on her knees and lays her arms on either side of* THE
    DOVE.) I hate the chimneys on the houses, I hate the doorways, I hate you, I
    hate Vera, but most of all I hate my red heels!
THE DOVE: (*Almost inaudibly.*) Now, now!
AMELIA: (*In high excitement.*) Give me the sword! It has been sharpened long
    enough, give it to me, give it to me! (*She makes a blind effort to find the
    sword; finding* THE DOVE'S *hand instead, she clutches it convulsively.
    Slowly* THE DOVE *bares Amelia's left shoulder and breast, and leaning
    down, sets her teeth in.*) (*AB*, 162–63)

This is what can happen when the surface cracks. Things get out of hand, out of proportion—more than can be accommodated by the scale of the one-act play. Later Barnes will attempt to contain this kind of fury between mother and daughter figures in the Shakespearean/Jacobean rhythms and knotty archaicisms of *The Antiphon*, a more than full-length drama.

There are no ominous undercurrents in the mock-Irish plays Djuna Barnes wrote during this period under the influence of Synge. In *Maggie of the Saints, An Irish Triangle,* and *Kurzy of the Sea* a kind of mellow sentimentality is indulged. Distance is insured by the blarneyness of it all:

KATHLEEN: And how are you this fine day, Shiela, and the winter scarcely over and the spring coming?
SHIELA: It's grand, fine I am, and glad to see yourself my eyes have not been clapped on since last October, and me watching your man going down into the woods quiet like, and it the poaching season.[1]

In *Kurzy of the Sea* where a father has attempted to trick his son into believing a local barmaid is actually a tailless mermaid—a miracle thrown up by the sea on his behalf—the confrontation between father and son after the truth has been discovered peaks emotionally when the parents utter sotto voce, "The prayers of the saints," and cross themselves. The (for Barnes) artificial language and literal displacement to small Irish villages (as far as I know she had not been to Ireland) seem to liberate her from the personal agon lurking so painfully in plays like *To the Dogs, The Dove,* and *Three from the Earth*, but these Irish effects don't work, either in literary or theatrical terms. These quaint dramas are the geographical and linguistic equivalent of period pieces—embarrassing imitations. One can imagine Barnes attracted to the exotic nature of Synge's language, characters, and settings as she was attracted only a few years later to Paris, seeking some sort of refuge from her demons in the initial anonymity, the promise of a fresh start that is the condition of the expatriate.

Barnes luxuriates in a language that is most her own in the descriptive passages which identify characters and in the interiors at the beginnings of plays. She seems often to have expended herself just at the point when the "drama" begins. The description of Gheid Storm which precedes the dialogue in *To the Dogs* is far more interesting than anything he says or does thereafter:

He is . . . a well-to-do man of property, brought up very carefully by upright women, the son of a conscientious physician, the kind of man who commutes with an almost religious fervour, and who keeps his wife and his lawns in the best possible trim, without any particular pleasure. . . . He walks deliberately, getting all the use possible out of his boot-leather, his belt-strap and hat-bands. His face is one of those, which for fear of misuse, has not been used at all. (*AB,* 45)

Of Helena's house in Cornwall-on-Hudson, Barnes writes, "there is perhaps

just a little too much of a certain kind of frail beauty of object" (AB, 44–45).
The undernourished artifice of the conversation between Helena and Gheid
Storm (whom she once kissed, pathetically, fallaciously when "a storm was
coming up") is anticlimactic to the rich suggestiveness of these passages.

This is true also of the perfunctory comedy which follows a playful
setting of the scene in the "Ten-Minute Play," *The Beauty*—one of a number
of short-short plays which appeared in magazines such as *Shadowland*,
Parisienne, and *Vanity Fair*:

The boudoir of Katrina Malevolitch. It is spacious and luxurious, enflamed by
highly colored cushions and dangerous-looking ikons, in front of which burn
candles with steady red flames. A jeweled samovar stands beside a couch. . . . Prince
Ivan Volovain is in the room. He is strapped into as many military garments as
possible, and he walks up and down rapidly, dragging a sword behind him. As he
walks he twirls, with sensitive and nervous fingers, a moustache no less sensitive
and nervous.[2]

There is a density of texture here which the plays themselves fail to achieve.
One wants the lush power of this surface brilliance to continue: "The
interior of a handsomely decorated drawing-room. It is paneled in brocaded
heron-blue satin. Twisted glass and candlesticks throw a shower of sparks
into the cool surfaces of many mirrors. . . . The studied odor of tiger lilies
pervades the air."[3] It is certain we learn more about Madame Deerfont, and
are more seduced by the momentum of the language, than we are about to be
as we become privy to the "near-confession" which begins and ends in stiff,
enervated dialogue:

MADAME DEERFONT: My dear, you have reached maturity. It is time that I should
    talk to you seriously.
ELLEN LOUISE THERESA: But I know all about it mother. . . . You were born in
    England, you fell in love with a fellow named Percy. . . .
MADAME DEERFONT: . . . I want you to know me, not as I appear to the audience or
    those who accept the hospitality of my home, but as I am, dark, obscure,
    terrible—[4]

The formal ambivalence that shows up in these disjunctions between
prose that is fecund and alive and dialogue that is typically moribund is most
obvious in the many stage directions which sabotage the form itself since
they are impossible to execute on the stage. They follow the logic of
description, which for Barnes is most compelling, rather than the logic of the
theater. The odor of tiger lilies, for instance, is hardly a feasible effect. In
The Beauty we are told, "A smoking cigaret butt in an ash-tray at the foot of
this couch, proclaims the recent presence of the mistress."[5] Of course, it
proclaims no such thing on stage. What it does tell us is that the writer is
reluctant to retire to the wings. She would like to continue as omnipotent
author—moderating, mitigating, titrating, measuring, and controlling—

filtering her passion through a style more subtly evocative than the stripped-down dialogue which is about to interrupt her pungent observations.

The surface is the true object of desire—to linger there, exploring its baroque intricacies while avoiding inevitabilities, catastrophes associated with forays which bring on the future tense. Better to stop it with the chemistry of language before the negative gets overdeveloped, to arrest the scene in just the right light:

Early in 1880, in spite of a well-founded suspicion as to the advisability of perpetuating that race which has the sanction of the Lord and the disapproval of the people, Hedvig Volkbein—a Viennese woman of great strength and military beauty, lying upon a canopied bed of a rich spectacular crimson, the valance stamped with the bifurcated wings of the House of Hapsburg, the feather coverlet an envelope of satin on which, in massive and tarnished gold threads, stood the Volkbein arms— gave birth, at the age of forty-five, to an only child, a son, seven days after her physician predicted that she would be taken. (N, 1)

This is, of course, the opening of *Nightwood*, where the descriptive act we identify as Barnes' is strangely predatory, generative, even orgiastic, emanating as it does out of the mind of a raging voluptuary-cum-metaphysician. There is room and distance for all of it in the novel—the contradictions, the gentle brutalities, the gruff sensitivies; love, hate; elegance, squalor. There is expanse enough for linguistic play that can balance contraries in delicious tension, an expansiveness which, oddly enough, eludes Barnes in the kind of play that is the drama. Her dramatis personae, deprived of the sheltering interstices, the heat and energy of her descriptive language, are standard—for all the attention to decor—on an empty stage with more to say to one another than is tolerable. In their exposed and undernourished state they are dead serious, unable to sport and feint in eloquent patterns of obliquity and silence.

It might be questioned whether Barnes was simply incompetent as a playwright, unaware of the particular exigencies of the form. But the problem is more interesting than that. She botched it despite the fact that she was, prior to and during the time of her brief one-act career, quite extensively involved with the Provincetown Players (and to a lesser extent with the Washington Square Players and the Theatre Guild), having performed in some minor roles and written numerous newspaper reviews demonstrating appropriate attention to theatrical effect. She was, moreover, an ardent fan of Synge and Strindberg and generally in touch with the contemporary theater, as well as a personal friend of Eugene O'Neill. In the 1919–20 season, Barnes' *Three from the Earth* and O'Neill's *The Dreamy Kid* shared a bill at the Provincetown Playhouse. *Kurzy of the Sea* and *Irish Triangle* were also produced that season.

Barnes has, obviously and really not so oddly, resisted the medium with its treacherous flow of events through time—the undeniable instrument of doom. (Undeniable, that is, to a consummate pessimist such as she is.) Her most frequent device for quelling anxiety is a cachectic irony entirely too close to the bone to enlarge or enrich perspective, much less to slow down or divert the insistence of time. Barnes' characters are declining into a terminal literalness (an incapacity for playfulness) devoid of lively figuration and, thus, the possibility of transfiguration. Without epicycles and erotics of linguistic play, they confirm her (and our) worst fears: they are speeding on a monorail along the shortest distance between two points—birth and death. As in all failed art, what should have been a divertimento becomes a memento mori.

A compatriot in pessimism, Samuel Beckett, suffering from many of the same misgivings, reinvented the dramatic medium. Djuna Barnes chose instead to move on and transform the novel. When she returned to dramatic form almost forty years later in *The Antiphon*, it was with the heavy machinery of a dense poetic style. It would be a disservice, even in the present atmosphere of redressing undeserved neglect, to count the early plays among her best works. In exploring the one-act no further, she herself was probably aware that it had been a misalliance.

¶ Please do not think of it—I was not offended in the least to be thought lesbian—it's simply that I'm very reticent about my personal life. . . .

> —Djuna Barnes,
> letter to Ottoline Morrell,
> 12 November 1936 (Harry Ransom
> Humanities Research Center,
> University of Texas at Austin)

¶ The only time I was a doormat was to Thelma, and then I was a damned good doormat.

> —Djuna Barnes,
> letter to Emily Coleman,
> 4 February 1939

¶ darling, should have sent the photographs earlier, but anything to do with us bothers me, the pain is so unequal that i just naturally avoid it when possible, its been so long a time too its too much. i have kept the pictures i love and that belong to me alone.

i have a trembly right hand so the typing, no hangover havent had a drink about ten years—spring is here but as rachel carson said it is silent, the people have taken everything.

i love you as always.

> —Thelma Wood,
> Fan Hill Road,
> Monroe, Connecticut,
> letter to Djuna Barnes,
> 14 April 1969

Writing toward <u>Nightwood</u>:
Djuna Barnes' Seduction Stories

Carolyn Allen

Djuna Barnes' status as a lesbian culture hero has shifted dramatically over the last decade. In 1973 Bertha Harris lovingly celebrated Barnes and her Paris circle as models for Harris' own life as a lesbian; in 1984 Tee Corinne characterized Barnes as homophobic.[1] There is, of course, evidence for both positions. Barnes herself said she was not a lesbian, that she "just loved Thelma,"[2] and as she grew older and more isolated, she had a low tolerance for her female admirers.[3] Nevertheless, Harris is right to honor her as a representative of "practically the only available expressions of lesbian culture we have in the modern western world" since Sappho.[4] Even though Barnes' denial of her lesbianism, reinforced as it was by a homophobic dominant culture and a new literature of sexology,[5] emerges in what little biographical information we now have, *Nightwood* and *Ladies Almanack* remain classics of lesbian imagination. I will argue further that three of her stories, linked by the "little girl" who narrates them, also belong to that imaginative tradition.

While *Nightwood* may be what Catharine Stimpson calls a lesbian narrative of damnation,[6] it portrays in Robin and Nora's relationship currents of lesbian sexuality still being debated in recent feminist work. Both its references to mother-daughter dynamics and its mixing of "pleasure and danger" anticipate recent discussion.[7] In less overt but equally powerful ways, Barnes' "little girl" stories have in their textual shadows these same configurations. These stories—called "little girl" stories because of the original titles of two, "A Little Girl Tells a Story to a Lady" and "The Little Girl Continues"—culminate in a third that is a direct precursor to *Nightwood*, "Dusie." All three interrogate gender identity and homosexuality. In my reading of them I look to shadows rather than to surfaces, and I read in the context of recent work on "difference," work which provides the light necessary for the play of these shadows.

The history of feminism's "second wave" is in part a history of the shifting value placed on difference. Beginning with a realization that the stress on difference between men and women has resulted in unequal separate spheres, feminist thinkers moved first against sexual difference toward a stress on abilities and talents shared by women and men. In the 1970s the tenets of liberal feminism came under attack by radical feminists who celebrated woman as different from — and superior to — men. Recently many feminists have argued from a position that stresses differences among women, in recognition of the danger inherent in obliterating factors of race and class in discussions of oppression.[8]

Alongside this feminist dialogue on difference and oppression developed another on difference and repression,[9] growing primarily out of Freudian and neo-Freudian psychoanalysis and centered on the oedipal/castration crisis in the formation of sexuality. In this novel, especially as it is reformulated by Lacan reading back through Lévi-Strauss and Saussure, woman is Other, lack, the means by which man knows what he is. French feminist scholars have criticized this theory because it does not permit woman to have difference of her own, to occupy anything more than a negative space. A growing number of feminists revising these models are focusing on possibilities for investigating the preoedipal, and thus the role of the mother rather than the father. In different revisionist ways, French psychoanalysts Julia Kristeva and Luce Irigaray both make the mother prominent in their work, though both still write with the father of psychoanalysis and his son, Lacan, looming over them.[10] Others acknowledge directly that the model is simply inadequate for understanding the construction of the female subject. In her reinterpretation of object-relations theory, American sociologist Nancy Chodorow argues further that the stress on sexual difference by male psychoanalysts demonstrates their own male need to remain as differentiated as possible from the feminine in light of the problematics of separation from the mother as first caretaker.[11]

Both *Nightwood* and the "little girl" stories explode the binary structure underlying Western thought from Plato forward that recent feminist theorists like Irigaray and Chodorow so radically question. By refusing the categories male and female, by shifting terms of sexual difference, Barnes' texts become radical examinations of dichotomous difference. By refusing to take maleness and the phallus as the norm, by questioning the construction of gender and the nature of sexuality, they rupture the surface of convention and illuminate the world of night. While Barnes may have denied her lesbian relationships, her texts question the dichotomous presence of sameness and difference in their presentation of lesbian sexuality.

Nightwood's seventh chapter, "Go Down Matthew," contains the novel's most extended discussion of gender and sexuality. Together Nora and Matthew give us a portrait of the invert, the third sex. In that portrait we recognize the boy in the girl, the girl in the Prince; not a mixing of gendered behaviors, but the creation of a new gender, "neither one and half the other" (N, 136). A woman loving someone of the third sex loves her as herself and her child. It is clear throughout the chapter that both these dynamics are at work in Nora's relation to Robin. Thus the Lacanian insistence on sexual difference is overturned here in favor of likeness: "she is myself" (N, 127). Here there is no Other; there is only oneself: "A man is another person—a woman is yourself caught as you turn in panic; on her mouth you kiss your own" (N, 143). The lover is not only like the self; she is the self.

But the chapter takes up difference as well. A man lies bejeweled in a velvet-lined box staring into a mirror to contemplate his own difference. Here he sees not a recognition of himself as differentiated subject, but himself as like the figure in the mirror and unlike the rest of the world. He celebrates his nonconformity. As such he resembles Matthew, Nora, and Robin, whose sexuality is "an honorific reappropriation of sexual difference."[12] That is, in their love of the same sex, they, like the man in the box, admire their nonconformity, their sexual difference from the rest of the world. Barnes is particularly clear about this difference in *Ladies Almanack*:

This is the part about Heaven that has never been told. After the fall of Satan . . . all the Angels . . . gathered together, so close that they were not recognizable, one from the other. And not nine Months later, there was heard under the Dome of Heaven a great Crowing, and from the Midst, an Egg, as incredible as a thing forgotten, fell to the Earth, and striking, split and hatched, and from out of it stepped one saying, "Pardon me, I must be going!" and this was the first Woman born with a Difference.

After this the Angels parted, and on the Face of each was the Mother look. (*LA*, 26)

The angels merge and give birth to the woman with a difference, the lesbian whose manners and mores as seen in the Natalie Barney circle are the subject of the book's fond wit.

So, although Robin and Nora are alike because they are both women, they are also lesbians, women with a Difference. And even in their likeness, they are different people, a differentiation marked especially in the text's casting of Nora as mother, Robin as child. Here is the second dynamic in *Nightwood*'s lesbian relationships—one's lover is not only one's self but also one's child: "Robin is incest too" (N, 156), a girl-child dressed as a boy who plays with toy trains and soldiers. The lovers' relationship is infused with an imbalance of power of mother to child righted when Robin the lover expresses her adult autonomy by leaving Nora to sleep with other women. At the same time the mother-child relationship is shot through with eroticism since mother and child are also lovers. As lovers they cannot conceive, so they share a doll to mark their union. Here is another turn on sameness and difference, for the doll resembles the child, yet is not alive: "The doll and the immature have something right about them, the doll because it resembles but does not contain life, and the third sex because it contains life but resembles the doll" (*N*, 148). Robin is like the doll, but different from it, just as Nora is like Robin, but different from her, just as Matthew, Nora, and Robin are like each other in their sexuality, but different from the world at large.

Neither of these currents is startlingly new in lesbian fiction; Barnes' French contemporary Colette, for example, also focused on the mother-daughter dynamics in lesbianism. Nor is either unexplored by psychoanalysis. Recent work, however, leaves aside nineteenth-century sexology's emphasis on sickness to celebrate the same kind of ambiguities that emerge in Barnes' novel. This recent work directly or indirectly attacks the phallocentric insistence on sexual difference and opens the way for alternative theorizing.

Luce Irigaray's two companion essays, "Quand nos levres se parlent" ("When Our Lips Speak Together") and "Et l'une ne bouge pas sans l'autre" ("And the One Doesn't Stir without the Other"), both rupture the Lacanian model of sexual difference and provide a text against which to read Barnes' "little girl" stories.[13] The first essay is, among other things, a dialogue between two women lovers who acknowledge their likeness ("When you say I love you . . . you also say I love myself").[14] What earlier psychoanalysts dismiss as narcissism becomes self-affirming because it is not an embrace of sameness and closure, which Irigaray identifies with maleness, but a lyric of multiplicity. Like Barnes' texts, Irigaray's undermines what she calls the "currency of alternatives and oppositions." She writes in the shadow of Lacan and, without naming him, disputes his view of sexual difference that negates woman.

The second essay, as its translator notes, echoes the first in its continuing meditation on woman-to-woman relationships, now shifted from lovers to mother and daughter. The daughter speaks to the mother from her undifferentiated state (in male psychoanalytic terms, the preoedipal): "I would like us to play together at being the same and different. You/I echoing endlessly and each staying herself." Here as in the earlier essay, the question of sameness and difference has parameters quite removed from standard models that pass over the preoedipal to concentrate on the role of the Father in the construction of sexual difference. It allows for difference in the context of resemblance, just as lesbian discourse does. Irigaray's essay fills a descriptive gap in male theory, then deliberates on the damage done when the woman is "trapped in a single function—mothering."[15] She both stresses the complexities and the sensuality of the mother-daughter connection and acknowledges the limiting dichotomy, mother-woman, in the referential world.

Chodorow also ruptures the Freudian/Lacanian insistence on the primacy of the father's role in structuring female sexuality. Unlike Irigaray, however, she is less interested in reformulating difference than in delineating differentiation. She connects difference with a model that reduces the mother to the "not-me," thus obliterating her as a subject. She stresses instead the process of the daughter's struggle to differentiate herself from the mother, the fluidity rather than the fixity of gender difference, and the potential slippage in heterosexual orientation for women because of their bonds with the mother.

Beneath the surface of their conventional prose, the three "little girl" stories anticipate a number of these contemporary feminist currents. The stories are held together not only by their common narrator, but also by the common interrogation of gender and sexuality that shadows the text. In all three stories a young woman tells a story to a lady. The narratives themselves are stories of one kind of seduction or another, seductions that have one younger and one older participant. The stories about seduction imprint on the narrative situation a forbidden atmosphere—the seduction of female by female, by older or younger, with incest shadowing the shadows. The narrator herself has the absolute autonomy usually reserved for men. She travels all over Europe, alone or with her sister; she decides how long she will stay, how she will live, when she wants to leave one place and move on to another. We know less about the auditor, the mysterious "Madame." But the narrator wants her to listen. "*Nicht wahr*," she says; "*n'est-ce pas*," "is it not so?" always seeking confirmation, looking for assent. Even in the midst of the stories themselves, the narrator intrudes with direct addresses or little asides to her listener so that we never forget she is a "little girl" telling her stories to "a lady": "Then this last autumn, before the last winter set in (you were not here then, Madame)," or "Sometimes it is beautiful in Berlin, Madame, *nicht wahr*?"[16] Of course the narrator is not a little girl at all, but a precocious young woman who implicates herself and her sexuality even as she seems with innocent nonchalance to be recounting some other woman's story to the presumably attentive "Madame." Her three stories, increasingly overt in their sexual content, are themselves a fictional seduction of the older "Madame" by the younger narrator, Katya.

In "Cassation" a mysterious older woman tries to convince Katya to come and live with her and take care of her child. Literally, that is—sexually, it is not a seduction story, yet there hangs over it an atmosphere of eroticism not unlike that of *Nightwood*. Originally titled "A Little Girl Tells a Story to a Lady" and first published in 1925, the story was revised and retitled "Cassation" for *Spillway*. The new title, come upon long after Barnes' Paris days and her denial of her own involvement with women, stresses what is now the standard reading of all the *Spillway* stories: the fascination with the void, with negativity, with the abyss at the heart of the world. Such a reading also connects "Cassation" to *Nightwood*, but it misses the radical nature of the text's questioning of conventional gender difference and sexuality. As usual in Barnes' fiction, plot is a minimal pretext. Several times Katya sees a mysterious and dramatic woman in a café; one day they are drawn together, and the woman invites the girl home. After they have lived together for a year, the woman, Gaya, asks Katya to stay forever to care for her mentally vacant child. Katya refuses, leaves, returns to say good-bye, and finds Gaya in bed with the child, both making the same wordless sound of vacancy.

The plot operates in a world of unconventionally marked gender and sexual likeness. The only man in the story is Gaya's husband, a sort of feminized ghost. He is little, dainty, dreamy, uncertain, appears infrequently, and does not participate in the action. Gaya does attribute to him what several generations later would be called "the power of the weak," the mark of woman. Conversely, the women, both Katya and Gaya, are independent and autonomous. In their year together they walk out, admire military cannons, hold intellectual conversations about philosophy and the state of civilization. During these brief scenes in the first half of the story, the women generally occupy masculine rather than feminine positions. But within this reversed gender structure, there are still differences in power. The older woman has the active/male role, the younger the passive/female role. Katya does what Gaya asks.

Halfway through the story, however, there is a shift in power. In the first half of the story Gaya has been the stronger force, leading the girl home, ensconcing her in a bedroom for a year, treating her in part as a child, in part as an intellectual equal. When in the story's second half Gaya must finally become a mother to her vacant child because of the child's growing need for care, the power shifts to the participant narrator. Katya exercises a masculine power of refusal in ignoring Gaya's pleas for her to stay, and Gaya, in turn, is reduced to childlike helplessness.

This then is the gendered structure of the story: the women marked by traditional masculine traits, the man by traditional feminine ones; the women present, the man absent. The reversal that drives the narrative comes when the older woman must assume the "trap" that Irigaray describes, the most institutionalized female role possible—the role of the mother. When she does so, the power dynamic shifts and with it the positions both filled by the two women. The "little girl" now controls the action. The mother cannot prevent her going and collapses into madness. This gendered narrative is written in language charged with sexual meaning that complements and complicates the structure. Throughout the story the two women, though never lovers, act out child-mother relationships like those referenced in the passages of "Go Down Matthew." Reading particular scenes and particular turns of phrase in the light of that chapter illuminates the sexual subtext of the narrative.

Early in the story, the women go home together:

Then one evening we came into the garden at the same moment. It was late and the fiddles were already playing. We sat together without speaking, just listening to the music, and admiring the playing of the only woman member of the orchestra. She was very intent on the movements of her fingers, and seemed to be leaning over her chin to watch. Then suddenly the lady got up, leaving a small rain of coin, and I followed her until we came to a big house and she let herself in with a key. She turned to the left and went into a dark room and switched on the lights and sat down and said: "This is where we sleep; this is how it is." (*SW*, 14)

This scene resembles one in *Nightwood* when Robin and Nora first meet, brought wordlessly together at a circus with a lioness bowing in recognition. In "Cassation" the women's first meeting begins with Katya walking elsewhere, looking at the statues of emperors (who look like widows, in keeping with the story's gender reversals), when she suddenly thinks of the café and the tall woman she has seen there. She returns; Gaya is there and speaks to her for the first time in a "voice that touched the heart" about her home with its Venetian paintings "where young girls lie dreaming of the Virgin" (*SW*, 13). The narrator sums up for Madame: "I said I would meet her again some day in the garden, and we could go 'home' together, and she seemed pleased, but did not show surprise" (*SW*, 14). Then follows the passage quoted above. Like the *Nightwood* scene, the two women come together silently; one leaves suddenly, and the other follows. In between, they focus not on a lioness but on the intensity of the only woman member of the orchestra. Here it is not the recognition of the animal appropriate to Robin's beast-self, but sexual difference, that only woman musician, that sends them home to the bedroom. Once there, the narrator takes time to describe the massive dimensions and great disorder of the room but saves her most lavish description for a great war painting which runs together "in encounter" with the bed. In it "generals, with foreign helmets and dripping swords, raging through rolling smoke and the bleeding ranks of the dying, seemed to be charging the bed, so large, so rumpled, so devastated" (*SW*, 14). So much for men in the bedroom.

In this narrative preparation, the two women have been drawn together by the repetitions of chance and the power of a woman's music; conventional expectations lead the reader to expect a sexual encounter. Here they are in front of the bed; the narrative action has been stopped to point to male violence and then? In any throwaway lesbian novel they might fall onto the bed, overwhelmed by Destiny. In "Cassation" they are prevented from so doing; a child lies in the center of the pillows, "making a thin noise, like the buzzing of a fly" (*SW*, 14). The charged atmosphere shifts from incipient sexuality to the needs of the child. But Gaya does nothing except drink a little wine, insist that Katya stay, throw herself on the bed, her hair spread around her, and fall asleep. Later that night she puts Katya to bed as she might a child or a young lover, loosening and braiding her hair. Katya stays a year.

After that year together, when the condition of Gaya's child worsens, Gaya, in the central monologue of the story, tries to convince Katya to stay and care for the child. She promises to be like her mother, her servant, she denies their previously intellectual sharing:

Now you will stay here safely, and you will see. You will like it, you will learn to like to the very best of all. I will bring you breakfast, and luncheon, and supper. I will bring it to you both, myself. I will hold you on my lap, I will feed you like the birds. I will rock you to sleep. You must not argue with me—above all we must have not arguments, no talk about man and his destiny. (*SW*, 18)

The sexual undercurrents of their coming together have earlier been bound up with Gaya's playing at the mother's role. Faced with actually mothering her own helpless child, the woman of power has become the suppliant who wishes to make her friend into her child's caretaker. As she continues her plea, she literally confuses her own child with Katya; friend and child become the same, as if Katya could fill in the vacancy of Gaya's daughter. Her actual daughter cannot provide the companionship that both Chodorow and Irigaray stress is basic to the mother-daughter relation; instead, the child's mental absence calls only for the mother's caretaking role. Not only is Gaya confronted with the institution of motherhood, but experientially she must mother a child who can never be her companion.[17] To avoid such mothering, Gaya tries to convince Katya to become her child's caretaker; in her speech, she merges Katya as caretaker with Katya as daughter-substitute. Were she successful, she, like Nora in *Nightwood*, could have her intimate as her child and be both her companion and her caretaker. Her independence threatened by Gaya's attempt to make her a dependent "daughter" rather than a playful intimate, Katya refuses. Her need for differentiation, as Chodorow might say, is as great as Gaya's confusion between her desire not to mother at all and her need for a daughter-companion. Their parting, like their meeting, is shadowed by longing:

Then Madame, I got up. It was very cold in the room. I went to the window and pulled the curtains, it was a bright and starry night, and I stood leaning my head against the frame, saying nothing. When I turned around, she was regarding me, her hands held apart, and I knew that I had to go away and leave her. So I came up to her and said, "Good-bye my Lady." And I went and put on my street clothes, and when I came back she was leaning against the battle picture, her hands hanging. I said to her, without approaching her, "Good-bye my love" and went away. (*SW*, 19)

Katya now has the power that initially was Gaya's. In the final scene, Gaya is no longer differentiated from her vacant daughter. She sits beside her child, imitating her mad sound, the seductive woman-turned-mother-turned-child fallen into the void.

Read in the context of "Go Down Matthew," this story confirms its configuration both of difference in likeness and mother-child dynamics between women intimates. Of course the story is "about" cassation, as

Gaya's long monologue and the ending indicate. But it is also about a little girl telling a story to a lady, one woman speaking to another about attraction, the power of women, the devastation of motherhood, and the conflation of child and intimate. It assumes a female world, then gives up the shifts in power, conventionally marked masculine and feminine, as a comment on the consequence of the ultimate female role—mothering.

The second story in the sequence, "The Grande Malade" continues the subtexts of gender and of sexuality/nurturance. Its original title, "The Little Girl Continues," connects it to "The Little Girl Tells a Story to a Lady," just as its revised *Spillway* title, "The Grande Malade," is linked to "Cassation" in its implication of annulment by disease. Unlike the earlier story, however, its unconventional structuring of gender implicates the male as well as the female characters. Again the story involves pairs of the same sex. Significantly, although the plot purports to be about a heterosexual couple, Moydia and Monsieur X, we never see them alone as a couple or hear anything of their relationship. Instead, the narrative construction subverts the ostensible focus of the plot by concentrating on the couples, Moydia and her sister Katya, and Monsieur X and his patron, the Baron. Katya, here again active and autonomous, is both narrator and participant. The story is of a cap, a cape, and a pair of boots, all marking transgression of gender and blurring of lines of difference. Katya has given up flowered hats in favor of a cap like her father's and Chinese trousers. Only the women listen to her, whereas men adore her sister Moydia. Moydia is feminine difference in this pair marked by female likeness. If "Cassation" is shadowed by the incestuous potential between women intimates, "The Grande Malade" suggests instead the sexuality of father-daughter couples. Moydia chooses as her lover Monsieur X, who himself is paired with the Baron, a man of "aged immaturity" who taps around after Moydia with his cane. With the Baron she is a gamine, teasing him in her childlikeness, sitting in his lap, playing either "the kitten or the great lady as occasion demanded" (*SW*, 24). He plays the passive but receptive older "father" to her spoiled child-flirt.

The story opens with Katya's description of Moydia's physical beauty. Its first half establishes them as a pair, always together, walking in the Tuilleries, hanging lace curtains over their beds to smoke and talk of lovers. They differ in their appearance; Moydia is clearly feminine, while Katya has her trousers and her cap. The sisters are like, an inseparable "we," but different not only in their appearance, but in their relation to father figures. Katya wants to be her absent father; Moydia wants to take him as a lover, substituting for him the available presence of the old Baron.

The males in the story, however, spend more time with each other than with the sisters. Monsieur X seems particularly unsuited as a lover for Moydia: "He was the protege of a Baron. The Baron liked him very much and called him his '*Poupon prodigieux*,' and they played farces together for the amusement of the Fauborg. That was the way it was with Monsieur X, at least in his season when he was, shall we say, the *belle-d'un-jour* and was occupied in writing fables on mice and men, but he always ended the stories with paragraphs *très acre* against women" (*SW*, 24). Moydia leaves town to visit her actual father, the one who lives so strongly in the imagination of Katya. During her absence Monsieur X dies with the Baron at his side. The narrative's only repeated passage, its doubling appropriate in a story where likeness defeats conventions of sexual difference, recounts Monsieur X's death and refers obliquely to the unconventional strains of the story. Katya tells Madame of Monsieur X's death: "When the Baron saw that Monsieur X was truly going to die, he made him drink. They drank together all night and into the morning. The Baron wanted it that way. 'For that,' he said, 'he might die as he was born, without knowing'" (*SW*, 27). A page later, Katya repeats the scene and the quote for Moydia when she returns from her visit. What is it that Monsieur X doesn't know? Among other things, surely, that his ties to the Baron were greater than those to Moydia.

Katya asked the Baron for something belonging to Monsieur X to give as a remembrance to Moydia. He gives her Monsieur X's cape. Given the fame of Djuna Barnes' own cape, familiar to all who knew her in Paris at the time of the story's publication in *This Quarter*, it is difficult not to see the story's cape as something of a private joke. But more than that, it marks a further transgression of gender identity, passing from a man of uncertain sexuality to a woman who in wearing it, as the story tells us, comes to resemble her dead lover. By wearing his cape, she becomes not only a masculinized woman who replaces the feminized man but also the "protege" of the old Baron-father with whom she earlier has had such a sexually coy relationship. Meanwhile, the boots that Monsieur X had earlier promised Katya are quite forgotten. So while Moydia puts on a man's cape, Katya must forego her man's boots; for both, clothes mark their move away from boundaries of gender identity toward an ambiguous center, "neither one and half the other," as Matthew O'Connor says. The matrix of gender and sexuality in "The Grande Malade" is not that of "Cassation," yet both stories are shadowed by outlawed transgression of difference boundaries. In their undercurrent of incest and their fascination with likeness and difference within that likeness, they anticipate the overt emergence of these ideas in *Nightwood*.

"Dusie," like *Nightwood*, brings the undercurrents to the surface. Published in a collection called *American Esoterica* and not included in *Spillway*, perhaps because of its unambiguous lesbian subject matter, "Dusie" directly anticipates many of *Nightwood*'s preoccupations. Like other homosexual texts, the story's very existence challenges theories of sexual difference. Within its theoretical structure of sameness, difference appears at the textual level in the variety of women presented, but particularly in the condemnation of one who commits an act of violence. Like *Nightwood*'s Jenny, Clarissa disappears before the narrative closes. The women who remain, like Nora and Robin, participate in the familiar mother-daughter-lover configuration.

The story is set entirely in a world of likeness. In Madame K's lesbian salon there are no men, only women with different roles. Questions of conventional gender give way to an explicit focus on sexuality. Dusie is the prototype of *Nightwood*'s Robin. She dresses in trousers, plays with dolls and toy soldiers, has many women lovers who call her pet or beast "according to their feelings."[18] In a description that looks forward to Matthew's *Nightwood* speech on the third sex as "uninhabited angels," the narrator says, "You felt that you must talk to Dusie, tell her everything, because all her beauty was there, but uninhabited, like a church, *n'est-ce pas*, Madame?" ("Dusie," 78). Like Robin she has brief outbursts of temper coupled with an unheeding absence. She has a "strong bodily odor" not yet elaborated as the earth-flesh, fungi perfume of *Nightwood*. Her movements are "like vines growing over a ruin" just as Robin recalls the "way back" of prehistory ("Dusie," 78). Others talk in front of her about her death. But she doesn't notice and "that made it sorrowful and ridiculous, as if they were anticipating a doom that had fallen already a hundred years" ("Dusie," 79). Other descriptions look forward just as directly both to the character and the language of *Nightwood*.

Clarissa anticipates Jenny just as Dusie does Robin. Both Clarissa and Jenny are thieves of others' lovers. Both mark difference in their female worlds; they counterpoint the other pairs of women lovers by their acts of violence and their narrative disappearances. Both are completely dependent on everyone they know. Jenny, the squatter, lives by appropriating others' words and loves. Clarissa seems "as if she lived only because so many people had seen and spoken to her and of her. If she had been forgotten for a month, entirely by everyone, I'm sure she would have died" ("Dusie," 77). She knows how to teach evil, just as Jenny does, and the story's brief action, Clarissa's mutilation of Dusie's foot, shares the power of physical violence with *Nightwood*'s carriage scene in which Jenny attacks Robin, making bloody scratches on her face. In both scenes the violence has a sexual context: after the carriage ride, Robin goes with Jenny as lover to America. Clarissa says to Dusie, "You must think, too, about the most terrible virtue, which is to be undefiled because one has no way for it; there are women like that, grown women, there should be an end . . ." ("Dusie," 81). These are the last words "the little girl" overhears before she falls asleep. When she awakes, Dusie is asking her to leave the bedroom. When she returns, Clarissa is gone and Dusie's foot is crushed. In this context, it is difficult not to hear the sexual implications of "defiled."

Set against this violence, the mother-daughter-lover dynamic in Dusie's relation with Madame K is warmer, but no less problematic. Though the story does not address the dynamic as directly as *Nightwood* does, it shares the novel's ambivalence about mothering one's lover. Dusie's dolls and tin soldiers, her vulnerability, and her self-absorbed absence signal her childlikeness. She clings to her lover, Madame K, as "the only reality." Madame K is mistress of the house, a large, very full blonde Frenchwoman who, the narrator reminds us, is childless. When she is with Dusie, she looks "like a precaution all at once" ("Dusie," 77). The narrator says she does not fear for either of them because of the way they "were with each other always" ("Dusie," 81). In the final moments of the story when Madame K returns from a visit to her own mother[19] and finds Dusie with her foot crushed, she takes the foot in her lap and says to the narrator: "You see how it is, she can think no evil for others, she can only hurt herself. You must go away now" ("Dusie," 82). Her maternal protectiveness, like Nora's of Robin, is unable to prevent Dusie's defilement. Despite this failure, this story, like "Cassation" before it and *Nightwood* after, makes clear how bound up with sexuality women's attempts to nurture are in Barnes' work.

With its discourse on the third sex as uninhabited angels, "Go Down Matthew" works out more elaborately what we see in Dusie as a character just as *Nightwood* contains the story of Dusie, Clarissa, and Madame K writ large. What is missing in *Nightwood* is the "little girl" as narrator. Indeed, the little girl's role in "Dusie" is considerably reduced from what it was in her first story, "Cassation," where she is half of the pair central to the story, and in "The Grand Malade," where she puts the story of Moydia in relief by her difference from her. In "Dusie" she is more strictly a narrator and less a participant, though she does consent to stay with Dusie when Madame K goes off and thus can report something of the goings-on between Dusie and Clarissa. But clearly her role is fading. In "Dusie" she no longer has a name; in *Nightwood* she disappears altogether. The novel's narrative voice sounds like that of the unseen birds in Robin's hotel room—present but not assigned to a character.

"Dusie" has a related figure for its narrative and that of the other "little girl" stories. In Dusie's room are two canaries, "the one who sang and the one who listened" ("Dusie," 76). As the "little girl," the one who is only a year younger than Dusie, sings her stories to "Madame," she becomes increasingly explicit in the sexual nature of her tales. We never learn how Madame responds, but we listen as Barnes works her way toward the exploration of gender and sexuality that is most fully presented in "Go Down Matthew." From "Cassation" with its shadow story about mothering through "The Grande Malade" and its sexual uncertainty to "Dusie" and *Nightwood*, in which lesbianism and meditation on inversion preoccupy the central characters, Barnes puzzles over likeness and difference, self and other, sexuality and gender. That these same puzzles are now crucial to feminist theory makes Barnes' place in a lesbian canon less important than her prescient raising of issues still hotly debated sixty years after she wrote her stories of seduction.

¶ In 1929, in Paris, I decided that the time had come to end the *Little Review*. Our mission was accomplished; contemporary art had "arrived"; for a hundred years, perhaps, the literary world would produce only: repetition.

I didn't want the *Little Review* to die a conventional death, so I discarded all the material that had been amassed for a Last Number and decided, instead, to ask the artists of the world what they were thinking and feeling about their lives and work. We drew up a questionnaire—ten simple, but essential questions—and sent it out to all our contributors.

QUESTIONNAIRE

1. What should you most like to do, to know, to be? (In case you are not satisfied.)

2. Why wouldn't you change places with any other human being?

3. What do you look forward to?

4. What do you fear most from the future?

5. What has been the happiest moment of your life? The unhappiest? (If you care to tell.)

6. What do you consider your weakest characteristic? Your strongest? What do you like most about yourself? Dislike most?

7. What things do you really like? Dislike? (Nature, people, ideas, objects, etc. Answer in a phrase or a page, as you will.)

8. What is your attitude toward art today?

9. What is your world view? (Are you a reasonable being in a reasonable scheme?)

10. Why do you go on living?

—Margaret Anderson,
The Little Review Anthology (1953)

¶ Dear Little Review:
I am sorry but the list of questions does not interest me to answer. Nor have I that respect for the public.
—Djuna Barnes

5

"Accidental Aloofness": Barnes, Loy, and Modernism

Carolyn Burke

In any reconsideration of modernism from our own (postmodern?) perspective, Djuna Barnes and Mina Loy should stand out. Standard accounts of modernism, however, fail to consider an issue that preoccupied their generation in ways that still put pressure on our thinking today—namely, the representation of gender. Yet another perspective is possible. For example, according to poet and critic Hayden Carruth, the women writers of their generation exhibit "the primary elements in the literature of their time": specifically, a post-Symbolist attention to craft and language, the use of psychoanalysis as a structure of understanding, and a preoccupation with metaphysical questions insofar as they examine the darker aspects of the human condition.[1] Furthermore, it is crucial to understand that Barnes and Loy both wrote from an awareness of the difficulty and the urgency of representing sexual difference from a woman's perspective. This essay will discuss the interwoven thematics of modernism and gender at three stages in their work and speculate about the impasses to which the aesthetics of their (female) modernisms may have led them.

Barnes' withdrawal into "practically complete silence" is well known. For her last forty years, she was a self-described recluse, "a form of Trappist" in penance for the time when she had been "rather the life of the party."[2] That her close friend Mina Loy also withdrew from the glittering artistic life that they enjoyed together in New York and Paris is less well known but equally suggestive. Possibly their celebrated wit masked in both a similar pull toward concision and silence, an affinity that had always been present in the psychic economies of their preferred formal units, the aphorism and the epigram. It is my contention that their lapidary language actually prefigures their reclusiveness, and that, for this reason, both their work and lives illustrate tensions inherent in modernism for women of their generation. One could, of course, argue that Barnes and Loy were eccentrics,

due to the peculiarities of their familial, social, and educational backgrounds. Yet the fact they wrote as ex-centrics or outsiders, doubly different
because of sex as well as personal background, paradoxically provided both
writers with an independent, decentered perspective. This complex eccentricity in turn ensured that they would be classed as inaccessible or coterie
authors, while equally difficult writers like Joyce and Pound were soon
canonized as the exemplars of modernist experimentation.

If one compares Barnes and Loy with their contemporaries Gertrude
Stein, Marianne Moore, H.D., and even Virginia Woolf, their greater social
marginality and educational eccentricity are immediately apparent. Neither
had any consistent education, although in Barnes' somewhat bohemian
family, literature and art were not ridiculed as they were in Loy's more
middle-class English household. Loy escaped from the tensions of her
Victorian upbringing at a series of academic art schools in London, in
Munich, and, from 1903 until 1907, in Paris. The positive influence in
Barnes' private education derived from her paternal grandmother, a suffra-
gist, abolitionist, and salonnière with spiritualist inclinations, while the
negative example of her father, a failed artist, may have provided her with the
determination to acquire some training that would allow her to earn a
living. Consequently, once she became a journalist, she put her years at art
school to use by doing her own illustrations. Unlike Barnes, Loy never
managed to earn a consistent living although she painted and designed hats,
lampshades, clothing, and covers for fashion magazines. But in spite of
differences in their artistic output—for Loy was a painter who wrote a
highly visual poetry, and Barnes a writer who knew the limits of the image
firsthand—their familiarity with both arts made possible a sympathetic
understanding for each other's work that could only have deepened their
friendship. And both women, moreover, inherited from their early training
in the arts a suspicion that not all could be said in words, that the silence of
the visual image was an ideal that language could emulate but never attain.

New York: "Stunning Subjects"

One finds their names linked for the first time about 1920 in the memoirs of
Man Ray, who remembered "two handsome young women writers, Mina
Loy and Djuna Barnes, the one in light tan clothers of her own design, the
other all in black with a veil." He added, "They were stunning subjects—I
photographed them together and the contrast made a fine picture."[3] It may
strike us as ironic that Man Ray remembered them chiefly as complemen-
tary aesthetic images at a time when both women were preoccupied with the
uses of artistic images to express a modern woman's subjectivity. How to
represent the new woman's perspective was, in fact, very much at issue in
Greenwich Village artistic circles during the 1910s.

Barnes frequently interviewed women whose activities did not fit into traditionally feminine categories: her subjects included Mother Jones, the suffragettes who endured force-feeding, women boxers, and a police-woman who wrote poetry. Soon after Loy's arrival in New York (1916), she was herself interviewed by a journalist as a representative New Woman, declaring that no one who had not lived in New York could pretend to understand the modern spirit.⁴ Although not without a satirical note, this article suggests that the question of how to reconcile the claims of gender and modernity was thought to interest readers even beyond Greenwich Village. Similarly, their joint involvement in the Provincetown Playhouse kept both writers in touch with experimentalist drama in which proto-Freudian explorations of the tensions between the sexes were featured on the playbill. (Barnes may, in fact, have met Loy for the first time there, after her 1916 performance as William Carlos Williams' wife in Alfred Kreymbourg's absurdist send-up of bourgeois marriage, *Lima Beans*.) It is worth noting that their friendship developed in a cultural context in which an awareness of sexual difference permeated experimental art and writing by both sexes, not without a certain ambivalence on the part of the participants.

Their friendship probably depended, however, upon affinities that went deeper than a rapid survey of the immediate cultural context can suggest. Barnes had read Loy's poetry in *Trend, Others, Camera Work,* and *Rogue* (where she also published) while Loy was still living in Florence. By 1916, both writers were known for daringly antisentimental stances toward traditional views of romance and relations between the sexes. When Loy's poems first appeared in *Others* (1915), they caused a mild outrage in the New York newspapers: her disillusioned "Love Songs" not only analyzed sexual love from a woman's perspective but did so in unpunctuated free verse. Similarly, Barnes' chapbook, *The Book of Repulsive Women*, appeared in the same year and gained even greater notoriety because of its Beardsleyesque illustrations and allusions to unusual sexual practices. Both authors focused on the predicament of the modern woman adrift in the urban wasteland, where her new freedoms (which proved to be only relative) culminated in psychic disillusionment, spiritual lassitude, or, as the final poems of *Repulsive Women* imply, in real or imagined suicide. Each must have recognized in the other's poetry an implicit critique of the pre-Raphaelite and Symbolist aesthetics that they had imbibed at art school, and in particular, a demystification of stock images for the representation of women.

Their situation at this point may be suggested as follows: if the role of women was to appear in art and poetry as pre-Raphaelite "stunners" (the term for women like Jane Burden and Elizabeth Siddal, whose unusual beauty inspired the work of Morris and Rossetti), or in more contemporary guise as the modernists' "stunning subjects," then female artists could not help seeing themselves as signs or counters within a symbolic system not of their own making. Before they could hope to represent their own subjectivity, both Barnes and Loy had to perform a critique of fin de siècle attitudes toward the female as artistic subject as seen through the eyes of their male mentors. Stock images of femininity from the artistic repertoires had to be demystified, reclaimed, or simply abandoned.

Loy's first published poems frequently problematize the question of looking at women through the images traditionally used for this purpose; these poems reflect upon the ways in which the tradition of the masculine look determines what one is able to see. Loy's poetic sequence, "Three Moments in Paris," for example, treats masculinity and femininity as perceptual and conceptual constructs; specifically, the sequence dramatizes moments of revelation when an unnamed speaker realizes that women see their own images through men's eyes and are thus deprived of an adequate self vision. In "Café du Néant," the central female figure attempts to see through "eyes that are full of love/And eyes that are full of kohl."[5] Although this woman plays her part well according to the decadent conventions of her lover's script, the speaker's irony implies that the couple's blindness is accidental, a product of their cultural conditioning.

Similarly, in Loy's "Magasins du Louvre," the glass-eyed mannequins in the department-store windows and the shopgirls and streetwalkers inside represent the range of cultural images of women: they are either blindly innocent or self-consciously aware of their availability as erotic objects. The female speaker, however, happens to observe the cocottes' visual response to the dolls, as well as their embarrassed recollection of their lost innocence. This momentary revelation brings the speaker to a realization of her own resemblance to the self-conscious "dolls," in spite of her wider vision. Unless she acknowledges her sisterhood with other women, one who sees with the eyes of the mind finds herself in the untenable position of the exceptional woman, a sort of honorary man. Similarly, other poems envision a female subjectivity based on a recognition of sexual difference that has been reimagined by a female consciousness rather than defined by traditional concepts of masculinity and femininity.

Although as a journalist Djuna Barnes wrote about a variety of modern women, as a poet she was, even in 1915, still immersed in the cultural ambience of the fin de siècle. She published *The Book of Repulsive Women* almost as if it were necessary to kill off the old images of women before a different vision might become possible. This sardonic chapbook of eight poems and five drawings reveals the speaker's response to the "short sharp modern Babylonic cries" of the new woman. In poems with titles like "From Third Avenue On" and "Seen from the 'L'," the anonymity of urban life simultaneously provides her nameless female subjects with the freedom of movement and the solitude that lead them to spiritual death. Frequently these depraved females are identified with New York itself, the modern Babylon. The woman is prostituted by city life, and as always in Barnes' writing, her illicit sexuality is, in turn, associated with mortality and death.

Of course, one must add that Barnes was aware of the decadent component of her own melancholy vision. She made satiric use of rhyme and verse patterns whose repetitions mock the very subject matter that they are in the process of unfolding:

> *Those living dead up in their rooms*
> *Must note how partial are the tombs,*
> *That take men back into their wombs*
> *   While theirs must fast.*
> *And those who have their blooms in jars*
> *No longer stare into the stars,*
> *Instead, they watch the dinky cars—*
> *   And live aghast.* (BRW, 94)

Her lurid depiction of the modern woman reveals an ambivalence toward her subject matter that would only deepen as she grew older. It is impossible, at this point, to separate Barnes' fascination with decadence from her implicit critique of the very attitudes she would satirize.

The imagery of earlier poems in the chapbook generates the final poem, "Suicide," in which two dead women are on display in the morgue. The sexual neutrality of "Corpse A" and "Corpse B" suggests Barnes' ambivalence about the possibility of even representing the female in the modern Babylon. "Corpse A," the narrator implies, had a spiritual potential: dead, she is "a small shattered/Cocoon,/. . ./all the subtle symphonies of her/A twilight rune." The fate of the second corpse is deflated, however, first in the description of her body "shock-abbreviated/As a city cat," then in the clichéd summation of her fate: "She lay out listlessly like some small mug/Of beer gone flat" (BRW, 100). The luridness of these images, with which *The Book of Repulsive Women* also concludes, causes one to wonder whether Barnes was also writing, in part, to *épater le bourgeois* and live up to her reputation as "the American Beardsley."⁶ In any case, at this point in her development, Barnes took the decadents' images of women to an even more unpleasant extreme and then disposed of them as so many mugs of beer gone flat. Similarly, her stylized illustrations, which feature a familiar repertoire of mesmerized or vampirish females in commerce with a variety of unclean spirits, also take Beardsleyesque technique to an extreme that Barnes subsequently abandoned in illustrations of her own writing. *The Book of Repulsive Women* reveals its author's awareness that she had, in fact, reached a dead end in the New York of 1915.

Paris: "Expatriate Pens Stood Still"

Mina Loy had traveled from Europe to New York during World War I in the hope that the new world would prove hospitable. She found, however, that although the avant-garde welcomed her as the poet who delineated the psychosexual dimensions of their generation's "crisis in consciousness,"[7] she could not conciliate her personal and professional lives or even live there on her modest income. According to one observer, by 1920 her cynicism on the subject of romance concealed "the real discouragement, almost despair, behind her trifling."[8] Her poetry, in any case, turned from the attempt to represent a modern woman's consciousness to the only slightly less problematic subject of modernist aesthetics. By 1923, she had resettled in Paris. Barnes, in turn, having exhausted her vein as the American Beardsley, also looked for new sources of inspiration in Paris, where (according to Ezra Pound) more that was new in arts and letters was being produced than at home, in the new world.

The two writers renewed their friendship in Paris during the early 1920s. For Loy, it was a homecoming, although under changed circumstances. Hoping to supplement her income through the sale of her art, she returned to the Montparnasse neighborhood where she had lived as an art student in the 1900s, until she could move into the building where Barnes had bought an apartment. Together, they visited James Joyce to collaborate on an interview for *Vanity Fair*, attended parties with Robert McAlmon and the *Contact* crowd, took part in Natalie Barney's salon, and discussed in private the inevitable failure of most love affairs, whatever their sexual choreographies. If, as Barnes implied in a subsequent article about Joyce, she had come there with the attitude of one who says "I know that all philosophies contradict themselves in the end, so I have made it a point never to do anything about it, until I visited Paris,"[9] her tentative conclusion may have been that there was nothing to be done about it, except to write.

Less certain than Loy about modernism as an alternative source of inspiration, however, Barnes evaluated the rival claims of the Old World and the new writing in the work of James Joyce. Implicit in her published comments is Barnes' awed respect. When *Ulysses* began to appear in the *Little Review*, she is said to have exclaimed, "I shall never write another line. Who has the nerve to after this?" She observed some years later that "expatriate pens stood still" when *Ulysses* appeared in final form at Shakespeare & Company.[10] Although she never kowtowed to Joyce, unlike other American writers determined to worship at his knee, Barnes numbered him among the major monuments of Paris, along with Notre Dame and various Left Bank churches. If, as Barnes observed, "Notre Dame somehow leaves you comparatively untouched," since "she is a lonely creature by preference," so too was Joyce enveloped in the self-sufficiency of what she called his "accidental aloofness."[11] But just as the cathedral provided a visual and spiritual summa for the depiction of the human condition, so, in Barnes' view, *Ulysses* offered a model of verbal and stylistic completion that summed up the possibilities for contemporary verbal expression.

Furthermore, in Barnes' view, Joyce's writing drew on his deeply musical sense and his ear for "the great talkers," those who spoke "in the

language of Sterne, Swift, or of the Restoration."[12] The Irish lyricism of
Joyce's great talkers undoubtedly pointed the way toward the stylistic
variety of *Ryder* and *Nightwood*, and more specifically, to the grandilo-
quent monologues of the latter's Doctor O'Connor. It is not necessary,
however, to rehearse here the variety of Barnes' indebtedness to Joyce, as
others have commented on the ways in which his inventive use of historical
styles, genres, and allusions served as a liberating influence on Barnes'
novels of the late 1920s and 1930s.[13] What is important, however, is that
Ulysses and *Finnegans Wake*, which she followed closely as *Work in
Progress*, confirmed Barnes in her own idiosyncratic modernism, which
reinvents the styles of past centuries to evoke modern dilemmas of the spirit.
Joyce's example encouraged her to explore the metaphysics of the human
condition in all its dimensions, from erotic to spiritual, and particularly, the
connections between these two. Barnes recalled that their many conversations considered the subjects "of rivers and of religion, of the instinctive
genius of the church which chose, for the singing of its hymns, the voice
without 'overtones'—the voice of the eunuch."[14] But Joyce, for whom all
was language in interaction with human consciousness, cared more about
the church's music than its appeal to the spiritual dimension, and so left "the
voice of the eunuch" or the transsexual to his attentive interlocutor. From
then on through *Nightwood*, the possibility of imagining a way out of
sexual dichotomies haunted Barnes' writing.

A critic has observed that although Barnes' 1928 novels were clearly
stimulated by Joyce's example, they also differ from *Ulysses* by lacking what
he calls "a single grand coordinating principle." One might reply that both
Ryder and *Ladies Almanack* depend upon a very unJoycean kind of modernism which disrupts this notion of "grand coordinating principles" from a
decentered "female" perspective. The same critic nevertheless observes that
in this literally ex-centric moral universe, "the pain in the world is rooted in
sexual difference"; furthermore, the problem of what Barnes calls "loneliness estranged in all human relationships" is revealed "primarily through
the condition of women."[15] When Barnes spoke with Joyce on the subject of
women, she noted, "He seems a bit disinterested," and added, "Were I vain I
should say he is afraid of them, but I am certain he is only a little skeptical of
their existence." In his commitment to recreate in writing "what a man says,
sees, thinks, and what such seeing, thinking, and saying does to what you
Freudians call the subconscious,"[16] women were of lesser importance.
Observing Joyce's lack of interest, Barnes adopted the terrain as her own.
She could take up her pen after all, and use it more freely because of both the
presences and absences in Joyce's writing.

Mina Loy, on the other hand, responded to Joyce not so much as a
source of inspiration but as an emblem of the principles she defended in her
1922 "Apology of Genius," a poem published in the same year as *Ulysses*.
Joyce was for her a companion outcast, one whose life and work were made

ex-centric by his Irish (i.e., non-English) birth. Both were outsiders in permanent opposition to the centralizing English tradition. With her own scores to settle against England as motherland and her English mother, Loy upholds the artist against the uncomprehending philistines of England and America in a related work, "Joyce's *Ulysses*": this poetic homage stresses the music of his "Celtic noises" and his defiance of "England/the sadistic mother." Although the poem also exalts Joyce as "Master/of metric idiom" and "recreator/rejector" of language, it emphasizes his role as celebrant of a new religion, one in which "The loquent consciousness/of living things/pours in torrential languages." For Loy, the modernist impiety of *Ulysses* shocks traditionalists: the novel unveils "The word made flesh/and feeding upon itself/with erudite fangs."[17] Joyce has been condemned because, like all truly creative artists, he is in advance of his time and therefore offensive to the retrograde public.

Loy's homage to *Ulysses* redresses in modernist terms the Symbolist commonplace of the artist's oppositional stance. She fully agreed with the famous quotation from *Portrait of the Artist* with which the *Vanity Fair* interview concluded: "I will not serve that which I no longer believe whether it call itself my home, my fatherland, or my church: and I will try to express myself in my art as freely as I can and as wholly as I can, using for my defense the only arms I allow myself to use, silence, exile and cunning."[18] Even in modernist disguise, art was still a kind of alternative religion, and its devotees still had to defend themselves against the official representatives of family, nationality, and religion.

"Joyce's *Ulysses*" follows "Apology of Genius" in *Lunar Baedeker*, Loy's 1923 collection of poems, as if to illustrate the predicament of the exiled artistic sensibility. "Apology of Genius" is, however, addressed to a "you," the unsympathetic public, and thus constructs an oppositional "we," the creative artists:

> *Ostracized as we are with God—*
> *the watchers of the civilized wastes*
> *reverse their signals on our track*
> *Lepers of the moon*
> *all magically diseased*
> *we come among you*
> *innocent*
> *of our luminous sores*

Although artists may be "ostracized" by traditional religion, their work resembles the divine creation: "we forge the dusk of Chaos/to that imperious jewelry of the Universe/—the Beautiful—." It is worth noting, moreover, that Barnes had used similar imagery to describe Joyce's writing in *Vanity Fair* one year earlier: "He turned to quill and paper, for so he could arrange, in the necessary silence, the abundant inadequacies of life, as a laying out of jewels—jewels with a will to decay."[19] "Apology of Genius" concludes, however, with the image of creative art as vulnerable flowers that miraculously survive the censor's lack of comprehension: "A delicate crop/of criminal mystic immortels/stands to the censor's scythe."[20] Although artists like Joyce, Barnes, and herself might be outlaws in the eyes of society, their alternative religion confers on them its own version of immortality.

Paris: *"The flight of/Eros obsolete"*

For the next decade, Barnes and Loy explored the rather different implications of the idiosyncratic modernisms that each had adopted during the early 1920s. Having decided that romance was no longer available as a legitimate subject, Loy declared "the flight/of Eros obsolete"—and wrote for the most part in a deliberately unmarked or asexual poetic voice.[21] She turned instead to the spare geometric constructions of Brancusi, Wyndham Lewis, and the cubists in an increasingly abstract investigation of the sources of creativity. Barnes, on the other hand, pursued the subject of sexual difference from the perspective of a female consciousness for whom Eros was, in fact, far from obsolete.[22] Seeking visual complements to the linguistically inventive *Ryder* and *Ladies Almanack*, she abandoned the fin de siècle stylization of her earlier illustrations and began to adapt old French engravings and popular images. By the late 1920s (when Loy gave most of her energy to the design of art deco lamps for her Paris shop while Barnes had more time to devote to writing), both had worked out characteristic solutions to their shared preoccupation with the possible relations between words and images.

Using the pared-down vocabulary of her modernist contemporaries, Loy reformulated the Symbolist idea of the work of art's silent perfection. A poem might emulate the "gorgeous reticence" of painting or sculpture if the poet dug down through layers of verbiage to reach what she called "the radium of the word."[23] In either poetry or prose, in fact, one could strip away layers of circumlocution to get to the heart of the matter, as artists were doing in their own medium. "Brancusi's Golden Bird," another homage to a fellow artist, reveals Loy's own aesthetic while celebrating the sculptor's accomplishment:

> *A naked orientation*
> *unwinged unplumed*
> *the ultimate rhythm*
> *has lopped the extremities*
> *of crest and claw*
> *from the*
> *the nucleus of flight*

This "inaudible bird" lays bare "the Alpha and Omega/of Form": it is the aesthetic archetype that the poem hopes to attain. Throughout her evocation of the silent objet d'art, however, Loy betrays her awareness of the contradictions inherent in such poetry: its aesthetic inevitably leads one to the abandonment of writing. In fact, "Brancusi's Golden Bird" concludes by recreating in modernist language the predicament of Mallarmé's silent swan (his figure for the poet in "Le vierge, le vivace et le bel aujourd'hui"). Loy hovered on the brink of a mystic's quiescence in her attempt to reformulate the old idea of artistic creation as a spiritual act.

Her quest for the "radium of the word" was, it seems, subverted by her skepticism about the efficacy of language compared with the visual arts' modes of signification. Given the multiple connotations of language, not to mention its linearity and syntactic logic, words could never free themselves from the excrescences that covered over pure significance (the "radium") in layers of meaning. The sculptural quality of her own poems, their thin columns of words (noted by T.S. Eliot and Yvor Winters),[24] express her awareness of the ambiguities underlying the use of language to evoke the mystery of artistic creation. The modernist wager of increasing purification as a means to convey the energies of the sensory world led her to an impasse as far as poetry was concerned. When *Lunar Baedeker* was published, it contained only eight of her poems from 1914–15 and eleven from 1921–22: Loy had omitted as many as she included. Paradoxically, during the 1920s, when she was recognized as one of the most original contemporary poets, she wrote little and returned instead to her quasispiritual exploration of the visual arts.

By contrast with Loy's increasingly spare poetry, Barnes' novels of the late 1920s and 1930s, *Ryder, Ladies Almanack*, and *Nightwood*, overflow with visual and verbal inventiveness. It is as if the story has to be told in every possible way and include the maximum number of illustrative allusions. (Again one can point to the example of *Ulysses*, but Barnes' speakers often keep talking to ward off some impending silence.) Similarly, although her earlier drawings were composed of little more than stylized silhouettes against sharply contrasted black-and-white backgrounds, the illustrations for *Ryder* and *Ladies Almanack* are full of details delineated with the apparently naive perspective and technique of the "ancient chapbooks, broadsheets and *Images populaires*" which Barnes acknowledges as her sources (*LA*, 3). Just as the example of *Ulysses* suggested a liberating approach to the styles of the past, so Barnes' discovery of Pierre Louis Duchartre and René Saulnier's 1925 collection of engravings and woodcuts, *L'imagerie populaire*, opened a new vein of visual imagery (see plates 14, 22). Barnes was inspired by the strong linearity, clear compositional principles, and bright, primary colors used by the eighteenth- and nineteenth-century *imagiers* (mass producers of graphic illustrations), but also by their atemporal quality. Reproduced with only slight variations since the Middle Ages, such images complemented her reversion to the prose styles of earlier periods.

Like Notre Dame, *L'imagerie populaire* offered a complete visual world, including saints and soldiers, virgins and amazons, which she could adapt to her own purposes. The cover for *Ryder*, for example, parodies popular images of the Virgin and child by reversing the sexes, so that a small female sleeps precariously on a patriarchal figure's knee. (This illustration also precedes chapter 47, "In which Wendell tells the authorities about the unaccountable children," and thereby raises the central Barnesian question of uncertain parentage and ambiguous father-daughter relationships.) Similarly, Barnes adapted an early nineteenth-century image called "L'Arbre de l'amour"[25] for the frontispiece, which depicts "The Tree of Ryder" (plates 14 and 15). Although in Barnes' illustration the patriarch stands solidly beneath his family tree as if he were master of all he surveyed, in "L'Arbre de l'amour" women are sawing or pulling down the branches on which the male figures are perched: Barnes' palimpsestic adaptation suggests that the ongoing decline of heterosexual romance has undermined apparently solid paternal claims to genealogical certainty. Although several images of serried cavalrymen charging behind their sword-flourishing captain may have inspired the cover of *Ladies Almanack*, one image in particular—the Saint-Simoniennes or "la nouvelle armée française de femmes"[26]—provided the model for its row of lesbian ladies galloping after their female leader (plate 22). For this affectionate satire of Natalie Barney's "Académie des femmes," Barnes must have taken pleasure in transforming images of female saints into the followers of Dame Evangeline Musset's sapphism. Similarly, the image of "Theodolina, Reine des Amazones,"[27] could not have failed to amuse her as a precursor of Barney, whose pride in her reputation as "L'Amazone" was well known. Barnes' deliberately anachronistic choice of this popular imagery (whose occasional bawdiness caused her some difficulty with the American censors) implies a refusal of the nonhuman art deco forms that captivated Mina Loy. Rather than abstractions, Barnes sought as complements to her prose images that would enhance its stylistic invention and narrative abundance.

But the self-conscious quality of Barnes' illustrations also suggests that, like many modernists, she was operating with tongue in cheek in these "quotations" from naive sources. In fact, her complex, doubled attitude toward these materials was soon brought into focus in *Nightwood*'s reflections upon the impasses of representation and interpretation. However, scattered comments on the nature of the image, and especially on the impossibility of conveying adequate images of women, are already evident in *Ryder*. For example, the walls of the matriarchal Sophia's salon present an emblem of Barnes' attitude toward her artistic materials. Sophia's room constitutes a museum crowded with powerful images: of the men and women whom she admires, as well as "prints of all she abhorred." Like the collector of images, however, Sophia keeps on adding to her visual anthology, until the original pictures are covered over by successive layers, chiefly of the man who has won her heart. Romance appears to complicate, even obliterate the possibility of consistent (self-) representation, for by the time Sophia reaches sixty, the top layer stands "a good two inches from the walls; the originals were, as she herself was, nothing erased but much submerged." Yet "this is the secret of the amusing woman," she tells her son Wendell, to keep her images about her "all in a conglomerate juxtaposition" (R, 14–16). Although Ryder's prophetic introduction adjures the reader to "reach not beyond the image," as if it could provide a reliable ground of meaning, the novel also reveals its author's awareness that our comprehension of visual images is no more certain than our interpretation of language.

New York: Moral Hermits

In the years to come, Loy and Barnes both kept their images about them "in a conglomerate juxtaposition," as if to see what unexpected combinations they might design among themselves. But soon, in Nightwood, an image would be called only "a stop the mind makes between uncertainties" (N, 111). Although as painterly poets, they intended "to rescue illuminating images from transience and hold them in memorable and revealing juxtaposition,"[28] the image had come to seem as ambiguous as language itself. But neither Barnes nor Loy stopped writing after the 1930s, when Nightwood appeared and Loy completed an unpublished novella about a surrealist artist. By the 1940s both writers had relocated to New York, where Barnes withdrew into seclusion and Loy confirmed her tendency to live as "a sort of moral hermit."[29] Although they were considered eccentrics by their contemporaries and legendary figures by the younger generations who sought them out, usually without success, they were occupied with their work: Barnes with her densely epigrammatic verse and Loy with constructions made of objets trouvés picked up in the Bowery or with poems about society's outcasts. Both reached the state of "accidental aloofness" that Barnes had ascribed to Joyce, for they were engaged in private spiritual quests that few could understand.

Two poems written about women in old age reveal some dimensions of their shared spiritual isolation. In Loy's "Chiffon Velours" (1947), an old woman is described as "sere./Her features,/verging on a shriek/reviling age,/flee from death in odd directions." Yet, although her ragged clothes are "skimpy even for a skeleton," she is momentarily transformed by her reflection in the gutter, where her black skirt glows as in "a soiled mirror." This fleeting vision of beauty is available, however, only to the speaker who observes her; the old woman remains an unconscious image of mortality, "the last creation,/original design/of destitution."[30] Although Barnes' "The Walking-Mort" (1971) may be read as a companion poem to Loy's "Chiffon Velours," it does not provide even the momentary release that illuminating images, however unstable, offered Loy. The subject of "The Walking-Mort" is a female other who may be a mirror image of the self. The identities of "I," the speaker, and "she," the image of death-in-life, become intertwined yet remain ambiguous:

> *Call her walking-mort; say where she goes*
> *She squalls her bush with blood. I slam the gate.*
> *Report her axis bone it gigs the rose.*
> *What say of mine? It turns a grinning grate.*

The poem concludes with a set of alternatives that hint enigmatically at both spiritual salvation and its opposite:

> *So, shall we stand, or shall we tread and wait*
> *The mantled lumber of the buzzard's fall*
> *(That maiden resurrection and the freight),*
> *Or shall we freeze and wrangle by the wall?*[31]

Although both poems envision the female image in extremis as varieties of "walking-mortes," Barnes' grim vision refuses even the limited consolations of aesthetic illumination.

One could apply to both writers the remark of a critic who is said to have pleased Barnes when he observed, "Her work has not fallen into oblivion, it was predestined for it."[32] Indeed, we are still catching up with the reasons behind the strangeness of their work. An important basis of their friendship undoubtedly derived from their conviction of living on the margins of existence and writing out of an aesthetics of crisis. Both in spite of and because of their eccentricities, Barnes and Loy deserve their place in the history of modernism, for they point to gaps at the heart of representation while attempting to convey new images of that familiar enigma, "woman."

¶ Mr Arthur Pell
‖ Liveright
386 Fourth Avenue
New York

13 April 1953

My dear Mr. Pell,

You do not pay "every six months" when the sum is so small? What a sense of humour. There has been no payment on *Ryder* for something like twenty years, that book being out of print. Will you please let me know how many copies remain, if any.

Sincerely,
D.B.

¶ I was very stupid about getting copyrights in my youth.
‖   —Djuna Barnes,
                    letter to Wolfgang Hildesheimer,
                    19 January 1969

¶ *Ryder* is a remarkable and ingenious *olla podrida*, harking back, in its ‖ style and its outspoken quality, to Sterne and Fielding, though these are only two of the writers parodied. The central figure is conceived too much in the stock Cabell manner to be very amusing, but the two wives are richly eighteenth century. The jacket states that the book is written in "the great picaresque tradition." This is true as far as its vigorous masculine coarseness is concerned; but it fails of the one picaresque quality in that the scenes and characters and dialogue are not tied down to one definite homely locality, as in "Don Quixote." They are abstracted so that in the end the impression given is of an allegory, which is in a sense the very antithesis of the picaresque novel. However, the particular name one gives to the form of "Ryder" is not half so important as the fact that it is a witty and original book, fat with rich phrasing and written with an almost too facile brilliance.

—"Fiction Shorts,"
The Nation,
5 December 1928

Writing the Grotesque Body:
Djuna Barnes' Carnival Parody

Sheryl Stevenson

In the early 1920s, Djuna Barnes hailed *Ulysses* as a "great Rabelaisian flower" and claimed that after it she would "never write another line."[1] Not surprisingly, then, Barnes' own censored extravaganza of literary styles, her 1928 novel *Ryder*, has been seen as a derivative work, written in the manner of the great bawdy parodists — Rabelais, Fielding, Sterne, and Joyce.[2] Combining close imitation of pre-twentieth-century styles with modernist disruptions of plot and conventional narrative structure, *Ryder* does indeed repeat a Joycean strategy: the virtuoso's trick of encompassing the literary past while breaking through restrictions binding art to realistic representation. And in its concentrated images of bodily processes, sexuality, and childbearing, Barnes' asterisk-pocked novel also incorporates major features of the Rabelaisian, "carnivalesque" tradition, which has been given current prominence through the work of Mikhail Bakhtin.

Yet attention to the feminist direction of Barnes' parodies suggests ways in which *Ryder* is not derivative but analytic: a reseeing of carnivalesque writing from the woman's angle and a reworking of carnivalesque procedures for feminist purposes. Read in this way, the history of Wendell Ryder becomes an anatomy of sexual ideology, turning critical attention back upon the novel's antecedents. Primarily imitating a family chronicle spiced with picaresque figures and Rabelaisian moments, *Ryder* details the rhetoric, adventures, and consequences of Wendell's grandly patriarchal project: to extend "his race" through mighty and illegally prodigal dissemination. Barnes then further extends the targets of her analysis, breaking up her racy eighteenth-century narrative with quasi-antique illustrations and a series of diverse, often chapter-length stylistic imitations ranging from Chaucer to Dante Gabriel Rossetti. Foregrounding the way each parodied discourse is saturated with conceptions of sexuality and gender, these parodies present not only Wendell's exploits and myths, but also female characters' resistance and countermyths. In this manner, *Ryder* illustrates two distinct feminist uses of parody: to encourage analysis of a culture's ideologies, ensconced within literary and mythic discourses, and to offer "female" versions of those discourses.

According to Andrew Field, Barnes described *Ryder* itself in such terms, telling friends, "I am writing the female Tom Jones."[3] Though often read as an admiring imitation (*Tom Jones* by a woman), Barnes' novel resembles the many countertexts by female characters that it incorporates. Like these "female" parodies, *Ryder* repeats male pre-texts in order to add a dimension of critical difference that is analytic and countercreative.[4] Yet this feminist parody-novel not only revises the carnivalesque tradition, but also suggests crucial qualifications for Bakhtin's compelling, useful, but afeminist reading of that tradition.[5] Adding a feminist perspective to the carnivalesque mode, *Ryder* shows the necessity of that addition.

The Father Unfathered

For Bakhtin, the crowning and uncrowning of a jester-king epitomizes the carnival's mocking reversal of established hierarchies of authorities (*Rabelais*, 10–11, 81–82). Barnes' feminist recasting of the carnivalesque starts from her use of this motif to set up Wendell Ryder as the ultimate (though excessive) patriarch, the "philosopher" of polygamy and self-proclaimed "Father of All Things" (*R*, 67, 277).

Barnes initiates this carnivalesque procedure in her illustration for the novel's first chapter, "Jesus Mundane." In the center of this picture, a man (identifiable as Wendell) sits astride a horse, which in turn apparently strides a cloud. With one arm the man seems to point ahead, while at his side an object dangles—the wonderful sponge later described (*R*, 76–77), a sign of Wendell's meticulous efforts and ever-readiness to appease "nature." Ten women, split five and five, face Wendell, each with one uplifted arm waving a handkerchief, forming an arch behind and over the man, with the inmost two handkerchiefs seeming to crown his head. In this drawing, Wendell appears as inspired guide—his idealized self-image, exposed to laughter. Separating Man from women, suggesting his desire for patriarchal authority and dominance, the picture hints that this desire may lie behind Wendell's repeated emphasis on sexual difference. The drawing even points from Wendell's fundamentally traditional sexual ideology to his renegade polygamous practice, which enmeshes many ambivalently admiring women: his mother, his wife, his live-in mistress, and countless female lovers. Elevating a fleshly mock-divinity, this early illustration prepares Wendell for pratfalls and largely female opposition—the uncrownings and comic debasements of the carnivalesque mode.

The novel sustains this mockery of the patriarch (and his discourse) by means of its multiple stylistic parodies. Chapters focusing upon Wendell frequently imitate robust or weighty styles associated with male writers. Through his depiction in jaunty Chaucerian verse, picaresque episodes, and biblical cadences, Wendell emerges as the "swashbuckling super-male"[6] and all-engendering creator—one who mimics Old Testament prophecies and genealogical catalogues in order to enumerate his own innumerably teeming offspring (*R*, 277–79). Wendell's portrait even confuses the bawdy and the biblical. Hence, in "The Coming of Kate-Careless, a Rude Chapter," the arrival of Wendell's future concubine leads up to the moment when he first reveals himself to Kate. Appearing above her and his family, "standing as he was born," astride the opening to his log cabin's second floor, Wendell makes his body itself a sign, glossed by his earthy prophecy, "That you may know your destiny!" (*R*, 107). While indeed bolstering Wendell's status as Father and swashbuckler, Barnes' parodies of Old Testament prophets and "rude" picaros expose the patriarchal ideology connecting seemingly diverse discourses.[7]

On one level, then, *Ryder* emphasizes sexual difference, through parodies that create a super-male and, in the process, echo a culture's conceptions of masculinity and femininity. Yet the novel seems to flourish these categories in order to throw them into carnivalesque confusion, a procedure most clearly represented in Wendell's uncrowning: the feminizing and unfathering of the patriarch.[8] This process begins hard upon the first chapter's pictorial crowning of Wendell, as Barnes introduces her apparent stud into the Ryder family history by comparing him to a girl: "In the cradle he looked much as he would look in the grave, a hawk nose, a long lip that upon the nipple seemed too purposeful, and a body like a girl's" (*R*, 20). The novel's manipulation of Wendell's image in order to confuse categories of gender is especially striking in the Old Testament parody, "Wendell Dresses His Child." With biblical precision and repetition, this chapter details (for more than three pages) the man's manner of caring for his dying infant, an illegitimate girl, outside patriarchal genealogies:

And he made her a diaper of the finest bird's-eye, and he washed it and hung it out in the sun three days, and saw that it was dry and sweet smelling. . . . And over its head he drew a shirt of exceeding soft wool, and fastened it with three buttons, that it might not choke, or ruck, or tighten, or cause discomfort of any kind, and over that also he drew a gown that reached three cubits below the feet. . . . And the tears fell from his eyes continually, like to a soft rain, for that it spoke not nor heard, nor showed confusion in the muscle, nor the eye, nor the ear, nor the mouth, nor in any of the openings of the body whatsoever; that it knew not joy or sorrow separately, for that it was born feet first, amid wailing and crying and great lamentation, from the midst of its mother. (*R*, 126–28)

Bringing out the man's tenderness, this passage illuminates Barnes' frontispiece, *The Tree of Ryder*, in which she chose to depict Wendell cradling an infant—an image which parodies countless representations of the Madonna and Child. Though he frequently appears in the garb of "masculine" styles, this man who would be Father is thrust within the quintessential image of Mother.

Down to Earth

The uncrowning of Wendell is connected with a second aspect of the carnival which Barnes adapts: carnivalesque degradation. For Bakhtin, this motif involves the bringing of all that is idealized "down to earth," the realm of the grave and the womb. To degrade is therefore to emphasize the processes of eating and defecation, copulation and pregnancy, childbirth and physical decay. Carnivalesque writing achieves this effect by representing the body as grotesque, the violative opposite of classical canons which produce a smoothed-over, idealized body in its prime. The grotesque body is instead shown at extremes of age—near birth or death—with an emphasis on the body's openings and protuberances. Images of this body are "ugly, monstrous, hideous"—contradictory and profoundly ambivalent.[9]

Yet Bakhtin insists upon the "deeply positive," even utopian philosophical content of grotesque images and the degradation they effect (*Rabelais*, 19). Such images, he finds, convey a sense of human life in a vital, holistic relation to the world: "Contrary to modern canons, the grotesque body is not separated from the rest of the world. It is not a closed, completed unit; it is unfinished, outgrows itself, transgresses its own limits" (*Rabelais*, 26). And in his brilliant defense of the "indecent" elements of carnivalesque writing, Bakhtin argues that such motifs as coarse verbal abuse and its physical equivalents—besmirching with excrement, drenching in urine— are means of a revitalizing reconnection with the earth and larger processes of change and renewal (see, for example, *Rabelais*, 147–52, 175–76).

Ryder offers impressive evidence supporting Bakhtin's argument. Filled with scatological imagery and depictions of taboo sexual practices, the novel obtrudes physical convexities (noses, breasts, codpieces and their contents, Kate's tremendous belly) and inspects the body's openings, as when one character describes how another "spends herself at both ends" (*R*, 199).[10] This ribaldry is glossed by Matthew O'Connor (who, in *Ryder*, plays the role of homosexual sage or debased Tiresias). Acutely aware of man as a creature with "two holes given him by the good Lord" (*R*, 309), O'Connor thus describes his life as a physician,

staring down into and up through the cavities and openings and fissures and entrances of my fellowmen, and following some, and continuing others, and increasing many, and them swelling and opening and contracting and pinching like the tides of the sea, and me a mortal like the sea with my ebb and flow, and my good heart, and my thundering parts and my appetites and my hungers. (*R*, 173)

With this awareness of the fully open, incomplete body, O'Connor envisions all things borne "down to earth," his repetitions of that phrase duplicating those of Bakhtin:

Sorrow burst and the seeds fell and took root, and climbed about the stations of the cross and bore Him down to earth, and climbed on and on and bore Matthew and Nora and Jacob down to earth, . . . and climbed on and bore their children and their children's children down to earth, and the children of them begotten, and were not appeased, and climbed and bore man down utterly, and stretched out and took his works and bore them down also, and there was Nothing, and this, too, they reached for and closed on, trembling terribly and gently. . . . (*R*, 177–78; Barnes' terminal ellipsis)

Emphasizing transience and mortality, this passage presents the reverse, tragic side of carnivalesque images. The more typical ambivalent and ironic humor of the carnivalesque pervades Barnes' comic rendition of the same vision, through the stiltsman who visits Wendell in his youth. A figure straight out of the carnival, this man displays his wisdom in the oblique fashion of a Shakespearean fool, asserting that "the world and his wife . . . pass between my legs, but Messalina could have said as much" (*R*, 24). Equating such "arches" as his (and Messalina's "arch most prone") with monuments men erect to their accomplishments, the stiltsman hints at the rickety instability of all such phenomena: "it is the arch that stands for the achievements of man" (*R*, 25). These last words of chapter 4 are followed by the first page and illustration of "Rape and Repining!"—a drawing of five women dispersed upon the ground, examples of the "arch most prone" and signs of the downward-tending changeability of human fortunes.[11]

Like the stiltsman, Wendell puts on the carnival motley, often bringing down to earth all that is stuffy, official, sanctimonious, and repressive. When summoned to defend keeping his children from school, this self-styled "outlaw" disrupts the public hearing, directing the community's attention down to earth, into the school's well, where three rats and a cat float in the children's drinking water (*R*, 167). And as he widely propagates myths, metaphors, and theories of human sexuality, Wendell also keeps his auditors focused upon that earthy "mystery."[12] These exploits and explanations stem from the master plan of a picaresque renegade, which Wendell annunciates in the prophecy of his progeny-to-be: "Now this is the Race that shall be Ryder—those who can sing like the lark, coo like the dove, moo like the cow, buzz like the bee. . . . Some shall be prophets, some sophists, some scoundrels, some virgins, some bawds, some priests" (*R*, 277–78). With a body image that is strongly grotesque (in Bakhtin's terms), Wendell breaks down barriers between human and animal, celebrating the abundance and fertility of the earth itself, epitomized in his own body.

Ryder includes all the defining features of carnivalesque degradation: emphasis on the grotesque body, deflation of idealized conceptions, ambivalence, and contradiction (conflating the womb and grave, life-giving and death-tending processes).[13] Yet while imitating the Rabelaisian manner, Barnes parts company with Bakhtin's carnivalesque by questioning Wendell's (and implicitly Bakhtin's) *positive* view of the grotesque body and its movement down to earth. Considered from the standpoint of women, the emphasis falls differently—not on fecund abundance and utopian becoming, but inescapable decay, pain, debasement, and death. As one female character remarks, Wendell "paints a rosy picture . . . of polygamy for—. . . the *man*" (R, 49). Bringing idealization of sexuality down to the womb-grave of the female body, *Ryder* then illustrates a peculiarly female carnivalesque, and one that uncrowns Bakhtin as carnival king of a "rosy" physicality.

Messalina's Arch

The image of Messalina points toward Barnes' creation of female picaros who pull down powerful men and their ideas. The story of Kate-Cast-Pot (R, 111–12) exemplifies this carnivalesque procedure. From her upper-floor window, Kate dumps the "perry-coloured contents" of her chamber pot "upon the periwigged pate of some good father of the law" (who is lost in thought about harshly punishing a female thief). And Kate "cap[s] the jest by seasoning the act with learning": she appears at her window as "a pure maid reading from a great morocco tome"—surely a metafictional self-image of the implied female author, as jestering reader of the Great (male-authored) Books.

In *Ryder*, female laughter and abuse consistently undermine male authority. Wendell's wife, Amelia, thus tells a degrading "just so" story to explain how women came to have the task of "dunging" (or cleaning up after birds). Placing men's ideas beneath the excrement of beasts, Amelia implies that the words of man are a poor substitute for the weighty, earth-enriching "turds" of prehistoric animals (which she treats as a form of tribute, "coin new minted" and prayerlike praise [R, 145–46]). Explicitly deriding Wendell's "faulty fancies"—"a dog at heel and a floor beneath his birds"—this parodic story of origins suggests that women's lowly roles may be traced to men's disruption of a natural economy.

Amelia's role as one of Wendell's female degraders is outlined by Wendell himself when he tells his children of their parents' first meeting:

> "Love, 'tis said, has been known to bloom at first sight. Be that as it may, your good mother, to become better acquainted, pulled me down from a wall in Shepherd's Bush (for our yards adjoined) and here," he pursued, "be it recorded that she had never looked me in the face, but, seeing something in my posterior that tempted her to play with the future, she gave me a goodly jerk, whereupon I found myself sprawling, white rats and all (I was very fond of them)—on her side of the coping.
>
> "'Bottoms-up!'" she cried. I liked her well, I was never one to hesitate. I went to the business like a carpenter's apprentice, who, having learned to lathe well and to take the round, manages the subtler niceties of jointure.

"'Braggart-the-Britches!' says she, 'All-Woman's-Thumbs' and 'Bird-of-all-Bushes!' and any number of catch-words that I have lost from the bottomless pit of my memory, and very sorry I am for it," said Wendell. "So then I laid about me in other ways, and catching her soundly about the waist, kissed her fairly.

"'Pluck-of-my-Luck,' she cried, 'Try-Again-Thomas, Hot-Put-and-Hurry-o!'

"Now she might have said any dozen of things more to my liking; there are some that make a better creature of a man, but she kept at it in this vein, a scavenger, tossing words about my head like so many cudgels." (*R*, 158–59)

Amelia's word-cudgels are part of a consummate carnivalesque degradation, in which she pulls the man down to earth, thwarts his attempts at control, and refuses to "make a better creature of" him, keeping him instead in a reversed, "Bottoms-up" state.[14]

Among the women who throw Wendell and his master plan into arrears, Molly Dance most fully combines parodic and erotic degradation. She first sets Wendell's mind reeling with her story of creation, a wacky Genesis which jumbles Jonah "out of a whale's mouth" (her First Man) and a lady of the lake, "hee-hawing like an ass, which is the sirens' song" (her new Eve), Norsemen and Romans, Cain killing Abel, and the birth of poetry from "Cain's frontal bone split asunder" (*R*, 255–57). Liking "all things, of all kinds, all at once, in the same place," Molly cares nothing for "arrangements," including determinations of good and evil, or truth and falsehood (*R*, 252–53). Her flexibility dismays Wendell: "How is a man to have pride of his ways in you, when he cannot find them ten minutes later?" (*R*, 260). He therefore decides to establish some "certainty" in Molly by becoming the father of her next child—an issue she has never, in ten childbearings, cared to sort out. And yet, after the fact, Molly informs him of the "one thing that might make something uncertain of this certainty": that "Dan, the corner policeman . . . had the same idea" two nights before (*R*, 261). ("'And that only goes to show you,' she added, 'that one man's thoughts are not worth much more than another's.'")

Molly commences this degrading of men's ideas with her alternative cosmogony, a strategy typical of Barnes' unruly females. Like Amelia's story of origins, Molly's begins "In the beginning," and both women author a counter-Genesis, eliding Eve and tracing original sin to men. Similarly, to dissect Wendell's overly "rosy" ideas, another female storyteller merges pornography with biblical iconography in her own unique revision of the Fall myth. This mocking portrait of polygamy starts with the patriarch's view, outlined in porn: "There was Tessie, aged forty, all pure and lean and waxing haughty; with her was one Mazie, a girl of twenty" (*R*, 49). The account then shifts to envision these women in a lesbian paradise, which is lost through Wendell's introduction of heterosexuality and rivalry among women.[15] Hence, *Ryder* repeatedly shows female parodists countering the phenomenon of Wendell and his "faulty fancies" by creating their own revised versions of dominant Western texts and myths.

Yet Barnes' women also use a second method—clear in Molly Dance—for overturning patriarchal authority: the trick of unfathering their children. Thus Molly, like her mother before her, does not distinguish much between possible fathers (her own or those of her children), and Kate-Careless has a similarly "uncertain background," so that she is called "No-Man's-Daughter" (R, 249–50, 101, 188). Wendell's mother unfathers him twice-over (through dislike of her first husband) by giving him her maiden name and claiming his conception was immaculate (R, 20, 46–47). And the novel's fifth chapter, "Rape and Repining!" adopts a variety of Renaissance styles to anatomize the woman who makes her child "Fatherless by too fast Fathering" (R, 35). With a tellingly economic metaphor, this chapter's "speaker" (possibly one of many) informs the "Wanton" that she has "pilfer[ed] from the Community, which has honoured you as True Coin, only to discover you Counterfeit, thereby changing a Known Sum into a Sum needing Recount" (R, 33). Casting doubt upon women and upon the legitimacy of children, the transgressive female introduces uncertainty into an economic system, making "of Society an Unknown Quantity" (R, 33). The novel's female mock-picaros capitalize upon this ability, displaying and actively promoting the biological uncertainty of paternity which vexes a patriarchal system.

Barnes multiplies these female outlaws who flaunt the "open" body, connected to processes outside legalistic paternity.[16] This condition of the "grotesque" female body thus emerges even in the thoughts of Kate-Cast-Pot's "good father of the law" (and victim), who at the moment of his crowning/uncrowning by Kate is pondering

on the case . . . of a bawd who . . . was by birth half Welsh and half of Ireland's briny soil, for she was born supine upon the boundary (she said, having little exact knowledge of matters pertaining to possibilities) of the two countries, thus giving her, she testified, the only uncertainty of her otherwise downright life, viz., to wit, whether or no her middle was good No-man's Land, or All Souls', and held to the latter with a tenacity becoming, etc., for, said she, when in doubt, give the gentlemen the benefit. . . . (R, 111–12)

Giving the gentlemen the benefit (of doubt, a degrading, perhaps salubrious uncertainty), the women of *Ryder* often reveal a body like this one, in a borderline state, oscillating between No-man's Land and All Souls': Messalina's arch most prone, erected to paternalistic authority.

Pregnant Death

Ryder highlights ambiguous, borderline phenomena, like the maternal patriarch whom the novel mocks, applauds, laments, derides, and even vindicates.[17] Barnes' portrait of Wendell then exemplifies carnivalesque ambivalence—for Bakhtin, a result of the carnival's concentration on physi-

cal processes, in which life and death, change and renewal, are contradic-
torily entwined (*Rabelais*, 24–26). Reworking a carnivalesque tradition
(shown outstandingly in Swift and Sterne), Barnes focuses this ambivalence
upon female sexuality and childrearing. The second chapter of *Ryder*, for
example, revolves around a dual, contradictory image of the marriage bed.
To the husband the site of his bride's "sweet terror," this bed bears the
woman's fourteenth childbearing, becoming for her "a terrible suffering
centre without extremities" (*R*, 7, 8). Cries and laments of women in
childbirth echo through the novel and are doubly pronounced in "Amelia
and Kate Taken to Bed," a chapter dominated by "the voices of two women
screaming their children in" (*R*, 117). Amelia's childbed soliloquies then
eloquently express (in rich, Shakespearean paradoxes) her love-hate for the
"mole" and monster-child digging its way out of her (*R*, 120).[18]

Barnes concentrates her ambivalent, contradictory images of sexuality and childbirth within the mythic story which Wendell tells his children,
describing the experience of love for the "great Beast," Thingumbob:

> Now [Thingumbob] was stricken for the love of a strange creature indeed.
> All through the hot night in the topmost branches of the greenwood tree, where was
> his next—for he had wings, you remember, as well as paws, feathers as well as fur,
> and compassion as well as wrath—he dreamed of her whom he loved. And this was
> the likeness of his love: she was, as he was also, of large limbs and of a beauty
> outside of the imagination and quite beside what men would call the point. She was
> terrible in her ways, which simply means that her ways were not our ways,—and she
> was fettered to the earth for a season of harvesting, after which she was to return to
> the gods. Her feet were thinly hoofed, and her hair was many coils, and her face was
> not yet, and her breasts were ten. (*R*, 150)

As rain falls upon her orchard, wheat, and corn, the beast-woman tells
Thingumbob, "I shall die beneath you, yet from my body you shall garner
ten sons. . . ." After their love is consummated, Thingumbob "plucked his
sons from her belly" and remains in sorrow, "for he knows her gift to him
was the useless gift of love" (*R*, 153). Beginning "Once upon a time"
and retelling fertility myths, this story foregrounds an archetypal female
who gives herself in love and undergoes, in the same moment, birthing and
death.

Barnes' drawing of Thingumbob and the "strange creature"—which
has been excluded from editions of *Ryder*—illuminates Wendell's beast fable
and brings out its resemblance to Bakhtin's idea of the carnivalesque.[19] In
this drawing, the Beast appears as a composite animal, combining a ram's
head, a massive bird's wings, and a lion's paws, hindquarters, and tail. The
hindquarters extend in the reverse direction from the torso and one wing,
while the second wing is nearly disconnected from the Beast's body, extending down from the clouds above him and touching the rest of him only by the
wing tips. These disjunctions emphasize the separable creatures joined in

Thingumbob, while the drawing effects an ambiguous merging at each juncture—blending lion's mane with ram's coat, the upper wing with the clouds, the line of the leonine back with that of the land's horizon. The beast sits above the female creature, touching her body prone upon the ground—a body which is predominantly that of a human female, but with ten breasts, no face, and hooves instead of feet. Like Thingumbob (though less strikingly), the beast-woman merges with her surroundings, so that her hair, for example, is nearly indistinguishable from the grass growing around it.

This story and illustration encapsulate key features of the carnivalesque both as a specific conception of physical life and as a parodic, ambivalent mode of representation. Barnes' versions of the hideous/beautiful beast-woman especially render the grotesque body, incorporating two of Bakhtin's specific attributes of the grotesque: emphasis on the maternal breasts (through multiplication) and deemphasis of the individualizing face and eyes (*Rabelais*, 316). Together, the monstrous lovers convey the porous quality of the grotesque body. Rooted to the earth and seasonal changes, the beast-woman merges the female, animal, and vegetable realms, while Thingumbob is situated between her and the clouds, joining earth, woman, animals, and the mineral realm of fecund rain. Strongly suggesting the water cycle, his upper wing's feathers seem to pour down from the clouds, part of a continuous circuit which reaches the prostrate female body, with grass springing up all around it.

Thingumbob and the beast-woman incarnate the grotesque body imagined by Bakhtin:

> The unfinished and open body (dying, bringing forth and being born) is not separated from the world by clearly defined boundaries; it is blended with the world, with animals, with objects. It is cosmic, it represents the entire material bodily world in all its elements. It is an incarnation of this world at the absolute lower stratum, as the swallowing up and generating principle, as the bodily grave and bosom, as a field which has been sown and in which new shoots are preparing to sprout. (*Rabelais*, 26–27)

Thingumbob as the fertilizing rain, the beast-woman as the sprouting-dying field: these emerging figures underscore sexual difference even while they undermine all such distinctions. Barnes' grotesque representation of these "female" and "male" bodies resembles the laughing "senile pregnant hags," which for Bakhtin epitomize the grotesque. Describing the impact of these sculpted figures, Bakhtin stresses that the image they present "is ambivalent. It is pregnant death, a death that gives birth. . . . Life is shown in its two-fold contradictory process; it is the epitome of incompleteness" (*Rabelais*, 25–26). Close to this image, Wendell's mythic representation of sexuality abstracts death in childbirth, highlighting the larger "contradictory process" rather than the individual woman's pain. Yet where Wendell and Bakhtin emphasize the cyclic renewal of life, Barnes—in recurring, haunting portraits—shows women tied to the earth, part of a process which betrays them at once to pleasure, maternity, physical suffering, and death.[20]

Ryder opposes the "rosy," utopian physicality of Wendell and (by extension) Bakhtin through parody of the carnivalesque tradition coming down from Rabelais and Chaucer. More truly ambivalent then Bakhtin's idealization of the flesh, the novel flaunts, anatomizes, but does not necessarily celebrate the transient, mortal body. For this reason, Barnes points toward ways in which Bakhtin's ideas must be revised as they are assimilated, especially by feminist critics. Yet her "female" version of Bakhtin's favorite tradition also shows that the carnivalesque offers women writers a rich source of critical tools—to focus on sexuality and childbearing, question hierarchical authority, and dissect dominant ideologies. Giving a feminist direction to the carnivalesque mode, *Ryder* promotes a reorientation of both critical and creative practice.

¶ Djuna Barnes, author of *Ryder*, returned to Montparnasse for a glimpse and fled to Vienna. She laughed at the Carey tale. "Montparnasse," she said, "has ceased to exist. There is nothing left but a big crowd."

"Don't put it that way," I said. "I love the Quarter." Then we rested our heads on each other's shoulders and wept for a minute. Djuna is well built and has a rich, red ocean of hair. We swapped anecdotes and had tea.

"Do you remember—?" she said.

"Yes. And how about—?"

That went on for about an hour.

Djuna took an apartment in the Rue St. Romain, far from the present bluster. She told me it was all over. "Montparnasse is all over. And Greenwich Village is all over. It's all over."

I protested. "You're teasing me," I said.

"It's all over in New York," she added. "Two weeks before the end of the *World*, I was spreading a high class Winchell. For what? That is all over now."

Everything is all over. Djuna heard me with frigidity. Everybody knows that that was all over before it started. We had more tea. A girl I once knew in Chicago came into the room. "Is this interview all over?" she said.

Then the three of us had more tea and we talked about the post-war days when Bohemians pranced in circles and no one cared. I look upon Djuna as recovered hope. We agreed that it was all over.

> —Wambly Bald,
> "La Vie de Bohême," Paris *Tribune*,
> 2 September 1931 (quoted in
> *The Left Bank Revisited*, ed.
> Hugh Douglas Ford)

¶ What are we going to have dear, snow or war? Everyone expecting bombs and fury or communism, which is worse—imagine living in a house with everyone you don't like, and making tin cans for the country or something! Mary Reynolds back and as sweet as ever—poor Walter no better off—Janet [Flanner] the only one of us with 3 jobs! She seems quite gay. Daniel [Mahoney] wandering about with me or going to bridge parties as loud as possible, Jo Milward sailed this a.m. but will be back in a month to live for a while in Italy—Thelma [Wood] writes that Firenze is divine, Charles [Henri Ford] that Maroc is sunny & cheap—but I say the hell with it, its a terrible world!!

> —Djuna Barnes,
> letter to Allan Ross MacDougall
> ("Dougie"), 8 March 1933

¶ . . . you must get somebody to give you a push or you'll never stop writing your poems long enough to translate some of your memorabilia.

> —Janet Flanner ("Jannie"),
> letter to Djuna Barnes,
> 4 September 1969

7

A Reader's <u>Ryder</u>

Marie Ponsot

The most evident qualities of Djuna Barnes' *Ryder* are superficial—style and styles so bright they shadow the structure, and structure so crystalline it shadows the story. The reader, caught up in the high panache of English on a rampage, absorbs without reflection the large cast of characters, their many points of view and actions, and the range of the author's authority. Even to realize that there is a plot takes rereadings that gradually reveal who is really who and how the story works both to reveal and to distract us from their identities. Yet it is the structure, with its nuclear story, that sustains the work and justifies its flamboyances.

It is not a book that yields much to those who begin with a linear examination. Until a reader knows the whole book well enough to distinguish its voices and where each speaker stands, the antics of the text are susceptible to false or mistaken readings. So *Ryder* is sometimes thought apprentice work, obscure or arbitrary, a training ground for *Nightwood* and *The Antiphon*. Claiming for it a substantial place of its own in Barnes' oeuvre means taking everything it offers into one account—coherent and (for all its broken sequences) consequential.

Here is a set of assumptions about the shape of *Ryder*. Starting with the onion's outer skin, the whole appears to be the history of a family over half of a century—fiction in the form of a partial chronicle of a tribe. Members of the family group and their many outriders, friends and acquaintances, are seen, sometimes with omniscience, both solo and in counterpoint, rarely in harmony, never in symphony.

The next layer displays a proliferation of smaller forms within the whole. In and around the chronicle, *Ryder* incorporates the sermon, anecdote, tall tale, riddling, fable, elegy, dream, epigram, vision, parable, tirade, bedtime story, lullaby, satiric couplet, parallel structuring, ghost story, debate, sententia or aphorism, and emblem or epitome activated as epiphany. They fit nicely in a family chronicle, for they are oral forms, and family life is the matrix of language and the powerful verbal structures of oral literature.

94

Since the defining quality of oral literature is its mere memorability, achieved through the strength of its structures, many bravura sections of *Ryder* appear detachable and stand up well when read on their own.[1]

Barnes' willingness to mix structures in this way is accounted for by Andrew Field in his timely biography, when he says that the "specific . . . form" she follows is that of the operatic spectacle "Bow Down," which mixes mime, singing, speaking, and instrumental performance.[2] This information properly situates Barnes among her modernist contemporaries in all the arts, then experimenting with freshly broken conventions. (Who were the friends of her work? Joyce, Eliot.) My interest is in the literary structures she mixes or juxtaposes and what effect their presence has on the novel as a whole. Oral literature provides her with a large percentage of the separable forms *Ryder* embodies.

The anthology of oral forms expressed in many different styles engages the chronicle and carries it forward. If Barnes needed literary precedents, the most eminent composition of chronicle through oral forms is the Bible—to which a loose link forms readily in the mind because the diction of *Ryder*'s sometime narrator, flavored by Renaissance and seventeenth-century prose, often echoes the King James version closely. The charm and independence of the oral forms has persuaded many readers to neglect the plot and its deeper continuity, with its few but telling inconsistencies, which the forms both amplify and conceal.

A further revealing concealment of what goes on among the Ryders is the marvelously varied diction. First, it is not often the same from one chapter to the next, since the speaker changes frequently. For instance, in chapter 5 an omniscient narrator recounts Wendell Ryder's boyhood, while in chapter 6 an otherwise unidentified Council of Women explode in a tirade on rape to some lords and an unidentified victim.[3]

Second, those experimental parts which echo the experimental beginnings of English prose are so wittily well contrived that even an attentive reader may stop short of noting their implications for the plot. When Barnes takes her objective reporter's look at the ordinary, we perceive it in all its freakishness. Levels of low and high diction mix. Events and lexicon show the bizarre and the outrageous; pages of Rabelaisian raciness shade the plot's slow subterranean coming to grief. Unmentionable acts and bits of anatomy are both mentioned in ribald circumlocution and signaled in their absence by asterisks indicating censored material. The Doctor's confession is full of puns as he sheds tears in his drawers. Wendell's bum-swob is enshrined in Chaucerian couplets.

Third, the diction of some passages, studded with unexpected abstractions, is extraordinarily concrete and keeps the imagination busy picturing the scene "down to its *finest* detail" (*R*, 51). The exercise of Barnes' customary skilled pleasure in evoking nineteenth-century costume has this effect on several occasions.

The fourth onion layer is marked by the diffusion of principal parts. Some chapters have a central figure — but some of these never appear again. Careful reading suggests that the characters for whom the plot turns are Sophia, Amelia, Kate, and Wendell, but we can never settle on a central figure. The title seems to point out Wendell. But the text which investigates his ancestors and youth gives equal time to Amelia's ancestors, youth, and life before she met Wendell, so that our expectations move through their parents and them to encompass their progeny. And, though the women of his household are presented as his mother Sophia, his wife Amelia, his mistress Kate-Careless, and his daughter Julie, we first meet Sophia as daughter, Amelia and Kate as daughters and sisters, Julie as granddaughter. The first action for both Sophia and Amelia, a generation and an ocean apart, is attendance on their mothers in childbed. For Kate the first action is playing the street organ to accompany her contralto mother. The external dependence of the women on Wendell is painful, not profound. Though Wendell alone is free to come and go, he is without responsibility and so is an opposite or absence of hero.

Nor is any of the other singular individuals the main character. Even the outrider, Dr. Matthew O'Connor, perhaps Barnes' most gorgeously realized invention, is not the main man. In the place of a hero are persons who, isolated in their mental lives, perform the haunting dance of family generation unto generation, dynamic, thick-booted, insubstantial. Their steps and acts are original, a mix of good, best, poor, worst; echoes of judgment shake the air. The unlikely often happens unexplained, and every anecdote works overtime as sign, signal, and symbol. A great mother-figure has an idle, tawdry son; a self-respecting Englishwoman shares her bed with husband and mistress; a stupid woman, meanly treated, is merry and generous-minded; a randy, talkative, pious M.D. practices wisdom and spends his life taking care of children. No hierarchy of interest or power sorts them all out. The inability to use our habitual focus on a central figure in a hierarchy of character serves as another distractor from the shaping plot.

But the plot is there, a fifth layer, in among the star-turns and the comet-tail language. It is essential. For one thing, without it, the turns are merely clever or brilliant, not a constellation of ironies — since the plot is what the turns and the turning speakers are distant from. I want to describe it as the text gives it, since discussions of *Ryder* often skimp it and sometimes read it inconsistently. Here it is, in the briefest possible terms.

Sophia, divorced, is reduced to sharing country poverty with her idle son Wendell. She begs many to call her Mother and give her money. Two women join them: Amelia as wife in 1887, Kate-Careless as resident mistress in 1897. Wendell preaches and lives by a "great thought": wide, free intercourse. Accused of polygamy, begetting bastards, and raising truants, he avoids prosecution by claiming that the children are truant because the school is intolerably bad and by telling fictional lies which legitimize Kate's progeny—two verbal triumphs. But to avoid arrest, he or Kate-and-her-brood or Amelia-and-hers must go. At Sophia's suggestion he invites Amelia to sacrifice herself.

Amelia, unskilled, has quit school, given Sophia her funds, wed Wendell, borne children, done hated housework and farmwork; she believes his claim to "great thought." Ex-actress Kate meets Sophia, joins Wendell, bears children and a share of the work. She and Amelia quarrel but converse. In 1913 Amelia saves Wendell by leaving with her children—having seen him, threatened, drop the "thought" she has suffered for.

This is the skeletal plot which all the poems, songs, and other discrete fireworks amplify and fitfully illluminate. It not only dispenses with a hero but proposes a plot line deeply submerged in action taken from many perspectives, so that we are borne forward by a sixth layer, of a suspense we can hardly account for. The usual suspenseful rise of a question through obstacles to an answer is present, but barely, the least visible of devices. (It might be phrased: *Question:* Can this family continue both to overextend itself and to flourish? *Obstacles:* Poverty, idleness, greed, sexual eccentricity. *Answer:* No; it will transform itself by the sacrifice of its most innocent members.)

Yet the thin thread of suspense is strong, kept taut in several ways. The reader generates some of the suspense by keeping alert. One stimulus is the rapid, high-spirited play of wit; one is the strong closure of each oral form and its rupture as another form succeeds it. Another rises from those narrator's remarks which evaluate a character; they are unequally trustworthy. In regard to Sophia, Wendell, and Kate they say things about characters whose deeds show something quite different; in regard to Amelia, Dr. O'Connor, and Julie, they say things which events confirm. So the narrator's irony sometimes but not always acts as a double agent, and shakes us awake. Once the reader foregoes the comforts of a steady focus, the mental exercise produces exhilarating suspense.

Tension of another kind rises within a few of the chronicle chapters. They are similarly constructed. As they draw to an end, the perspective shifts dramatically. A character will suddenly cast shadows larger than life as a family parable dissolves into mystery and emerges on a more exalted level of cosmic vision, with tiny beings toppling out of place or time.[4]

Exactly the opposite strategy—a chiastic stroke—is followed in chapter 24. It begins and continues with dream, nightmare, and vision flowing in Julie's mind, and ends in an absolutely abrupt leap to brief realistic dialogue between Sophia and Wendell, who are suddenly beside Julie as she sleeps. It's not the beginning, but the end, of an event *Ryder* nowhere describes. If we ask, "What happened?" we get no answer. That blank enlivens the question and makes it, though hidden, central to the novel.

Both these strategies augment suspense and suggest how far the plot is intended to resonate. However, the plot is not the very heart of the onion, as I see it if I look at Julie, oldest daughter of the youngest generation. From that perspective *Ryder* has as its nucleus the story of Julie's ancestry, childhood, and early identity. That story, underlying the plot and all the divagations, casts a most steadying light on the anecdotal record of all the Ryders.

Why Julie? First, she is a child, a *tabula* others mark without cunning, almost by accident; and so is an intensifying reflector of others' behavior. To irony is added dramatic irony; we are both distant and engaged as we watch her move in the adult world about which we have been told more than she has. From that engaging distance we notice that she, unlike others, changes in the course of the book. She is in suspense and suspense is in her, as she becomes herself because of the plot and its actions.

Second, it is for an event in Julie's experience that *Ryder*, in chapter 24, shows a gap, a moment left pointedly blank and unexplained, which leaves the reader questioning in dataless emptiness. There are many dissociative passages but only one blank, and it is best observed from Julie's point of view.

Then, too, Julie is a figure of the childhood of Nora in *Nightwood* and Miranda in *The Antiphon* and so of special interest to those who see Barnes' work as a large and diverse but interconnected literary whole. As a Portrait of the Artist as a Young Girl, *Ryder* is a big, bold book successfully struggling to open the conventions of literature to new and metamorphic experiences.

Julie is mentioned or present in twelve of *Ryder*'s fifty chapters. She is front-and-center in four of these, clustered at the center of the text. Here is a bald summary of the infraplot around her.

Julie, child of Amelia and Wendell, helps her mother in labor by calling a doctor whom she assists. Wendell gives her work, tells her stories, shows her a corpse, nags and ignores her. Unschooled, she reads; Sophia, who says she loves her, reads to her. Waking from dreams of guilt expiated by death, she sees, as Sophia cries, her father looming over her. When one day, for Amelia's sake, she tackles Kate, Wendell encourages the fight. Kate later reports that Julie has refused her apology. Four major characters reveal themselves by defining her.

Though we are told little, that little is telling as soon as we give it our attention. The first appearance of Julie's name is in a metonymic phrase, in a story about Sophia and her set of chamber pots, each inscribed with a line of verse. Julie comes to Sophia, "confessing, 'Alas, alas! there goes "Do what you will"'" (*R*, 12). "Confessing" to the accidental breakage of the vessel suggests that Julie has found herself guilty of offense. "Alas" expresses regret and distress, and the loss in fact of "Do what you will" as the pot collapses into shards may imply an end to some larger license of the innocent.

The narrator in this same chapter 3, describing Sophia as nurturing

but controlling grandmother, says, "To Julie she turned her best love, and
. . . would take her up on her knee, lying to her . . . calm in the wisdom that
realism is no food for a child" (*R*, 18). The narrator assures us that later
"Julie held her grandmother's lies as the best of a capacious soul," and
"loved her most," but Julie also "gave this queen her mortal hurt . . . Sophia
offering her heart for food, Julie spewed it out . . . and said, 'I taste a lie!'
And Sophia hearing, cried in agony, but Julie went apart" (*R*, 19). Through
the portrait of Sophia we see her: a cherished grandchild, who is loving; who
inclines to judgment, most severely of herself; who wants the language of
truth; and who, deprived of it, does not stop loving but isolates herself.

The next mention of Julie is just a phrase, in chapter 14, confirming
the affectional connection to her grandmother. It is a clause in Sophia's will,
which leaves nothing to anyone but leaves orders for her burial beside Alex, her
adored former husband, with her jewelry and mementoes, including a "pince-
nez presented to me on my natal day by my granddaughter Julie" (*R*, 97).

By chapter 16, the family context is thick. We've met the generations
of Amelia Grier Ryder and Wendell Ryder. We know the voices of Sophia's
long-gone salon, of Amelia's sister, of the sisters Louise debating Wendell's
"great thought," of Tittencote villagers outraged by a rape committed
among them. We've just learned of Sophia's new convert to foster-daughter-
hood, Kate-Careless. Kate now comes to Storm King where Amelia, Wendell, their children Julie and Timothy, and Sophia live. On the property of
Sophia's successful elder son, they have a one-room cabin with a loft
overhead. To receive Kate, the women and children are assembled; Wendell
announces as he straddles the loft's trap door, buck naked, ". . . know your
destiny!" Julie is the first to look up, then her brother Timothy, as Wendell
looks down and laughs; "and the eyes of Timothy came down, and the eyes
of Julie came down" (*R*, 107). The Julie we see here is noticing, silent,
exposed to the unusual, and a child—that is, the family is her world. Mostly
indifferent and much preoccupied, the family fills her field of vision.

Amelia's preoccupation in chapter 19 is overwhelming. Julie listens as
her mother, in difficult labor and terrified, tells her, "I shall die this time, and
there's no doubt about it, my darling" (*R*, 117). The endearment measures
Amelia's fear; only in this chapter, and here only twice, is Julie affectionately
addressed; the family enjoys epithets and nicknames but not those of
tenderness. In a direct quotation of her own mother's advice to her (*R*, 40),
Amelia goes on to say, "Don't let a man touch you"; to call her gravidity
"doom and damnation"; and to paraphrase more of her mother's advice
against having children with, ". . . screaming yourself into a mother is no
pleasure at all" (*R*, 117).

Kate is gravid, too, in another room. On the hill outside, a workman
glances at the cows, "a little cow within," as he listens to the women's cries
and to the young voice of Julie, who is playing at imitating their labor as her
brother tosses her a rag doll.

When Sophia finally asks Wendell if a doctor is expected, he shakes his head and says two things with no sense of contradiction: "I am sufficient," and, to Julie, "Go to your mother." She obeys, "trembling" (*R*, 118). Amelia again says that this time she will die; she and Julie cry. The narrator's report of this passage between Amelia and Julie is exceptionally vivid and economical. Julie, through the window, sends Timothy running for Dr. O'Connor. She then stands by, afraid, holding her dress. (She is ten.) The doctor comes; he asks Julie for scissors and silk twine. "Why was that? Julie brought them. He was in the trouble now" (*R*, 119). These three sentences, and a few more in chapter 27, are meant to be direct and unself-conscious, overtly in Julie's true inner voice. (And, to my ear at least, Barnes turns to her own uses the diction of Joyce's portrait of Stephen at Clongowes.) Amelia asks if she will die. Dr. O'Connor reassures her, listens to her wandering monologue of distress and effort, and helps her at last (in a text asterisked to show deletion of censorable matter) to deliver the baby, feet first: "Out, monster, this is love!" (*R*, 120). Amelia takes Julie's hand and apologizes that the baby is not a girl.

In this chapter Julie encounters the major Barnes motif of childbirth. She and Amelia endure the unstoppable process under fear of death. (All Barnes' works are about an era before World War II introduced antibiotics against puerperal fever and techniques of natural childbirth against helpless ignorance.) The naturalistic diction, during home birth undergone by an ill-prepared woman helped by an unprepared child, is full of intimate dread. Julie's witnessing of Amelia's labor and delivery has an immediacy unlike, say, the concern of Bloom or the unconcern of the jolly medical gents in *Ulysses*. The scene takes place much as it might have in Barnes' own rural childhood. (Julie is ten; Barnes had a brother born in her tenth year.) These few pages are a memorial and a reminder.

Brief as they are, they change Julie; we see her grow toward identity. Though Amelia comes through safely, her psychological anguish equals her physical distress. Out of that anguish she gives her daughter the warning against touching men that her own mother gave her. In the event, it is a reasonable warning. Julie, terrified, is in an ideal state of readiness to hear and believe her.

Julie's education has entered a new phase. She is a little girl playing, as the chapter begins. By the end of it, she has expected to watch her mother die; stood by her in fear and trembling as she suffered; known her own incompetence and ignorance; increased in competence and knowledge; replaced her father by sending for the doctor; observed the power skill can bestow (power her father does not have) and learned both from Amelia's words and face to face what it is to bring a child into the world.

Just in case Julie has failed to be sufficiently disturbed, in chapter 23 Wendell Tells the Mystery to Julie and to Timothy. He describes with lofty circumlocution, in biblical rhythms and parallel structures, the conception and birth of Timothy, then of Julie. Given the recent work as assistant in obstetrics to which Wendell left Julie while he went strolling, the description seems a classic case of parental sexual instruction which informs knowing children too little and too late. The terms Wendell emphasizes in his remarks on birth are not reassuring: "It came upon its mother in every place, and she was brought to great pain and to bed, and she was in labor, and her belly was emptied . . . in the time of cries and blood, and that which was a bond was cut, and there was wailing and no one anywhere" (*R*, 131). In chapter 19 the girl and the woman undertook the experience. Now that the labor is done, the father adds the thoughts of himself as cause, "bestowing a little instinct" (*R*, 131). He subsumes the event in this page of instruction which re-presents Julie's life-against-death day of drama, diminished into generalities, quite as if he had authority to do so. Timothy and Julie are incidentally taught to view themselves—like their newborn brother—as occasions of their mother's suffering. Perhaps Wendell never notices what happens to other people, and so sees no disparity between Julie's experience and his discourse. Perhaps Julie in the moment simply takes him at his word. The text gives no clue here; it provides only Wendell's monologue. Only the chapter title tells us whom he is addressing.

But it's no surprise that in chapter 24 when Julie Becomes What She Had Read, she isn't Pollyanna or Little Goody Two-Shoes. In parody, pastiche, and dead earnest Julie ruminates a story like a melodramatic children's tract out of *Tom Sawyer*—haunted by a crisis theology of guilt and stories of Jesus' betrayal, replete with a false morality of inescapable infant faults and sins. Its heroine is Arabella Lynn, her exquisite blonde appearance fully described. She is a five-year-old saint-sinner, holy and self-convicted of impious crimes, begging her mother's and heaven's forgiveness. For all but the end of the chapter, we are overhearing Julie's thoughts as they elide into reverie and nightmare. In the dream, Arabella Lynn suddenly dies: "Poor tortured soul! She is set upon by corruption and the icy forces of death even as she prays" (*R*, 135). Her death is for the best, for "what foul demon might have weakened that structure had it reared into full womanhood? What sin might have battened on that edifice, dragging it down into inevitable ruin?" (*R*, 135). Julie pictures the throng of children at the funeral and the outbreak of storm, rain, and thunder as Arabella is buried. She becomes all of the mourners in a fugue of self-forgetting; they are "Julie in multitude. . . . It is Julie now lying on her bed, it is Julie snatched up and flung down into the marketplace, where they are selling Jesus for a price. It is Julie all horror, and terror, and great history, . . . the shudder of the condemned . . . screaming the scream incredible. The shadows of foreshortened destinies . . . pray beside her . . . and she stands turning among them" (*R*, 136). The bookish reverie has darkened into nightmare; Arabella in mortal anguish has given place to Julie. When the nightmare modulates, it is to a dream of being sixteen and voluptuous: "Love shall be, never being, and life . . . a fine queen on a black mare, breathing like a man." The dream quickly darkens again: "Or . . . life like an idiot girl, smelling of nether puberty, shall finger the hem of her reverses" (R, 137). The perspective shifts briefly to that of a rabbit somewhere fleetly pawing the earth.

And Julie again is multiplied into the whole crowd of mourning children, then into their metamorphoses, as "they become mothers and are laden and are large, and the embedded face some this way and some that way. . . . And they are falling slowly . . . silent and soft and docile, scourged and blasphemed . . . uncoiling their destiny" (R, 137).

The dream dissipates. "And the company grows old and whispers among themselves and Julie lies and looks up at Wendell, and Sophia running, weeping and crying: 'Do not strike her, do not strike her! I had no daughter ever, and she is that daughter!' 'Keep her,' says Wendell, 'she is none of mine. Did I not hear her deriding me greatly?'" (R, 138).

Thus the text; it tells us no more. The leap from dream to dramatic event is not explained. It leaves us to ask, as it must in the moment leave Julie to ask, what is happening? What is Wendell doing there, looming over the girl who has fallen dozing and musing into dream and nightmare? To what is Sophia making such vehement response? What has she seen or heard or suspected that brings her running? Why is she weeping? Why does she cry to Wendell to spare Julie for her sake — and not for Julie's — so far unmothering her as to claim Julie as daughter? When has Wendell heard Julie deriding him greatly? What has Julie said or done in derision, and why does Wendell react to Sophia's intervention by denying Julie her paternity, implying that she deserves to be cut off? In the two sentences of their dialogue Julie hears she has lost her rights in both mother and father. Was Wendell about to attack a sleeping child? Of what nature was the attack?

We do not know because Julie does not know. What we know is what Julie knows. If her perceptions inform her, then the relating of her perceptions informs us about her in a particularly intimate way.

There is always every reason to take Barnes at her every word. So we need to notice that the big piece of information this chapter contributes is in the shape of a nothing: a gap in the action, an important gap, a gap that corresponds to a gap in the consciousness of Julie, who is the speaker of most of the chapter.

Julie is plainly too alone and too little articulate to have found anyone to talk to about the recent and unforgotten fear and confusion of her mother's childbed. She finds symbolic expression for them in the self-sacrificial tale she meditatively tells herself and carries over into metamorphic dreaming. She first muses, saving and damned, begging her parents' pardon. Turning and turning among the principal beings of her family, she changes again, this time into her unimagined sexual future. Briefly she hears "birds sing for all she has yet to learn" (R, 137). Her lapse back into dreaming herself as split and multiple persons reflects what she has learned from her father's telling of the mystery: the fate of a "voluptuous" woman is pregnancy.

All these matters flood her mind, receding as she swims into consciousness to see her father over her and to hear her grandmother running, crying, weeping. Julie hears herself, without accusation or trial, judged guilty and cast out. She is not even directly addressed as her grandmother cries out and her father disowns and accuses her.

The few sentences of direct speech that conclude this chapter are symptomatic of a constant in Wendell's life, in that none of the three speakers is engaged in conversational exchange. Julie speaks to the self of her reverie and sleep; Sophia's plea to Wendell is couched in terms of Sophia's, not Julie's distress, and elicits only an oblique response; Wendell's self-bound edict is the chapter's last word.

Though dissociated from each other, these sentences work on several levels, like most of *Ryder*. They have taken us through new phases in Julie's identity and demonstrated again the unconversing isolation of these highly verbal people. They also develop further, symbolically and all at once, the biographies of the other participants. Sophia, too late to prevent a scene (whatever its content) from developing, claims the privileges of maternity based on her notion of herself, never considering this an intrusion on the rights of Julie's true mother, Amelia, or a usurpation and uninvited invasion of Julie's archetypical world. Wendell asserts pique at having been found (thought of? dreamed of?) less than perfect and abolishes his relation to his daughter for what he evaluates as her treachery.

This complex chapter is full of details worth noticing. One small aspect of its first part, as Julie fantasizes, telling herself a story, is its descriptiveness. Elsewhere the material which reveals Julie to us is more often active and narrative than static and descriptive. Julie's own perceptions, too, are expressed concretely as active, responsive, ethical, unmirrored. In this chapter, however, Julie's mental language includes that characteristic specialty of Djuna Barnes' concreteness: description of appearance, frequently undertaken with the meticulousness of a theatrical costume designer. Julie's fantasy and dream give us Arabella Lynn with "a cross of water diamonds set in a sweet bezelled ring" as she "kneels in her figure-haunted gown" (*R*, 133). And at Arabella Lynn's funeral, Julie describes a fantasy which becomes not herself but her selves, as she tells about the crowd of a hundred little-girl mourners whom she becomes as she dreams: "The long file of white-clad children in their smallest laces, with three-button, white cotton gloves, therein holding the diminutive prayer books, the fair head and the dark bowed together in immature grief. The black shoes with the shin bones rounded, the fluttering pale ribbons at wrist and waist, the solemn octave of their falling feet, as they wend . . ." (*R*, 135).

The one other description we have of Julie's appearance is not fantasized; it is in the third chapter which concerns her nearly, chapter 27.

There, as she goes fishing with her father and her brother Timothy, she is seen in action, "her three-ply stockings off and laid aside, and her skirts rolled up, and her panties crotched to sticking" as she bottoms "backward into the brine, feeling it come up over her with a round edge" (*R*, 148).

Wendell makes reed whistles for the children; Julie plays hers "as if it were a thing of beauty" (*R*, 149). For the length of a sentence, Julie's young life follows the convention of that fabled rosy light around childhood in American Eden. Her father stops her short: "That's no way to hold it, and why don't you keep step?" (*R*, 148). The nagging voice breaks off Julie's confident tooting to say she is wrong again, twice wrong, in her spontaneous play and in her very walk, not intentionally but intrinsically wrong.

The next sentences are, like the sentences at the end of chapter 24, presented in the voice of Julie's perception: what we see is what she is identified by seeing. "And away he went, walking, tearing, at the pot of crabs and unhooking my-ladies'-chamber from their insides, and 'Come here and see,' he said, and Timothy got there first, so that Julie could not see. And 'Oh!' he said, and 'Oh! she is sitting on her throne, and she has yellow hair!' And Wendell said, 'Yes, that is the ladies' chamber'" (*R*, 149).

Wendell has passed judgment on Julie with the casualness of paternal authority. He now extends that authority to the crabs he has caught live; the image is packed with a violence that is ordinary, easy, useless to turn from or resist. Timothy, preventing Julie, sees the throne in the ladies' chamber before it is torn from the crab's abdomen; his father confirms what he sees. Admitted to the mystery, Timothy is recognized as right, just as Julie is excluded, wrong.[5]

Julie is, however, not established in defeat, not silenced; she asks her father to tell a story. There follows the centerpiece of the chapter, Wendell's tale of the Beast Thingumbob. The Beast dreams of his love (who remains unnamed), a creature born of the underworld to live 1010 years and then return to the gods. In response to his longing, she tells him—as creatures copulate around them—to take her ten sons from her body, and bury her. He does, takes the sons home, and sits in the smoke of his grief because "her gift to him is the useless gift of love" (*R*, 153). Julie asks him, "Is that all?"

On the way home, Wendell is able, accidentally, to offer Timothy and Julie another of his free entertainments: a walk through big, unlaid sewer pipes, where they happen on a dead body. Wendell says it's probably a tramp who has starved to death, "white belly up" (*R*, 154), and keeps going. Here, too, we know what Julie knows; no narrator's comment distracts us from her unframed perception of an abandoned corpse and a calm father.

When Sophia reads to them that evening, Wendell reminds her to spare his sensibilities by skipping any death scenes. She does so, but later, with Julie on her lap, reads in all its detail the death of Emily, "and the darkness pulled at Julie and tore her away from her beloved while yet she lay upon her breast" (*R*, 154).

The chapter then ends in another of *Ryder*'s remarkable mythic perspective-shifting flights which (among other things) prepare us for the perspective of the final paragraphs of the book. In this one, a cat leaps into a tree, leaps again, and the places of the world vanish, and the cat falls "down falling, surprised, falling surprised forever, and no one to tell it to" (*R*, 154).

This chapter clearly exhibits Barnes' strategy throughout *Ryder* of hiding what she shows. Wendell's story of the Beast Thingumbob takes up most of the pages and is vivid enough in language and characters to be memorable. As a father's choice of tale for his children, and as a reflection of his interests, it tells us a good deal about Wendell. But it is present also as a distractor, a conjuror's gesture; the three brief Julie events or anecdotes are the payoff, slipped past our guard: Julie sees the crabs aborted and herself prevented from looking at the ladies' chamber. Julie hears her father's inconclusive story of death and love, then sees the corpse and her father's cold dismissal of it. Warm in Sophia's lap, with the girl's death scene in her ears, Julie falls out of consciousness of safety into sleep. And the cat falls forever with no one to tell it to.

Julie is present—not just discussed by others—for the last time in chapter 33. Her younger brother and one of Kate's sons are at odds. Their mothers insult each other. Wendell intervenes "mildly" to berate the innocent and reward the guilty child. Julie, now fourteen, rushes from the house and throws herself "tooth, foot, and nail on to Kate, crying loudly and wildly, 'You and you and you,' to her father" (*R*, 182) because of the torment to her mother that Kate represents. Julie fights hard, still crying "You!" at her father, seeing Kate as the "manifestation" of a disease which comes directly from him. Wendell is charmed by the spectacle. He imprisons Amelia by the apron to hold her away; Sophia wrings her hands, afraid to move, as three-hundred-pound Kate, "like a horse flicking a fly" (*R*, 183), knocks Julie sprawling. It is Kate's son who speaks up to stop the fight, by admitting his guilt. Amelia then praises him, and Kate as his mother. How Julie gets up is not mentioned.

This chapter is Julie's one clear moment of protest against her father, and in defense of her mother. Though she attacks Wendell only indirectly, in the form of Kate, it is to him she addresses herself, out of indignation at Amelia's "torment" and possibly out of imperious distaste for Amelia's acceptance of it. (By the time of *The Antiphon*, Julie/Miranda expresses her distaste for Amelia/Augusta's collusion in Wendell/Titus' acts. Among memories of her family, only the memory of Sophia/Victoria is nowhere examined for evidence of collusion with Wendell/Titus.) Amelia, whose ethical posture is unexplained before the final chapter, relaxes her stern belief in Wendell's exculpatory greatness and tries to help Julie but is physically impeded, as Wendell holds her back by her apron strings. She is differently impeded by her middle-class, marble-mouthed, English inhibition against praising her own child. Wendell, intact, as self-bound and regal as an infant, is not drawn into the conflict; he keeps his usual freedom from the concerns of his women and children, only preventing Amelia from interrupting a sporting conflict he is disposed to enjoy. Though his injustice is a cause of the fight, he is unmoved. His distance is the opposite of Kate's hot-blooded, shouting involvement; the blow she gives Julie is by clumsy accident.

Julie is both concerned and aloof. A social principle of justice bids her leap into action that is expressive of larger anger against larger unfairness; and, though her physical target is Kate, she seethes as she recognizes Wendell, almost openly, as enemy. Yet it is by herself that she decides, fights, and falls.

Chapter 35 is the third of four letters to Amelia from her sister, Ann, in Britain; from that ironically remote point of view, Ann comments on the news, in Amelia's latest letter, of Julie pulling at Sophia's diaper ends to get them out of sight and remarks that such activity is not conducive to "woman's splendor" (*R*, 199).

Chapter 36 is a bedtime story Amelia tells, perhaps to Julie, her only daughter. It is about two sisters, one of *Ryder*'s perfect bravura set pieces of wit and elegance, deliciously told. It is yet another tale of death in childbed.

Chapter 37 gives us a woman who, before going off to bed with Wendell (in a house which is not the family cabin though Amelia and Sophia are both there), chats about Julie: "You have a little daughter and she has no breasts. Now where are those jujubes I wanted to bring her?" (*R*, 206). As she chatters, in amorous delay, about unseen wonders, spirits made visible seem to throng the farmhouse. Among them, "foremost, a prince" cradling in his arms "the supine form of a girl-child with the blood of the rape flowing in a thin, fine, ever-widening stream, the slotted insertion of her communal dress, petal by petal, falling, the bride's bouquet in her betrayed hands" (*R*, 207). The vision continues with a child's hand, held "downward, holding the india red fountain-of-all-ladies'-hope" just after Wendell expresses his hope in his children: "I shall come to memory from time to time, if not with words of praise, why then of calumny" (*R*, 208). This passage, like chapters 5 and 24, is also interesting for the remote light it sheds on the doll's-house episode at the end of act 2 in *The Antiphon* (*A*, 94).

The final mention of Julie in *Ryder* occurs in chapter 39, "Wendell Discusses Himself with His Mother." Wendell having described at length some of his doings with women, Sophia describes how she has told all the children she loves them and will care for them; but when she told Julie, she "could not kiss her . . . because she was thinking something outside the family. Therefore I leaned my head upon her little breast, and she said 'You have betrayed me,' and . . . I shall remember her always, and she will walk to my grave, and will doubt me long, until I am a memory with her . . . and then she will condemn herself" (*R*, 222). Wendell says, "But she has always been a hussy and a stubborn girl." Sophia says, "She has always been you . . . except that she is unhung and you are slung like a man; it will make the difference" (*R*, 223). Wendell's next remark is characteristically nonresponsive; he says, twice, "To get back to me."

But Kate interrupts them, furious at knowing that both she and Amelia are pregnant again. She asserts her idea of motherhood: "It makes me ill, and there's no pleasure at either end, but I'm addict, and it's your fault, keeper of the shop, and madame of the keeper" (*R*, 224). She says that after the fight with Julie, she went to find her and beg her forgiveness. "And because she is decent, she . . . hid her face, and would not kiss me, and would not forgive; because she has a spirit and a clean heart and would not soil herself with the conditions of an imperfect soul" (*R*, 225).

Julie has been summed up three times, in views as unlike as the characters who express them. They agree chiefly in finding her different, distinct, identifiable. They show three facets cut by her child-life. Their reflections cast sight lines that take off from yet guard her unexpressed sense of self.

Sophia's version is the least simple. It is dominated by Sophia as an inextricable strand of Julie's character and future and her son as the original of which Julie is a replica changed only in sex. Wendell's version is authoritative and dismissive; he wants to resume his discourse; Julie is "always" what he's decided she is, and not worth further speculation. His and Sophia's discourse is, as usual, more a taking of turns at self-expression than an interactive exchange. It is Kate, oddly enough, who seems to see a side of the Julie the reader of *Ryder* has seen in action—young, powerless, private yet still spirited, and given to intensely principled acts.

Though Julie is not named in chapter 50, the Julie-minded reader recognizes that Amelia's self-sacrifice to Sophia's and Wendell's demands means that Julie and her four brothers will accompany their mother. They are headed for exile from the family and for whatever independence they can contrive.

Ryder offers us a world of antiphonal events. They call each other forth as the characters move between the extremes of life that are Barnes' motifs—life and death. Barnes treats them not as dual but as polar. Between them action is electric and current; between them the novel's world turns on itself and around a center. We see Julie begin to become herself through her fluent experience of new life hoped for, loss and death dreaded, new life hoped for. Without such uncanceling contraries there would be no progression.

A mythic apprehension of reality surrounds the turning world of literature like a sky or light reflective space, intangible and imagined. Literature precipitates such mythic thinking (mythic in this literary sense) in the forms of stories about absolute power.[6] Ideas about absolute power are both original and inherited, for they are *in* the power of language. On the grand scale the stories are of genesis or of apocalypse.

On the human scale, only two acts reflect the concept of absolute power. They are human creation, or birth; and human dissolution, or death—with the concept of resurrection as a mediator. In these acts, human beings intersect space and time.

The big motifs of birth and death inform Barnes' moral concern, her perception, and her lexicon. The mediating concepts she finds to show transaction between them is usually resurrection in the derived form of life-threatening childbirth—especially as it may appear to an onlooker—agonizing, bloody, and invasive. (Do Field's remarks about Barnes' "deep belief" in childlessness perhaps follow from this?) Women giving life and fearing death, women giving life and dying, women giving life and shamed by bastardy recur in her work, sometimes as principal characters, often as images and as (giveaway) throwaway phrases.

Examples abound. The earliest are in *The Book of Repulsive Women*; its second poem describes tombs as wombs; its sixth poem addresses the first of Barnes' many Kate-figures: "in your living [are] all grimaces of the dead . . . you, the massive mother of illicit spawn/staring in the sun a few more years" (*BRW*, 97). *Nightwood* opens with the death of a woman in childbirth on page one. The latest images go from *The Antiphon*'s last-page question about the death of Augusta and Miranda, "Could I know/which would be brought to childbed of the other?" (*A*, 126), to the stunning late poem "Quarry," whose speaker holds off death by striking at the face of the soul "that it fetch breath," a gesture as clinical as the slap on a baby's "most unaccustomed bottom" that makes it gasp.

Throughout *Ryder* the current between birth and death overflows in images of childbed. In "The Midwife's Lament," a perfectly measured blank-verse elegy which constitutes chapter 13, "The Horrid Outcome of Wendell's First Infidelity" is death in childbirth of a girl "who dies as women die, unequally/Impaled upon a death that crawls within;/For men die otherwise. . . ./But women on a sword they scabbard to" (*R*, 93). The jocular title does not impair, though it may be intended to undercut, the noble economy of the lines.

The second chapter of *Ryder* introduces the Ryder family in the person of Sophia's gravid mother. She is in bed, "the terrible suffering center without extremities" (*R*, 8); at the story's climax she leaves her newborn son to pregnant Sophia and dies. And Sophia "remembered her mother when she was beginning that she had finished" (*R*, 9)—a play on pronouns that sets the spiral of generative women spinning.

When Amelia meets Sophia she learns that Sophia's youngest child died an infant. When one of the sisters Louise discusses Wendell's "great thought," she has a vision of many peaceful women turned against each other, rabid, once they are aware of his "thundering male parts hung like a terrible anvil, whereon one beats out the resurrection and the death" (*R*, 51).

Soon after we meet Amelia, her mother tells her about her Aunt Nelly's suffering and disgrace when, pregnant out of wedlock and married off to a guard, she rides her horse unflinching before him as he whips her for her beauty and her state. Her advice to Amelia is: "Never let a man touch you, never show anything, keep your legs in your own life, and when you grow to be a woman keep that a secret, even from yourself. Never, never have children. . . . If you live you will be a fool. It takes a strong woman to die before she has been a fool. No one has the imagination. I did not; you will not" (*R*, 40).

Having repeated to Julie part of her mother's advice, "Don't let a man touch you," Amelia in childbed says, in her distress, "No mother would be mother ever an she could, in mid-fight, throw herself a moment out of scent" (*R*, 120).

When it is her turn to invent a lullaby and a bedtime story, Amelia uses the death of a child for one and the death of two gravid women for the other. A lost boy's mother finds him

> *Head-first in the water-butt*
> *And as the most of him was in,*
> *(Indeed, naught dry but his small chin!)*
> *. . . three-quarters lost*
> *She would make whole at any cost*
> *. . . So down she thrust the lagging heels/. . . all complete*
> *by simply pushing on the feet! (R, 130)*

The bedtime story is about Felice and Alix, delicious sisters, who expect to deliver babies at twenty and twenty-one minutes past ten on 4 April. "And at twenty minutes past ten, Felice died. One minute later Alix died. And that's the end of the two little sisters" (*R*, 202).

One chapter is a list of fantasized definitions of who Kate might have been were she not Kate. It closes with a possible Kate whose karma "overcame the custom of childbed" until the day she harbors a fallopian fetus that "burst the retort and dying unborn took with him that which had so hemmed him about" (*R*, 114). The Kate who is Kate, in fury over her pregnancy, says, "I'll kill it the minute it's born, but I'll bear it . . . you can't prevent me! I'll stand over it like a bitch before a wailing litter, and I'll stamp it to the ground, and be done with your filth! . . . I'll spew out my heart in my own way" (*R*, 224). She scouts Wendell's notion that women must "wail under the same doom, with skeletons got from the same box" (*R*, 225).

Wendell, elaborating his self-image for his mother, assures her, "my real glory is in the merry music I've struck up with my spherical, timbersome pipe of a single stop. How many notes fly through a woman at its orchestration! . . . all clinging to the beam of her interior, and ripening after the nine months, to fly forth duly harmonized, or, stillborn like a rush of grace notes, too hurried for the voice to catch, and then silence and a Christian burial" (*R*, 216). He adds that polygamy puts "a man in fettle for the midwife or the grave-digger" (*R*, 219).

When the authorities confront him and demand an account of Kate's children, Wendell tells flimflam; the second is about Moll and Eva, two fine women who live together, one always going to and the other always coming from church. They are found at the tale's end in bed "and a babe between them. Eva moved . . . a little, and Moll moved never at all" (*R*, 289), having died and left Eva a mother.

The tale he invents for Julie and Timothy has the beloved of the Beast Thingumbob say, "I began a long way before the beginning of your love, and there's that in my blood will cry halt when your blood but gets the whip, and go whining down a thin wind . . . and bed in dirt, and rot. I shall die beneath you yet from my body you shall garner ten sons. I am burst asunder at their way within me, for they come marching" (*R*, 153).

Dr. O'Connor gets Wendell to talk about faith. Wendell says, "All women are equal, until one dies in childbed, then she becomes as near to saints as my mind can conceive. Why is that? you ask; because they died at the apex of their ability" (*R*, 265).

O'Connor talks to children too, for in his *Ryder* incarnation he excels both in soaring soliloquy and in conversation. He has asked several of them about their futures. Amelia's son Hannel replies by quoting Wendell, that instructive father: "Observe that slaughter makes the shoulders rise and the head descend. See . . . the little girls stumbling to school; it's their future maternity makes them stare into the hedges" (*R*, 211).

A lyric passage, lapsing into vision, shifts the perspective around Wendell at the end of the book. He is discovered in the dark of an open field where all the beings of the earth encircle and eye him, flowing and pulsing close, far, then close again. In the wave of alien beings, he drowns and arises again—looking for someone else to disappoint.

Timothy's apostrophe to his Light-o'-Love builds to a penultimate paragraph: "I know thee as harmful, as sick and unstable, as mortal and ailing, as deadly as death, as tough and enduring, as fatal as life" (*R*, 170).

Elisha, Kate's son, preparing a piano recital, muses: "Death and the Maiden. So painfully mingled, two wings folded over her feet, and two over her eyes, and two that would not fly. . . . He thought of his mother's experiment-shocked body, heavy of belly, the stiff legs, a distorted shape of death. . . . Who can doubt the word of the mother when she is shameless in her nakedness before you, to show you how a body goes down in death?" (*R*, 293; 295–96).

From these few examples of text, we can see how the life-and-death image of childbed is the knife that cuts across the onion layers of family chronicle, oral forms, absence of heroism, leaps of diction, plot, and diffused suspense. What about Julie, the heart of the matter?

The four Julie stories—Amelia's childbed; Julie's nightmare and waking; crab-catching day; the fight with Wendell through Kate—are not accidental in order or substance.

As the responsible onlooker at Amelia's labor and delivery, Julie is terrified, then horrified. What she sees does not look at all like the triumphal delivery of new life through willing obedience to intuition and its primeval pattern of action. She sees Amelia's terrible fear and assists the doctor in Amelia's struggle with a feetfirst presentation. The delivery is not described. But as I imagine it (with what authority my own six easy experiences with natural childbirth afford), Julie would suppose that the placental blood she sees is flowing from deep inner wounds, and that Amelia's screams, grunts, and sweat flow from despair. Women, even well prepared, do not give birth as neatly as do the farm animals Julie may be supposed to have seen. Julie's image of birth is full of the fear of death and framed by the sight of her mother's sprung and bloody pelvic floor.

Wendell's post facto explanation of the mystery is also an onlooker's view, and most damaging in that it nowhere speaks to Julie's experience.

Just before Julie wakes to find her father above her and her grandmother running to her in tears, her nightmare takes its worst last turn. The many mourning children who are herself change into women with babies embedded in them, women who float and tumble in a slow coil, headed implacably for labor and delivery.

Julie's day out with Wendell and Timothy goes from torn female crabs, through the Beast's beloved packed with sons and dead beneath him, to the dead tramp, to the heard story of death, to the solitude of far-falling sleep. Nothing comes, however painfully, to birth.

Finally, Julie fights Wendell through Kate and expresses her savage indignation with the conditions of her life. The explosive action is not something being done to her; it is her deed, her vivid interference against injustice. For that moment she breaks herself free of nightmare, fear, and others' crowding confusion. She falls. She picks herself up and goes off to be alone. Unlike Wendell, she does not back down.

One way to describe Julie's role in *Ryder*, that profoundly original book, is to read it as a portrait of the artist as a young girl. Her mother's faith and belief are in patriarch and family — extended, and tangentially including the many women her father impregnates. Julie lives within the faith; she does her best to serve it, even as an acolyte at childbed, the locus of holy dread, until she says to Sophia, "You have betrayed me." Her fight with Kate shows her identifying move away from it, confirmed later by her spirited refusal to be reconciled: *non serviat*.

Field notes that Barnes' interview with Joyce is the first published citation of the great phrase, "silence, exile, and cunning"—and why not, since Barnes came to live by it? If we look at some of the matters *Ryder* shows as long or short verticals to Julie's life at home — childbed; rape; miscarriage; missed abortion; sexual activity wretched or pleasant, personal or fortituous, hetero- or homosexual; incest and threat of incest; vague implications of bestiality; child abuse; experiment-shocked women; domestic tyranny;

transvestism; sadomasochism; bastardy; struggle to survive injustice; poverty, cadging, begging, and helplessness as the lot of hard-worked women unable to work for money — we may even want to say (as Barnes would not) that at the last, as Julie goes from her first faith which has betrayed her into exile, she goes toward forging the uncreated conscience of her sex.

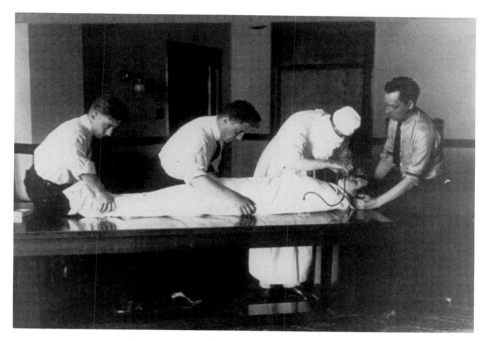

1. Barnes undergoing force-feeding; from her article "How It Feels to Be Forcibly Fed," New York *World Magazine*, 6 September 1914. Courtesy Special Collections, University of Maryland at College Park Libraries.

2. *Twirling a Mustache, He Watches the Death Pang*; illustration by Barnes for "When the Puppets Come to Town," *New York Morning Telegraph*, 8 July 1917. Courtesy Special Collections, University of Maryland at College Park Libraries.

3. Early newspaper illustration by Barnes. Courtesy Special Collections, University
of Maryland at College Park Libraries.

4. *Because the Road He Took Was Wrong*; early newspaper illustration by Barnes. Brooklyn *Daily Eagle*, 27 August 1913. Courtesy Special Collections, University of Maryland at College Park Libraries.

5. Early painting by Barnes (*The Doughboy*), exhibited 1915. Courtesy Special Collections, University of Maryland at College Park Libraries.

6. James Light; pencil sketch by Barnes, late 1910s or early 1920s. Courtesy Special Collections, University of Maryland at College Park Libraries.

7. Helen Westley; illustration by Barnes from *A Book* (1923). Courtesy Special Collections, University of Maryland at College Park Libraries.

8. Head of a Polish girl by Barnes (tearsheet); *Dial*, March 1920. Courtesy Special Collections, University of Maryland at College Park Libraries.

9. Mary Pyne; illustration by Barnes from *A Book*. Courtesy Special Collections, University of Maryland at College Park Libraries.

10. Mary Pyne of the Provincetown Players. Courtesy Special Collections, University of Maryland at College Park Libraries.

CHAUFFAGE CENTRAL
SALLES DE BAINS
EAU COURANTE
Froide et Chaude
—
TÉL.FLEURUS 29·40

11. Thelma Wood; sketch by Barnes on Grand Hôtel stationery. Courtesy
Special Collections, University of Maryland at College Park Libraries.

12. Silverpoint drawing by Thelma Wood. Courtesy Special Collections, University of Maryland at College Park Libraries.

13. James Joyce; pencil sketch by Barnes. Courtesy Special Collections, University of Maryland at College Park Libraries.

14. *L'arbre d'amour*, from Pierre Duchartre and René Saulnier, *L'imagerie populaire* (1926). From the Avery Architectural and Fine Arts Library, Columbia University.

15. The Ryder family tree; frontispiece from *Ryder* (1928). Courtesy Special Collections, University of Maryland at College Park Libraries.

16. Detail of Julie from the Ryder family tree (plate 15). Courtesy Special Collections, University of Maryland at College Park Libraries.

17. *The Sisters Louise*; unpublished drawing by Barnes for *Ryder*. Courtesy Special Collections, University of Maryland at College Park Libraries.

18. *Amen*; unpublished drawing by Barnes for *Ryder*. Courtesy Special Collections, University of Maryland at College Park Libraries.

19. *Ye Olde Wives' Tail*; unpublished drawing by Barnes for *Ryder*. Courtesy Special Collections, University of Maryland at College Park Libraries.

20. Young Natalie Barney. Courtesy of the Natalie Barney Papers, Bibliotheque Jacques Doucet, Paris.

21. Natalie Barney at age fifty, 1926. Courtesy of the Natalie Barney Papers, Bibliotheque Jacques Doucet, Paris.

22. *H U S*, from Duchartre and Saulnier, *L'imagerie populaire*. From the Avery Architectural and Fine Arts Library, Columbia University.

23. Drawing of a bull by Barnes, late 1920s. Courtesy Special Collections, University of Maryland at College Park Libraries.

24. Title page vignette for *Ladies Almanack*. Courtesy Special Collections, University of Maryland at College Park Libraries.

25. Cordelia Coker Pearson; photograph of painting by Barnes, signed and dated 1947. Location of original unknown. Courtesy Special Collections, University of Maryland at College Park Libraries.

26. Alice Rohrer; oil painting by Barnes; 1934. Courtesy Special
Collections, University of Maryland at College Park Libraries.

¶ . . . Somewhere I met André Germain, who at the time was much excited by the vitality of young Americans; and he used occasionally to appear to look us all over. Generally he saw to it that he paid all the bills, as Monsieur Germain was a man of great wealth, though very careful with his money.

Like Ronald Firbank, André was different. His voice was thin and high; his hands showed age, but they were delicately scrawny, like a small, blue-blooded old lady's. . . . One night at the Boeuf sur le Toit with Djuna Barnes and Sarah Kelly, Monsieur Germain was made very unhappy. He dearly loved beautiful and elegant people, particularly women, and both Sarah and Djuna were looking so that night. Djuna had on a gown with a ruff about the neck and looked very elegantly Victorian; Sarah was elegant with a smartness that I shall not try to describe. Thelma Wood came in with Margot Van Schuyler, both looking neatly tailored and handsome boyish girls. The party grew. We ordered food, starting with caviar, on to roast duck. Afterwards there was a fine old brandy with coffee, and André paid the bill without demur. He was looking admiringly at Djuna who, handsome to look upon, was also being very much the lady.

André showed her a collapsible diamond ring, of platinum. Djuna took it to admire and then, turning naughty-girl, shook her finger at Monsieur Germain and said, "André, where did you get that ring?"

Monsieur Germain looked thunder struck, and answered, "Honorably, Miss Barnes." I doubt that he ever forgave her. At the time I was hopeful about getting Monsieur Germain to have some of Djuna's stories translated into French and published in a magazine or by a publishing house which he virtually controlled. Instead, Monsieur Germain shortly fled into the night.

—Robert McAlmon and Kay Boyle,
Being Geniuses Together,
1920–1930 (1968)

Gilt on Cardboard:
Djuna Barnes as Illustrator
of Her Life and Work

Frances M. Doughty

To tell, not to tell, to tell in disguise? A central tension in Barnes' work is her effort to transform, to tell her story while keeping it secret. It is as if Barnes were stuck, able neither to let go of the effort nor to complete it. The telling is hidden and encoded, buried under a heavy brocade of style, never finished, never forthright.

"Notre Dame . . . a lonely creature by preference . . . is not disturbed by those devotees who fall into two classes; those going toward, and those coming from, faith. She is in the centre condition, where there is no going and no coming. Perhaps this is why, for me, there was something more possible in the church of Saint Germain de Pres."[1] This image of perpetual going to and coming from vividly conveys Barnes' obsessive struggle with her material, the perpetual motion itself a paralysis. The inability to come to rest is also reflected in Barnes' presentation of women's sexuality, which embraces neither heterosexuality nor lesbianism. Reminiscent of an entry in her brother's journal for 1900,[2] the image is expanded from the passing reference above, published in 1922, to an entire chapter in *Ryder* and recurs in *Ladies Almanack*, both written when Barnes was in her late twenties and early thirties and both published in 1928.[3] The recurrence of the theme throughout the 1920s and its possible origin in Barnes' childhood indicate its importance.

In both the language and the illustrations of *Ryder* and *Ladies Almanack*, Barnes' strategy to resolve the powerful and conflicting desires to tell and not to tell is to "hide" pieces of experience, quite literal and untransformed, in an intricate weave of borrowed styles. The original experience lurks beneath the surface, a stubborn, intractable datum skulking in its lair.[4] Although Barnes has been classified as a modernist and was deeply influenced by Joyce,[5] she turned to the past for her literary and visual sources and used them to disguise her experience rather than to create forms whose experiential referent was the creative process itself.

Judging by her surviving work, Barnes does not seem to have used visual art as a primary means of expression but as a means of illustrating something preexisting, whether a concept, as in her antiwar work; a text, as in the illustrations to her fiction; or a person, as in the portrait sketches accompanying her interviews. In addition to the illustrations to *Ryder* and *Ladies Almanack*, not all of which are encoded, Barnes' published visual work includes many illustrations to her journalism, both fiction and nonfiction, in the 1910s and early 1920s and again in the early 1930s, as well as the illustrations to *The Book of Repulsive Women*, published in 1915, and to *A Book*, published in 1923.[6] She also painted several portraits in oil in the early 1930s.

In 1913 alone, in six months, Barnes produced thirty-eight articles accompanied by eighty-eight drawings, as well as more than twenty drawings apparently not associated with any text. Some of these newspaper illustrations are densely patterned renditions of figures in a style reminiscent of Beardsley (e.g., plates 2 and 3). Although some faces of these illustrations seem to have individual features, their elaborate costumes and strange postures contribute to an effect of remoteness and detachment from ordinary human life. Other drawings, on the other hand, use a loose, flowing, outline style that seems to capture the essence of the moment and of the person being portrayed (e.g., plate 4). She was not above visual puns, as in her drawing of Diamond Jim Brady, which is a series of mainly triangular rectilinear shapes, arranged to give an impression of diamonds, and set in a black circle with a diamond-shaped cravat hanging down below.

In 1915, the same year that *The Book of Repulsive Women* appeared, Guido Bruno exhibited a group of Barnes' antiwar paintings and drawings.[7] Two items in the Barnes Collection were probably part of that exhibition, *The Bullet* and *The Doughboy*.[8] Both pieces are among the most emotionally powerful and direct visual work by Barnes that has survived. The colors are somber, the backgrounds dark; the forms are highly expressive. *The Bullet* portrays a skull-like head looming out of a black background with stark white spaces denoting eyes and teeth, and a vivid slash of red lips. *The Doughboy* (plate 5) is a standing male nude in a murky battlefield, holding a phallic rifle with bayonet while an elongated hand rises surrealistically from the ground. These two works, Barnes' most unambiguous and direct visual statements, are self-explanatory, self-contained, and immediately comprehensible without any accompanying text.

In the late 1910s and early 1920s, in addition to the lively, straightforward black-and-white outline drawings illustrating her interviews of prominent literary and theatrical personalities, Barnes produced more detailed portrait drawings, primarily in pencil and using color and shading. Her subjects were her friends and acquaintances, many of them connected with the Provincetown Players.[9] Barnes labeled three of these drawings, probably at the time she was preparing her papers for the University of Maryland, judging by the infirm state of her handwriting.[10]

The most impressive of them is that of James Light (plate 6), with whom, according to Field, Barnes had a brief affair after his marriage to Susan Light ended.[11] He stares intensely out at the viewer, his face framed by a mass of hair touched with red. On the back, Barnes wrote, "James Light of Provincetown Players—first producer of Jean O'Neil [sic]." Barnes also drew a pen-and-ink portrait of O'Neill himself that continues the black-and-white, highly textured style of her earlier, more Beardsleyesque work. A reptile is growing out of his shoulder, but the drawing is empathetic and sensitive.[12]

The other two drawings identified by Barnes were published as illustrations to *A Book*. The first, appearing after "Song in Autumn," carries on its reverse the note "Louise Hellstrome" [sic] in Barnes' hand and is also stamped "Harper's Bazaar," as if it had been submitted for publication. The second appears after *Three from the Earth*. It is identified as Helen Westley by an inscription on the lower border (plate 7). The drawing originally appeared in 1919, illustrating a review of Westley in the play "John Ferguson" that was published in *Vanity Fair*.[13] Barnes had interviewed Westley in 1917, two years prior to the review, and preserved a photo of her, now in the Barnes Collection at the University of Maryland.[14] It seems likely that there was a personal as well as a professional connection between them.[15]

There are two remaining drawings in *A Book*, neither identified by Barnes, that are clearly of women. One portrays a woman with strong cheekbones, exuberant hair, narrow eyes, and a large prominent nose, following the story "Oscar"; the second is of a woman with staring eyes, a long, thin, beaklike nose, and a small, pursed mouth.[16] The first of these two unidentified drawings is probably of Ida Rauh, one of the founders of the Provincetown Players and a woman whose talents ranged from the law to sculpting.[17]

The second unidentified drawing of a woman (plate 9) precedes "Six Songs of Kahlidine (To the Memory of Mary Pyne)." Mary Pyne, also connected with the Provincetown Players, "had Titian red hair, gray-blue eyes . . . creamy skin and red lips (plate 10). She combined the charm of Mimi in *La Bohême* with the spiritual beauty of a Della Robbia Madonna."[18] Charles Norman, who describes her as "frail and beautiful," states in his memoirs, "There is a drawing of her in Djuna Barnes' first book."[19] Barnes kept a photograph of Pyne taken at Saranac, New York, where she had been sent to recover from a severe hemorrhage and where she eventually died of tuberculosis. The original drawing is in pencil, with red lips and marked round red areas, signs of fever, carefully colored on the cheekbones.[20] The overall expression is of someone profoundly disappointed. Like the later oil portrait of Emily Coleman, with whom Barnes had a long, close friendship, the image seems deformed. One feels no one could look like that, yet it has the power of psychological truth.

The position of the illustration, immediately preceding the poems dedicated to Pyne; the deformation parallel to the painting of Coleman; the lack of resemblance between the first unidentified drawing and photographs of Mary Pyne in the Barnes papers at the University of Maryland—all suggest that this is Barnes' representation of Mary Pyne, a woman whom she apparently loved. Is this transformation that is both revealing and deforming what Barnes made of those whom she loved?

The portrait shocks the viewer, who wants to deny that anyone could look like the vision Barnes has created. The portrait of Emily Coleman, which also appears frighteningly distorted, is the most extreme example of this portraiture, yet comparison with photographs and verbal descriptions of the subject shows that Barnes' portrayal of Coleman contains a psychological truth. Nonetheless, these images are a peculiarly bleak and Barnesian view of a human being. The more emotionally involved Barnes was with her subject, the more likely she was to represent that person in the idiom of her own inner world, producing an image at once deformed and transformed, horrifying and true.

If it was the very act of loving, the fact of intimacy, that caused Barnes to reshape, to deform, those she loved, the roots of this process may be seen in her own early experience of intimacy. In creating the illustrations and text of *Ryder*, Barnes concealed bits of her autobiography amid the tropical exuberance of her profusion of styles and genres. With such a dense and concealing cover, the autobiographical information is perceived only by those with enough information or intuition to apprehend it.

The illustrations for *Ryder* and *Ladies Almanack* show a marked break from Barnes' prior work. The volume of her published drawings diminished from thirteen (not including those in *A Book*) in 1923 to none in 1924, with three (all in one article) in 1925, then none until the appearance of *Ryder* and *Ladies Almanack* in 1928.[21] Within this five-year period, Barnes moved to Paris and became the lover of Thelma Wood (plates 11, 38, 39, 45), who was herself an artist. Wood's work consisted of sculpture and etchings. The few images by Wood that are accessible in Field's *Djuna* and in the Barnes Collection are fluid and sensual and contain interesting juxtapositions—a lady's boot with a lush flower, a cutaway view of the ocean: a ship and tiny sailors above the surface, the depths populated by highly expressive sea creatures in various relations to each other (plate 12).[22] Did the fact that Wood was an artist contribute to Barnes' decision to derive her illustrations from existing images?

This strategy of literal representation hidden by borrowed and highly stylized form that seems to have no experiential referent is especially clear in these illustrations, which contain direct copies of folk images from popular culture into which Barnes inserted the faces of her family and friends. *L'imagerie populaire*, the source of many images in *Ryder* and *Ladies Almanack*, appeared in 1926; Barnes was apparently working on the drawings to both texts between 1926 and 1928.[23]

Neither part of the image is transformed by Barnes, but the combination itself, by "hiding" the experiential referent in the copied image, encodes her experience, making it unrecognizable to anyone who does not know the original sources for both parts of the image. Because the faces in the published drawings, much reduced from their original size, are so small, because most readers are not trained to look for the telling detail that indicates portrayal of a specific individual,[24] and because fewer readers, if any, know the individuals represented, the drawing is read as a whole simply illustrating the text with which is it associated.

The first illustration in *Ryder* is the frontispiece, the Ryder family tree, copied from the Tree of Love reproduced in *L'imagerie populaire* (plate 14). Barnes has removed the gender distinction between the ladies on the ground and the men in the tree whom the ladies are seeking to capture and has added branches enough to accommodate the Ryder family, as well as identifying banners for each character (plates 15, 16). In her original drawing at least five faces of Barnes' family can be seen: Barnes' paternal grandmother, Zadel Barnes Gustafson (Sophia Ryder); Zadel's second husband, Axel Gustafson (Alex Alexson); Barnes' mother, Elizabeth Chappell Barnes (Amelia Ryder; plates 31, 32); and Barnes' father, Wald Barnes (Wendell Ryder; plate 30).

The tree also represents Barnes' image of her family. Wendell and Amelia sit on opposite sides of the tree, in contrast to the happier pair of Sophia/Zadel and Alex/Axel, who sit facing each other. Amelia is hunched, sitting sideways. She is smaller and more remote than Wendell, who sits facing squarely forward, holding a small figure in a long skirt like that held by the figure in the illustration to chapter 47, "Going To, and Coming From." The smallest, most gathered-in person in the tree is the figure of Julie on the top left branch of the tree, above her mother, below her brother, and on the other side of the tree from her father. In Barnes' own portrait of her family she has given the figure representing herself the least amount of space. She has also made clear her distinction between the legitimate and illegitimate members of the family by placing the other women and the children Ryder sired by them on the ground at the foot of the tree: Molly Dance with her dogs and children of unknown fathers, Laura Twelvetree, and Kate Careless and her children. Dr. Matthew O'Connor, in a younger, pre-*Nightwood* version of himself, stands off to the right and at the rightmost edge of the drawing is a small tombstone bearing the legend, "Like Any Ewe," referring to the woman who died in childbirth in chapter 13, "The Horrid Outcome of Wendell's First Infidelity."

The same combination of a real face in a borrowed image appears in the illustration to chapter 1, "Jesus Mundane." Wendell again wears a coat with a fur collar. His nose, the set of his mouth, and the way his hair curls all resemble the photograph of Wald Barnes cited above. The rest of the image is in the style of *L'imagerie populaire*. (The sponge he carries, which "Hither and thither about his bum y-swoped" [*R*, 76], hangs from his saddle. Even this sponge may refer to an incident in 1900, described by Djuna's older brother Thurn in an exercise book held in the Barnes Collection in the McKeldin Library.)

The third illustration in *Ryder* shows five women in a minimal landscape with tufted trees, lying on the ground. This apparently strange scene in fact exactly represents the sentence, "Ear to the Ground my Gossips!" (*R*, 29), which is written as a caption on the lower border of the original.[25] Drawings that seem inexplicable by themselves turn out to be exact representations of the text. They seem bizarre not because of their style but because the viewer cannot imagine the scenes that would explain them. Barnes, however, can and has described them in words which the illustrations match exactly.

Another literal representation of a bizarre scene in the text is found in the illustration to chapter 8, "Pro and Con, Or the Sisters Louise," in which the women are tearing each other's hair and rolling over each other, matching Barnes' description of the fight over Wendell. The landscape and composition come from the fifth row, second column of a set of pictures in *L'imagerie populaire* showing "Le Monde renversé" (the world turned topsy-turvy), in which mice are chasing a cat uphill.[26] Barnes makes a number of visual references to the topsy-turvy theme, a common series in *L'imagerie populaire*.

An unfinished drawing of two women playing the piano side by side apparently was intended to illustrate the same chapter, which opens with the two sisters Louise playing the piano together (plate 17). There are other unfinished sketches of heads on the same sheet in pencil. The sisters are outlined in ink, the outlines having been traced, with yellow and pink coloring in their hair and dresses respectively.

L'imagerie populaire again provides the source for the illustration to chapter 13, "Midwives Lament, or the Horrid Outcome of Wendell's First Infidelity."[27] The deceased's nightgown is held upside down, as if it were the shape of a tombstone, and on it is written the lament for the woman who died in childbirth. The volume and stiffness of the nightgown resemble that of the breeches in the "Partage de la culotte" (the dividing of the breeches), a widespread theme in the popular art of the French provinces.[28]

In addition to the unfinished illustration to chapter 8, "Pro and Con, Or the Sisters Louise," there are four other drawings that were not included in the published version of *Ryder*. The first shows a double bed in the center of the drawing, with a man entering through a door on the left and the back of a seated woman to the right (plate 18). Close inspection reveals that the woman is seated on a chamber pot labeled "Amen." She, therefore, is identified as Sophia and the drawing as illustrating chapter 3, "Sophia and the Five Fine Chamber-pots."

The second of these unpublished drawings seems upside down until one reads the banner at the top, whose legend is "Woman Upsidedown." The theme, if not the image, comes again from the world-turned-topsy-turvy drawings in *L'imagerie populaire*. These drawings, which were important enough to Barnes that she mounted a page of them and saved it,[29] were done in sets with each item showing a different reversal of the natural order, such as mice chasing cats, fish flying in the air, land animals living under the water, animals flogging human beings, and so forth. The natural versus the unnatural and the disturbance of the natural order are major themes in both *Ryder* and *Ladies Almanack*. The original drawing for "Women Upsidedown" is not in the Barnes Collection, but there are two reproductions of it, made in Paris, one of which is annotated on the back in Barnes' hand, "Amelia hears from Ann,"[30] indicating that it was intended for chapter 12, "Amelia Hears from Her Sister in re Hisodalgus, That Fine Horse," in which Amelia's sister Ann decries the changes she observes in the world around her.

The Beast Thingumbob, illustrating the chapter of the same name, is more sophisticated and complex than the image of a monster devouring a human shown in *L'imagerie populaire*, but Barnes may have used that image as one of her sources. The drawing is a frightening image: the creature seems to be a woman but has hooves, no face, and a prostrate naked body, over which stands the beast. Like other unnerving illustrations in *Ryder*, it exactly represents what is described in the text: "she was . . . of large limbs and of beauty outside the imagination. . . . Her feet were thinly hoofed, and her hair was many coils, and her face was not yet, and her breasts were ten" (*R*, 150). Love and death are interwoven in this story of two strange beings, told by Wendell to his daughter Julie and her brother.

In contrast to the Beast Thingumbob, the last of the unpublished illustrations is homey and humorous (plate 19). Captioned "Ye Olde Wives Tail," it shows Amelia and Kate cozily knitting, each on her side of the fireplace, each lovingly handcrafting a knit codpiece for Wendell. What is most interesting about the drawing is the exactness of its portraits of Elizabeth Chappell Barnes, Djuna's mother, as Amelia and of Fanny Faulkner, the Mrs. F. of Thurn's journals, as Kate Careless.[31] Although the chapter starts off happily enough with a discussion of the difficulty of fitting a body part so variable in size, the two women soon begin fighting "till blood flowed, and hair fell, and there were tears amid the equal anger" (*R*, 228). The fighting that actually went on in Djuna's childhood is portrayed in Thurn's journal entry for 5 June 1901 (in the Barnes Collection). Both the tone and the scenario, the enmity between the women, their attitudes toward the children, and the man who is both central to and detached from the battle, are similar to the incident in which Elisha hits his brother on the head (chapter 33, "Be She What She May"), showing how closely parts of *Ryder* reproduce Barnes' own experience. Like the bizarre drawings, a literal rendition that the reader finds unbelievable is as good a disguise as fiction.

Despite the constant ill-will between Amelia and Kate, when it is time for Wendell's dinner they put aside their differences and, functioning like a pair of well-trained plowhorses, produce dinner for the man whose bed they share and whose children they bear. This subservience of women to Wendell's needs recurs throughout *Ryder*, which is a book about (male) sexuality: fecund, "natural," indiscriminate.

In the tradition in which Barnes placed herself, sexuality has been a male domain: in an androcentric world, that which lacks a marker for "female" (e.g., "female sexuality") is assumed to be male. The "hero," Wendell Ryder, is portrayed as a natural force, male, female, child, all in one. Wendell's sexuality is rampant, overflowing, one with the great stream of Nature's procreation, a broadcast sowing of seed. And, like seed, the result of Wendell's sexual impulse falls where it may, with no further connection between its source and its growing place.

Is it in fact desire that drives him? Volume rather than satisfaction from pleasure in the act itself appears to be the predominant motif, along with a certain smugness at his insatiability. In discussing Wendell's sexuality, one of the sisters Louise observes, "He paints a rosy picture . . . of polygamy for — . . . the *man*" (*R*, 48, 49).

And the picture of polygamy for the woman? Barnes portrays female sexuality as "the undulating ground, bursting with pea-pod, bean-pod and chicory . . . here the eyes of the potatoes looking forth, and there the deep-banked fires of many a mound of manure, a perfect prostrate tapestry of fecundity . . ." (*R*, 50). And six women in like mode, "pinching and pushing their fertile fingers into ribs and buttocks. . . . Panting, they flung themselves in threes beside the murmuring fountains . . . hair dishevelled, clothes awry, hot and with leaping heart and pelvis, and fell over upon each other, laughing and limp" (*R*, 50). Then, breaking through the Firbankian rhythm, the comedic distance of mannered prose, the image comes upon the women "of Wendell setting forth from the earth with stupendous great wings, outstripping the cornfield and the mountains, and rising up into the clouds, like an enormous and beloved insect, with strong hands upward and arched feet downward, and thundering male parts hung like a terrible anvil, whereon one beats out the resurrection and the death" (*R*, 50, 51).

The women, like cats, begin to fight, "writhing, biting, tearing, scratching, screaming, crying, over and over they rolled in blood and tears" (*R*, 51). They finally come to "the ravine . . . where between tall rank grasses the rubbish blooms" (*R*, 51).

Of all the women in *Ryder*, only four are portrayed as taking pleasure in sex: Sophia, Wendell's mother; prolific Molly Dance;[32] the anonymous

Haymarket drummer of Wendell's youth who was, "very simple, very lewd" (*R*, 265); and Lady Terrance Bridesleep, in her sixties. These women are also, each in her own way, self-sufficient, and each, in her own way, has diverged from respectable womanhood.

The dubious pleasures of sex for the women of *Ryder* include pregnancy and death in childbirth, in addition to jealousy, lack of autonomy, and rape. The mother of Wendell's wife Amelia warns her when she is a girl, "'Never let a man touch you, never show anything, keep your legs in your own life, and when you grow to be a woman, keep that a secret even from yourself.' She shuddered. 'Never, never, have children . . .'" (*R*, 40). Wendell's first extramarital affair causes pregnancy and death.

> [She] died as women die, unequally
> Impaled upon a death that crawls within;
> For men die otherwise, of man unsheathed
> But women on a sword they scabbard to. (R, 93)

(The word "vagina" is exactly the Latin word meaning "sword sheath.")

Barnes, writing about (male) sexuality, is often broad, open, humorous, seemingly relaxed, certainly a phenomenon for a woman writer, even in the 1920s. Yet there is a bitter aftertaste, an uneasiness in the fun, a hollowness in its pleasure. Sex is only a momentary satisfaction for Wendell. A trail of women leads to the novel's ultimate question and its last sentence, the repeated refrain, "Whom should he disappoint now?" Under the pastiche, the play of genre, are we to seek some other meaning; and if we do, will Barnes slide out from under, saying from her elusive distance that we missed the joke?[33] The style is a mixture of parody and passion, making fun of itself by the use of alliteration, interruption, irony, and pastiche. Yet occasional passages of raw power, such as the image of the anvil or the venom of the gossips in "Rape and Repining!" break through. The reader responds to those passages Barnes has written with direct and powerful emotion, then feels foolish when she returns to parody.

This uneasiness is particularly acute in the passages in which Barnes deals with women and sexuality. Is she mocking the stereotypes of women — that women ask to be raped; that women are "catty" — or women ourselves? The voices of women, the gossips in "Rape and Repining!" say that women *do* ask to be raped, that women *are* hypocritical, that women *do* tear each other apart for a man. What is Barnes' own stance towards these voices?

There is a lack of congruence between Barnes' sexual humor and freedom of sexual language, her apparently Rabelaisian sexual zest and her underlying story, which tells of women damaged by heterosexuality, childbirth, death, gossip, and each other. Moreover, even Wendell, the perpetual picaresque hero, derives only self-satisfaction from his sexuality, not pleasure in the act itself. There is a lack of volition: even his sexual perpetual motion apparently results from Wendell's passivity, his complacent view of himself as part of the forces of nature over which he has no control. He remains ever the son, carried by his mother's energy. It is she who raises money for his ménage, and it is she who procures the two women who compose it. Significantly, she does not invite them for Wendell's sake, but to be daughters to her. (Is that invitation part of family history? Is it something Barnes wanted a woman to say to her?) Even in his mates, Wendell is the passive recipient of his mother's going forth.

Dame Musset, the heroine of *Ladies Almanack*, on the other hand, has always been the agent of her own pleasure. The opposite of passive, she looks back on a life well spent. "'Still,' she remarked, sipping a little hot tea, 'they were dear Creatures, and they have paced me to a contented and knowing fifty. I am well pleased. Upon my Sword there is no Rust, and upon my Escutcheon so many Stains that I have, in this manner, created my own banner and my own Badge'" (*LA*, 35). She is noted, we are told, for "her Genius at bringing up by Hand. . . . [and] her Slips of the Tongue" (*LA*, 9). Like the coat of arms on the title page, Musset's skill at the two staples of lesbian lovemaking is only slightly disguised, though the reader must make some effort to decode it.

As in *Ryder*, the reader would not know without other sources of information that both the illustrations and the text contain accurate presentations of actual people: Natalie Barney and her friends. Barnes makes very little effort to disguise the women who were her originals for *Ladies Almanack*. She made a greater effort in *Ryder* to conceal the autobiographical sources of her characters, but since *Ladies Almanack* is a satire, it is important that its subjects be recognizable through their coded nicknames.

The face of Dame Musset in the frontispiece and in the illustration on page 16 ("For these reasons sainted") is clearly copied from photographs of Natalie Barney (plate 20). In the original drawing for the latter illustration, Barnes reworked the face by cutting out a second version and pasting it over the old one.[34] And again, as in *Ryder*, Barnes inserted these likenesses into images drawn from folk art, so that the reader will see the illustration simply as a single entity done in the style of popular art. The cover is adapted from *L'imagerie populaire* by making ladies out of the soldiers following their leader and by putting a skirt on the leader's coat.[35]

Barnes uses the same technique in her drawing of the sainted Dame Musset's tongue playing upon the seated Senorita Fly-About after Musset's death. The features of Senorita Fly-About are not individualized, but the hair is indicated by short, wavy lines—a shorthand portrayal of Mimi Franchetti, who was known for her lustrous short curly hair. Natalie Barney and Mimi Franchetti were lovers in 1926, as recorded by Liane de Pougy in her memoirs:[36] "during the summer Nathalie wrote me a line saying that she was in love, madly in love with a woman, and that this love outstripped all her other loves by a long way. Rather vexed, I answered: 'The best in your life was me! Me! Me!'" (de Pougy, *My Blue Notebooks*, 202).

Like *Ryder, Ladies Almanack* contains illustrations that seem inexplicable without their accompanying text. The illustration for April, for example, depicts a banner broken by a hand-lettered star, under which sits a lady wearing a hat and urinating onto a cloud, at the other end of which is a small female figure running to the right and carrying a pitchfork on which sits a disproportionately large bee. The text explains: "as in the old Days when a Person in the last stages of Hydrophobia sometimes found small Whelps in the Urine, in the Waters of such [a woman in love] is seen the fully Robed on-marching Figure of Venus no larger than a Caraway Seed, a Trident in one Hand and a Gos-Wasp on the left Fist" (*LA*, 28).

Urination, bare buttocks, and spanking are popular themes in Barnes' drawings. In addition to this drawing of a woman urinating in "April" of *Ladies Almanack*, there are two illustrations of women peeing in *Ryder*, that for chapter 3, "Sophia and the Five Fine Chamber-pots," in which Sophia is shown sitting upon the fifth fine chamber pot, marked 'Amen' (unpublished), and for chapter 15, "Who Was the Girl," in which the voluminous mother of Kate Careless pisses copiously into the street while hitting a high note (published only in the reprint edition of *Ryder*); a third drawing, also unpublished but apparently not associated with either *Ryder* or *Ladies Almanack*, exists in which a huge bull stands in the middle of the street (plate 23). The animal is shitting, farting, peeing, and belching all at the same time. Children are flying kites in the breeze from the fart, sailing boats in the puddle of urine, and trying to hold their skirts down in the wind from the animal's mouth.[37]

Drawings depicting bare buttocks and/or spankings include four from *Ladies Almanack*, illustrating "March," "June," "August," and "November," and one from *Ryder*, in which Horace Chubble, with a feather in his own bottom, looks under the skirts of the angels, as described in a letter to Amelia from her sister Ann (chapter 12, "Amelia Hears from Her Sister in re Hisodalgus, That Fine Horse.") These drawings are the visual equivalent of Barnes' apparently sexually free writing. Like the writing, however, they seem more like adolescent sexual humor than the bawdiness of sexual pleasure which is comfortable with itself.

In addition to direct borrowing from the drawings of *L'imagerie populaire*, reference to its illustrations of the theme of the world turned topsy-turvy exists in *Ladies Almanack* also, in the illustration for "September," "She Is a Fish of Earth." A mermaid is shown heaving up out of the earth with small wings growing out of her temples, corresponding to the statement in the text describing the deterioration of woman's condition, "She was not fashioned to swim in Heaven, she is a Fish of Earth, she swims in Terra-firma" (*LA*, 56). Woman is by nature caught in a contradiction, unable to transcend or adapt.

Whereas several unpublished illustrations for *Ryder* exist in the Barnes Collection, none has been identified for *Ladies Almanack*, perhaps because it was privately financed and printed, giving Barnes complete control over its publication.[38]

The world portrayed in *Ladies Almanack* is a world of women, with the lone voice of Patience Scalpel interjecting the heterosexual point of view, complete with the stereotypical "I wouldn't want my daughter to marry one": "'Methinks,' she mused . . . 'they love the striking Hour, nor would breed the Moments that go to it. Sluts!' she said pleasantly after a little thought, 'Are good Mothers to supply them with Luxuries in the next Generation; for they themselves will have no Shes, unless some Her puts them forth! Well I'm not the Woman for it! They well [*sic*] have to pluck where they may. My Daughters shall go amarrying!'" (*LA*, 13). Scalpel's voice and Barnes' own introduction of the *Ladies Almanack* as a "slight satiric wigging" (*LA*, foreword), allow Barnes to keep her distance from the reader. Like the gossips of *Ryder*, Patience Scalpel introduces doubt in the reader's mind as to what Barnes' own views are.[39] As in *Ryder*, Barnes' presentation of women's sexuality is ambiguous, although the ambiguity has different terms. Unlike respectable heterosexual women, the lesbians of *Ladies Almanack* are not punished for their sexuality by rape and pregnancy. Having already stepped to the other side of the line identifying the nice and the good, they enjoy their lust, despite a broken heart every so often.

> *Casting to the Winds all common Care*
> *Like a Bell that throws its Nature to the Air.*
> *Of such is then the high and gaming Pride*
> *of Woman by a Woman's girlish Side! (LA, 40)*

They are autonomous and independent; they like sex. "I would . . . that there were one Woman somewhere that one could take to task for Lethargy," says Dame Musset (*LA*, 34).

But are they to be taken seriously? No. Barnes' stance in her foreword to the reprinted edition of *Ladies Almanack* is that the work is something tossed off in her youth; she does not disavow its lesbianism, however. In writing the book, Barnes interwove her "neap-tide to the Proustian chronicle" (*LA*, foreword) with reflections on lesbian mores and on the nature of man, of woman, and of time.

Ladies Almanack is considerably shorter than *Ryder*; perhaps for that reason Barnes did not mix so wide a range of genres so outrageously as in *Ryder*, but she is equally ambiguous in her intent toward the reader. Her comments on lesbians and women are less than adulatory. The hatred of gossip—especially in "Rape and Repining!" for example—recurs in *Ladies Almanack* in Barnes' comments on a woman who "snaps Grace in twain with a bragging Tongue, . . . sad chronicling this that all Women are not tidy and neat of Perch, for when a Woman is sick she is sicker sick than any Man, as a rotten Plover is more stincking [*sic*] than a rotten Stick" (*LA*, 48, 49).

Women are more prone to jealousy than men: "Yet do this Fire rage as hotly here in the Garden of Venus, yea, with an even more licorous and tempestuous flame, than in the very Camp of Nature; and where one Man is cut down from a Rope's End for the sake of his dishonest Wife, two Maids will that same day be found swinging to that Same Beam for that same Girl" (*LA*, 57). Women don't reason, are caught in a maze (*LA*, 58):

We shake the Tree, till there be no Leaves, and cry out at the Sticks; we trouble the Earth and we shall not cease to eat of it until the easing Bone. Our Peace is not skin deep, but to the Marrow, we are not wide this side of *rigor mortis*; we go down to no River of Wisdom, but swim alone in Jordan. We have few Philosophers among us for our Blood was stewed too thick to bear up Wisdom, which is a little Craft, and floats only when the way is prepared, and the Winds are calm. (*LA*, 59)

Unlike the passages used to create distance between the author and reader in *Ryder*, Barnes here directly speaks in the first person of the pain of women who love women.

Yet there are also zest and pleasure in *Ladies Almanack*, and its description of women who are sexual with other women, especially of Dame Musset, conveys a satisfaction lacking among the heterosexual women of *Ryder*, and even lacking for its hero, Wendell Ryder. This difference between Dame Musset and Wendell Ryder reflects the difference between Natalie Barney and Wald Barnes, the people whom Barnes took as her sources for those characters. Dame Musset is described as "a Person well pleased a long time" (*LA*, 23), as one who is her own revenge (*LA*, 26), which characterization could be written with equal truth of Natalie Barney, who may have loved and left, but who did not disappoint.

Although Barnes' account of Natalie Barney and her friends is notably more sympathetic than her portrayal of heterosexuality in *Ryder*, in later life she disowned the world of women, denying that she was a lesbian — she just loved a woman (Thelma Wood) — and protesting the use of the name her father gave her by Djunabooks, a women's bookstore in New York City.[40] It is as if, in the end, she could not let go of her need for the power of the male to validate her, especially as a writer.

The issue is not whether Barnes was a lesbian or a heterosexual, but that she was neither. What is described by the words "sexuality" or "sexual preference" is not a simple matter of the physical construction of those with whom one has sex; it also conveys a sense of tribe and tribal allegiance, and it is the issue of tribe that most people find threatening about sexual difference, especially in a society in which sexual allegiance is a matter of intertribal warfare. A third element in sexual preference is the issue of public self-identification, or social identity, since identity as a member of a sexual minority creates a social persona in and of itself.

The image of coming and going, with its corollary of never being at rest, describes Barnes' sexuality as well as her conflicts about telling. It is as if she were incapable of being a member of any tribe, of settling in any place. The constant motion of coming and going, in the paradoxical manner of human emotions, represents in fact a paralysis in which it is impossible to integrate and resolve the conflict of polar opposites. In the construction of sexuality in our society, male and female are set against each other. For some women, the choice of a specific sexual preference represents a choice of loyalty to one or the other, heterosexuality representing loyalty to the male, lesbianism representing loyalty to the female. Barnes gave her loyalty to neither.

It is possible that the origins of her unwillingness and/or inability to claim a tribal sexual identity lay in Barnes' perception of her family structure, in which her father was both a failed human being and a man with sexual power over several women, a self-proclaimed deviant and a failure in the larger world; and in which her mother failed to fight back against the father powerfully enough to give her daughter a sense of refuge or safety. It is also possible that Barnes, never having escaped from the tangled history of her original family, could not bear to re-enmesh herself in any social unit that had any hint of familial or tribal feeling. Given Barnes' background, it seems likely that her refusal to take on a lesbian social identity comes not from fear of stigma but from fear of suffocation. In her later years, however, as she narrowed her identity increasingly to that of a writer, she may have, in addition, been afraid of being stereotyped as a lesbian writer, rather than as a great writer.

Yet, despite her rejection of lesbianism as a social identity, Barnes was a member of lesbian social networks. These networks have remained virtually invisible in biography and history for several reasons. Lesbianism has usually been seen as a stigma, so that biographers have until recently been reluctant to identify their subjects as lesbians. This view of lesbianism as a stigma has also resulted in a discrepancy in historiographic standards: no specific evidence of sexual activity is required to prove heterosexuality, whereas such proof is demanded if lesbianism is the issue. A further and even more basic cause of the absence of lesbian social networks from the historical record is the invisibility of women in history. Women find a place in history mainly through their connection with great men or because they were active in an arena usually dominated by men; friendships between women who meet neither of these criteria are doubly discounted.[41]

It is necessary, therefore, to reconstruct these networks from individual biographies, from primary sources such as letters and snapshots, and from bits of evidence scattered through secondary sources. The network of which Natalie Barney was the center is the best documented. Barnes had an affair with Barney but did not become part of her inner circle of friends, although Barnes knew them well enough to parody them in *Ladies Almanack*.[42]

Another group of lesbians, with whom Barnes was closer, included Janet Flanner and Solita Solano, writers and lovers from the late 1910s to World War II; Solita's closest friend Margaret Anderson and her lover at the time, Georgette Leblanc (Djuna had incurred Margaret's ill-will by going to bed with her previous lover, Jane Heap);[43] and Kathryn Hulme and her lover Alice Rohrer. In her recollections of her days at the Hotel Napoleon Bonaparte with Janet Flanner, Solita Solano puts Barnes first in her list of those who spent time at the hotel: "Djuna Barnes when in trouble (the year of 'Nightwood' [*sic*] or 'Bowed Down' [*sic*]) slept in my room and Janet and I took her to the American Hospital when she had appendicitis and fetched her back as well."[44] Kathryn Hulme, who came to Paris in 1930 with Alice Rohrer, a wealthy milliner from San Francisco, describes her first sight of Flanner, Solano, and Barnes, whom she met at the Cafe Flore:

[They were] sitting in a row like three Fates . . . they all wore black tailored suits, white satin scarves folded ascot style, and all were hatless. Three pairs of white gloves and three martinis were on the marble-topped table before them. Janet Flanner of the *New Yorker* arose and put forth her tiny hand, introducing herself, then her friend Solita Solano for whom the roadster [belonging to Rohrer] was destined, then Djuna Barnes who had come along to see it. I looked at their faces and felt as if I had come home to my kind.[45]

Hulme remained in touch with Flanner, Solano, Anderson, and their lovers over the years, writing them a group letter on the death of her former lover Alice Rohrer in 1958.[46] A copy of *Ladies Almanack* containing Alice Rohrer's bookplate carries an inscription from Barnes to Rohrer, "Alice dear—there are birds of another wing!, Love, Djuna, Paris, Sept. 1931."[47] The book was underlined and had notes in Rohrer's hand, many of which are now erased. A surviving note on the margin of page 59 refers to the phrase "We have few Philosophers" with the comment, "Great thing for new Lesbian Books," evidence that the women of this circle did identify themselves as lesbians, at least in private.

Some of the illustrations in *Ladies Almanack* are clearly lesbian, such as the two women lying together in the illustration to "May" (*LA*, 30); some are direct references to sexual passages in the text, such as the drawing of Dame Musset's funeral urn and its flame (*LA*, 80); and some are covertly sexual in their own right, as in the title page ornament, ostensibly of a heraldic flavor, but actually a slightly stylized representation of female genitals, with Dame Musset, busby and all, at the entrance, appropriately enough, to the vagina (plate 24). It is a multilevel visual play. The raised arm, holding a flower, not a sword, is a play both on a rampant heraldic animal and on the engorgement of the clitoris; the buxom mermaids framing the device also form the labia majora, while the foliage at the top can be seen as lifted and parted inner lips. The disguise makes it a game, without which the reader would lose the pleasure of recognition, the little self-congratulatory moment when she "gets it" (the book, of course, was originally written for the circle of English-speaking lesbians connected with Barney).

The sexual language, like the drawing on the title page, is also in disguise, and all of *Ladies Almanack*, in a sense, is about "getting it," because to be a lesbian is to live in a subculture which must maintain a selective visibility by being both visible to itself and invisible to the larger society. Most of the women in this particular group did not hide their lesbianism, but coding and signaling—and thus "getting it"—are generally crucial to lesbian survival and have therefore become part of lesbian literary tradition.[48]

With the exception of the illustrations to her *Theatre Guild Magazine* columns from 1929 to 1931, done in the same style as the illustrations to *Ryder* and *Ladies Almanack*, Barnes produced no more known illustrations. A few drawings in the Barnes Collection (for instance, the self-portrait in Folder B-18 which seems to be of Barnes older than she would have been in the early 1930s), probably were done after the *Theatre Guild Magazine* illustrations, but the last major surviving visual work consists of a series of portraits in oil with gilt background on cardboard. The discrepancy in her choice of materials is striking: the elegance of gilt; the shoddiness of cardboard. Did Barnes think so little of her work that she put it on highly perishable cardboard? Did she believe that she couldn't afford canvas? Her painting in oil conveys a struggle with the medium. Perhaps she thought it unworthy of canvas.

Three of these portraits and photographs of two others are located in the Barnes Collection. Subjects of two of the original portraits are identified as Emily Coleman and Alice Rohrer; the third is unidentified. Of the portraits represented by photographs, one has been identified as Cordelia Coker Pearson by Mary Lynn Broe, and the second is unidentified. Douglas Messerli identified the titles of five paintings in his bibliography of Barnes' visual work, a list he knew to be incomplete: *Cordelia Pearson, Emily Coleman, The Giants, Portrait of Alice*, and *Thelma Wood*.

One of the two photographs has a note on the back in Barnes' hand: "Oil painting on cardboard by Djuna Barnes. Now in possession of Rudolph Glossop of Penzance, England. Date of painting forgotten. Background was gold leaf, *chaise longue* was burgundy" (folder B-5, the Barnes Collection). The photograph shows a man on a chaise longue, his legs stretched out to the right, his torso full-front, and his head turned three-quarters to the left. The same chaise longue appears in a colored drawing of a woman who sits on it with a man on the floor beside her.[49]

The second portrait is represented in the Barnes Collection by a sepia-toned photograph mounted on cardboard (plate 25). In the lower right corner of the painting is the signature "Djuna Barnes," below which is the date, 1947.[50] The materials, colors, and provenance of this work are unknown at this time. The signature is less angular than the signature in

Barnes' earlier work. The subject has been identified as Cordelia Pearson. A woman wearing a hat with a rounded crown and upturned brim, probably a riding hat, stands in three-quarter view looking sardonically out at her audience. The head seems to dominate the slender body, which appears short by comparison. Strong lines run under the cheekbones; the nose is long and sharp; the chin pointed, jutting slightly forward. The eye facing the viewer is large and tilts down, looking down and slightly to the subject's right. The expression is—bitter? slightly contemptuous? haughty? It is not the face of youthful expectancy.

Horizontal bands run across the jacket, possibly indicating strips of thicker material or stripes of color. In the breast pocket of the jacket is folded a handkerchief, and the woman wears what appears to be a pleated formal shirt with a bow tie. Her arms are behind her back, hands hidden and holding what appears to be a crop, or possibly a cane. The angle at which the crop or cane sticks out from the body gives it almost a taillike appearance. The legs are remarkably insubstantial and end in small, pointed, shiny, high-heeled boots that look almost like hooves. The stance is open and the knees hyperextended, so the legs appear to curve backwards. The modeling of the cloth of the pants, especially over the thighs, does not seem related to the muscles under it, thus adding to the somewhat animal quality of the legs. The overall effect of the painting conveys a curious mixture of dominatrix and Pan.

Of the three paintings actually at the University of Maryland, one portrays the head of a man who is unidentified, while the other two are of Alice Rohrer and of Emily Coleman. The portrait of Alice Rohrer, signed and dated 1934 (plate 26), is quite like her photographs, in which she is strikingly slender: in the Gurdjieff work she participated in with Hulme, Solano, Anderson, and Leblanc she was known as The Thin One.[51] A preliminary drawing of her face shows Barnes at her most careful in a detailed, realistic representation similar to the style of her drawings of her friends a decade and a half previously. The finished portrait was exhibited in an all-woman show mounted by Peggy Guggenheim, Barnes' grudging benefactor, in 1943.[52]

The third portrait at the University of Maryland is that of Emily Coleman. Emily Coleman and Djuna Barnes were friends for many years. They were both guests of Peggy Guggenheim at Hayford Hall in England in the summers of 1932 and of 1933. Guggenheim's description of Emily's behavior, in which Emily appears as violently emotional, lends credibility to Barnes' otherwise shocking portrayal of a monstrous-appearing woman.[53] In this painting, as opposed to the encoding of her illustrations to *Ryder* and *Ladies Almanack*, Barnes has made a direct and powerful, though clumsy, emotional statement. It is frightening to the viewer. What did Barnes make of those close to her? Did she merely make visible their inner lives or did she add her own vision of the desolation of the human condition?

The question of what proportion of Barnes' total visual work is represented by the material now at the University of Maryland is unanswered. The number of paintings and drawings in the Barnes Collection drops significantly after 1940. This decrease may be an accident of preservation or it may indicate that Barnes increasingly chose writing as her medium. Barnes' writing in *Nightwood* and *Antiphon* deepened and contracted as she struggled more directly with her material, letting go of the protective cover afforded by parody and other devices to create distance in *Ryder* and *Ladies Almanack*. The visual style she had adopted to illustrate *Ryder* and *Ladies Almanack* seems inappropriate to the greater emotional depth and more unified verbal style of the later writing.

Barnes, who always was primarily a writer rather than a visual artist, seems to have decided to jettison her role as illustrator and to concentrate on her struggle to resolve in her writing the continual going-to and coming-from of the relationship between her life and her work. If Barnes, trapped in her need to speak the unspeakable, had allowed herself to give it full voice; if her creative process had resolved and completed the transformation of her experience, would the result have been a re-formation as frightening and yet as true as the vision her portraits give us of those with whom she was most intimate? It may be here, rather than in the illustrations to her written work, that we find Barnes' clearest visual statement of her inner world.

¶ Djuna Barnes was the most important woman writer we had in Paris. She was famous among us for her great short story, "A Night among the Horses." Within a short time after the publication of her novel *Nightwood* (brought out in London before publication in New York) it became available in a paperback edition and attained enormous popularity among young European intellectuals all the way from Rome to Berlin. I wrote of it at the time as a "difficult book to describe, since the only proper way of dealing with its strange, nocturnal elements is to have written it in the first place, which surely no one but Miss Barnes could have done." Djuna was tall, quite handsome, bold-voiced, and a remarkable talker, full of reminiscences of her Washington Square New York life and her eccentric childhood somewhere up the Hudson. My favorite story of hers dealt with a period when her father, who entertained odd ideas of nourishment, decided that since chickens ate pebbles to aid their digestion, a few pebbles in the diet of his children might be equally salubrious. I was devoted to Djuna and she was quite fond of me, too, in her superior way. She wrote a chapbook called *The Little Ladies' Almanac* [sic], and illustrated it boldly. It was a take-off of many ladies in the American colony, published privately, I think by Miss Natalie Barney, *doyenne* of the Left Bank, who appeared in it as a leading character under the guise of Dame Musset. I was one of a pair of journalists called Nip and Tuck. Djuna wrote a play that she showed to T.S. Eliot; he told her that it contained the most splendid archaic language he had ever had the pleasure of reading but that, frankly, he couldn't make head or tail of its drama. She gave it to me to read, and I told her, with equal candor, that it was the most sonorous vocabulary I had ever read but that I did not understand a jot or tittle of what it was saying. With withering scorn, she said, "I never expected to find that you were as stupid as Tom Eliot." I thanked her for the only compliment she had ever given me.

—Janet Flanner,
Paris Was Yesterday: 1925–1939 (1972)

¶ Marianne Moore said: "Reading Djuna Barnes is like reading a foreign language, which you understand."

—Note in Barnes' hand,
n.d. (Barnes Collection)

Speaking in Tongues:
Ladies Almanack and the
Discourse of Desire

Susan Sniader Lanser

Its author calls it a "slight satiric wigging" (even as she sets it next to Proust); its 1972 publishers claim she regarded it as "a simple piece of fun, in no way to be considered among her serious works." Its original, anonymous, and private publication, though in a foreign tongue, was so threatening that its distributor withdrew and the book was sold by its author's friends on Paris streets. It has confounded critics, intimidated readers, enticed feminists, outraged conservatives, and delighted for decades the people it parodies. But mostly it has been unnoticed and unread: only now is *Ladies Almanack* beginning to assume a place of distinction in the complicated corpus of Djuna Barnes and the differently complicated intertext of lesbian literature. In both canons, *Ladies Almanack* stands apart, posing a challenge to questions of writing, reading, and authorship.

It is at once a book that reaches forward and a book intimately tied to time (1928) and place (expatriate Left Bank). Barnes' slim volume is the most audacious of a body of texts produced by and about the lesbian society that flourished in Paris between the turn of the century and World War II. *Ladies Almanack* was allegedly created for the amusement of Barnes' lesbian friends, who persuaded her to publish it and financed the venture. Its actual and implied readers were its own cast of characters: the circle of Natalie Clifford Barney, *l'Amazone* whose Paris salon was a center of culture in the first decades of the century. The Barney whom Barnes creates is a savior of women, pictured in Barney's favorite of the drawings "carrying a pole" and

This essay originally appeared in somewhat different form as "Speaking in Tongues: *Ladies Almanack* and the Language of Celebration," *Frontiers* 4 (1979): 39–46; reprinted by permission.

"stepping out upon that exceedingly thin ice to which it has pleased God, more and more, to call frail woman, there so conducting herself that none were put to the chagrin of sinking for the third time!" (*LA*, frontispiece). This "wonderworker" becomes the centerpiece of a bawdy *discours à clef* that eludes classification and inscribes a world in which the lesbian is normative. And though Djuna Barnes was apparently unwilling to associate herself with the women's movement of the 1970s and 1980s, the vision of her *Almanack* finds its surest resonance in contemporary lesbian-feminist wit.

Ladies Almanack is also a linguistic and literary experiment, a dense and sometimes barely coherent discourse that spurns the conventions of realism, wanders far from the story it is supposed to tell, adopts and parodies a host of forms and norms, evokes a spectrum of times and texts. Its surface form is the monthly chronicle, a medium that Barnes used with some frequency, but the book resembles the picaresque fable in structure, the mock epic in tone; it uses or parodies the saint's life, the ode, the prayer, the lullaby, the allegory, the myth, as well as specific works from the Bible to *Finnegans Wake*. Some have suggested that the form of *Ladies Almanack* was inspired by the legend that Barnes' friend James Joyce "was never without his book of saints"[1] (Barnes' ladies are never to be without their almanack); perhaps Barnes knew the eighteenth-century English journal called "LADIES Diary and Woman's ALMANACK," which has a subtitle almost as elaborate as her own. Placing it "neap-tide to the Proustian chronicle," Barnes herself suggests in the 1972 foreword that *Ladies Almanack* is a corrective to *Sodome et Gomorrhe*, which the Barney circle apparently criticized for its portrayal of lesbians.[2] She may have been revising *The Well of Loneliness*, which also features Natalie Barney in the persona of Valerie Seymour and which had appeared in July of that year, or rewriting her own *Ryder*, which had been published just three months earlier. She might, by the same token, have been responding to a famous line from her favorite book, Burton's *Anatomy of Melancholy*, as if to show just what would happen in his future-possible where "women wear the breeches" in "a world turned upside downward."[3] Barnes identifies herself on the title page of *Ladies Almanack* only as a "Lady of Fashion," thereby ironizing not only the dutiful writers of sentimental novels but the classic denotation of female chastity in a virtual conflation of "lady" and "lesbian": *all* "ladies" should carry this book, "as the Priest his Breviary, as the Cook his Recipes, as the Doctor his Physic, as the Bride her Fears, and as the Lion his Roar!" (*LA*, 9). The book is illustrated by its author with baroque cherubs, medieval grotesques, parodic iconography, feminized zodiacs, sexual caricature, and other emblems archaic and arcane. The result is a pastiche that defies generic definition; perhaps "satiric wigging" is classification enough.

The discourse of *Ladies Almanack*, similarly, is a dense and highly allusive prose through which almost nothing is made clear; the text speaks cryptically, figurally, and evasively. Sentences are winding, inverted, unfinished or impossibly long. Antecedents get misplaced, verbs dangle, pronouns lose their source. Key words are sometimes elided from sentences whose meanings remain forever indeterminate, as in "I came to it as other Women, and I never a Woman before nor since" (*LA*, 24). Archaisms are common—some as old as Chaucer, some barely obsolete; neologisms are frequent; grammatical forms are resurrected from the Renaissance or invented on the spot. There is a continual mingling of registers as well as lexicons: plain modern English coexists with fancy Elizabethan; obscure terms are juxtaposed with blunt Anglo-Saxon unpleasantries. Metaphors often make one strain desperately and still end up not quite making sense: "the anomaly . . . that, affronted, eats its shadow" (*LA*, foreword); "she thaws nothing but Facts" (*LA*, 37); "Outrunners in the Thickets of prehistoric probability" (*LA*, 43); "two Creatures sitting in Skull" (*LA*, 51) are frustratingly typical. And enshrouding the whole are the Capital Letters: most nouns and a few adjectives and verbs are capitalized, so that the text seems at once Ancient and Fantastical.

The perspective and tone of *Ladies Almanack* are sometimes equally indeterminate, clouded by indirect discourse, rhetorical questions, oxymorons, and maxims of uncertain intent. Lesbian sexuality is called a "Distemper" and a "Beatitude" in the same paragraph; women who love women are like "a tree cut of life" yet they make "a Garden of Ecstasy" (*LA*, 12); "Love in Man is Fear of Fear," but "Love in Woman is Hope without Hope" (*LA*, 23). These contradictory and coded messages generate a narrative voice that is evasive, devious, playfully indirect. There are moments when the narrator does say or imply "I" and "we," but never in a context that commits her to a single, coherent textual identity. The result is "a Maze, nor will we have a way out of it" (*LA*, 58): a text that speaks in tongues.

At least three different modes of discourse combine to create this maze. First and most prominent are the narrative segments that tell the story of Dame Musset and her coterie of allegorically named characters (each with a historical counterpart). These narrative passages are the most ribald sections of the book and the most accessible. A second set of sequences fashions a fanciful amazonian lore, using song and poetry, illustration and myth, to turn patriarchal discourse to gynocentric ends, as if anticipating Monique Wittig's call to women in *Les guérillères* to "remember, or failing that, invent."[4] The third and least common mode of discourse in *Ladies Almanack* is expository, pondering questions of a social and philosophical sort; perhaps because these passages cannot rely on fictional visions, they are the most ambiguous and ambivalent segments of the text, yielding much of its contradiction and its few moments of gloom. These three kinds of discourse are usually interwoven and interspersed rather than sequential and discrete: a myth about woman's Edenic origins slides into the story line as Eve becomes Daisy Downpour; Dame Musset's friends take on the philosopher's role and shift narrative to essay-in-dialogue; a single page juxtaposes poem and picaresque. Though each chapter is named for a month of the year and is headed by apt illustration, the segments vary in length, mode, and formal composition: some tell the story of Dame Musset; others are essays; several are composites of poetry, story, and inquiry.

This mélange of modes and media permits an exploration of lesbian culture and female experience from multiple points of view, each form or voice carrying another shade of difference, another piece of the prism that constitutes the book's elusive rhetorical stance. The interweaving of philosophic, mythic, and narrative modes, each with its particular tendencies of mood, creates a sense of motion in the text: not a beeline or a circle, but an uneven, irregular expedition, now meandering, now dashing, now turning back, like one of Dame Musset's romps through the Bois. Like all almanacs, this one allows time to be both cyclic and linear. (It is no accident that Barnes used the almanac form on several occasions:[5] given her preoccupation with time, the almanac may have afforded her a way to mark its passage without despair.)[6] As it progresses the text becomes at once more radical and more covert, until clarity is restored as narrative turns mythic in a climactic account of Dame Musset's death.

Dame Evangeline Musset is herself a figure of intertextuality. Her last name (evoking the romantic poet Alfred de Musset) marks her as individualist and celebrant of love, her first evangelist and faithful American heroine. Her title, "Dame," like the author's pseudonymous "Lady of Fashion," redefines ladyhood and reclaims it from the Victorians. No ordinary lesbian, Musset is "one Grand Red Cross" for the succor of women. And though the text suggests that some women discard "Duster, Offspring and Spouse" to become lesbians in middle age, Dame Musset herself is a born lesbian: she was intended by nature, says the narrator with tongue in cheek, to be a boy, but when she "came forth an Inch or so less than this, she paid no Heed to the Error" (*LA*, 7). To her father's worries that her behavior will "by no Road, lead her to the Altar," Evangeline retorts, "Thou . . . wast expecting a Son. . . . why then be so mortal wounded when you perceive that you have your Wish? Am I not doing after your very Desire, and is it not the more commendable, seeing that I do it without the Tools for the Trade, and yet nothing complain?" (*LA*, 8). For Evangeline, then, the phallic Lack is as much the signifier of superiority as it is the site of feminine tragedy.[7]

If Dame Musset provides one pole around which the discourse circulates and through which its monthly episodes chart themselves, at the other pole stands Patience Scalpel, the book's one staunch heterosexual (all the named characters in the book are female), introduced (pointedly, in "cold January") as she who "could not understand Women and their Ways" (*LA*, 11)—in a semiotic slippage common to the text in which the word "Woman" substitutes for the censored "Lesbian." Her "Scalpel" is her voice, "as cutting in its derision as a surgical instrument" (*LA*, 12); its sharp proclamation: "my daughters shall go a'marrying" (*LA*, 13). With the other characters occupying mediate points, Musset and Scalpel clash head-on over issues from psychology to politics. In the "March" section, for example, when Lady Buck-and-Balk calls for legalized homosexual marriage in order that "Alimony might be collected, and that straying be nipped in the Bud," the discussion turns to the value of men. In parody of the philosophical and theological tradition that asks whether women are of any use at all, one woman would "do away with Man altogether" while another finds men useful for "carrying of Coals" and "lifting of Beams." Patience, however, wishes one of "the dears" were "hereabouts" and argues that were it not for men, lesbianism would be less enticing; in her view, "Delight is always a little running of the Blood in Channels astray!" (*LA*, 24). Dame Musset presents the most extreme and the most political position as she describes a crime for which symbolic castration becomes the only fit punishment: "'When I wish to contemplate the highest Pitch to which Irony has climbed, and when I really desire to *wallow* in impersonal Tragedy,' said Dame Musset, 'I think of that day, forty years ago, when I, a Child of ten, was deflowered by the Hand of a Surgeon!'" (*LA*, 24). Musset's love for women is poetic justice; when her friends swear revenge, she can stop them by proclaiming:

"I am my Revenge!"
    "I had not thought of that," said Tilly happily, "You have, verily, hanged, cut down, and re-hung Judas a thousand times!"
    "And shall again, please God!" said Dame Musset. (*LA*, 26)

The designation of surgeon as rapist implicates the name Patience Scalpel as well, linking her voice even more firmly to a violent heterosexuality.

As the book's monthly chronicle continues its loosely linear development, however, the poles of archlesbian and archheterosexual begin to meet in a new conception of lesbian identity. A major sign of this movement is that the Scalpel's voice begins to lose its cutting edge. The "May" section shows her still holding forth, but in "the Voice of one whose Ankles are nibbled by the Cherubs," looking on in dismay while "amid the Rugs Dame Musset brought Doll Furious to a certainty" (*LA*, 30). Patience is still wondering what "you women see in each other," while Dame Musset, for her part, is complaining that lesbianism has become all too blatant and too popular:

"In my days I was a Pioneer and a Menace, it was not then as it is now, *chic* and pointless to a degree, but as daring as a Crusade, for where now it leaves a woman talkative, so that we have not a Secret among us, then it left her in Tears and Trepidation. . . . What joy has the missionary," she added . . . "when all the Heathen greet her with Glory Halleluja! before she opens her Mouth, and with an Amen! before she shuts it!" (*LA*, 34)

For (ostensibly) opposite reasons, Patience and Evangeline are both lamenting the blurred lines between "woman" and "lesbian." Indeed, as the text continues, these lines begin to converge, creating a kind of "lesbian continuum," as Adrienne Rich calls the myriad "forms of primary intensity between and among women," bonds both personal and political, whether or not explicitly sexual.[8] This is precisely the continuum that works such as *The Well of Loneliness* or *Sodome et Gommorrhe* deny when they designate homosexuals as a "third sex" or as "hommes-femmes." Here is then another crucial way in which *Ladies Almanack* rewrites both Hall and Proust.

The "August" chapter marks a climactic point in this convergence of sex and sexuality on both the narrative and philosophical planes. The essay that opens the chapter discourses about a "they" whose identity seems to slide from heterosexual women, to all women, to lesbians. This confusion is reinforced by the plot, for it is in August that Patience Scalpel herself begins to yield. Dryly, the narrator reveals:

> though it is sadly against me to report it of one so curing to the Wound as Patience Scalpel, yet did she . . . hint, then aver, and finally boast that she herself, though all Thumbs at the business and an Amateur, never having gone to so much as a Nose-length into the Matter, could mean as much to a Woman as another. (*LA*, 50)

If she has not become a lesbian, Patience has at least felt it necessary to declare, in a neat cultural reversal, her lesbian capabilities. And by "November" Dame Musset has further sealed the heterosexual/lesbian rift by recruiting women who have "gone a'marrying." Though at first most ignore her, Musset can finally boast that "ten Girls I had tried vainly for but a Month gone, were all tearing at my shutters" (*LA*, 78–79).

As Musset's proselytizing promenade through the months brings more and more women into the lesbian fold, there comes also an increased attention to the oppression of all women. In the "September" section, one of the most broadly political, the narrator complains that woman's "very Condition" is "so subject to Hazard, so complex, and so grievous" (*LA*, 55) that by middle age her body has been distorted and her mind "corrupt with the Cash of a pick-thank existence" (*LA*, 56). In this light, lesbianism becomes a rejection of the roles a patriarchal society has imposed upon women. The message is reinforced by a poem called "Lists and Likelihoods" that names virtually everyone in its catalogue of those likely to become lesbians: vixens, hussies, athletes, virgins, even

> *The Queen, who in the Night turned down*
> *The Spikes of her Husband's Crown*
> *Therein to sit her Wench of Bliss. (LA, 60)*

Such a passage neatly redefines both the divine right of queens and the symbols of kingship. And the *Almanack* goes farther: in keeping with its name, it delineates the universe itself as a female Anatomy, sisterhood as the cosmic choice:

> *all the Planets, Stars and Zones*
> *Run girlish to their Marrow-bones!*
> *And all the Tides prognosticate*
> *Not much of any other state!* (LA, 60)

It should be evident by now that throughout the text, this movement to feminize encompasses a gynocentric sexual rhetoric. Many of *Ladies Almanack*'s terms for the female body—furrow, nook, path, keyhole, whorl, crevice, conch shell (terms which would be at home in a contemporary work like Wittig's *Les guérilleres*)—are clearly designed to counteract emerging Freudian notions of phallic supremacy and clitoral insufficiency. Sexual innuendo pervades the text: when the "July" section, for example, claims that lesbian love language is "more dripping, more lush, more lavender, more mid-mauve, more honeyed, more Flower-casting" than the Narrator dare say (*LA*, 46), she has of course managed to say it all anyway. When "a woman snaps Grace in twain with a bragging Tongue" (*LA*, 48), she is always both verbal and sexual.

The *Almanack* revises not only language but the bases of culture itself, creating alternatives to patriarchal ritual, dogma, and myth. The "February" section, for instance, presents an outsized icon of Musset, "For These 12 Reasons Sainted," with a heart in one hand and a rose in the other, standing upon a tasseled pillow, a glowing crown atop her head, angels surrounding, and supplicants kneeling at her feet. In the "June" entry Musset tells Doll Furious about the "Fourth Great Moment of History," revising the three great moments Matthew O'Connor posits in Barnes' own *Ryder*[9] and recasting the Old Testament to unite the Queen of Sheba and Jezebel:

Jezebel, that flighty forthright, used to spend much of her Time in angling from her Window and crying "Uoo Hoo!" to the Kings thatway wending to War and Death. And some turned in at her Door, and others went on, though not a many 'tis true. Thus was Jezebel employed, when the Queen of Sheba passed beneath her Window, and Jezebel leaning outward called "Uoo Hoo!"
And that was Jezebel's last "Uoo Hoo!" (LA, 41)

An even bolder challenge to culture appears in the "March" section, where the question of whether men are needed is given a fanciful solution in a myth of all-female birth that rather pointedly parodies the *Summa Theologiae*'s discussion of "Whether Women Should Have Been Made in the First Production of Things." Aquinas, whose work Barnes owned and read, concluded that the value of woman is in her role as man's helper in reproduction, but *Ladies Almanack* offers another version of the generative act:

This is the part about Heaven that has never been told. After the Fall of Satan (and as he fell, Lucifer uttered a loud Cry, heard from one End of Forever-and-no-end to the other), all the Angels, Aries, Taurus, Gemini, Cancer, Leo, Virgo, Libra, Scorpio, Sagittarius, Capricornus, Aquarius, Pisces, all, all gathered together, so close that they were not recognizable, one from the other. And not nine Months later, there was heard under the Dome of Heaven a great Crowing, and from the Midst, an Egg, as incredible as a thing forgotten, fell to Earth, and striking, split and hatched, and from out of it stepped one saying "Pardon me, I must be going!" And this was the first Woman born with a Difference. (*LA*, 25–26)

Here we have female myth making at the "origin": a fable of angelic parthenogenesis within a paradise from which the last male angel has been cast.

All of these audacious and subversive stories prepare the way for the *Almanack*'s final entry, in which the three modes of discourse—narrative, philosophic, mythic—converge in religious parody. By "December" Dame Musset has lived ninety-nine years, and her missionary activities have lost their usefulness: "she had blossomed on Sap's need, and when need's Sap found such easy flowing in the year of our Lord 19— what more was there for her to do?" (*LA*, 81). As she lies dying, as it were, of her success, St. Musset asks her followers "of many Races and many Tempers" to honor her death each in her own way, as each "loved me differently in Life" (*LA*, 82). The funeral rituals once again conflate "women" with "lesbian" as "Women who had not told their Husbands everything, joined them" (*LA*, 83). Finally it is lesbian sexuality that remains, taking its stand against canonized chastity as a miracle proves Evangeline's sainthood and the pentecostal "tongue of flame" becomes the double signature of sexuality and textuality: "They put her upon a great Pyre, and burned her to the Heart . . . And when they came to the ash that was left of her, all had burned but the Tongue, and this flamed, and would not suffer Ash, and it played about the handful that had been she indeed" (*LA*, 84).

Dame Musset is to be the same tireless lover in death as in life, as the women pay their last respects at the Temple of Love (named for the Temple à l'Amitie that stood in Barney's garden):

And seeing this, there was a great Commotion, and the sound of Skirts swirled in haste, and the Patter of much running in feet, but Senorita Fly-About came down upon that Urn first, and beatitude played and flickered upon her Face, and from under her Skirts a slow smoke issued, though no thing burned, and the Mourners barked about her covetously, and all the Night through . . . And as the day came some hundred Women were seen bent in Prayer. And yet a little later between them in its Urn on high, they took the Ashes and the Fire, and placed in on the Altar in the Temple of Love. There, it is said, it flickers to this day, and one may still decipher the Line, beneath its handles, "Oh ye of little Faith." (*LA*, 84)

Echoing and revising a story Dr. O'Connor tells in *Ryder*, in which the male member outlives the man,[10] this (ri)bald finale, surely one of the boldest by a woman writ, bespeaks a serious intent: a refusal of phallocentrism that stops short neither of religion nor of sexuality nor of a conjoining of the two. In transforming death to sexual resurrection, *Ladies Almanack* reclaims the positivity of the female body and the lesbian experience.[11] But this reclamation of the Tongue is also the reclamation of female voice; "censor the body," says Hélène Cixous, "and you censor breath and speech at the same time."[12] Female sexuality and female word thus coalesce in the Last Signifier that displaces the Phallus in preeminence. At the same time, this verbal play is metaplay: the Tongue—and Text—outlives the flesh.

But a text that speaks in tongues cannot, finally, be read as singularly as I have been doing in these pages. It is not a naive critical blindness but a troubling nexus of textual, biographical, and theoretical constraints that has led to divergent critical responses to *Ladies Almanack*. In direct contrast to my reading, for example, James Scott calls the book a protest against "the absurdity of female promiscuity," "the sterility of the sisterhood," and "the absence of decent restraints of privacy" (as if it were, finally, a document of Victorian morality).[13] Louis Kannenstine sees moments of "Sapphic manifesto" in the text but claims the book's humor to be only "surface levity" concealing "a pain-racked comedy" and documenting the "horror" of "coming back upon oneself."[14] Andrew Field, while giving greater stress to the positive vision, still calls it "a queer little book" whose "finest portions . . . are about melancholy."[15] In strong contrast, Bertha Harris names the text "a document of lesbian revolution,"[16] while a reviewer, disappointed that it is *not* such a document, lambasts it for a tone that is "hard to fix" and a "playfulness" she deems "irresponsible."[17] Such a confusing mélange of judgments has plagued the criticism of all Barnes' work, but *Ladies Almanack* has been subjected to contradictions of particular intensity.

This is partly because Barnes herself was demonstrably ambivalent about both the book and the personal questions it raised. Although fame and fortune (understandably) preoccupied her rather strongly in her later years, and although *Ladies Almanack* had been unavailable since its initial private printing of 1,050 copies, Barnes was reluctant to reissue it and did not include it in the 1962 edition of her *Selected Works*. Natalie Barney and others in the group urged her repeatedly to reprint it. "Why not let that side of us appear in your complete works?" Barney wrote to her in 1963; "Why not open the eyes of 'Seuil' [French publishers of *Nightwood*] to this masterpiece?" she asked again in 1968.[18] Barnes' responses are always ambivalent, claiming that *Ladies Almanack* was a work "of another kind," one meant for "the private domaine [*sic*], . . . written as a jollity and distributed to a very special audience," though she promised it would be included in any "collection of the entire corpus" that might appear. She also feared charges of "salacious[ness]" even as she demurred that *Ladies*

Almanack was "much too mild" for "present taste."[19] It was probably with complex emotions, then, that Barnes gave reprint rights to Harper and Row in 1972, allegedly fearing the kind of literary piracy that had already occurred with *The Book of Repulsive Women*.

Barnes' "codedness" about *Ladies Almanack* mirrors, of course, the codedness within the text itself. There are political explanations for both Barnes' own reticence and the ambiguous discourse and perspective of *Ladies Almanack*, beyond the particular resonance of modernist discourse and the Barney circle's delight in innuendo and obscurity, beyond the fact too that *Ladies Almanack* was first a private document that probably embeds a host of private references. Barnes did not reveal her personal life to her reading public and was displeased at the claims on her identity made by lesbian historiographers. Literary biography—that dangerous, irresistible game—does tell us that Barnes had relationships with both women and men, and that probably the major love of her life was Thelma Wood, with whom she was stormily involved for the decade surrounding the writing of *Ladies Almanack*. Her biographer Andrew Field considers her "basically heterosexual," accepting all too readily, I think, Barnes' own reported comment, "I'm not a lesbian; I just loved Thelma."[20] For Thelma Wood was not the only woman with whom Djuna Barnes was involved; she had a profound and possibly sexual relationship with Mary Pyne, and at least a brief affair with Natalie Barney. Indeed, it is possible to read *Ladies Almanack* itself as a love letter to Natalie: the February section calls itself a "Love Letter for a Present," and claims that its author has nothing original except her words to give the legendary lover Dame Musset; if she cannot "make a New Path where there be no Wilderness," then "Fancy" will be her "only craft" (*LA*, 15–17). Barnes' ambivalence about declaring her sexuality may have played a role in the elision, from various collections of her short works, of texts with lesbian implications such as "Dove," "Khalidine," and "Paprika Johnson." It may also be significant that while Barnes usually identifies those to whom she dedicates her work (her mother, Peggy Guggenheim, and Mary Pyne, for example), in the dedication to *Ryder* Thelma Wood is discreetly coded as "T.W."

Barnes' reticence is a "problem" only because so many critics seem reluctant even to contemplate a lesbian-centered reading of *Ladies Almanack* without a definitive "corroboration" from Barnes' own life. The shape of critical controversy over the perspective of *Ladies Almanack* suggests the degree to which literary criticism can bathe itself in both biography and intentionality, especially when a discourse is ambiguous or politically sensitive. For whatever Barnes' own attitudes, and however elusive and shifting the narrative perspective of this book, the rhetorical stance of *Ladies Almanack* is an inside stance. The charged word "lesbian" is mentioned only once in the entire text—a significant sign of self-censorship—but its context, interestingly, is a reference to the "Lesbian Eye," which suggests a lesbian point of view and, homonymically, the affirmations "I" and "aye."[21] Were there no information whatever to suggest a biography of lesbian experience, the *textual* perspective would remain.

There is another important reason for the ambiguity and codedness of *Ladies Almanack*: the constraints on sexual discourse, especially by and about women, still prevailing in 1928. A journalist, Barnes must have understood that lesbian material, as the book itself puts it, "could be printed nowhere and in no Country, for Life is represented in no City by a Journal dedicated to the Undercurrents, or for that matter to any real Fact whatsoever" (*LA*, 34). Better to shroud the Undercurrents in obscurity, generating a prose whose meanings dissolve beneath a torrent of difficult words and sentences. The political implications of Barnes' discourse would surely "loom the bigger if stripped of its Jangle, but no, drugged such it must go. As foggy as a Mere, as drenched as a Pump; twittering so loud upon the wire that one cannot hear the message. And yet!" (*LA*, 46). The "Jangle"—a common strategy in the artistic performances of women and other outsiders[22]—protects the discourse from those whose understanding would be dangerous, while providing a signal to those whose understanding the writer seeks. Without Barnes' "Jangle," even private publication in a foreign land might have been impossible; after all, the much more accessible and far more decorous *Well of Loneliness* was subjected to legal censorship in just that year.

Indeed, it is especially illuminating to see the *Almanack* against this more conventional and chaste counterpart, for together these texts—respectively the most infamous and most obscure lesbian writings of 1928—frame the borders of the textually possible in their moment of history. Hall's novel offers a clear, carefully plotted psychological narrative in the (conservative, for 1928) nineteenth-century realist mode. Although the plot engages the reader in a mimesis of lesbian life, the story is otherwise a conventional Bildungsroman with a tragic denouement. Radclyffe Hall understood *The Well of Loneliness* to be a compromise; she consciously cramped her politics inside the conventions of the realistic novel and the Victorian mind in order to reach a wide audience of heterosexual, middle-class intellectuals, with the express purpose of portraying lesbian existence and identity in a voice that would plead for "tolerance." A passionate plea and a cry of rage, audacious enough in theme, *The Well of Loneliness* could not afford to dare in structure, language, or tone. *Ladies Almanack*, in contrast, takes lesbian existence almost for granted, eschews realism and even readability, and seeks to "reach" only the already converted audience of Barnes' own friends. Its purpose is not to plead but to delight. In *Ladies Almanack* there is no question of a tragic denouement, because there is neither a plot nor an audience that would demand or even tolerate it. Yet only in privacy could *Ladies Almanack* exist in 1928. (One can measure the distance lesbian discourse has traveled simply by noting Harper and Row's decision to publish *Ladies Almanack* in 1972, a decision that as far as I know was not a controversial one.)

What *Ladies Almanack* may finally tell us, then, is the degree to which reading and even writing becomes a function of the reader's desires, and the degree to which desire, in turn, creates both the frustrations and the pleasures of the text. In this context it is worth remembering that *Ladies Almanack* was written for an audience both lesbian and modernist, and that it presupposes a specific world view. As Bertha Harris explains, the multinational lesbian society in Paris during the 1920s was complacently elitist, extending hierarchies of social class to sexual caste:

The world, as they saw it, was quite naturally divided into rigid class systems and into gay and straight; and, in their extension of such logic, to be upperclass was at its finest to be also gay.... [L]esbianism gave [one] automatic rank as an aristocrat: to be lesbian was at its finest also to be upper class. In general, all that was heterosexual was "ugliness" and all that was lesbian, "beautiful"; and they spent their time in refined enactment of that which was beautiful and fleeing from that which they knew as ugliness.... They directed their energies toward the recreation of what they wanted to be their ancestry, an age of Sappho delightful with lyric paganism, attic abandonment.[23]

Whatever Barnes' response to this lesbian chauvinism, such a circle would hardly fail to fascinate a woman who once defined depravity as "the ability to enjoy what others shudder at, and to shudder at what others enjoy."

There is perhaps no greater testimony to the readerly pleasures of *Ladies Almanack* than the lifelong responses of its own "characters." Janet Flanner reportedly boasted often of being represented in the book. Solita Solano wrote to Barnes in the 1960s that she had "reread '*Ladies Almanack*' and had nearly forgotten how charming and amusing it is—in fact, has improved with *my* age."[24] Natalie Barney writes constantly to Barnes during the 1960s that *Ladies Almanack* is "a constant joy to me," a solace when she has not had news from Barnes herself. She rereads it, she says, "with new finds and delights."[25] If interpretation is fullest when it encompasses its readers' own desires, then a reading of *Ladies Almanack* through the audience of its desire may unveil the pleasures that a conventional discourse cannot afford. "Honour[ing] the creature slowly," as Barnes advises in the 1972 foreword, makes of *Ladies Almanack*'s linguistic complexity an invitation to explore rather than a barrier to surmount, turning parody to celebration and doubt to display.

Read inside its author's own intertext, *Ladies Almanack* also becomes a commentary on the Barnesian corpus, that body of darkness upon which the two 1928 parodies, *Ryder* and *Ladies Almanack*, dance a light and often playful melody. In a language as ribald as *Ryder*'s, *Ladies Almanack* counters *Ryder*'s heterosexual mythology—with Dame Musset the lesbian counterpart to Wendell Ryder—even as it amplifies the feminist

elements already present in *Ryder*. Like *The Book of Repulsive Women*
before it, which opens with a blatantly sexual lesbian poem,[26] *Ladies
Almanack* dares a discourse of desire; like *Nightwood* after it, *Ladies
Almanack* creates a problematics of that desire. But by the time of *Nightwood*, where hope has died not only politically with the imminence of fascist
plague but personally for Barnes in the final rupture with her own Night
Wood, love has lost its enchantment if not its force, and sexuality has
become more bondange than bond. The 1928 books offer one moment in
Barnes' work in which the troublesome questions of gender, love, and sex
converge with at least the hope of happiness. Perhaps *Ladies Almanack* and
Ryder are parodic works because they mock not only a particular literary
tradition, but the inward and tormented tendencies of Barnes' own consciousness.

For *Ladies Almanack* is finally an extraordinary text in the Barnesian
chronicle (as in all its canons—lesbian, female, modernist), sharing theme
and form with other works, yet far more radical in its politics, far more
gynocentric in its consciousness.[27] As such, *Ladies Almanack* suggests the
power of a moment—of an intersection of cultural circumstances—virtually
to overpower personal "identity" in shaping the voice and vision of a text.
There is finally no authorization from Barnes herself—from her public
statements, her private correspondence or her published works—for the
radical implications of *Ladies Almanack*, no moment in Barnesian discourse
that matches the vision of this text. And had Djuna Barnes been presented
with the political implications of her work as I have drawn them here, she
might well have disavowed them entirely.

Barnes may finally, then, have been articulating a universe less of her
own desire than of the desires of those who were at once her friends, readers,
and characters. Such a concept challenges notions of the unitary writing
subject and traditional images of the nature of writing in relationship to
authorial identity. We may then have to account for the radical vision of
Ladies Almanack in the euphoria and daring of a cultural moment of which
Barnes found herself the articulating voice. And if context is able so
profoundly to shape discourse, virtually to generate its vision, then the
notion of "author" becomes inconceivable or irrelevant apart from "text."
The problem lies, then, not in attempting to reconcile the historical Barnes
with the textual voice of *Ladies Almanack* but in having thought the two
equivalent. It is within the freedom of this more complex vision of reading
and writing, of *Ladies Almanack* and Djuna Barnes, that one may discover
the pleasures and perils of speaking in tongues.

¶ . . . What is my dear Paris like now? People tell me it is the same, but it can't be—nothing is the same—they are used to it—probably I would be as shocked as any friend who comes upon a friend too suddenly. Is Natalie still about—and all of as old as God? Looking back in this day is a very precarious position—what a world we have of it now—alreading computing carefare [*sic*] to Mars—or for you, Hesperus—the morning star!—the ancient amenities out the window, and sins more bloody awful, free and pointless. I'd give my teeth for a day or two back in time, in Paris, at a sidewalk bistro (there's a word's got away!) for the purpose of correcting, no reinforcing the apprehensions of memory—as say Proust. All my public is talking Royal Jelly . . . I do not write letters anymore myself, but writing to you is like that Proustian *madeleine*—and that uneven courtyard stone that set him pitching headfirst into his past. I hope you are not too somber, that you have some of your former hilarious sorrow. . . .

—Djuna Barnes,
letter to Dan Mahoney,
14 November 1958

¶ "No personal life, and now no home." I don't know what to say, that is, what could be said to comfort you. What comfort is there for a person when they feel life falling away. Only the old advice, so old no one believes it, or believing partially still does not care about it, or feels it inaplicable [*sic*] to his or her case etc, etc as the King of Siam said. In the end, as far as I can see there's exactly nothing left for it but the *mind* and the *spirit*. Faith and books . . . one at least, two if possible . . . and a hobby. That you have, bookbinding. Its at least merciful you have an income. What an aging woman does without that I'll surely find out.

—Djuna Barnes,
letter to Mary Reynolds,
14 June 1949

All Women Are Not Women All:
Ladies Almanack and Feminine Writing

Frann Michel

> The very Condition of Woman is so subject to Hazard, so complex, and so grievous, that to place her at one Moment is but to displace her at the next.
> —Djuna Barnes, *Ladies Almanack*

> In "woman" I see something that cannot be represented, something that is not said, something above and beyond nomenclatures and ideologies.
> —Julia Kristeva, "La femme, ce n'est jamais ça"

The very condition of Djuna Barnes' corpus is so subject to dismissal, so complex and so grievous, that to read her at one moment may be to misread her at the next. Readers have found Barnes' work "elusive," "queer," "less than inviting," and "blubbery."[1] Even in an eccentric body of work, *Ladies Almanack* is an eccentric text: one that has another center, that deviates from conventional patterns. But the awakening attention to Barnes that this volume represents reflects in part the availability of new theoretical frameworks to guide the often puzzling process of reading her work. *Ladies Almanack* is challenging because its formal complexity is also a complex dialogue with the masculine cultural hegemony. Yet until recently the various formalisms by which one might decipher the stylistic peculiarities of Barnes' works have tended to bracket the questions of cultural content, including issues of gender. Barnes' inscriptions of gender and sexuality become more accessible when one notices that Barnes shares with postmodern writers on the feminine the assertion that Woman has no single,

This essay appeared in somewhat different form as "Displacing Castration: *Nightwood, Ladies Almanack*, and Feminine Writing," *Contemporary Literature* 30 (Spring 1989): 33–58; used by permission of The University of Wisconsin Press.

stable place, but rather is multiple, indefinable, outside or beyond ordered systems of representation and thought.

Hélène Cixous notes that the dominant modes of symbolic discourse are organized by binary oppositions: active/passive, culture/nature, logos/pathos, Man/Woman. As Alice Jardine observes, representation itself "confirms the possibility of an imitation (mimesis) based on the dichotomy of presence and absence." For all of these couples, the first term is valorized. Thus, thought in patriarchal society is focused through sameness: because the opposition Man/Woman defines Woman only as not-Man, Woman's difference remains radically elsewhere. Cixous suggests that because masculine/feminine is the founding couple in the dominant symbolic order, then that order can be designated "masculine." Clearly this is a static and monological view of language. Descended from a structuralism that detaches language from social process (and then reabsorbs social process into a reified language), it yields the view that all representation has been appropriated by dominant masculine modes of thought (which are not just masculine but white, European, bourgeois, and, perhaps most importantly here, heterosexual). Hence, in Kristeva's view, "woman" — a term, not a condition — "cannot be represented." Woman cannot be placed, even to be displaced, because the oppositional position from which Cixous and Kristeva themselves write has been discounted. Yet their project demonstrates the tremendous power of dominant modes of thought, and it is explicitly a project that seeks to disrupt that power.[2]

For Cixous, Kristeva, and Luce Irigaray, order itself — coherence, unity, identity — is coded as masculine, so that the feminine is not another identity but is instead nonidentity. With the authority of unity and order coded as masculine, the feminine becomes nonauthoritative, disruptive of authority or mastery. Because Woman functions in the masculine socio-cultural economy as the gift, and because she who is given or exchanged cannot be assigned a stable place, cannot fully be accommodated by or assimilated into the masculine economy, then she is seen as disruptive of — indeed, becomes the term for all that is disruptive of — ordered and ordering systems, including systems of gender.[3]

Despite numerous and significant dissimilarities in their work, Kristeva, Irigaray, and Cixous share the view that the feminine's disruption or disordering of a repressive and oppressive order is potentially liberating. Cixous notes that psychoanalytic theory provides the alibi for the founding of the dominant order of symbolic discourse in the couple masculine/feminine.[4] Psychoanalytic theory depends for the security of this foundation on the notion of woman as a castrated man (or as lacking the lack, the phallic passkey to language: for Lacan, ~~The~~ Woman does not exist). The inadequacy and consequent instability of this definition of Woman thus puts her in a subversively exterior relation to the system it supports.

In this view, syntactical, ordered, representational writings — that is, most, if not all, modern Western writings—are masculine. In naming a writing "feminine," we would call attention to the ways it inscribes Woman's exteriority and continue its implicit project of subverting existing systems of signification—the phallogocentrism they signify and the patriarchy that phallogocentrism supports.[5] In such a spirit I will argue that *Ladies Almanack* foregrounds the contradictions of gender definitions, questioning the myth of castration and displacing masculine language with a woman's writing.

Cixous, Irigaray, and Kristeva differ on just how feminine writing would inscribe Woman's exteriority and escape the strictures of phallogocentric thought. Cixous stresses the importance of releasing from the masculine economy the heretofore repressed female unconscious by writing female sexual pleasure. Irigaray too focuses on the masculine sociocultural economy with its structure of sameness and singleness and consequent exclusion of the multiplicity of specifically female sexuality. Cixous and Irigaray's emphasis on body and voice demonstrates their sense of the importance of material experience eccentric to the abstracted linguistic system of phallogocentrism. Irigaray suggests that the disruption of this phallogocentric system is to be achieved from within, by the feminine entering it through a "playful repetition," a kind of parodic or ironic mimesis (*This Sex*, 76). Such a parody or irony calls attention to language as language, as material. Further, the possibility of irony implies an alternative perspective from which to critique masculine language, even if that perspective can never be definitively located because "there is no feminine meta-language."[6]

According to Kristeva, the feminine occurs in language in the semiotic, which becomes apparent when discourse is guided by the sound values of words rather than by their logical, symbolic signification in the order of the sentence. The eruption of the semiotic into the symbolic would subvert existing systems of signification; by disrupting syntax, logical system, and the practice of representation, such feminine writing would disrupt the patriarchal order of phallogocentrism.

Thus, while Cixous implies the possibility of a feminine affirmation, Kristeva sees writing the feminine as an inherently negative practice, a rejection of "everything finite, definite, structured, loaded with meaning, in the existing state of society," a continual process of saying "that's not it" and "that's still not it."[7] While Cixous stresses the importance for women of "the 'mother' as nonname and as source of goods,"[8] Kristeva states,

If the archetype of the belief in a good and pure substance, that of utopias, is the belief in the omnipotence of an archaic, full, total, englobing mother with no frustration, no separation, with no break-producing symbolism (with no castration, in other words), then it becomes evident that we will never be able to defuse the violences mobilized through the counterinvestment necessary to carrying out this phantasm, unless one challenges precisely this myth of the archaic mother.[9]

Where Cixous sees a possibility of reuniting word and object and, like Irigaray, rejects the notion of castration (which both consider in a primarily physical sense), Kristeva emphasizes the need to refute the possibility of such a reunion, to accept the notion of the symbolic or metaphorical castration of all subjects. Designating as "castration" this split that marks entry into the symbolic both stabilizes the symbolic and calls attention to Woman's exclusion from it (since, in Lacan's view, women lack the lack).

Kristeva's view, as well as Cixous's and Irigaray's, postulates feminine writing as distinct or distinguishable from masculine writing. Yet deconstructive theory and practice demonstrate that order, the coherence of system, is always illusory. Any text, examined closely enough, will reveal an uncertainty, an undecidability, an aporia. If feminine writing displays this uncertainty more readily than does masculine writing, still the difference is not qualitative; it depends rather upon how far one is, so to speak, standing from the text. The qualitative difference lies instead in the direction from which the parody approaches the language it renders. Irigaray suggests that women's parody of masculine language is possible because women are "not simply reabsorbed in this function. *They also remain elsewhere.*"[10] Thus, feminine writing would seem to be as much a matter of subversive perspective as of disruptive form.

Nonetheless, the conceptual subversion of feminine writing materializes as disruptive form, and some writing seems more readily to undercut its own authority, to challenge the idea of order and the order of its own language. Feminine writing, with its disruptions of conventional or expected order, its wordplay, parody, attention to language and the materiality of language, sounds like what is usually described as modernist writing or the writing of modernity. The frequency with which Joyce, for instance, is cited as an example would seem to confirm that feminine and modernist writing are, if not synonymous terms, at least overlapping categories. Alternatively, in the work of Mikhail Bakhtin, that which disrupts hierarchical order (specifically of genre, but also, by implication, any hierarchical ordering system in writing), that which is multiple, undefinable, parodic is the novel or novelized writing.[11] Both "novelized" and "modernist" can be useful terms; each is linked to a particular code; each raises a particular complex of issues. Thus, in a literary-historical study, one might refer to such writing as "modernist"; in a genre study or a study of the languages of a work or works, one might designate such writing as "novelized." The term "feminine writing" foregrounds the problematic issues of gender and sexuality, examining them through the matrix of language and illuminating the perspective from which masculine language is disrupted in *Ladies Almanack*.

But while the ideas of the feminine and feminine writing may be critically useful, their usefulness for feminist criticism is not initially evident. Naming that which subverts the conceptual couple Man/Woman or

masculine/feminine either "Woman" or "the feminine" retains the terminology and thus much of the force of the binary order of the masculine. Though
Woman, the feminine, is not to be confused with women, female human
beings, there is, as Irigaray points out, a "complicity between the values
recognized in discourse, and those admitted for sexuality. These values are,
in fact, the same."[12] The structure of discourse which represses Woman is
consonant with the structure of the sociocultural economy which oppresses
women. In valorizing Woman as the figure of disorder, nonidentity, radical
alterity, one risks reasserting and reinforcing the traditional associations
that have funded patriarchy and have been used as justifications for the
oppression of women, since a mere reversal of value can only "repeat the
traditional scheme . . . in which the hierarchy of duality is always recon-
stituted." Radically to change this, according to Derrida, requires "a
transformation or general deformation of logic."[13] Deconstructive activity
can deform logic, ordering systems, but nonetheless it cannot fully extirpate
these systems; as Roland Barthes notes, "a code cannot be destroyed, only
'played off.'"[14] Cixous acknowledges that work on and of the feminine has
just begun; she looks toward "another time (in two or three hundred
years?)" when the "general logic of difference would no longer fit into the
opposition that still dominates," but she does note that "we are still
floundering about—with certain exceptions—in the Old order."[15] The
utopianism of this view arises from the absolute division of feminine and
masculine language, but the exceptions to the dominant order are those
oppositional perspectives from which it can be critiqued—perspectives thus
in dialogue with the dominant order.

Given this old order, the distinction between Woman and women
poses a problem for feminist critics and thinkers. Despite the implication
that the repression of Woman oppresses women, the terms cannot be
conflated, precisely because the feminine has been repressed, while females,
by most accounts, do exist. Though writers on the feminine at times suggest
that women are closer to the feminine than men are, women are also, as
subjects constructed in masculine discourse, at least potentially masculine.[16] Thus, Cixous asserts, "to be signed with a woman's name doesn't
necessarily make a piece of writing feminine."[17] However, since the scheme
of hierarchical opposition still dominates, divorcing the gender of the text
from the gender of the author implicitly sanctions history's neglect and
devaluation of writing by women. Indeed, many of the writers most often
cited as having produced feminine texts are male (e.g., Joyce, Artaud,
Genet).[18]

Clearly, then, ideas of feminine writing do not in themselves constitute a feminist criticism. Feminine writing has not yet liberated women and
men from phallogocentrism; the "exceptions" Cixous refers to are contex-
tualized within the old order. Mary Jacobus notes that to "label a text as that
of a woman, and to write about it for that reason, makes vividly legible what

the critical institution has either ignored or acknowledged only under the sign of inferiority. We need the term 'women's writing' if only to remind us of the social conditions under which women wrote and still write."[19] Woman has no essence, no essential nature, but women do occupy particularized places within the social structure. The disruptive form characteristic of feminine writing is one manifestation of women's potentially oppositional perspectives. Women can write as women without writing as Woman.

Yet the system of thought founded on the dualism of masculine/feminine exerts great power. For instance, the notion that Woman has no place in language may be a symbolic or theoretical expression of the forces that also give rise to what Gilbert and Gubar have called women's "anxiety of authorship."[20] Because of this power, because of the complicity between systems of discursive repression and systems of social oppression, women writers are likely to engage with the order of discourse that excludes them. Barnes' engagement with the order of discourse that would exclude the woman writer places her both inside that order, to the extent that she confronts its terms and myths, and outside, to the extent that her position as subject in the act of engagement would be impossible within such an order.

The contradictory positioning of the woman writer both inside and outside phallogocentrism finds a correlative in the "place" of feminine writing. "Woman" and "the feminine" are terms for that which is excluded from the symbolic order; yet they function as terms and ideas within that order. Examining the feminine in the works of a woman writer can thus reveal the effects of the woman writer's engagement with a masculine-oriented language.

Because the dominant masculine-oriented conceptual order is founded on the heterosexual binary Man/Woman, the erotic couple woman/woman can confound that order. Not all conceptualizations of women's desire for women exploit this effect: sexologists' codification of homosexuality as inversion preserves a notion of desire as heterosexual, suggesting that if both lovers are women, one must still be masculine.[21] But writing can confound the binaries Man/Woman or masculine/feminine by the process of speaking from the elsewhere of women's desire for women. Indeed, Irigaray's work on the question of the feminine in the 1970s often emphasized the role that speaking/writing women's desire for women plays in disrupting phallogo-centrism (e.g., "When Our Lips Speak Together"). Lanser argues that the convergence of the terms "woman" and "lesbian" in *Ladies Almanack* creates a version of what Adrienne Rich has called the "lesbian continuum."[22] But by disrupting the construction of "Woman" within the dominant order, it also disrupts what might look like the ends of that continuum, and perhaps the very possibility of linearity.

Ladies Almanack is structured by the calendar form and is to some extent linear and representational, but it is so in multiplex fashion: it includes stories of St. Evangeline Musset and her sect, as well as of other women, and stories that rewrite history and myths. Thus, it is not an example of a feminine writing entirely unlike any writing we have known; indeed, it challenges the notion of a completely alien feminine. The book's representations are stylized, its structures arbitrary rather than definitive; a modernist work, the book calls attention to its own artificiality. Because Barnes uses potentially feminine aspects of writing to write female sexual pleasure and to interrogate masculine representations of Woman and desire between women, calling the book "feminine" allows us to foreground its engagements with this masculine order. The style and form of *Ladies Almanack*, multiple, parodic, of indefinite genre, allow Barnes to displace masculine writing to make way for her own, to explore and disrupt definitions of Woman. By including the masculine, feminine writing can undermine and perhaps escape it.

Privately printed and circulated, *Ladies Almanack* falls, even in the circumstances of its publication, between the masculine economy and Luce Irigaray's utopian vision of "Exchange without identifiable terms of trade, without accounts, without end. . . . Where use and exchange would mingle" when the "goods" get together.[23] Similarly, in form and content *Ladies Almanack* "takes place" in the feminine no-man's-land between the masculine and the feminine, takes its place by being unplaceable and by simultaneously rejecting what it also appropriates. The effects of Barnes' complex engagement with the dominant order have been read differently by different readers; male, heterosexual critics seem to have noticed the appropriation, but not the rejection. As Lanser notes, *Ladies Almanack* has evoked a range of responses, from the delight of Natalie Barney and others about and for whom it was written, to the dismissive reactions of heterosexual male critics who have seen the book as a statement against lesbian sisterhood.[24]

The book's author has on the one hand many predecessors: "Shall one stumble on a Nuance that twenty Centuries have not pounced upon, yea, worried and made a Kill of?" (*LA*, 15), and on the other hand no predecessors, "for Life is represented in no City by a Journal dedicated to the Undercurrents, or for that matter to any fact whatsoever" (*LA*, 34). The book does revise texts on theology, sexology, psychoanalysis, and even evolution: "whelks whispered in the bunk of the Night," and "some billion of improving Years later . . . became Queen-Man and King-Woman" (*LA*, 69). But the male writers known for these theories were not writing from the point of view of the author of *Ladies Almanack* and so do not constitute her predecessors. Her forerunners are, instead, women-desiring-women, but she is as plural as her forerunners. The narrative voice is not singular but multiple, alternately "I" or "we" or not designated in the text (e.g., February, October, May); it is finally, not an isolated subject but a fluid perspective which informs and deflates masculine discourses that pretend to stability and authority.

Barnes' use of the capitalized Woman and her repeated, contradictory, parodic definitions of Woman both raise and parody the question of definition. Lesbian self-definition occurs in parodic or ironic dialogue with the hegemonic masculine order. As Lanser notes, there are at least three modes of disclosure in *Ladies Almanack*: narrative, "fanciful amazonian lore," and expository, and these encompass verse, music, illustrations, double columns of text.[25] The multiplicity of forms and definitions in *Ladies Almanack* both highlights the conflicts within the masculine order and makes the book's own in-definitions of Woman more supple and fluid than any single definition.

As Irigaray, among (many) others, has pointed out, the ideas of Woman generated by masculine systems—ideas of Woman as castrated man and of the lesbian as masculine woman—are clearly worse than inadequate. Such ideas can account for relations between women only "by affirming that as soon as she desires (herself), as soon as she speaks (herself, to herself), the woman is a man."[26] Yet a simple rejection or negation of these ideas would leave them in place. *Ladies Almanack*, like the works of Cixous and Irigaray, engages with and disrupts the myth of castration as a physical "fact," as a reference to the idea that the female body is a mutilated version of the male body, and thus that Woman is simply an inadequate version of Man.[27]

In the opening section of *Ladies Almanack*, the narrator reports that Evangeline says, "'never . . . has that Greek Mystery occurred to me, which is known as the Dashing out of the Testicles, and all that goes with it!' Which is said to have happened to a Byzantine Baggage of the Trojan Period, more to her Surprise than her Pleasure. Yet it is an agreeable Circumstance that the Ages thought fit to hand down this Miracle, for Hope springs eternal in the human Breast" (*LA*, 7). Evangeline asserts that she has never experienced castration, perhaps never thought of it. Yet her very negation suggests that she does think of it, and the narrator certainly does. The displeasure of the "Byzantine Baggage" might seem to imply that what lesbians (or women in general) want is to be men. But the exaggerated tone of the passage is clearly ironic. Castration here is not simply the loss of the singular male member; the penis is a mere adjunct to the testicles. The nature of the hope that the story of this mystery supplies is not entirely unequivocal. Is it women's hope that they may become male? Or men's hope that they may become female? Or women's hope that men may become female? Rather than simply ignore or reject the myth of penis envy and of the Woman as castrated Man, Barnes undermines it with mockery, exposing its absurdity.

Barnes is not merely mocking the psychoanalytic focus on castration; by reinvoking the classical course of many of Freud's theories, she is demonstrating some of the gaps in the dominant masculine order. Rather than privileging the metaphorical and punitive castration of Oedipus, Barnes' equivocal formulation seems to invoke actual and chosen castra-

tions. Male followers of the cult of the mother-goddess Rhea or Kybele
would castrate themselves, offering their genitals as a sacrifice; survivors
dressed thenceforward as women.[28] Irigaray notes that in feminine writing
"the issue is not one of elaborating a new theory of which woman would be
the *subject* or the *object*, but of jamming the theoretical machinery itself."
By retrieving some of the multiple meanings of classical castration, Barnes
suspends, in Irigaray's words, Freud's "pretension to the production of a
truth and of a meaning that are excessively univocal."[29]

Later, the myth of Woman as variant or deviant male is given a further
twist, when one character comments, "what have These Scriveners said of
her but that she must have had a Testes of sorts, however wried and awander;
that indeed she was called forth a Man, and when answering, by some
Mischance, or monstrous Fury of Fate, stumbled over a Womb, and was
damned then and forever to drag it about, like a Prisoner his Ball and Chain,
whether she would or no" (*LA*, 53). Thus the myth of castration is reversed:
the "man" becomes a woman not by loss but by addition, and again, the
agency of transformation is female: the Furies. But even this version of how
Woman came to be Woman is described as the construct of male writers. The
speaker's companion concurs that "they cannot let her be . . . but will admit
her to sense through the masculine Door only," but points out "near to a
Man or far from a Man, she will not be of him!" (*LA*, 53).

In addition to these undercuttings and rejections of the idea of
castration or Woman as variant of Man, Barnes displaces the myth of
castration, of Woman as made from Man, by replacing it with her own
account of Woman's genesis. Lanser suggests that the account of "the first
Woman born with a difference" is a parody of Aquinas, but it also speaks to
any theological account of Woman's origin and resonates in dialogue with
psychoanalytic, sexological, and evolutionary accounts.[30] Postdating the
Miltonic account of Satan's fall, the biblical parody nonetheless escapes, by
inscribing within itself, masculine theology. Far from being exclusively
fathered (by God and Adam), this "Eve" is exclusively, and multiply, moth-
ered. Barnes' account, printed in a column to one side of the "main" text but
accorded a full-page illustration, graphically indicates that though marginalized by a dominant discourse, the force of the feminine asserts itself
elsewhere.

Barnes' tactics for dealing with the issue of castration here accord
with Derrida's description of the hymen's graphic, a graphic of the undecidable associated with Woman, "which describes a margin where the control
over meaning or code is without recourse." Barnes' styles make possible her
affirmation of Woman, the affirmation beyond negation in which, as Derrida writes, "la castration n'a pas lieu."[31] Ideas of castration are included
within *Ladies Almanack* but are undermined; castration does not "have
place," has no determinate place, because it is only part of a feminine play of
style. The idea cannot simply be negated, for women do have to deal with its

effects (for instance, the objectionable and limiting ideas of male writers), but it is not finally definitive: it does not define Woman, and, when explored, it begins to point to the impossibility of defining Woman. According to Derrida, "had it ever taken place, castration will have been a sort of syntax which, in its annulment and equalization of any discourse in the mode of *pro et contra*, would have stabilized its undecidable."[32] The illusion of castration is what makes possible the simple opposition Man/Wo-man; but *Ladies Almanack*'s inscription of the destabilization of castration marks the undecidability of the definition of Woman.

Commenting on women's "distempers," the text informs us, "there have been some and several who hold the Sickness and Signs of such are diverse to the Point where Classification becomes almost impossible. . . . Others be of a temper that nothing will discountenance them save Vanity" (*LA*, 28–29). The text thus raises the problem of definition or classification, yet it presents the problem of classification as itself only one possibility (others don't care about it), thus demonstrating that it is a constructed problem, a problem of received definitions and not necessary to women even if constitutive of lesbian experience. Rather than simply accept or reject these classificatory systems or definitions, the text creates new signs out of them, like Evangeline Musset, who says she has "upon my Escutcheon so many Stains that I have, in this manner, created my own Banner and my own Badge" (*LA*, 35).

Woman is not, therefore, simply undefined; rather, as Irigaray observes, she "renders any definition inadequate."[33] Evangeline Musset's observation that "All Women . . . are not Women all" suggests not simply that not all women are "all Woman," but further that every woman is not entirely Woman; women are not encompassed by the masculine order that defines Woman in opposition to Man. Like the Queen-Man and King-Woman, "never is she one, either male or female."[34] Barnes goes further than Irigaray when Miss Nip speculates that she might—or might not—have known Cynic Sal as Timid Tom or Most-Infirm-of-Purpose and notes, "no Man could be both one and neither like us" (*LA*, 37). Women are and are not women, and are and are not men, and are women because they are and are not. When an unnamed Eve figure is finally specified as Daisy Downpour, "for so she might as well be called as any other" (*LA*, 63), Barnes highlights the contingency of naming: Daisy Downpour might be called any other name; any other woman might be called Daisy Downpour. Nomination is never definitive or assured; the "stains" of use upon an authoritative and hierarchical language and upon the stains themselves create a new and fluid approach to the definition of Woman.

Thus, *Ladies Almanack* displaces masculine definitions of woman by giving place to such definitions, by allowing them to displace each other. It includes, for instance, the notion of the lesbian as masculine woman: Evangeline Musset "had been developed in the Womb of her most gentle

Mother to be a Boy, when therefore, she came forth an Inch or so less than this, she paid no Heed to the Error" (*LA*, 7). Gender here is defined not by physiology but by sexual orientation. But while the lesbian is a woman who is a man, she is not an inadequate man; the lack of such a little thing as a penis is less than an inconvenience. Yet the lesbian is also defined not as man but as woman. The heterosexual Patience Scalpel "could not understand Women" (*LA*, 11), and the women she cannot understand are lesbians. Here it is the female who enters into heterosexual relations, into the hom(m)osexual sociocultural economy, who is not a woman (for Woman does not exist within that system).[35] If the lesbian is distinguished from other women by being the woman who is a (castrated) man, she is not a woman, and Woman is not a castrated man. If, however, the lesbian is the woman with a difference, who originates outside the phallogocentric system, then heterosexual women are not women but castrated men. Either way (and the either/or structure is neither comprehensive nor conclusive), Woman both participates in the masculine system of definition and escapes it—indeed, escapes it by participating in it.

But where Woman has been repressed, excluded from partcipating in the system of definition, women have not escaped its effects. "What they have in their Heads, Hearts, Stomachs, Pockets, Flaps, Tabs and Plackets, have one and all been some and severally commented on, by way of hint or harsh Harangue, praised, blamed, epicked, poemed and pastoraled, pamphleted, prodded and pushed, made a Spring-board for every sort of Conjecture whatsoever, good, bad and indifferent" (*LA*, 47–48). Woman is thus already singularly multiple even within masculine writing, which, however, thus dismembers and objectifies her. She provides "material" for the masculine text, to which she herself nonetheless always remains exterior. Within the masculine sociocultural economy, each single definition can impinge upon women, shaping self-definitions and relations with each other. For instance, one couple in *Ladies Almanack* wants to legitimize lesbian relations on the model of heterosexual marriage (*LA*, 19). Irigaray states that her critique of Freud's account of female homosexuality does not mean "that what Freud describes does not fit a certain 'reality,' or that his commentaries or explanations are simply 'wrong.' Many homosexual women can recognize themselves in this story or could at least try to find their bearings in it." The point is rather that masculine definitions are inadequate, that female desire also escapes these explanations, for in them "nothing of the special nature of desire *between women* has been unveiled or stated. That a woman might desire a woman 'like' herself, someone of the 'same' sex . . . is simply incomprehensible to Freud, and indeed inadmissible" within phallogocentric thought.[36] Just as *Ladies Almanack* acknowledges (by mockery) masculine accounts of the origin of Woman by castration and supplies its own account, it not only acknowledges but also supplements masculine accounts of desire between women; one character comments that love of woman for woman is "'a Kiss in the Mirror'" (*LA*, 23). Further, the text recognizes the quotation marks Irigaray places around "like" and "same": a lesbian unhappy in love "tears her Shift for Likeness in a Shift, and a Mystery that is lost to the proportion of Mystery" (*LA*, 57). Relations between women are precisely those which turn sameness into the difference of nonhierarchical likeness, into a mystery which, being lost to the proportioning of the masculine order, is all the more mysterious.

The parodic styles of *Ladies Almanack* make possible, even inevitable, this indeterminate, mysterious nondefinition of Woman and relations between women. What Derrida calls the "vertiginous non-mastery" of parody can never be pinned down, and thus no definitive account of Woman can be found in the text.[37] But though the parodist or ironist undermines masculine mastery or authority, there is nonetheless a certain "authority" implicit in this activity: the nonlocatable authority of the right to parody, the unknown (here unknowable) greater knowledge of the ironist. Thus, *Ladies Almanack* challenges the notion of a feminine that would be entirely excluded from authority. To the extent that it is masculine (asserting the authority to challenge), it is feminist (challenging the masculine), though its feminism is made possible by its femininity (destabilizing/undermining authority), which also, in turn, challenges its feminism (because feminism asserts an authority): the femininity and feminism of the text both enable and question each other.

Irony and parody generate a (feminine) surplus which cannot be fully reassimilated to any (masculine) system; but the direction of this surplus in *Ladies Almanack* seems primarily affirmative; it becomes a feminist feminine. The best example of this might be the chapter-long complaint about women's love letters to each other, which ends, "twittering so loud upon the Wire that one cannot hear the Message. And yet!" (*LA*, 46). The narrator's complaint implicitly includes the love letter of her own text; her own final message here is left unstated or incompletely stated, pushed to the edge or margin of the chapter by her virtuoso linguistic performance. But precisely because the signifier overwhelms the signified, the book's criticisms of women are never wholly criticisms: that "And yet!" points elsewhere. Further, the very excess of the praise of women (for instance, labeling Evangeline Musset a saint) leaves a residue of real praise, while protecting both praiser and praised by preempting the extratextual parody to which they might otherwise be subject. The affirmative direction of the excess of *Ladies Almanack* seems to be confirmed in the text's feminist closure, which is itself made available by the masculine structure of the calendar. In "December," Evangeline Musset dies, and after multiple funeral services, multiple internments, and multiple rituals of mourning (in keeping with the multiple natures of Woman), she is finally cremated. Her tongue, however, "would not suffer Ash," but "flickers to this day . . . on the Altar in the Temple of Love" (*LA*, 84). Like *Ladies Almanack* as a whole, this final image symbolically links specifically female, lesbian passion and the power of women's language.

Yet for all its symbolic affirmation, the image of the tongue remains troublingly ambiguous on a literal level: a tongue without a mouth may (and in the text does) give sexual pleasure (*LA*, 84), but it cannot speak. Similarly, *Ladies Almanack* inscribes women's sexual pleasure, but must do so equivocally. Male, heterosexual critics have read *Ladies Almanack* as antilesbian. Because the feminine is the difference between the masculine and the feminine, feminine writing leaves the reader, one way or another, on the boundary between the masculine and the feminine. *Ladies Almanack* can be read as profoundly affirmative, but its affirmation depends upon an unstable irony that also invokes the masculine: the text is always potentially compromised by that which it subverts. The transformational power of this feminine writing is thus a function of reading this full ambiguity: what is potentially revolutionary is not simply feminine writing but feminine reading.

Through this heuristic lens, Barnes' work can be seen to explore and explode the illusive, exclusive hegemony of the masculine order, displacing its organization-through-castration by encoding and inscribing the elusive feminine in language, replacing its decapitated Woman with a woman writing. Barnes' work suggests that the value of ideas of the feminine and feminine writing consists less in their postulation of a new language or their call for a revolutionary future than in the possibilities they offer for new ways of thinking language, ways that recognize the subversive and potentially revolutionary elements already operative within the languages of the past and present. The postulate that all language is masculine and represses the feminine hypostatizes language, itself repressing the feminine that has been put into language, but it can help us recognize the power of the masculine in language as that through and against which the woman writer inscribes the feminine of her own text. The assumption that Woman is always outside language situates itself within the very system of binary thought it wishes to subvert, and thus it represses the multiplicity of the conditions of women; and yet it not only obscures but also alludes to the conditions of the woman writer's subversive engagement with language.

¶ . . . I was, I believe, the first American to be sent to Europe for the purpose of interviewing Mr. Gurdjieff, his dancers and disciples. Gurdjieff is an unmitigated scoundrel precisely because he does (or is it did?) know something of the wisdom of the East, a sort of Greek, Roman, Russian, God-knows-what-quick-lunch-counter method for expiring ancient ladies of the old Regime and the younger who could be used fore and aft in prayer, particularly if they had diamonds or other forceful finger rings. I have yet to see one of his people who walked out any better for his addiction to large cigars, Armagnac, groaning larder and "self observation." . . . He got a great deal of ground work done and a slice of kitchen work by this method, but all that it ended in, so far as I can judge, were wanderers enflated [sic] with deprivation. Ouspensky left him. Orage, who was said to be a very intelligent editor, ended up with women and more women. Women seem to be idiotic oftener and more profitably than Daddy Browning.

His dancers were remarkable. So are trained seals. . . .
  —Djuna Barnes,
  letter to Allen Tate,
  June–July 1946

¶ —I lay awake last night and could not think what in the world the world is about—old women starving (my aunt), Elsa [the Baroness] out of a mad house—my mother soon to be left son-less—you without your love—and I could think of what how many pairs of gloves were bought last week by wealthy bitches, without a worry!! And then people's characters! My God, their awful states of mind, their dreadful pettiness— their ghostly ghostly souls—the best of them occasionally think up things too incredible to believe!"
  —Djuna Barnes,
  letter to Eleanor Fitzgerald,
  10 May 1926

11

The Outsider among the Expatriates: Djuna Barnes' Satire on the Ladies of the <u>Almanack</u>

Karla Jay

When Djuna Barnes died on 19 June 1982, we lost not only a noteworthy writer but also the last witness to that fabulous era of American expatriates in Paris in the early 1900s. With her demise, the curtain fell on that great stage; far from having opened the show, however, Barnes made the last entrance when she disembarked in France in the early 1920s. Natalie Clifford Barney and Gertrude Stein had arrived and set up their salons more than a decade earlier, and the avalanche of American and British expatriate writers and artists, including Radclyffe Hall, Una Troubridge, Mina Loy, Sylvia Beach, Janet Flanner, Alice B. Toklas, and Romaine Brooks, had solidly landed. The party was firmly underway.

It was not merely the timing of her arrival that distinguished Barnes from most of her sister expatriates. Unlike most of the other women, Barnes had to work for a living and had little enough to get by on comfortably, since she lacked the fortune of Natalie Barney or Peggy Guggenheim or even the relative security of Gertrude Stein or Romaine Brooks. If others wrote or painted, it was because they *chose* to: Barnes *had* to. Whereas her peers could overlook the drearier economic aspects of writing, Barnes could not. Barney could take her literary output lightly and quip that her "only books/ Were women's looks,"[1] and Stein could play the brilliant hostess while awaiting her discovery by American audiences. Barnes had to earn her living as a journalist and illustrator, at which she had more than a modicum of success. Her work was published in most of New York's important news-

This essay also appears in *Lesbian Texts and Contexts: Radical Revisions*, edited by Karla Jay and Joanne Glasgow (New York: New York Univ. Press, 1990).

papers. Therefore, when Barnes began in Paris to venture into long, hermetic, and uncommercial fiction, she was risking a starvation that none of the others would ever have to contemplate. As a consequence, she ultimately wound up at the economic mercy of other women, not just Peggy Guggenheim, as Andrew Field reports in his biography, but also Natalie Clifford Barney, who frequently sent Barnes checks for one hundred dollars and paid bills for repairs in Barnes' apartments. Once she even sent her own housekeeper, Berthe Cleyrergue (who owed her position in Barney's household to Barnes' introduction), to tend Barnes when the latter was ill at the Hôtel d'Angleterre.[2] Sometime in the late 1920s another unnamed "rich American woman" provided Barnes with a monthly stipend of fifty dollars.[3]

Rather than inspiring gratitude, occasional handouts of fifty or one hundred dollars from the generous who have millions tend to create bitterness, resentment, and anguish in the recipient, negative reactions usually not perceived by the donor. Barnes' letters to Natalie Barney are filled with complaints about finances and problems with her living quarters; they were likely veiled requests for additional funds. The wealthy clique of expatriates in Paris would probably not have understood the emotional toll of poverty on Barnes, who was perpetually placed in the role of the beggar at the feast, the celebrant in the borrowed gown, the one to partake of others' hospitality without being able to return it in kind. With Barnes' elegant looks and stylishness, it was probably easy for them to overlook her impoverishment. But it was not easy for Barnes to live with it, and much of her bitterness emerged when she depicted her wealthy friends in *Ladies Almanack*.

In addition to aiding Barnes financially in an extremely modest way, Natalie Barney included her friend in her literary circle. Barney's Academy of Women attempted to create a milieu in which elite women artists would nurture one another, provide supportive criticism for each other's work, and publish one another when necessary.[4] Still, this salon was not for everyone; Barney deeply detested the masses and envisioned herself as writing for and surrounding herself with the chosen few. She attempted to reify this dream, first by going to Lesbos in 1904 with poetess Renée Vivien (Pauline Mary Tarn) and later, in 1927, by establishing the Academy of Women as an addition to her already prestigious Paris salon. Certainly, Barney considered Djuna Barnes one of the select few qualified to breathe her rarefied air. But did Barnes feel comfortable breathing it? The biting satire, verging on viciousness, found in *Ladies Almanack* strongly suggests that she did not; instead, she bit the very hands that brought *Ladies Almanack* into existence.

As part of the cultural mission of her salon, Barney subsidized anonymous publication of *Ladies Almanack* in 1928. Though Barnes' name did not appear on the book for several decades, it was commonly known that she was the "Lady of Fashion" who had penned the wicked satire of Barney and her circle. Barney, in her role as "patroness" of the arts, never admitted directly to Barnes that she saw any ill intent in Barnes' portrayal of her as the seductive Evangeline Musset; in fact, in 1935, Barney wrote Barnes a letter in which she called the work "a never failing delight" and thanked Barnes for the "many new admirers" the work had attracted to her.[5] Friendly letters were exchanged between the two until Barney's death in 1972. However, in a rough draft of an essay on Barnes, Natalie Barney wrote, "Djuna Barnes [*sic*] pistol has too easy a trigger with no safety catch."[6] In other words, Barnes wrote too quickly without perceiving the consequences, but Barney obviously noticed the bullets. It would be consonant with Barney's character to choose to overlook publicly (in the published version of the essay in *Aventures de l'espirit*) and privately (in her letters to Barnes) the poison in the barbs. If she confessed Barnes had wounded her, she would violate the codes of knightly chivalry that she tried to emulate.

While Barney and some of the others—such as Solita Solano, who also reacted positively (in public at least) to the *Almanack*—preferred to ignore the more venomous side of Barnes' humor, it is nevertheless there, commencing with the title. Although Barney admired knights and virgins, she never labeled herself a "lady," preferring to be called a "woman"; in her epigrams, she said that a lady was no more than an "expurgated woman."[7] Yet Barney was very much a lady—a lady of leisure and a lady who ran a salon in the tradition of the best noblewomen in France, such as Mlle de Scudéry or Mme de Staël. It was only at the beginning of the twentieth century, with the advent of rich Americans such as Gertrude Stein, Mina Loy, and Natalie Barney, that salon hostesses reflected such bourgeois origins. In the *Almanack*, Barney is called Dame Evangeline Musset, the term *dame* underscoring her generational claims, if not to a title, at least to wealth. Without a doubt, Barney was much more of a grand dame than was the "Lady of Fashion" who penned the work. If Barnes were a "dame," she was so only in the coarse American usage of the word.

The book begins with the unflattering account of Barney/Musset and her father, Albert (called "Father" in the *Almanack*), who is perturbed because his daughter Evangeline has not turned out quite to his liking.

He had Words with her enough, saying: "Daughter, daughter, I perceive in you most fatherly Sentiments. What am I to do?" And she answered him High enough. "Thou, good Governor, wast expecting a Son when you lay atop of your Choosing, why then be so mortal wounded when you perceive that you have your Wish? Am I not doing after your very Desire, and is it not the more commendable, seeing that I do it without the Tools for the Trade, and yet nothing complain?" (*LA*, 8)

The belief that lesbianism was caused by parents who strongly desired a son during or after the child's conception would have been disputed by Barney, who believed herself to be "naturally unnatural."[8] She thought herself very much a woman, not a "pseudo-man," as she is portrayed here in the beginning of the *Almanack*, especially when Barnes proclaims Musset's sexual anatomy to be lacking only an inch (*LA*, 15). Such a description of Barney was insulting on several levels. To begin with, Barney not only considered herself to be completely feminine, but she also pursued beauty in its myriad feminine forms, as Liane de Pougy later described: "We loved long hair, pretty breasts, pouts, simpers, charm, grace, not boyishness. 'Why try to resemble our enemies?' Nathalie-Flossie [Barney] used to murmur in her little nasal voice."[9]

Moreover, the idea that a lesbian was a woman whose anatomy was similar but not equal to that of a man's was a negative stereotype that had long been present in the laws of Great Britain and other countries. It was erroneously believed that lesbians engaged in sex by penetrating other women with unnaturally elongated clitorises. This widely believed but biologically unproven premise had been brought into the public eye a century earlier (1811) in the notorious slander case in Edinburgh, Scotland, brought by schoolmistresses Marianne Woods and Jane Pirie against Dame Cumming Gordon, whose niece had accused the two of engaging in lesbian practices in the boarding school they ran. The teachers were vindicated by the court in part because the judges believed that no such deformed women existed in Scotland![10] While feminist critics, such as Susan Sniader Lanser, defend *Ladies Almanack* partly as a celebration of oral sexuality,[11] they fail to explain this demeaning definition of lesbianism created by patriarchal, misogynistic law courts which could not conceive of sexuality without a phallus or a substitute for one. The deformation of Musset's/Barney's anatomy undercuts the prowess attributed to her tongue, which superficially at least outweighs all other forms of sexual techniques referred to in the *Almanack*.

Barnes may have gone so far as to mock Barney's renowned sexual prowess. For instance, it is claimed that at the age of thirty, Musset "made a Harlot a good woman by making her Mistress" (*LA*, 17). This deed, of course, is a direct reference to Barney's love affair in 1898–99 with Liane de Pougy, who was the most famous courtesan of her day, and whom Barney did succeed in seducing. However, the rest of the story contradicts the facts as Barney and her circle would have known them. Barney, who was only twenty-two or so when her affair with de Pougy transpired, failed to "reform" her: that transformation was accomplished by a man, Prince Georges Ghika, whom Liane de Pougy married. Barney desperately tried but did not succeed in persuading de Pougy to abandon her life in the demimonde. In other words, what is on the surface related as one of Barney's greatest triumphs was in fact one of her greatest failures. Barney was unable to accomplish what a "real" man did. Barnes is not so much rewriting history as holding up failure in the guise of success, a tactic which might be intended to irritate Barney but go unnoticed by the unwary reader.

Nor is Barney portrayed as the kindest of lovers. In one episode,

Musset leaves Doll Furious (Dolly Wilde, with whom Barney was lovers during the 1920s) in the middle of their lovemaking in order to pursue another woman, Bounding Bess (Esther Murphy),[12] despite the protests of Doll Furious (*LA*, 31–32). "Fickle" would be a euphemism for the way in which Musset leaves her, despite her rationale of converting another woman to the "cause." Dolly Wilde, the niece of Oscar Wilde, was known to be as witty as he; she once remarked, "I am more Oscar-like than he was like himself."[13] It is not her wit, however, which is exhibited in the *Almanack*; rather, she is portrayed as a "slave" to Musset's sexual prowess, begging her to stay and continue their lovemaking. Not only does she ignore the presence of Nip and Tuck (Janet Flanner and Solita Solano respectively), but in addition she clearly has no qualms about making love on the carpet in front of her acquaintances.

Barney/Musset pursues not only Bounding Bess, but several other women as well. Nevertheless, her primary relationship during this era was with American artist Romaine Brooks, with whom Barney was involved for over half a century. Although Brooks is not sexually satirized as is Dolly Wilde, Barnes also manages to attack Brooks on the points she felt most sensitive about. In the *Almanack*, Brooks, thinly disguised as Cynic Sal, is reduced to the role of a servant: "She dressed like a Coachman of the period of Pecksniff, but she drives an empty Hack" (*LA*, 36), a clear reference to Brooks' mode of dressing in somber suits with black top hats. Brooks was insecure about her social standing within Barney's circle and with herself in general: Brooks' mother had treated her much like a servant (and by some accounts gave her away to be raised by one) until her sickly brother, St. Mar, whom her mother greatly preferred, finally died. As a result, Brooks suffered emotional and economic scars from her childhood, which Barnes does not refrain from digging up (or into). The empty hack might refer to a loveless life, and Barnes' remark that Brooks "still cracks as sharp a Whip" (*LA*, 26) is a comment upon Brooks' reputedly dour and antisocial personality, which caused her often to remain alone in her own apartment or studio rather than attending Barney's salon. Brooks is further described as "the Woman . . . who is of so vain and jealous a Nature that do what you will you cannot please her" (*LA*, 36), a comment that alludes to Brooks' well-known jealousy over Barney's love affairs with other women, especially Dolly Wilde, whom Brooks finally drove from Barney's bed after nearly a decade of struggle. Thus, Brooks was a "servant" in another regard—that is, she was a slave to her love for Barney and to her own jealous nature.

Barnes does not linger long on each of Barney's lovers; instead, she rushes Barney quickly towards eternity and her elevation to lesboerotic sainthood. In the book, Dame Musset dies at the age of ninety-nine— ironically, just a bit older than Barney was at her death in 1972, when she was ninety-five. When Musset dies, her followers carry her body here and there and finally cremate it:

And when they came to the ash that was left of her, all had burned but the Tongue, and this flamed, and would not suffer Ash, and it played about upon the handful that had been she indeed. And seeing this, there was a great Commotion, and the sound of Skirts swirled in haste, and the Patter of much running in feet, but Señorita Fly-About [Mimi Franchetti] came down upon that Urn first, and beatitude played and flickered upon her Face, and from under her Skirts a slow Smoke issued, though no thing burned, and the Mourners barked about her covetously. (*LA*, 84)

Finally, after all the mourners have taken their turn over the tongue, they place Musset's ashes "on the Altar in the Temple of Love" (*LA*, 84).

Barney/Musset appears to have been elevated to sainthood, but on closer analysis, she has been reduced to a sexual acrobat in life and beyond. Barney's tongue gives pleasure in life and is hotter than the flames of cremation, but only the sexual talents of her tongue transcend mortality. She is not portrayed in the book as the charismatic salon hostess, witty speaker, and creative writer that she was. In her postmortem state, she mechanically gives pleasure to others because her eyes and brain have not risen from the flames along with her tongue. The fact that Musset is interred in a Temple of *Love* is ironic, for what can the nature of such an indiscriminate love be? The fact that Musset's posthumous prowess delights as well as amazes her devoted followers reduces them to Musset's level, for their adoration of the mobile relic seems to them more than an adequate replacement for the deceased woman or at least metonymy for what she was. Barney could hardly have been thrilled to see all her intellectual accomplishments forgotten—despite her pose of anti-intellectualism she was a prolific writer—while her sexual athleticism alone is immortal.

Furthermore, this reductionist vision of Barney as a conscienceless nymphomaniac negates much of what she most valued in life: friendship. Barney prided herself on being a fine friend as well as an outstanding lover, and the fact that almost all of Barney's lovers remained close friends with her when the sexual aspect of their relationship ceased seems to prove that she attained her goal. Barney detested Don Juanism and emphasized the "Platonic" element of her relationships (in both the modern and original meaning of the concept). The shift from the Temple of Friendship to the Temple of Love may seem slight, but it drastically alters the scale of values Barney upheld throughout her writing, where the former held the higher place. In the final analysis, Barnes does not elevate Barney; rather, she flattens her into a one-dimensional, slightly pornographic caricature. Even if Musset does attain sainthood in the *Almanack*, what does her immortal state consist of? The lives of the saints often begin with accounts of sinning that lead to a visitation, transformation, or rebirth, any of which creates a higher, purer self. Musset in the end is reduced to ashes, and what has risen is the relic of her most carnal self, a testament to unrestrained, undirected, uncontrolled, and indiscriminate cunnilingus.

Barney and her lovers are not the only ones to be sniped by Barnes' bullets; others become targets as well, most notably Radclyffe Hall and Una Troubridge, presented as Tilly Tweed-in-Blood and Lady Buck-and-Balk respectively. According to Barnes, Troubridge "sported a Monocle and believed in Spirits." Hall "sported a Stetson and believed in Marriage" (*LA*, 18). Unlike some of the more obscure references in this roman à clef, there can be no doubt about the identity of these two women, for Troubridge did indeed favor a monocle, and Hall a stetson. Both Troubridge and Hall were greatly devoted to Catholicism and believed that they would be reunited in heaven, despite the teachings of the Church on the subject of homosexuality. When the two have tea with Musset, the pair insists that English law should legalize their union: "For the equal gold Bands . . . shall make of one a Wife, and the other a Bride" (*LA*, 19).

After the publication of *The Well of Loneliness*, Radclyffe Hall was tried on charges of obscenity in both England and the United States because of the novel's lesbian subject matter (although Stephen Gordon is portrayed as so self-sacrificing and helpless in her sexual preferences that one can hardly blame her for her "deformity" as it is presented). It is illogical for Hall and Troubridge to expect the privilege of marriage, considering the legal consequences of merely writing about the topic. In view of their satirized dress—especially that of the masculine Radclyffe Hall, who liked to be called "John" and who cropped her hair like a man—their demand for the legalization of their union both within the *Almanack* and against the mores of their time can only serve to make the readers guffaw at Hall and Troubridge, not sympathize with them. The couple certainly forms a vivid contrast to Barney's infidelities, but they do not emerge in a sympathetic light, and the pity Hall hoped to evoke from the public in her novel is totally lacking in Barnes' cruel satire of her. Even Musset, upon hearing their pleas for marriage, proclaims that one might do equally well to take the law into one's own hands: "But there are Duels to take the place of the Law," she facetiously proclaims (*LA*, 20).

Satire and caricature by definition exaggerate and flatten the people they depict, but other bawdy characters (one thinks of Chaucer's Wife of Bath) manage to retain their humanity while Barnes' characters do not. Some might argue that the work is an almanac, not a tale or a novel, but it does not belong to the first genre, either. Despite organizing the book by months, Barnes' work does not fit the traditional description of an almanac, which usually contains such items as weather forecasts, tide tables, and lists of facts. Nor is it for a specific profession, such as farmers. Neither can the *Almanack* be classified as a novel, for the only plot is a rather sketchy biography of Musset.

Perhaps by placing the work beyond recognizable genres, Barnes also hoped to escape the limitations or expectations of such forms, but the structure of the *Almanack* itself does not explain the heartlessness of the joke. Part of the explanation, of course, lies in Barnes' monetary situation discussed earlier. She resented being poor, and the willingness of the others to support her work financially may have ironically increased her anger at them. *The Antiphon* strongly suggests that Barnes had been bought or sold at least once in her youth, and she might have perceived well-meaning gestures of literary admiration and financial backing as having hidden strings or ill intent.

A further irony is that Barnes' satire was so extreme that most of the women in the *Almanack* failed or refused to identify themselves, though the work was purportedly an "in-joke," written for and subsidized in part by the other women in the work. Even Natalie Barney, who provided most of the characters' identities in the margins of her own copy of the *Almanack*, was unable to name all the figures in the book, though they were all supposedly either her lovers or intimate members of her circle. For example, Barney could not identify the three women who were the sources for Maizie and the two Doxies.[14] Similarly, Janet Flanner, who admitted in *Paris Was Yesterday* that she was depicted in the *Almanack*, was not sure whether she was Nip or Tuck.[15] Barney, however, was sure that Flanner was Nip, a journalist who "could not let a Morsel go, though she knew well that it could be printed nowhere in no Country" (*LA*, 34). We can only assume that members of the café circle among whom the book was circulated were even further afield in their speculations about the identities of the wild ladies of Barnes' Sapphic calendar.

Humor, it is traditionally suggested, is based on, among other things, recognition. But if the members of Barney's coterie did not recognize themselves or one another, even in a caricatured form, one wonders what they were laughing at. The bawdy humor was most likely the source of laughter and praise. The *Almanack*'s ribald Joycean humor and puns have sold copies of the book to admiring readers who most likely are unable to identify *any* of the characters in the book.

If one were to attribute kindness to Barnes (a trait that never seems conjoined with her name), one might suggest that in her satire she hermetically protected the identities of her friends. However, through the veneer, those somewhat acquainted with the period and the group can easily recognize Barney, Brooks, Wilde, Hall, and Troubridge. It is not, however, the witty Barney or Wilde, the artistic Brooks, or the brave Hall and Troubridge who are depicted; instead, Barnes presents a reductionist vision of them which flattens them to a one-dimensional level, usually sexual, in which their lifetime achievements are diminished or omitted. It is questionable whether Saint Musset's followers are liberated lesbians or sexual slaves.

Several critics, including Susan Lanser and Gayle Rubin, have described the book as a joyous celebration of lesbianism, but they have somehow overlooked this reductionist element, and most importantly, Barnes' sexual alienation from the other members of the circle.[16] For one thing, Barnes seems to identify most closely with the character of Patience

Scalpel, whom Barney identified as Mina Loy. Loy, who was a poet and salon hostess in Paris at the time, provides a distinct counterpoint to the lesbians. In contrast to Barney's lusty sexuality, Loy is described as being frigid and is represented by the month of January (*LA*, 10).

Yet it is too simplistic to label Loy as a "foil" to Barney/Musset, as does Louis Kannenstine.[17] Loy's position in the group is unique. Though she had dabbled in Sapphic love, she is a heterosexually identified woman, and as such she is forever an outsider of some sort, no matter how deeply she shares the literary preoccupations of the others. She "could not understand Women and their Ways" (*LA*, 11), and her liberalism and sympathy for the group have obvious limits. She rejects the lifestyle of Barney and her circle for her own daughters, whom, she insists, "shall go a'marrying" (*LA*, 13).

Therefore, Loy was in some fashion simultaneously within and outside the group, intellectually in one camp and sexually in the other. Her position strongly reflects that of Barnes herself. While their economic situations were not analogous, Loy was Barnes' closest friend within the circle, the one with whom she identified. Like Loy, Barnes refused to label herself a lesbian. Despite her decade-long affair with artist Thelma Wood, she insisted, "I'm not a lesbian. I just loved Thelma."[18] Since her relationship with Wood appears to have been longer than any other relationship in her life and since she also had affairs with other lesbians, including Natalie Barney,[19] there is quite obviously a strong element of self-denial here—not that Barnes or Loy would be the first woman to be a lesbian yet thoroughly and totally deny it. The negation comes across clearest when we note who is *not* in the *Almanack*. Barnes manages to mention, if only in passing, almost all the members of Barney's intimate circle during this era *except* herself and Thelma Wood. Their absence from the sensual circle seems more telling than their presence, even if briefly noted, would have been.[20]

Although the narrative voice occasionally uses "I" and "we," the effect of omitting herself from the cast of characters is to create a chasm between "I" and "they." The text has been traditionally interpreted as being about the Barnes/Barney circle, but the curious lack of the encompassing "we" and Barnes' absence undercut this possibility and suggest another intention. Barnes' role is that of an outsider, an observer of a "sexual and social institution" to which she does not claim membership. Her choice of signature may provide the clue here: she is the "Lady of Fashion." As previously noted, the "ladies" represent Barney and other elite, upper-class lesbians of her coterie. The "Lady of Fashion" is thus either the one who participates solely because it is the rage at the time (the "fashion") or perhaps the one who dresses for a role she plays rather than being a real lesbian (as in a lesbian "after a fashion" or someone masquerading as a lesbian but who is not truly one).

From her own perspective, Barnes must have found herself in a historically and otherwise unique situation. Usually, lesbians were persecuted by the church or the state, sometimes both. In traditional social circumstances, a woman like Barnes, who was trying to make her way in the world, would go out of her way to avoid the scandal associated with such women. For a variety of reasons, lesbians moved to the forefront of the literary and artistic movements in Paris in the 1920s. To make her way among the literary denizens, Barnes had to ingratiate herself with a group she might be expected to shun under other circumstances. She was torn, therefore, between two sets of mores, and I believe she managed to accommodate both by joining the group on one hand and mocking and denouncing it on the other.

Even had Barnes wanted to join wholeheartedly in the Sapphic circle, she was not a "real" lady like the others, who were economically independent women, free to choose not only where they lived but how they lived, sexually and otherwise. On the contrary, Barnes was not financially free to be a lesbian and could not afford to live like the salon set. She was at the mercy of a phallocentric literary establishment in the United States, from which she earned her living as a journalist and illustrator. She knew too well that the fortunes of publishing are more fickle than Barney's trust or Brooks' inheritance. She did not sign the *Almanack* because of a fear of scandal; the book is no more obscene than Joyce's *Ulysses* or Gide's *Corydon*. Rather, she did not sign it because she could not afford to be publicly identified as a lesbian or to identify herself as one. And if the world should discover the identity of the "Lady of Fashion," the negative relationship to the set portrayed within the *Almanack* would protect her reputation. After all, there were limits, even to bohemianism.

Thus, Barnes underscores her economic and sexual isolation from the rest of the circle by removing herself from the family album. Had Barnes been willing or able to accept her lesbianism, the *Almanack* might not have existed or might have been different. The same could probably be said for *Nightwood* and some of her other works. And were some critics not so eager to salvage whatever positive lesbian material that can be gleaned from this era to counterbalance the pits of solitude and despair into which other authors disparagingly tossed us, then they might see that *Ladies Almanack* is not quite the lighthearted prolesbian romp we would like to embrace without reservation. What is contained within the book is problematic at best because of its reductionist vision of lesbianism, and what is missing is perhaps even more so because of all the questions we must ask about Barnes' absence. Barnes left us no final answer as to whether her barbs were meant to vex or to please and whether the trigger went off accidentally or on purpose. But unlike Dame Musset, whose tongue survived even death, Barnes left us only silence for the last half of her life and an only partially solvable enigma of an intriguing roman à clef, which in its fun-house mirror reflects not only Barney's Paris coterie but fragments of the expatriate Barnes herself, who stood on the doorstep, half in and half out of the club.

¶ Back in 1930 I had published poems in a little magazine called *blues*, jointly edited by Charles Henri Ford and Parker Tyler. . . .

Later I had run into Ford in Paris with Tchelitchew, the painter. Now suddenly he was in Tangiers, awaiting the arrival of Djuna Barnes from Devonshire, where she had been visiting Peggy Guggenheim. Until her arrival Ford had been staying with a young Spanish couple, Pita and Carmita. Djuna came and explained that she wanted to find a house. Someone suggested that since I used my house on the Marshan only to work in, it was logical that she should use it to sleep in. Charles Henri Ford moved in with her, on the understanding that after one thirty in the afternoon I could always count on their being out of it. Before she would unpack, Djuna insisted on removing all seventeen jackal pelts [acquired in Lagouhat] from the walls where I had hung them; she also rolled up the python skin and put it away.

Soon Djuna and Charles Henri found a more comfortable house in the middle of an orchard a few hundred feet up the lane. They lived Moroccan-style, on the floor. She was typing a manuscript called *Bow Down*; the title was later changed to *Nightwood*. We use to sit at the Café Central in the Zoco Chico, and because Djuna's makeup was blue, purple, and green in a day when no one used such colors, she was an object of interest to everyone. She did not at all mind being stared at; a brief imitation of Sir Francis Rose she did one day galvanized the spectators in the café, as well as the passersby.

—Paul Bowles,
Without Stopping

Mousemeat:
Contemporary Reviews of <u>Nightwood</u>

Jane Marcus

Reading Djuna Barnes' clipping books in the University of Maryland library, one is struck by the richness of the literary world of the thirties. Any novelist writing today would give her eyeteeth (or at least her first edition of *Nightwood*) to be reviewed at great length by Dylan Thomas, Alfred Kazin, Graham Green, Philip Toynbee, Carl Van Doren, and Mark Van Doren. Oh, to be trashed as decadent by the righteous left wing (represented by Philip Rahv in the *New Masses*), to be called dirty and disgusting by literary ladies in the South and Midwest, and to be championed by the intrepid socialist-feminist journal, *Time and Tide!* Many reviewers printed strings of quotations from the novel and most, predictably, judged it according to their opinion of T.S. Eliot and his introduction. The length of the reviews and the number of literary journals and Sunday book review sections reveal how impoverished is our present world of books and readers. Miss Barnes may have been annoyed at the misreading of *Nightwood*, but it was given the kind of press coverage which only cookbooks get today, from serious intellectuals who took reviewing seriously and wrote elegant, if often malicious, essays for an enormous reading public.

Reviewing *Selected Works* (*New Leader*, 16 April 1962), Stanley Edgar Hyman recalled that the wildly enthusiastic *New Yorker* review by Clifton Fadiman was retracted later the same year. As a college freshman, Hyman was left "holding the bag of Fadiman's former opinion"; on re-reading, he found it "just as great as I remembered, or as Fadiman ever said." "Go Down, Matthew is a chapter title, and it is at once a homosexual joke, a

---

Ed.'s Note: References to the many reviews of *Nightwood* mentioned here by Jane Marcus may be located in Douglas Messerli's *Djuna Barnes: A Bibliography*. New York: David Lewis, 1975.

call to prayer and a command to descend into Inferno," and "the key image is one of the agonized heart." Mr. Hyman, one of the most perceptive readers of *Nightwood*, compares the novel to *Miss Lonelyhearts* and finds it unequal to that "fully achieved tragedy," but nevertheless "a masterpiece." Roger Shattuck wrote a similar piece for the *Village Voice* on the same occasion (22 May 1962). He shared Hyman's preference for Nathanael West and for the beginning of the novel over the end, and found the language "as far ranging as Shakespeare's," as he compared Barnes to Tolstoy, Proust, Joyce, and Lawrence. Groucho Marx, Shattuck insists, could have played his greatest role as Dr. O'Connor.

Graham Greene (*Tablet*, 14 November 1936) read *Nightwood* as a Catholic novel of spiritual experience by "a major poet," as horrible as Webster and Tourneur, "obscene, though never pornographic" like *Ulysses*. Carl Van Doren recommended it as "a work of art like a poem, to be read with attention to each word and consideration of its ideas and its structure." The *TLS* review, an author's dream, was titled "Nightmare of the Soul":

It carries upon all its lineaments the symptoms of an indigestion or sickness of the soul so deep and pervasive as to seem irremediable, like M. Celine's otherwise quite different book "Voyage au Bout de la Nuit," or like a passionate exercise in *Memento Mori*, calling up a grotesque or hideous obverse to what, in moral pride, we call beautiful—to love especially, to life and even to hope. Yet it is a book that, once opened, one cannot throw down in impatience, for one is aware immediately of a new author with an unusual and impressive power of expression. The plastic qualities of this imaginative work are of a very high order—an eloquence that seems to come from an inexhaustible spring, a descriptive clarity, a wealth of imagery and allusion that seems far more spontaneous than that of Mr. James Joyce, a kind of dark and dithyrambic fecundity as alarming and irrepressible as an angry sea.

The *Tribune* praised its "superb character analysis," while in the *Listener* it was proclaimed as "an undeniable work of genius," and Barnes was hailed as "like a fresh mountain wind" in the *Spectator*. But the *Oakland Post Enquirer* (22 May 1937) found it "flashy," "forced," "brittle," so "morbid and unwholesome" that it reminded the reader of night-worms. Osbert Burdett agreed in the London *Post* (3 November 1936), patronizing the novel as "an American fantasy." "Written in pretentious and sometimes meaningless prose, its chief characters are a garrulous doctor, a Jew, and three inverted women." "This book will be read and reread for reasons other than its plot," Rose C. Feld predicted in the prestigious *New York Herald Tribune* (7 March 1937):

For character portrayal such as this, for a philosophy and a wisdom convoluted and complicated with a knowledge of good and evil, for language that has deep-flowing rhythm and Saxon hardihood, for the maintenance of a mood that is strange and dark, Djuna Barnes achieves distinction. If flaw there is in the volume, it lies in the final pages of horror, sinister and incomprehensible in implication.

Feld compares Barnes to Baudelaire and Proust for their "quality of moonlight over dissolution," combined with the "corrosive bluntness of James Joyce." She praises Barnes' genius wrought of "intellectual flagellation" and the mixture of the lyrical and the earthy in her style. But Alfred Kazin (*New York Times Book Review*, 7 March 1937) hedges. He opens with the famous passage on stream-of-consciousness from Virginia Woolf, on the "luminous halo" and "transparent envelope":

It was Virginia Woolf who delivered that challenge in one of her numerous attacks on realism in the novel, but Miss Barnes has gone beyond Mrs. Woolf's practice of her own theory. For Miss Barnes is not even concerned with the immediate in time that fascinated the stream-of-consciousness novelists. In her novel poetry is the bloodstream of the universal organism, a poetry that derives its coherence from the meeting of kindred spirits.

He finds O'Connor's speeches reckless with bad poetry, romantic tragedy, and a "desperate lyricism" in which "joy must be grotesque in its extravagance and exquisite self-torture is one of the conditions of existence, a background against which people move in a kind of angry stupor, without love, without trust."

In "Mr. Eliot Presents Miss Barnes" in the *Brooklyn Eagle* (7 March 1937), C.L. Watson argues that only readers who share Eliot's world view still like *Nightwood*, but he admires her "distinction and virtuosity" despite her "exotic limitations":

Mr. Eliot derived a certain moral uplift from not disapproving, and he has another phrase about "the human misery and bondage which is universal," suggesting that the book helps to substantiate Mr. Eliot's faith in Christianity. It seems unfortunate that a critic as scrupulous as Mr. Eliot should intrude his religious beliefs into the most ordinary kind of literary criticism, and on that account I feel his introduction is in one respect unreliable. The merits of Miss Barnes' work are sufficient, without mixing them up with religion. Among other things, in fact, her book is an excellent companion piece for "The Waste Land."

The review in the *Newstatesman and Nation* (17 October 1936) is unsigned but its tone is remarkably like Rebecca West:

Lesbos has never been a happy island. While the suburbs of a certain Mesopotamian city (during Biblical days reputed to have been destroyed by fire from Heaven, but since rebuilt on an even more magnificent scale) enclose many pleasantly embowered retreats where one-time lovers, now the best of friends, continue to pluck their eyebrows, paint pictures or cultivate their herbaceous borders in perfect amity, the airs of Lesbos are sharp with sighs, there is an undertone of jealous girding in every breeze, the foliage of its Swinburnian coppices is "sodden with tears." Rarely are the prospects it affords agreeable. Not every modern citizen may have the spirit to emulate its most distinguished classical inhabitant; but, should the tourist who approaches its shores care to look over the rail any fine afternoon, there are few creeks, bays or romantic fiords in which he will not catch sight of some solid, well-tailored figure pacing distractedly up and down, rearranging a bow tie, angrily shooting her striped cuffs, furiously glancing at a masculine wrist-watch, as she expects in vain the absent and faithless beloved. Perhaps because there is something inherently baren about its soil, Lesbos—Mère des jeux latins et des voluptés grecques—has received surprisingly little attention from contemporary poets and story-tellers, and, when described, has been described briefly and gloomily. True, we have Baudelaire's poem, Balzac's *Fille aux Yeux d'Or*, a very bad novel by Colette and long passages of *A La Recherche du Temps Perdu* (which suffer, like other episodes of that prodigious book, from Proust's inability to make up his mind whether Albertine is a boyish girl or a girlish boy); but, on the whole, it has never been explored effectively, and if Miss Djuna Barnes' book had no additional merit it would be worth reading inasmuch as it attempts to portray the peculiarly distressful atmosphere of the haunted island—the wild nerve-storms that are perpetually laying it waste.

But *Night Wood* (though not exactly a book one would read for pleasure) is, in many respects, a very remarkable production. Miss Barnes has an almost Elizabethan flow of words. She is the kind of modern writer whose prose-style appears to have been founded on a close study of the mad-speeches in Webster and Tourneur; for she has the same gusto, the same topsy-turvy eloquence, the same wealth of grotesque and lively imagery. No, *Night Wood* is not a comforting book to read. Imagine the worst of hangovers, complicated by acute remorse and extreme retrospective jealousy—all thickened into a view of modern civilisation and contemporary social life that, for bitterness and crazy violence, leaves the darkest chapters of *Ulysses* far behind. There is not a single "sane" character in the entire story; and a narrative peopled by one uncommonly neurasthenic Jew, three unusually dotty Lesbians and a drunken, melancholic Irish doctor who, in his spare time, retires to his squalid attic bedroom and there lies in misery and solitude, wearing a thick mask of paint and powder, a feminine nightgown and a curly Mary Pickford wig, is bound to make heavy demands on the reader's tolerance. Nevertheless, the book has a curious force; and it is to be hoped that no puritanical busybody will take umbrage at its unconventional background and occasionally shocking references. The test of a book's obscenity is said to be its power of corrupting those who are open to corruption; and, had I a daughter whose passions for mistresses and older girls were beginning to cause scandal and alarm, I should certainly insist that she read *Night Wood*. If, after observing the awful fate of Robin, Nora and that particularly horrible woman, Jenny Petherbridge, she did not enter a religious retreat or immediately announce her engagement to some thoroughly eligible young man, I should realise that the time had come to say good-bye: that all I could do was to buy her a dinner-jacket and turn her loose.

A more thorough-going deterrent it would be hard to imagine. Normal jealousy, heaven knows, can be bad enough; but the jealousy of homosexual lovers seems, for some reason, doubly excruciating; and the best and most painful passages of *Night Wood* have to do with Nora's efforts to hold the faithless and irresponsible Robin who leaves her friend's roof to roister round the cafes and night-boxes of Montparnasse, and who, in the end, is entrapped by the grasping, foolish, shallow Jenny Petherbridge, Miss Barnes shows just how well she could write if she were content always to write directly and unpretentiously. A great deal of *Night Wood* is neither direct nor unpretentious; and there are moments when the novelist descends to an exceedingly low level of sentimental verbiage. But, elsewhere, though one may be bored, repelled or exasperated, one must needs admit that she shows remarkable fertility of invention, a very uncommon skill in the management of words. *Night Wood* is not only a strangely original but (as I have already indicated) an extremely moral work; and I was not surprised to learn that it appears under the aegis of the most eminent Anglo-Catholic poet of the present day.

Mark Van Doren in *The Nation* (3 April 1937) claims

for brilliance and formal beauty few novels of any age can compare with it. But one must also say how desperate it is. Mr. Eliot condemns in advance any reader who feels superior to the three chief persons of the narrative, all of whom belong to the third sex. That, however, is not the point. The point is that Miss Barnes has strained rather than enriched our sensibilities. "Nightwood" is more fascinating than interesting. The marvelous doctor who speaks so many lines . . . has another aria about the women of the world who scurry out from doors at night with lamps in their hands. "Like a thousand mice they go this way and that, now fast, now slow, some halting behind doors, some trying to find the stairs, all approaching or leaving their misplaced mouse meat that lies in some cranny, on some couch, down on some floor, behind some cupboard." "Nightwood" is mouse meat at which we nibble page after page with a special kind of joy. But great fiction is more ordinary than this, and ultimately more nourishing. Beefsteak and apple pie.

Dylan Thomas' review in the Oxford and Cambridge journal *Light and Dark* (March 1937) lets quotations from the novel speak for themselves:

There should be two reviews of this book, and both written with the intention of selling it: the first to attract the intellectual flippity-gibbits, who read everything new and nasties have read it before; and one to attract by quotation, the honest people who like beautiful writing. The first review should say what an evil book it is, that it's about homosexuality, and that it's very bawdy; also that Mr. Eliot, certainly not new or nasty, has written an enthusiastic preface to the American edition. This review for the chi-chi people could have any sort of title like "A Bible of Evil," could describe the principal character, a gargantuan doctor with a lot of surrealist club-room stories, as a symbol of utter degradation made utterly wise; it could comment on the fact that, as far as evil goes, the characters of the American, Miss Kay Boyle—with whom Miss Barnes has been compared—represents a little girl's conception of Paris. And it would sell a hundred copies in Cambridge.

The second review is, I think, this review. "Night Wood" was turned down by every publisher in America. It can't be called a novel, because it only has a sort-of-a-plot; the characters don't as in the actual life of fiction, develop and change from mood to mood, sentence, etcetera; they talk witty, passionate dialogues on dirty mountaintops (making, that is, the comparative unimportance of the fact of level dirt into a mountainous truth). It isn't a lah-de-dah prose poem, because it's about what some very real human people feel, think, and do. It's "Nightwood," by Djuna Barnes, and one of the three great prose books ever written by a woman.

He doesn't say who the other two are. However, Philip Rahv in the *New Masses* was sure of the novel's decadence and political incorrectness as Thomas was of its genius. "Its people are ghosts, its theme a mere string for the aphorisms of literary despair." He finds her "pitiful" and "quixotic" for trying to revive the dead decadence of the twenties, imitating Joyce's "night mind," in a "fog of *Weltschmerz.*" It's not perversion that bothers him for he admires Proust's "realistic" homosexuals:

But the trouble with Miss Barnes is that she has not really written about perversion; she has merely exploited perversion to create an atmosphere of general mystification and psychic disorder that will permit her to transcend reality and make plausible a certain modernist attitude whose essence is a tragic pose and a learned metaphysical sneer. And in his mannered preface to the novel, Mr. Eliot, ever on the alert for new proofs of original sin, only confuses the issue when he suggests that the book has "a quality of horror and doom very nearly related to that of Elizabethan tragedy." Nothing, it seems to me, could be further from the truth. One must, indeed, be adept at fantasies to mistake a trickle of literarious despair for a heaving sea of Elizabethan poetry. It is not the doom of a world reeling to its destruction that Miss Barnes expresses, but those minute shudders of decadence developed in certain small in-grown cliques of intellectuals and their patrons cliques in which the reciprocal workings of society decay and sexual perversion have destroyed all response to genuine values and actual things.

In the *Saturday Review* (27 March 1937), Theodore Purdy wrote:

Passing over Mr. Eliot's assertion that the book is not a psychopathic study, one can only wonder at his failure to perceive that the atmosphere of decay in "Nightwood" stems from the fin-de-siècle Frenchmen rather than from the Elizabethans. The early chapters even recall Wilde and Pater with due modern improvements in frankness. It is this element which renders "Nightwood" coterie literature in spite of its imaginative scope and occasional verbal felicity. Such a book has value as an interesting literary sport, aptly conceived to convulse the Bloomsburys of the world.

Peter Burra in *The Spectator* (27 November 1936) called it:

A completely undressed book. A grim, sordid, and depressing story, it will be called. That is necessarily the side of the picture that will catch most attention, and there will not be wanting persons to deplore it as unhealthy. . . . Yet the characters of *Nightwood* are complete, rare and astonishing individuals every one of them carved out in words with genius. The story is told swiftly and with immense vigour, while commonplace incidents and the repartee of salon or café are absorbed into the style with perfect aptness. . . . One cannot recommend *Nightwood* indiscriminately to the novel-reading public any more than one can describe it plainly as a novel.

Edwin Muir raved about its brilliance and imagination in *The Listener* (28 October 1936) comparing *Nightwood* to

those disquisitions on human life which were more common in the seventeenth century than they are now, and which were always enlivened by imaginative illustrations: in this book the disquisition completely disappears into those imaginative illustrations which form a symbolical picture of the human state as Miss Barnes sees it.

Lewis Gannett in the *New York Herald Tribune* (20 March 1937) found "a magic of phrase and an integrity of style, a phosphorescent wit and an acid etching of character" but judged it a Gothic horror written in the poetry of death.

One of the most interesting reviews was A. Desmond Hawkins' in *The New English Weekly* (29 April 1937):

Miss Barnes's method is curious. A brilliant opening of concrete description presents the Volkbein family, but this in some ways loses momentum and for the rest of the book Volkbein is always in danger of being forgotten. The centre of the stage is taken over by the lesbians and the Doctor, an oracular figure who exists to be consulted. The book goes into a stream of prodigious analysis, the characters sitting like bridge-fiends in an elaborate post-mortem on how the cards were played. But the cards have been played, that is the point. Whatever action there is occurs as something now being relived in dialogue. The book is a work of sibylline sensibility, a relentless confession counterpointed with oracular pronouncement. Once the stage is set we do not know what has happened until the characters involved begin their post-mortem.

It is a method to which we are not accustomed. "Lord Jim" is perhaps the nearest in English, but other differences weaken this as an analogy. If there is any worthwhile comparison it is with Hugo von Hofmannsthal, whose "Andreas" is very close in conception to "Nightwood." Von Hofmannsthal has the same sense of individual isolation in unapproachable misery, the same deliberate refinement of character out of the action of Life to a point where it becomes archetypal, a pure symbol of some facet of metaphysical experience. The Knight in "Andreas" also, like Miss Barnes's Doctor, is the "omniscient passive" about whom the other characters revolve. It is a much more self-conscious and abstract performance than the Jacobethans, with the possible exception of Webster. Webster has this in common with Miss Barnes: he liked to arrest his action as quickly as possible and open it up. "The White Devil" and the "Duchess of Malfi" both have tableaux of action followed by a dialogue in tragic idiom which seems to strain away from the tableaux. Webster is a genius of the individual sentence, a master of vocabulary. Von Hofmannsthal shows the same difficulty of constructing an action into which he can integrate his tragic vocabulary.

I think this is true of Miss Barnes also. Her characters suffer lavishly on the minimum of misfortune. Any vulgar tendency to well-being is repressed, the sources of suffering are removed to second-hand, and we have a stream of superb sentences, of penetrating epigrams lighting up an essentially static scene. There is no change in any character, and the only major occasion when action overweighs analysis is in the brief last chapter which seems to me to fail.

Miss Barnes is faced with the problem of finding in the contemporary world some "action" which can submit to the ordering of her metaphysic without diffusing it. In the absence of that, it is necessary to tell parables in the Henry James manner or to use eccentric "masks" in order to speak a deliberate commentary. Miss Barnes chooses the latter method, and "Nightwood" is a terrific "aside" on a drama which does not exist independently.

Of the quality of this commentary there can be no doubt. It conveys a more intensive concentration of experience than any woman in this century has achieved. There is very little diffuseness, very little irrelevant sensitivity. Miss Barnes is throughout in control of the instruments of language. The only reservation I make is that tragic idiom has to some considerable extent been stolen from tragic circumstances. Of this there can be neither law nor demonstration, but its effect may be described as "Hamlet" without everyone but the Prince.

Nevertheless, whatever uncertainty one may feel about the degree of its magnitude, "Nightwood" undoubtedly dwarfs all recent fiction. It is the work of a first-rate mind in its maturity, and as such it demands attention. For my own part, I have never been so impressed by a novelist hitherto unknown to me.

Helen Fletcher in *Time and Tide* (14 November 1936) also wrote a review as brilliant as the novel:

The manufacturers of a well-disguised chocolate laxative, traduced by their own cunning, and stricken with a vision of Greedy Gregory in a worse plight than any cautionary tale imagined, have inserted in each packet the warning: "Stop! This is not really a chocolate. Kindly place beyond children's reach." Similarly, Messrs. Faber & Faber, by publishing *Nightwood* (a short book) at 10s. 6d., by robing it in pale grey and by printing a tart warning to optimists inside its cover, have done all that any human publishers could do to keep this novel from the hands of that over-protected child, the average reader, and themselves from the wrath of his governesses—The Mother's Union and the Public Morality Council.

"I am confident," said Keats, "of nothing but of the holiness of the Heart's affections and the truth of Imagination." It is odd that there should still be people whose appreciation of *Nightwood* will be spoilt by the fact that to them Nora's affection for Robin seems less holy because Robin should be spelt Robina. Odd, and irrelevant. What is important is that, unlike her colleagues Graves, Day Lewis and Dunsany, Djuna Barnes has written a book of imaginative truth. Read *Nightwood* not to learn that Lesbians, like other lovers are often unhappy, not to emit righteous "so there's!" at Robin's final degradation, but to hear how prose sounds in the moment when it seems to write itself and become "emotion recollected in tranquillity." I do not mean that Miss Barnes writes in the Sparkenbroke Fakir-in-family-pew tradition. She is capable of inspired sense and inspired nonsense, never of high-up thinking.

Nora loves Robin with her life and when Robin leaves her to go to America with the odious Jenny, she climbs to the attic of the mad doctor, hoping to tell him of her distress. But her grief is new and has no words and his is old and has many, so instead of talking she finds herself listening to a monologue which for wit, beauty and bawdiness, is unexcelled by any I have found in modern fiction. I regret that the last quality should make much of the best of it unquotable; quotations have a deterrent as well as an attractive value, and Dr. O'Connor's words would tell you much better than any words of mine could whether or no you can read *Nightwood* with pleasure. And remember, there is no other reason for reading it. A great deal of trouble is caused by people reading books that they know they cannot possibly enjoy and then complaining afterwards. *Nightwood*, despite much over-writing and some nonsense, is a work of art. . . . The Doctor's description of Jenny from which it comes, is to my mind worthy of an honourable place in the literature of hate. . . .

The important question is whether Girl meets Boy, Boy marries Girl is to continue to be the sole topic for the novel in England, or whether we are to emerge from the nursery and apply Keats' wisdom to literature.

The famous Fadiman review in the *New Yorker* (13 March 1937) contained these remarks:

One hopes devoutly that Djuna Barnes' "Nightwood" may not be visited with a succès de snobisme or served up as caviar to the general. The portents, however, are dire: it arrives upborne on the rare incense of such intellectual English critics as Edwin Muir and T.S. Eliot; its pitiless concision may make it seem obscure, and therefore destined only for the lofty-browed; its language is on occasion scatological; the central character is a homosexual, and the three chief female characters are dominantly sapphic. Only by a miracle, it would seem, can "Nightwood" escape the affectionate, destroying hands of some twittering literary cult.

I don't want to be banally arty about this, but obviously some books approach the non-representative condition of pure music, in that they defy description in other terms. Everything that they are is immovably contained in and identical with the original phrasing of the author. "Nightwood" is like that, just as "Ulysses" is, and "The Waste Land," and the best of Hart Crane. . . .

By conventional standards, all the people in "Nightwood" are mad, but it would be madder still to judge them by conventional standards. Yet though they are akin to Faulkner's nocturnal grotesques, they do not add up to an Eden Musée, but settle in the reader's shuddering, remembering blood like the black souls of Ford's dramas. I think Dr. O'Connor, particularly, will stand beside Stephen Dedalus and Christina Stead's Marpurgo (in "The Beauties and Furies") as one of the great, bitter, eaten characters of modern fiction. He crouches in the mind, depraved, obscene, sibylline, clad in a woman's dirty flannel nightgown, rouged and faded, releasing the spate of his fearful wisdom, his talk a medley of wild, precise images drawn from the operating room, the privy, the nightmare, lust's bed, and yet he is a religious man whose bile is but the souring of love, whose jests and maledictions thinly curtain his true seriousness and melancholy.

The reviews were long, detailed, and serious. *Nightwood*, whether it was understood or not, was regarded as a great work of art. Philip Toynbee reflects its status, reviewing the reprint in *The Observer* (15 December 1963) called "The Power and the Glory":

Nightwood is one of those great books of its period which had the courage to embrace a decadence so extreme that it became a fresh start, a revivification. Miss Barnes is no Proust and no Joyce, but she shares with them this readiness to take the whole burden of an overweighted age, to see clearly that "the road of excess leads to the palace of wisdom." This is a highly mannered work, and like so many books written in an overweighted age it constantly teeters on the edge of gross affectation, bluster and grandiloquence. . . .

This is a book which seems made for the mockery of that cowardly modern spirit which sticks out its tongue at all "written" books and giggles at the paradoxes of deep feeling. But a new reader must not be put off by the sheer unfamiliar brilliance of the book's surface. Most of these lucidly obscure sentences yield, on a harder reading, that pure lucidity which could not have been devised by any other method. "Nightwood" is a small masterpiece which has been allowed to lie to one side of the general attenton. I hope this edition will place it where it belongs—full in the eye of anyone who is devoted to the literature of our century.

¶ An unpublished novel, *Nightwood*, by Djuna Barnes, was recently published here before its appearance in America. In an unsigned paragraph on the jacket, T.S. Eliot praises it as a book which "has nothing to offer readers whose temperament attaches them to either an easy or a frightened optimism," and the not easily placed *Sunday Times* eulogized the volume in a similar serious vein. . . . Certainly only she would have so thoroughly and deliberately steeped herself in the eighteenth century in order to have conveniently at hand its richer vocabulary, and to grasp, without reaching too far across time, those early novel-patterns in which the amative, ribald, and melancholy states of man's mind were plot enough and to spare. The period of the book is 1925. The principal characters are a Viennese Jew who is posing as a baron; two American girls, one of whom becomes a hound of hell to the other, who is her doomed adorer; and a San Francisco–born Irishman, Dr. Matthew O'Connor. His fantastic monologues—the conversation becomes a dialogue only when his listener can squeeze a word in sideways—are the pulse of the book. Sometimes he touches on subjects which have rarely been treated with such freedom. In his final oration, which he starts while on his sinful attic cot, and attired in a woman's nightgown and wig, he becomes an unforgettable spokesman for liars and lovers of all genders and generations.

Miss Barnes's verbal talent at times goes into a trance, then wakes again to phrases of amazing beauty. If you enjoy remarkable reading and writing, *Nightwood* is not to be missed.

—Janet Flanner, *London Was Yesterday,*
1934–1939 (10 February 1937)

¶ It seems pretty obvious that they, the Italians, think my writings frightful. It is also sure the readings are not very careful, Eugenio Montale has the doctor from Dublin, the dog as *Jenny's*, Robin *abandoned* by her husband—and then he gets into the business of "Robin meaning red-breast, and *blood*—." O well, I've gone through all of this before. . . .

—Djuna Barnes,
letter to Mrs. Pellegrini
(Italian translator), 6 December 1968

¶ . . . By the by, the French translation made an error in translating the heading of the chapter "Go Down Matthew," he has it "A genoux, Matthieu" . . . it is not to the knees, it refers to the song "Go down Moses, let my people go."

—Djuna Barnes,
letter to Wolfgang Hildesheimer, 25 July 1959

¶ I read *Nightwood* back in the 1930's and was very taken with it. I consider it one of the great books of the twentieth century. At that time I even tried a few writing experiments, consciously imitating her style. It is an entirely unique style: one sentence, and you know it is Djuna. It is a pity if, merely because her literary output was relatively small, she is not more widely recognized and read today.

—William Burroughs,
letter to Mary Lynn Broe, 14 January 1985

¶ I have read *Nightwood,* as did everyone I know, soon after it appeared around 1937, in Chicago. We were all fourteen or fifteen. Today at sixty, after another dozen readings, I'm as caught up as ever by the novel's gorgeous claustrophobia. If I still don't "understand" it, I *am* more critical. *Nightwood*'s a mess, an enthralling mess redeemed by contagious obsession (the author's) and sheer chutzpah (her chief character's). I'm referring, of course, to the content, especially the doctor's arias, which today as yesterday is original and to a point of genius but, well, unmanageable. The form, however, is not chaotic; indeed, it seems, in its accumulation, quite pristine, even musical. Off and on for decades I've thought of making the book into an opera. (It could once have been a good movie—with Garbo, maybe?—but now it's too late.)

I never met or even saw Djuna Barnes, although in the 1940s I lived just around the corner from Patchin Place. But Norris Embry used to describe how he haunted her hallway leaving homages of gin, and I'd drink that up. (The description, not the gin. The gin too.) Virgil Thompson too still talks of her, but not in the hushed tones of her younger fans, or even of such mature artists as Charles Henri Ford.

In the Village, and later in Paris during the fifties, I more than once ran across elderly male "eccentrics" (Dante Pavone, Alan Ross MacDougall, Robert LeMasle) who professed to be, if not the actual model, at least a *layer* of Doctor O'Connor. They were a cult, like the cult a generation earlier of French adolescents who all claimed to be Cocteau's original *enfants terribles.*

If I have to name ten favorite books *Nightwood* would be among them. Its very flaws are its force—which can be claimed by none of her other books which I find wilful, affected, weakish. Still, Djuna is not a generally shared taste, never being listed (anymore than Jane Bowles is listed, or Purdy, or the Tennessee Williams of the early stories, or indeed any American homosexual) in annual tottings by, say, the *New York Times* which inevitably embrace the predictable Mailers and Bellows and Updikes. Even among the lunatic fringe there are those who can't buy Barnes.

Yet I can never stroll through the Place Saint Sulpice (I was just there last April) without being invaded by a sense of the past so intense that the *quartier* seems to have been invented by Djuna rather than the reverse.

Ned Rorem,
letter to Mary Lynn Broe,
23 September 1984

13

Nightwood: "The Sweetest Lie"

Judith Lee

I'm not a lesbian. I just loved Thelma.
—Djuna Barnes

Women's practice can only be negative, in opposition to that which exists, to say that "this is not it" and "it is not yet."
—Julia Kristeva

Most critical discussion of *Nightwood* has centered on questions of genre, style, and structure.[1] Barnes' use of caricature and her virtuosity of language invite us to trace the patterns of imagery and allusion that are clearly central to *Nightwood*'s meaning. But this is also, as Andrew Field has demonstrated, an intensely personal book, and its "necessary excesses," in Louis Kannenstine's words, constitute a strategy of disguise as much as a "rhetoric of lamentation," as Kenneth Burke has suggested.[2] This ambivalence between disguise and revelation makes *Nightwood* both intriguing and problematic. In showing that female experience, specifically lesbian love, proves false our assumptions about both love and gender, it promises a new form of meaning, but it then denies the possibility of making meaning.

Nightwood is distinctively modern not only in its subject and form, but in its consideration of what our concepts of masculine and feminine imply. It has become a truism that the opposition between masculine and feminine shapes our conceptions of identity and meaning. Masculine and feminine are metaphysical constructs, categories with which we organize and interpret the differences we perceive in the world. Because we live in a patriarchal culture, we tend to label as masculine those aspects of our experience and those qualities that are closest to the existing forms of power (autonomy, reason, speech, culture), and we tend to label as feminine what cannot be accommodated by, is contrary to, or threatens the existing forms of power (passivity, emotion, silence, nature).[3] These abstractions are, as

Djuna Barnes was aware, inseparable from our psychosocial experience. We tend to formulate our values and to define our assumptions about the world in terms of the meanings we have invested in masculine and feminine. In our cultural mythology, therefore, sexual difference represents the primary experience of our individual difference.

In *Nightwood* Djuna Barnes treats this mythology ironically. In portraying the inversion of experience, depicting a world of darkness, irrationality, and degeneration, she tells four "anti–fairy tales" in which she caricatures the qualities opposed in masculine and feminine to show that they are inherently incompatible. In addition, she deconstructs the opposition between masculine and feminine because it does not define the most fundamental experience of difference: the difference between the identity one imagines (the self as Subject) and the identity one experiences in relationship with someone else (the self as Other). In defining this difference, central to the experience of women, in terms of the opposition between mother and child, Barnes raises the possibility for a new figuration of female identity.[4]

Because the significance of *Nightwood* as a modern text derives largely from its reworking of our assumptions about masculine and feminine, the following reading will focus on the three ways in which Barnes exposes the inadequacy of our cultural myths: her retelling of the fairy-tale romance in the first four sections of *Nightwood*; her depiction of the love shared by Nora and Robin; and her characterization of Robin and Matthew as members of "the third sex." Despite her incisive irony, however, we shall find that in the opposition between speech and silence Barnes fails to resolve the contradiction that is at the heart of *Nightwood*: if the most profound experience is unspeakable, and every interpretation is a distortion, how can any story have meaning?

Matthew O'Connor tells the version of the fairy-tale romance that is the basis for Barnes' ironic treatment of the opposition between masculine and feminine:

What is this love we have for the invert, boy or girl? It was they who were spoken of in every romance that we ever read. The girl lost, what is she but the Prince found? The Prince on the white horse that we have always been seeking. And the pretty lad who is a girl, what but the prince-princess in point lace—neither one and half the other, the painting on the fan! We love them for that reason. We were impaled upon them as they rode through our primers, the sweetest lie of all, now come to be in boy and girl, for in the girl it is the prince, and in the boy it is the girl that makes a prince a prince—and not a man. They go far back in our lost distance where what we never had stands waiting; it was inevitable that we should come upon them, for our miscalculated longing has created them. They are our answer to what our grand-mothers were told love was, and what it never came to be; they the living lie of our centuries. (*N*, 136–37)

This is a tale of narcissistic love, the love for oneself in another. Matthew's version of the fairy-tale romance is a "child's dream" because in ignoring the dichotomy between masculine and feminine it ignores the obstacles posed by sexual difference. The prince-princess in this tale figures not androgyny (the resolution of sexual difference) but narcissism (the rejection of sexual difference).[5] As retold in *Nightwood*, this fairy-tale romance is "the sweetest lie of all" because for Barnes' characters love leads not to an experience of wholeness but to the discovery that such an experience is irrecoverable. Felix, Nora, and Jenny are would-be princes who fail to "rescue" their princess from oblivion.

The story of Hedvig and Guido Volkbein is the most straightforward parody of the fairy-tale romance, beginning as it does with an account of the deaths of this "prince and princess" rather than ending with the promise that they "lived happily ever after." Guido is the "prince" who rescues Hedvig from oblivion by offering her a name: "The thing that she stalked, though she herself had not been conscious of it, was Guido's assurance that he was a Baron" (N, 5). Hedvig is the "princess" who promises Guido both a son and the possibility of assimilation. Their "fairy tale castle" in Vienna is a "fantastic museum" that preserves the spurious and romanticized chronicle of Guido's past, the centerpiece of which is the pair of portraits of "two intrepid and ancient actors" dressed as a romantic lady and her knight purported to be his parents. The marble statues represent stylized art at its most grotesque: "a runner's leg, the chilly half-turned head of a matron stricken at the bosom, the blind sockets of the eyes given a pupil by every act of the sun" (N, 5). These fragments are grotesque because they, like the myth of romantic love, represent an idea, an image that is divorced from experience.

In Hedvig and Guido Volkbein, Barnes also parodies the stereotypes of male and female. Each is a comic prince-princess. Hedvig is a woman "of great strength and military beauty" (N, 1) who has "the same bearing, the same though more condensed power of the hand" as a general (N, 6); she dances as if demonstrating "a tactical maneuver" (N, 4) and plays the piano "with the masterly stroke of a man" (N, 5); Guido is "small, rotund, and hautily timid" (N, 1). Hedvig prefigures Robin as a caricature of the feminine: she is "held up to nature, precise, deep-bosomed and gay" (N, 4). And Guido is made a caricature of the masculine in his obsession to identify himself with the line of power: "He had said that he was an Austrian of an old, almost extinct line, producing, to uphold his story, the most amazing and inaccurate proofs: a coat of arms that he had no right to and a list of progenitors . . . who had never existed" (N, 3).

The story of the second Volkbein marriage follows the same pattern as the story of the first. Like his father Felix is a "prince" who rescues Robin from oblivion by providing her with a name; like Hedvig, Robin is a "princess" who offers the promise of a son. Like the figures of fairy tale, Felix and Robin have no interiority, gravitating toward each other without choice; for Felix "it was as if the weight of his life had amassed in one precipitation" (*N*, 42), and "Robin's life held no volition for refusal" (*N*, 43). Ironically, at the moment when Robin awakens to the fact that she can choose she does refuse the destiny that Felix has chosen for her.

In the story of Robin and Felix, Barnes intensifies her parody of conventional conceptions of masculine and feminine. While in Hedvig and Guido she parodies their complementarity, in Felix and Robin she shows them to be inherently incompatible. Felix is a comic figure, not only because his attempts to ingratiate himself and be assimilated are so obviously futile, but because he represents the falsity of the values embedded in the masculine. His reverence for culture is a reverence for military and economic power, and he turns the accident of meeting Robin into the messianic purpose of siring a son who would redeem the past: "To pay homage to our past is the only gesture that also includes the future," he tells Matthew (*N*, 39). For Felix "redemption" would be the recuperation of a sense of teleology, a triumph of the masculine over the feminine.[6]

The irony is, of course, that although he was born to this mission and moves easily through the countries of Europe, Felix is, less by nature than by destiny, a figure of the Wandering Jew, a figure of betrayal and of the unredeemed. We last see him, moreover, having returned to Vienna a kind of drunken somnambulist, bowing before a man he believes to be the Grand Duke of Russia, "his head in his confusion making a complete half-swing, as an animal will turn its head away from a human, as if in mortal shame" (*N*, 123). This last image of Felix prefigures our last image of Robin: their sexual difference makes little difference in the end.

Robin is portrayed in this "fairy tale" as a similarly exaggerated representation of the values embedded in the feminine. She is a caricature of the "sleeping beauty" who awakens in the presence of the prince and whose destiny is determined by his. She parodies "feminine" passivity and emotion in her dependence upon someone else for her very existence and in her habit of acting only out of blind instinct. Her very experience of temporality is incomprehensible to Felix;[7] she represents to him all that cannot be accommodated or tainted by historical time. "He felt that her attention somehow in spite of him, had already been taken by something not yet in history" (*N*, 44). She is identified with nature in its wildest and most primitive form, utterly different from the landscaped gardens to which Felix takes her. Her room is like "a jungle trapped in a drawing room" and the "perfume that her body exhaled was of the quality of that earth—flesh, fungi. . . . Her flesh was the texture of plant life. . . . About her head there was an effulgence as of phosphorous glowing about the circumference of a body of water" (*N*, 34). Even when, after the birth of her son, Robin wanders through Europe alone, she is attracted not to cultural artifacts but to Catholic churches, and the historical figures of interest to her are not emperors and generals but women who were never tamed by their culture: "Louise de la Valliere,

Catherine of Russia, Madame de Maintenon, Catherine de'Medici, and two women out of literature, Anna Karenina and Catherine Heathcliff" (*N*, 47). This list suggests that in the history and culture for which Felix has chosen Robin, the life of women is a death sentence; Robin's choice to leave him is an alternative to a form of suicide.

While the stories of Hedvig and Guido and of Felix and Robin parody the fairy-tale romance and the values mythologized in it, the story of Jenny and Robin tells of the perversion of idealized love and of the violation of the values it represents. This version of the fairy-tale romance tells of an evil "prince" who kidnaps the "princess," who "escapes" when she returns to her homeland. This prince and princess meet not by chance but through Jenny's machinations and, sharing no "castle," they meet in cafés and stay in hotels.

Guido and Felix are pathetic and comic because they are so clearly and inherently "out of step" in their attempt to participate through imitation in a culture from which they are categorically excluded; Jenny is evil, however, because she attempts to manipulate without participating in a culture and history from which she is categorically excluded: "She was one of the most unimportantly wicked women of her time—because she could not let her time alone, and yet could never be part of it" (*N*, 67). Like Felix and his father, Jenny reveres the past ("absorbing time, she held herself responsible for historic characters" [*N*, 67]); but while the Volkbeins construct their own fantastic history, Jenny steals: her love of history is "a continual rapacity for other people's facts" (*N*, 67). And unlike the possessions of Hedvig and Guido, Jenny's possessions do not reflect her life, real or imagined; rather, they are "second-hand dealings with life" (*N*, 66), selected and given value by people who possessed them before her. Jenny is a "squatter" because she appropriates the masculine values that will always be alien to her, and in so doing she denies her own (feminine) nature.

The story of Nora and Robin also follows the pattern of the fairy-tale romance. Like *Nightwood*'s other "princes," Nora attempts to "rescue" Robin when, at the circus, she is threatened by her lack of difference from the beasts. Robin and Nora's apartment, like Hedvig and Guido Volkbein's home, is a "fairy tale castle" which represents their dreamed-of life. But with a difference. The objects which decorate Nora and Robin's apartment— circus chairs, wooden horses from a ring of an old merry-go-round, a collection of music boxes—are icons not of a fantastic history but of an escape from history.

Like Felix's home, Nora's apartment becomes a womblike retreat to which Robin returns only when she is drunk and only to sleep. And this womb becomes a tomb when Nora, like Felix, insists on awakening Robin:

I said, "It is over now"; she was asleep and I struck her awake. I saw her come awake

and turn befouled before me, she who had managed in that sleep to keep whole. . . .
No rot had touched her until then, and there before my eyes I saw her corrupt all at
once and withering because I had struck her sleep away. (N, 145)

With Felix, Robin had awakened to her cultural and historical difference;
with Nora, she awakens to the loss of the (narcissistic) world of which she is
sole and omnipotent proprietor—the world of dream. She leaves both her
"princes" because she experiences her own difference as a form of death.

Of *Nightwood*'s "princes," Nora alone is identified with the feminine rather than the masculine. Her house "in the centre of a mass of tangled
grass and weeds" is set against both Austria's castles with their landscaped
gardens and the Volkbeins' urban homes, her "decaying chapel" against the
European cathedrals. Her "democratic" love is the opposite of the Volkbeins' worship of the aristocracy, moreover, and in contrast to the historical
and cultural center of Vienna, Nora's salon provides a haven for the
marginal and disenfranchised: "poets, radicals, beggars, artists, and people
in love" (N, 50) and people of every creed.

Where Barnes reworks the opposition between masculine and feminine, she proves the myth of romantic love to be "the sweetest lie" because
male and female are inherently and inevitably incompatible and because the
values mythologized in the masculine are based on illusion. But in the story
of Nora and Robin, Barnes proves the myth of romantic love to be "the
sweetest lie" because it does not tell of the experience of difference specific
and inevitable in female experience. In this version of the fairy-tale romance,
Barnes replaces the dialectic between masculine and feminine with the
dialectic between mother and child. In doing so, she shifts the locus of
meaning from the struggle to overcome difference to the struggle to establish
difference; in addition, she de-emphasizes the difference between self and
other and emphasizes the (internal) difference between self as Subject—the
self one feels onself to be—and self as other—the self as perceived by
someone else. In the story of Nora and Robin, Barnes shows that, paradoxically, to love someone is to become aware of how very different one may be
from the other's image. She does not merely imply that "the love of a woman
for a woman" is narcissistic, but that it leads to the discovery of an
insurmountable difference that precludes the possibility of any relationship.

The relationship between Nora and Robin is repeatedly compared to
that shared by a mother and child. Matthew calls the "love of woman for
woman" an "insane passion for unmitigated anguish and motherhood" (N,
75), and Nora herself thinks of Robin as her child: "I saw her always like a
tall child who had grown up the length of the infant's gown, walking and
needing help and safety" (N, 145). In the central image of their relationship
Robin is described as a kind of fetus: "In Nora's heart lay the fossil of Robin,
intaglio of her identity, and about it for its maintenance ran Nora's blood.
Thus the body of Robin was now beyond timely changes, except in the blood

that animated her" (N, 56). Nora and Robin thus share a symbiotic bond; Nora's identity depends upon Robin's presence as much as Robin's existence depends upon Nora.

At the same time, the presence of Robin changes Nora's identity. Before meeting Robin, she was self-contained, "unidentified, endlessly embroiled in a predicament without a problem" (N, 53); after meeting Robin, however, she experiences a split within herself, a double identity as both child and mother. This split is dramatized in her two dreams of her grandmother.

In the first dream (N, 62–63), her grandmother and Robin (who determine her own identities as child and as mother) remain distinct. She dreams that she is in a room that, at least within the dream, is her grandmother's room; seeing Robin below her, she calls to her to come up even though she knows that this room is taboo. The dream reminds Nora of a memory of her grandmother dressed in a military outfit, surprising her with a seductive smile. In the eternal present of dream, what was promised—or threatened—by Nora's grandmother is renewed in Robin, and the child's desire to be loved is both validated and fulfilled by her (maternal) love for her own "child."

In the second dream (N, 148–49), the difference between Nora's grandmother and Robin is collapsed, and the two figures merge as one. In this dream her grandmother is lying in a grave, and her father is flying above, into and out of the grave, while Nora stands by as witness. Nora has this dream while she is half awake, so she experiences a double identity as dreamer and dream-figure. As dreamer, she has the power to make her grandmother present over and over again, but as dream-figure she must reexperience the pain of her loss and separation repeatedly: "for all of us die over again in somebody's sleep. And this, I have done to Robin: it is only through me that she will die over and over" (N, 149). As dreamer, Nora experiences herself as Subject; as dream-figure she experiences herself as Other. As dreamer she is "mother" bringing into existence her "child" Robin; as dream-figure, she is "child," witnessing the death of her "mother." In this dream, birth is indistinguishable from death; both represent forms of permanent separation, but when they are conflated they represent the (narcissistic) denial of separation. In this "waking dream" the figures of her grandmother and Robin mediate against Nora's experience of her own difference.

Barnes' shift from the external difference between masculine and feminine to the internal difference between self as Subject and self as Object, a difference inherent in the bond between women, generates the image of the Madonna.[8] By making her into a Madonna-figure, Robin denies Nora's subjectivity, her internal difference, which would require—or enable— reciprocal interaction. As Matthew tells Nora, "You almost caught hold of her, but she put you cleverly away by making you the Madonna" (N, 146).

Paradoxically, by idealizing Nora, Robin reifies her, and by making her thus inaccessible, she allows her own, self-defined (narcissistic) identity to remain inviolable. As Nora puts it: "I knew that the image [of the Madonna] was what I had been to Robin, not a saint at all, but a fixed dismay; the space between the human and the holy head, the arena of the 'indecent' eternal" (N, 157). As "Madonna," Nora provides a boundary for Robin against the "non-Being" she would face were she to acknowledge the difference within herself between her identity as Subject and her identity as Other—between, that is, the self she can create and the self she must be.

In the final scene of *Nightwood*, Barnes invests the bond between Robin and Nora with a mythological importance that both enlarges its meaning and intensifies its irony. This "prince and princess" will indeed live together "ever after," but their "marriage" is a mating and a curse. In portraying this "second coming" that denies the possibility of ending, Barnes makes the mother-child bond an ironic version of the Mother-Son heurosis that is the central Christian image for redemption, and in Nora she combines the figures of Demeter (mother of life) and Hecate (mother of death) from pagan myths of resurrection.

Robin's ritual is a sacrificial act. She begins her prayer by standing before the statue of the Virgin (a figure of Nora) and she completes it by submitting to Nora's dog (also a figure of Nora). The "space between the human and the holy" disappears: Robin sacrifices the possibility for making meaning out of the difference between the sacred and the profane, between human and beast, between self as Subject and self as Other.

As the fulfillment of Matthew O'Connor's prophecy, Robin's return to Nora marks the end of both the cyclic movement that outlines the "fairy tale" of Nora and Robin and the linear movement from east to west and from morning to night. The time span—from 1885 to the late 1930s—corresponds to the "fifty-odd years" of Matthew's lifetime, a lifetime that is an inexorable (linear) descent into silence that counterpoints Robin's Dantean (cyclic) descent into sleep. These two members of the "third sex" provide the two centers around which *Nightwood* turns: Matthew's speech substitutes for Robin's absence. In these two figures Barnes parodies the idea of redemption; in Robin she treats ironically the idea of redemption through innocence, and in Matthew she treats ironically the idea of redemption through knowledge. The "curse" from which they promise redemption is the experience of sexual difference.[9]

Matthew and Robin appear most clearly as two forms of a single mode of consciousness in the one scene in which they are both present: Robin's awakening. Each is represented as having two natures. In Robin these two natures remain undifferentiated; she is "meet of child and desperado" and "beast turning human." She is described in images of incomplete transformation. Even her pose as a dancer, her "thick-lacquered

pumps looking too lively for the arrested step" (N, 34), suggests an unfinished movement. She prompts a response that is an interruption, a gap in
consciousness:

Sometimes one meets a woman who is beast turning human. Such a person's every
movement will reduce to an image of a forgotten experience; a mirage of an eternal
wedding cast on the racial memory. . . . Such a woman is an infected carrier of the
past. . . . We feel we could eat her, she who is eaten death returning, for only then do
we put our face close to the blood on the lips of our forefathers. (N, 37)

Calling to mind a moment that is preverbal, prerational, almost prehuman, a
moment after death and before birth, Robin represents a consciousness
which cannot be understood in terms of ordinary modes of differentiation.[10]

   In contrast to Robin, Matthew reveals two natures—masculine and
feminine—that remain unintegrated. His use of Robin's powder and perfume, as surreptitious as "the movements common to the 'dumbfounder,' or
man of magic" (N, 35), reveal his feminine nature, its lawlessness under-
scored when he steals Robin's money; his authority derives from his overt
(masculine) actions as a doctor who cures Robin and as a priest who
"baptizes" her. Here, as when Nora later visits him in his room, Matthew
uses makeup to mask and mute his masculine nature, and he uses his power
as a male to indulge in the pleasure and desire he experiences in his feminine
nature.

   Just as Robin seeks to preserve her lack of difference through
remaining a "somnambule," Matthew struggles to reconcile his divided
nature through his interactions with others. He seeks to drown out his
"prehistoric memory" of the time when he was his true self—a woman:

The wise men say that the remembrance of things past is all that we have for a
future, and am I to blame if I've turned up this time as I shouldn't have been, when it
was a high soprano I wanted, and deep corn curls to my bum, with a womb as big as
the King's Kettle, and a bosom as high as the bowsprit of a fishing schooner. . . . I've
given my destiny away by garrulity, like ninety per cent of everybody else—for no
matter what I may be doing, in my heart is the wish for children and knitting.
(N, 91)

Matthew's speech is a way of suppressing his feminine nature and the desire
it represents, just as Robin's silence is a way of rejecting the experience of her
own difference.

   Matthew and Robin also offer Felix and Nora different forms of
healing. Robin is "an incurable yet to be stricken with its malady" (N, 41)—
the malady of her own (sexual) difference. In her silence and her self-
containment, Robin offers to Felix and Nora the possibility that their
experience of difference (their incurable malady) is an illusion, the possi-

bility that there may be no such thing as salvation or damnation. Living and speaking his own experience of difference, Matthew offers them the possibility that the difference they experience with Robin's departure can be resolved, that though the (narcissistic) "innocence" she promised is illusory, its irrevocable loss might be healed. They fail to realize their "child's dream" with Robin because she is incapable of interaction, an innocent who "can't do anything in relation to anyone but herself" (N, 146); they fail to be healed by Matthew because he is capable only of interaction. His messianic effort proves him a liar who offers only "a sweet lie" because the "malady" of their difference is incurable. As he responds to Nora's claim to a "horrid love" for honesty":

Do you know what has made me the greatest liar this side of the moon, telling my stories to people like you, to take the moral agony out of their guts, and to stop them from rolling about, and drawing up their feet, and screaming, with their eyes staring over their knuckles with misery which they are trying to keep off, saying "Say something, Doctor, for the love of God!" And me talking away like mad. Well that, and nothing else, has made me the liar I am. (N, 135)

The point is that one's identity, one's sense of oneself as Subject, depends upon the experience of one's own difference; thus, while Felix and Nora scream in pain at the "wound" of the love through which they discover that difference, in the end they both nevertheless separate themselves from Matthew.

Throughout *Nightwood*, the power of speech is associated with the experience of separation and difference. Felix is "a master of seven tongues" (N, 41), and Robin speaks only when she leaves her lovers or awakens. Even Jenny, the only storyteller other than Matthew, tells only borrowed tales; indeed, she alone never tells her own version of her story; instead, we hear it (secondhand) from Felix, Nora, and Matthew (and the narrator). Her very ease with language is appropriated: "The words that fell from her mouth seemed to have been lent to her; had she been forced to invent a vocabulary for herself it would have been a vocabulary of two words, 'ah' and 'oh'" (N, 66), the infantile language of response.

As a would-be doctor, priest, magician, and alchemist, Matthew is a representation of the Word ("And then in his loudest voice he roared: 'Mother of God! I wanted to be your son—the unknown beloved second would have done!'" [N, 149–50]). Through language, Matthew tries and fails to heal, to absolve, to entertain, and to transform experience. Yet Matthew's power of speech noticeably decreases in each of the dialogues that constitute the second half of *Nightwood*. He speaks most powerfully, and with the widest range, when he appears as a woman in Nora's presence in the middle of the night. This section is essentially a long monologue, punctuated by Nora's questions and responses. When Felix comes to Matthew, the doctor speaks only in response to Felix, and he offers no answers to the questions that Felix poses. Finally, when Matthew meets with Nora for the last time, at her home rather than his, the scene is structured as a dialogue of alternating speeches. Nora has found the power of speech herself, and seeks there healing for her own divided nature: "I don't know how to talk, and I've got to. I've got to talk to somebody. I can't live this way" (N, 129). Indeed, when Matthew chides Nora, he speaks of Robin as if he were speaking of himself: "What did she [Robin] have? Only your faith in her—then you took that faith away! You should have kept it always seeing that it was a myth; no myth is safely broken. . . . The trouble with you is you are not just a myth-maker, you are also a destroyer" (N, 140). Matthew refers here to Nora's refusal to be a "madonna," to her demand that Robin "awaken" and acknowledge her own subjectivity; but he also refers to Nora's appropriation of the power of speech, to her refusal to rely solely on the "myth" of his own healing powers. As he leaves Nora, he stands "in confused and unhappy silence" (N, 158).

Matthew's final descent to a drunken sleep, sprawled across a table in an unmistakable image of the crucified Christ, foreshadows Robin's sacrificial offering of herself. His final incoherent speech echoes Christ's last words on the cross, although ironically this "messiah" gives into the temptation to despair and dismisses his followers with a curse. He also rejects the possibility of making meaning through speech: "Now that you have all heard what you wanted to hear, can't you let me loose now, let me go? I've not only lived my life for nothing, but I've told it for nothing" (N, 165–66).

Barnes makes Matthew O'Connor a counterpart storyteller; his asides to Nora during his first long monologue might be her own challenges to the reader. "And must I, perchance, like careful writers, guard myself against the conclusions of my readers?" (N, 94); "I have a narrative, but you will be hard put to it to find it" (N, 97). "Life is not to be told, call it as loud as you like, it will not tell itself" (N, 129). Like *Nightwood* itself, Matthew's speeches do not follow the syntactic logic of conventional narrative (of the fairy-tale romance, for instance), and they too constitute a response to an experience (an unexpected love) which has meaning only in the fact that it remains inexplicable. When *Nightwood* closes, however, with Robin's silence replacing Matthew's speech and her lack of differentiation prevailing despite his experience of separation, Barnes reclaims her provenance over both her story and her experience.

Therein lies the problem. Barnes completes her story with a scene that represents Matthew's final vision of "nothing but wrath and weeping." She shows that the dichotomy between masculine and feminine does not define the most profound experience of difference, but she denies the signifying value of her own deconstruction. She exposes the failure of values embedded in the masculine, and yet she does not counter that failure, for she denies that her "feminine" text has meaning beyond itself. It is as if she followed the advice she has Matthew give Nora: "No one will be much or little except in someone else's mind, so be careful of the minds you get into" (N, 129). For *Nightwood* is designed to thwart interpretation, to resist becoming in the reader's mind something other than what Barnes wants it to be. It becomes "the sweetest lie of all" because it remains a virtuoso performance that denies, in the end, the possibility of giving voice to (feminine) silence.

¶ . . . I am also pleased that you so much like the doctor. Yes he was a real man, he did indeed exist. Everyone of my generation who were in Paris at that time knew him, though no one had the idea that he would make a great figure for a novel, except me, fortunately for me, and for him while he lived, for he had pride in being Dr. Mighty-Grain-Of-Salt, though a little put out that his gun-metal chin was mentioned. He died only a little while back, I think I wrote you, and as to his age I have no idea, it was one of those pieces of information that he guarded more carefully than the most idle and vain of women, but he must have been seventy or thereabouts.

—Djuna Barnes,
letter to Wolfgang Hildesheimer,
20 August 1959

¶ Hildesheimer: "Page 32, line 7 from the bottom: 'Tiny M'Caffrey'—Is that someone special?"

Barnes: "page 32 . . . just *what* word, undoubtedly short and improper the Tudor king said I've now forgotten, but Tiny M'Caffrey is a word the doctor uses for both himself and his member, if you recall, he took out 'Tiny' in the scene in the church, asking God 'which' was the true Matthew; . . . it is also a sort of 'cant' word among certain homosexuals of that day, and in Paris, a 'camping word' . . . passing for a number of things."

—Djuna Barnes,
letter to Wolfgang Hildesheimer,
(German translator), 17 July 1959

¶ The Gypsy Bar was a little foul-smelling boîte on the boulevard Edgar-Quinet, full of hardfaced young lesbians and desperate looking old women whose spotted, sinewy arms rattled with jewelled bracelets. We were hailed by a tableful of the latter, one of whom, rather younger than the rest, was wearing male evening dress and a monocle. . . . A new arrival suddenly evoked screams of joy. A curvaceous squat man in black, with blue shaven jowls covered with violet talcum-powder and eyes loaded with mascara, he held his hands in front of him like a dancing dog.

"Dan! Dan!" everyone shouted.

This was the famous Dr. Maloney [*sic*], the most-quoted homosexual in Paris, a man who combined the professions of pathic, abortionist, professional boxer and quasi-confessor to literary women. He waddled forward and a place at our table was made for him at once.

"I have just had a marvellous experience," he murmured to the old woman in the purple velvet hat who was our hostess. "Such a divine piece of rough trade, my dear, with wooden shoes, velveteen trousers *and* a gorgeous three days' beard. Not until our encounter—if you will pardon the expression—was over did I learn he was a genuine grave-digger! I was furious. If I had only known . . ." He snapped his fingers with extraordinary force, and two waiters came running. "Champagne, champagne, to celebrate the victory of vice over the grave!"

Dr. Maloney then treated us to an astonishing harangue revolving around unmentionable subjects and indescribable practices.

Angela, with her big moronic eyes fixed on him, was laughing compulsively. Daphne seized her arm. "Come on," she said to me over her shoulder, "we're going home."

"Bitch!" said the old woman in the purple hat. "Boy-lover, cradle-snatcher, peep-hole woman, *flagellante manquée* . . ."

"Have a good time," said the lady with the monocle.

"While there is yet time," roared Dr. Maloney. "But in the hour of your utmost abandon, think of me, Dr. God Almighty Maloney, the irrepressible backwoodsman, the original Irish tenor!"

—John Glassco,
Memoirs of Montparnasse (1970)

Laughing at Leviticus:
<u>Nightwood</u> as Woman's Circus Epic

Jane Marcus

Lion and woman and the Lord knows what
        —W.B. Yeats

    O monsters, do not leave me alone. . . . I do not confide in you except to tell you about my fear of being alone, you are the most human people I know, the most reassuring in the world. If I call you monsters, then what name can I give to the so-called normal conditions that were foisted upon me? Look there, on the wall, the shadow of that frightful shoulder, the expression of that vast back and neck swollen with blood. . . . O monsters, do not leave me alone. . . .

        —Colette, *The Pure and the Impure*

Djuna Barnes' great Rabelaisian comic epic novel, *Nightwood* (1936), is beginning to excite the critical attention it deserves. As a contribution to that effort this essay is a feminist interpretation that argues, among other readings, that *Nightwood* is a brilliant and hilarious feminist critique of Freudian psychoanalysis and a parody of the discourse of diagnosis of female hysteria. Using Julia Kristeva's *Powers of Horror*, I argue that *Nightwood*, in its original title of "Bow Down" and its continual reference to submission and bowing or lowering of the self, is a study in *abjection*, and that by its concentration on the figure of The One Who Is Slapped, the downtrodden victim, it figures by absence the authoritarian dominators of Europe in the 1930s, the sexual and political fascists. While Kristeva studies abjection as a pathology, I maintain that Barnes' portraits of the abject constitute a political case, a kind of feminist-anarchist call for freedom from fascism. Looking at Nikka's tattoo as a defiance of the Levitical taboo against writing on the body, I see the body of the Other—the black, lesbian, transvestite, or Jew—presented as a text in the novel, a book of communal resistances of underworld outsiders to domination. Its weapon is laughter, a form of folk grotesque derived from Rabelais and surviving in circus.

With Bakhtin's *Rabelais* as model methodology, I see *Nightwood*'s extravagant language and imagery as a direct descendant of medieval "grotesque realism" (as *Ladies Almanack* is certainly a descendant of the Rabelaisian almanac hawked about in Paris street fairs). In this "reversible world" or "world turned upside down," Barnes moves from high to low culture, from opera to circus, and even expands Bakhtin's categories from their base in the material to include the mystical and mental grotesqueries that he excluded.

I would also argue that the status of *Nightwood* as a lesbian novel or a cult text of high modernism has obscured the ways in which it is a French novel, indebted as much to Victor Hugo and Eugène Sue as it is to Rabelais. My purpose in reviving *Nightwood* is political. Strangely canonized and unread, it cannot function as a critique of fascism. The revision of modernism in which this essay participates is an effort to read race, class, and gender back into the discussion. Unlike most expatriate writing from this period, *Nightwood* paints the Paris underworld and demimonde with its own colors, not a specifically American palette. Its characters are Barnes' modern "misérables," brothers and sisters to the hunchback of Notre Dame. *Nightwood*, like modernism itself, begins in Vienna in the 1880s. Freud, fascism, Hitler, "high art," and the lumpen proletariat haunt the text as a potent "political unconscious." *Nightwood*'s hysterical heteroglossia is a perverse and almost postmodern folk-text in which language and its possibility for figuration is as potent and explosive as it is in Shakespeare or Joyce.

Tattoo as Taboo

Ye shall not make any cuttings in your flesh for the dead, nor print any marks upon you . . .
—Leviticus 19:27–28

In order to be pure and symbolic, Kristeva argues, the patriarchal body may have only one mark, the circumcision, a cut that duplicates in the symbolic order the natural cut of the umbilical cord that separates mother and son. The ritual cut replaces the natural cut: "the identity of the speaking being (with his God) is based on the separation of the son from the mother."[1] In political terms, patriarchal identity is established by marking the body to distinguish it not only from the unclean mother, but from the polytheistic worshippers of the mother goddess who threaten the tribe. The establishment of marked sexual difference with rigid boundaries differentiates the people of the Bible from those of other religious cults, such as the worshippers of Dionysius in Greece, for whom the erasure of sexual difference is the point of ritual activity. (The Jews were neither the first nor the only people to use circumcision, a practice some anthropologists see as a form of menstruation envy.)

Writing on the body, I would argue, is breaking a powerful patriarchal taboo for the inheritors of the Judeo-Christian ethos in which the possession of the Logos is indicated by writing on the holy tablets. Making human skin into a page or a text violates the symbolic order. A body covered with marks is too close to the natural "unclean" state of the newborn's body, which bears the marks of the "unclean" placenta, the traces of its mother's blood. A tattoo, then, is not only taboo; it is also the birthmark of the born-again—the self-created person who denies his or her birth identity. This "monster" is a carnivalesque figure who reveals in the taboo-shattering act of making the body a book, dissolving the difference between spirit and matter.[2] (The Levitical taboos include incest and homosexuality and mark out any aberrant or physically blemished person as unpleasing to God. While the prohibition extends to prevent the union of same and same or human and animal, it also extends to the mixing of things: seeds should not be mingled, nor breeds of cattle; clothing should not be made of both linen and wool.)

In this context, Djuna Barnes' *Nightwood* might be called "The Lamentations of the Levitically Impure." Leviticus is about separation; *Nightwood* is about merging, dissolution, and, above all, hybridization— mixed metaphors, mixed genres, mixed levels of discourse from the lofty to the low, mixed "languages" from medical practice, circus argot, church dogma, and homosexual slang. Barnes' revision of the Old Testament parallels Joyce's revision of Homer in *Ulysses*. By making hybrids of the sacred texts of Western culture, both writers revitalize "high" culture, carnivalizing the dead bodies of the old texts, engorging them in a sacred/ profane cannibalism. *Nightwood* is also a dangerous novel, if we use Mary Douglas' concept of "purity and danger," for the whole social order of this novel is "impure."[3] The world is turned upside down for carnival; it is the reversible world of the circus, the night world of lesbian, homosexual, and transvestite Paris. Leviticus writes the rules for purity of blood. Ironically, it is Felix, the wandering Jew, marked as impure by a world that has incorporated his culture's ethic of purity and named Jews themselves as impure, who searches hopelessly for a "pure" aristocratic European bloodline: "With the fury of a fanatic, he hunted down his own disqualification" (N, 9). *Nightwood* makes a modernism of marginality. Its "danger" is that the excluded object of its rage, the white Christian male, might read it. The Aryan Superman is absent from the text, but his "uprightness" is the ethic that the characters' abjection opposes.

At a party in Vienna in the 1920s echoing act 2 of *Die Fledermaus* the characters of *Nightwood* meet. Count Ontario Altamonte is entertaining "the living statues," collecting for his amusement—as some European aristocrats did—circus people, Jews, transvestites, exiled Americans. I take one passage as my example here, but the whole novel encourages close reading. Dr. Matthew O'Connor tells Felix the story of "Nikka the nigger," whose name not only mimics the obscenity of the word, like a Middle European mispronunciation of the racist epithet, but has a feminine ending. He "used to fight the bear at the Cirque de Paris." His role is that of the savage male battling the beast for the thrill of an effete audience. But O'Connor exposes the myth of the fascist projection of savage sexuality on to the black man:

"There he was, crouching all over the arena without a stitch on, except an ill-concealed loin-cloth all abulge as if with a deep-sea catch, tattooed from head to heel with all the *ameublement* of depravity! Garlanded with rosebuds and hack-word of the devil—was he a sight to see! Though he couldn't have done a thing (and I know what I am talking about in spite of all that has been said about the black boys) if you had stood him in a gig-mill for a week, though (it's said) at a stretch it spelled Desdemona. Well, then, over his belly was an angel from Chartres; on each buttock, half public, half private, a quotation from the book of magic, a confirma-tion of the Jansenist theory, I'm sorry to say and here to say it. Across his knees, I give you my word, 'I' on one and on the other, 'can,' put those together! Across his chest, beneath a beautiful caravel in full sail, two clasped hands, the wrist bones fretted with point lace. On each bosom an arrow-speared heart, each with different initials but with equal drops of blood. . . .

"The legs," said Doctor O'Connor, "were devoted to vine work, topped by the swart rambler rose copied from the coping of the Hamburg house of Rothschild. Over his *dos*, believe it or not and I shouldn't, a terse account in early monkish script—called by some people indecent, by others Gothic—of the really deplorable condition of Paris before hygiene was introduced, and nature had its way up to the knees. And just above what you mustn't mention, a bird flew carrying a streamer on which was incised, '*Garde tout*!' I asked him why all this barbarity; he answered he loved beauty and would have it about him." (N, 16–17)

O'Connor exposes in his tale ("at a stretch it spelled Desdemona") the white man's projection of desire for the white woman on to the black man, the white's naming of the black's genitals as "rapist," the white man's desire to rape and kill woman. The pun on the word "spell" suggests that his penis is *named* Desdemona, as O'Connor's penis is *named* Tiny O'Toole, but "spell" could also be read sexually as "to satisfy" Desdemona or, in another meaning, to take someone's place. The name concealed by Nikka's knickers is Verdi's Desdemona more than Shakespeare's, as Nikka acts an operatic Othello. The miscegenation and murder suggested by "Desdemona" are also in the tattoo's "confirmation of the Jansenist theory," defined by the *Oxford English Dictionary* as the heresy of belief in the eternal battle of good and evil, the belief in the "perverseness and inability for good of the natural human will." Nikka's tattooed body is like one of Lambroso's drawings of criminals or Djuna Barnes' drawings for *Ryder* or *Ladies Almanack*. There are no margins; the text and illustrations devour the page; every inch of space is covered with drawings and writings, breaking both the Levitical taboo of writing on the body and the taboo on mixing objects, for text and drawings clash with each other, mixing the sacred and profane, the vulgar and the reverenced, the popular and the learned. The texts of each breast and buttock contradict each other as the ferociously oxymoronic frenzy of Barnes' prose style, like her painting style, continually yokes opposites in violent opposition, mocking Levitical prohibitions in an endless play at dissolving and reconstituting difference.

The length of the name, Desdemona, suggests a gigantic penis and is part of an age-old tradition of sexual jokes. But it also suggests Othello and "savage" jealousy and murder. Victor Hugo's *Notre Dame de Paris,* with its famous digression on the criminal underworld and the sewers, is invoked in the line "Paris before hygiene was introduced."[4] Hugo's earlier novel *Bug-Jargal* (1818 and 1826) was, like Aphra Behn's *Oronooko,* a study of a figure of "the royal slave."[5] This figure, a projection of a "phallic negro," is the white man's archetypal erotic animalization of the black. The white's spelling of desire on the black's penis, the pricking of the "prick" in what must have been a very painful operation, renders him impotent as a man while it mythologizes him as savage maleness. The black man's body is a text of Western culture's historical projections and myths about race. The angel from Chartres represents the myth of the black as angelic, innocent, and childlike during the early days of slavery; the book of magic refers to Europeans' fears of African religions. The Rothschild rose from Hamburg may suggest money made in the slave trade. The caravel suggests a slave ship, and the elegant wrists the ladies who benefited from slavery. In a further description of the tattoo, O'Connor claims that an obscene word runs down one side into the armpit, a word uttered by Prince Arthur Tudor on his wedding night, "one word so wholly epigrammatic and in no way befitting the great and noble British Empire" (*N,* 16). We may assume that that word, *merde,* is the Doctor's favorite and the author's too, since the text is as full of references to bird droppings as Paris itself is.

We know from Barnes' long response to Emily Coleman's essay on *Nightwood* that she expected readers to understand the references to Victor Hugo in the novel and to see it as part of the comic tradition of grotesque realism reaching back through Hugo to Rabelais.[6] In *Les Misérables,* Jean Valjean's fellow convict Cochepaille is tattooed with the date of the defeat at Waterloo, 1815. In *Nightwood,* Robin wanders from church "monstrously unfulfilled" with her large monk's feet, and the nuns at the convent of Perpetual Adoration give her a sprig from their rosebush and show her "where Jean Valjean had kept his rakes" (*N,* 46). Hugo describes the way in which the basest word in the French language, *merde,* became the finest word, as General Cambronne hurled it at his enemy on the battlefield. Hugo says that the expression of the excremental equals the soul, and in a note about the novel he claims that *merde* was the "misérable de mot," the outcast word, as his *misérables* were outcast people.[7] The fecal motif in Hugo's sewer chapters is continued in Barnes' *pissoir* passages and in her description of O'Connor's chamber pot.[8] For Hugo, the person who says *merde* is Prometheus, expressing the obscene laughter of the oppressed. The language of the latrine, which O'Connor speaks in the novel, is regenerative and Rabelaisian, as voiding is cleansing. Gutter language, *fex urbis*, is the voice of outcast people. In these chapters Hugo explores the argot of the underworld, its special culture, and defines it as "verbe devenu forçat," the word becomes a convict.[9]

Similar convict words are chained together in Dr. O'Connor's speeches, his stories of grotesque and painful suffering, the intensely overdetermined figures banging against the bars of the prison-house of language. His swearing, the mixture of prayer, oath, and profanity, the inclusion of the Virgin Mary and shit in the same sentence—all this goes back to Rabelais, reminding us of Gargantua arriving in Paris and drenching the crowd with urine, his "Mère de ... merde ... shit, Mother of God." Dung and defecation, in the Rabelaisian tradition described by Bakhtin, are part of carnival's reversal of authoritarian values, the eruption of folk humor in a bawdy acceptance of decay as renewal, of death as part of life. The language of this irrepressible force, as Bakhtin says, privileges the lower parts of the body. Critics who have described *Nightwood* as modernist decadence or the product of perversity have missed its deep roots in folk culture via Hugo and Rabelais. For Barnes is the female Rabelais, the articulator of woman's body/bawdy language. Like Hugo and Rabelais before her, Barnes writes scatology as ontology. She affirms being by celebrating the Below, the belly, the bowels, the big feet of Robin Vote and Nikka, who is a natural black man only to the knees.

Nikka's tattooed body, to return to the text, is a cabalistic ritual object put on display at the circus. Fighting the bear, he reminds us of Eugène Sue's Morok and Hugo's bizarre *L'homme qui rit*, whose monstrous and maimed characters resemble those of *Nightwood*. The friendship between the bearlike man Ursus and the civilized wolf Homo reminds us of Robin Vote as "the beast turning human" and the novel's controversial last scene with the dog; and Hugo's circus wagon as a universe of human, animal, and divine monsters is an earlier version of the circus world of *Nightwood*. "Garlanded with rosebuds and hack-work of the devil," Nikka's body is also a journalist's page (hack; Barnes as a brilliant journalist and "hack" writer; printer's devil). The tattoos, with their combination of text, vines, flowers, gothic script, and so forth, are an exact version of the early definition of the grotesque. In *Rabelais*, Bakhtin describes the bold infringement of borders in early grotesque art, in which forms "seemed to be interwoven as if giving birth to each other," animal, vegetable, and human passing uncannily one into another (*Rabelais*, 32). Nikka's body is like one of Djuna Barnes' drawings for *Ryder*, which I describe as "Pennsylvania Dutch surrealism" to capture their combination of folk naïveté and vitality with mythical beasts, texts, human figures, and grotesque vines.

But the art of tattooing is also a kind of bloody needlework. Thelma Wood, Djuna Barnes' lover and the model for Robin Vote, was an artist who did silverpoint etchings, a genre that one might call, with its dangerous, uncorrectable pinpricks, a "high art" form of tattoo. These etchings are also tabooed objects, studies of cannibalistic flowers and fetishistic shoes. (Thelma Wood's Berlin sketchbook is in the McKeldin Library.)

In the body of Nikka, Barnes creates an aesthetic of the Modernist Grotesque, a delicate and exotic refinement of the gross Rabelaisian realistic grotesque and the romantic intellectual grotesque of E.T.A. Hoffmann. Nikka's body as ritual object asserts the real and unalterable grotesquerie of the human body. In *The Painted Body*, Michel Thévoz follows Lacan in seeing the marking of the body as primitive human grappling with the mirror stage of development and identity formation, so that human skin is humanity's "first ground and surface of sign-making."[10] In other words, the body is our first book, the primal blank page on which our ancestors wrote. Anthropological evidence places the most ancient tattoos on the genitals, a tattooed or decorated phallus or voluptuous female body decorated on breast, buttocks, and genital areas being among the first human artifacts. Our own bodies were our first works of art, a remaking of the self. *Nightwood*'s project is a remaking of gender and race categories of selfhood, and it is preoccupied with skin as a blank page. In Nikka's case, the tattoo so graphically described is another of Barnes' reversals: Africans seldom tattoo the body, preferring scarification or body painting, while light-skinned peoples, notably Asians, use tattoos. Marking the body seems to enact opposite meanings, suggesting first a symbolic separation from the mother as in Kristeva's use of the terms "semiotic" and "symbolic," where "semiotic" means all that Plato excluded from art—circus, carnival, festival, music, laughter, and dance. But it also marks the return of the repressed savage and unconscious desire. *Nightwood*'s language is a perfect example of this "semiotic" in practice.

Thévoz sees the original tattoo as a symbolic mark of the human being's social relation to culture and circumcision as a representation of the taboo against incest with the mother. In Western culture, tattoo has been used to mark the subject as a slave or convict and has lost its ritual social origins in inclusion rather than exclusion from culture. The modern tattoo is like the mark of Cain, a sign of exclusion. But it also identifies the body with a certain class or group. The meaning of tattoo has changed historically from embodying symbolic law in "primitive" societies to marking the outlaw in modern societies—hence the figure in the modern novel of the lesbian feels that she has the mark of Cain on her forehead. (Cain seems to survive as a figure for the prepatriarchal, driven out because he will not slaughter an animal for a patriarchal god.) Nikka in *Nightwood* is like the convicts in Kafka's *The Penal Colony*, their bodies tattooed by the infernal machine that inscribes each criminal with the text of the law he has infringed. French soldiers in the nineteenth century often tattooed the side of the hand with the word "merde" so that it would deliver a message when they saluted their superiors.

Djuna Barnes was fascinated with *maquillage*. Body painting, makeup, extravagant costuming, and cross-dressing are part of the style of what Shari Benstock calls "Sapphic Modernism."[11] Figuring Nikka as abjection, his skin a text on which the dominant culture writes him as other, Barnes writes from the place of exclusion as woman, exile, and lesbian, juggling the double message of the memory of body marking as beautiful and social and its present meaning as sinister and shameful. Thévoz relates the angry or erotic tattoos of modern convicts and mental patients as the outcasts' defiance of logocentric society's exclusion of them—hence the body and hair painting of contemporary "punk" culture. The answer to the question raised by Nikka's tattoos in *Nightwood* may be found in Ilse Koch's barbaric collection of tattoos cut from the skin of victims of Nazi persecutions at Buchenwald. Given the Levitical prohibition against writing on the body, these "works of art" were taken not from the bodies of Jews but from other outsiders; they represent the moment when culture ceases to laugh at Leviticus and begins to shudder.

Since so many readings of *Nightwood* situate the reader as "normal" and the characters as perverse and "damned," reading against the grain of the text's privileging of the oppressed as "us," I propose this reading as a sisterhood under the skin with the victimized, as the "fluid blue" under Robin's skin allies her with Nikka. In a similar way, many studies of the Nazis (aside from the brilliant film *Our Hitler*) emphasize the perversity of individual sadists rather than the complicity of a whole nation in genocide. Such readings deny not only history and reality but also the power of art, expressed in fiction like *Nightwood*, to change us.

Modernism, then, if we take *Nightwood* as its most representative text, is a tattoo on the backside of a black homosexual circus performer. The non-Aryan, nonheterosexual body is a book inscribed with the modern failure to understand or assimilate the difference of race, class, and gender. Sexuality, liminality, and color are textualities written on the body in thousands of pinpricks, little dots that make a language of bloody ellipses, a dot-dot-dot or code of absences as presence. The representation of taboo in tattoo is a fierce example of the display of the body as other, a ritual hieroglyphic of pleasure and pain, an invitation to read the body of the Other as a book. What is absent is the Nazi who will burn this book.

If Joyce in *Ulysses* writes ancient and modern patriarchy, mythologizes woman and Others the mother, Djuna Barnes in *Nightwood* laughs at Leviticus, bringing all the wandering Jews, blacks, lesbians, outsiders, and transvestites together in a narrative that mothers the Other. While Joyce privileges the fertility of the modern mother-goddess and her private parts, Barnes privileges the penis. But she celebrates the nonphallic penis, the limp member of the transvestite Dr. O'Connor—who masturbates in church like the Jongleur of Notre Dame doing tricks for the Virgin Mary—and the black man's impotent genitals that bear the white man's sexual burden.

The symbolic phallus as law is absent from *Nightwood*, replaced by the wayward penis of outlaw and transvestite. But its presence is brilliantly conveyed in the person of a woman, Hedvig Volkbein, Felix's mother, who dies in childbirth, not quite convinced by Guido, an Italian Jew masquerading as a German aristocrat, that his blood is untainted. Hedvig is German militarism. With her "massive chic," her goose step, her "hand, patterned on seizure," she dances in "a tactical manoeuvre" with shoulders conscious of braid and a turn of head that holds "the cold vigilance of a sentry." Like Lina Wertmüller's daring representation of a Nazi concentration camp commandant as a woman in her powerful film *Seven Beauties*, Barnes breaks taboo by representing absent Aryan patriarchal power in the person of a woman. In the film, Italy is to Germany as woman is to man, the Other. So the Italian male is Other to the German woman, feminized by fascism.

Kenneth Burke says *Nightwood* is not political, that it has nothing to do with the Nazis.[12] Burke's discomfort with the seeming anti-Semitism of *Nightwood* is understandable. The scholar working on the text is confronted with T.S. Eliot's editorial cuts of passages that seem overtly homosexual or questionably anti-Semitic. But Djuna Barnes identifies with all outsiders. She was originally named Djalma, after Eugène Sue's *Wandering Jew*. Sue's Djalma is tattooed by a "thug" in Java during his sleep, and his killing of the panther onstage in chapter 14 is surely a source for Robin's scene with the lion in *Nightwood*.[13] But I would argue that the "political unconscious" of *Nightwood* is located in its supposedly irrelevant first chapter, meant to disguise its existence as a lesbian novel.

As *Nightwood* is not only a lesbian novel, its antifascism is apparent only when its triumphs over its own anti-Semitism, when we realize that its characters—Jews, homosexuals, lesbians, transvestites, gypsies, blacks, and circus performers—were all to perish in the Holocaust. Felix Volkbein is named for his role as wandering Jew (and the Yiddish Theatre in New York?), his middle European sadness contradicting the happiness of the Italian "Felix." As "Volkbein" he is the foot soldier of history, the portable slave, the legman of disaster, the unofficial "advance man" of the Paris circus, as Nora Flood is in reality the legwoman of the Denckman Circus. Like the Roman fragment of a runner's leg in his parent's plush Vienna flat, Felix is "disassociated" from his past. As his ancestor's black-and-yellow handkerchief reminds him of the medieval Roman circus in which Jews were forced to run around the arena with ropes around their necks, his restless search for "pure" racial nobility to which to "bow down" signifies his internalization of racial difference while underscoring the reality of a Europe in which racial purity has been obscured by mixed marriages and false credentials. The dismemberment and fragmentation of the Roman statues, the runner's leg, and the "chilly half-turned head of matron stricken at the bosom" recall early Roman circuses that sacrificed outcast Christians to the lions and medieval circuses in which outcast Jews were terrorized and prophesy with chilling accuracy the Nazi destruction of millions of Jews and other outcasts, devoured by their modern technological lions, the gas chambers and ovens of the concentration camps.

The blond Aryan beast slouching toward Buchenwald is present in this novel only in Hedvig's resemblance to him in 1880, but Felix's uneasiness, his attraction to the Catholic church, his scholarly labors, and his devotion to the past, to his sick child, and to the topsy-turvy world of the circus are reminders of what was destroyed by fascism's ugly fist. Felix is literally the foot of the folk, the embodiment of Bakhtin's carnivalesque, the preserver of circus culture and history.

Joyce's Night Town with cross-dressed Bella-Bello played against Bloom in a corset, like Tiresias in Eliot's *Waste Land*, suggests emasculation, not the ancient and powerful life-force of mythical transvestite figures. Barnes' doctor-transvestite is only posing as a gynecologist, and he identifies with the maternal principle. He lampoons all of the male sex doctors whose own sexual identity was so troubled, from the mad Otto Weininger to Havelock Ellis (who was aroused only by women urinating) to the Freud of the Fleiss letters. Unlike Joyce's Night Town, Barnes' *Nightwood* privileges the female world of night, magic, and ritual in the last scene in the chapel in the forest (Dante's darkwood), suggesting that "culture," in the primitive figure of Robin as racial memory, survives in America as Europe is destroyed by fascism.

The exiled Felix with his monocle reminds one of Djuna Barnes' sketch of Joyce (plate 13), as *Nightwood* in its static structure reflects Stephen Dedalus' aesthetic of stasis and proves it wrong, for fiction can be just as "impure" standing still as it can be while wandering. Joyce is recalled in O'Connor's chamber pot, in the naming of Nora, and in Nora's flat in the rue de Cherche-Midi, the home of the eye clinic where Barnes visited Joyce after his many operations. Did he give the printer's copy of *Ulysses* with hand corrections to the author of *Nightwood* in tribute to a writer of one of the few modernist texts to rival his phallogocentrism? Or, by giving the logos to a woman-identified man, does Barnes rob it of patriarchal privilege? Since O'Connor, "the Old Woman who lives in the closet," defines the female as only the maternal and womb-centered, his is a matriarchal phallogocentrism, a gynologos, not a cliterologos. Molly's "yes" is answered by Robin Vote's "no" to marriage, "no" to motherhood, "no" to monogamous lesbianism. Robin's "no" is a preverbal, prepatriarchal, primitive bark—as the novel ends in America and she ritually acts the bear before her Madonna-Artemis, goddess of autonomous sexuality, owner of her body and her self. As Europe bows down to fascism, O'Connor asks, "Why doesn't anyone know when everything is over, except me? . . . I've not only lived my life for nothing, but I've told it for nothing—abominable among the filthy people" (*N*, 165).

Despite Burke's denial of its political awareness, I believe *Nightwood* is the representative modernist text, a prose poem of abjection, tracing the political unconscious of the rise of fascism, as lesbians, blacks, circus people, Jews, and transvestites—outsiders all—*bow down* before Hitler's truly perverted Levitical prescriptions for racial purity.

We might also see the "political unconscious" at work in the other meanings of "tattoo."[14] After the Doctor finishes telling the story of Nikka, Felix asks him about Vienna's "military superiority." For a tattoo is also a military drum signal or call to alarm, as well as a symbolic drama or masque performed by soldiers by torchlight to act out the victory of valor over the forces of the night. The rosy-faced German boys the doctor recalls will soon be at the gates of the night world of Paris. The drumbeats of racial "purity" will sound against Nikka, O'Connor, and Volkbein. The evening of the "living statues" and outcasts at the Count's is a museum of soon-to-be-exterminated human types, like Hitler's Jewish Museum at Prague, meant to be all that was left of Jewish culture after the Holocaust. As Hugo's *Notre Dame de Paris* is an antihistorical novel prefiguring the Revolution, *Nightwood* is an ahistorical novel anticipating the Holocaust.

When the "living statues" are expelled from the party, the scene anticipates uncannily all the Expulsions from the Party of modern European history. Their refuge is a café in Unter den Linden, the traditional meeting place of homosexuals and political aliens. O'Connor explains the Count's action as fear of impotence: he "suspected that he had come upon his last erection" (N, 25). The erection is a signifier of order and uprightness. And the remark is uncanny in the light of subsequent political events, as in Frau Mann's lament, "I've an album of my own . . . and everyone in it looks like a soldier—even though they are dead" (N, 27). The narrator may say with Doctor O'Connor: "Oh, *papalero*, have I not summed up my time! I shall rest myself someday by the brim of Saxon-les-Bains and drink it dry, or go to pieces in Hamburg at the gambling table, or end up like Madame de Staël—with an affinity for Germany" (N, 126).

Ritual as Instruction: Barnes Critiques Freud

My voice cracked on the word "difference"; soaring up divinely. . . . (N, 92)

Nightwood is problematic for the woman reader and unusual for modernism because it is such a tightly closed text and because the narration is so distant and detached. Its heteroglossia resides in the doctor's multi-voices stories of abjection; its carnivalesque is not open to the audience but stylized and ritualized in the performative mode. *Nightwood* avoids the intimacy of a Colette or Woolf novel in which narration is shared with the reader so that she feels cocreative in the making of the text. The narrative voice here seems to have no gender except in the vitriolic description of Jenny Petherbridge, which privileges Nora's pain. Jenny, as the most abject character (because her author hates her), might be Barnes' portrait of the voyeuristic reader or literary critic, collecting other women's clothes and discarded loves. Strictly cast in the role of "audience," the reader is forced to "bow down" to the text, to replicate the anxiety of abjection. The reader reads at the site of what Naomi Schor calls the "bisextuality" of female fetishism. As a lesbian novel *Nightwood* dramatizes illicit love in a patriarchy, and some readers may find Nora's possessive infantilization of Robin as patriarchal as Hedvig's militarism or Felix's fixation on Germany. Despite the fact that its plot is a lesbian love story, *Nightwood* does not write the lesbian body as *Ladies Almanack* does, nor does it dramatize female desire, except insofar as it voices victimization, sets the alienated subjectivity of all outsiders, and flouts bourgeois concepts of normality by privileging the private pain of a panoply of "monsters." The indeterminate desire of transvestite, Jew, lesbian, and black makes the forbidden erotic into a political cry for freedom. Racism, sexism, anti-Semitism, and homophobia are challenged by this text. Mademoiselle Basquette, raped on her wheeled board, is the archetypal sexual victim as "basket case," humiliated and used by male sadism as Nikka is abused by male masochism. The desire of the disabled like Mademoiselle Basquette, "a girl without legs, built like a medieval abuse" (N, 26), for love and freedom *as they are*, rather than to be made "normal," cannot be made into a universal principle of natural law. As Hans Mayer writes in *Outsiders*, "The light of the categorical imperative does not shine for them,"[15] and O'Connor says, "even the greatest generality has a little particular" (N, 89). Mademoiselle Basquette, who looks like the figurehead of a ship and is raped by a sailor, is the disabled woman, hostage to men, of Hans Christian Andersen's "The Little Mermaid," as brilliantly analyzed by Nina Auerbach in *Women and the Demon*. There is always another Other.

By centering the marginal, *Nightwood* provides a spectacle of human bondage that articulates the angst of the abject so well that the absent upright, the pillars of society, are experienced unconsciously by the reader as the enemies of the human spirit. Figuring plot as plight in the tradition of the great nineteenth-century French realist fictions of Victor Hugo and Eugène Sue, Barnes modernizes the story of the oppressed hunchback or Jew to include sexual outcasts. As a melodrama of beset "perverts," *Nightwood* transcends its models by its refusal to play on the reader's pity. The human dignity of the aberrant is maintained by the narrator's objectivity, the irrepressible comic carnivalesque tone, and the exuberant vitality of obscene language.

The linguistic richness of *Nightwood*—its choked abundance of puns and plays on words, its fierce allusiveness to medieval and Jacobean high and low art, the extraordinary range of its learned reach across the history of Western culture—marks it as the logos-loving match of *Ulysses*. We are not accustomed to thinking of Djuna Barnes as a learned woman, a scholar as well as a writer. Nor does *Nightwood* arrange itself neatly next to other modernist, experimental works by women in an antilogocentric act. Gertrude Stein robs words of meaning, objectifies them, empties them, and fills them again out of her own ego. Woolf and Colette experiment with an intimate and flexible female sentence. The narratives of Jean Rhys, H.D., or Elizabeth Bowen are inescabably women's novels. If we place *Nightwood* among female antifascist fiction of the 1930s—Christina Stead's *The House of All Nations*, Virginia Woolf's *The Years*, and Marguerite Yourçenar's *Coup de Grâce*—it fits thematically. Woolf's novel traces the rise of fascism from the 1880s to the 1930s by concentrating on its origin in the patriarchal family. Stead condemns capitalism for its collaboration with fascism. Yourçenar brilliantly exposes German militarism and its patriarchal code of honor by privileging the ruthless and ethically bankrupt officer-narrator, leaving the reader the work of judging his self-serving narrative. In light of these antifascist texts, *Nightwood*'s project is to expose the collaboration of Freudian psychoanalysis with fascism in its desire to "civilize" and make "normal" the sexually aberrant misfit. *Nightwood* asserts that the outcast is normal and truly human. Freud and fascism, by labeling deviance medically and politically, expose the inhumanity of the madness for order in every denial of difference from Leviticus to the sex doctors, Kraft-Ebbing, Havelock Ellis, Otto Weininger, and even Freud himself. Barnes makes us all misfits, claiming that in human misery we can find the animal and the divine in ourselves.

In this reading Nora is the archetypal Dora or female hysteric, and Dr. Freud is brilliantly parodied in the figure of Dr. Matthew-Mighty-grain-of-salt-Dante-O'Connor. The lesbian patient chooses as doctor a transvestite whose most passionate desire is to be a woman, whose womb envy is so strong that it parodies Freudian penis envy mercilessly. The psychoanalyst's office is a filthy bedroom with a reeking chamber pot. Freud's famous totems, the sacred objects from ancient cultures that people his shelves and tables in H.D.'s famous tribute, are mocked by O'Connor's rusty forceps, broken scalpel, perfume bottles, ladies' underclothing, and abdominal brace. The psychoanalytic structure is ruptured as the patient asks the question and the doctor answers. The doctor is in bed in a granny nightgown and wig, powdered and rouged, and the patient stands by his bed; it is three in the morning, not three in the afternoon. The patient is rational, puritanical, and analytical; the doctor is mad. When Nora complains of heartbreak at the loss of Robin, Matthew mocks her: "A broken heart have you! I have falling arches, flying dandruff, a floating kidney, shattered nerves *and* a broken heart! But do I scream that an eagle has me by the balls or has dropped his oyster on my heart?" (*N*, 154).

But he proves to be a brilliant feminist psychoanalyst and he devastatingly deconstructs her dream. Floating in a Chagall-like dreamscape, her grandmother, "whom I loved more than anyone," is in a glass coffin with her father circling the grave struggling with her death. In the dream she watches, unable to do anything; then her father's body stops circling and drifts immobile beside the grandmother's body.

O'Connor detects the absence of the mother in Nora's dream. "'It's my mother without argument I want!' And then in his loudest voice he roared: 'Mother of God! I wanted to be your son—the unknown beloved second would have done!'" (N, 149–50). The two grandmother incest dreams constitute a revisionary psychological constitution of the female self, which we may call a *nonology*. The *nona* or grandmother may well become a young woman's role model and beloved in cases of real or imagined incest, when the mother has not protected the daughter from the father's assaults. Nora refuses to deal with the relationship between her love for Robin and her own role as daughter in the family. She begs the doctor to tell Robin never to forget her. O'Connor's psychological advice to the upright Nora is that she must bend, bow down, experience the body and get out of herself in ritual or carnival, let herself go, deal with the animal in herself:

> "Tell her yourself," said the doctor, "or sit in your own trouble silently if you like; it's the same with ermines—those fine yellow ermines that women pay such a great price for—how did they get that valuable colour? By sitting in bed and pissing the sheets, or weeping in their own way. It's the same with persons; they are only of value when they have laid themselves open to 'nuisance'—their own and the world's. *Ritual itself constitutes an instruction.* So we come back to the place from which I set out; pray to the good God; she will keep you. Personally, I call her 'she' because of the way she made me; it somehow balances the mistake. . . . That priceless galaxy of misinformation called the mind, harnessed to that stupendous and threadbare glomerate compulsion called the soul, ambling down the almost obliterated bridle path of Well and Ill, fortuitously planned—is the holy Habeus Corpus, the manner in which the body is brought before the judge. . . ." (N, 150; emphasis added)

The doctor continually points out to Nora that the rigidity of her American Protestant consciousness, her fear of the body, of drink, promiscuity, and dirt, make her love for Robin destructive, possessive, patriarchal in its insistence on monogamy and control of the beloved. He mocks her romantic possessiveness: "there you were sitting up high and fine, with a rose-bush up your arse" (N, 151).

Like Freud, O'Connor has an inexhaustible fund of case histories of aberrant behaviour, and he has a great deal to say about the art of writing. "I have a narrative, but you will be put to it to find it" (N, 97), he tells his "patient." He begs Nora to stop writing letters tormenting Robin: "Can't you rest now, lay down the pen?" Since he has no one to write to, he takes in "a little light laundry known as the Wash of the World" (N, 126), the psychoanalyst as Irish washerwoman, the writer as producer of dirty linen.

"Haven't I eaten a book too? Like the angels and prophets? And wasn't it a bitter book to eat? . . . And didn't I eat a page and tear a page and stamp on others and flay some and toss some into the toilet for relief's sake—then think of Jenny without a comma to eat, and Robin with nothing but a pet name—your pet name to sustain her . . ." (*N*, 127). Telling one of his homosexual stories in which he claims that he can tell the district and nationality of every penis he encounters like a gourmet, he asks, "Must I, perchance, like careful writers, guard myself against the conclusions of my readers?" (*N*, 94). He rails against American cleanliness, praising "the good dirt"; because a European bathes in "true dust," he can trace the history of his actions. His body is his page. "*L'Echo de Paris* and his bed sheets were run off the same press. One may read in both the travail life has had with him—he reeks with the essential wit necessary to the 'sale' of both editions, night edition and day" (*N*, 89). Nora's problem is the body/mind split. "The Anglo-Saxon has made the literal error; using water, he has washed away his page" (*N*, 90). The doctor wants Nora to recognize her animality, to face her desire for Robin as physical, and to stop seeing herself as "saving" a lost soul.

The great writer writes from the body. The dirty bedsheet is the writer's page. Patriarchal culture has traditionally seen women as a blank page on which to write. So Nora sees Robin, and projects herself on to that page. Djuna Barnes' genius lies in her ability to overcome Nora's anxieties, and she is one of the few women writers whose novel was run off the same press as her bed sheets. Contemporary novels such as Gabriel Garcia Marquez' *A Hundred Years of Solitude* or Günter Grass' *The Flounder* owe a great deal to the fantastic realism of *Nightwood*. Feminist fantastic realism has its own as yet critically uncharted history, but certainly *Nightwood* may be read in the context of Sylvia Townsend Warner's *Lolly Willowes*, Rebecca West's *Harriet Hume*, Joanna Russ' *The Female Man*, and their brilliant successor, Angela Carter's *Night at the Circus*. I have argued in "A Wilderness of One's Own" that these novels often appear after a period of realism in fiction reflecting political activism on the part of women, like Woolf's *Orlando* and *Flush*, where the writer is frustrated at the failure of struggle to change the power structure.[16]

Nightwood differs from its sister texts in its anticipation of historical horror, its proleptic impulse. Women writers have traditionally been forced to wash away from their page any mention of desire. It is as if Djuna Barnes had decided to include in *Nightwood* every word, image, and story that women have never been able to tell, to flout every possible taboo from the excretory to the sexual, and to invent, in Nora's grandmother incest dreams, her *nonology*, taboos uncatalogued even by Freud. Her boldness is remarkable. Even H.D., in her *Tribute to Freud*, was sly and subtle in her critique of "the master." She undermines his authority by greeting his dog first, by getting him to complain that she won't love him, by pretending that he treats her as an equal, by claiming that he approves of her relationship with Bryher, by describing him as a fellow student of myth and the collective unconscious. In short, H.D. fictionalizes Freud as Jung. Her "tribute" is really to woman's power to make the analyst collaborate with her, to save her "abnormality" for her art.

Djuna Barnes' critique of Freud is less directly personal than H.D.'s, but both are part of a modernist feminist insistence on woman-centeredness and partnership between doctor and patient. *Nightwood* challenges not only Freud, but the whole history of the treatment of female hysteria. Dr. O'Connor's lies seem to Felix "to be the framework of a forgotten but imposing plan"; "the great doctor, he's a divine idiot and a wise man" (*N*, 30, 31). Matthew says, "the only people who really *know* anything about medical science are the nurses, and they never tell; they'd get slapped if they did" (*N*, 31). (The nurse is a major icon of European modernism. See the brilliant story by Barnes' friend Antonia White, "The House of Clouds," and one of many novels about nursing in World War I, Irene Rathbone's *We That Were Young*.)

O'Connor claims that he is not neurasthenic and pronounces, "No man needs curing of his individual sickness; his universal malady is what he should look to" (*N*, 32). These remarks are part of the slapstick dialogue, with Felix as "straight man," which introduces "La Somnambule." Stage Irishman and stage Jew mock each other's racial traits as liars and meddlers and make fun of doctors. The comic pair then wake Sleeping Beauty, in the person of Robin Vote, "meet of child and desperado" (*N*, 35). In keeping with the carnival spirit of their "act," O'Connor plays magician or "dumb-founder" at a street fair and turns his back on the patient to make up his hairy face with her powder and rouge and steal a hundred-franc note. The reader "watches" this scene as a cabaret act and "reads" it as a pantomine of Sleeping Beauty woken by the wrong prince as well as a classic joke about a crooked apothecary or quack doctor.

The narrator tells us that "the woman who presents herself to the spectator as a 'picture' forever arranged is, for the contemplative mind, the chiefest danger" (*N*, 37). The "picture" of the disheveled Robin flung like a dancer on the bed, in a scene like Rousseau's "jungle trapped in a drawing room," emphasizes her legs and feet in men's white flannel trousers and dancing pumps. Extraordinarily cinematic, the scene reverses the reader's picture of Marlene Dietrich in 1930s vamp films such as *The Blue Angel* or *Blonde Venus* (which even has a gorilla, a "beast turning human"). We remember Dietrich "transvested" from the waist up in top hat and tails, pointing the contrast to very feminine legs. In a famous essay Kenneth Tynan wrote of Dietrich what might be said of Robin Vote: "She has sex but no particular gender. They say . . . that she was the only woman allowed to attend the annual ball for male transvestites in pre-Hitler Berlin. . . . [T]his Marlene lives in a sexual no man's land—and no-woman's either. . . . [S]he is every man's mistress and mother, every woman's lover and aunt. . . ."[17] In the context of *Nightwood*, one would say, "Every woman's lover and grandmother."

Lesbian subculture in Paris in the 1920s and 1930s affords many examples of the woman in a tuxedo. (Rebecca West once described Radclyffe Hall and Una Troubridge as looking in their male attire and cropped hair like "a distant prospect of Eton College.")[18] As tattoo is a form of the general Levitical taboo against transvestism, Robin's appearance in men's trousers is another version of writing on the body, or rewriting the body. The carnival of cross-dressing destabilizes identity, keeping bisexuality from being anchored to one pole and acting out a "female fetishism," denying Freud's assumption that fetishism is exclusively male. Naomi Schor's argument — "that ultimately *female travesty*, in the sense of women dressing up as or impersonating other women, constitutes by far the most disruptive form of *bisextuality*" — applies more fully to *Nightwood* than to any other novel I can think of, though it is characteristic of the lives and work of the whole movement of "Sapphic Modernism." If "female fetishism is an oxymoron," then one may argue that Djuna Barnes' style itself is a form of fetishism which allows the reader free play in the riddle of sexuality.

Even Robin's skin participates in tattoo and links her to Nikka and to Nora's obsession with her as "purity's black backside." Consoling Felix for the loss of Robin, O'Connor later compares her to a horse whose "hide was a river of sorrow. . . . Her eyelashes were gray-black, like the eyelashes of a nigger, and at her buttocks' soft centre a pulse throbbed like a fiddle. . . . Yes, oh God, Robin was beautiful. . . . Sort of fluid blue under her skin, as if the hide of time had been stripped from her." Robin's "hide," her "flayed body," is "the infected carrier of the past"; she is "eaten death returning" (N, 37), exactly Bakhtin's construction of the material body as the memory of culture. The "fluid blue" under Robin's skin is like Nikka's tattoo. The scene at the circus when Robin is lionized by the lion's eyes reminds us of Mae West's brilliant articulation of female animal desire in the classic 1930s film *I'm No Angel*. As a heroine, Robin rescues libido from the exclusive possession of men. The agency of her desire and its refusal to be fixed as the desired object of lesbian lovers or husband, contained in motherhood, or controlled by T.S. Eliot's or other critics' reading of her as doomed, damned, or pathologically placed as a medical case study is a textual triumph. Even Robin's voice (reported, for she only speaks twice) resembles Marlene Dietrich's: "In the tones of this girl's voice was the pitch of one enchanted with the gift of postponed abandon: the low drawling 'aside' voice of the actor who, in the soft usury of his speech, withholds a vocabulary until the profitable moment when he shall be facing his audience" (N, 38). It is precisely that pitch of postponed abandon that characterizes the art of Dietrich: the "low drawl," the slight catch in the phrasing, the way she sang the sensual as if it were a lullaby, and, above all, the sense that every song was sung as if she were remembering it from a long time ago—these are the things that constitute her appeal. So Robin's "soft usury" of speech is related to her archetypal resemblance to the ancient past. There is a nonthreatening animal growl to this voice; O'Connor would call it the voice of the dream prince, the "uninhabited angel," the genderless or empty sign of her body in which child and desperado meet. Robin is a speechless picture for much of the novel, but her outburst at Nora (the fetish talks back?) when she is drunk in the street is telling: "You are a devil! You make everything dirty! . . . You make me feel dirty and tired and old!" (N, 143). She makes Nora give money to an old prostitute: "'These women—they are all like her,' she said with fury. 'They are all good—they want to save us!'" (N, 144). Robin's sisterhood with the downtrodden, crawling in the gutter with outcasts, is the way in which "ritual constitutes an instruction for her. Her abjection is the reverse of Nora's uprightness, and it is privileged in the novel as the more *humane condition*. She doesn't want to be saved; she wants to be free.

There is an ironic message for Nora in Matthew's tale of the London "Tupenny Upright": "ladies of the *haute* sewer . . . holding up their badgered flounces, or standing still, letting you do it, silent and indifferent as the dead. . . . [T]heir poor damned dresses hiked up and falling away over the rump, all gathers and braid, like a Crusader's mount, with all the trappings gone sideways with misery" (N, 130–31).

At the very heart of the novel the twin *pissoir* passages condemn the upright. A woman curses her lover in the toilet: "May you die standing upright! May you be damned upward!" She curses her lover's genitals: "May this be damned, terrible and damned spot! May it wither into the grin of the dead, may this draw back, low riding mouth in an empty snarl of the groin" (N, 95). The rest of this passage anticipates Robin on all fours at the end of the novel. "For what do you know of me, man's meat? I'm an angel on all fours, with a child's feet behind me, *seeking my people that have never been made*, going down face foremost, drinking the waters of night at the water hole of the damned . . ." (N, 95; emphasis added). The lesbian curse on the clitoris in the *pissoir* is terrifying. Why does Barnes set it next to the rollicking tales of happy homosexual cruising ("cottaging") and O'Connor's domestication of the Parisian *pissoir* as his cottage ("my only fireside is the outhouse" [N, 91])? What is missing from the casual sex of the men is the possessiveness of "love." (These passages couldn't be written after AIDS.) Yet when Nora seeks solace in the arms of other women she misses Robin even more. Barnes seems to suggest that the dynamics of lesbian sexuality are different from those of homosexuality. Matthew longs to be someone's wife while Robin rejects Nora's wifely domestic ways and her infantalization of her. In Latin "infans" means speechless, and *Nightwood* creates the sex object as the silent subject.

Between them, O'Connor and Nora try to analyze lesbianism, though she cannot give up her posture, derived from patriarchal conceptions of love, of the abandoned wife. The discussion centers on the figure of the doll as the lesbian's child, Robin's smashing the doll, Jenny Petherbridge's gift of another doll to Robin and the figure of the prince. Robin says she chose a girl who resembles a boy as a lover from the figures of the prince and princess in romances. "We were impaled in our childhood upon them as they rose through our primers, the sweetest lie of all . . ." (N, 137). When the love that one has been told to expect never arrives, one chooses the androgynous figure of the prince.

Nora tells the doctor that the doll she shared with Robin was "their child," but she also says, "We give death to a child when we give it a doll — it's the effigy and the shroud" (N, 142). O'Connor tells Nora that she really wanted Robin to *be* a doll, an "uninhabited angel," an object onto which she could project "sexless misgiving." But she does not really listen to him or respond to his analysis.

Do you think that Robin had no right to fight you with her only weapon? She saw in you the fearful eye that would make her a target forever. Have not girls done as much for the doll? The last doll, given to age, is the girl who should have been a boy, and the boy who should have been a girl! The love of that last doll was foreshadowed in the love of the first. The doll and the immature have something right about them, the doll because it resembles but does not contain life, and the third sex because it contains life but resembles the doll. (N, 148)

So sleeping Robin is not really the princess but the prince.[19]

The scene in which Robin raises her child over her head as if to smash it, but doesn't, and the later scene in which she smashes and kicks the doll — her "child" — with Nora have an element of the uncanny in them. We may compare the treatment of the doll figure in *Nightwood* to Freud's essay "The Uncanny."[20] When O'Connor tells Nora that she has "dressed the unknowable in the garments of the known" (N, 136), he is giving a definition of the uncanny much like Freud's definition of a species of the horrifying that is also very familiar. Freud's essay is a peculiar example of the analyst as literary critic, or rather, as father of patriarchal aesthetic theory. Like some contemporary theorists, he begins, "I have not made a very thorough examination of the bibliography" ("Uncanny," 123). He then claims that he himself is not susceptible to the uncanny but will nevertheless write the essay since most aesthetic theory deals only with "the sublime." Freud fills the gap with several pages from dictionaries in various languages defining *unheimlich*. *Heimlich* comes to mean not only *homely* in some cases, but its opposite, and magic is associated with it as well as the secret parts of the body. It never occurs to Freud that *heimlich* refers to the female world of the home with safety and comfort provided by woman. The transition of the word's meaning from holy to unholy, from the domestic to the horrific, clearly marks the historical change from male pleasure in the female to his fear of woman, her body and her space. Freud, albeit unwittingly, is one of the best examples of this ideological reversal. While Freud's definition is a workable one, there is a great discrepancy between his definition and his examples, most of which come from E.T.A. Hoffmann's *Tales*.

I maintain that Freud's notion of the uncanny, as developed in his examples, is gender-biased: only certain men would experience the uncanny in the cases he cites, and women do not find these situations uncanny. Therefore, they are not universal. It seems perfectly reasonable to suppose that male and female versions of the uncanny should be different from each other and to examine the female versions of the uncanny offered by *Nightwood* in contrast to Freud's analysis. Since women have been the providers of *heimlichkeit* or domestic bliss, it is obvious that their experiences of the uncanny will be different. Freud, quoting Jentsch, starts his inquiry by finding the uncanny in our doubt as to whether something that appears animate is really alive or whether a lifeless object might really be alive ("Uncanny," 132), as in waxwork figures or dolls.[21] Freud is at some pains to deny the importance of the figure of the doll, Olympia, in the uncanny effect of Hoffmann's "The Sand-Man," the first act of Offenbach's opera *Tales of Hoffmann*.[22] (I wonder if one could read Manet's famous painting *Olimpia* as another participant in the Freud-Hoffmann doll-making paradigm, the reduction of women to the passive object of the male gaze. The painting seems to invoke an order of objecthood: white woman—doll, black woman—dog.)

Hoffmann's fantastic realism and grotesquerie were a direct influence on Djuna Barnes. While Bakhtin regards Hoffmann as too alienated and morbid to participate in the Rabelaisian folk tradition of grotesque, Djuna Barnes was influenced by and participates in both traditions. The romantic concern with the sick self, the move of fairy-tale fantasy from pastoral forest to metropolitan café, the concern with night and dream and with Mesmer's experiments with hypnotism, "the science of the soul," as proof of the existence of the supernatural—these concerns come from Hoffmann to Barnes and are part of the intellectual origins of *Nightwood*. "The Sand-Man" was originally published in *Night Pieces*, and Hoffmann shared Barnes' love of Callot, the seventeenth-century grotesque engraver of creatures part beast and part human. Like Barnes, Hoffmann had an amazon grandmother, and he enjoyed disfiguring the margins of her Bible with images of satyrs and hell. His portrait of Olympia seems to have come from his mother, described as rigid, cold, hysterical, and given to staring vacantly into space (*Tales*, 18, 19). Nathaniel's obsession with Olympia, the automaton, is based on her passivity: "Never before had he such a splendid listener. She neither embroidered nor knitted; she did not look out of the window nor feed a bird nor play with a lapdog or kitten . . . she sat for hours on end without moving, staring directly into his eyes, and her gaze grew ever more ardent and animated" (*Tales*, 162). Through the spyglass he buys from Coppelius, Nathaniel sees his real lover, Clara, as a doll and tries to kill her.

Eyes are the heart of the story, and Freud insists on reading through men's eyes a tale of fear of castration in the loss of eyes and the hero's relation with his father and Coppelius as a good father/bad father drama.

I suggest that Freud's analysis represses his own interest in the collaboration of Professor Spalanzini with the mysterious charlatan Dr. Coppelius/Coppola (Italian for "eye-socket") in which he may have seen his own collaboration with the eventually discredited Fliess, though the part of the body in question was the nose. The two doctors "create" a woman. (The womb envy of the Freud-Fliess letters is obvious; Fliess believed that men had cycles like women, and Freud appeared to accept this idea.)[23] What is at issue in the story is the male doctors' creation and destruction of the woman patient. Hoffmann's Olympia is mechanical, "La Somnambule." The intellectual history of "somnambulism," which meant hypnotism (not merely sleepwalking), is the direct forerunner of Freud's definition of the unconscious. In this history the line between science and charlatanism was very thin. For Fourier, Eugène Sue, Victor Hugo, Mesmer, and Hoffmann, somnambulism proved the existence of the human spirit, the collective unconscious, or God. This antienlightenment, antimaterialist doctrine of "illuminism" was also the mother of modern socialism; metempsychosis (Joyce's "met him pike hoses") and animal magnetism were some of its tenets, as were an adrogynous god, a sexed universe, and a division of the world into animal, human, and angel.[24] Since so many of these ideas animate the world of *Nightwood*, I suspect that Djuna Barnes' intellectual origins are to be found here.[25]

When she labels Robin Vote "La Somnambule," Djuna Barnes is not aligning her with Lady Macbeth but with the innocent heroine of Bellini's opera *La somnambula*, whose romantic story was written to prove the existence of the soul to atheists and rationalists. People are not simply "living statues," material automatons, it was argued, but animated by spirit. The count in the opera was a "scientist" who proved to the unbelieving folk that the heroine's unconscious spirit caused her to walk in her sleep and that her rational self had no control over her actions. Unlike *Tales of Hoffmann, La somnambula* no longer commands the immense popularity it had in the nineteenth century, largely because intellectual historians have not been willing to see the roots of modern thought, either socialism or psychoanalysis, in these romantic, irrational experiments. At a production of *La somnambula* in Washington, D.C. (December 1984), the audience laughed through the scene in which the heroine sings of her love for her fiancé while sleepwalking to the count's bed. The unconscious power of her desire is the point of the opera, as it is the point of Robin's nightwalks into promiscuity in *Nightwood*: she retains her innocence, her association with the virgin Diana of Epheseus. We interpret Robin's virginity as control over her own sexuality; as a sleepwalker she is the collective unconscious of undifferentiated female desire. Felix says she has the "odour of memory"; her speech is "heavy and unclarified"; "there was in her every movement a slight drag, as if the past were a web about her" (N, 118, 119).

Nightwood plays operatic allusions against circus allusions in a dialectic between folk and highbrow art on the subject of desire. O'Connor introduces Robin to Jenny Petherbridge at the opera, the powerful *Rigoletto* (also based on a Victor Hugo plot), in which the father murders his daughter while trying to avenge her rape, refusing to accept the fact that she loves the count who raped her. O'Connor mocks the Diva: "there's something wrong with any art that makes a woman all bust!" (N, 103).

Though Felix asks for Wagner's music to be played in cafés, O'Connor turns Wagner's heroic chaste male ideal of brotherhood, as well as the medieval patriarchal theme of the quest (used to great effect by the Nazis), into a joke and a feminist critique of Wagner: "one woman went down through the ages for sitting through *Parsifal* up to the point where the swan got his death, whereupon she screamed out, 'Godamercy, they have shot the Holy Grail!'" (N, 96). Barnes is taking potshots at the repressive ideal of male celibacy articulated by Wagner, an ideal that displaces desire onto evil figures of seductive females. The operatic *motives* are also "answered" in the dialogue of the novel with lines from music-hall and popular songs. This pastiche of fragmented pieces from the past of Western culture that we now associate with the postmodern is also practiced by Barnes in her painting and drawing: *faux* woodcuts, parodies of the Beardsleyesque, copies of folk-art cartoons in which the faces are made into realistic portraits while the rest of the drawing is derivative, oil paintings on cardboard.

The doctor tells the story of Don Anticolo, the tenor from Beirut, who mourns his dead son while drinking with a dozen sailors and throwing up and down the box of his ashes "no bigger than a doll's crate" in a scene that recalls Robin smashing the doll. The whole of the chapter "The Squatter" mimics the opera as well as a commedia dell'arte Punch and Judy show. When Jenny dresses up in costume and takes Robin and her guests in old-fashioned carriages to the Bois, the grand masquerade scene is an abduction from the lesbian seraglio; the fighting and scratching of the lovers are like a puppet show at a fair where Punch and Judy are both women; and the child Sylvia, who is caught in the quarrel, adds a melodramatic *frisson*. Djuna Barnes' father composed operas, including the comic and melodramatic "Allan Castle," whose heroine is stabbed as she poses inside a picture frame, anticipating Nora's "framing" in the window as she observes Robin with another woman and in the doorway of the chapel in the last scene.[26]

To return to Freud, Hoffmann, and the uncanny, one may say that the (woman) reader (though "woman" is not a universal category) does not experience a chill when the mechanical doll is smashed and the eyes roll on the floor, whereas some women do have such a response to Robin smashing the doll in *Nightwood*. The (woman) reader of "The Sand-Man" knows that Nathaniel will reject Clara precisely because she is not a doll, because she has a mind and uses it to analyze his obsessions as well as to criticize the poem in which he predicts that he will kill her. Hoffmann pictures the patriarchy in the persons of the two doctors, constructing "woman" as a passive, mindless doll and passing on this "ideal" to a young man who accepts the image, sees through the patriarchy's lens, its dark glass, and cannot relate to a real woman. "The Sand-Man" is, in fact, about the construction of the male gaze and the oedipal initiation of the son into the father's dominating I/Eye. Coppola's doll does not move the reader because she is so patently not of woman born, so clearly a creature of male science and male desire. When Robin smashes the doll the horror is caused by the erasure of the difference between sign and signified. Western culture has socialized girls by giving them dolls to develop their maternal instincts. A doll *is* a baby, they are told. It is precious and must not be broken. The uncanny moment is caused by Robin killing her and Nora's baby, the symbol of their union. The doll signifies as well the unnatural and illegitimate in their relationship.

The smashing of the doll is a recurrent scene in women's writing. The mathematician Sophie Kovalevsky tells in *A Russian Childhood* of her pathological fear of dolls; in *Smile Please* Jean Rhys almost defines her writing self as the doll breaker. Fear of objectification and abjection seem to be at work here, as well as fear of motherhood. The classic story is that of Maggie, deliberately working out her anger on a doll in George Eliot's *The Mill on the Floss*. Eliot calls the doll "a fetish which she punished for all her misfortunes." She has banged three nails into the doll's head in her fury, and the trunk is "defaced by a long career of vicarious suffering." What is interesting is that Maggie never really destroys the doll, for in order to go through her ritual of comforting it after she has beaten it, she has to leave it some semblance of likeness to herself. The doll as a toy or "baby" is a relatively recent cultural phenomenon, but there is a long history of the doll as a magical ritual object. In the Russian version of Cinderella, it is the doll that brings Baba Yaga to save the heroine.

Freud claims that the doll Olympia is "nothing else but a personification of Nathaniel's feminine attitude toward his father in infancy" and "a dissociated complex of Nathaniel's which confronts him as a person" ("Uncanny," 139). I suggest that she is Freud's patient, the female hysteric, who is hypnotized and forced into "good" and wooden behavior and eventually destroyed by quarreling male "doctors." Freud claims that one of his patients believed that her dolls would come to life if she looked at them with enough concentration, but that "the idea of the living doll excites no fear at all" ("Uncanny," 140).[27] For a woman who is socialized to be looked at, who even objectifies herself in the mirror, the uncanny is not figured in symbolic castration of the eyes—for she is the object being gazed at—but in the fear of becoming a living doll or statue, of becoming only an object. Robin and Nora act as *kores* (in Greek, *kore* means "pupil of the eye") or "living statues" of the lesbian as eternal maiden while looking at a representation of such abjection in the statue with the blank, protruding eyes; as pupils (in the other meaning of the word) of the eye, they deconstruct the process of objectification/abjection of woman. Felix, with his monocle and false portraits of ancestors as blank-eyed actors, returns the gaze of the Aryan at the Jew.

Djuna Barnes' articulation of the female uncanny and its relation to writing in a complex of signs around images of dolls and eyeless statues participates in female modernism's larger interrogation of gender and the writing self under the male gaze, which also includes the problem of the struggle between the needle and the pen. (In "Il vole," set to music by Poulenc in "Fiancailles pour rire" [1939], French poet Louise de Vilmorin writes, "I should like to sew but a magnet/Attracts all my needles.") Jean Rhys uncannily suggests in *Smile Please* the relation of the woman's eye to her "I."

Before I could read, almost a baby, I imagined that God, this strange thing or person I had heard about, was a book. Sometimes it was a large book standing upright and half open and I could see the print inside but it made no sense to me. Other times the book was smaller and inside were sharp flashing things. The smaller book was, I am sure now, my mother's needle book, and the sharp flashing things were her needles with the sun on them.

Her nurse forbade her to read and told her a version of the sand-man story:

"If all you read so much, you know what will happen to you? Your eyes will drop out and they will look at you from the page."

"If my eyes dropped out I wouldn't see," I argued.

She said, "They drop out except the little black points you see with."

I half believed her and imagined my pupils like heads of black pins and all the rest gone. But I went on reading.[28]

The relationship between the woman reader and the woman writer often reproduces the uncanny feeling of your own eyes looking up at you from the page. God/father/book is indecipherable, but in reading a sympathetic writer and in writing for a sympathetic reader, the woman can look at herself and be looked at without fear. The eye of God is the big book, but in the little book the needles (pens) connect with the eyes of the mother as the daughter's mirror. When the book is the mother's eye, the daughter writing finds her "I."

Freud asks, "Who would be so bold as to call it an uncanny moment, for instance, when Snow-White opens her eyes once more?" ("Uncanny," 154). Many women would be so bold. Certainly we may read Nora's dream of her dead grandmother in a glass coffin as her wish to be the prince who wakes Sleeping Beauty or Snow White. Her anxiety is caused by her wish to kill her father, who is already playing that role and standing in her way in the dream. The dream, with its absent mother and hovering father, also enacts the struggle to maintain female connection within the patriarchy, the desire to remove the possessive father and incorporate the magic grandmother, to erase the boundaries imposed by patriarchal culture. Robin, lying prone on the bed, acting as a "picture" for others to look at in the chapter "La Somnambule," is the proverbial woman patient. By exposing the erotics of the doctor-patient relationship, its voyeurism and quackery, Barnes brilliantly parodies the famous scene in which Charcot and a group of upright doctors hypnotize the horizontal female hysteric. We see psychoanalysis as circus in Matthew "I am my own charlatan" O'Connor, whose womb envy is openly expressed: "it was a high soprano I wanted, and deep corn curls to my bum, with a womb as big as the King's Kettle. . . . [I]n my heart is the wish for children and knitting. God, I never asked better than to boil some good man's potatoes and toss up a child for him every nine months by the calendar" (N, 91). As transvestite-shaman, O'Connor knows by vicarious experience what certain women want. His analysis of Nora and his advice that "ritual constitutes an instruction" amount to a feminist critique of patriarchal psychoanalysis. "And do you need a doctor to tell you that it is a bad strange hour for a woman? If all women could have it all at once, you could beat them in flocks like a school of scorpions; but they come eternally, one after the other . . ." (N, 101). He recognizes female desire as different from men's and urges difference on Nora. He claims to be "the last woman left in this world" (N, 100), though he is "the bearded lady." O'Connor's transvestism is a positive force in *Nightwood*. The most powerful representation of the uncanny in the novel occurs when Nora sees him in bed in his flannel nightgown and curly wig and says, "God, children know something they can't tell; they like Red Riding Hood and the wolf in bed" (N, 79). In the typescript of the novel the following lines are crossed out: "with what cunning had his brain directed not only the womanly, but the incestuous garment? For a flannel night dress is our mother."[29] In fragments from the chapter "Go Down, Matthew" Barnes wrote: "What sense is there in saying the girl went wrong at twenty, that she wore a bowler hat by preference when but eight months old and showed a liking for kissing her grandmother's ~~button~~ left elbow; it's not that she did so that needs explanation, its what it seemed like while she was about it."

Children liking Red Riding Hood and the wolf in bed is uncanny because O'Connor is acting the role of Nora's grandmother in the other dream, the version that is "well-dreamt" because Robin enters it "like a relative found in another generation." Nora is looking down into the house "as if from a scaffold" at her grandmother's high room "bereft as the nest of a bird which will not return" (Nora is mocked by O'Connor as "Turdus musicus," or The European singing thrush); Robin is lying below in fear with a disk of light (obviously a spotlight) on her. Nora keeps calling her to come into the "taboo" room, but "the louder she cried out the farther away went the floor below, as if Robin and she, in their extremity, were a pair of opera glasses turned to the wrong end, diminishing in their painful love" (*N*, 62).

The house is *unheimlich* because, though it has all her grandmother's things, it is the opposite of her real room and "is saturated with the lost presence of her grandmother, who seemed in the continual process of leaving it." It is a house of incest, and if Robin enters it she joins the incestuous family. There are two grandmothers, a beautiful feminine one and one "dressed as a man, wearing a billy cock and a corked moustache, ridiculous and plump in tight trousers and a red waistcoat, her arms spread saying with a leer of love 'My little sweetheart.'" Nora had wanted to put her hands on something in this room but in the past "the dream had never permitted her to do so." I suggest that she wants to put her hands on "the plume and the inkwell" and the pictures of her ancestors mentioned in the beginning of the dream: that is, she wants to take up her grandmother's profession of writing.

The costume her grandmother wears is that of the master of ceremonies at the circus, precisely the role of the narrator of *Nightwood*. Robin is in fear because she is being written about. Nora experiences the dream as "something being done to Robin, Robin disfigured and eternalized by the hieroglyphics of sleep and pain" (*N*, 63)—that is, being made into La Somnambule. As publicist for the circus, Nora is dreaming herself into the male role of master of ceremonies, Djuna Barnes writing this novel as circus. Her grandmother is herself in drag. The grandmother is cross-dressed as herself, the writer. This role of narrator as master of ceremonies at the circus is spelled out in "La Somnambule" in the description of Robin's room as like a jungle trapped in a drawing room: "the set, the property of an unseen *dompteur*, half lord, half promoter, over which one expects to hear the strains of an orchestra of wood-winds render a serenade which will popularize the wilderness" (*N*, 35).

The performative structure of *Nightwood* is like an eight-ring circus, brilliantly controlled by the grandmother-narrator-*dompteur* as each "act" is performed and the living statues speak their lines. As Paul Bouissac argues in *Circus and Culture*, circus acts progress in a dialectic of control and disturbance, culminating in a triumphant assertion of the performer's mastery. The reader is never allowed to play a participatory role but is eternally cast as "audience" at the circus or cabaret.[30]

In her dream Nora sees her grandmother as a "wolf," in both senses, and recognizes the ill-fitting male costume she must don as granddaughter-writer; when she constructs the doctor as her grandmother, a fine feminist transference for a workable psychoanalysis begins. Like Felix watching O'Connor's tricks at Robin's bedside, the reader experiences "a double confusion" (*N*, 35) as the narrator alternates between *dompteur* and "dumbfounder," providing a sideshow and "preparing the audience for a miracle" (*N*, 35). Barnes' rhetorical tricks are like the magician's feints with back and elbows, "honesties" to distract the audience from his hoax. Is *Nightwood* a hoax or a profoundly humanistic and political novel? When the woman acts the beast and the beast turns human in the last scene, do we laugh or weep?[31]

Bakhtin would argue that Barnes, like Rabelais, does not reverse the world for carnival as political therapy or release, in the steam-engine model of social behavior; but that Barnes' characters represent the revolutionary potential in folk culture.[32] That is, *Nightwood* reveals that gays and outcasts *have* a culture, a linguistically and philosophically rich culture, encompassing high and low art, opera and circus, psychoanalysis and religion, and that this culture is a vital political force.

Inversion reveals the essence of the particular historical moment that we construct as the "rise of fascism" in the "upright" defining their differences from the abject by race, gender, or sexual practice. At this historical moment the outcasts constitute the essence of human culture. Fascism chooses to eliminate from "civilization" those very figures who are the "symbolic forms" of humanity in ancient traditions: circus folk, lesbians, homosexuals, transvestites, and the Jew who is the recorder of history and culture.

The "splendid and reeking falsification" of the world of carnival and circus in *Nightwood*'s reversals is redemptive. As in Rabelais, the circus folk take royal titles: Princess Nadja, Baron von Tink, Principessa Stasera y Stasero, King Buffo, and the Duchess of Broadback. In carnival, enthronement of the fool implies dethronement of hierarchy. They are "gaudy, cheap cuts from the beast life" (*N*, 11) as the butcher is a stock figure in old European carnival. (O'Connor compares penises to mortadellas, and carnival parades often featured enormous phallic salamis.) Nadja's spine curves like a lion's, and Frau Mann's costume is like Nikka's tattoo:

She seemed to have a skin that was the pattern of her costume: a bodice of lozenges, red and yellow . . . one felt they ran through her as the design runs through hard holiday candies, and the bulge in the groin where she took the bar, one foot caught in the flex of the calf, was as solid, specialized and as polished as oak. The stuff of the tights was no longer a covering, it was herself; the span of the tightly-stitched crotch was so much her own flesh that she was as unsexed as a doll. The needle that had made one the property of the child made the other the property of no man. (*N*, 13)

Here the novel's themes converge: circus performer = doll = lesbian. In *Fires* Marguerite Yourçenar imagines Sappho as an aging lesbian trapeze artist, in a mode described by Susan Gubar as preserving "the utopian grandeur of the lesbian aesthetic project in the modernist period."[33] Memoirs of Paris in the 1920s and 1930s recall the circus, the elegant trapeze act of Barbette, the Texas Transvestite, the human gorilla.[34] In *Nightwood* the lovers meet at the circus and mix circus figurines with ecclesiastical hangings in their flat, continuing carnival's tradition of mixing the sacred and the profane. Robin laughs in church and goes home to read de Sade on the day she gives birth, and O'Connor masturbates in church as the Transvestite of Notre Dame in one of the novel's most hilarious scenes. Bouissac defines circus as a *language*, "a set of rules for cultural transformations, displayed in a ritualistic manner that tempers this transgressive aspect." It enacts freedom from culture and inverts the ordinary. He claims that "individuals who have not been fully integrated into a culture find it more acceptable to enjoy this type of performance, as do individuals with a marginal or unique status, such as poets and artists."[35] As Lévi-Strauss says, we see the circus as supernatural, a place where human beings can still communicate with animals and with our own "higher powers." One of *Nightwood*'s most fascinating aspects is that it has more animal characters than people, from lions to mouse-meat, cows, horses, fish, and an extraordinary number of birds, adding to its archetypal qualities.

Like the circus, *Nightwood* is polycentric; it makes the reader uneasy with time and history for political purposes. Robin Vote, Nora Flood, and O'Connor (whose names intersect in their o's, r's, and n's) are performers of archetypal roles. The hybrid form of the fiction reinforces the hybrid experience of the characters. O'Connor says, "Take away a man's conformity and you take away his remedy," and tells of the paralyzed man in a velvet box at Coney Island: "suspended over him where he could never take his eyes off, a sky-blue mounted mirror, for he wanted to enjoy his own difference" (N, 146). Robin is the androgynous ideal, the archetype of the savage virgin Diana, a feminist version of the Noble Savage; *Nightwood* is her "sacred grove." The name "Vote" signifies the suffragettes, often martyrs and victims of police and government brutality. As a young reporter, Barnes investigated the violent force-feeding of hunger-striking suffragettes by having herself forcibly fed: "If I, play-acting, felt my being burning with revolt at this brute usupration of my own functions, how they who actually suffered the ordeal in its acutest horror must have flamed at the violation of the sanctuaries of their spirit?"[36] The accompanying photograph, which shows Barnes, the prone victim, being violated by a group of doctors (plate 1), echoes the picture of the hysterical woman being hypnotized by Charcot and the French doctors. The image conflates the subordination of the politically independent woman with that of the medical model of the aberrant woman. Barnes experienced force-feeding as a kind of rape, as did many of the brave women of the movement. Christabel Pankhurst was figured as Joan of Arc on the front page of *The Suffragette*. Martyrdom, sainthood, and the androgynous militant figure of the woman in men's clothes were part of the mythology of this feminist modernism, and Barnes draws on its culture for Robin.

But *Nightwood*'s uniqueness lies in its language, its billingsgate and—to use a phrase Freud coined for the analysis of dreams in his letters to Fleiss, a nice combination of Yiddish and Greek—its "dreckology," the continual use of animal and human excremental imagery, from "whale shit" to "dinosaur droppings" to bird turds. Djuna Barnes is the female Rabelais. Only ribaldry is powerful enough to carry *Nightwood*'s political vision. For she was writing, like Nora in the dream of her grandmother, at what Victor Hugo calls "noir ceur sublime de l'écritoire," the sublime blackness of the inkstand.[37] Despite fascism or political repression, folk art survives among the marginal and in the circus: "Clowns in red, white and yellow, with the traditional smears on their faces, were rolling over the sawdust as if they were in the belly of a great mother where there was yet room to play" (*N*, 54).

If I am right in reading *Nightwood* as a prophecy of the Holocaust, an attack on the doctors and politicians who defined deviance and set up a world view of us and them, the normal and abnormal, in political, racial, and sexual terms, a world that was divided into the upright and the downcast, the horror that in fact took place is still very difficult for us to contemplate. In *Colette: A Taste for Life*, Yvonne Mitchell describes Sarassani, the "great circus king" who invited the European press to performances in Berlin in the early 1930s in order to get bookings in France for his troupe of five hundred animals. Djuna Barnes and Thelma Wood may well have been there with Colette and other journalists. Because the circus performers were Jews, Yugoslavs, and blacks, and because Sarassini chose expatriation over firing his crew, they were scapegoated by the Nazis. The night before he left Antwerp for South America, "the tent housing his twenty-two elephants caught fire, and most of them were burned to death."[38]

The abjection Barnes figured in *Nightwood* is mild compared to the murder and dehumanization (including medical experimentation) of the Nazi concentration camps. When American soldiers liberated the camps, the stench of excrement and death overpowered them. They could not identify with the tortured, starved prisoners as fellow human beings. One soldier wrote of them as a "horde of gnomes and trolls. . . . Some hop on crutches. Some hobble on stumps of feet. Some run with angular movements. Some glide like Oriental genies." Another described the emaciated victims as "huge, lethargic spiders," and others described the "absent-minded apes" of Buchenwald, while many said the scenes were like a bestial circus nightmare.[39] While the soldiers had difficulty identifying with the humanity of the Nazi's victims, civilians refused to believe the newsreel evidence of the massacres. Eventually the press began to focus on individual perverse Germans as perpetrators of the crimes, since people could not deal with the idea of sadism on such an immense scale, involving an entire nation. Interestingly, the press focused on two women, "Irme Grese, the Bitch of Belsen," and "Ilse Koch, the Beast of Buchenwald." It seems to me immensely significant, though it has not been noted before, that the press singled out individual women as symbols of Nazi sadism and cruelty, as objects of hate, when nazism itself was such a patriarchal ideology and the crimes were committed almost entirely by men. Ilse Koch is significant for us, for she collected pieces of tattooed human skin from camp prisoners. Did she write on the skin as a direct challenge to Leviticus? Were Felix and Guido among her victims? Certainly Nikka's body as the black backside of Western culture and the mutilated body of Mademoiselle Basquette challenge us to remember the inexpressible horror of the Holocaust. *Nightwood* reminds us that the human condition is a sister- and brotherhood of difference, and that ideologies that seek to erase those differences and define only themselves as human are indescribably dangerous.

¶ Dan [Mahoney] always clapped his hands when anyone died. When I asked why, he looked at me as tho I were mad.

> —Djuna Barnes,
> letter to Laurence Vail,
> 14 May 1966

¶ I feel it a grave disservice to letters to reissue merely because one may have a name for later work or for the unfortunately praised earlier work, or for purpose of nostalgia or "history" which might more happily be left interred.

> —Djuna Barnes,
> letter to Margaret Anderson,
> 30 April 1952

¶ I wish I could write you as I used to, it is not because of lack of "frankness" (which, if you think it over, is rather a ridiculous thing to say about me)—not because of my "lack of honesty" about myself . . . writing intimately to a person is something that is so AGAINST MY NATURE . . . contrary to you I am happier in silence . . . I cannot (as I well knew) have any peace of mind when continually attacked; and as after all I am well on in my life, I must try to use the rest of it to do something of my own again.

> —Djuna Barnes,
> letter to Emily Coleman,
> 5 January 1939

15

"Woman, Remember You": Djuna Barnes and History

Julie L. Abraham

"Looking at her," Djuna Barnes began her description of *Nightwood*'s Nora Flood, "foreigners remembered stories they had heard of covered wagons" (*N*, 51). Of the salon Nora presided over before the action of the novel has begun, she wrote,

> At these incredible meetings one felt that early American history was being re-enacted. The Drummer Boy, Fort Sumpter, Lincoln, Booth, all somehow came to mind; Whigs and Tories were in the air; bunting and its stripes and stars, the swarm increasing slowly and accurately on the hive of blue; Boston tea tragedies, carbines, and the sound of a boy's wild calling; Puritan feet, long upright in the grave, striking the earth again, walking up and out of their custom; the calk of prayers thrust in the heart. And in the midst of this, Nora. (*N*, 51)

Barnes' work is dense with such references to history, from the narrator's proposition in the *Ladies Almanack* "that Priscilla herself was prone to a Distaff, and garbled her John for her Jenny" (*LA*, 71), via the hallways of the Viennese home of Guido and Hedwig Volkbein, "peopled with Roman fragments, white and disassociated" (*N*, 5), to Augusta's declaration, in *The Antiphon*, "I would be Helen/Forgotten, day by day, for ever and for ever!" These allusions to historical epochs, events, and characters are accompanied by a stream of comments about "history" made by Barnes as narrator or by her characters.

The evocations of historical detail and the discussions of "history" as such are however only part of a complex historical presence in Barnes' writing. Her characters are frequently as concerned about their relation to history as they are about their responses to each other. History is also the source of an additional cast (Helen of Troy, Catherine the Great, Dante, Sappho) who move in and out of her work, as well as a smaller group of more contemporary public figures (Dreyfus, Oscar Wilde, Radclyffe Hall) who

252

are present only by implication but whose individual histories shape Barnes'
own.¹ Dreyfus, Wilde, and Hall represent the historical context in which
standard fictional conventions could not accommodate Barnes' stories;
Helen of Troy, Catherine the Great, Dante, and Sappho provide her textual
world with its own alternative location and resonances.² Barnes used history
as a framework for her texts, within which she could situate both her
practice as a writer and her anxieties about that practice. At the same time,
implicit throughout her work is the sense that her texts are themselves
additions to history, recording characters, experiences, and perspectives
that history usually prefers to ignore.

Djuna Barnes was a lesbian writer: a woman writer for whom
"looking at her" was potentially a prelude to sexual desire and emotional
vulnerability.³ She inverted history to record what was at the time often
referred to as inversion, "the part about history that has never been told" as
she describes the conception and birth of the first "woman born with a
difference" in the *Ladies Almanack* (*LA*, 24–25). The first three of the
"great moments of history" are recounted by Dr. O'Connor to one of
Wendell Ryder's bastard children in *Ryder* (*R*, 302–14). But the fourth, final,
and lesbian moment, the story of Jezebel and the Queen of Sheba which
rebukes the authority of biblical history itself, is told by one of a pair of
women lovers to the other, Doll Furious to Dame Musset, in the *Ladies
Almanack* (*LA*, 41). The interest in history prefigured in *Ryder* and in such
early stories as "Cassation" was fully developed in the *Ladies Almanack*, as
well as in Barnes's two major works, *Nightwood* and *The Antiphon*. The
gesture of turning toward "women in history" is repeated by one of the
women in each of these works: Bounding Bess in the *Almanack* (*LA*, 32),
Robin Vote in *Nightwood* (*N*, 47), and Augusta in *The Antiphon*. Of all of
the women whose memories they could invoke (including Catherine of
Russia, Sappho, Louise de la Vallière, Madame de Maintenon, Cleopatra,
and Lillie Langtry) only one, Sappho, offers an obviously applicable lesson.
However, although her characters might look uncritically to these inappropriate models, the tenor of Barnes' own overall turning to history was
more accurately represented by the critical spirit of the *Almanack*'s narrator,
who asks: "Was there a whisper of Ellen or Mary, of Rachel or Gretchen . . .
or of Wives whispering a thing to a Wife? What's in a name before Christ?
Were all Giants' doings a Man's . . . No Time without God, no end without
Christ!" (*LA*, 70).

For Djuna Barnes history always had at least a double meaning.
History was fixed, exact, monumental, the source of power. It was also
chaotic, fragmentary, constantly under construction. History was the story
of both the Christians and the Jews, the source of innocence and depravity, a
false lesson of male authority and an only superficially fantastic account of
the lives of lesbian women "with a difference" (*LA*, 26). This multiplicity
was possible because Barnes' sense of "history" incorporated both the

official record and the stories of those who were either marginal to or completely excluded from that record.

Throughout her work Barnes maintained the distinction between what might be recorded if historians told "the story of the world to the world" (*N*, 161), as the Doctor advocates at the conclusion of *Nightwood*, and what actually is set down, history as a "commodity," as she refers to that Jewish history recognized by a Christian-dominated society (*N*, 10). She was not, however, consistent in her labeling of the terms of this opposition. Sometimes she would define the official record as "history," in opposition to the stories of those who are politically powerless. Dr. O'Connor is in the process of drawing such a distinction as he is introduced into *Nightwood*:

"We may all be nature's noblemen," he was saying . . . "but think of the stories that do not amount to much! That is, that are forgotten in spite of all man remembers (unless he remembers himself) merely because they befell him without distinction of office or title—that's what we call legend and it's the best a poor man may do with his fate; the other . . . we call history, the best the high and mighty can do with theirs. Legend is unexpurgated, but history, because of its actors, is deflowered." (*N*, 15)

Later in the same work the Doctor reverses his terms, describing all that is excluded from the record as "history" and the record itself as "faulty." He tells Felix that "Man is born as he dies, rebuking cleanliness," and identifies "cleanliness" with "neatness and "conformity" as well as with the history of the official record: "So the reason for our cleanliness becomes apparent; cleanliness is a form of apprehension; our faulty racial memory is fathered by fear. Destiny and history are untidy; we fear memory of that disorder" (*N*, 118).

Barnes could not be consistent about which of these she defined as the true history because her project was founded on a challenge to the idea of a limited "history proper." She did not need to be consistent in this respect because both were necessary parts of her own stories, each requiring the other. The history of those marginalized or excluded by the official record is shaped by their relation to that record, as Felix Volkbein in *Nightwood* and Augusta in *The Antiphon* are obsessively concerned with their relations to history. At the same time, the official record, "our faulty racial memory," the Doctor has explained, is comprehensible only in conjunction with what it fears and therefore marginalizes or excludes. But this understanding of the official record was only a secondary effect of Barnes' stories. The idea of a definitive history figures so significantly, and there had to be at least two "histories" contending (whichever is defined as "history" at any given moment), so that she could establish the negative relation of those excluded to the official record. Barnes' understanding of the effect of exclusion from the record, despite the fact that the effect itself is negative, provided her with a means of gaining access to the position of recorder herself. She was concerned with the stories of those whose lives were not usually recorded; those stories included the experience of that exclusion. By taking on the possibility of writing about that experience of exclusion Barnes was able to situate her own work relative to the official record, circumventing the initial fact of her subjects' historical and, by extension, literary disqualification.

Within this framework she traced the overlapping social divisions between genders, classes, races, and sexual persuasions that mark the limits of the history of the official record. She identified those for whose benefit that history is written: the aristocracy, the military, Christians, fathers, heterosexuals. But her account of the "high and mighty" is strictly contingent. She focuses on those who are outside the circle of power that the official history bestows and legitimates: Jews, wives, daughters, homosexual men, and lesbians.4

The story of Felix Volkbein functions as a paradigm of Barnes' understanding of the relation of the powerless to the record of the "high and mighty." From the first sentence of *Nightwood* she establishes both the Jewishness of the child about to be born and the fact of the historical persecution of the Jews. In the following pages the child's father, Guido Volkbein, is described as an "outcast" even in the arms of his Christian wife (*N*, 3). This negative status is only emphasized by his concern for his place in history, his manufactured genealogy and title, and the ancestral portraits that are really studies of a forgotten actor and actress. Felix inherits his father's place and his preoccupation: his race and his relation to history will be his two most important characteristics. Around the stories of Guido and Felix Volkbein, Barnes constructs an account of the relation of Jews and Christians; she describes a subject people as historically marginalized by the social order that scorns them. To the extent that they enter the history of the official record it is as victims, for the entertainment of the dominant group. Guido remembers

the ordinance of 1468, issued by one Pietro Barbo, demanding that, with a rope around its neck, Guido's race should run in the Corso for the amusement of the Christian populace, while ladies of noble birth, sitting upon spines too refined for rest, arose from their seats, and, with the red-gowned cardinals and the *Monsignori*, applauded with that cold yet hysterical abandon of a people that is at once unjust and happy, the very Pope himself shaken down from his hold on heaven with the laughter of a man who forgoes his angels that he may recapture the beast. (*N*, 2)

Even "four centuries later" this history ties Guido and his son to the role of outsiders. It also contains a threat that is not confined to the past; the victims of this history have to be aware that "history" is never ended. So, although Felix appears to be committed to a definition of history that is tied to the past, the history of anciens régimes, his own continuing sense of disqualification as a Jew, and his attempts to remedy that condition reflect his functional sense of an ongoing history. Acting on that understanding, Felix devotes his life to the hope that he can overcome his "outcast" status through reverence for the history, Christian and aristocratic, that excludes him. Barnes describes such submission as necessary and almost automatic: she refers to "the degradation by which his people had survived. . . . [T]he genuflexion the hunted body makes from muscular contraction, going down before the impending and inaccessible, as before a great heat" (*N*, 2) and describes Felix as "heavy with impermissible blood" (*N*, 3).

This history of social marginality and its accompaniment of persecution that Barnes invokes at the beginning of *Nightwood* provide a framework within which the social positions of all of the characters in the book are circumscribed: Frau Mann and the other circus performers; Matthew O'Connor, transvestite homosexual and doctor of dubious credentials; and the lesbians, Nora Flood, Robin Vote, and Jenny Petherbridge. Felix's position as a member of a group that appears in the history of the official record, even though only to be recorded as marginal and persecuted, offers a clarifying pattern. This pattern allows Barnes to elaborate her account of the parallel but more complete disqualification of her lesbian and gay characters from that record and, at the same time, to connect them to its history. With the bridge provided by the paradigm of Felix's story, their part of the "story of the world" can also be recorded.

She uses Jewish history and the relation of Jews to the dominant Christian culture to suggest something for which there was then almost no trace of a record, the history of lesbians and homosexual men. Such a connection of the experience of Jews and homosexuals was obviously not without its historical precedents. *Nightwood* indicates that Barnes was aware of the parallel between anti-Semitism and hostility toward gays in the European social context in which she was living and writing.[5] The work of Marcel Proust also provides a major contemporary intertext to *Nightwood*. J.E. Rivers has argued that *A la récherche du temps perdu* (1913–29) is structured around a parallel between Jewish and homosexual experience within a society dominated by Christianity and heterosexuality and hostile to both minorities.[6] Proust explicitly compared the social and historical experiences of Jews and gays in the first part of *Sodome et Gomorrhe* (1921), using Jewish stereotypes and history as analogies to illustrate his account of homosexuality.[7] Barnes was familiar with this work and particularly interested in Proust's account of homosexuality.[8] In *Nightwood* her account of the relation of Jews to the dominant culture, expressed through their relation to the history of that culture, is completely interwoven with her account of her lesbian and gay characters. When Guido Volkbein is described as an "outcast" and when she refers to Felix's "impermissible blood" (*N*, 3), these terms must also be credited to her history of the Doctor, Robin Vote, and Nora Flood. The story of Guido and Felix Volkbein and their obsession with history is thus integral to *Nightwood*, not in real or false competition with but as a contribution to the central concern with Robin and Nora.⁹

Both women are explicitly located outside the history of the official record. Barnes concludes her only extended description of Nora with the observation that "the world and its history were to Nora like a ship in a bottle; she herself was outside and unidentified" (*N*, 53). Felix observes Robin after their marriage: "He felt that her attention, somehow in spite of him, had already been taken by some thing not yet in history. Always she seemed to be listening to the echo of some foray in the blood that had no known setting" (*N*, 44). The explanation of a "foray in the blood" to which Robin is listening recalls Felix's "impermissible blood" (*N*, 3), the cargo of the "hunted body," and is also implicitly a sexual suggestion. The official record has no setting for these women because they are lesbians.

At the same time they are both presented in the context of detailed historical trappings, from Nora's salon where "early American history was being re-enacted" (*N*, 51) to the antique cloth from which Robin initially has her dresses made. This is in part Barnes' acknowledgment of the fundamental paradox of their relation to history, as outsiders whose stories are nevertheless being recorded. It is also an indication within the text of her consciousness of dependence on the official history that these trappings all invoke, the necessity of establishing some relation to that record in order to be recorded. She makes this point overtly as part of her explanation of Felix, arguing that Jews only exist in a Christian-dominated society as outcasts from, and at the same time dependents on, the religion and therefore the history that denies them:

A Jew's undoing is never his own, it is God's; his rehabilitation is never his own, it is a Christian's. The Christian traffic in retribution has made the Jew's history a commodity; it is the medium through which he receives, at the necessary moment, the serum of his own past that he may offer it again as his blood. In this manner the Jew participates in the two conditions; and in like manner Felix took the breast of this wet nurse whose milk was his being but which could never be his birthright. (*N*, 10)

Christian control of Jewish history is a function of the politics of cultural domination. But given this, Felix's relation to history, even though it is negative, is the necessary basis for his existence within the dominant culture, and by extension, the only means through which his story can be told within that culture. Similarly, the fact that Robin and Nora's story can be told at all is contingent on a relation to the official record, in this case the relation that Barnes establishes within her own text, superficially with historical trappings but critically through the framework of Jewish history.

Felix's relation to history is also a focus for the inevitable tensions within this project. As Nora and Robin can only be brought into the record by analogy with those who are officially recognized as marginal and potentially persecuted, they will also be locked into that role. But the contradiction of this marginal position is acted out to its conclusion within the novel by Felix. His gestures of reverence toward "history," toward those individuals and institutions legitimized by the official record, become the definitive sign of his own disqualification from that history.

Barnes was also aware of the implications of the actions she recorded for her own practice. The glimpse of Jewish history that we are given at the beginning of the novel—Guido's memory of the fifteenth century—indicates more than the persecution of the Jews, which is, paradoxically, the means by which they enter the dominant history. As a graphic image of the fate of those outcasts whose stories are partially recorded (objects of ridicule whose pain is entertaining to those whom history routinely secures), it also expresses the anxiety about the result of her own record that pervades Barnes' text. At the beginning of *Nightwood* she says of Felix, "He felt that the great past might mend a little if he bowed low enough, if he succumbed and gave homage" (N, 9). The original title for the whole of *Nightwood* was to have been "Bow Down."[10] That became instead the title of the opening chapter, which is predominantly Felix's story. It is an explicit reference to Felix's abasement before the history of the official record. It also recalls the experience of the "hunted body" that made such abasement inevitable. That Barnes was willing to consider a description of abasement as representative of the whole book is indicative of the anxiety at the center of *Nightwood*. Barnes' fundamental defiance of "history" is accompanied by her own consciousness of the "hunted body." Felix Volkbein, with his "impermissible blood," provides a paradigm for the relation of the author, as well as her characters, to the official record. Barnes' apprehension of the meanings, the effects, and history's interpretation of her own insistence on the place of these stories in the record can be seen behind her clear account of the abasement that Felix accepts in order to establish his own relation to history and thus his existence. This is an apprehension that echoes also in *The Antiphon*, where Dudley describes Miranda as a child:

> You had her so convinced she was the devil,
> At seven, she was cutting down the hedges,
> To furnish brier to beat her to your favour;
> All time since, been hunting for the crime. (A, 164)

Augusta responds later in the play with the charge against her daughter, "She gives her weapons to the enemy" (A, 162).

These images of humiliation, these charges and countercharges, are the expression of an anxiety based on history in the most concrete sense. If you announce your "impermissible blood," your "disqualification," to the world, perhaps especially in the process of asserting your right to a record, to history, then you are telling those whose power history always confirms where to find you. Such a consciousness would hardly have been excessive in the Europe of the 1930s. Given that Barnes was recording experience that was historically condemned, it is not possible to separate the conditions of her writing from history. But she was also faced with specifically literary difficulties: the absence of literary conventions for writing about lesbianism as other than sickness or evil, as well as the fundamental prohibition against the subject that that absence represented. By choosing to locate her writing explicitly within the framework of history she was then able to deal with those literary difficulties, as well as the political situation they reflect, by translating them from literary into historical problems and shifting the burden from her own shoulders onto her characters. The marginality of the Jews within the history of a Christian-dominated society, and the conflict that could generate in people required to humiliate themselves in order to survive, was more accessible as a subject to writer and readers than was the exclusion of homosexuals from a heterosexist history, the social and political humiliation exacted from the lesbian if she is to survive. Also, the exclusions, persecutions, and humiliations of history were easier to map than the exclusions, persecutions, and humiliations reflected in or required by literary history and conventions: the difficulties of political-historical survival are easier to record than the difficulties of writing. But the anxiety within Barnes' text reflects the difficulty of her literary as well as her historical situation.

The pervasive connection between literature and history operating within *Nightwood* appears on the most superficial level in the number of historical references that are also literary references: Helen of Troy and Catherine of Russia are touchstones of equal value. But the actual link is forged through her interchangeable use of "history" and "stories," which leads into a refrain of statements about "telling" and its conditions. The Doctor's initial discussion of history in *Nightwood* is about stories, "stories that do not amount to much" because they befall people who may be "nature's noblemen" but who are not history's aristocrats. In the Doctor's final speeches, when he seems to be making a narrator's apology despite the fact that he is not the narrator, he defends the alternative histories Barnes has recorded before an imaginary "normal" audience whom he assumes would scorn and ridicule his friends: "Only the scorned and the ridiculous make good stories . . . so you can imagine when you'll get told!" (N, 159). He denies that this record is a betrayal in the same terms: "Nora, beating her head against her heart . . . rotten to the bone for love of Robin. . . . And that old sandpiper, Jenny! Oh, it's a grand bad story, and who says I'm a betrayer? I say, tell the story of the world to the world" (N, 161). On the one hand, the insistent references to telling implicitly deny the fact that the story is being written. They also make the Doctor's self-defense possible: "I wouldn't be telling you about it if I weren't talking to myself" (N, 163). The implied refusal to acknowledge the permanence of the record that is being made is inextricable from the anxiety also expressed in the references to scorn, ridicule, and betrayal. This apprehension is produced by the telling of the story itself, as well as the real pain that is the subject of the story. It is this anxiety that ultimately underscores the fact that the record is irreversible, the story is being told "to the world," that is, is being written.

Anxiety about the stories being told, about her own challenging of history, especially as expressed through the Doctor's framing statements, is more than a self-conscious context within the text for the production of its alternative record. This conflict about whether these stories should be told is part of the story Barnes records, in *Nightwood* and in *The Antiphon*. The question of history, the record, incorporating both history and writing, is a framework and also a central concern of both texts. Toward the conclusion of *Nightwood* Dr. O'Connor argues with Nora's grief: "If you, who are blood-thirsty with love, had left her alone, what? Would a lost girl in Dante's time have been a lost girl still, and he had turned his eyes on her? She would have been remembered, and the remembered put on the dress of immunity. Do you think that Robin had no right to fight you with her only weapon? She saw in you that fearful eye that would make her a target forever" (N, 148). Barnes is referring to history, Dante's time, by means of a literary figure, Dante. As Dante was a writer, the implied connection between his having seen the lost girl and her being remembered is that he would have written about her. The conclusion is that to have been recorded by Dante, and so to become part of the official literature and history he represents, would be to become immune, safe. But safe from what? The fact that immunity is described as a dress is indicative. The lost girl, Robin, described elsewhere as a "girl with the body of a boy" (N, 46), would have been certified as heterosexual, as the object of a male poet's gaze. The shift in the center of the passage, to the negative fate that Nora's love for Robin implies, is the shift from the safety of being recorded as a heterosexual love object, to the prospect of being loved, and recorded, by a woman, being made a "target forever" by a woman's gaze.

There is an underlying ambiguity: the distinction between the possibility of being remembered/recorded by Dante and by Nora/Barnes is not clear-cut. Dante is the poet of heterosexual love, in the *Vita Nuova*, but is also the poet of religious and social judgment, in the *Divina Commedia*. As such, he represents a literature and a history that are strictly ordered and that are based throughout on an elaborate system of reward and damnation, of which one of the subjects is sexual behavior. Dante, seeing a lost *girl*, might have made her Beatrice, the object of his love poetry, forever narrowly and safely defined. Or, seeing a *lost* girl, he might have remembered her only to record her as a lesbian, a sinner, making her a "target forever" in the appropriate circle of Hell. The question of which gaze, which record, would damn or save a woman, remains unanswered. But it is clear that being made part of a lesbian record is "fearful." The Doctor is pointing to a struggle between Nora and Robin over the question of whether or not there would be a record, and indicating that that struggle was fundamental to the destruction of their relationship, and so to the story Barnes is recording.

Yet the question of a record is presented only indirectly in this passage, through the reference to a writer. And instead of saying explicitly that Dante would have desired and then written about the lost girl, and in his writing secured her reputation, Barnes uses the term "remembered" to indicate both the desire and the record. Throughout this passage Barnes equates the gaze, "looking at her," with memory, memory with love, and love and memory with writing, being remembered with being both loved and recorded.

"Memory" subsumes both history and literature, becoming the material of history and the means of writing. Barnes' anxiety about writing is worked out within her stories through the values of remembering and forgetting and the conflicts between them. The Doctor does not say that the stories of the common people will not be written into history; he says they will be forgotten. The stories of the "high and mighty" will also not explicitly be written; they will be remembered. He tells us that we fear "memory" of the "disorder" of "destiny and history" (*N*, 118). The history of the official record becomes "our faulty racial memory" (*N*, 118). Doctor O'Connor initially declares that the only effort that can be made against exclusion from history is individual, to remember oneself.

Memory is the basis of Barnes' attempt to challenge the history of the official record, the source of the alternative stories she is recording. Memory is the fundamental mode of her texts themselves: *Nightwood* and *The Antiphon* are in part Barnes' personal acts of memory. She was writing against the absorption of her own history into the simple negatives used to define a woman without a man, the voice of the son and brother in *The Antiphon* who decries his sister Miranda as a "manless, childless, safeless document" (*A*, 179). Memory is also an action taken by characters within the text, especially Nora in *Nightwood* and Miranda in *The Antiphon*.

As Barnes' history has little relation to the conventional distinctions between past and present, Barnes' memory has no usual relation to forgetting. Augusta declares in *The Antiphon*, "I would be Helen / Forgotten, day by day, for ever and for ever!" (*A*, 207). In *Nightwood* the Doctor explains to Nora, "because you forget Robin the best, it's to you she turns. She comes trembling, and defiant, and belligerent, all right—that you may give her back to herself again as you have forgotten her" (*N*, 152–53). But Helen is manifestly not forgotten. And Nora has just been telling the Doctor that her love means she cannot forget Robin: "Robin can go anywhere, do anything . . . because she forgets, and I nowhere because I remember" (*N*, 152). Memory encompasses forgetting, because a person or story must come within the frame of memory before she or it can be forgotten. To remember is the definitive gesture, because memory, identified with both history and writing, shares attributes of both. It functions like the history of the official record to the extent that whatever is outside the range of memory might as well not exist. It is necessary to come within the range of memory, as it is necessary to come or be brought into the range of history. At the same time, memory is synonymous with writing. Because of the potential historical seriousness of any record, Barnes is very aware that what has been written cannot be unwritten, as what is remembered cannot be forgotten in the sense that it could be beyond recall or consequence.

Memory is a source of conflict, between Robin and Nora in *Nightwood* and between Augusta and Miranda in *The Antiphon*. Nora remembered Robin, which meant remembering her drunkenness and nighttime world as well as their love. After Robin has gone Nora tells the Doctor, "She turned bitter because I made her fate colossal. She wanted darkness in her mind—to throw a shadow over what she was powerless to alter—her dissolute life, her life at night; and I, I dashed it down" (*N*, 156). In *The Antiphon* the ostensible source of the conflict between Augusta and Miranda is the daughter's denial of the mother's false version of history in general and family history in particular. When the facts of Miranda's childhood are revealed Augusta curses: "Wolves! Mountebanks! Historians!" (*A*, 186).

Memory is such a source of conflict because it bears the weight of writing, of history as record. It is the connection between the events within the text and the construction of the text. So when Robin fights Nora or Augusta resists Miranda it is in part because of the written record that is pending, that Nora and Miranda represent, couched in the terms of memory. But memory is, as writing, a source of conflict chiefly because of what would be remembered/written, which is the other attribute of memory, love. Robin might not want her drunkenness recorded. Augusta has reason to want the story of her husband's cruelty to her daughter suppressed. But it is not Robin's alcoholism which, recorded, will make her a "target forever." Augusta, struggling against Miranda's knowledge of family history and against Miranda's warnings about the murderous intentions of the sons her mother prefers to her daughter, is also struggling against her daughter's love. "Who's Miranda?" she asks: "I can't afford her / She's only me" (*A*, 162). This echoes Nora's explanation of love between women in the previous work: "A man is another person—a woman is yourself, caught as you turn in panic; on her mouth you kiss your own. If she is taken you cry that you have been robbed of yourself. God laughs at me, but his laughter is my love" (*N*, 143). Memory is fought because it is the memory, the record of a love that can be described as "God's laughter," that could make the lovers "scorned and ridiculous" (*N*, 159).

Memory, as an act of love, is a sexual act. Felix, talking of Robin's sexual attractiveness, comments, "The Baronin had an undefinable disorder, or sort of 'odour of memory,' like a person who has come from some place that we have forgotten and would give our life to recall" (*N*, 118). Nora remembers and describes to the Doctor a specific scene: "and I knew that in that bed Robin should have put me down. In that bed we would have forgotten our lives in the extremity of memory, moulted our parts, as figures in the waxworks who are moulted down to their story, so we would have broken down to our love" (*N*, 158). Memory becomes sex. The story becomes love. But the lovers are represented as figures in waxworks, that is, as figures from history, historical characters. Memory is a sexual act, and the story that would have been remembered is a story of love which is identified with history.

As a lesbian Barnes has every reason to see a connection between sex and history. In the *Ladies Almanack* she records in comic terms very real historical changes in social attitudes and sexual possibility for lesbians. She recounts how in the 1920s Dame Musset had almost to fight off women who in the 1880s she would have had to coax and cajole into her embrace. The narrator laments that what was once a matter of secrecy and trembling is now talked abroad at every slightest opportunity. Although only part of any full account of the times, these observations indicate that the *Almanack* was grounded in an accurate historical understanding of lesbian experience.[11] Decades later *The Antiphon*, with its account of the rape of the daughter ordered by the father and attended by the complicitous silence of the mother, suggests a very specific sexual secret at the heart of its history of the family.

The difference between the lesbian sexual assumption of the *Almanack* and the domination of heterosexuality in *The Antiphon* produced very different accounts of history and uses of history in each work. In the *Almanack* the chronology of many years is inverted into the chronology of one year; the passage of time from the 1880s to the 1920s and from birth to death in Dame Musset's ninety-nine-year lifetime is recorded between a January and the next December. Barnes then scatters through her text a lesbian genesis story that takes place after the fall of Satan, as well as references to such diverse historical locations as the Old Testament and colonial America. She also records changing attitudes towards lesbianism between the 1880s and the 1920s while failing to mention World War I. But such disruptions of any official record of history, which seem to be the product of the *Almanack*'s lesbian sexual energy, are very distant from *The Antiphon*. Although Barnes was writing in the late 1940s and early 1950s, the later work is very clearly located in the history of the official record by its setting at the beginning of World War II. This wartime setting is emphasized by the presence of passing refugees who are frequently referred to and occasionally directed to appear. The play begins when Miranda and Jack arrive as refugees themselves from the Nazi invasion of Paris. The house to which they have come, the immediate setting of the play, is described in detail as the historic family residence. Although the play is full of other references to history, it is the history of the official record: Tudors, Nazis, courtesans, and warriors.

In both the *Ladies Almanack* and *Nightwood* Barnes had already identified the history of the official record as male. As already noted, the narrator of the *Almanack*, looking for a lesbian history, protests, "Were all Giants' doings a Man's? . . . No time without God, no end without Christ!" (*LA*, 70). At the beginning of *Nightwood* the institutions of the official record—the aristocracy, the military, and Christianity—are temporarily embodied in the female figure of Hedvig Volkbein. But this has the effect of masculinizing the woman: " When she danced, a little heady with wine, the dance floor had become a tactical manoeuvre; her heels had come down staccato and trained, her shoulders as conscious at the tips as those which carry the braid and tassels of promotion; the turn of her head had held the cold vigilance of a sentry whose rounds are not without apprehension" (*N*, 4). Her Jewish husband, Guido, sees that Hedvig "had the same bearing" as "a general in creaking leather," and "looking at the two he had become confused as if he were about to receive a reprimand, not the officer's but his wife's" (*N*, 4.)

The oppositional relation of both the *Almanack* and *Nightwood* to the history of the official record, as well as such statements as the Doctor's that "history, because of its actors, is deflowered" (*N*, 15), imply that history is also heterosexual. By the time she wrote *The Antiphon* Barnes was willing to identify heterosexuality and masculinity overtly with the history of the aristocracy, Christianity, and the military—the Nazis who had driven Miranda from Paris. Jack/Jeremy describes the war at the beginning of the play in terms of an attack on the histories of Barnes' previous works:

> *I expect to see myopic conquerors*
> *With pebbled monocles and rowel'd heels,*
> *In a damned and horrid clutch of gluttony*
> *Dredging the Seine of our inheritance.*
> *Or dragging from the Tiber and the Thames*
> *Cruppers, bridles, bits and casket handles;*
> *Rocking-horses and sabres from the fair.*
> *Trawling the Hellespont for log and legend*
> *And all things whatsoever out of grasp.* (*A*, 91)

"Legend" is one of the terms the Doctor uses in *Nightwood* to describe the stories of those who are excluded from the history of the "high and mighty." Carousel horses, "rocking horses . . . from the fair," are part of the furnishings of the house that Nora and Robin create as a monument to their love (*N*, 58).

In *The Antiphon* this war is enacted within the family. Masculinity and heterosexuality are united with history in the person of the father. Augusta makes this identification explicit when she sees the image of Titus, her husband, reduced to a doll figure and is able to indulge in a moment of temporary repudiation:

> *How do we thaw from history. How many*
> *To this splinter have, like porcupines,*
> *Made careful love? What apes our eyes were*
> *Saw him great because he said so. (A, 183)*

The act of accepting that history is sexual. This is illustrated in the course of the play by Augusta. Her position relative to the history of the official record is parallel to that of Felix in *Nightwood*; like Felix she is obsessed with her relation to history and unable to recognize the humiliation this forces on her. She "would be Helen," "Empress Josephine," or "Lily Langtry . . . waiting on the inert Prince of somewhere" (A, 199). Her sexual relation, real or fantasy, with the "Prince of somewhere," is a heterosexual woman's claim on history. When her daughter remains obdurately skeptical, Augusta becomes only more frantic in her reconstructions:

> *Never checked a visitor's knobs and bosses*
> *On any field of any Marathon?*
> *Nor never, in great joy, kissed on the mouth*
> *By a mouth deposed between me and the kissing? (A, 200)*

Miranda comments on the futility of Augusta's history, summarizing all of the roles her mother imagines and uniting them with the domestic service that is their corollary: "O unhappy wanderer—/I've seen you dig for Antony/With a kitchen spoon" (A, 200).

In *The Antiphon* the opposition to that history of the official record finally vested in the father and his sexual authority (to which the mother's sexual submission is tribute) is carried on by the dissident daughter.[12] The fact that the father is dead only reinforces the lesson of his power, as the authority he embodied and the patterns of male power and female submission it created are replicated even in his absence in the relations to his wife and sons, and their joint rejections of the daughter. The absence of the father also makes it clear that the mother is the ground of the daughter's struggle. In this context the lesson at the center of history becomes the first lesson the daughter learns, and it is a sexual lesson, that of her father's favored access to her mother and of her own female inferiority. Her own existence is proof of the first part of this lesson. The proof of its corollary is that the mother will never be for her. Unlike the Freudian daughter, this girl-child does not agree to transfer her desire from her mother to her father. Unlike the Freudian son, waiting until adulthood will not change her situation, will not provide her with a wife/mother of her own. "History" begins with the heterosexual "facts of life." So history, whether explicitly identified with the father or not, is the first and ultimate antagonist, and the battle—to love, to remember, to write—is inescapably within history, and always in part a sexual contest.

When Bounding Bess in the *Ladies Almanack* and Robin Vote in *Nightwood* look to the women of history, even women they have "come to connect with women" (*N*, 47), as Barnes explains the quality that attracts Robin's attention, most of the women they look to are renowned as heterosexual lovers. That Sappho, "singing over the limp Bodies of Girls" (*LA*, 32), is the only obviously appropriate model recalled seems to predicate Barnes' own defeat, to lead directly to Augusta's "kitchen spoon" and the lesson of the father's sexual authority in *The Antiphon*.

Barnes was not, however, defeated by the limits of the official record. As suggested by her presentation of both Sappho and Catherine of Russia, "twittering over a Man at ten" (*LA*, 32), as models for Bounding Bess, she did not distinguish between female sexuality and specifically lesbian sexuality. Despite the fact that the ladies of the *Ladies Almanack* are indirectly referred to as women "born with a Difference" (*LA*, 26), one such woman explains:

"from where, say you, come such Women? Up from the Cellar, down from the Bed of Matrimony, under Sleep and over come. Past watching Eye and seeking Hand and well over Hedge. From Pantry and Bride's-sleep, in Mid-conception and old Age, from Bank and Culvert, from Bog's Dutch and Fen's marrow, from all walks and all paths, from round Doors and drop Lofts, from Hayricks and Cabbage-patch, from King's Thrones and Clerks' Stools. . . . Indeed, some of all sorts, to swarm in that wide Acre where, beside some brawling March, the first of shes turned up a Hem with the Hand of Combat."

"Too true for you, perchance," admitted her Love. "But nevertheless, did not some and several return to their Posts?" "Indeed, and a few . . . but *how*!" (*LA*, 53–54)

Because such women can come "from the Bed of Matrimony," the mother retains a powerful promise. In *Nightwood* Robin chooses the apartment she and Nora will live in in Paris, it is implied, because, "Looking from the long windows one saw a fountain figure, a tall granite woman bending forward with lifted head; one hand was held over the pelvic round as if to warn a child who goes incautiously" (*N*, 55). Perhaps to redeem the mother would be to redeem all of the women of history, Helen, Cleopatra, and Catherine. So Miranda struggles wither her mother even as Barnes illustrates, through Augusta's continuing hostility to her daughter, the strength of the father's power.

Barnes' writing is predicated on such contradictions. She records for history what she acknowledges is not part of history, insists on remembering what she defines as the forgotten. She incorporates the potential denial of her texts into the texts themselves. She subverts her own recognition of the limits and conditions of history and literature. Dr. O'Connor confronts Nora with the contrast between the security that Dante's heterosexual gaze would convey, and the fearful fate that her own lesbian gaze implies, for the lost girl, Robin. But this lesson is undercut finally because the Doctor, Matthew-Mighty-grain-of-salt-Dante-O'Connor, is also Dante himself, and this Dante does assume the role of narrator within the text. The debate has been decided in that the story is being recorded. Such contradictions are necessary because contradiction is fundamental to Barnes' work. As she acknowledged in the *Ladies Almanack*, she was writing stories that "could be printed nowhere and in no Country" (*LA*, 34). In *Nightwood* the Doctor insists, "Life is not to be told, call it as loud as you like, it will not tell itself" (*N*, 129). Yet her stories were told and were printed.[13]

The author herself is finally in a contradictory relationship to such work. Barnes made a gesture toward anonymity in her most explicitly lesbian work: the title page of the *Ladies Almanack* bears the legend, "By a Lady of Fashion." But as she began her alternative history of the love between Nora Flood and Robin Vote she wrote of Robin, "Two spirits were working in her, love and anonymity" (*N*, 55). The logic and the tension of this pairing—love and anonymity—depend on history, the prohibition against lesbianism. They also depend on Barnes' own identification of love, by means of memory, with writing. If love must be written, the writer is faced with the difficulties of writing this love and at the same time with the danger of losing the beloved, a beloved "fearful" of being made a "target forever" within history. If love and anonymity are set in opposition, for the beloved—by the connections between love, memory, and writing—they are also opposed for the lover/writer. Loving and therefore remembering and writing love inevitably brings the lover/writer back to telling the self. There is the fear that the only response will be scorn and ridicule, or alternatively that history will respond. As the Doctor, brought to bay, declares, "And What am I? I'm damned, and carefully public!" (*N*, 163).

As Barnes' connection of writing and loving may cost the writer her beloved, the difficulties of writing, behind the tension between love and anonymity, are also the difficulties of loving. So in *Nightwood* memory is an attempt to hold love. Nora's last message to Robin is, as she advises the Doctor: "Tell her, if you ever see her, that it is always with her in my arms—forever it will be that way until we die. Tell her to do what she must, but not to forget" (*N*, 150). From the beginning of their love, Barnes records, "Robin . . . kept repeating . . . her wish for a home, as if she were afraid she would be lost again, as if she were aware, without conscious knowledge, that she belonged to Nora, and that if Nora did not make it permanent by her own strength, she would forget" (*N*, 55). This need is re-emphasized by the Doctor's delivery of Robin's last message: "She says, 'Remember me.' Probably because she has difficulty remembering herself" (*N*, 121). Barnes records this history to make it easier for the lesbian Robin to remember herself.

The connection between sexuality and history that Barnes eventually elaborated was starkly presented in an early story, "Cassation":

A great war painting hung over the bed; the painting and the bed ran together in encounter, the huge rumps of the stallions reined into the pillows. The generals, with foreign helmets and dripping swords, raging through rolling smoke and the bleeding ranks of the dying, seemed to be charging the bed, so large, so rumpled, so devastated. The sheets were trailing, the counterpane hung torn, and the feathers shivered along the floor, trembling in the slight wind from the open window. (*SW*, 14)

By the beginning of *Nightwood* the bed has itself become a battlefield, on which Hedvig Volkbein, exhausted by struggling against the unspoken alienation of her "outcast" Jewish husband, gives birth to the son who will carry on his father's struggle with history:

. . . a canopied bed of a rich spectacular crimson, the valance stamped with the bifurcated wings of the House of Hapsburg, the feather coverlet an envelope of satin on which, in massive and tarnished gold threads, stood the Volkbein arms. . . . Turning upon this field, which shook to the clatter of morning horses in the street beyond, with the gross splendour of a general saluting the flag, she named . . . [the child] Felix, thrust him from her, and died. (*N*, 1)

In the final work, *The Antiphon*, Miranda is given a bed made from a carousel car, and shaped like a mythical animal, a gryphon. Her mother—refusing to deny the father, denying instead Miranda's account of history—will neither let her sleep there nor make love to her. Across that bed the women, struggling, die.

Earlier in the play Barnes had drawn on an echo of *King Lear*:

AUGUSTA: You won't even tell me how you are, or what.
MIRANDA: Trappist—sprung—and of an hard-won silence.
AUGUSTA: Nothing else about your history?
MIRANDA: Nothing.
AUGUSTA: Nothing at all?
MIRANDA: Nothing at all. (*A*, 202–3)

Lear asked his daughter for a protestation of her love for him, which she refused to make. Augusta, asking for Miranda's history, is also asking for an avowal of her love, as her "history" is her love for women, the lesbian memory never explicitly spoken in this play. What the mother expects is a statement of love for the father. What she cannot hear is a statement of love for herself. In their final struggle Augusta accuses her daughter: "I know you. You are the one would lay / Me ticking down, ten cities deep!" (*A*, 222). To be laid ticking down, to be buried alive, is the fate of Antigone. Ten cities deep is the site of the history of Helen of Troy. To be buried alive beneath a myth is the fate of women within the history of the official record, the history of the father. Miranda denies that history, offering instead an alternative sexual fate as an alternative history. "Nay, sparrow," she protests, "I'd lay you in the journey of your bed, / And un-bed you, and I could, in paradise" (*A*, 222).

¶ Another attractive institution in Cambridge was the Poet's Theatre, which held about eighty people. It was a jewel of a small theatre, with a proper stage, wings, footlights and all. The actors were students and the performances were put on of an evening. Here, one evening, we came upon T.S. Eliot and Djuna Barnes, at a performance of Dick Wilbur's translation of Molière's *Misanthrope*. Djuna Barnes, who had known Eliot since he was a very young man in Paris, was treating him with easy, affectionate camraderie and he was responding with an equally easy gaiety that I had never seen in him before. As I put it to myself: Tom Eliot is much more human here than in England. He was less deliberate, less cautious, smiling more easily, spontaneous in repartee, enjoying the teasing he was getting from Djuna. Neither Edwin nor I had met Djuna before and we were both drawn to her on sight: a tall, gallant, high-spirited woman with a faint suggestion of rakish adventure and fun about her, difficult to define but very likeable. In her company Eliot seemed to have shed some English drilling and become more American. This impression was only confirmed when we met two aunts of his, little old ladies who told us: "Tom is so good to us, he has taken us to Schrafft's and given us steaks."

—Willa Muir,
Belonging (1968)

¶ . . . It [*The Antiphon*] is a work that has had a strange reception; liked by the best people, at once or slowly, others being so silent, you could hear it! Some damning it on Monday to come back to praise it on Tuesday, some praising it on Tuesday to return on the day-after to tear its head off. Eliot said it was a "cosmic explosion," and the curator of the British Museum, or was it the London University Library, said it was of the "greatest magnitude," etc. etc. and then there is of course the fact that Mr. Hammarskjold liked it enough to get it on the stage in Sweden, and the heart warming appreciation of Edwin Muir . . . in this wretched world, as near to a saint as you are like to meet.

—Djuna Barnes,
letter to Wolfgang Hildesheimer,
28 March 1966

¶ . . . I told the newspaper man how pleased I was with the startling insight shown by that particular reviewer [of *The Antiphon*], but that he, the writer, had the play's motivations (in part) wrong, as "Miranda did complete the guilt of her mother . . . Miranda accuses herself of lascivious desires by accusing Augusta . . ."! That Jack was trying to "redeem Miranda while attacking Augusta"! Jack is not trying to redeem anyone, Miranda did not complete the guilt of her mother, her act was vindication of her mother for "belief" in the father's "crusade"—and nowhere does Miranda accuse herself of lasciviousness, or for that matter her mothers . . . she exclaimed against her mothers effort to live her life through her . . . I'm afraid it's a very difficult play.

> —Djuna Barnes,
> letter to James Burns Singer
> (reviewer of *The Antiphon* for *TLS*),
> 25 May 1959

The Antiphon: "No Audience at All"?

Meryl Altman

> Courtesy requires that when you speak
> You make it more than silence.
> —Burley, *The Antiphon*

The Antiphon, Djuna Barnes' only full-length drama, is intimately concerned with questions of speech and silence, with the use of the dramatic mask and the histrionic voice both to reveal and to conceal.[1] It is quite a different proposition, however, to claim as some critics have done that *The Antiphon* is itself silent: inscrutable, unplayable, inviolably private by accident or by design. *The Antiphon* is, to be sure, an extremely complicated work, both verbally and emotionally. Like the late, high-modernist works of Joyce, Pound, and Beckett, the play is dense with words and phrases—and with feelings—that point in many directions at once, that demand a close and committed reading, a carefully attuned ear. Unraveling a Barnes text to discover her intentions is never a simple task, and since her intentions are complex and multiple, such unraveling would be reductive and unsatisfying. But it is insufficient and unfair to claim for this reason that the drama is so intensely personal that the author intended it to speak of and to only one person, and that it is interesting to us only as an example of pathology;[2] or, alternately, to claim that it is purely an exercise in vocabulary or verbal "tricks," interesting to us only as an example of modernism gone haywire.[3] Like the gryphon that is central to its stage decor and also to its metaphorical structure, *The Antiphon* synthesizes aspects of many preexisting forms and types; but the reader who complains that it is not, therefore, a "good" example of one of them, that the "average" audience would have been unable to place or understand it, is in the absurd position of calling a gryphon a failure because it is not a serviceable horse. Rather, we need to understand Barnes' expectations of the dramatic form by looking at her experience of the twentieth-century theater, and to listen to what *The Antiphon* itself tells us about the dangers, uses, and adaptations of the dramatic form.

271

It is important first of all to understand that *The Antiphon* is not a closet drama. Closet dramas at their most successful draw on a conception of character which is dramatic and not lyric; but they themselves are really long poems and not plays.[4] This distinction was well understood by authors such as Edna St. Vincent Millay, T.S. Eliot, and Gertrude Stein, who attempted, at different times, both closet drama and "real drama."

Barnes, who conceived *The Antiphon* in the hope that actors would someday realize it, also understood the difference.[5] The most cursory examination of the text of *The Antiphon* as we have it shows that it is a script and not a poem. More than a set of images to guide the imagination of a reader, her detailed physical settings can be seen as instructions to a designer, for realizing carefully thought-out, appropriate visual correlatives to the mood and action of the play. Her plan for the decor includes a gallery which various of the main characters ascend and descend, and upon which an "audience" of unrelated "strangers" occasionally and momentarily appears; this both enables the actors to use stage distances effectively to develop character and provides a symbolic frame for their action.[6] Barnes also provides descriptions of characters' gestures and manner of delivery, which, while they do guide us as readers in picturing actions we are not witnessing, were clearly intended to function as instructions to actors. Her introductory "Cautionary Note" explains the physical appearances and the motivations of her characters and the intended tone of dialogue (*A*, 79). And stage directions throughout—"hurriedly turning the prow end of the gryphon," "seating herself," "searching her pocket," "peering about," "spitting out shells"—explain what physical movement is attending the dialogue, while constant parenthetical adjectives and phrases—"spitefully," "ignoring this with contemptuous pity," "appraising Jack," "with troubled modesty"—suggest the manner in which Barnes wanted the lines to be delivered.[7]

For us readers, these directions function as hints or clues to help us imagine a play taking place as we read; to real actors or directors, they would be clues toward a fully realized interpretation. Perhaps critics who complain that *The Antiphon* is "static"[8] have failed to make this imaginative leap from script to performance, from reading about a woman named Augusta who says certain things to visualizing Augusta on a stage removing Miranda's shoes and putting them on her own feet while saying these things in a particular tone of voice. Moreover, these bits of business are not simply busyness; they illustrate character motivation and contribute to the symbolic intensity of the play. So, as Augusta step by step strips Miranda of her costume and, with Miranda's consent and help, assumes it herself—rings, shoes, hat—we watch the mother assuming the daughter's identity as her own, both compensating vicariously for her own disappointments and attacking the daughter for the very accomplishments and experiences she envies and wishes to usurp, and we understand that Miranda permits and colludes in this as well. Similarly, Miranda's slow descent from the gallery correlates to her unwilling, but finally total, abandonment of the detached or "silent" position of the writer/observer, placed among the audience, and her final reengagement with the emotional issues of the family battle. The very existence of this gallery, the provision for the vantage point of the spectator within the play, is crucial to *The Antiphon*'s self-referentiality, for this is a piece about theater as well as a piece of theater.

It should be remembered that Barnes' ideas about performance and staging were not the naive idealism of a poet or novelist who suddenly turns to writing for the stage. Rather they were the result of half a lifetime of practical experience and training, including involvement as both writer and actress with the Provincetown Playhouse and the Theatre Guild, and a short but intensive stint as drama critic and columnist for *Theatre Guild Magazine*. Barnes' ideas about the theater were formed in the early days of American experimental drama; she knew this movement not just as an observer, but as a participant.[9]

The Provincetown Playhouse, also called the "Playwright's Theatre," is best remembered for discovering and launching the career of Eugene O'Neill. But, as conceived of by Susan Glaspell and George Cram "Jig" Cook and remembered by Djuna Barnes in the first of her *Theatre Guild Magazine* articles,[10] the Provincetown was originally an idealistic and a collective enterprise. The early Provincetown group of which Barnes was a part did not foresee that they would later be fostering talent and creating productions that would move to Broadway as O'Neill soon did. Rather, they saw themselves as an experimental alternative, constituted in opposition to the commercial values of Broadway. While they sought constantly to improve their production values, they were proud of their status as "amateurs." The focus was, at least initially, on the play and the playwright—not the actors—and it was an integral part of the scheme that a member of the company might wear many hats: a playwright might also act, an actress might also design sets, a director might also take tickets.[11] Those who wrote for the Provincetown imagined an audience of like-minded Greenwich Villagers, people much like themselves, who would be willing to suspend expectations for an evening, to try on something new and argue passionately about it afterwards. Early experimental groups such as the Provincetown, the Washington Square Players, and the Actor's Group Theatre freed writers like O'Neill and Odets—and Barnes—to develop truly modern and experimental dramatic forms.

The irony with which the Provincetown was soon forced to struggle was that these forms could, after all, be commercially successful; and some would argue that in moving productions to larger houses and more general audiences the experimental theater movement lost its initial idealistic impulses. A later group like the Theatre Guild found itself straddling the gap between experiment and success in just this way, by employing professional actors like the Lunts to perform both "experimental classics" (Shaw, Chekhov, Ibsen, O'Neill) and new plays by unknowns, with the never-realized goal of becoming a true repertory theater. *Theatre Guild Magazine* in the years Barnes wrote for it reflects this paradox (or as some chose to regard it, this compromise) neatly; articles attacking censorship and setting out the latest trends in experimental set design run side by side with advertisements for expensive furs, country homes, and Packard automobiles. But it bears reiterating that the initial impulse behind all this was one of tolerance, experiment, the search for the new.[12]

This understanding of Barnes' background in the theater helps answer the hostile rhetorical question, "Whatever can Djuna Barnes have been thinking of when she wrote *The Antiphon*?" Remembering the context of her dramatic development can help us see why Barnes, in the 1950s, wrote an emotionally and intellectually taxing play, in verse, and expected not only that it would be performed by a company equal to its demands but that it would find an audience and perhaps make money. Who, after all, would have predicted the tremendous success achieved by *The Emperor Jones*? Despite the pessimism for which Barnes is famous, the form of *The Antiphon* argues, I believe, a probably unjustified optimism about the seriousness and engagement of American theater professionals and American audiences.

But Barnes turned her attention back to the theater for other reasons as well. By convention, a dramatic character gradually reveals himself or herself by the presentation of a series of poses or fictions, with the audience in the position of voyeur. This form, Barnes realized, was particularly appropriate to her final examination of the poses, fictions, deceptions, and self-deceptions that she believed characterized the relations between the sexes and within the family. In 1929 she had remembered the days when her first plays were written, the "Days of Jig Cook," in this way:

We used to sit in groups and recall our earlier and divergent histories. One would say, "I was well smacked by my mother for chewing the paint off the gate post"; another maintained that he had learned the value of madness when his father jumped from a window in an effort to prove gravity, and was picked up convinced. So we talked, and so we went our separate ways home, there to write out of that confusion which is biography when it is wedded to fact, confession and fancy in any assembly of friends versus friend and still friends.

Of such things were our plays made. Eugene O'Neill wrote out of a dark suspicion that there was injustice in fatherly love. Floyd Dell wrote archly out of a conviction that he was Anatole France. I wrote out of a certitude that I was my father's daughter.[13]

Barnes was returning to a core of autobiographical material — "confusion . . . wedded to fact, confession and fancy" — on which she had drawn before, first in her one-act play *Three from the Earth*, and then in *Ryder*, and which she had previously interpreted in very different ways. As Burley, in *The Antiphon*, recognizes, "The lily, onion, and confessional/Have many layers. Pare on" (*SW*, 110). And in returning to this material she also returned to the theater. What better way to set forth and then pare away a many-layered deception and mystery than through the medium of actors, themselves mask-wearers by profession?

A clue to this motivation is provided by another of Barnes' *Theatre Guild* pieces, "Why Actors? Brother Sumac Searches for an Answer." In this piece, a sort of mock interview, Brother Sumac (who sounds rather like Dr. Matthew Mighty-grain-of-sand O'Connor) makes a pilgrimage to Rome to ask the Bearded Wonder, Dona Barbetta del Rabis, some questions about morality and the stage. The wise woman does not answer, but the questions are themselves revealing:

Dona Barbetta, I ask you, why are actors and actresses, and for what are they good?

Because I am a holy man, Dona Barbetta, I have seen many sorrowful things. Men wanting to be Napoleon, and women wanting to be Helen of Troy, and little children wanting to be policemen. Therefore this passion in the human heart to be something it is not, is no secret to me, yet it troubles me, for I am not sure if it is true aspiration or a terrible and unholy criticism of the Most High, and this I must know, for I myself have wanted to be other than I am. . . .

How sinful then is an actress, Dona Barbetta del Rabis, and how sinful an actor? Are they not much of the time persons that they have not even thought of, but have been invented by those other mad people, the playwrights? This is insane, Dona Barbetta, surely it is insane.[14]

If actors merely dramatize the sinfulness of human pride—the desire to appear what we are not, to mock God by recreating ourselves in a fictional image—what better medium than the theater could Barnes have found for her final anatomy of the deceptions and manipulations women and men practice upon those closest to them, and upon themselves? And so she has given us in *The Antiphon* the tragedy of a man—Titus—who wished to be Napoleon, his wife, Augusta, who wished, as she says in act 3, to be Helen of Troy, and their two sons, Dudley and Elisha, who in retaliation have wished to be policemen.

It is in this light that we must understand the self-referentiality of *The Antiphon*, its constant allusion to role, scene, and costume, its controlling metaphor—constantly drawing attention to itself—that all the stage is a stage. The play's exposition, in act 1, reveals that the entire scheme of action encloses itself; it is a performance, managed and orchestrated by Jeremy/Jack, who has called his family together, assembled the cast, and proceeds to make them dance in various ways, performing a sort of private family morality play. He is, however, only imperfectly in control.

Over the balustrade hang flags, gonfalons, bonnets, ribbons and all manner of stage

costumes . . . [on the table] a gilt mardi gras crown. . . . Miranda, a tall woman in
her late fifties, enters from the cloister. She has a distinguished but failing air,
wearing an elegant but rusty costume, obviously of the theatre, a long cloak,
buckled shoes and a dashing tricorne. . . .

 She is followed, at a respectful distance, by Jack Blow, a bearded fellow. . . . At his entrance he is holding his billycock straight up over his head, as
though he expected applause from the gallery. His manner during this act is . . .
clowning. (A, 81–82)

Miranda and Jack enter almost in the manner of circus performers entering
a ring. Jack in particular ignores the "fourth wall" of realistic theater from
the first instant, presenting an outright caricature of the principle of male
dominance in the exaggerated and incongruous fashion of a clown. The two
begin by characterizing, antiphonally, the scene in which they find themselves—"rudeness once was home"; almost immediately, Jack does so by
"metaphorical" reference to the theater.

> JACK: . . . But where's your Uncle Jonathan?
>   You said you came to kiss him fond farewell.
>   The scene is set but seems the actor gone.
>   No tither, weeper, wait or *cicerone*;
>   No beadle, bailiff, barrister, no clerk;
>   In short no audience at all.
>   My hands will have to be your clamour, lady.
> MIRANDA: Not so fast. (A, 83)

Is Jack, as he facetiously suggests, the only viewer present to applaud
Miranda's farewell performance? She suspects otherwise.

 Left alone for a minute, Jack soliloquizes; but he uses this opportunity not to communicate private thoughts to the audience, but to reflect
upon the theatrical nature of what he is doing:

> They say soliloquy is out of fashion,
> It being a kind of talking to your betters.
> (*He climbs into the chair*)
> But then what motion but betrays oneself? . . .
> Do I unplot my head by plucking hairs?
> Or throw my lines away between my teeth? . . .
> (*He stiffens, hearing a noise in the gallery, but does not turn.*)
> Do I hear the world approaching at my back?
> Then though the world be present, I'll be proctor—
> (*with increasing bravado, calling, like a barker*)
> Hurry! Hurry! This way for the toymen:
> This way, strutters, for the bearded lady,
> The human skeleton, the fussy dwarf,
> The fat girl with a planet in her lap;

> The swallower of swords whose hidden lunge
> Has not brought up his adversary yet! (A, 93–94)

Jack wonders not about his actions or feelings, but about the nature and quality of his performance and about his degree of mastery over the show that is about to take place. Is his style of speech appropriate? Is he the ringmaster or merely another clown?

As these two examples, and many others, show, reference to the theatricality of what is taking place is usually accompanied by some anxiety about the possibilty of human communication. *Is* there an audience? Characters seem to fear both that someone is listening and that no one is listening. And who *are* these oddly costumed people? Burley, the voice of rationality throughout the play, quite reasonably wants to know.

> BURLEY: Less skipping, if you please.
> JACK: Suspect *her* as a member of the Odeon;
>   A dresser to the opera—and say,
>   She swept the Comedie Francaise for tragedy.
>   Me—plain Jack—who followed close behind,
>   The whipper-in, the prudent ferryman.
> BURLEY: Courtesy requires that when you speak,
>   You make it more than silence. (A, 102–3)

But Jack refuses to honor Burley's request for an honest explanation in simple, representational language. He goes on to describe Miranda, on the occasion when he "first met" her, as behaving like an actress before "her public, her herd in hobble":

> *her hands dropped and thoroughly performed—*
> *The tension lost as in tragediennes*
> *Who've left the tragic gesture to the stage*
> *And so go forth alone to meet disaster.* (A, 104)

Again the ambiguity: is Miranda more powerful because of her "herd in hobble" or audience, or does she stand before them like a sacrificial victim?

Burley regards Jack's obscurity of reference and refusal to tell his story straight as a dangerous sign of theatricality, a characterization to which Jack assents:

> BURLEY *(to himself)*: Fantastick—Scapin!
>   *(to Jack)*: You should have been an actor!
> JACK: I was, I am, the company unseen;
>   I think they call it "carrying the spear." (A, 106–7)

He admits to being a performer but, in keeping with his disguise as "Jack Blow," denies that he is a major character or full participant in the moral drama that is about to unfold. He describes himself as simply encouraging

Miranda to performance, which he sees as appropriate to the apocalyptic
extremity in which they find themselves:

> *We're all at profile in this session, girl—*
> *Whip up your splendours and your consternations,*
> *Stand to the trumpets and the terrors;*
> *(Bank to performance;) give tongue for tongue,*
> *All the tapestries have thrown their spears!* (A, 112)

Finally, Jack in this act performs his function as "proctor" or
"whipper-in." When Burley asks, "Shall we get on with it?" Jack responds
"It can't be halted, as I'm well aware" (A, 104). At the end of act 1, as all the
characters, including Augusta, head offstage, finally assemble for what
seems an imminent collision, he remarks, "Therefore, let us begin it," as
though the first act were merely a prologue he had finished delivering. And
Miranda, from the balcony, answers futilely, "No, no, no, no, no, no!"—
unable to prevent the collision between characters which gives rise to
dramatic plot (A, 114). What is at issue in act 1's constant reference to itself as
theater is not simply deception (who are these people?) and anxiety about
audience (who is listening?) but control over the unrolling of a plot which
Jack has the power to set in motion but which neither he nor any other
character has the power to halt.

Barnes, however, is in complete, consistent control of both plot and
language. Act 2 continues to develop the theatrical metaphor as it fleshes out
the bare characterizations and outline of family history sketched by the
prologue/exposition. The psychological action begins with a concerted
family attack on the poses of the father, Titus, who is not present to defend
himself and who therefore functions initially as a scapegoat for the hostili-
ties and failures of his family. This attack develops in two directions: the
group attacks Augusta for her complicity with Titus, and the mother and
brothers attack Miranda for her nonconformity and disobedience to the
revised family standard of conduct, under which success is measured purely
by material gain. The attacks on Miranda are posed metaphorically in terms
of the role—and the costume—she has chosen for herself. She has committed
the sin of appearing "dressed as though there were no God," compared with
which actual disbelief in God would be a minor infraction.

> AUGUSTA (*nervous on finding herself alone with her sons*):
> I wonder what it is Miranda's dressed for.
> Though compounded of a thousand ills,
> Embroidered, and embossed for some high scandal,
> She is, all in all, magnanimous—
> ELISHA: So? The whole fool's present in Miranda.
> DUDLEY: If rigged for anything it's trouble.
> A strolling player indeed! Without Protector,
> Husband, son, or bank-account? Phizz, phizz!

> She'd better been a traveling salesman,
> With all that *tutti* and *continuo*,
> And walking round creation once a day,
> And been no menace to our purse. (*A*, 168)

Miranda is criticized for being an actress, for dressing a part. Yet Augusta, in attempting to justify her own past behavior and throw the blame on Titus and his mother more effectively, recalls her own youthful costume in elaborate nostalgic detail; and almost every character by the end of the act has been accused of, or laid claim to, playing the role of the fool.

"Fool" in *The Antiphon* has a Shakespearean resonance. Jack, calling himself "Tom O'Bedlam" and "plain Jack, juggler," lays claim to a role similar to that of Kent in *King Lear*: under cover of anonymity and bizarre behavior, he brings forth the truth about the past in at attempt to heal old wounds or, as he says in a particularly Shakespearean phrase, "to medecine contumely" (*A*, 224).[15] Dudley and Elisha attempt a similar trick, but less successfully.

Act 2 closes with two "plays within the play" which, again as in Shakespeare, push the self-referentiality yet another step, as though we saw the action reflected in a small mirror within a larger mirror. In the first of these smaller plays, Dudley and Elisha, who have earlier admonished one another, "Patience. (Keep it fast,) Keep it funny" (*A*, 150), like one comedian aside to another, put on masks which paradoxically enable them to express their sexual hostility toward their mother and sister in a more undisguised way:

(*Exeunt Burley and Jack. They are no sooner gone than silently and swiftly the two sons—*DUDLEY *donning a pig's mask,* ELISHA *an ass's, as if the playthings would make them anonymous—rush the two women.* ELISHA *knocks* MIRANDA'S *cane away, seizing her and pinning her arms behind her.* DUDLEY *pushing* AUGUSTA *about in an attempt to make her dance.*)
DUDLEY: I'll huff, and I'll puff, and I'll blow your house down!
AUGUSTA (*thinking they are really playing*): A game! A game! (*A*, 175)

The play or game seems to give permission both for actual physical violence and for extreme verbal cruelty. The brothers beat, trip, kick, and maul Miranda; they taunt her with her age, her infirmity, and their concept for what they see as her failures: lack of man and child, lack of traditional female role, poverty, profession as writer and intellectual, expatriation. And Augusta also seizes the opportunity of the carnivalesque "game" to wound Miranda. The tragedy of Augusta's uncomprehending complicity, in favoring her sons and standing with them against Miranda ("You never would—you know you never would/Listen to your brothers" [*A*, 177]) is revealed here. Augusta never does understand that the brothers wish for her own death and that only Miranda's presence prevents them from accomplishing their purpose. Augusta has failed, in other words, to recognize that "playing" is an extremely serious matter.

But the second play within the play—Jack's—while it is static and more artificial, involving a sort of puppet show with dolls and a dollhouse rather than masks on live actors, brings Augusta to an inescapable sense of her own guilt and complicity, her own responsibility, as an adult, for her husband's rape of Miranda by proxy.[16] Here Jack plays Hamlet as well, catching the "conscience of the king" (in this case, the queen) by means of a play. And Augusta, confirming her guilt by shrieking out a denial and a refusal to know—"I did not see it! I did not hear it!"—cries out also against the theatrical situation in which she finds herself:

> AUGUSTA (*Looking wildly about, and seeing stray travellers who have climbed up the back way into the gallery, staring down, she throws herself over the doll house, beating at it with both hands*):
> No, no! Stop it! Enough! Away!
> Wolves! Mountebanks! Historians! (*A*, 186)

This last word is one of the few significant variants from Barnes' earlier published version of the play: in the 1958 text, the word is not "historians" but "histrions."

For Barnes, the meaning of these two words converged in an awesome and terrible way when she came to depict her own family history. Without knowing—and I argue we cannot possibly know—to what extent Barnes was drawing on specific actual experiences, to what extent she created and recreated character and situation to tell the subjective emotional truth about her childhood, we can understand that *The Antiphon* is a revenge tragedy in a double sense. In writing it, Barnes both depicted and carried out symbolic revenge, so that *The Antiphon* itself acts like a play within a play, a corrective investigation and remirroring, if the larger play is life. "I wonder what you'll write when I am dead and gone," says Augusta (*A*, 209). Within *The Antiphon*, the ironic answer would be "nothing," for the two die in the same moment, and Miranda has no chance to remember or record her history. But in a larger sense, Barnes went on to write *The Antiphon*, without which Augusta would never have lived to have the opportunity for that comment. Another mirror within a mirror—or is it outside?

The tragedy of tragedy—the dark and violent potential of the drama—has already been revealed by the beginning of act 3. But this last act is far from anticlimactic, for it is here, alone with Miranda, that Augusta gets *her* chance to "play the fool," to justify her moral stance by role playing.

The act opens after a gap in time: intermission for the audience, "dinner" for the characters. Augusta pronounces the gryphon "a solid beast, an excellent stage, fit for a play" (*A*, 192) and goes on to suggest that she and Miranda "pretend" to take on the roles of mother and daughter they have been playing all along.

> AUGUSTA: So, let us play. The epilogue is over,
> The boys asleep, and we are girls again,
> Nor need not think of them this part of night. . . .
> Now the animals are put up in their box,
> Let's be young again and tell of our lives. . . .
> Come, play me daughter. (*A*, 193)

Augusta behaves as though her colloquy with her daughter were outside the play, after the epilogue, outside of history and judgment.

> AUGUSTA: Let's jump the day of wrath. Let us pretend.
> The play is over and the boys are put to bed.
> Let's play at being Miranda and Augusta.
> Say we're at home hunting-box with lords—
> Say duck-sniping—on a lake, or snaring
> Woodcock in the hills—shooting and kissing—
> Your father wore the trappings, but his aim—
> MIRANDA: Was wild.
> AUGUSTA: So let us both forget him.
> I think the gryphon moved. We have a carriage! (*A*, 197)

Treating the terrible revelations of act 2 as fictions, or as the result of a male world of responsibility from which she cuts herself off, Augusta proceeds to write her own imagined role, to indulge her fantasy of being a young woman, beloved and therefore famous. She imagines herself into traditional scenes of romance, imagines herself present as feminine on-looker to great moments of history, sees herself as the Empress Josephine, Lillie Langtry, Helen of Troy, and makes use of her envious guesses about Miranda's sexual experiences to imagine herself living all these things through Miranda, to the point of assuming her very own costume. As Miranda says, "Love puts forth her foot, and in my shoes" (*A*, 198).

But Miranda refuses to cooperate with this fantasy. Throughout the play, she is rarely and very reluctantly drawn into discourse, and never in order to defend, justify, or explain herself. Now, too, she remains for the most part silent or unromantic about her experiences, and she checks her mother's enthusiasm at every point.

> MIRANDA (*smiling*): No fountains, no flambeaux, no music nor no gallants.
> . . . .
> O unhappy wanderer,
> I've seen you dig for Antony
> With a kitchen spoon.
> . . . .
> Blow less hard about the stage. Be still. (*A*, 197, 202)

Miranda moreover refuses to participate in the illusion that by playing or pretending women can wish their history away. She insistently calls her mother back to the truth of their family life, to the sins of Titus, Dudley, and Elisha, to Augusta's complicity and failure to protect Miranda or even herself.

> *Be not your own pathetic fallacy, but be*
> *Your own dark measure in the vein,*
> *For we're about a tragic business, mother.* (A, 205)

It is Miranda's refusal to help her mother tell the other, sweeter story—her refusal to "play"—that hastens Augusta's inevitable casting off of her momentary alliance with her daughter in favor of her deeper preference for her sons. Miranda's refusal to share in the illusion also catalyzes the "excellent arrangement of catastrophe" (A, 219) in which the women quite literally do each other in as the men escape.

What is at issue here for Miranda—and for Barnes—is the exposure of the deadly fictions of femininity by which women are deceived into colluding with, and loving, their oppressors. "In my day we did not leave our husbands," says Augusta early on (A, 160); it also seems natural to her to treat her sons as valuable property, as clues to her identity, but to "cast the privy look of dogs/Who turn to quiz their droppings" on her one girl child (A, 87). Augusta agrees with Dudley and Elisha in finding Miranda finally valueless because she has neither husband nor son, refusing to understand that she herself has gained nothing from the so-called protection of either her sons or their father. Miranda will not allow her mother to forgive herself too easily, will not allow her to take refuge in childlike, "feminine" irresponsibility and fantasy, for Miranda understands that Augusta's early fantasies of feminine power are responsible for the family tragedies of rape, ruin, exploitation, and betrayal.

Barnes had taken up this theme earlier in a *Theatre Guild* piece called "The Dear Dead Days: Love Is Done Differently on Our Current Stage." By way of reviewing a play called *Young Love*, which presented the "modern attitude" toward relations between the sexes, Barnes investigated theatrical fictions about women through the ages and reported, among other things: "I discovered that Marguerite—she of Gounod's opera—was a phrase. She was created and destroyed verbally. She was a virgin because people told her she was a virgin, and she was destroyed because people told her she was destroyed." And about the theory of modern behavior presented in "Young Love," she commented: "It makes amusing reading, laughable drama and dreadful homecoming; but it is far better than that one Bronte should be sacrificed to the brother, which was traditional when love was love and sin was sin and never the two could mix and mingle. Sin led to Hades, and love to a lot of male children doted upon by a mother who bore a sufficient number of girls to clean up after them."[17]

Barnes understood very well how a woman could be destroyed verbally—the chapter "Rape and Repining!" in *Ryder* provides a series of vivid examples. She has Augusta in *The Antiphon* cry out against "the whole of love's debris/The horrid holocaust that is the price/Of passion's seizure" (*A,* 207), but it is left to Miranda to reply to her mother's anguished "Say, who *is* Sylvia/That all the swains adored her" with a cold "Indeed, who" (*A,* 206). The final service to which self-referentiality and self-conscious theatricality are put in *The Antiphon* is an exploration of the dangerous and damaging effects of "female" roles and "feminine" role playing upon both women who accept such roles and women who do not.

We may finally understand *The Antiphon*'s supposed obscurity or unintelligibility, its reliance on archaic language and formal verse patterns, in the light of the play's thematic distrust of conventional "realistic" language. Miranda, who like the early participants in the Provincetown Playhouse is at the same time writer, actress, heroine, and "wardrobe mistress, tiring many parts" (*A,* 210), is distinguished by her silence: that is to say, her refusal to acquiesce to any easy, comfortable rendering of the truth about her experience and her family. And she herself provides an explanation of the play's difficulty, toward the end of act 3.

> MIRANDA: Rebuke me less, for we are face to face
> With this the fadged up ends up discontent:
> But tie and hold us in that dear estrangement
> That we may like before we too much lose us.
> As the blacksmith hammers out his savage metal,
> So is the infant hammered to the dance.
> But if not wrapped in metric, hugged in discipline,
> Rehearsed in familiarity reproved;
> Grappled in the mortise of the ritual,
> And turning in the spirit of the play,
> Then equilibrium will be the fall;
> Abide it. (*A,* 213)

The very extremity of the family's emotional situation (the "fadged-up ends of discontent") make necessary a formal, "disciplined" solution, a "metric," a "ritual," a "dance," avoiding and "reproving" the "familiarity" of conventional wisdom, conventional realistic presentation. Only in the "spirit" of this "play"—Miranda's play—with all its gaps, silences, and difficulties, is any connection or "tie" between human beings possible.

In a play about the artificiality and theatricality of human interchange the difficulty of finding a language in which the truth can be told, artificiality and difficulty ought not to be held up as weaknesses, for they are precisely the point of the excursion. Rather, we should understand the play's carefully wrought complexity as a triumph of integration between manner and matter and look for a company of modern-day theater idealists—

perhaps a feminist theater company—with sufficient grasp of the play's depth and its politics to surmount apparent technical obstacles to production. We can return finally to Miranda's response to Jack's doubt about the whole enterprise of the play they are about to undertake:

> JACK: In short, no audience at all. . . .
> MIRANDA: Not so fast.

¶ . . . Augusta is a fury, not a policeman, a fury but not sophisticated.
—Djuna Barnes,
letter to Wolfgang Hildesheimer,
14 September 1969

¶ . . . I was upset when asked to explain exactly what the plot was, what the meaning was. I felt I did not know how to go about it; that I'd have to write another play to explain the play.
—Djuna Barnes,
letter to Wolfgang Hildesheimer,
17 May 1961

¶ 76 — "Yet in abandon of variety" Augusta is voicing her general anxiety, disapproval, and suspicion (as usual) of her daughter and her supposed "gay" life, or "abandon" which Augusta is always hinting at (and as shown in the last act, *trying to take over* for her *own* lost life, which was without excitement of sentiment, love or worldly knowledge) which considering her hinted censure is a monstrous sad thing—so here she hints that her daughter has a life so full of "adventures" she has forgotten it, as the owl is said to have lost the awareness of what it has been looking at, because its head is supposed to turn all the way around on its neck, and come back to the place from which it started.
—Djuna Barnes,
answer to query from Wolfgang
Hildesheimer concerning *The Antiphon*

¶ . . . I must re-read *The Antiphon*. Miss Koschel [one of a team of two German translators] thought that Titus raped his daughter Miranda. I am very much afraid that play is too difficult, unless I am right over-the-shoulder, which is impossible. I hate re-reading my work, but it has to be. I have exclaimed with horror to the poor young lady for her thought, and alerted my publisher to watch over the thing.
—Djuna Barnes,
letter to Wolfgang Hildesheimer,
19 January 1969

17

"Tom, Take Mercy": Djuna Barnes' Drafts of <u>The Antiphon</u>

Lynda Curry

During the 1950s, T.S. Eliot, editor and close friend of Djuna Barnes, was on the board of Faber and Faber in London, where he had already published *Nightwood*. Eliot was helping Barnes with her verse tragedy, *The Antiphon*, reading consecutive drafts as she mailed them to him and suggesting changes. By 1956 the play had gone through four complete rewrites since Barnes began writing in 1937; both Eliot and Barnes were anxious to see its completion. In February, Barnes (in New York) sent the newly completed fourth draft to Eliot and followed it up with a letter:

> I am sorry that the typescript is now in some scratch about. I did not think you would mind if I did not retype the whole thing all over again, as undoubtedly you, or someone at Faber and Faber, will see occasion to further pencil it, when and if, I will this time have it attacked by a proper stenographer, if it calls for it.
>
> And Tom, do take mercy on the author who has been twenty months in a fairly gruesome state of tension. (Barnes to Eliot, 21 February 1956)[1]

Eliot did not "take mercy." He continued to make severe demands on Barnes, asking her to accept his editing and to make further cuts of her own. In August 1956, Eliot wrote that he was satisfied with acts 1 and 3, but that act 2 was still far too long; he advised further editing:

> It seems to me what is needed is much more drastic cutting, twelve to fifteen pages. Don't cut anything at the beginning, and don't cut anything at the end, but I

Ed.'s Note: Shortly after submitting her essay for inclusion in this volume, Lynda Curry died. Her pioneering work on *The Antiphon* has proved to be an important resource for many contributors to this volume. In her memory, and with the permission of her executor, Chris Langlois, we dedicate this essay to her daughters, Rachel and Ann.

feel sure there are pages in the middle which can be disposed of. I know it is painful to sacrifice what one feels to be good lines, but you had to cut a good deal, you will remember, out of "Nightwood," stuff which was quite good enough to stay in, except that there was *too much of it*, and with a play, still more than with prose fiction form, it is undesirable far to overstep the limits of the essential. Will you have another shot at it? (Eliot to Barnes, 10 August 1956)

On the basis of this letter, Barnes began the fifth and last major revision of *The Antiphon*.[2] She literally slashed her way through act 2, saving only what she considered essential information and her best poetry, excising nearly three hundred lines.

The Antiphon never recovered from this final revision; since the first moment it appeared in print, it has been subjected to vehement critical attack and has been produced only twice in the last twenty-six years.[3] As a result, the literary world continues to underestimate and undervalue this play. In the following pages, a few of the most important cuts will be returned to their original places in order that the reader may see the play as its author envisioned it before her editor forced her to make these final, drastic cuts.

In order that the reader may more easily follow the textual alterations as they are introduced and discussed, a brief summary of the plot will be given here with special emphasis on act 2, where most of the changes in the fifth (final) draft occurred.

The action takes place in England in the fictional township Beewick, near Dover. The family members gather at the ancestral home; at present in ruin, it was once a college of chantry priests and still bears remnants of the former religion on its crumbling walls. The action takes place in the late afternoon (act 1), evening (act 2), and night (act 3) on a day in October 1939, shortly after the start of World War II. During the second act, strangers pass through Burley Hall, the ancestral home, on their way to port. They are fleeing the country, as are most of the characters in the play. This setting lends a sense of decay and doom to *The Antiphon* from the very beginning.

Act 1 is devoted to establishing motivation and giving background information on the six characters. The play opens with Miranda and Jack entering their former home after an extended absence. The brother and sister discuss their childhood memories and their adult fears. Each has a premonition of impending disaster but is unsure of its source and direction. Jack is disguised; he intends to behave as an outsider throughout the play, never revealing his identity nor the fact that he has called the family together for this important reunion. Miranda expresses a fear of her younger brothers, American businessmen, and checks nervously about the house for intruders. While she is offstage, Jack voices his doubts about his own position in the family and in life.

His monologue is interrupted by Jonathan Burley, Jack and Miranda's maternal uncle and caretaker of Burley Hall. Jack and Jonathan establish that Miranda has been back to visit her uncle and her early home several times in the last twenty years, but that she has always come in costume and with a group of actors or traveling musicians or vagabonds of some sort. Jonathan Burley shows himself to be a steady, thoughtful, gentle character in his comments about the family members and his actions toward them.

After Jack and Jonathan leave the stage, Dudley and Elisha, Jack and Miranda's younger brothers, sneak on. Harsh, unsympathetic, and selfish individuals, they are interested in acquiring more wealth and in disposing of their aged mother, Augusta, and their older sister, Miranda, in any way they can. However, they are too cowardly to kill the women outright and so speculate about the possibility of arranging for them to kill each other. Dudley and Elisha are intelligent as well as evil and would be even more dangerous than they are if it were not for their somewhat ambivalent feelings about their mother and sister. Both brothers stand in awe of Miranda's articulateness and aristocratic bearing, and Elisha especially is rather fond of her. Dudley admires his mother's regal attitude and biting wit and even in his adulthood can be admonished by her. Thus they hesitate to do the deed. They duck quickly out of sight at the sound of approaching footsteps.

Jack and Jonathan reenter, give further information about how Jack and Miranda met in Paris, what they did there, and why they then came on to Burley Hall together. During the first act, four of the five characters state their intention to leave England in the morning on the last ship out for America; Jonathan will stay in England, guarding the house, for the rest of his life. The act ends with all five characters on stage, listening apprehensively to the approaching steps of the queenly Augusta.

Much of act 2 is devoted to Augusta and her relationship with each of the other characters. She also gives much information about her dead husband's (Titus') sexual escapades and his own mother's freewheeling, sociopolitical activities, so that the audience begins to see the kind of family chaos and destruction that were wrought in the past and must be dealt with in the present. All the characters, except Jonathan, demonstrate why they have reason to hate and mistrust the others; yet each shows, in some way, that familial ties are still important and that love has not been completely destroyed. Jack goes out to get food for dinner and, with Jonathan's help, sets up the meal. The two men then step outside to bring in a handmade toy of Jack's. While they are gone, Dudley and Elisha don masks and attack their mother and sister. A gruesome free-for-all ensues in which the women are roughed up, insulted, struck, and abused. Elisha threatens to rape Miranda but is weeping as he does so, and she controls him with punishing observations of his character. Eventually Miranda defends Augusta by focusing the attention on Dudley's "lost innocence" and thus drawing the men off her mother and herself.

Jack and Burley reenter with Jack's handcarved toy, a miniature dollhouse and dolls, an exact replica of the family dwelling in New York State where all except Jonathan were forced to go when Beewick banished Titus. Augusta is lifted onto the table and placed before the house. Made to relive the more vivid incidents of her children's history, she is handed various dolls and told to look in certain windows. The lurid and undeniable past rises slowly before her, and she is at last driven to guilty hysteria while a crowd of travellers on the balcony looks down on her. She screams and beats on the house with her fists until the strangers withdraw, and Miranda helps her down from the table. As the family goes in to dinner at the close of the second act, the younger brothers accede to Jack, saying that he has accomplished far more in his attack on Augusta than they themselves had ever hoped to do. Miranda draws Jonathan aside as the others leave the stage and expresses her love for him and her anxiety that he not be hurt in the conflict she believes is sure to follow.

Act 3 consists of a lyrical battle between mother and daughter. Augusta shows yet another aspect of her personality by becoming a frightened lonely child in the presence of Miranda's angry maternal love. Miranda finally reveals herself fully, accusing and excusing Augusta, whose thoughtless instinctual drives resulted in Miranda's birth and the beginning of the daughter's unhappiness. In the darkness that has fallen around them, the women try to soothe their own deep wounds while defending themselves from one another. It proves impossible.

At the height of the argument, Augusta hears her younger sons running away from her. She blames Miranda for this estrangement as she has blamed her for all the abandonments of the past, while Miranda offers to stay with Augusta and keep her safe at Burley Hall with Jonathan. But Augusta does not listen and instead responds by attacking her daughter with a heavy brass bell. Miranda, choosing neither to flee nor fight back, falls under the repeated blows, and Augusta collapses beside her. Jack and Jonathan enter to make the final ambiguous statements about the action, Jonathan asking Jack why he caused the deaths and Jack responding that he could not possibly have known what would happen. Jack refuses to take the blame for what, in fact, his father has done. Jack reveals his identity, admits his mistake in thinking he could "medicine contumely with a dolls' hutch," and leaves Jonathan alone with the bodies as the final curtain descends.

The first major cut to consider occurs in the second act. In the fifth draft and the published versions of act 2, Jack goes out to "fetch supper," and, before he returns, Miranda and Burley leave the stage to get lamps (A, 163, 167). Augusta, anxious because she is alone with Dudley and Elisha, begins speculating about Miranda—her dress, her manner. The brothers suggest that their sister would be more presentable and less of a threat to their own incomes if she were working for a living. Augusta first defends

Miranda, then (in the next breath) accuses her of not having kept the addresses of all the famous people she once knew. Elisha's following words to Augusta make little sense. The audience would have to hear the speeches again in order to understand what is happening; the reader would have to reread them:

> AUGUSTA: Don't falsify. She never whined your purses.
>   What I find strange is that she is not famous.
>   I really thought she'd get into the papers.
>   She's met everyone of any consequence.
>   Would she make a note of their addresses?
>   No, she would not.
> ELISHA: Still you swept the strings, and still she cried
>   "My mother, oh my mother!"

After rereading this passage, one assumes that Augusta nagged her daughter about becoming famous—that is, played the same song over and over ("Still swept the strings")—and that Miranda kept saying she wanted to be let alone. However, this reasoning is not quite satisfactory either: Miranda's words are too strong for that kind of response.

The fourth draft clears up this problem by showing that a major cut was made at this point. It also contains the kind of historical detail—here about Titus—lost in the fifth draft.

> AUGUSTA: She almost amounted once—and I have said so.
>   I really thought that she'd get in the papers.
>   She'd met everyone of any sort of consequence,
>   But she would not make a note of their addresses.
> DUDLEY: She's been knocked into the stubborn ever since
>   The hour she drove between our father and the gate,
>   Where he tried to make her mutton at sixteen—
>   Initiated vestal to his "cause"!
>   Self-anointed Titus, Little Corporal,
>   Horn mad after false gods; madder still
>   For her wild teeth and even wilder kicking.
>   And having failed in that, what did he then?
>   Hauled her, in an hay-hook, to the barn;
>   Left her dangling; while in the field below
>   He offered to exchange her for a goat
>   With that old farm-hand, Jacobsen.
> AUGUSTA: Atrocious, outrageous, monstrous Dudley!
> ELISHA: And still you swept the strings, and still *she* cried
>   "My mother, oh my mother!"
> AUGUSTA: Don't you dare talk like that before my brother!
> DUDLEY: No? I've observed the more Miranda lives
>   Up to the general precepts of her scruples,
>   The more she is abandoned.
> AUGUSTA: What? What?⁴

When this hayhook scene is put back in the script, Elisha's response makes complete and coherent sense. In the past Augusta had acquiesced to Titus' outlandish demands (sometimes even cooperating with him) as he collected women, "cored" the dog, and horsewhipped the babies. In this context, "still swept the strings" implies that Augusta continued to accompany Titus even in the extreme case of attempted incest and rape. Elisha's lines also suggest that Augusta bemoaned her situation at times of crisis, concentrating on her own pain to the exclusion of her children's, while Miranda thought more about her mother than herself.[5]

In the second draft of this hayhook speech there are two more lines at the end. I will quote Dudley's last five lines so the reader may see the alteration more fully:

> *Hauled her in an hay-hook to the barn*
> *Left her dangling, while in the field below*
> *He offered to give her, to the farm-hand, for a goat,—*
> *You know, I've seen heifers dangling from an halter*
> *Just like that, while he charged the rape-blade in.*

Because the background given here has been eliminated in the fifth draft and published versions, the audience has to get most of its information from Jack's crystal speech in the dollhouse scene of act 2. That passage, so significant in the published version, appears for the first time in the second draft in a rudimentary form. As a result of Jack's words and actions during this speech, the past is relived, and Augusta is accused as accessory to the crime. Therefore, it is important to be able to see this revealing speech at its inception. Here is a rendering of it which includes all corrections and marginalia—Jack is speaking to his mother:

> JACK: The crystal, like a pregnant girl, in hour
> Is delivered of her phantom figure, image passenger
> Giving room to later prophesy   [cancelled]
> Giving up/the room to younger spectre
> And a newer prophecy,//, and image.
> But   The eye-baby that you're pregnant with
> You'll carry/to the grave.
> You made you, madame, *madame* by submission
> With apron over head, yet strewing salt
>   All up the stairs, and down the hall,
> Did you think to catch your villany and his
> Counting in the salt, how many feet were whose or hers
> Walked that last mile?
>   That small time cockney
> Thrown in with a/cockney, thrice her age
> Indeed, to be correct, Matilda's brother,—
> And left/to it, tho she cried out like the ewe

"Do not let it be, but if he will it—!"
Showing what a hash her mind/was made of.
Lemmings? an abbatoir where like reindeer stretch out the throat for
    slashing[6]
So I say, both you and your husband Titus
In the setting, and denying of her,
Made of that doll's room a babes *bordel*.

   If this speech is combined with the hayhook passage, quoted above, the past comes together suddenly to reveal character motivation and to clarify the plot. After the Titus Hobbs family had been driven out of England because Titus refused to send his children to public school, spent all the family money, and practiced polygamy, they fled to upstate New York where they settled on a farm. There Titus added a new religion to his other practices, making himself the godhead and high priest; and because he had always resented Miranda, he tried to rape his daughter when she was sixteen. He wrestled her up against the pasture gate where she struggled in angry silence, biting and kicking, and eventually managed to fight him off. Titus then grappled her to a hayhook in the barn and hoisted her into the air. The farmhands and the family members gathered to look up at her swinging above them, while he offered to exchange her for a goat, saying he would make her the first virginal sacrifice of his new religion. Eventually, Titus chose an older man to perform the "ceremony," a cockney about fifty-eight years old, and lowered Miranda to the ground. She was dragged into the house and up to a top-floor bedroom, the brothers watching, the mother acquiescing, and locked in with the older man. With both parents so obviously determined that it should take place, the child eventually succumbed, comprehending only in part what was happening. While the older man raped her, Miranda cried out against it, "Do not let him, but if it will atone" (A, 186), Titus happily rubbed his hands together in a lower room, and Augusta put her apron over her head and threw salt on the stairs outside the bedroom door. Then Miranda, harshly violated, crawled across the floor toward the door, bleeding and crying, "My mother, O my mother." Jeremy, utterly terrorized, watched it happen and never forgot it.
   In the fifth draft, the hayhook scene is cut, Augusta's guilty reaction eliminated, and Dudley's observations given to Augusta. The most important excision is the background information on Titus' sexual attempts against Miranda. Besides losing that, we lose Augusta's sense of guilt by association (demonstrated in her overreaction to both sons' words) and Dudley's momentary sympathy with Miranda. The characters in the fifth draft are not as close as in the former versions; each seems less aware of the others, more intent upon himself. The brothers no longer seem to be defending Miranda.
   Next, various bits and pieces of information are lost in the cutting of

act 2, especially those concerned with "Miranda's scruples" and the filling out of her character. For example, the travellers who had speaking parts as early as the first full draft of act 2 (1954) are reduced to silent figures, passing behind the stage and along the balcony in the fifth draft. In the fourth draft, some of their words are given to Dudley and Elisha, but in the final rewrite all their speeches that had contributed information on Titus and Miranda are removed. The reference to Titus as "Old Baron Ox" was retained in the final typescript and the published editions (*A*, 146), but all the other phrases, descriptions of Miranda, are gone.

For our sense of Miranda, these cuts are a serious loss. In most of the early versions, the travellers said she was a "lapsed patrician, [who] drank the toll oil of dead philosophers"; and "Out of plain caution, never married/ A toff, so rare and choice of mind—/You could push her, boots and all, under a door," to which Elisha felt moved to add, "Except the door stands open in astonishment/For the rest to follow." This kind of information about Miranda—that she is tall, thin, aristocratic, and philosophically inclined— can be gathered from seeing her on the stage or hearing the comments of her family. She and Augusta both carry themselves with a certain "classic" bearing that strongly affects those around them.

However, no one can be sure about Miranda's adult past, and it is helpful to hear from outsiders how the world saw her. That she chose not to marry and apparently not to reproduce suggests that she lived according to the standards she voices in act 3 when she says the parents sin against the child in giving birth to it. They also suggest that her childhood experiences with her father warned her away from contractual relationships with men. Her parents' marriage was a disaster, destructive to every living thing that came within the sphere of its influence, and Miranda has apparently chosen not to repeat the mistake. She senses the danger inherent in coupling and from this knowledge derives her ideas about death in birth (*A*, 219). When the audience loses these fragments of information, it loses a little more knowledge about the background of the characters (especially Miranda), knowledge that must be gathered elsewhere or surmised.

Another piece of information lost in cutting is the brief description of Augusta as a child. It is important because it leads into one of Augusta's crucial lines on confusion of identity with her daughter (*A*, 219). In the fourth draft, the image of a carefree childhood is built smoothly, with various family members contributing (act 2):

> ELISHA: Father's browsing fall. Who else?
> VOICE DUDLEY: [handcorrected] Old Baron Ox—
> AUGUSTA: We speak in pride and not now of your father.
> DUDLEY: And weren't you, for the very devil of it,
>   Wearing tongue-slit stems of dandelion,
>   The meadow curls, rung out upon the ear

Either side the head, like country brats?
AUGUSTA: That was Miranda too, and let it be so.
Miranda's all Augusta, laid up in Miranda
As myself, discharged among my follies;
Born again to be Augusta's new account,
And all her candidature. There's that about Miranda
Is profit, though the cash seems spent.
Miranda, when I die I charge you lay me in a tree;
Remember it among my sons who dare
Remember less.
DUDLEY: Back to trees again!

The rewritten version of this exchange (very similar to the published version; A, 146–47) leaves out Augusta's revealing remark on Titus, the childhood games with dandelions, Augusta's begrudging admiration of Miranda, and her acknowledgment that the sons do not understand or love their mother as the daughter does. Seventeen lines have been reduced to nine, resulting in a blurred image of familial relationships.

A third example of lost information concerns Augusta's musings on Titus (A, 164–65). She is on the stage with Dudley and Elisha; the latter is giving his vivid description of Titus' firing his wife's letters into a dog, thus destroying both the dog and Augusta's self-respect with one shot:

ELISHA: That reminds me, what of that stray dog,
That half-wild cur you held down with both hands
While father cored him, with his blunderbus
Rammed down in a bolt of your own letters—
To kill two prides a throw.
AUGUSTA (*Pretending to have missed the point*):
Your father, unlike the finch or dauber,
Pulled his house apart while weaving—a Penelope.
I wonder what it was he waited for.

Augusta pretends to miss the point that her pride and spirit were killed by Titus; however, she makes another point by demonstrating how deeply confused her husband was. The man had no great plan, did not, in fact, know for sure what he was doing, and consequently brought about his own destruction ("Pulled his house apart while weaving"). Augusta suggests that Penelope knew what she was waiting for and had an excellent reason for pulling apart at night what she had woven in the day. She wonders aloud what Titus was waiting for; her musing lines imply that Titus didn't know either. Thus his recantation and subsequent betrayal of the family are anticipated and do not surprise the audience. It is what one might expect of "an eager, timorous, faulty man" (A, 144).

When brief but clear speeches such as Augusta's are cut, the problems that the family has inherited seem less specifically overpowering. Unless the audience has a strong idea of Titus' influence and his actions, his children will appear obsessed with trivia, struggling with shadows, arguing with a dead man.

In summary then, during July and August 1956, Barnes rewrote and substantially shortened the first two-thirds of the second act of *The Antiphon*, leaving only the masked attack scene and the dollhouse scene uncut. Her severe editing in this fifth draft cost the play a great deal in character development, theme, and general information; but it succeeded in getting the work close to the size Eliot had recommended. Barnes followed her manuscript with a letter: "On the thirty-first of August I mailed (registered) you back the fair copy of THE ANTIPHON that you had returned to me for cutting of act II. I have now brought the act down by some twenty odd pages. I think now it will do." This letter marks the end of the draft stages of the play.

To look back from this vantage point, with the writing virtually finished, is to see *The Antiphon* from a unique point of view that strongly influences one's ideas about the growth and nature of the play.

First, although the length of the play is approximately the same in the original and final drafts, it changes radically in the middle drafts. This change is a result of the movement of historical information from act 1 to act 2 in the second, third, and fourth drafts and the subsequent cutting of much of it in the fifth. These fluctuations in length, while significant, reveal little in comparison to the changes in the play's nature. If *The Antiphon* begins as a tragicomedy, it ends as a modern verse tragedy. The drafts show that it was not originally pure comedy or tragedy, but a mixture of both with the stress on comedy in the first two acts, tragedy in the third, allowing the audience to slowly acquire a deepening sense of the problems portrayed as entirely serious and far-reaching in their implications.

The Antiphon has much in common with *Ryder*, Barnes' popular novel of the late 1920s. The novel depicts farm life in New York, which in the play is depicted by character reminiscences. That is, *Ryder* deals with all of the humor inherent in an unconventional marriage and family situation, *The Antiphon* with all the agony. The two stories overlap at the end when the women together face the terror of loneliness, hunger, and approaching death.

The early drafts of *The Antiphon* contain silly jokes, an abundance of physical activity, and the casual development apparent in *Ryder*. Jack and Jonathan succumb to obvious puns, while Dudley and Elisha are even more gross and physically abusive. They roughhouse with their mother and sister through most of act 2, play for a long time on a wide variety of instruments and march-dance all over the stage. Miranda is so relaxed in the opening scene of the early drafts that she tells the audience who Jack really is, and Jonathan tells them again in act 1 when he recognizes Jeremy's disguise. Jack asks Miranda questions and then proceeds to embellish and augment her answers until she finds it necessary to caution him that he knows too much, rather than to *suspect* him of knowing too much as in the later drafts. She broadly states that his disguise will fool no one if he continues to give all the answers. In the early drafts Jonathan, too, raised all the Burley-Hobbs children and could recognize their separate voices singing in the chapel by the whistling of the missing teeth. He quickly recognizes Jeremy and talks about his childhood at Burley.

There are other significant changes in detail occurring in the later drafts. At the beginning Dudley is the oldest child with Miranda second, Elisha third, and Jeremy last, but as the play progresses, Barnes removes all the references to Jeremy as the youngest and gives him knowledge and information that had earlier been Dudley's. For example, it was originally Dudley who discovered Titus wrestling in the reeds with Trudy (one of Titus' additional wives), whereas in the last version Jeremy calls his father a "seducer" (A, 159), thereby helping to set in motion the process that ends in a general exodus from Burley. Also in the early drafts are lines that suggest Jeremy's usurped position (see his soliloquy, [A, 92–94] and allow Augusta to mourn his departure in such a way as to suggest that her romantic view of the past includes the return of her eldest son to do battle for his rights and hers, according to the ancient laws of primogeniture.

In general, then, there is more movement, openness, ease, and activity in the early drafts; and in the midst of the "hurly-Burley" all the information necessary for an understanding of the plot gets dispensed in a rather lusty fashion. Even at the end of the second act, when she has been severely reminded of her past sins and sharply accused by her children, Augusta calls for a judgment rather than a curse. Her final statement of act 2 opens up the whole gaudy situation to the world for its better judgment, rather than hiding the truth and turning it in on the ill-fated house as in the later version. A kind of purge by public witness is invited and the guilt, like the other incidents of the past, is dealt with in a vigorous and straightforward manner.7

Next, the characters are more outspoken about their emotional states in the early drafts. Miranda says that she must be Augusta since Augusta says so; Jack in his soliloquy wishes he could stop shaking with fear and get on with whatever it is he plans to do, now that he has gotten himself to Burley, and in act 2 he displays open hostility toward his mother. As a result, his and Miranda's whole plan of action seems more casual, even fragmented.

Most important, the central theme of the human antiphon is introduced earlier and more obviously in the early drafts. When Augusta passes harsh judgment on her daughter (A, 163), Jonathan answers:

> BURLEY: I think you much mistaken.
> Your daughter is yourself,
> But only more offended.
> She's not you alone; she's also what you called for;
> She is response.

This is a remarkably clear statement of the response theme and of the mother-daughter identity that will be demonstrated in act 3. In later drafts and the published versions, only the first and third lines are retained, the others are removed.

Throughout the early drafts, the one in act 3 is quieter, lyrical but somber, and the burst of hysterical anger followed by the beating death at the end is quite shocking. As the play develops, however, darker qualities begin to permeate the other two acts, changing them over the course of four draft stages with the addition of elements of fear, dread, suspicion, danger, and long-harbored hatred. The merry carelessness is gradually toned down or eliminated as night descends, literally and figuratively, over the stage.

This slow development toward the tragic and away from the comic, toward the subtle and away from the obvious, continued into the fourth draft stage, when the reading at Cambridge occurred.[8] Because of the cool reception of the play and the actors' confusion, Barnes backtracked slightly and made changes intended to remove some of the verbal ambiguity or further explain the action. It was also in the fourth draft that Barnes first labeled her play "a tragedy in verse," thereby acknowledging the direction in which *The Antiphon* was moving.

But the major alteration that deeply affected the nature of *The Antiphon* was the severe cutting it underwent in the fifth draft stage. This was an alteration of a different kind, abrupt and final. The editing in the fourth draft may have been for the best, but the excising in the fifth was too much. Gaps appeared in the play that the uninitiated reader would be hard-pressed to fill. Language and logic became condensed, even abbreviated to such an extent that in some passages the words turned into a kind of shorthand, indecipherable for a first-time reader, impossible for a listening audience.

By the time this cutting took place, Barnes had been working continuously on the play for six years or more. Eliot had read and discussed it many times; it had acquired a familiarity for them that no longer allowed them to see it as difficult or dense. Eliot was thinking of playing time, the attention span of the audience, reader interest, and the reluctant board at Faber and Faber; Barnes was thinking of publication. All her time and effort would be lost if the play were never to be published. When Eliot told her to cut the second act, she gave up trying to salvage the hayhook scene, the descriptions of Augusta as a child, many of Jonathan's observations, and the travellers' comments on Titus and Miranda, saving only the most essential information and the best poetry. The result was one long, intricate, complex image after another. Such images, encountered for the first time without knowledge of their original form or intent, can be very discouraging, as many critics were later to insist. However, read in the context of the drafts and their cumulative development, these images become much more accessible and intelligible. They can be seen not as complicated insults directed to an ignorant audience, but as the collective efforts of author, editor, and publisher struggling to get the work into print.

To conclude, I would like to make one personal note. Of the three hundred lines removed from the final edition of the play, this article has considered only about thirty, a mere fraction of what Barnes had included in her original conception. If these cuts could be put back into the text of the play, especially act 2, the original *Antiphon* would emerge as the beautifully coherent and poignant tragedy that its author had envisioned.

¶ What a dreadful thing (excepting for Valerie) the whole history of that poor wretched man [Eliot], the gifted and mourning. And was that a grim last joke? The "damp corner" of St. Michaels, under a dreadful window beam, riddled by watch beetles, the floor boards gaping, the church boiler cracked, the carrillon broken. I don't know what to make of it, do you? Anymore than I understand his cultivation of Groucho Marx, (his picture on Tom's office wall, and mine, if you noticed, just above it—Tom told me it was there so, and remarked that "undoubtedly I'd not be as pleased as I should"—all thing strange things. . . . The rather stuffy, and I presume completely accurate assessment (from the obituary, *Times*) was, as you suggest, probably written by Mr. Hayward, now in that "after death mood," that falsifies, just as surely as it falsifies in the case of too much living fame. Cyril Connolly, with his querulous acerbity, and his somewhat androgynous sword play, sticks Tom "wriggling on the wall," with "we were sapped and ruined by the contagion of his despair!" . . . the "veritable brainwashing" . . . perfect! And Hugh Kenner has made an acute observation; "This withdrawal of any affirmative personality, has allowed his work to be discussed, and like such a legacy, it invades the reader's mind and there undergoes an assimilation which soon persuades us that we have always possessed it." I consider this one of the most fog-clearing insights on the Eliot influence to date.

—Djuna Barnes,
letter to Peter Hoare,
18 January 1965

"To Make Her Mutton at Sixteen": Rape, Incest, and Child Abuse in <u>The Antiphon</u>

Louise A. DeSalvo

Djuna Barnes' *The Antiphon*, a tragic drama in three acts, is a chilling, utterly realistic, and highly accurate portrayal of the psychodynamics and sexual pathology that operate within a family organized so that each child (but especially Miranda, the daughter) will be available for routinized and ritualized sexual molestation that their father, Titus Higby Hobbs, disguises (with the collusion of his dim-witted wife, Augusta) as religious ceremony.

The Antiphon is an early and extremely overt and courageous example of the literary exploration of a girl's victimization by incest, a subject that, according to Judith Herman's landmark study, *Father-Daughter Incest*, was not usually treated in literature, until recently, until "the resurgence of the women's liberation movement" even by "the most courageous explorers of sexual mores" who "simply refused to deal with the fact that many men, including fathers, feel entitled to use children for their sexual enjoyment."[1]

Barnes inverts the usual process of narrative progression by presenting the reader or the viewer with the *effect* of Miranda's history on her character, before she recounts its cause in Titus Higby Hobbs' rape of his daughter.[2] The effect of reading the play or seeing it is shattering. From the moment that Barnes' central character, Miranda, sets foot on the stage, as she enters Burley Hall in England, her ancestral home, we enter the cracked cosmology of a woman who has been raped by her father, although this fact is withheld from us until much later in the play. As her brother Dudley puts it, "She's afraid of life" (*A*, 137). It is first necessary that we behold the world

---

This essay was written in memory of my sister, Jilda Calabrese.

as Miranda beholds it; that we see the effect of his act on the way she perceives the world; that we live through her terror, fear, and self-loathing, moment by moment; that we learn her language, the language of the incest victim, which simultaneously masks and reveals; and that we experience her extraordinary bravery in simply continuing to live, instead of doing away with herself, which would be far simpler, far less painful. Only after we enter Miranda's world are we given the cause for her seeming pathology in her father's barbarous misuse of her at sixteen, when "he tried to make her mutton,"[3] nothing more than a piece of meat, to be devoured, to be used sexually, by any man that he has allowed to have access to her, including her brothers.

The effect of this form is extraordinarily realistic, because it duplicates the need of the incest victim to maintain her silence, to maintain her dignity, to hide behind a cloak of normalcy. Miranda presents herself to us at first as just any woman, although she comes to represent for us all women who have been sexually abused as children—up to one-third of *all* women.[4]

Act 1 introduces all of the participants in the tragedy, with the exception of Augusta, the mother, who makes her entrance during act 2. Because her father has ripped her open, Miranda, wherever she goes, perceives "a rip in nature" (*A*, 82): "The world is cracked—and in the breach/My fathers mew" (*A*, 83). Because she can never get past that moment of her desecration, the rape has robbed her of her present, and so for Miranda all time is past time, "This lichen bridled face of time" (*A*, 84). For Miranda all time is rape-time, and rape is the ultimate act of ownership, for what the rapist wants to do is to own his victim's psyche: he wants to imprint his image onto his victim's consciousness for every single moment of her waking life.

Miranda understands that when her mother married her father, she too was victimized. The ceremony of marriage was also the ceremony of Augusta's obliteration, and Barnes suggests that *any* marriage, not only Augusta's marriage, insists upon the extinction of the woman: "Hopping and singing went she, when in one/Scant scything instant was gaffed down. . . ./in passion's clabber drowned,—/Holding a single flower upright" (*A*, 87).

The act of sexual intercourse, for Augusta, is described by her daughter as "the tragic ballet," "that sprawl" (*A*, 87). Instead of portraying the act of giving birth as a dignified act, Miranda describes it in bestial terms, seeing her mother as a dog who "pupped truncated grief" (*A*, 87). This description not only conveys Miranda's disgust with all things sexual; it also indicates her feelings of revulsion, loathing, and hatred of her mother.

From the moment of their birth Augusta regards her male children very differently from the way she regards her female child, having internalized her husband's and society's loathing of her own gender. At the moment of Miranda's birth, there has been no celebration: "Yet in her hour, her either end being terror,/The one head on the other stared, and wept" (*A*, 87). Whereas she has had "three sons [whom] she leaned to fairly," on Miranda "she cast the privy look of dogs/Who turn to quiz their droppings" (*A*, 87).

Barnes establishes, therefore, that from the moment of Miranda's birth her mother regards her as shit. Whereas her brothers have been "pupped," she has been excreted. Because she is excrement, it is no wonder that she has been abused: she does not even possess the status of beast, which is the image which is reserved for her brothers; she does not possess even the status of human excrement—she is beneath even that image.

This image of the girl-child as nothing more than dog excrement is repeated again and again in *The Antiphon*, and Miranda's language, a kind of lyric coprolalia, is completely understandable given the fact of how she has been regarded. Barnes also implies that her mother's birth canal is reserved for male children; a girl-child emerges from her mother's anus. Barnes therefore transforms the culture's preference for male children into this stunning and powerful image which answers why women are treated like shit: they are treated like shit, because, to the patriarchy, they *are* shit.

Because her brothers have a privileged position within the society and within the family hierarchy, Miranda, with good cause, states: "I fear brothers" (*A*, 90). Her brothers are violent barbarous men, true sons of Titus Higby Hobbs: they are their "father's blasphemy" (*A*, 100). Soon after Dudley appears, he announces "when I don't understand a thing—/I *kick it!*" (*A*, 98), and we know instantly that one of the things that he has kicked has been Miranda. In fact, we realize soon after their entrance that both Dudley and Elisha count, as their right and privilege, access to Miranda's body, so that in addition to having been violated by her father, she has also been violated by her brothers, which is in keeping with recent research that has determined that once other male members of a family learn that a girl has been sexually abused, they will also begin to abuse her. Dudley indicates this, when he says, "we loved the lamb—/Till she turned mutton" (*A*, 147). When Dudley first sees her, he calls her "Our deadly beloved vixen, in the flesh," and he says, "What more could two good brothers want?" (*A*, 99). Dudley uses the word "want" as a double entendre, a form of discourse used again and again, obsessively, by each of the characters throughout the play. It indicates quite clearly that this family is fixated on sex, preoccupied with it as a weapon of power that forces the status of victim upon women.

We know that Miranda is fair game for her brothers; whatever they want from her, they get. The name Miranda—which in Latin means "to be admired"—is brilliantly and savagely ironic. Miranda is all too much admired by each male member of the family, even as each member of the family, including her mother, reviles her and victimizes her. And we soon learn that both Elisha and Dudley prefer to degrade Miranda through sodomy—the ultimate expression of their revulsion of her and their sexual domination of her — because they do not even need to see her face. The act of sodomy also serves as a reminder of her status in the family as no better than excrement. When he sees Miranda and Augusta, Elisha says, "Turn them to the wall" (*A*, 99). As Burley, Augusta's brother and witness to the family interaction, puts it, Elisha "walks behind his love, to kick her down" (*A*, 139). In describing how he "teases" members of his family — although it is clear that he is referring to Miranda — Elisha says, "I gouge my chin into the shoulder bone,/And whiz my thumb into the buttock joint" (*A*, 139). All family "play" in the Hobbs family is sexual "play" that involves sexual degradation. And the Hobbs boys describe their behavior as a form of sport. It is important to note that this use of sodomy both to "own" Miranda and to degrade her illuminates the fact that these men so despise women that they prefer anal intercourse to entering a woman through the vagina.[5] This both denies her essential nature as woman and suggests as well that they use Miranda as a replacement for their unacknowledged homoerotic desires or (even more likely) their desire to vent their rage on their father by raping him — but because they believe he is more powerful than they are, they find a substitute in Miranda and in other women.

Even Jeremy, the preferred son, disguised as Jack, has used Miranda. As he states, "Being vertical is one of her positions" (*A*, 107) — being on her back, being sexually available to any male member of the family who wants to use her, is in the nature of things as far as these sons of Titus Higby Hobbs are concerned. And he colludes with his brothers in their plan to murder their mother by playing on Augusta's jealousy of Miranda and Miranda's deep-seated rage at her mother for not having protected her.

After meeting Jack in Paris, and without knowing that he is her brother, she has probably been involved in a sexual relationship with him, and she has let him accompany her to their ancestral home, and Jack/Jeremy describes the meeting in language that transforms Miranda into tragic hero:

> *Say I fell in, a time ago in Paris.*
> *I, with the single, she, the compound eye*
> *Met back to back — a kind of paradox.*
> *Descending the terraces of Sacre Coeur*
> *I saw her stand before the city literal,*
> *Tall, withdrawn, intent and nothing cunning;*
> *. . . Her hands dropped and thoroughly performed —*
> *The tension lost, as in tragediennes*
> *Who've left the tragic gesture to the stage,*
> *And so go forth alone to meet disaster — (A, 104)*

It seems as if Jack/Jeremy has enjoyed knowing that he is committing incest, even as he keeps this knowledge from his sister. And he tells Burley the history of her life in the demimonde and how he has seduced her. He describes to Burley a woman, her "hip well stapled back, the thigh/In its cup

full quartered, lay and couched/Where she sat checking on her gap in time—"
(*A*, 111). Throughout the play, "gap," "rip," "tear," and other words that
denote forcible entry or opening refer to Miranda's vagina, which has been
forcibly entered first by Titus and then again and again and again throughout her life. Jack/Jeremy tells Burley, who wants to hear all the details, how at
"the apex [climax]" he cried out "lady, do not scream" (*A*, 111). Although at
first we are not sure that he is referring to Miranda, when Burley asks Jack/
Jeremy to name the woman he is describing, he says "Miranda" (*A*, 112).

Even as Miranda fears her brothers, Jack articulates his fear of his
sister: as Jack puts it, "I became her man—/Out of the high fear" (*A*, 113).
But Jack/Jeremy also understands that Miranda, because of how she has
been misused, is potentially deadly, and he describes her leaving Paris "As
the leopard in a land made desolate . . . forsaking covert for some prowl" (*A*,
104). Miranda is potentially deadly because she has nothing left to lose,
because her very existence is testimony to the bestiality of each of the male
members of her family. As her mother sees it, her status as victim has
degraded her, but it has also ennobled her, and her very existence reminds
them of their own degradation: "She's one of awful virtue," says Augusta,
"and the Devil" (*A*, 140). Until she is safely dead, she just might tell her story,
which would defame each of them, would unmask the fraud of Titus Higby
Hobbs. Simply because Miranda exists, simply because she can bear witness
to the atrocities she has experienced, she is a threat. What *The Antiphon*
enacts in its concluding scenes is the horrifying consequences to the incest
victim of the silence being broken.

Like every victim of incest, Miranda has internalized a sense of
worthlessness, a compulsion to repeat the degrading experiences that gave
her both the only attention that she has had as a child and the only power
that she has known. When Burley asks Jack if he will betray her, Jack states
that he won't have to: all he will have to do is set up a situation so that she
will destroy herself: "It won't be necessary; she is her own collision./. . . She
has rash fortitude; she will undo herself,/Meeting herself but totally un-
armed" (*A*, 114). Her father's rape has initiated her into prostitution, as
every act of incest is an initiation into prostitution,[6] and it is highly likely
that Miranda has spent her life in the care of "patrons" who pay her for her
sexual services. Later in the play, her sons describe how Augusta has sent
Miranda into prostitution to support her after Titus has abandoned his
family.

Act 2 is an increasingly terrifying litany of the perverse and sadistic
behavior of Titus Hobbs and the complicity of his wife, Augusta. In the
course of this act, which begins in sardonic humor but which ends in the
brutalization of Augusta and Miranda, we learn that Titus has practiced
polygamy, that he was a believer in "Free-love," "Free lunch," "Free
everything" (*A*, 127–28), and that, for the most part, Augusta has condoned
his behavior. Even now she seems to miss the time when her husband's

"wenches" roamed the countryside: "I almost wish/They walked again, I'd have a fourth at bridge—" (*A*, 124).

When the family settled in New York after having taken a ship at Plymouth, it was in a house "he liked to call 'Hobbs Ark'" (*A*, 128), a house surrounded by a high wall that afforded him the kind of protection that he needed to carry out his utter domination of his family—a wall "Which he'd built up high for fear of tongues—" (*A*, 159). It is clear that he believed his role, like Noah's, was to father a whole new race: "He said he was the stud to breed a kingdom" (*A*, 161). And Augusta was enthralled by him: "A very autumn cone he was, all scaled in medals;/Braced in knocking points; ribboned, buckled—/I do love a man who jangles!" (*A*, 135).

Unfortunately, not only did Titus jangle, he also beat his children and quite possibly even murdered a "bastard child" (*A*, 165). Dudley recalls, "even as a baby in your arms/You let him lash me with his carriage whip"; "I have against my father that he whipped me/*Before I knew him*" (*A*, 143). In response to this accusation of her lack of maternal protection, Augusta can only respond, "That puzzles children—" (*A*, 143), which is a completely inappropriate response given the atrocities she has permitted her husband to engage in—as completely inappropriate as her description of him as "an eager, timorous, faulty man" (*A*, 144). Augusta has learned to use a language which excuses men for their behavior, which does not hold them accountable for their actions, which romanticizes them or makes them tragic heroes, rather than one which describes them as reprehensible when they are reprehensible, as in this case. Titus is no religious prophet, no hero, no saint, as his wife sees him; rather, he is a sadistic monster who destroyed his children, made perverts of his sons and a prostitute out of his daughter. As Elisha says, "You also did exactly what he told you,/And let him get away with anything" (*A*, 143), while Augusta lived with the masquerade that they were living a good Christian life and that she was the good Christian wife, "Knitting 'little things' for the Swahili" (*A*, 144). Barnes suggests that the brutalization of children, polygamy, and incest can all be carried on within the context of civilization, provided those practices are disguised as the practice of a religion; indeed, Barnes suggests that one of the prime functions of religion is to provide a shield behind which these practices *can* be carried out.

When confronted with her complicity, Augusta remarks, "I was a victim" (*A*, 159), and she states, "In my day we did not leave our husbands" (*A*, 160). In fact, Titus' total domination is made possible by the unlikelihood that Augusta could support herself without him. Although her behavior is indefensible, it accords with the behavior of many mothers who are trapped into complying with their husband's victimization of their children because there is no way for them to support themselves and their children outside the patriarchal household. Indeed, men's control of the economic power structure of a society results in women and children having to choose between going hungry and enduring any behavior that the head of the household chooses to engage in. Barnes suggests that any society that does not allow women access to economic well-being is a society that covertly clings to the right of the father to behave as he pleases within his own household, even if his behavior is like that of Titus Hobbs. In fact, when Titus abandons his family, Augusta finds that she cannot support herself, and she pushes Miranda into prostitution to support her: "When you, grass-widow, were set out to pasture,/. . . Pushed her, into the dark, as sole provider" (A, 169).

There is considerable evidence in the play that Augusta has engaged in some of her husband's practices herself. She calls Elisha an "unnatural, brutish boy"; she says "you nursed me standing!" (A, 173). And although it is unclear whether that act was forced upon her, by Titus or by Elisha, it is likely that she initiated her own incestuous relationship with Jeremy, who fled the household when he tired of it. Augusta remarks that Jeremy left her "stranded on an high bad bed,/. . . Shedding the airy tears of age, and rocking/My one and happy memory, the hour/We went hunting, all alone together,/In the Catskill mountains" (A, 133).[7]

The result of their having been beaten by their father and sexually abused by their mother is that all three of Augusta's sons exact a deadly vengeance upon women in general, and their mother and sister in particular. Theirs is the psychopathology of the sex offender, for, as Elisha puts it, "There's only one kind inch on any woman—/Between her tot and tail—" (A, 141). And rather than seeing Miranda as an equal sufferer within their family, they turn their rage at their mother for not having protected them from Titus—and their rage at Titus for abusing them—onto all women, including Miranda. And although they have been victimized by their father, they have also internalized his idea that men are superior to women, which is another reason that they cannot include Miranda within their number so that, although each of them has the comradeship of his brothers, Miranda is completely alone. If they decide to join together to attack her, as they do by the end of the act and as they surely did during her childhood, she cannot possibly fight back.

The whole family seems to perceive Miranda's incestuous relationship with Titus as a privileged status. Elisha refers to Titus as Miranda's "first cadet" (A, 135). And Augusta says that "Titus overwhelmed all but Miranda" (A, 147). As the act progresses, it becomes clear that, despite what has happened to Miranda, every member of the family is jealous of her and envies her. Augusta envies her youth and feels enormous rivalry with her daughter. She asks her brother Burley to tell them "How I was handsomer than she" (A, 142) and she tells Miranda that Titus' "acts to me/Were never gentle, fond nor kind;/Nor he never held nor stroked me anywhere" (A, 212), implying that Titus fondled, held, and stroked Miranda. And rather than blaming Titus for destroying the family and perverting the relationships within it, she blames Miranda: "I pushed four children from my list," she says, "One stayed in the web to pull it down—" (*A,* 117).

At the end of act 2, after Jack and Burley exit, Dudley and Elisha begin to enact a debauched scenario in which Dudley dons a pig's mask, and Elisha an ass's. Augusta, whose major defense mechanism seems to be a denial of what goes on about her, gleefully chortles, "A game! A game!" (*A,* 175). Dudley, "striking out in light rapid taps" at Augusta, taunts her, "Going to play with baby?" (*A,* 176), and it becomes clear that Augusta and Titus have foisted their episodes of sexual abuse onto their children by introducing them as play, as game.

Elisha tells Miranda that she'll "be crawling in my gutters yet"; he calls her an "abominable slug of vengeance," and he refers to her "starving puss" (*A,* 178), and, as he mauls her, he calls her "dog" (*A,* 179). Dudley cheers Elisha on and urges sodomy: "Slap her rump, and stand her on four feet!/That's her best position!" (*A,* 176). Throughout this deadly serious scene of sexual attack which is disguised as sexual play, Miranda asks her mother to join forces with her as a woman against her sons, but Augusta will not; in fact, Augusta trivializes the impact of what is happening to Miranda and what has happened to her: "I've seen my daughter die before, and make it" (*A,* 180).

What they all fear most is Miranda telling her tale. Elisha states, "If we take her home and loose her on our ledgers,/She'll blot us up" (*A,* 180). He calls her "Manless, childless, safeless document—" (*A,* 179), and what seems to enrage him as well is that as much as they torment her, she is bound to no man.

When Jack and Burley reenter with a model of Hobbs Ark, a "beast-box, doll's house" (*A,* 181), we realize that it is a prop that will be used to split Augusta from Miranda even further; it will, in fact, be used to turn Augusta's envy of Miranda into murderous rage.

The dollhouse scene is one of the most brilliantly orchestrated scenes in modern drama. In it, Titus Hobbs is reduced to the size of a tiny doll; this monster, who has destroyed the lives of this whole family, becomes "A chip, a doll, a toy, a pawn,/. . . A nothing!" (*A,* 182). Augusta ruefully states that if Titus had been the size of the doll in real life, "I could have jumped him, and have been/Happily unacquainted with you all" (*A,* 182). The use of the dollhouse and the Titus-doll to symbolically deflate Titus' power exposes the fact that the father's power, depends upon the fact that he is perceived as having absolute power, absolute authority. This is what the institution of the patriarchy depends upon: that a "little man," a "midge, a tick, a peg, . . . a gnat" (*A,* 182), is perceived by the members of his family as all-powerful, and more than anything else, it is this perception of the father's power that keeps him in power. Jack reinforces this when he gives the Titus-doll to Miranda and says: "You have an husband in the hand,/A slave, a fit of pine to do your bidding./Was this the inch that set you out at hack?/Then 'tis a kissing splinter for a catch,/And you can game again!" (*A,* 182).

But rather than being relieved that this monster-man has been whittled down to his proper size, Augusta is furious: "Whose malice was it hacked him down?" she asks (*A*, 183), and she is furious precisely because she can excuse her utter enslavement to a man of heroic stature, but the fact that she has been enslaved by "A midge, a tick, . . . a gnat" deflates her own status as well. Barnes' dollhouse scene is a brilliant depiction of how women who have been dominated by men need to make heroes of them in order to rationalize their having been dominated. It is too risky to see them as they really are, because then the enormous self-sacrifice, the self-annihilation that comes from serving their needs and their wishes will have counted for naught. To be the slave of a hero is one thing; to be the slave of "this splinter" (*A*, 183) is quite another. Augusta's great awakening, forced upon her by her sons, is that she "saw him [Titus] great because he said so" (*A*, 183). And once Augusta realizes this, she will never be the same again.

But the revelations do not end there. Jack/Jeremy pushes Augusta against the attic window of the doll's house and asks her what she sees. She replies, "A bedroom, no bigger than my hand" (*A*, 184). Miranda asks her mother if she remembers the scene that was enacted in that attic room, and Augusta replies, in a superbly crafted phrase that reveals her solipsism, "I don't care what you've done, I forgive me" (*A*, 184). But Jack forces Augusta to look again, and she sees, as "in a glass darkly," the "fighting shadow of the Devil and the Daughter" (*A*, 185). Miranda counters, telling her that what she sees is "Miranda damned, . . ./Dragging rape-blood behind her, like the snail—" (*A*, 185).

In refusing to use the word "incest" to refer to what Titus has done to her, Miranda calls incest by its proper name: rape. She refuses to protect Augusta any further by denying the impact of Titus' act upon her. She refuses to protect Augusta any further by denying the role that she has played in paving the way for Titus' rape.

Although in this scene it seems as if Augusta is calling Titus "Devil," earlier in the act Dudley reminds Augusta that when Miranda was a little girl, "You had her so convinced she was the devil,/At seven, she was cutting down the hedges,/To furnish brier to beat her to your favour;/All time since, been hunting for her crime" (*A*, 164). Thus, Augusta has blamed Miranda for her own rape; *she* is the Devil, not Titus, who is a member of the elect and who can do no wrong.

But Jack states that any mother of an incest victim is nothing more than a madam running a house of prostitution: "You made yourself a *madam* by submission/With, no doubt, your apron over head" (*A*, 185); "between you both, you made/Of that slaughter house a babe's *bordel*" (*A*, 186). Even Augusta is forced to admit, "I liked her most when she looked wanted" (*A*, 164). Although it is not stated clearly—because, of course, it is a family secret—it is highly likely that Miranda has become pregnant from the rape: as Burley states, "There towered an infant on her face!" (*A*, 185). It seems, however, that Miranda has never delivered the child because she is referred to as "childless." Indeed, it is even possible that the bastard child whom Titus murdered was Miranda's child.

To protect the family's reputation, Miranda is given or sold to a man who agrees to marry her: "A girl who'd barely walked away sixteen—/Tipped to a travelling cockney thrice that age,/. . . . Why?/Titus had him handy—" (*A*, 186). And Miranda has been so seduced by her father's claims to being an instrument of God's will that she submits: "Though Miranda cried at first, like the ewe,/'Do not let him—but if it will atone—'/Offering up her silly throat for slashing" (*A*, 186).

An earlier version of the scene is even more graphic, even more barbaric, although it deflects attention from Miranda's rape to Titus' insane mutilation of the heifers. In this version of the scene, Dudley says: "Hauled her in an hay-hook to the barn/Left her dangling, while in the field below/He offered to give her, to the farm-hand, for a goat,—/You know, I've seen heifers dangling from an halter/Just like that, while he charged the rape-blade in."[8]

In act 3, Augusta and Miranda confront one another in a scene that makes the confrontation at the end of Edward Albee's *Who's Afraid of Virginia Woolf?* appear tame by comparison. In fact, in the history of women's literature, it has no parallel in its graphic depiction of the hatred that a mother had for her daughter and the violence that a daughter can expect from her mother. In this act, Barnes tackles a topic that is even more taboo than the topic of rape: she unflinchingly explores the fact that daughters are alone in the universe and that mothers are often the instruments of the patriarchy's need to annihilate its daughters when it can, or mutilate them when it cannot. As Miranda puts it, she is "Carrion Eve" (*A*, 193).

Throughout her life Miranda has had to choose to believe either that her mother *didn't* know that she was raped by her father, and that she must face her life knowing that she had not had the protection of a mother who should have been there to take care of her, or that her mother *did* know that she was raped by her father, and that she must face her life knowing that she has not had the protection of a mother whom society says should have been there to take care of her. Either way, she has been betrayed. This is the horrifying dilemma of the incest victim: whichever alternative she chooses to believe, the consequences for her psyche are the same—she is alone in a universe of male lust with no one to protect her; she is totally alone in a universe that she knows, on evidence, is out to destroy her and will destroy her whether she submits or whether she fights. As Miranda puts it, "By the unrecording axis of my eye/It should be observed I have no people:/But on the dark side, there I entertain" (*A*, 205).

And that betrayal by her mother, even more than the act of rape itself, is what she often fixes upon. As Miranda puts it: "To think I had a mother should betray me!/Tax me guilty both of audit and default;/Tot me up, as idiots their droppings,/And as indifferently, tick off the count" (*A*, 195). This, of course, deflects the blame from the father onto the mother. Rather than understanding that the father should have stopped himself, the daughter in her own way also colludes in absolving him, no matter how much she may hate him, for she chooses to believe that her mother should have stopped her father, rather than blaming the father for not stopping himself.

What Barnes understands as well is that the mother will also inevitably blame the daughter for what has transpired and that this will also exonerate the father. When the mother enacts her revenge, it will not be against the father, but against her daughter, her father's "scapegoat" (*A*, 198). As she beats Miranda to death with the bell at the end of *The Antiphon*, Augusta shouts, "You are to blame, to blame, you are to blame—" (*A*, 223).

Augusta is a pathetic, deadly prisoner of the patriarchy, and when she is confronted with the knowledge of what has happened to her daughter, she can do nothing but enact the revenge decreed by a patriarchal ideology embedded in the roles established for women in fairy tales. Barnes understands that Augusta has internalized the notion that after you find your Prince Charming, you live happily ever after, immobilized in a universe of being loved and being cared for, and it is precisely her belief in the cosmology established in fairy tales that sets Augusta up to be Hobbs' prisoner. She never wants to grow up, to become a woman, to assume the responsibilities required of a mother. At the end of *The Antiphon*, she pleads with Miranda to play with her: "Do let's pretend we're girls again; let's play" (*A*, 210). One of the reasons for this, of course, is that in fairy tales there are only beautiful girls and beastly mothers; there are no role models which teach women how to become responsible adults who care for their daughters: for the power of the male to remain absolute, a woman must be immobilized by her love for a man. "Was I ever princess in a legend?/... *Did I sleep a hundred years?*" (*A*, 199). She kills Miranda, a "bloody Cinderella" (*A*, 193), rather than join with her in recognizing that each, in her own way, has been victimized. Augusta can never get beyond a solipsistic concern for her own pain to truly see what has happened to her children. She says, "God have mercy on me!" but it takes Miranda to say, "God have mercy on us all" (*A*, 216).

Augusta wants to be forgiven by Miranda: "Do not stamp me down for tally in the earth," she says. "Be merciful" (*A*, 204). Barnes understands that, in addition to suffering the torment of being victimized, Miranda is expected to pardon those who have degraded her. If she refuses; if she will not take care of their guilt for them; if she does not tell the rapist father that it really *was* all right; if she does not tell the colluding mother that she really could not have staved off her husband's attacks—then, in addition to suffering the rape and the effects of incest, she will be punished even more severely. Thus the most abused member of the family is expected to be the most forgiving; the most defenseless member of the family is expected to assume the burden of guilt of all its members. Her simple existence bears witness to their bestiality. If they can snuff her out, they can reclaim their own pretence to civilization. The greatest threat to the façade that is civilization is Miranda alive to tell her history.

Thus, in *The Antiphon* civilization and culture become nothing more than the high wall which Titus builds around his compound—the screen of silence behind which the screams accompanying the daily atrocities cannot be heard; it is the blind which prevents us from seeing that the norm in a patriarchal family is brutality and victimization. In setting her play during 1939, Barnes suggests that the events of that year were not an aberration in the history of the human race; rather, Hitler's behavior is reinterpreted for us, through Barnes, as normal behavior for a well-socialized male. The only problem with Hitler, as Barnes sees it, is that he has co-opted the right of the father to behave like a Hitler (as Titus does) within the confines of his own household. Barnes takes the word "holocaust" and applies it to the goings-on within the Hobbs household to underscore the devastation that Titus wreaked there: "Fie upon the whole of love's debris," says Augusta, "That horrid holocaust that is the price/Of passion's seizure" (*A*, 206). And Barnes suggests as well that had Hitler confined his attention to women only, his atrocities would have occupied nothing more than a footnote in the pages of the history of our times. The wall around Hobbs Ark reminds us of the walls around Hitler's death camps: Hitler has practiced one form of extermination; Titus Hobbs has practiced another. And the wall around Hobbs Ark is nothing more, nothing less than the picket fence or the privet hedge that delineates the boundary of the household in which the father as fascist reigns supreme.

But Barnes does not permit us to cling for one moment to the romanticized notion that women are protectors, that women are inherently more loving than men. As Miranda tells Augusta, "had [you] been a man/ you'd been the bloodiest villain of us all" (*A*, 201). And Barnes also unmasks the mythology that surrounds motherhood. Miranda states: "Every mother, in extortion for her milk—/ . . . Draws blood" (*A*, 210). Augusta expresses the fact that mothers are expected to nurture everyone, without getting any support themselves: "What's never been remarked is that the mother,/ Fearing what it is a spirit eats,/Goes headlong through her children's guts,/ Looking for bread" (*A*, 205).

The end of *The Antiphon*, in which Augusta beats Miranda to death with the curfew bell and Miranda submits to the beating, is so shattering precisely because it announces Barnes' understanding that a woman like Augusta will exact retribution for her husband's deed from her husband's victim—Miranda—which is the fate of the incest victim who is at great risk, especially from her mother, if the incest is discovered. Augusta can forgive Titus, but she can never forgive her daughter: "If you are speaking of your father, I forgive him" (*A*, 208). Moreover, it articulates that the daughter has no defense because the very notion that she has the potential power to defend the integrity of her person has never been taught to her; in fact, she has been taught the reverse. Jack says, "I might have known, being weary of the world,/. . . She'd not defend herself" (*A*, 223).

Barnes understands that the life of the victim of incest, if she is to survive, must be the life of silence, the life of a "Trappist, . . . an hard-won silence" (*A*, 202). For the incest victim to survive, she must keep her secret to herself. The penalty for the breaking of the silence, even if you do not break it yourself, is death. In killing Miranda, Augusta obliterates Miranda's (and paradoxically, her own) history. One major reason for her murdering her daughter is that she is terrified that her daughter will write her life, that her daughter will write something like *The Antiphon*: "May God protect us! I wonder what you'll write/When I am dead and gone!" (*A*, 209).

Barnes' tale is horrifyingly real, for she does not permit us to believe in the romance of the possibility of reconciliation between the abused daughter and her mother. Rather, she forces us to watch Miranda's murder at the hands of her mother. In this moment, Augusta becomes every woman bound to life-threatening patriarchal rites: she is every mother who has bound her daughter's feet; she is every mother who has held her daughter down for the ritual incision of clitoredectomy; she is every mother who has dressed her daughter in a wedding gown; she is every mother who has bound her daughter's behavior into the rigid, gender-proscribed constraints of silence, self-annihilation, and submission.

Barnes has chosen the name of her heroine carefully: Miranda in *The Antiphon* is twin sister to Shakespeare's Miranda,[9] and *The Antiphon* provides a cipher with which to reinterpret *The Tempest*. What Prospero has created on his island, the island to which he has escaped with his three-year-old daughter, is no different from Hobbs Ark. It is the fantasy kingdom of every incestuous father: a world without adult women who might intervene to protect his daughter from his total control over her. Prospero's language, like Titus', is the language of the seductive father: "No harm./I have done nothing but in care of thee,/Of thee, my dear one, thee, my daughter" (1.2.15).

Miranda's mother, "a piece of virtue" (1.2.55), conveniently disappears from Shakespeare's narrative after she has fulfilled her reproductive function of giving birth to Miranda. *The Tempest* therefore actualizes the absence of a mother's protection, which in *The Antiphon* is a reality, even though the mother herself is present. Shakespeare even usurps Miranda's mother's birthing function, creating a moment in which Prospero symbolically gives birth to Miranda, having on board the ship that takes them to the island "Infused with a fortitude from Heaven,/. . . Under my burden groaned, which raised in me/An undergoing stomach to bear up" (1.2.154).[10]

So unimportant is the function of Miranda's mother in this text that Shakespeare obliterates her history: we never hear how she died, or when she died, or if she died. Although Miranda vaguely remembers a world with

women ("Had I not/Four or five women once that tended me?" [1.2.46]), the
world that Prospero has created is the ultimate incestuous fantasyland, a
world without mature women. Like *The Antiphon*, *The Tempest* is in fact a
variation on the theme of Persephone being separated from her mother,
Ceres, and being carried to the underworld by Pluto. It is described by Ceres
in the masque in act 4 in which Ceres appears, mourning the loss of her
daughter and reviling Venus and Cupid who plotted her abduction. But in
Barnes' text there is no mother mourning the male possession of the
daughter's body. In the incestuous subtext of *The Tempest*, the uninhabited
island is the underworld, Miranda's mother is Ceres, Miranda is Persephone,
and Prospero is Pluto, Miranda's father/husband. And because the masque
which is performed to celebrate Miranda's betrothal to Ferdinand is described as Prospero's "present fanc[y]" (4.1.120), it becomes clear that
Miranda's being taken to the island by Prospero has been, in fact, the
correlative of Persephone's abduction.

In Prospero's world, the only woman allowed is daddy's little girl,
fifteen-year-old Miranda, who has been without the company of women for
twelve long years. And like all seductive fathers, instead of being parent to
his daughter, he expects his daughter to provide *him* with emotional
sustenance and support, which, of course, Miranda does: "Oh, my heart
bleeds/To think o' the teen [sorrow] that I have turned you to" (1.2.63).

Like Titus, Prospero has total control over what Miranda knows
about the world, and it is this control that makes it possible for him to
dominate her. Shakespeare's Miranda's knowledge of the world has come
from her father, her "schoolmaster" (1.2.172). When he doesn't want her to
ask any more questions, when he doesn't want her to know what is going on,
he simply puts her to sleep: "Here cease more questions./Thou art inclined to
sleep, 'tis a good dullness,/And give it way. I know you canst choose"
(1.2.185).[11]

Both Titus and Prospero are sadists. But in *The Tempest*, because
Prospero defines Caliban as less than human, the audience tolerates, even
laughs at, Prospero's brutality: "For this, be sure, tonight thou shalt have
cramps,/Side stitches, that shall pen they breath up. . . ./Thou shalt be
pinched" (1.1.324). Prospero excuses his treatment of Caliban by stating,
"In mine own cell . . . thou [Caliban] didst seek to violate/The honor of my
child" (1.2.345).

There is an enormous similarity between the way Elisha and Dudley
brutalize Miranda in *The Antiphon* and the scene in which Caliban has tried
to violate Miranda. Just as Titus has brutalized his sons, so, throughout *The
Tempest*, Caliban describes how he has been tortured by Prospero. "For
every trifle are they set upon me—/Sometime like apes, that mow and chatter
at me,/And after bite me" (2.2.8). Caliban attempts to rape Miranda to get
his revenge against his master; yet Caliban and the sons in *The Antiphon*
collude with the male in power in the domination and sexual degradation of

a woman—he is powerless to enact his revenge on the male who dominates him; but he does have the power to sexually defile a woman.

Ariel tells us that Prospero can see the future. If Prospero can see the future, then we must assume that he foresaw Caliban's attempted rape of Miranda and that he did not stop it—that he chose not to stop it. Prospero allows Caliban to attempt to rape Miranda for many of the same reasons that Titus has sold or given his daughter to the cockney in *The Antiphon*: using a lower-class, barbaric "other" to rape a daughter demeans her, degrades her even more than when he does it himself; it allows the incestuous father to enact his belief that women are worthless instruments to be defiled. Indeed, even when Miranda is under his thrall and is falling in love with Ferdinand, Prospero describes it in the following terms: "Poor worm [Miranda], thou art infected!" (3.1.31). When he turns Miranda over to Ferdinand, Prospero treats her as if she were a prostitute: Miranda is Ferdinand's "own acquisition/Worthily purchased" (4.1.13), as Barnes' Miranda is sold to the highest bidder.

Having Caliban attempt to rape her also satisfies a deep-seated voyeuristic desire, a desire to witness someone else engaging in a vulgar act, a bestial act; it establishes, moreover, the father's complete domination over his daughter's sexuality by demonstrating that he also controls the sexual behavior of every other man in his domain. Thus she learns the crucial lesson that the incestuous father seeks to teach his daughter: that every sexual encounter that she will ever have is really a sexual encounter with him. He totally controls her sexuality; her sexuality is his and not hers.

Prospero's setting up the love affair between Ferdinand and Miranda later in the play is different in degree but not in kind from his allowing Caliban to nearly rape his daughter, or from Titus selling Miranda to the farmer. Prospero, the ultimate voyeur, watches Ferdinand and Miranda just as he had watched Caliban and Miranda. Although Ferdinand and Miranda might think they are courting in private, and although they believe that they have freely chosen to love the other, they are, in fact, merely puppets in a drama that Prospero has scripted: "It goes on, I see,/As my soul prompts it" (1.2.419), he says, when he sees that Miranda thinks that Ferdinand is "A thing divine, for nothing natural/I ever saw so noble" (1.2.417). Prospero can see whatever they are doing any time that he chooses. In act 5, scene 1, he draws back the curtain to expose them as they are playing chess: not only does he use his powers to watch them himself, but he also uses his powers to expose their lovemaking to other male eyes.

Prospero's Miranda is "my gift, and thine own [Ferdinand's] acquisition" (4.1.14), just as Titus' Miranda is his gift to the farmer and the farmer's own acquisition. And it is clear why, at the end of *The Tempest*, Prospero is so world-weary, so depressed, so vexed. He has lost his possession, his Miranda. He has demonstrated to his satisfaction his utter control of Miranda's sexuality by using his powers to have her fall in love with

Ferdinand, he has transferred his ownership of her to a man whom he has chosen; yet this very act has removed her from him, and now she belongs to another man who will exert his right of ownership over her. In the incestuous subtext of the drama, his statement "Our revels now are ended" (4.1.147) takes on new meaning, and his statement that "We are such stuff/As dreams are made on" (4.1.156) becomes bitterly ironic, for Miranda is nothing more and nothing less than the physical embodiment of her father's fantasies, her father's dreams, her father's wishes. And we, as audience, become coconspirators to Miranda's enslavement because we choose to misapprehend her marriage to Ferdinand as cause for joyful celebration.

Miranda's enslavement in Prospero's kingdom is precisely the enslavement experienced by a daughter in an incestuous household like Hobbs Ark—and, to a lesser extent, by any girl in a patriarchal household. Prospero's world and Titus' world are the same world: the kingdom of the patriarchal family where the sexuality of girl children is controlled absolutely by the father; where initiation into sexuality is the right and prerogative of the father, unless he is stopped by a strong wife; where a girl is an object of sexual exchange, to be used to bring the father fame, fortune, or privilege; where girls are mesmerized into submission and held in thrall by their father's absolute power over them. Barnes' allusions to *The Tempest* (and to a score of other tragedies) serve to redefine the function of tragedy in a patriarchy, and she claims that form for women dramatists. She suggests that the tragic form forces us to elevate to the status of hero the most reprehensible males our society has produced. On one very important level, Shakespeare's *The Tempest*, like Barnes' *The Antiphon*, enacts the takeover of every woman's power by a man; it teaches the culture's ideal of total male dominance over women. And whereas Barnes criticizes this idea, *The Tempest* supports the idea that usurping a woman's power is a man's right, an event to be celebrated within the cultural form of comedy rather than criticized and deplored through tragedy, which Barnes uses to treat the same issue. Indeed, Barnes suggests that if a play enacts the takeover or diminution of feminine power (as through marriage), the patriarchy will celebrate it through comedy; but if a play enacts the loss of male power, the patriarchy will mourn the loss through tragedy.

The title of *The Antiphon* is apt: when a girl cries out for a mother's aid, the only response she can expect, the only antiphon she will ever receive, is betrayal. And in the Black Mass that is the climax of *The Antiphon*, Barnes substitutes the murdered and molested body and rape-blood of Miranda for the body and blood of Christ.

The Antiphon is Barnes' antiphon to *The Tempest*, and to every other patriarchal text in which the drama of the submission of daughters to fathers is celebrated rather than condemned. Barnes' tale is Shakespeare's tale told from Miranda's point of view. It is a woman's text; it is Miranda's text. It is the antiphon.

27. "For Mother from Djuna, May 20, 1906." Courtesy Special Collections, University of Maryland at College Park Libraries.

28. Zadel Barnes Gustafson, grandmother of Djuna Barnes. Courtesy of Duane F. and Kerron Barnes.

29. Wald Barnes, Djuna Barnes' father, and his second wife, Fanny Faulkner. Courtesy of Duane F. and Kerron Barnes.

30. Brian "Wald" Barnes, father of Djuna Barnes; inscribed "To Dear Sue from Wald," 31 October 1888. Courtesy Special Collections, University of Maryland at College Park Libraries.

31. Elizabeth Chappell Barnes, mother of Djuna Barnes. Courtesy Special Collections, University of Maryland at College Park Libraries.

32. Elizabeth Chappel Barnes, April 1936. Courtesy Special Collections, University of Maryland at College Park Libraries.

33. "The chalet, Cornwall-on-Hudson, where I was born June 12, 1892"; inscription on back in Barnes' handwriting. Courtesy Special Collections, University of Maryland at College Park Libraries.

34. "Djuna at about 20–22"; inscription on back. Courtesy Special Collections, University of Maryland at College Park Libraries.

35. Profile of Barnes, circa 1917. Courtesy Special Collections, University of Maryland at College Park Libraries.

DJUNA LITTLE   DJUNA BIG

36. *Djuna Little, Djuna Big*; self-caricature by Barnes. Courtesy Special Collections, University of Maryland at College Park Libraries.

37. Barnes and the Baroness, Elsa von Freytag-Loringhoven. Courtesy Special Collections, University of Maryland at College Park Libraries.

38. Thelma Wood. Courtesy Special Collections, University of Maryland at College Park Libraries.

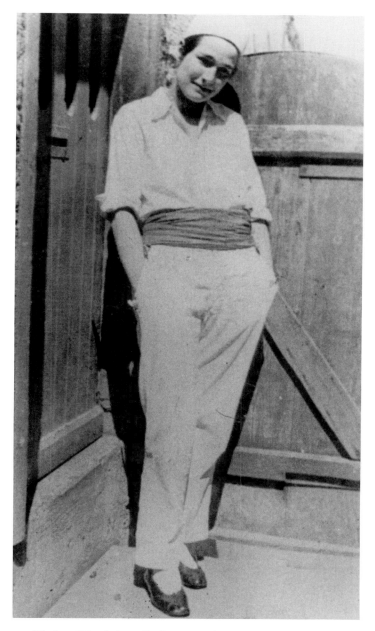

39. Thelma Wood; inscribed "Remember Me?". Courtesy Special
Collections, University of Maryland at College Park Libraries.

40. "To Dearest Mother, Christmas 1919, Djuna." Courtesy Special Collections, University of Maryland at College Park Libraries.

41. Djuna Barnes (*left*) and Mina Loy, Nice, France. Courtesy Special Collections, University of Maryland at College Park Libraries.

42. Eleanor Fitzgerald, director of the Provincetown Players, with
dog, Buffy. Courtesy Special Collections, University of Maryland at
College Park Libraries.

43. Ernest "Putzi" Hanfstaengl, Barnes, and Charles Henri Ford, Munich, 1931. Courtesy of the Harry Ransom Research Center, University of Texas at Austin.

44. Barnes and Charlie Chaplin (*center*) in front of the Aldon Hotel, Berlin, 1921. Courtesy Special Collections, University of Maryland at College Park Libraries.

45. Thelma Wood and Djuna Barnes on beach, Provincetown, Mass.
Courtesy Special Collections, University of Maryland at College Park
Libraries.

46. Photograph of oil painting of Barnes; artist, date, and location of original unknown. Courtesy Special Collections, University of Maryland at College Park Libraries.

47. Djuna Barnes at Gotham
Book Mart, early 1950s. Courtesy
Special Collections, University of
Maryland at College Park Li-
braries.

48. *Madame Majeska;* oil painting of Emily Holmes Coleman by Djuna Barnes. Courtesy Special Collections, University of Maryland at College Park Libraries.

49. Djuna Barnes in front of Patchen Place gates, 14 April 1962. Photograph taken by Marion Morehouse (Mrs. e.e. cummings). Courtesy Special Collections, University of Maryland at College Park Libraries.

50. Sif Ruud as Augusta in Stockholm production of *The Antiphon*, 17 February 1961. Courtesy Special Collections, University of Maryland at College Park Libraries.

¶ . . . For myself, I am occasionally attacked by the birds of paradise . . . the falling away of the heart . . . and the gripping of the midriff, upper, by the belt so to say, the rest of the time, in sweltering heat, trying to keep disorder at bay.

> —Djuna Barnes,
> letter to Marion Bouche,
> 26 July 1962

¶ "It's a damn spring again!" . . . and so it is, and nothing done, or all to be done again (for that 'glow,' accomplishment!) with smaller means, and less stomach. I've been harried in and out of hospitals, so turned, broiled, basted, punctured, poked and generally read down, that what's the matter, can only be what's the matter still.

> —Djuna Barnes,
> letter to Peter Hoare,
> 13 May 1963

¶ How does one arrange for life . . . how do writers keep on writing? Professional ones do, I don't see how my kind can—the "passion spent," and even the fury—the passion made into *Nightwood* the fury (nearly) exhausted in *The Antiphon* . . . what is left? "The horror," as Conrad put it.

> —Djuna Barnes,
> letter to Peter Hoare,
> 18 July 1963

¶ We have known, for some time now, that we are the vestiges of an ancient and lost line, tho the youth of today I'm told, find the *"twenties"* utterly fascinating,—and the days pull out and go off to somewhere I have no interest in. . . .

> —Djuna Barnes,
> letter to Peter Hoare,
> 19 September 1964

¶ Me? An old lady working against time like an idiot . . . Photo of your humble servant (near 77) looking like Holbein's Erasmus, also there. To realize your age truly, you have to see your *latest* photograph held up in PUBLIC, but *PUBLIC*! The privacy of one's home tells you nothing; you still *think* you felt young . . .

> —Djuna Barnes,
> letter to Silas Glossup,
> 20 April 1969

¶ . . . I no longer have any idea when, or if, the poems [late poems] will please me enough to go on re-writing and endlessly tearing up . . . a thing I have noticed in the old . . . Nancy Cunard burned her manuscripts in the middle of her room, my father demanded that all his works be sent to sea, and of the famous, isn't Kafka, for one, and hundreds of others, including St. Thomas and a staggering number of other craftsmen . . . all, all walking away into the horizon (the camera carefully focused on the small of their backs). My old friend Marcel Duchamp for one, and last night a view of Henry Miller peddling off (in impeccable scotch tweeds) into *Great Sur* (spelling?), in short, if you let the beast live long enough, he takes up tail, and makes for the woods. So one should certainly die young.

> —Djuna Barnes,
> letter to Wolfgang Hildesheimer,
> 23 June 1969

¶ Difficult for me to write, particularly now. Absolutely life has changed for everyone, and so for me . . .

About Emily I can tell you nothing. She does not answer the phone, or at least the phone does not get answered. She does not write. The last time I saw her, the first time in twenty odd years, she seemed erased. I dare say I seemed the same to her. I said would you have known me? She answered "No, except for the eyes." I don't think, had I passed her on the street, that I would have known her at all. She was colour dun, carrying a Rip Van Winkle staff, a fur pelt, in *baret* style on her head, her hair lank and to the turn of the cheek, the coat, capsized wool, the feet well apart. She said since her head operation she found it difficult to balance. How can I say this? How can I tell anyone about anything anymore: She was cheerful, seemed obscurely amused, and only Emily like when I put a bowl of excellent chicken soup before her. She did not seem mournful, but neither did she seem to have listed (in her mind) the passing of her, life. She spoke of nursing (pushing about in a cart I take it) a cancer case. I asked her how could she stand it? She answered "God had intended it." Simple, like that . . . She is another phantom in my spirit, well haunted as I am. I would have liked to show her, and the "public" my "thanks" to her for her part in my "career." Obviously we are too late with it.

—Djuna Barnes,
letter to Peter Hoare,
27 May 1970

¶ . . . the time of the twenties and thirties seems the property of someone else, to be observed, in the mind, with Greta Garbo's murmur, when sitting through Camille, or Anna, etc. "Watch, see *her* now, *she* is going to—" When you look up, you are sitting in your particular house number—No one can stand it, that's certain . . . but one can parry, parry, or try to foil . . . or draw a measure—

—Djuna Barnes,
letter to Peter Hoare,
5 January 1974

Reminiscences

Ruth Ford

My poet brother, Charles Henri Ford, introduced me to Djuna in the late 1930s. He loved her and admired her genius.

   She was formidable in the best sense of the word, that rare person with so many gifts that put you in awe of her: stunning in appearance; tall; dashing; with a certain arrogant posture; elegant; short and wavy reddish hair combed back off her face; green-blue eyes (tempting and taunting); and dressed with great style, romantic capes and turbans. Her voice was attention getting—softly guttural. She had a quick tongue and could be witty, humorous, confounding, and devastating. Sure of herself. She was aware of her specialness without a show of ego; eccentric, yes. She was *not* a gypsy. She was an ultra sophisticate.

   When I met her, she had returned from Paris. Her apartment on Waverly Place looked French. Everything in it had a French flavor—pale blue walls, red velvet draperies, paintings and objets d'art, and intoxicating French perfume. Hanging on the wall, unfurled like a Chinese scroll, was the full-length portrait she painted (on a gold background) of her friend Alice Rohrer.

   She taught me to love Mozart. She told me of her brother, Saxon, that he was a Greek god. Handsome. Tall. Blond hair. Blue eyes. And she had plans for us to get together. Well, Saxon was all Djuna claimed him to be, but it didn't jell, except for a friendship (which has lasted to the present time). He lives on a farm in Pennsylvania with his wife. So next in line was her half brother, Charlie—not *quite* the Greek god that Saxon was but pretty close. Our relationship was closer but had a short life.

   Djuna called me one day in the early 1940s, nervous and irritable and depressed and rather desperate, saying her mother, Elizabeth, was staying with her. She couldn't sleep at night because her mother read the Bible aloud all night long. I had a small guest room. I told her she was welcome to come over and stay as long as she liked. She did come, but didn't stay long. Her mother finally went back to her home and Charlie came and took Djuna back to hers.

After the 1940s I didn't see Djuna anymore. By then she had become a confirmed recluse at Patchin Place. But she did for a long time send me Christmas cards with sweet messages.

I was at a party one night in the late 1940s—at Harold Clurman's—with a lot of bright, creative people, and we were talking about art and artists. Someone said there was no such thing as a really talented artist being unknown and not being recognized. I promptly spoke up and said, "Oh yes there is." To the question "Who?" I said, "Djuna Barnes." Harold Clurman was the only person in the room who had even *heard* of her!

Djuna was *sui generis*.

James B. Scott

"Would you like a drink, Mr. Scott? I have some sherry in the refrigerator," Djuna Barnes offered. She had not herself had a drink, she said, in twenty years, or smoked a cigarette in eight. On that April afternoon of 1971 she was seventy-eight years old.

"Tea?"

If she was having tea I would have some, I said. She boiled water on an apartment-size gas stove in a kitchen so tiny one did not so much enter it as stand in front of it. She put a tea bag in the cup and made a shaky negotiation of the few steps to where I sat in an overstuffed chair. Behind me, leaning against the wall and staring straight ahead, stood *Alice*, painted by Miss Barnes in 1934 and exhibited in Peggy Guggenheim's showing of the work of women artists at the Art of This Century gallery in 1943. The cup rattled on the saucer over my new suit. Then I had the tea on the arm of the chair. From the refrigerator she took chocolate cookies, which she offered me out of the bag. I took one. She bent over me in her blue bathrobe and pajamas, insisting that I take another. I hadn't wanted even the first, hadn't wanted anything but to talk; but I reached again into the wrinkled sack. That is when I realized that she was smiling. Not at me. She was looking away and smiling to herself. It slowly came to me that she was playing "Hostess," and was finding some laconic amusement in my discomfort. Here she had this fortyish man sunken into the chair and trying to balance the cup of gentility, his suit fairly shining in her eyes, and I suppose she could not resist the temptation—this woman whose entire life from infancy on had been so exclusively bohemian.

We had not yet begun to talk about the book I was to write about her works. I was balancing a teacup and two unwanted chocolate cookies above my lap, and Djuna had already established our relationship. It would continue for several more years, mostly by correspondence, on pretty much the same terms. I would be dogged, determined, "sincere," as I tried to balance the demands of my editors against those of this "most famous unknown author in the world" (a phrase I learned that afternoon). For her part, she would be eternally maneuvering, outflanking, challenging, and retreating to the higher ground of a loftier conception. Over the next couple of years she would read every word of my manuscript, at least in its earlier forms. "Do better" would be her most commonly penciled remark. "Let's knock the spots off criticism," she would challenge me. Then turn right around and assure me that if I managed to get just two good sentences written that would be enough. Few could write even one, she said. Back and forth the manuscript went through the mails, ricocheting off the folding card table–work table in Patchin Place and into my hands for another look, another attempt to describe her writings without "reading into" them.

Miss Barnes was a faithful correspondent, and even when the words in a letter were angry, she would promptly reply. She was not afraid of whatever storm or strife came through the mails. To deal with words—any words—was all in a day's work. She spent a lot of time on that manuscript because she didn't like most critics and was looking to me to show the world how criticism *should be* written. Not just the large ideas, not just the accuracy of the data mattered. The sentences themselves must sing, she insisted—every phrase be examined and listened to for clarity, musicality, and concision.

Eventually the time came when the ricocheting back and forth was between the publishers and my desk. At about this time I learned that Miss Barnes had applied to my publishers to stop publication of the book. I was furious. Had I not slaved for six years on this slender offering, and had she not leaned into the project with a will, holding me to her highest standards, I demanded? Had I not balanced, finally, the contradictory demands of my editors and Miss Barnes? She replied matter of factly, as if nothing at all were wrong. Yes, she had tried to stop the book from coming out, but the publishers had the law on their side and would not be deterred. She denied that she had helped me, saying she had only offered "good advice" which I "persisted in refusing to take." She did not want anyone writing her "biography" and that was that. She knew, of course, that I had written a book of criticism with all biographical details rigidly suppressed.

The publishers did go ahead, and in March 1976 the first book-length study of Djuna Barnes' work was in print. Now Miss Barnes wrote me, querulously, as though nothing had happened. Why had she not received her copy of the new book, she wanted to know? I made arrangements.

Looking back, I am sorry that I could not rise to that Olympian high ground separating the fragile and by now very old artist in her rumpled one-room apartment (she lived very poorly) from the academic in the shiny suit who took everything so seriously.

She had a heart condition, arthritis, and severe emphysema. She had just (barely) survived a number of operations in one of New York's hospitals and had been prematurely signed out by a brother on the advice of an intern who told her, "They are killing you here. Get out if you have to go in a stretcher, a blanket, a wheelchair. But get out!" (Miss Barnes tended to speak in exclamation points.)

I had waited in the hallway at Patchin Place for our meeting while for long minutes she was racked by prolonged, deep, and obviously painful coughing—each attack followed by the gasping, choked, indrawing of breath of the asthmatic. She had quit smoking, but the damage was done.

Her voice had a harsh, hollow quality. "You can tell it's the voice of an asthmatic, can't you?" I hung fire. "Well, *can't* you?"

"A little bit," I admitted, not wanting to seem critical about a condition we smokers no doubt invite. Her voice was still strong, but she would not listen to Caedmon's urging that she record *Nightwood*, because the quality was "deteriorating." She thought "Tom's voice" was just right, though, for *The Wasteland*. Tom, I realized, must be T.S. Eliot. "But he recorded his poem in a monotone," I objected.

"Yes, that's just how I would read *Nightwood*—very controlled." She would not have let Robin say "anything at all" if she had that to do over again, she said. Dylan Thomas had a lovely voice, she thought, although somewhat damaged by the whiskey; but she was sure that *Under Milk Wood* was "ripped off" from *Nightwood*.

I remember a large flashlight on the stand by her narrow bed, and a sort of lazy susan on which were arranged her medications. By the bed was a stand of handsome ladies canes, but she did not need one in the small apartment. She stood very straight and must have been as tall as a medium-sized man when she was younger. When she wanted "a good look" at me I stood, removing my glasses, and six inches apart we studied each other, eyeball to eyeball. The eyes I saw were a faded blue and quick-moving, very alert. Her hair had become thin and white. Her cheeks had fallen, and her face, long and thin, was deeply furrowed.

Miss Barnes was looked after by three or four young men who lived nearby in this rather Old World Greenwich Village quarter. If she could not go out, she said, they shopped for her. If she needed something electrical fixed, or needed bookshelves (one whole wall was covered with books), these young mechanics and taxi drivers came in and wired and painted and carpentered for her. They moved heavy boxes of papers (these ended up at the University of Maryland, by the way, where Andrew Field used them for his gossipy biography *Djuna*), and they carried out the garbage. They would not take any money. Miss Barnes was "theirs" to take care of. They knew her work, she told me, and were fans. "I have no children to take care of me; my books are my children." I registered with interest that she did not speak of the young men as adoptive "sons." And it pleased me that it was these young blue-collar readers who cared for her. Why I was pleased I don't really know, but suspect that I too had become afflicted with a certain possessiveness. Djuna Barnes was *mine*—just as surely as the young men knew that she was theirs.

What an illusion this was! It is a great mistake to attempt to domesticate Djuna Barnes into the affable confines of the middle-class imagination. There are not very many truly bright women in the world. There are not very many truly bright men in the world, either, for that matter. One among millions gives us the light bulb and we all benefit. We can illuminate the dark we dread. After all these years there has still been but one Shakespeare. And we have something to read by that light bulb. Miss Barnes was also a singularity. She was born bright, and her education was a handmade, one-of-a-kind fitting, shaping, and adapting of the native intelligence to an aggressively literate family milieu. By the time grandmother Zadel Barnes was finished, she had shaped her granddaughter into a kind of literary-artistic monster who, turned loose upon the world, would be forever disappointed in that world's inability to measure up to any sort of enlightened behavior.

Herself the eternal, aggravating perfectionist, she watched the twentieth century, born full of fatuous optimism, slip deeper and deeper into its own disillusioned, enraged incompetence. Violence inevitably and repeatedly followed. Her own increasing outrage must explain why twenty years after delineating the inverted and introspective world of *Nightwood* she chose for her verse-drama *The Antiphon* a canvas large enough to reflect in the background the destructiveness of world war. That work's set, plot, and characters are what the world had come to: a bombed-out landscape (England during the 1939 blitz) populated by suicidal egomaniacs, inept would-be killers, and the odd, ineffectual do-gooder. The play embodied the author's exasperation with global degeneration, and did so in the highest, most demanding of artistic terms. One has to be truly civilized just to be able to read *The Antiphon*.

It was typical of her to make this most important statement about the modern world as impenetrable as she could. Speaking of its Swedish premier in 1961 (appropriately, one of the translators was Dag Hammarskjöld of the United Nations) she declared, "You can't act it. It wasn't meant for acting. I wrote it because I wanted to. I wrote it as a verse-drama because I like the form. But it can't be acted. I know that." Then she turned to me, puzzled: "Did you ever see anything flop like *Antiphon*? I can't understand it." Such contradictions were typical. I came to recognize the nearly simultaneous pride in the depth of her craftsmanship—her "obscurity"—and petulance at the same moment that her audience could not fathom the play, could not register her grim assessment of the modern world. The sudden reversals of thought and behavior, rather like Miranda (and her mother), are perhaps the price paid for talent of this level. For when she wrote, there was no Djuna Barnes. Of course she was there as the planner, the architect of the work. But mainly she was not there, having gone into a "trance" wherefrom she entered entirely into the subjectivity of each character. She herself became the whirling center of all the contradictions inherent in her inflamed cast.

Our conversation on this occasion dwindled, gradually, into the sort of literary gossip at which she was adept and I unable to respond. She had known everyone in Europe who wrote, painted, or talked about either art during the two decades prior to World War II. And she had opinions about all these artists and pretenders. The forcefulness of her declarations left me in no doubt that all this life, the Paris of the 1920s and 1930s, had ended only yesterday. About the present age she was equally certain. With what I took to be a very old person's crabbed irritation at a world gone mad, she condemned miniskirts ("It's not their *legs* the silly little things should be showing off") as well as the women's movement ("Why don't they all just *shut up?*"). Her attitudes, pretty solidly hostile to the modern ways, revealed again and again that she had always been a lone thinker and saw no other viable direction for any woman. Her mind simply refused to consider the possibility that *all* women could not be as smart as she was. She did not oppose women's *rights*, or, certainly, women finding fulfillment. Quite the contrary; she wanted women to do a great deal more than they ever had. But a "movement" by its very nature sought to raise unearned the conditions of its adherents. To succeed meant, for Djuna Barnes, to project oneself by force of wit and will upon the world, and "Damn the torpedoes, full speed ahead!" could be the only battle cry.

She was an overpowering person and she knew it. She correctly divined when my headache began, some hours later, and gave me two of her aspirin, shaking them out of a small bottle into my palm. Bending over, she put a trembling glass of water in my other hand. As I swallowed the pills I was conscious that she was staring at me very closely. But now with a direct smile. "I have been told that I give everyone I talk to a headache," she said.

"You're so intense!"

"Yes. I know."

Alex Gildzen

I first wrote to Djuna Barnes in the fall of 1969. I was teaching a writing class and had prepared a handout, "How Djuna Barnes Starts Stories," a short anthology of first lines. I sent a copy to Patchin Place—never expecting a reply from such a celebrated recluse. But answer she did: "I do hope your class enjoys the stories as much as yourself."

I was so overwhelmed to have a letter from the legend that I spent the night I received it among pines and mosquitoes, composing a response purpler than Dr. Mighty O'Connor's mascara.

It was two years before I had another letter from Barnes. This time it was in reaction to my idea of celebrating her four score years with a festschrift. (I presumed she had pitched my night letter and my name with it and was responding as if to a stranger.)

I no longer was teaching English but working as a special collections librarian and editing a series of Occasional Papers for the Kent State University Libraries.

"The proposal contained in your letter of the 20th seems very pleasing—but what is this festschrift, and what the Occasional paper series?" she wrote back.

I sent her copies of previous numbers and explained, "As I envision the festschrift, it would be a clustering of commentary, tributes and greetings from world leaders in the arts who have responded to your work." I requested a recent poem of hers for the publication.

"If it entails *no* effort on my part—I am as you note, eighty in June—I shall be properly astonished!" Barnes replied. She added a postscript, "I *deplore personal* data," and wrote on the back of the envelope, "*No* interviews."

Her next letter held no promise for a previously unpublished piece of writing but was firm on one point: "Certainly, if you will be so responsible, I would like to see what you intend to publish *before* you publish: these things can be most unfortunate."

In my riposte I pledged to send her proofs and notified her that I would begin writing letters to potential contributors. That initial letter of invitation was posted the last week of October 1971.

By the first week of November responses began to arrive. Edmund Wilson sent his notorious "regrets" card but wrote in the margin, "I like Djuna Barnes personally, but I don't care much for what she writes."

From Forty-one Doors Conrad Aiken explained, "My health hasn't been all it might be in the last two years, nor my energies up to much." He also had been asked to write an introduction to Barnes' new book. "I'm by no means sure I can undertake it, but if I do, that's ALL I can do, and in any event I wouldn't want to do both."

His one-time student Paul Metcalf reported not having read Barnes in years and when he tried rereading *Nightwood* was unable to finish.

Parker Tyler also felt the need to reread. And Charles Henri Ford, coauthor with Tyler of the 1933 novel *The Young and Evil* for which Barnes had written a blurb, wanted me to obtain permission from the camera-shy author for him to photograph her.

"I was delighted to hear that you are publishing a Festschrift for Djuna Barnes; no one deserves it more," wrote Malcolm Cowley. "For a month now I've held your letter, trying to think whether I had something to say and could find time to say it in, but the answer was No—I'm simply too tied up to embark on a new project." Cowley suggested I write to John Glassco in Canada.

"I've never lost my intense interest in her work," Jim Harrison wrote, adding he was leaving the next day for Ecuador and would write a short piece upon his return. He never did.

"Of course, I admire Djuna Barnes' work, but am simply not competent to discuss it," conceded W.H. Auden.

I personally asked John Ashbery to contribute. His response is recorded in *The Year Book*:

> *he said he adored Djuna Barnes when he was 18*
> *but when he reread her later he didn't know why*

Muriel Rukeyser agreed to write something but asked me to send her a copy of *Nightwood* and "the latest book" because hers were in her cellar. Months after the festschrift's publication her agent sent my personal copy of the novel to the poet's son in Canada by mistake.

Matthew Josephson wrote, "As I really did not know her well—I only saw her a few times long years ago in N.Y. and Paris—and as I haven't read her admirable works in forty years, it seems inappropriate for me to write about her."

Writers as disparate as John Updike and Iris Murdoch, Anne Sexton and Mark Van Doren sent regrets but none as stylish as Margaret Anderson's: "I used to like the things that Djuna Barnes sent us for the *Little Review*, but I loathe the kind of poetry she's writing today," Anderson retorted from France copying out "The Walking-Mort." "The *New Yorker* printed this masterpiece—which isn't astonishing to me since they now publish the world's most ghastly poetry."

She continued, "I've been tempted to write Djuna as follows: *Dear Djuna*, would you mind telling me what you're talking about? In exchange I'll send you a poem with real emotion in it:

> *My bonnie lies over the o-shun,*
> *My bonnie lies over the sea,*
> *Oh who will go over the o-shun*
> *And bring back my bonnie to me?*

"Of course, you won't want to use this letter, I'm sure, but I've sent it anyway, hoping at least that you will feel like laughing with me."

As the reader of the festschrift can attest not everyone said no. Anaïs Nin was particularly helpful, not only contributing but also introducing me to Louis Kannenstine, who wrote an essay which was incorporated in his book *The Art of Djuna Barnes: Duality and Damnation*. She also was willing to speak to Henry Miller but warned, "he is 80, not in good health and I never heard him praise Djuna Barnes."

The other great diarist of our time, Ned Rorem, once told me he read *Nightwood* every seven years. When he sent his contribution, he assured me that the writer's name "*is* from Arabic—not Welsh."

I first discussed Barnes with Joseph Chaikin on the floor at a party following one of the previews of *The Serpent*, performed in New York just before the Open Theater sailed to Rome for its official premiere. Long after the company disbanded I discovered in their archives a section of *Night-wood* which had been dramatized for a workshop. Surely the Open Theater's final piece, *Nightwalk*, owes at least its title to Barnes.

Lawrence Durrell returned my letter. On the verso he hastily typed his tribute. Its last line — "One is glad to be living in the same epoch as Djuna Barnes" — resurfaces with regularity.

Throughout work on the festschrift my only feel of the Barnes pulse came from her editor Frances McCullough, then with Harper and Row. Early on she advised me, "She'll snort about the festschrift but I think secretly she'll be delighted, as long as she doesn't have to *do* anything."

In April Barnes sent me "Quarry," which she claimed was her favorite poem. She made two changes from its initial appearance in *The New Yorker*. "I can't do better . . . nor can I, just now, send you an unpublished poem. I am too exhausted, as everything has come down upon my head at these last hours of my existance [*sic*]."

When 12 June arrived without the publication, Barnes phoned her editor: "Mrs. McCullough," she asked, "just where is my festschrift?"

The booklet with its die-cut cover revealing a previously unpublished Berenice Abbott portrait did arrive at Patchin Place before the month was out. The only response I received from the honoree was a postcard of Washington Arch on which she scrawled in green ink, "Thank you all. SORRY about fearful photo." I would never hear from Djuna Barnes again.

Hank O'Neal

19 September 1978

First meeting with Djuna Barnes. Late afternoon. Took Liza Stelle with me. The meeting had been set up by Berenice Abbott. Miss Barnes, she said, was having a difficult time getting about. She lives at 5 Patchin Place, apartment 2F. She is eighty-six, suffers from arthritis, emphysema, hardening of the arteries, and has cataracts on both eyes. The cataracts are sufficiently severe that she is blind in one eye and has only partial vision in the other. She reads with the aid of a large magnifying glass and is terrified of blindness. She said she was not afraid of death but was simply bored with the process that led up to it. Her circumstances are modest. She lives in a tiny one-room apartment that includes a small kitchen and bathroom. There is also an oversized walk-in closet used for storage. Her one room is filled with a bed, a large chair, a bureau, and two writing desks. Her only typewriter is a small portable that was given to her about 1963 by Peggy Guggenheim. The desks are piled with papers, mostly poetry that is being worked and reworked. It is all typed and looks as though it is undergoing rather severe editing. Under the desk are more piles of papers, apparently filed in some order.

Djuna Barnes remains an extremely handsome woman. Her physical problems have her down a bit, particularly the blindness, but her mind is sharp and she is as interesting a conversationalist as I have ever engaged. I planned to stay an hour and simply offer whatever help Liza and I could provide. We stayed and talked for over four hours.

Nightwood is on her mind. She says things like, "Isn't it a simply beautiful work," and "I wonder how I could have written it." She feels she would be unable to write it now. She says she has not looked at the book for years; in fact, she gives the distinct impression that she has not looked at much of her work for many years. She did say she had recently reread *A Night among the Horses* and didn't think it was very good. . . .

23 September

Second meeting with Djuna Barnes. . . . I took her a small cassette tape recorder and some cassettes of Dylan Thomas. She was very certain she did not want to listen to them, but I played one anyway. The moment she heard Thomas' voice she broke into a smile a mile wide and did not say a word until he had finished reading; in this instance it was "Fern Hill." It was apparent she knew the poem well. She waited a moment after it was finished and then expressed an interest in learning how to play the infernal little machine. . . .

She talked about her writing. She considers "Aller et Retour" and "The Passion" to be her best stories. She said someone issued two of her stories in a small book entitled *Vagaries Malicieux* but that she has never seen a copy and would like to. She said things like that happen to her all the time. Many of her stories were in newspapers and defunct magazines, and people just take them and do whatever they please. She said the same holds true for a 1948 edition of *The Book of Repulsive Women*. It is a pirate edition, and she hates it; she dislikes all these publications of her work. She is equally unhappy about all the people who are forever pestering her for information about herself. . . . At the same time she is even more unhappy that there are not many of her friends left to be asked questions.

She asked me about *The Antiphon* . . . adding that the U.K. edition is the first version, and the version in the *Selected Works* is the second. The second, she said, is far superior. She added she could not understand why so many people told her it was dull; Eliot told her he did not like the play very much, but he thought the last act was the best piece of theatrical writing he had ever read.

Then we talked about her poetry. She had been working very hard but had not made much progress. . . . She said she wants to get a book of poetry together, but her failing eyesight is a major problem. She added that there are pieces of poems scattered about; one part of a poem is here another part is there, and she can't see well enough to put all the pieces together. She holds some of the poetry in very low regard; in fact, there is little she feels is truly first rate. This may be an excuse to abandon the poems altogether. Still, she claims she works on the poems daily. . . .

27, 29 September
... She wanted to talk about Joyce; this was brought about by my playing a cassette of him reading "Anna Livia Plurabelle." The recording is not very good, but Miss Barnes enjoyed it. She said it is important to have Joyce reading it because he had told her *Finnegans Wake* is meant to be read aloud. ... Miss Barnes remarked that Joyce was not a very good poet, that his early work was romantic and sentimental. She added that Joyce's wife, Nora, used to tell her that she "should have known him when he was younger," indicating he was nothing like he was in the 1920s. ...

Miss Barnes then asked if I could find the cassette of Dylan Thomas reading *Nightwood*. ... Things move around in this room. She listened carefully as Thomas read the lines; she interrupted twice, when she said Thomas read them incorrectly. She must have a very clear memory of what she wrote so long ago. She likes Thomas, even though she feels he is a bit high-minded. She talked about her own voice and how bad it sounds, which is why she has never consented to make any recordings. ... She should at least consider the possibility. ...

I told her I had found a copy of *A Book* in a used book store and she asked that I bring it by. ... She was eager to look at the drawings, identifying all the people. ... One was an actress, another a "pansie," a third the wife of Max Eastman. I forgot the rest. She did say she felt the drawing of Eastman's wife was a good one, adding she had burned most of her early drawings because she didn't think they were very good. I asked her to sign the book and she did so, saying there was a man who wanted to put out one of her poems in a fancy edition and have her sign one hundred copies of it. He offered her one dollar for each signature, and she told the man to go to hell. Suddenly she stopped at one of the stories (or perhaps a poem) and said, "After I published this one they first accused me of being a lesbian." She added the accusation was nonsense. ...

6 October
... She is proud of the fact she never wrote anything for popular consumption and still refuses to have some of her work reprinted, even though people send her money for permission. She feels if she accepts the money it shows a measure of approval she does not wish to show. She needs money, like everyone, and has sold possessions, including a copy of *Ulysses* inscribed by Joyce for $150.

She spoke of Jean Cocteau. "He was a pansie, surrounded by a lot of other pansies but he was damn clever." She loves his movies and took the time to describe the ones she likes best; *Blood of a Poet* ranks at the top. This movie led to a discussion of Lee Miller and in turn Man Ray. She mentioned that Man Ray had once taken a good photograph of her with Mina Loy. ...

Then back to *Nightwood*; after she wrote it everyone thought she was a lesbian, that she is not, and if she had known what would have happened she would have never written it. I told her I thought it was unimportant what anybody thought, and she said I was probably right. . . .

18 October
. . . Talk about *Nightwood*. Robin is Thelma Wood (Berenice said the same thing); Nora is Henrietta Metcalf, the doctor is Dan Mahoney. Talk about Edwin Muir; has a little picture from a magazine of him framed, sitting next to a sixty year old Brownie camera.

25 October
Met with Miss Barnes 4:30–7:00. . . . Gave her the photographs of James Joyce and herself, a present from Berenice, and they please her very much.

Commented about how Berenice dressed her up for the photograph and this led to her telling how a magazine had photographed her for a cover in Paris. They retouched it, turning her dime-store ring into an emerald. This in turn led to a story about Joyce, who once asked her to buy him a particular iron ring, but she could not afford to do so at the time. She looked carefully at Berenice's photograph and said he was wearing a couple of rings, and he didn't need another one anyway. This led to a discussion of Nora Joyce, who she feels was a great marytr. She loves Joyce's books but says he was something of a burden to everyone who knew him well. . . . I had recently seen the Welsh National Theater Company do *Under "Night-wood."* I quickly caught my mistake and said *"Under Milk Wood."* She laughed loudly and said, "It's the same thing." She said Thomas once told her the only things he really liked to read were Shakespeare, Marlowe, and *Nightwood*. She was sure he didn't mean it, but it was nice to hear.

Then all the lesbian nonsense bubbled out. She said she hates lesbians and is rather unfeeling towards women in general, but she loved Thelma Wood in a very strong and passionate fashion, primarily because Thelma reminded her of her grandmother. She looked just like her, and the grandmother fended off Miss Barnes' father. . . . He beat her with a whip but the grandmother kept him from doing it too often. . . . It was clear she cared for Thelma Wood very much and lesbians in general very little. In fact, she said she felt all women were just a little too sentimental and sloppy for her and in general liked men more because they were not. . . .

26 October
Hart Crane came up. He was a little terror in Paris. She says the first time he called on her, he left a note on her door hanging from a dagger. She doesn't think he's that very good. . . . Thought it was funny how his parents always sent Margaret Anderson candies. I had a Walker Evans book in my bag and showed her his photograph of Crane, and she thought it was all right but not distinguished. Made a point to say he did not jump off that boat because of Peggy Cowley, that he was gay so she was of no concern.

A great deal of discussion about the Swiss production of *The An-*
tiphon. . . .

Man Ray came up. She claims to have had many photographs by him
but she threw them away. I told her this was foolish because they are
valuable. She feels Man Ray was very shallow. He was not serious, had no
training, and did silly bits of work like putting tacks on an iron. He charged
a great deal to do a portrait, and no one liked him but Kiki. So much for
Man Ray.

Then old people and how she hates them. She hated them when she was
young and she hates them now. Everybody hates old ladies; they aren't good for
anything. They aren't pretty and they can't screw so what good are they? . . .

Then she wanted to look at the Walker Evans book again. She says she
knew Evans but can't remember where or when. Looked at each photograph
very carefully and found them moderately interesting but only one exceptional; the one of the family plot in Kentucky taken from the rear. The side
view bothered her because the sun was not right. She thought it was only
proper that he wait until the sun was right to take the photograph. Then she
wanted me to compare Berenice and Walker Evans. An interesting conversation. She understood the difference. She did not like the photograph Evans
took of Berenice. . . . Talked about voices again. Does not want to record
because her voice is old and full of asthma. She only likes Dylan Thomas;
does not like Burton or Eliot or anyone else.

Then *Ryder*. Told me to take a copy and give it to Les Pockell at St.
Martins. It is only mildly dirty, so it probably will not sell. But she is willing
to try. *Nightwood*, she says, would make a great movie, but no one will be
allowed to do it unless they do it perfectly, and that is unlikely because there
are no good American directors. I suggested she contact Orson Welles. She
asked if I knew him. Negative. The movie, she feels should be black-and-
white, done in and around Paris. Once rejected $30,000 for a one-year
option. Her quote for the day: "If you can't be marvelous why bother, and
you can't be marvelous very often." She says the one good photograph in the
Evans book proves the point. Only one is truly marvelous.

27 October

An interesting day. We talked about *Ladies Almanack*. She simply did it as a
lark; never even bothered to get a copyright. Wrote it in the hospital while
tending Thelma. Didn't even plan to do anything with it but Robert
McAlmon saw it and said he would pay for the printing, which he did. She
paid for the printing of the illustrations. Got into a disagreement with the
publisher, Edward Titus, who wanted half of all the money made on the
book including the money Miss Barnes made when she sold them herself in
the cafés or to friends. She told him where to get off. The drawings are very
derivative, she says, and showed me a book to prove it, an old volume of
French folk drawings published in Paris about 1925. At the time of the book

she was bothered a great deal by a dreary old lesbian named Natalie Barney who was after her but she couldn't stand her. Barney was a failed writer who came from a wealthy family (toilet-seat monopoly) and couldn't stand it when any woman rejected her. She was, apparently, a rather successful lover of ladies and usually got whomever she went after. She didn't get Miss Barnes. [Barnes] signed my copy of the book, thinking it was interesting I had copy number 1000, the last one. Said there was a man who sent her a pile of bookplates to sign, but she threw them in the garbage can. "My signature is worth $10. Why should I send that money to him?" Spoke of the reissue version of the book; no changes in the book, just the new introduction.

Talked about her writing style. She thinks it is very amusing when people speak about her unique and wonderful style of punctuation. It is, she says, neither unique nor wonderful. She simply doesn't know any of the rules or how it is supposed to be done properly. She likes to use colons: they look nice. She used one in her poem "Quarry," which was published in *The New Yorker*. When the editor of the magazine looked at it he said the colon was not properly used, and it should be removed. She agreed, reluctantly, but when it was reprinted in another publication she made certain the colon was back in place. She talks a good deal about her inability to spell correctly and poor punctuation, but she does not question her ability to write. . . . "I wonder why I wrote so little?" Then she added, "But as Tom said, some of it was marvelous."

Then Eliot and how she is not very fond of his poetry but feels his literary criticism is better than anyone's. She liked him personally because he was very well read, well spoken, well dressed, and civilized. Auden came up for a moment. She does not like his poetry and feels sorry for him because he is so ugly; a face like an elephant's ass. Then to surrealist painters, spurred on by the dust cover of a book about Delvaux. She likes him a great deal. Dali was mentioned. He has become a prostitute. She recalled once having lunch at "21" with Janet Flanner and Anita Loos; Dali was two tables away. At one point he rose and in a flamboyant manner announced, "All hail Djuna Barnes!" She did not elaborate on the story other than to say she felt like hiding under the table. She did not.

Out of the blue she asked me, "Do you remember the ending of *Nightwood*?" I replied that I did. She then became very upset because of the way some people interpret this part of the book. People say Robin is making love to the dog. This is nonsense. There was nothing like that in her mind when she wrote the scene. In fact, it was taken from an actual scene she once observed: a lady named Fitzi was drunk as a hoot and crawling around on all fours and her dog, Buffy, was running around her, growling and barking. She talked about how animals get all worked up when they see their masters in an unusual state. She then spoke about how animals feel, how people feel, and how their reactions to certain situations are based on "things they really don't recall but simply know from long, long ago, like the way children really like to see the wolf in bed in 'Little Red Riding Hood.'" . . .

Eliot's introduction. How the book was rejected in the United States and finally taken in the U.K. because some people pushed very hard for it. Eliot's introduction helped a great deal, but he should have mentioned he didn't write one for the first edition. And why. (She didn't say.) Then into how it would make a great movie and maybe Igmar Bergman would be a good director. She likes his movies, particularly *The Virgin Spring* and *The Seventh Seal*. She added she had seen every one of his movies up through "five or six years ago, when I stopped going out." Says she thinks the rape scene in *The Virgin Spring* is the finest thing she has ever seen in a movie. Enjoys Bergman because so many of his ideas are about God; as are hers.

2 November
Showed me an old scrapbook. . . . At least eighty percent of the photographs are of Thelma Wood. A good copy of Berenice's photograph of Wood plus one of Berenice and Wood together with a notation of it being taken in 1921. A fine Man Ray portrait, a candid picture of Miss Barnes with Chaplin, assorted literary folks, a portrait of Brancusi, inscribed to Djuna Barnes, and some funny pictures of her during her newspaper days, being force-fed, hugging a gorilla, being carried down a building by firemen. She did all these things for the paper to earn money for her family, which was in those days, apparently, having a poor time of it. A nice one with Mina Loy and a poor one with Natalie Barney. A series of photographs of the place she lived in Algiers, "Where the rent was $5 a month and servants were 5 cents a day. . . ."

She told me about her animal poems. There are twenty-six verses, one for each letter of the alphabet. She has been working on them a long time, and they are about ready to go. . . . She showed me all the drafts; there are seventeen versions, and they need sorting. Will do this on Friday.

Talk about writers. She loves Sherlock Holmes and Conan Doyle. Told me I should read *Anatomy of Melancholy* and *Lady Windermere's Fan*. Wanted to know what I thought of Lawrence Durrell (not too much), John Hawkes (don't know), and Truman Capote (first things great, the rest average). Agrees about Capote and said they had once asked her to have a photograph taken with him but she wouldn't even consider it. . . . She is concerned about not being alive much longer. At one point said, "Don't think for a minute this is the real Djuna Barnes. The real Djuna Barnes is dead."

. . . Talked about piano-playing fiancé, Putzi, a six-foot-four German. He apparently later became Hitler's official pianist and wrote some sort of German anthem in the 1920s. Said he was the one who hid Hitler after the Munich affair. She wanted to interview Hitler but he wanted two dollars a word and no one would pay the bill. . . .

3 November
The animal poems—"A is for alas"—there is a pile of papers about three inches thick. We sorted it carefully down to the last two versions. It has been

worked and reworked. There must be fifty versions of each verse. In any event, it is sorted down to two versions, and Miss Barnes will go at it this weekend. She is interested in the poem; it is not marvelous, but it is at least charming, and she wants to see it issued. She says she is in no hurry, but this is probably a pose. Nonetheless it is underway; the final draft she is using is dated April 1971. She says Harpers wanted to issue it then but only if properly illustrated. . . .

Other incidentals: *once* offered the editorship of *Vanity Fair*. Turned it down. No big thing; everyone was offered that job at least once, and it only paid about fifteen dollars a week. Eliot once told her she is in *Finnegans Wake*. She asked if he recalled the page. He did not. She said she'd be damned if she would look through the entire thing for it. Talked about "Quarry" and how good she thinks it is. The first line, "While I unwind duration from the tongue-tied tree," is one of her favorites. She explained about the rings in a tree, one for each year of her life and how she is unwinding them in her mind during the course of the poem—or was unwinding them while writing the poem. Told me what "Sowl" means; if you don't know the word it is impossible to figure out the ending of the poem. She is distressed so few people understand what the poem is about; she thinks it is plain and to the point. But as Eliot used to say, "Miss Barnes, you are unique; there is no one like you." She will probably always have this problem. . . . Some people said that in a few hundred years she might be as important as Shakespeare. And she doubts it with hearty laughter. Talked about how she tries to inject as much humor as possible into what she writes. . . .

8 November

. . . Talk about the *Ryder* project and this led to a discussion about religion and *Ryder*. One reason she withheld its reissue is that she feels it treats religion very lightly through Dr. O'Connor. After the book was published she changed her mind and decided never to poke fun at religion, not because she is religious but because many people need religion. She does not care to offend them. She says she is a complete agnostic; all she believes in is her own ignorance. She feels she does not know enough to know whether there is a supreme being or not. She is very emphatic about this.

. . . Chat about funny incidents. Once interviewed Jack Johnson (who pinched her bottom) and Jack Dempsey (who didn't). Mentioned Joe Gould, a very dirty Village character who never wrote one sensible word. He used to hang out with e.e. cummings, and she could never understand how cummings allowed him to come around so often. Then she turned on other, older Village characters: Havel (who would often be found lying in the gutter but his collar would be clean), Carlin (who lived to be 104), and Hartman (who had babies by everyone in sight and wanted to have one with her). Talk about Proust. Loved the Atget/Proust book I left. Understands Atget but understands Proust better. She never met him and regrets it.

Jealous that Natalie Barney did manage to have a late-night meeting with him. Proust arrived very late, all bundled up, and Barney thought she was going to have a grand time telling Proust all her lesbian relationships, but it turned out Proust wanted to talk about his own homosexual relationships, so the lesbians had to wait for another day which never came. Added that it is best to read the later Proust and skip the earlier. . . .

17 November

. . . She does have a tendency to save everything that is on a piece of paper, and to compound the problem she is forever making notations on anything in sight, and it then must be saved for future reference. Poems on grocery lists. All these papers are just piled up on her desk in no apparent order. She said there are many good poems buried under the heaps and scraps, but a mine detector will be needed to find anything. We worked for a while on the animal poem. She is content with the first six verses but does not want any to be published unless they are all up to the seal and giraffe. Most of the work was on the letter "I," going through various dictionaries looking for animals and unusual words. . . .

19 November

Interesting day working on the animal poems. The flying fish is complete. Progress. Started organizing the papers. Found a pile of things about Eliot she had been looking for forever. They were all remembrances of her last meeting with him when he was very ill. She said at their last meeting he knew it was all over for him. His last words to her were, "Good-bye, my darling," and that was that. She never saw him again. There are many, many poems lying scattered bout her desk, all completely unorganized. There are dozens of versions of the same thing. . . .

Some discussions about Ezra Pound and how she first met him in Paris and interviewed him for the *Little Review*. He helped her find an apartment, but she refused to take it because the people next door were practicing black magic. Many years later when Pound returned to the U.S. and stopped talking she visited him at St. Elizabeth's. Much to her surprise he spoke to her about their first meeting in Paris. When he spoke to her she almost fell over. Never saw him after that Washington visit.

24 November

. . . She then went on to *The Antiphon* and mentioned the reading in Boston. "Tom Eliot was sitting on one side wiggling, and Muir was on the other side being very serious. It all went well enough, and then they read the last line improperly." At one point Herbert Berghof wanted to produce the play at his studio and sent a car around to call for Miss Barnes. She went over to his studio, took one look, and walked right out. There is a rumor the play was once produced in Germany, but she has no proof. After she wrote *The Antiphon* she wrote another play but tore it up because it was too close stylistically to *The Antiphon*, and it is very important not to repeat oneself. . . .

Talked a bit about *Ryder* and her family. Her mother threw *Ryder* out the window when she saw it, and one of her brothers would not speak to her after he read it. He felt a lady should not write such things. Talked about her father, that he was very stern but very talented. A man who could do so many things: play the violin, write novels, write an opera, farm. He could do anything he wanted to and was encouraged by his mother to do so. She mentioned two other relatives, a half brother and a half sister, still living in Philadelphia. She is not close to either but called them recently. She claims that once she was in the hospital dying, and two of her brothers came to call. They spent most of their time there arguing about missing a lunch date. . . . She spoke of Baroness Elsa and how she kept mice as pets and a small dog locked in a closet. The mice ran all over her bed and she fed them there, not thinking such behavior was in any way unusual. Comments about her interviews: Fanny Brice because she was living with a gangster and the papers wanted to know about him but she wouldn't tell; Duchess of Marlborough, who didn't see anyone but asked her to tea anyway where she asked if the Duke was interested in politics, and everyone roared with laughter. . . .

25 November

Hurried visit. . . . Talked about her days on the papers. She finally quit because she would not cover a rape case. A girl had been raped six times, and her editor at the *Journal American* suggested an interview and told her to contrive a story to gain access to the victim. She sneaked past the guards at the hospital and got in the room with the girl, made up some wild stories, and managed to get some answers out of the girl, but in the end felt very bad about what she had done. She told her editor she would never cover another rape case and would not give him the information about this one. He fired her on the spot. Once also interviewed a rough gangster named "Baby Face" (Nelson?) and his girlfriend in her apartment on Waverly Place while his bodyguards watched the doors and windows. Another time she was asked to interview the father of a woman who had been murdered. She went to the house, got in to see the body laid out in the living room. The outraged family threw her out. She then managed to get back into the house via an upstairs window and take a photograph of the dead girl. "This was the kind of thing that made me get out of the newspaper business." I'm not surprised.

27–28 December

Lots of contact over the last few days . . . A recent concern is the publication of a small book entitled *Greenwich Village as It Is*. The Phoenix Book Shop published it, and it is selling briskly for twenty dollars a copy. She is less than pleased with it; "a simple little article that appeared in a newspaper" is how she describes it. It distresses her to think someone might read it and think it is representative of her real work. "I did it to pay the rent; it costs twenty dollars and you can buy *Nightwood* for eighteen dollars less. What sort of fool would pay twenty dollars for this silly little book?" She threw it across the room at me and added, "This is worth about four cents." I offered her a nickel for it, and she accepted my offer. The people at the book store are trying to be honorable; they sent her $600 as a "royalty." She didn't want to take it, feeling her action might condone the printing. After much argument she agreed to keep the money and use it to have a masseuse come by to work on her legs, which are more and more numb every day.

She ripped into almost everyone today. Everyone will do you in for enough money. "Eliot even did," but she stopped there. The world is in a shabby state, and she is sorry about it; the Village is even worse than shabby. . . .

Talked about Berenice. Said Baroness Elsa wanted to leave all her possessions to her (Barnes) but she suggested they should be left to Berenice. Apparently they wound up with someone else. Berenice asked her to do *Greenwich Village Today and Yesterday* with her but she refused. Had no interest in the Village then or now. She tries to be very stern about Berenice, but it is very obvious she doesn't mean it.

Then the subject of ignorance again and how she only believes in her own ignorance. I said that was a valid thing to say, but I believed that some people possess a good deal more ignorance than others. She laughed, adding this was my noble thought for the day. Looked at me squarely and said she was convinced she has wasted her life and that one day she had said the same thing to Eliot. He apparently told her that she may have wasted most of it, but she should look very carefully at what she did when she was not wasting it.

This led to *Nightwood*. Told her I had reread it this week and she wanted to know everything I thought. She wants it to live very much. "I know it is very, very good but at times I cannot understand how I could have been good enough to have written it." She told a story about working on it and leaving the manuscript at the foot of her bed. The bed was covered with "handmade satin sheets, a comforter and religious vestments" but was very near a fireplace. She woke to find the bedclothes burning, and the fire was just reaching the manuscript. She snatched it out of the flames and then put out the fire. "If it had burned there would have been no *Nightwood*. I could never have written it again."

Talk of Dan Mahoney, the doctor in the book. He often told her she had ruined him because so many people came to him later wanting to write down everything he said, thinking it was possible to write a great novel by simply taking down Mahoney's remarks. This is not the way it happened at all; she often visited with Mahoney and listened to him and sometimes lost friends because of it. Her friends told her they didn't approve of her spending so much time with such a dirty person. She admits her friend did supply some keys to *Nightwood*. He would say something she would elaborate upon, but she never used long passages of Mahoney's dialogue. . . .

21 January

. . . She asked that I look at the papers of Baroness Elsa von Freytag-Loringhoven. She feels it is important that someone do something sensible with her poems and letters. She retains the literary rights to the papers; it is unclear why she has them, but she maintains this is the case. Barnes herself tried to make sense out of the material years ago, but she abandoned the Baroness for unstated reasons. She seemed relieved when I said I would look the papers over. . . . She is very concerned about Berenice's reaction to this because Berenice was once close to the Baroness and her letters are also mixed in with all the papers. . . .

22–27 January

. . . The scheme is to get the poems finished. There are many poems, well over forty, in various stages. . . . By 26 January all the different poems had been sorted into different folders and on the twenty-seventh DB worked all day on the one that begins, "Man cannot purge his body of its theme." We started at four o'clock and worked until midnight. She was up for it, feels she made great progress, and this is the most important poem of the lot. There are as many as five hundred different drafts of this poem, with many different titles. The most common are "Phantom Spring," "Viaticum," and "Rites of Passage." Something like the last one will probably be selected. It has also been significantly condensed; it is but one sheet of legal-sized paper. Some of the other longer poems include "Derelictions," "Rakehill," "The Ponder Rose," "Figures in an Alphabet," "Tom Fool," "The Laughing Lamentations of Dan Corbeau (The Book of Dan)," and then there are many shorter ones that are virtually complete. . . . There is also a very long poem with about two inches of manuscript entitled "Virgin Spring. . . ." She remembers the poems in her head. Give her a line and she can finish it. She was fibbing earlier when she said she did not remember one line of her poetry. It is also amazing how much she uses John Donne in her work; she likes him a great deal. One of her short poems is dedicated to Eliot's wife, Valerie. I mentioned I had been looking at the facsimile edition of *The Waste Land* and she said she had seen it. She does not like the poem very much and "neither did his wife."

At one point I went to get a dictionary, and next to it was a copy of the "What 290 Means to Me" issue of *Camera Work*. It had an inscription to DB from "The old man at 291." I asked why she had it, and she said she used to go to the gallery and look at pictures. She showed her own work to Stieglitz, and he expressed a strong hatred of it all, but he apparently liked DB and asked her to contribute something to the issue, which she did. . . . The poems I have seen are very religious in a mysterious, nonsecular fashion. I mentioned this, and she said she was rarely "consciously religious, except the mysteries of life and death and what everything means, if life means anything at all," fascinate her. There is also a profound hatred of her family in some of the poems. The primary source of evil is her father; there is more affection for the mother but a general dislike as well. We talked about this, and the conversation drifted to great hatred of mushy women, total intolerance for lesbians (especially the ones who bother her about it), and a general intolerance for the sexually indulgent. "You will find it is better to write one good line than to make love all night!"

Hates noisy babies and often displays a disparaging attitude towards men; one poem is about castration, and another begins speaking of the famine of a kiss from an old man's mouth. At the same time there is an affectionate poem about the need for a special park for old men to "piddle in." The papers are turning up some interesting things. There are two three-act plays that are complete. . . .

29 January–3 February

A very good week. Worked every day at least three hours on the poetry. All the papers have been sorted a second time, and many missing or misplaced manuscript pages have been found. There are about forty to fifty completed poems that just need a little work, so it appears it may be possible to put together a good, small book. The work is slow but DB is trying very hard, working steadily each day as best she can. . . .

It is too bad she does not want to be recorded; more stories keep pouring out. She has a natural wit and a slightly macabre sense of humor. She loves to tell a story, make a remark, and then laugh along with me. Example: "Henry James was a silly pansie but he didn't work at it." It appears almost all the men she knew were, as she calls them, "pansies," and she speaks of them in a condescending fashion. Most of the women were lesbians; she is less harsh with them, except for the ones who tried to get her into bed. She laughs at them because most of them failed. She goes from poignant to harsh. Of Robert McAlmon: "He was the saddest man I ever knew because he wasn't Joyce, and wanted to be so badly." Later she spoke of him as Bob McAlimony because the woman he married was also gay, and he just wanted her family's money. Spoke of Natalie Barney, admits she is Evangeline Musset in *Ladies Almanack*, but "I never gave her permission to say she was, and she said so all the time." Spoke of McAlmon selling copies of the book when he was pressed for funds. "He had every right to; he paid for it." Then spoke a bit about interviewing that old fraud Gurdjieff; she found him to be a very silly man. "He was of the opinion he could completely cure you of anything by simply looking at you, but he never cared to look." He would not allow her any photographs, so she had to draw him from memory.

DB is annoyed because I do not know a great deal about poetry. She is always asking what I think of this line or that, and the best I can do is offer gut reactions. "None of it is easy, and even the little throwaway lines are very difficult. Each word must be carefully crafted, and it is the hardest kind of writing there is." At this point she spoke of some of the things that pass as poems today and finally said, "If that stuff is poetry, I'll eat the floor."

This was the last entry. From this point on the meetings became increasingly regular, usually about four a week. . . .

The next two years saw a great deal of work accomplished, some significant, some not. Miss Barnes completed and approved about twenty-five poems, including the small book eventually published as *Creatures in an Alphabet*. Additionally, virtually all her books were reissued, in every language imaginable; it became possible to find *Nightwood* in Finnish and *Ladies Almanack* in Spanish. In fact, all her major work was available in English, Spanish, German, French, and Italian, and some titles found their way to more obscure locations. And, happily, she was financially secure.

In late 1980 Miss Barnes began to change; she tended to need almost constant attention and was unable to do any serious writing. She had, however, finished most of the poems she cared about and had made such notations on them and most of the publishing and other business matters were well in hand.

I was fascinated by the changes at first; I had never witnessed anything like it on a personal level. At the same time it was very sad and frustrating because slowly, often imperceptibly on a day-to-day basis, someone I once knew very well changed into someone else. Legally she was the same person—the same name and social security number—but mentally she was someone else, a person I scarcely knew and one who didn't know me. For the last six months I was with her, all the things she told me in the previous two and one-half years poured out in an almost unending stream of jumbled statements often directed at me with a vengeance.

As Miss Barnes became increasingly infirm and forgetful, it became necessary simply to take matters in hand and make certain her affairs were handled properly. Andrew Field, in *Djuna*, suggests I "presumed to exercise too much autonomy" with Miss Barnes' affairs. He is partially correct, but I didn't presume anything. I simply did what needed to be done, knowing full well it would probably lead to the difficulties between Miss Barnes and myself that came later in the year. We had a serious disagreement in late May, and the last time I ever saw her was during the following month.

Chester Page

On a spring afternoon in 1970, visiting Marianne Moore in her Ninth Street Manhattan apartment, I asked if she ever had news of Djuna Barnes, who lived nearby. Miss Moore seemed so concerned about her that I wrote to

Miss Barnes, asking if I might somehow be of help. A few days later a pale grey envelope bearing the imprint "Five Patchin Place" arrived in reply, with an invitation to come for tea.

At that time there was no bell she could ring to admit visitors. The downstairs door was open, and I climbed the narrow stairs one flight, found her door with a "Do Not Disturb" notice, knocked, identified myself when she looked through a peephole, heard the clanking of a police lock bar being removed. The door opened, and there stood the living, aged legend whose wit was the terror and joy of the Paris literati, straight as a spear shaft, eyes the blue of a Tiepolo sky or a Mediterranean seascape. She greeted me warmly, in such a friendly manner that some of my apprehensions were overcome.

She was then seventy-eight, not at all like the famous photographs of her in her youth. She wore a black dress with a bow at the neck, looking very French grande dame and quite marvelous as she half reclined Mme Recamier–fashion on her bed, beneath a blue-shaded lamp, her own books prominent on the bookshelves at her side. Her hair was grey and luxuriant. She was a most handsome and elegant figure.

Her voice, rich in the alto register, was that of a dramatic actress, with British overtones. For fear of being inadequate, she never made a recording of her reading. To hear her read, as I did, Miranda's great speech from the last act of *The Antiphon*, was very moving.

She could be hilarious. One might roar with laughter, or sit apprehensively in her large Victorian chair, depending on the mood of the moment. She was often bitter. She had been wounded by the world and had, as a consequence, built around herself an almost impenetrable barrier of reserve and distrust.

She felt she could trust no one. Eliot let her down. Only Edwin Muir had been loyal. "What a darling he was," she said. "You can't trust your dearest darling. They all betray you, perhaps even Muir had I been closer. I am the most famous unknown writer," she remarked wryly.

She spoke movingly of Marianne Moore as a person and of the perfection of her work, though "it's not poetry, you know," she commented. She had asked Marianne Moore what she thought of *Nightwood* and she claimed never to have read it. "I could scarcely believe that," she said, but gave her a copy. Miss Moore had said after reading it that it was like a foreign language suddenly made plain. With her own work, Miss Barnes said she was never satisfied.

She was indignant at misinterpretations of the final scene of *Nightwood*. "The dog is *not* being romantic towards Robin! It is furious at the mystery of her drunkenness, a kind of exorcism of what it does not understand." It was taken, she told me, from the experience of a friend of hers, whose dog, "frenzied because of her being drunk, beat its legs against the walls of the room."

At one time she was despondent over her failing vision and had had negative prognoses from several physicians. I persuaded her to see an eminent eye surgeon who gave a more optimistic opinion. In a moment of familiarity in his office, he patted her on the knee and said, "Ziegfeld would have admired those legs." Miss Barnes restrained herself at the time, but in the limousine returning to Patchin Place, she exclaimed, "What cheek! As a matter of fact, Ziegfeld did admire my legs and asked me to appear in one of his productions. I refused." She told of having gone on stage in nonspeaking roles for the Theatre Guild, once as a nun in a play by Claudel and once as Darkness in a Tolstoy play. She later had eye surgery with this doctor, and though she sometimes complained about the results, she had better vision from that time.

Our friendship, after a long interval of silence on my part in its beginning, resumed in earnest and we became, to our mutual surprise, rather close. Among memorable outings together were a shopping trip to Altman's on Fifth Avenue, where she was an awe-inspiring figure with her cape and cane and regal posture; a nearly disastrous afternoon at an Ingmar Bergman film, two hours of unrelenting gloom, from which we were rescued by having tea at the Palm Court of the Plaza. There a violinist played melodies from the 1920s and 1930s and ladies in cloche hats appeared as if on cue. "I never dreamed such things still existed," said Miss Barnes.

On occasions such as a rare luncheon at her favorite Chinese restaurant and countless afternoons at her apartment, she was a fascinating companion, telling about events in the past, of meeting the royal Wittelsbachs with Putzi Hanfstaengel in Munich, of Berlin, where she withdrew to write while other Americans like Marsden Hartley acquired fabulous things with meager American dollars. Her conversation and comments were breathtaking, both in content and language. The air crackled with electricity. Nothing she said was ever commonplace. She could be harsh at times, but underlying it all was a warmth, a sincerity, an adherence to principle, and a generosity that I have seldom encountered in any other person. When one left to nurse one's injured feelings for a time, one missed her enormously.

Near the end of her life she had long since ceased to go out except for hospital stays or visits to doctors. The loss of old friends like Janet Flanner and Peggy Guggenheim were hard blows. Years earlier, after Dag Hammarskjöld's death, she confessed she had "cried for a week." Her rather forbidding façade masked a vulnerable and sensitive soul. Her need to be loved was more and more apparent to her little band of faithful friends who endeavored, with slight success, to alleviate her miseries. The days when she might read aloud her Animal Alphabet with great bravura or talk about the past were gone. She then longed to die, to be out of her sufferings.

I saw her last just a few hours before the end, receiving a parting kiss and a wan smile that were a final farewell, though I did not know it. Even in that state, she remembered to ask about my mother, who was also very ill.

Djuna Barnes was incomparable. I consider all those afternoons
spent with her in her gloomy little apartment, listening to her fabulous wit,
or commiserating with her on the state of the world, feeling her affection and
concern, one of the great privileges of my life.

Andrew Field

Mary Lynn Broe has asked me to provide this collection with a brief piece
about my research experiences in preparing my 1983 book about Djuna
Barnes. I am happy to be doing this, not only because I feel that it is still early
days for the interest in Djuna Barnes, but also because I have been interested
in the previous writing of a fair number of contributors to this volume,
which I hope will be a milestone along the way. Barnes was a special sort of
person and writer, and it is important, since there are still so many who are
dismissive of her, that those who know her worth should make the effort to
avoid ideological and methodological division and instead follow their
various commitments to Barnes in a spirit of common cause.

Of course, the Barnes papers in the Katherine Anne Porter Room (a
lovely irony: they weren't too fond of one another) at the University of
Maryland provided me with the essential core of my knowledge of Barnes
outside of her printed books, which I had admired for many years. What I
did that no one else can now do to the same extent was to start from the
archive and track down those who had been close to Djuna in her time. Once
I had worked on Nabokov and enjoyed the luxury of an émigré culture that
was largely unknown and ignored. I was stunned to discover that the
situation was much the same for whole areas of the expatriation of the
1920s, and even more so for the culture of old Greenwich Village. It was a
privilege and responsibility to meet and talk with so many of the last
survivors of these times. A few lucky hunches (— *So you already know about
that?*) led people to assume that I knew more than I did, and gradually the
pieces fell into place. Until June 1985, there were still some closed archival files
at Maryland and at the Bibliothèque Litteraire Jacques Doucet in Paris which
may in time yield important information, and I shall be most curious in the
decades ahead to see if the general contours that I have mapped hold true.

I visited the past of Djuna Barnes in England, France, and North
America. I even tracked Charles Henri Ford to Nepal, where Meg and I were
"tested" by a visit to a native tea house where dogs drank from a water spout
over piles of freshly "washed" dishes and tea glasses (we asked for seconds,
passed the test, and were sick for a week). But for some reason, probably
exhaustion at the end of several years of work on the book, I didn't go to see
Paul Bowles, even though I was on vacation in Morocco. Someone should ask
him about Djuna Barnes. And Glenway Wescott, who was away when I
passed by, and James Stern in England, who declined to speak with me on the
grounds that he was writing his own memoirs.

There are, as readers of my book will know, many narrative islands which are essential to place and understand Barnes and which require some further exploration. Most important of all these stories is probably that of the grandmother, Zadel. What a wonderful and worthwhile book is there for someone with a number of years to spare and considerable determination. Have any of the operas of Wald Barnes survived in any attic? And will they tell us anything about *The Antiphon*? The archive of the Baronin, also at Maryland, had not been put in order when I visited the university; it, too, should be carefully examined. Thelma Wood will be someone's important story someday. I located an address for a sister in New Jersey, but the trail went cold there. Did Emily Coleman talk about her friend at the Catholic Workers' Farm in New York State where she ended her days? I'll bet she did — the only question is whether any of the listeners were wise enough to take notes of things she said. Guido Bruno's life has probably told us all that it needs to, but what a tremendous disappointment not to be able to find the hundreds of Village caricatures of Clara Tice. If found they will furnish a virtual telephone book to the past, for there will be scores of new names to follow, and, among other things, we will learn more about Djuna Barnes.

I would like to be able to warn future researchers about a friend of Barnes, a person still living at this writing, an admirer above all of truth who told me nothing but lies (fortunately, I discovered them in time); but I had better not. Last, I received an extraordinary letter from an old woman after my book appeared in which she said that Djuna *did* attend school, with her on Long Island, although it is true that she was frequently truant. School and town records must be checked, both there and at Cornwall-on-Hudson.

Implicit in all my remarks is the assumption that the life and work of Barnes will ultimately have the same fascination that people find in Edgar Allan Poe.

Frances McCullough

When I first went to see Djuna Barnes, shortly after she had broken a long silence by giving an interview to the *New York Times*, I has hoping to convince her to let us (us was three young ladies, two editors, and an art director from Harper & Row, all Barnes fans) publish her stories in paperback. Despite her reclusive nature and her thorny reputation, she was pleased to see us, pleased to be courted again by publishers. I think she was relieved that we were all women and well read in Barnes. We had a fine lunch in the Village while she entertained us with wild stories from the old days — despite the heat of early July and her emphysema, which gave her terrible coughing fits. We had a glorious time, laughing and laughing. Yes, she would love us to do the stories, and there were other things as well, to speak of later.

Then, back at her little atelier on Patchin Place, things were suddenly very serious: she *had* to have a new air conditioner, or get hers fixed, *now* — it was Friday before the Fourth of July; a heat wave had just begun, and temperatures in the 100s were arriving the next day. No one could help her. We tried calling all over town—no luck. Then I remembered someone in Brooklyn who owed me a favor, called him, pleaded, and the new air conditioner was installed that afternoon. And in that way I became immediately invaluable—I was, she kept saying, the one who could do anything. Or so it seemed to Barnes, in her increasingly fragile old age. And I, in my youth, shared the same illusion.

Our first project after the stories was to reprint *Ladies Almanack*, that enchanting document Barnes had virtually hand-printed in Paris. Of course this had to be done properly, and for some reason Harper indulged us in this, printing up several different dummy bindings—none quite right, of course, but that was inevitable. My idea was to have an introduction to this curious work, something that would give a modern reader a clue about how to enter its spirit. I thought someone who had been in Paris at the time and cared about Barnes' work would be right—but of course no one was; she fixed me with her fierce eye and pointed out that only Eliot and Hammarskjöld would do, and they were both dead. When I rejoined with a writer very up on Barnes who still breathed, she hit me in the ankle with her cane— "That man's not worth my little finger, Mrs. McCullough, how can you possibly even speak his name in this context. . . ." And so it went. In the end it was just a cryptic note Barnes herself wrote that served as introduction, and it was definitely pitched to the few, not the many.

Meanwhile, I had been busily setting up the publication as an event— after long discussion and argument, Barnes had finally agreed to an interview. I had the interviewer ready, excited interest from the book review editor at the *Times* and it looked very much as though we might have a front page review. And then, once the book was published, utter silence. It went on and on; I couldn't even get my connections to return my calls. Finally I learned, many months later, that the book had gone to three reviewers, none of whom could figure it out at all, and so the editor concluded there was no audience for this book. Barnes herself had just about reached the same conclusion—it was a terrifically painful experience for her; she used to say "All they want, Mrs. McCullough is me upside down on 42nd Street, with my skirt over my head and my bum in the air." I thought at first that perhaps Barnes had just outlived her potential readers, and that in my own infatuation with anything Barnesish I had completely misread the situation. Now I think it was just bad timing—a few years later and it would have been a celebration that greeted the book.

I was beginning to understand that I couldn't do everything. The next project was the selling of her papers, but of course before the papers could be sold they had to be properly examined and verified by a curator. I got one from Parke–Benet, but naturally it was impossible for him to work in Barnes' tiny quarters, sitting on her bed ("I don't like his beard and I don't like his bottom, which I see whenever he bends over—where *do* you find these people?") while Barnes naturally wanted to see everything he was looking at before he read it. So we moved with the help of Craig Novo, another of my authors, all the many boxes of letters, artwork, photographs, early drafts, etc. to Harper & Row, to the Document Room, where the humidity was controlled and the atmosphere of the pharaoh's tomb prevailed. There the work was finished, many months later. This was a relative success, and in fact the papers were sold, giving Barnes a nest egg for her old age—though of course everyone involved was at one time in a state of complete exasperation.

What saved us, always, from quarreling, was Barnes' great wit and her very real warmth. Then too, I had great sympathy for her current writing. Her dearest wish was for even a line of really brilliant verse—at the time of the republication of the *Almanack* she said she was "entertaining poetry," as indeed she was—and every now and then it came, but just a line or two, and nothing to hook them up. Over the years she abandoned the long sequence of "spiritual" poems she had hoped for, and began to concentrate on the bestiary, *Creatures in an Alphabet*, which also had some marvelous lines but wouldn't quite cohere. All this time, she was *saying* the most extraordinary things—the language was just amazing. Probably her best line was on Eliot—"Poor Eliot, he kept his organ in the Church," inexplicably given as "he left his Auden in the Church" in a biography—but there were lines almost as good, almost every day. Most of them had a good kick of the gutter in them, rendered in exalted but salty language. Then there was the wonderful little roar of Barnes' laughter, the merry light in her eyes that could so quickly go up in a blaze. She was possessed of an amazing personal force. I used to think of her as Shakespeare's sister, or possibly Dr. Jonson's, with a Rabelaisian ancestor thrown in.

Over the years I came to realize that of course I couldn't do it all, in fact I couldn't even do very much of it, and even that I couldn't do particularly well. And to undertake more would mean losing my relationship with the optimum Barnes and descending into the truculence of daily commerce. So she embarked on a long parade of other helpers, and I would fade in and out as a wild card, getting a housekeeper here or clearing up a reprint permission there. Perhaps the least chore came one day when her back was giving her terrific trouble—"Well, can't we *do* something for the poor Barnes, Mrs. McCullough?" and I responded with the offer of a backrub. This quickly became a lower backrub, and there before me lay a perfectly gorgeous backside, with the graceful slopes of a lioness gently defined. It was like one of Barnes' early voluptuous drawings, with a fresh, firm, luminous skin—altogether astonishing. In less than ten minutes she was asleep, and when I told her later how lovely she was she laughed—"Well of course I *used* be absolutely gorgeous *dear*, but that was before you were even born. . . ."

She began to focus more and more on publication: a last poem, something for *The New Yorker*, the bestiary. I felt she was keeping herself going for this last piece, that and her ninetieth birthday. The last scrap of poem—and very lovely—went to *Grand Street*, and we determined to force the issue of the bestiary, which by now lay in hundreds of versions in various untouchable piles of paper. Finally she let me go through them all and make up the variorum, and slowly we began to assemble a final text. Often she would catch just a glimpse of a connection, a line that might be gorgeous, and it would be instantly gone—she'd sink back on the pillows: "Damn, damn, damn." Then the lines wouldn't even tease anymore, and so we declared it finished.

I think all of us around her and Barnes herself felt any minute she would go during the last six months or so of her life; it seemed just incredible that she could hang on in great pain and losing so much stamina. But she really did want to have a ninetieth birthday. And on that day, something amazing happened: a Barnes fan from Germany, a beautiful young man with golden curls who loved her work passionately, flew in for the birthday. She lay sleeping deep into her pillows, helped by her pain drugs, but she roused herself for this young man and as he tenderly stroked her face and spoke to her about her work and her meaning in life, she grew completely radiant. It was a magical moment of the most intense intimacy—a writer and her reader.

¶ Recently *Time* magazine, pernicious as ever, dismissed the *Selected Writings* of Djuna Barnes by saying that the best of her work, *Nightwood*, offered little more than "the mysterioso effect that hides no mystery," and even Leslie Fiedler has described Djuna Barnes' vision of evil as effete. Yet all her myth and fear are mightily to be envied. Surely there is unpardonable distinction in this kind of writing, a certain incorrigible assumption of a prophetic role in reverse, when the most baffling of unsympathetic attitudes is turned upon the grudges, guilts, and renunciations harbored in the tangled seepage of our earliest recollections and originations. It is like quarreling at the moment of temptation. Or it is like working a few tangerines on a speedily driven lathe. Djuna Barnes is one of the "old poets," and there is no denying the certain balance of this "infected carrier" upon the high wire of the present. She had moved; she has gone out on a limb of light and indefinite sexuality and there remains unshakeable. She has free-wheeled the push bicycle into the cool air.

—John Hawkes,
"Fiction Today,"
Massachusetts Review (Summer 1962)

Afterword

Catharine Stimpson

Before Djuna Barnes died in 1982, her neighbors on Patchin Place in Greenwich Village were uneasy. For at least six months, they had smelled smoke coming from her apartment. As they waited and worried outside, Barnes was inside, destroying her correspondence.[1]

Because of the essays this Afterword follows, we will be able to read Barnes, her pages and person, far more closely, explosively, and reliably than before. These essays, lightning bolts and laser beams of critical intelligence, will cauterize and change our perceptions of Barnes and cultural modernism. Yet, Barnes' motives for burning her letters remain an enigma, as smoke must be to someone who has never seen fire or felt it near the skin. Did she wish to seal up her privacy even more hermetically? To block a hermeneutics of her life that might have ranged between prurient gossip and psychoanalysis? So doing, was she seeking her revenge on people who might want to study her and, by studying, possess her shadow? Or, was she consumed by anger and frustration with this world, a chaotic time and space she could not costume? Or, did she simply want to see and hear and feel a flame?

Whatever her reasons, the self-willed, self-incited immolation of Barnes' letters is a symbol of her contradictory relationship to language. Like Samuel Beckett, she regards it mordantly, playfully, and ambivalently. In 1915, when she was twenty-three, she published a collection of eight poems, *The Book of Repulsive Women*. One, "Seen from the 'L,'" records that mixture. A nude woman stands behind a window, "chain-stitched to her soul for time." She blooms there. Simultaneously, however, she ravels "grandly into vice" and drops "crooked into rhyme."

Barnes did boldly seize and commandeer language and its rhymes. In a similar commitment to words, Nora Flood, in *Nightwood*, sends letters to a fugitive Robin Vote. A hard-working journalist, Barnes also earned her precarious living by writing. She took on genre after genre. Violating notions of generic decorum as consistently as her Bohemian life did the social proprieties, she mixed those genres wildly. Like all outlaws, she took a rule as a mate with which she might play and then abandon. She was neither consistently likeable nor pleasing.

In part, Barnes went for language because she was aware of its tremendous powers as jeremiad, prophecy, history, confession, insult, and lyric. Like Nora Flood, before Nora's discovery of the night, Barnes wished she had been a Christian in Christianity's first days. She might then have freshly, purely believed in Logos, the Word that generates, orders, and regenerates, the Word that was with God in the beginning.

Barnes is too much in thrall to a cosmology of heaven and hell, of salvation and damnation, in which earth is both testing and killing ground, to be a post-structuralist. Nevertheless, she anticipates the post-structuralist anguish about letting loose a word, a sentence. As Derrida writes in one of his most famous essays: "Speaking frightens me because, by never saying enough, I also say too much. And if the necessity of becoming breath or speech restricts meaning—and our responsibility for it—writing restricts and constrains speech further still. . . . It is the moment at which we must decide whether we will engrave what we hear. And whether engraving preserves or betrays speech."[2]

In our damned and natural world, the powers of language have gone astray in multiple, twisted ways. Robustly, defiantly, Barnes ransacks literature's most rambunctious genres—satire, parody, scatology, burlesque—in order to expose these piggish, pokish, dangerous wanderings. This very ransacking of the past might have damaged Barnes. Apparently, she construed literary tradition and authority as masculine. She wanted the approval of a T.S. Eliot. Waiting for such endorsements, fearing they will never come, can restrain, even paralyze, the most limber word processor.

Wretchedly, language enables its speaker/engraver to lie and to deceive others and themselves. In Barnes' story "Smoke," terrorists cheerfully threaten to storm a town but fall asleep in drunken squalor. More painfully, in *Ryder*, Julie, Barnes' red-haired surrogate, learns that her grandmother Sophia has lied to her, a violation of the trusting love and loving trust between them.[3] No matter how harmful such deceptions are, they can be tempting and desirable. For lying, when it is the spinning of fantasies and fictions, allows us to enter into other worlds and to become other people. Of course, these actions then permit us to inhabit even more domains of pain. In one of the most difficult chapters of *Ryder*, "Julie Becomes What She Had Read," she takes on the identity of many children: "suffering the tortures of the damned, kneeling at the parent knee, in all ages, all times and all bindings, becoming what books make of a child."[4]

Sometimes, a speaker/engraver can use language accurately, stand up and be a straight-shooter of the sign. Barnes is clear-tongued about lesbianism. No one would mistake the ebullient *Ladies Almanack*, coeval with Woolf's *Orlando*, for a handbook about the joys of heterosexuality. Contrasting heterosexuality, lesbianism, and "the third sex," the man who would be woman, the woman who would be man, *Nightwood* is as sharply etched as *Gray's Anatomy*. Yet, another wretchedness, even the plainest of speech names foulness and death. Again and again, a Barnes' narrative stops with death. Even *Ladies Almanack* ends in death, the tribal funeral of Dame Evangeline Musset, that hearty evangelist for lesbian love and lore.

Barnes' sexual theories are sophisticated, her texts about homosexuality intricate, her affair with Thelma Wood passionate. Nevertheless, she does not place lesbian practices at the center of her universe. Indeed, perhaps diminishing their importance too drastically, she told her editor in New York after her return from Europe that she could not understand why "all these lesbians keep coming around."[5] Homosexuality is but one among several passages into the self and through history, this City of Man and Woman for which the City of God is an absence that mocks and tests faith. Thelma Wood is but one stand of nightwoods.

Barnes' texts reveal a great difficulty in being plain about family life, especially her own. Often, what she does write about families—for example, the polygamous groupings and troopings of *Ryder* or *The Antiphon*—can scald the heart. The legs of parents seem to form an arch-like entrance into the torture chambers of the damned. The more her narratives tell of families, the more complicated, flurried, and evasive they become. The metaphors and epigrams become more clotted. The jokes swing more furiously on the trapezes of her paragraphs. Characters speak on and on in monologue or dialogue. As if she were a listening, dependent child again, the author can do little more than to let their voices flow without her intervention. They go on and on, until their rhetoric floods over and drowns linguistic normalcies.

Yet, the heterosexual family is a linch-pin as the human species wheels on. As language replicates the world through the production of speech and writing, so this family regenerates the world through the reproduction of children. Homosexuals can speak and write. They can be virtuous or vicious. No matter which, they partake of futility, for they cannot breed with each other.

Barnes distinguishes male heterosexuality from female, as if she were compelled to deploy an amalgam of Christianity, Victorianism, and a wary feminism. Male sexuality, fathering, is necessary. Fathers, however, are egocentric and demanding. Female sexuality, mothering, is necessary and far more desirable. Morally superior to fathers, psychologically closer to their daughters, mothers are meant to nurture, extracting only the price of acclaim. Yet, being a mother is risky. She is often a sacrifice devoured by the cannibalistic tribe. Being a daughter is worse. For she is often a far more vulnerable sacrifice.

Barnes, who can blaspheme as well as any would-be believer, hints that God may be a woman writ unimaginably large, a "bag of tricks," a fecund womb. Our woe is that whatever illicit creature God drops may fall far away, and God will be indifferent to that distance.

Bowed down by such weights, seared by such contraries, Barnes surprises us. She wrote so much and burnt so little.

Notes
Selected Bibliography
Notes on Contributors
Index

Notes

Introduction

1. Emily Holmes Coleman, unprocessed diaries (1 July 1933), The Coleman Papers, Special Collections, University of Delaware–Newark Library, Newark.

2. For an analysis of the failures of incest discourse to include the complexities of the Barnes family relations, see Broe, "My Art Belongs to Daddy: Incest as Exile, the Textual Economics of Hayford Hall," in *Women's Writing in Exile*, edited by Broe and Angela Ingram (Chapel Hill: Univ. of North Carolina Press, 1989). While there are many gaps and omissions in the history of the "double household," the following information, derived from research at the McKeldin Library, was confirmed by Duane Barnes, Djuna's half-brother. Brian [Wald] Barnes was married to Djuna's mother, Elizabeth Chappell, from 3 July 1889 through 6 November 1912. On 22 February 1912, Elizabeth Chappell issued a summons to Wald, forcing him to respond within twenty days. On 2 August 1912, divorce papers were filed. The marriage was dissolved three months later. On 13 November 1912, a marriage certificate was issued to Fanny Faulkner and Wald Barnes. I am grateful to various members of the Barnes family for their generosity: Duane; his son, Kerron; Djuna's brother Saxon; and his wife, Eleanor. *Cold Comfort: A Biographical Portrait of Djuna Barnes in Letters*, edited by Mary Lynn Broe and Frances McCullough (New York: Random House, forthcoming), will present new material to help explain many puzzling gaps and omissions in the chronology of Barnes' first twenty years. This biographical portrait through letters will also correct errors in the only biography now available.

3. For a fuller portrait of Zadel Barnes and for a more detailed background on family life, see Broe and McCullough, *Cold Comfort.*

4. Most of Zadel's journalism was published in *Harper's Monthly Magazine*, 1870–85; see also Zadel Barnes Gustafson, ed. and introd., *Zophiel: or, The Bride of Seven* by Maria del Occidente [Maria Gowen Brooks] (Boston: Lee and Shepard, 1879); *Genevieve Ward* (Boston: James R. Osgood and Co., 1882); *Can the Old Love?* (Boston: James R. Osgood and Co., 1871); *Meg, A Pastoral and Other Poems* (Boston: Lee and Shepard, 1879).

5. In two private interviews with Duane Barnes over the past two years, his discussion of "visitors" to the farm (that is, Zadel as a practicing medium and spiritualist) confirmed the information in a family diary to which he referred: that the "Eaches" or spirits who used Zadel's body to "come through the dead" always seemed to be public men, mostly musicians or writers of note, who urged diligence on the children. As late as 1988, Duane Barnes still felt the power and accuracy of the visitors and never felt there was a "rigged" session.

6. See Broe, "Djuna Barnes," in *The Gender of Modernism*, ed. Bonnie Kime Scott (Bloomington: Indiana Univ. Press, 1990), for both a reprint and a critique of Barnes' interview with Helen Westley and the 1919 play *To the Dogs*.

7. See, in particular, letters from Barnes to Silas Glossup and Laurence Vail in the

377

Barnes papers, The McKeldin Library, Special Collections, University of Maryland–College Park. Selections from these and other Barnes letters will appear in *Cold Comfort*.

8. Djuna Barnes, letter to Casa Editrice Valentino Bompiani, 8 February 1951.

9. A constant revisionist with her own writing, Barnes left at least five copybooks (the most interesting from 1963 and 1964), each a compelling bricolage of found quotations, book references, definitions, and readerly marginalia. A modernist's museum of references, foods, names, printings, clothes, and architectures embroider works such as *Nightwood, Antiphon, Ryder*, and many of the early one-act plays. Here is a glimpse of one Barnes' sourcebook—elliptical things, meant to conceal as they reveal, adding to personal legends even as they encourage us to theorize the uses of marginalia and the production of her texts: "Eminence eats itself." "One writes as one deserves." "One says 'Oh God' for oneself, 'My God' of others!" "Why is a very hasty miscarriage and a late climatric admired by old women?" She saved a definition of "hucklebone" from *As You Like It* (2.7), and to the following—"Nero, that monster, slit his mother's womb to see from whence he came, and seeing it undid himself"—she penned in her familiar green ink, "Irreparable intimacy." Next to Francis Bacon's name, she wrote: "The care of posterity is greatest in them who have no posterity." Verse after verse of stanzaically structured poetry of notebook 3 dwindled to annotations such as the following: "One must escape from life by the slow and intelligent and honorable suicide (which is work), and I say live on your heels." It seems that whatever she wanted from this repository, she simply cut out with a scissors.

10. Kenneth Burke, "Version, Con-, Per-, and In-: Thoughts on Djuna Barnes' Novel *Nightwood*," *Southern Review* 2 (1966): 329–46. Rpt. in Kenneth Burke, *Language as Symbolic Action: Essays on Life, Literature and Method* (Berkeley: Univ. of California Press, 1968). 240–53.

11. Louis F. Kannenstine (*The Art of Djuna Barnes: Duality and Damnation*. New York: New York Univ. Press, 1977) calls this decline "a complex record of disunity and disharmony."

12. Joseph Frank, "Spatial Form in Modern Literature," in *The Widening Gyre: Crisis and Mastery in Modern Literature*. (Bloomington: Indiana Univ. Press, 1963).

13. See in particular essays by Joseph Frank and Kenneth Burke.

14. See recent dissertations by Elyse Blankley, "Daughters' Exile: Renee Vivien, Gertrude Stein and Djuna Barnes in Paris"; Sheryl Anne Stevenson, "The Never-Last Word: Parody, Ideology, and the Open Work;" and Susan Clark, "Misalliance: Djuna Barnes and the American Theatre," particularly her informed look at *all* Barnes' plays, not simply at those performed during the Provincetown Player's "season of youth" in 1919. Carl Herzig, who recovers much radical early journalism, reads a number of the "seemingly contradictory impulses which characterize *Nightwood*" in her writing of twenty years earlier (255), yet still dismisses this youthful writing as "essentially immature" (269). Cheryl Plumb's book, *Fancy's Craft*, remains a well-researched, definitive text on the early journalism.

15. Lawrence Schehr ("Djuna Barnes' *Nightwood*: Dismantling the Folds") suggests that we read *Nightwood* as an obvious presentation of the theory of semiosis with each of the first four chapters of the novel showing us how a sign is produced and implemented (38).

16. Marilyn Reizbaum ("A 'Modernism of Marginality': The Link Between James Joyce and Djuna Barnes" in Scott) challenges the notion of *Nightwood* and *Ulysses* as quintessential modernist texts, suggesting instead that both texts are better viewed as representations of the ongoing revision of modernism. See also essays by Frann Michel, Elizabeth Beranger, and Mairéad Hanrahan.

17. Barnes and some of her women journalist contemporaries—Agnes Duer Miller, Dorothy Parker, and Jane Grant—followed the footsteps of Margaret Fuller who, seventy years before, visited factories, insane asylums, and coal mines, writing dispatches to the *Tribune* about social and educational inequalities. Fuller was lowered on a bucket into a New-castle coal mine on 6 September 1914.

18. For lengthy treatment of the early journalism Cheryl Plumb, *Fancy's Craft*, and Louis Kannenstine, *Duality and Damnation*. See Carl Herzig "Roots of Night: Emerging Style and Vision in the Early Journalism," *Centennial Review* 30 (Autumn 1987): 255–69.

19. Ironically, among the first plays by the team of Susan Glaspell and Jig (George Cram) Cook were *Suppressed Desires* and *Fidelity*. *Suppressed Desires* parodied current fads of psychoanalysis by presenting on stage an amateur encounter session, but one that valorized, as the Cook/Glaspell liaison did for so many years, the powerful and cunning husband who tricks a very bright wife into submission.

20. For another view of this play see Broe, "Djuna Barnes."

21. See Elyse Blankley, "Daydreams and Nightmares: Djuna Barnes and the City of Visions," in *Daughter's Exile* for Barnes' "feminizing" this city of women hereafter represented by male memoirists such as Jimmy Charters, Malcolm Cowley, and others.

22. We are reminded of the disparity between Natalie Barney's wealth (she inherited $2.5 million from her father in 1902; later, when her mother died, she received another $1.5 million) and Barnes' poverty, a litany of economic despair that weaves in and out of the last fifty years of Barnes' life. The later years were very different from the 1920s, when she earned $15 an article, sometimes $5,000 a year. The pastiche of small gifts and bequests is extensive and certainly not limited to gifts from women: the 1927 advance of $250 from Donald Friede at Liveright (not the $1000 promised); the 1936 royalty check for thirty-three cents; in 1955, the $200 bequest from "Fitzi's" (Eleanor Fitzgerald's) will; Janet Flanner's $200 check to buy a typewriter in the 1960s; $500 from Marianne Moore; $2500 from Cordelia Coker Pearson in 1949; a $100 check from Mary Reynolds; the Albert Lewin bequest of $2500 in 1968; occasional checks from Eustace Seligman and others. In the 1940s, Barnes at times went without food for days. Her brother Zendon is on record giving $5 to Lizzie, Djuna's mother, and directing her *not* to give it to Djuna all at once.

1. *"Bringing Milkshakes to Bulldogs": The Early Journalism of Djuna Barnes*

1. Harry Payne Burton, letter to Djuna Barnes, 2 November 1925, the Djuna Barnes Collection, McKeldin Library, University of Maryland, College Park.

2. Matthew Josephson, in *Life among the Surrealists, a Memoir* (New York: Holt, Rinehart, 1962), 83, recalls that at one period Barnes was living on a monthly stipend of fifty dollars, given to her by a rich American woman (probably Natalie Clifford Barney).

3. "'Twingless [*sic*] Twitchell' and His Tantalizing Tweezers, etc.," Brooklyn *Daily Eagle*, 27 July 1913, 6.

4. "Ruth Royce, Greatest 'Nut' in Vaudeville," New York *Press*, 19 May 1915, sec. 4, p. 4.

5. "Found in the Bowery: The Italian Drama," New York *Morning Telegraph*, 21 January 1917, sec. 2, p. 1.

6. The prototype usually cited for Dr. Matthew O'Connor is Dr. Dan Mahoney. For accounts of this friend of Barnes' expatriate years, see John Glassco, *Memoirs of Montparnasse* (New York: Oxford Univ. Press, 1970); Robert McAlmon, *Being Geniuses Together* (Garden City, NY: Doubleday, 1968); and Andrew Field, *Djuna: The Life and Times of Djuna Barnes* (New York: Putnam's, 1983).

7. "Billy Sunday, a Fire-Eater in Pulpet, etc.," New York *Press*, 12 February 1915, sec. 5, p. 2.

8. "Training Seals in Stage Stunts, etc.," Brooklyn *Daily Eagle*, 31 August 1913, 30; "Roshanara, a Wraithlike Reincarnation of the Ancient East," New York *Press*, 14 June 1914, sec. 5 p. 3; "The Girl and the Gorilla; Dinah at the Bronx Zoo etc.," New York *World Magazine*, 18 October 1914, 9.

9. "If Noise Were Forbidden at Coney Island, a Lot of People Would Lose Their Jobs etc.," New York *Press*, 7 June 1914, sec. 5, p. 5.

10. "Surcease in Hurry and Whirl," New York *Morning Telegraph*, 15 July 1917, 2.

11. Louis Kannenstine, *The Art of Djuna Barnes: Duality and Damnation* (New York: New York Univ. Press, 1977), 5–6.

12. "The Songs of Synge: The Man Who Shaped His Life as He Shaped His Plays," New York *Morning Telegraph*, 18 February 1917, 8.

13. I am indebted to Hank O'Neal's memoirs (excerpted in this volume) for Barnes' account of her newspaper experiences and for her denial of Walter Winchell's "spittoon" anecdote.

14. Henry Raymont, "From the Avant-Garde of the '30's, Djuna Barnes," *New York Times*, 24 May 1971, 24.

15. "How It Feels to Be Forcibly Fed," New York *World Magazine*, 6 September 1914, sec. 5, p. 17.

16. "Vagaries Malicieux," *Double Dealer* 3 (1922): 253; reprinted in *Vagaries Malicieux: Two Stories by Djuna Barnes* (New York: Frank Hallman, 1974).

2. *The Early Attic Stage of Djuna Barnes*

1. Alexander Woollcott, "Second Thoughts on First Nights: The Provincetown Plays," *New York Times*, 9 November 1919, sec. 8, p. 2.

2. Djuna Barnes, *An Irish Triangle: A Play in One Act*, in *Playboy*, May 1921, 4.

3. Barnes, *An Irish Triangle*, 4.

4. Djuna Barnes, *Kurzy of the Sea*, typescript, the Djuna Barnes Collection, University of Maryland, College Park.

5. Carroll Smith-Rosenberg, "The New Woman as Androgyne," in *Disorderly Conduct: Visions of Gender in Victorian America* (New York: Knopf, 1985), 290.

6. Margaret Anderson, "Art and Anarchism," *Little Review*, March 1916, 3.

7. Anderson, "Art and Anarchism," 4.

8. Djuna Barnes, "The Days of Jig Cook," *Theatre Guild Magazine*, January 1929, 32.

9. Lydia Steptoe [Djuna Barnes], *She Tells Her Daughter*, in *Smart Set*, November 1923, 78.

10. Rebecca Drucker, "As We Were Saying," New York *Tribune*, 16 November 1919, sec. 4, p. 7.

11. Barnes, "The Days of Jig Cook," 32.

12. Lydia Steptoe [Djuna Barnes], *Little Drops of Rain*, in *Vanity Fair*, September 1922, 50.

13. Djuna Barnes, "How It Feels to Be Forcibly Fed," New York *World Magazine*, 6 September 1914, 5, 17.

14. Barnes, "How It Feels," 5.

15. Djuna Barnes, "The Girl and the Gorilla," New York *World Magazine*, 18 October 1914, 9.

16. Barnes, *She Tells Her Daughter*, 77.

17. Barnes, *She Tells Her Daughter*, 79.

18. Rachel Crothers, *A Man's World*, in *Plays by American Women: 1900–1930*, ed. Judith E. Barlow (New York: Applause, 1985), 1–69.

3. *One Acts: Early Plays of Djuna Barnes*

1. Djuna Barnes, *An Irish Triangle: A Play in One Act*, in *Playboy*, May 1921, 3.

2. Lydia Steptoe [Djuna Barnes], "Ten-Minute Plays VI. The Beauty," *Shadowland*, October 1923, 43.

3. Djuna Barnes, *She Tells Her Daughter*, in *Smart Set*, November 1923, 77.

4. Barnes, *She Tells Her Daughter*, 77.

5. Barnes, "The Beauty," 43

4. *Writing toward* Nightwood: *Djuna Barnes' Seduction Stories*

1. Harris, "The More Profound Nationality of Their Lesbianism: Lesbian Society in Paris in the 1920s," in *Amazon Expedition*, ed. Phyllis Birkby et al. (New York: Times Change Press, 1973), 77–88; Corinne, in a slide show on lesbian images in art at a panel, "Old Dyke Tales: The Diversity of Feminist Experience," National Women Studies Association Conference, Douglass College, June 1984. Not all recent assessments by lesbians have been negative, however. See, for example, Monique Wittig, "The Point of View," *Feminist Issues* 3 (Fall 1983): 63–69.

2. Andrew Field, *Djuna: The Life and Times of Djuna Barnes* (New York: Putnam's, 1983), 37. Since Field rarely documents the sources of information in this, to date the only book-length biography of Barnes, its scholarly usefulness is limited.

3. Field, *Djuna*, 233. For example, Anaïs Nin wrote her admiringly about how Nin's own work had been influenced by *Nightwood*, but Barnes didn't answer her letter.

4. Harris, "Profound Nationality," 87.

5. For a delineation of that literature in connection with Barnes' contemporary, Radclyffe Hall, see Esther Newton, "The Mythic Mannish Lesbian: Radclyffe Hall and the New Woman," *Signs* 9 (Summer 1984): 557–75.

6. Stimpson, "Zero Degree Deviancy: The Lesbian Novel in English," in *Writing and Sexual Difference*, ed. Elizabeth Abel (Chicago: Univ. of Chicago Press, 1982), 244.

7. For discussion of "pleasure and danger" in lesbian sexuality see Carole Vance, *Pleasure and Danger* (London: Routledge & Kegan Paul, 1984), especially essays by Gayle Rubin and Alice Echols. For mother-daughter dynamics, see below.

8. For details of this history see Hester Eisenstein, "Introduction," in *The Future of Difference*, ed. Hester Eisenstein and Alice Jardine (Boston: G.K. Hall, 1980) xv–xxiv; Hester Eisenstein, *Contemporary Feminist Thought* (Boston: G.K. Hall, 1983); and Alison Jaggar, *Feminist Politics and Human Nature* (Totowa, NJ: Rowman and Allanheld, 1983).

9. This distinction between oppression and repression has become shorthand for contrasts between recent American and French feminisms. See, for example, Alice Jardine, "Prelude: The Future of Difference," in *The Future of Difference*, xxv–xxvii; and Margaret Homans, "Her Very Own Howl," *Signs* 9 (Winter 1983): 186–205.

10. For a discussion of Kristeva and Irigaray in the context of French feminist theory, see Josette Feral, "Antigone or the Irony of the Tribe," *Diacritics* (Fall 1978): 2–14.

11. Chodorow, "Gender, Relation, and Difference in Psychoanalytic Perspective," in *The Future of Difference*, 3–19. For a full discussion of her ideas see *The Reproduction of Mothering* (Berkeley: Univ. of California Press, 1978).

12. Herbert Blau, "Disseminating Sodom," *Salmagundi* no. 58–59 (Fall 1982–Winter 1983), 237.

13. "When Our Lips Speak Together," trans. Carolyn Burke, *Signs* 6 (Autumn 1980): 66–79; "And One Doesn't Speak without the Other," translated and with an introduction by Helene Vivienne Wenzel, *Signs* 7 (Autumn 1981): 56–67. Both of these essays are very subtly wrought and deserve a full reading which space does not permit here. Irigaray's work also stresses woman and language and thus is a particularly promising intertext for Barnes.

14. Irigaray, "When Our Lips Speak Together," 70.

15. Irigaray, "And the One Doesn't Stir without the Other," 61, 66.

16. "The Grande Malade," *SW*, 25; "Cassation," *SW*, 19.

17. For a full delineation of the difference between mothering as "institution" and as "experience," see Adrienne Rich, *Of Women Born* (New York: Norton, 1976).

18. "Dusie," in *American Esoterica*, (New York: Macy-Masius, 1927), 78. Hereafter cited in text.

19. As in "The Grande Malade," actual parents are absent from the story proper. Barnes saved parental confrontation for *Ryder* and *The Antiphon*.

5. *"Accidental Aloofness": Barnes, Loy, and Modernism*

1. Hayden Carruth, "A Duesgiving: For Djuna Barnes and Others," in *A Festschrift for Djuna Barnes on Her Eightieth Birthday*, ed. Alex Gildzen (Kent, Ohio: Kent State University Libraries, 1972). Since the completion of this essay, an ongoing critical debate about the relations between gender and modernism has developed; see, among others, Shari Benstock, *Women of the Left Bank* (Austin: Univ. of Texas Press, 1986); Carolyn Burke, "Getting Spliced: Modernism and Sexual Difference," *American Quarterly* 39 (1987): 98–121; Sandra M. Gilbert and Susan Gubar, *No Man's Land: The Place of the Woman Writer in the Twentieth Century* (New Haven: Yale Univ. Press, 1988); Bonnie K. Scott, ed., *The Gender of Modernism* (Bloomington: Univ. of Indiana Press, forthcoming).

2. Barnes, quoted in Henry Raymont, "From the Avant-Garde of the Thirties, Djuna Barnes," *New York Times*, 24 May 1971, 24.

3. Man Ray, *Self Portrait* (Boston: Little, Brown, 1963), 98.

4. On this interview, "Do You Strive to Capture the Symbols of Your Reactions? If Not You Are Quite Old-Fashioned," New York *Evening Sun* (13 February 1917), 10, and the material in the next few paragraphs, cf. my "The New Woman and the New Poetry: Mina Loy," in *Coming to Light: American Women Poets in the Twentieth Century*, ed. D. Middlebrook and M. Yalom (Ann Arbor: Univ. of Michigan Press, 1985), 37–57.

5. Mina Loy, *The Last Lunar Baedeker*, ed. Roger L. Conover (Highlands, NC: Jargon Society, 1982), 39, henceforth abbreviated as *TLLB*.

6. Barnes' publisher, Guido Bruno, often referred to her in this way. Cf. Bruno, "In Our Village," *Bruno's Weekly* 1, no. 14 (21 October 1915), 143; quoted in Louis F. Kannenstine, *The Art of Djuna Barnes: Duality and Damnation* (New York: New York Univ. Press, 1977), 23.

7. The phrase comes from Loy's "Aphorisms on Futurism," a cross between a prose poem and a manifesto that calls for aesthetic and psychic liberation. Originally published in *Camera Work* (January 1914), it also appears in *TLLB*, 272–75.

8. Robert McAlmon, "Post-Adolescence: 1920–1921," in *McAlmon and the Lost Generation*, ed. Robert E. Knoll (Lincoln: Univ. of Nebraska Press, 1962), 136.

9. Barnes, "Vagaries Malicieux," in *Vagaries Malicieux: Two Stories by Djuna Barnes* (New York: Frank Hallman, 1974), 5. Originally published in *Double Dealer* 3, no. 17 (May 1922): 249–60.

10. Cf. Burton Rascoe, *A Bookman's Daybook*, ed. C. Hartley Grattan (New York: Horace Liveright, 1929), 27; and Barnes, "Lament for the Left Bank," *Town and Country* December 1941, 138.

11. Barnes "Vagaries Malicieux," 11, 12.

12. Barnes, "James Joyce," *Vanity Fair*, April 1922, 65.

13. Cf., among others, Jack A. Hirschman, "The Orchestrated Novel: A Study of Poetic Devices in the Novels of Djuna Barnes and Herman Broch and the Influences of the Works of James Joyce upon Them," Ph.D. diss., Indiana University, 1962; Kannenstine, *The Art of Djuna Barnes*, 47–49 and *passim*; and Jane Marcus in this volume.

14. Barnes, "James Joyce," 65.

15. Kannenstine, *The Art of Djuna Barnes*, 49, 53, 55.

16. Barnes, "James Joyce," 65.

17. Loy, *TLLB*, 20–22.

18. Barnes, "James Joyce," 104.

19. Barnes, "James Joyce," 65.

20. Loy, *TLLB*, 4–5.

21. The phrase occurs in Loy's "Lunar Baedeker" (*TLLB*, 9), a poem which satirizes the lush vision of the decadents. Loy figures, perhaps, as one of the "onyx-eyed odalisques" who observe the departure of Eros. An important exception to this "impersonal" current in Loy's poetry of the 1920s is her autobiographical "Anglo-Mongrels and the Rose."

22. Loy's turning away from the subject of heterosexual relations was undoubtedly related to the long mourning process she experienced after the death of Arthur Cravan, her husband, just as Barnes' intense preoccupation with lesbianism and sexual difference was surely deepened by her difficult love affair with Thelma Wood. During these years, Barnes and Loy fortunately enjoyed the friendship and support of Natalie Barney, in whose "Académie des femmes" they participated. On Barney's efforts on behalf of French, English, and American literary women, cf. Natalie Clifford Barney, *Aventures de l'espirit* (Paris: Emile Paul, 1929); and on her salon's erotic atmosphere, cf. George Wickes, *The Amazon of Letters* (New York: Putnam's, 1976); Susan Lanser, "Speaking in Tongues," in this volume; and of course, Djuna Barnes, *Ladies Almanack*, in which Mina Loy appears as Patience Scalpel, the only heterosexual among the sapphic novitiates of its heroine's religion.

23. "Gorgeous reticence" describes the silent perfection of a Brancusi sculpture in Loy's "Brancusi's Golden Bird," *TLLB*, 18–19. The phrase "radium of the word" occurs in Loy's poetic epigraph to her article, "Gertrude Stein," *Transatlantic Review* 2 (1924), 305; the epigraph is also published separately under the title "Gertrude Stein," in *TLLB*, 26. On Stein and Loy, cf. my "Without Commas: Gertrude Stein and Mina Loy," *Poetics Journal* 4 (1984), 43–52.

24. Cf. T.S. Apteryx [Eliot], "Observations," *Egoist* 5 (1918): 70; Yvor Winters, "Mina Loy," *Dial* 80 (1926) 496–99.

25. Cf. Pierre Louis Duchartre and René Saulnier, *L'imagerie populaire* (Paris: Librairie de France, 1925), 34.

26. Duchartre and Saulnier, *L'imagerie populaire*, 112.

27. Duchartre and Saulnier, *L'imagerie populaire*, between 214 and 215.

28. Kannenstine, *The Art of Djuna Barnes*, xvi.

29. Loy, *TLLB*, xv.

30. Loy, *TLLB*, 186.

31. Barnes, "The Walking-Mort," *New Yorker*, 15 May 1971, 34.

32. Quoted in Kannenstine, *The Art of Djuna Barnes*, 169. Cf. his helpful discussion of Barnes' late poems, 161–69.

6. *Writing the Grotesque Body: Djuna Barnes' Carnival Parody*

1. For Barnes' public homage to *Ulysses*, including the comparison to Rabelais, see her interview with Joyce: "James Joyce: A Portrait of the Man Who Is, at Present, One of the More Significant Figures in Literature," *Vanity Fair* April 1922, 65, 104; rpt. as "James Joyce," in *Interviews*, ed. Alyce Barry (Washington, D.C.: Sun & Moon, 1985), 288–96. Burton Rascoe reports her remark about never again daring to write; *A Bookman's Daybook*, ed. C. Hartley Grattan (New York: Horace Liveright, 1929), 27. These remarks about *Ulysses* are discussed by Louis F. Kannenstine, *The Art of Djuna Barnes: Duality and Damnation* (New York: New York Univ. Press, 1977), 48; and Andrew Field, *Djuna: The Formidable Miss Barnes* (1983; rpt. Austin: Univ. of Texas Press, 1985), 108, 126.

2. For an extremely negative evaluation along these lines, see the review of *Ryder* in

New Republic, 24 October 1923, 282. More balanced readings that still approach the novel as shaped by Joyce's (or Rabelais' or Sterne's) example include the review in the *Nation*, 5 December 1928; Ernest Sutherland Bates, "A Robust Tale," *Saturday Review*, 17 November 1928, 376; Field, *Djuna*, 35, 100–111; Kannenstine, *The Art of Djuna Barnes*, 47–49, 56; and James B. Scott, *Djuna Barnes* (Boston: Twayne, 1976), 84–85.

3. Field, *Djuna*, 127. Field's biography is occasionally inconsistent in its treatment of titles (as on 146), and Field does not italicize the Fielding title in the quotation cited here.

4. I am drawing upon Linda Hutcheon's definition of parody as "repetition with a critical difference"; *A Theory of Parody: The Teachings of Twentieth-Century Art Forms* (New York: Methuen, 1985), 7.

5. For studies of Bakhtin that emphasize his failure to consider social or linguistic issues related to gender, see Wayne C. Booth, "Freedom of Interpretation: Bakhtin and the Challenge of Feminist Criticism," *Critical Inquiry* 9 (1982): 45–76; Mary Russo, "Female Grotesques: Carnival and Theory," in *Feminist Studies/Critical Studies,* ed. Teresa de Lauretis, Theories of Contemporary Culture 8 (Bloomington: Indiana Univ. Press, 1986), 213–29, and Patricia S. Yaeger, "'Because a Fire Was in My Head': Eudora Welty and the Dialogic Imagination," *PMLA* 99 (1984): 955–73. Booth specifically treats Bakhtin's nonengagement with Rabelais' problematic portrayal of women. Russo draws upon Bakhtin's ideas about the carnival and the grotesque body in order to survey relations between carnivalesque motifs, representations of women, and contemporary critical theory. My own analysis concentrates on *Rabelais and His World*, trans. Helen Iswolsky (1968; Bloomington: Indiana Univ. Press, 1984), which offers Bakhtin's most extended study of the carnivalesque tradition that Barnes parodies (hereafter cited in text as *Rabelais*). Bakhtin's related (and often overlapping) discussions of the carnivalesque include *Problems of Dostoeskvy's Poetics*, trans. Caryl Emerson (Minneapolis: Univ. of Minnesota Press, 1984), 101–80, and in particular his discussion of the picaresque novel as a carnivalesque form, 157–58; his essay on parody, "From the Prehistory of Novelistic Discourse," in *The Dialogic Imagination: Four Essays*, trans. Caryl Emerson and Michael Holquist (Austin: Univ. of Texas Press, 1981), 48–83; and his scattered comments on Rabelais, Sterne, and the English comic novel in "Discourse in the Novel," in *The Dialogic Imagination*, 259–422.

6. Eugene Jolas, review of *Ryder, transition* 16–17 (1929): 326.

7. Barnes also works up contrastingly "feminine" chapters, which imitate romantic or sentimental styles imbued with notions of femininity. These include chapter 36, which exposes the clichés of popular girls' stories, and chapter 24, a stylistic medley presenting a range of icons, from the pious girl of sentimental pulp fiction to the "voluptuous" virgin (*R,* 137), a specific parody of Dante Gabriel Rossetti's *Blessed Damozel.*

8. Near the end of the novel, Wendell claims, "I have unfathered myself" (*R,* 318), a result of his attempt to go outside the system of legalized paternity. For a more detailed reading of how *Ryder* makes Wendell "androgynous man" rather than the "super-male," see Kannenstine, *The Art of Djuna Barnes*, 40–42, 49–50.

9. *Rabelais*, 25. Bakhtin defines "degradation" in *Rabelais*, 19–21; he repeats the phrase "down to earth" on pages 20, 21, and 22. Describing Barnes' use of the phrase "go down," Kannenstine comes close to Bakhtin's view of carnivalesque degradation; *The Art of Djuna Barnes*, 45. I have summarized Bakhtin's description of the grotesque in *Rabelais*, 19–30. For another view of the grotesque in Barnes, see Field, *Djuna*, 33.

10. Barnes' strongest scatological images occur in "Sophia and the Five Fine Chamber-pots" and "Kate and Amelia Go A-Dunging." Field states that the expurgated parts of *Ryder* were largely concerned with "bodily fluids," including urine (*Djuna*, 127), a confirmation of Bakhtin's idea that images of urine, as well as excrement, are characteristic means of carnivalesque degradation (*Rabelais*, 147–52). Taboo sexual practices include Wendell's sexual "experiments" (*R,* 70–71, 226) and Barnes' verbal and pictorial representations of both female and male homosexuality (*R,* 48–51, 172–76).

11. Scott notes a duplication of the stiltsman's arch in Wendell, naked above his women (an arch most erect); *Djuna Barnes*, 65.

12. For "the mystery," see *R*, 131. For Wendell's other theories and stories of sexuality, see *R*, 149–53, 216, 218–21, 226, 277–79, 297–300. Scott's reading of *Ryder* focuses on Wendell as the novel's true (nearly unquestioned) picaresque hero, in rebellion against restrictive morality and convention.

13. While I have concentrated on grotesque imagery and deflation of Wendell's ideas as patriarch, the last section of this essay will examine ambivalent and contradictory aspects of the grotesque body presented in *Ryder*.

14. Bakhtin's discussion of the carnivalesque nature of abusive language illuminates Amelia's ambivalent, teasing-repelling epithets; see especially *Rabelais*, 15–17, 146–48, 165–66. Bakhtin also uses the phrase "bottoms up" (*Rabelais*, 411) to describe carnival motifs of reversal (such as transvestism, garments turned inside out, and reversed gestures such as walking backward).

15. Describing the Hermetic tradition of a hermaphroditic Adam and a Fall into the two sexes, Alan Williamson argues that this revision of Genesis informs Barnes' oeuvre; "The Divided Image: The Quest for Identity in the Works of Djuna Barnes," *Critique* 7, no. 1 (1964): 58–74.

16. Lady Bridesleep and the "whore" of chapter 43 are other such unruly women, and they are overshadowed by Wendell's mother, Sophia, a prominent example I have only touched upon. For a semiotic cultural analysis of the transgressive female "as public spectacle," see Russo, "Female Grotesques," 217.

17. The chapter "Midwives' Lament"—a Blakean illustrated poem—sorrows over Wendell's ways, which lead to a girl's death in childbirth. Yet the novel seems to applaud his feat in getting the cat (and three rats) out of the school's well. And chapter 18, "Yet for Vindication of Wendell," presents a compelling defense of his prodigality.

18. The resemblance of Amelia's monologues to Shakespearean language is especially marked in the passage beginning, "What is this matter that kills me with his craft of being?" (*R*, 119).

19. This illustration is in the Barnes Collection, McKeldin Library, University of Maryland, College Park. The drawing is reproduced in Field, *Djuna*, 128.

20. Bakhtin's reading of the pregnant hags is criticized on similar grounds by Russo, "Female Grotesques," 219.

7. *A Reader's* Ryder

1. Chapter 5 of *Ryder*, "Rape and Repining!," did in fact appear separately. Louis F. Kannenstine says that it is "a bit of facetiae that is sufficiently independent of the main narrative to have appeared in *transition* in advance of the novel"; *The Art of Djuna Barnes* (New York: New York Univ. Press, 1977), 37.

2. Andrew Field, *Djuna: The Life and Times of Djuna Barnes* (New York: Putnam's, 1983). Field attributes "the main structure of all her major works" to her grandmother and "equally to her father," who composed opera in this form of "ritual folk music-theater" (183). Field reads *Ryder* loosely at the layer of "disconnected chronicle" and assumes that Wendell is the protagonist. His interest is, properly, in using *Ryder* to deepen his presentation of Barnes' life.

3. Kannenstine (*The Art of Djuna Barnes*, 44) reads this chapter as about Wendell; Field (*Djuna*, 43) as about Amelia. The text warrants neither assumption.

4. Such a heady shift in point of view is characteristic of Barnes; it first occurs in the first poem of *The Book of Repulsive Women*, "From Fifth Avenue Up" (91).

5. Some of Barnes' word-games develop in the manner of Joyce's impacted referenc-

ing. This passage, for example, increases in range if examined in the style of articles in the *Wake Newsletter*: 1. Event and words express Wendell's callous, destructive treatment of female genitalia. Wendell is, we know, promiscuous, idle, dependent on women. 2. Use of the plural form, "ladies' chamber," where we expect the singular, parallels Wendell's dominant trait, promiscuity. The commonest usage appears in the nursery rhyme—which also, in another way, extends the context of the passage:

> *Goosey, goosey, gander*
> *Whither shall I wander?*
> *Upstairs and downstairs*
> *And in my lady's chamber.*
>
> *There I met an old man*
> *Who wouldn't say his prayers.*
> *I took him by the left leg*
> *And threw him down the stairs.*

See William S. Baring-Gould and Cecil Baring-Gould, eds., *The Annotated Mother Goose* (Cleveland, Ohio: World Publishing, 1967), 70, 86. The second quatrain is openly angry at willful domestic callousness; anger at Wendell's gross behavior is the subsurface of *Ryder*, carefully unexpressed in the text. 3. The expression "ladies" or "lady's chamber" refers to the sponge of the sponge crab, *Dromiavulgaris* (*Oxford English Dictionary* [*OED*], compact edition, s.v. "sponge," 4.13.b, p. 2976). The female crab carries its eggs on the abdomen in a protruding sac called the *sponge* (*Encyclopedia Americana* [1957] 8:43). Another definition of "sponge" is "one who meanly lives at the expense of others; a parasite" (*OED*, s.v. "sponge," 4.10, p. 2976). Wendell has a sponge as attribute and as appendage of his promiscuity:

> *A sponge of fibers soft*
> *Which well before and well behind he oft*
> *Hither and thither about his bum y-swoped*
> *. . . So well he rode his sponge, his shirt was light*
> *And cleanly. . . . (R, 76–77)*

6. My perception of myth as structure, metaphor, and mode is wholly indebted to the large-minded work of Northrop Frye, from his *Anatomy of Criticism* through *The Great Code*.

8. *Gilt on Cardboard: Djuna Barnes as Illustrator of Her Life and Work*

Thanks to Natalie Robb for looking at my slides of Barnes' work with an artist's eye; to Carolyn Allen for sending me copies of the illustrations from *A Book*; to Douglas Messerli for his hospitality and a copy of his unpublished bibliography of Djuna Barnes' visual work; to Gayle Rubin for slides of her gorgeously hand-tinted edition of *Ladies Almanack*; to Judith Serin for kindly editing; to Lupe Rosenbaum for emergency express mailing; to Lisa Duggan for use of her *Frontiers*; to Carole Vance for research assistance and copies of *L'imagerie populaire* and a keen editorial pencil; to the staff of the McKeldin Library Special Collections at the University of Maryland, including Dr. Blanche Ebeling-Koning, Jessie Hinkle, and Loren Brown for seeing me through every folder of Barnes' drawings and photos, and Mary Bocaccio for her help in making the oil paintings accessible during my first visit; to Allan Bérubé for cheery encouragement and last-minute typing; and to Carole Vance, again, ever and always, for everything.

1. Djuna Barnes, "Vagaries Malicieux," *Double Dealer* 3, no. 17 (May 1922): 249–60. The unresolved thesis and antithesis in the form of dualistic oppositions have been

discussed by Louis Kannenstine, who includes Barnes' visual work as well as her writing in *The Art of Djuna Barnes: Duality and Damnation* (New York: New York Univ. Press, 1977).

2. A passage in the first of the two exercise books by her older brother Thurn, written in 1900, contains a parallel in his description of a golf game. The journals, which are held in the Barnes Collection at the University of Maryland, are dated 1900 and 1901, when the family was living in the Bronx. They give a vivid picture of family life for the Barneses at that time. It is sometimes difficult to reconstruct the words whose Barnesian versions Thurn has written. When did Barnes acquire the journals from her brother and why? Did she use them as sources during the writing of *Ryder*?

3. Chapter 5 of *Ryder*, "Rape and Repining!," appeared in *transition* 9 (December 1927). In *Ryder*, "Chapter Forty-seven: Going To, and Coming From" is devoted to the image. In *Ladies Almanack* it is alluded to in describing the voice of the prophet as one given to "those who go neither Hither nor Thither" (*LA*, 23) and in showing those women who "swing between two Conditions like a Bell's Clapper" (*LA*, 48) to be in no place, "for that which is always moving is in no settled State long enough to be either doomed or transfigured" (*LA*, 48).

4. Andrew Field cites evidence for the autobiographical basis of Barnes' work in his biography, especially chapter 4. Unfortunately, his statements of fact are not always accurate; *Djuna: The Life and Times of Djuna Barnes* (New York: Putman's, 1983), 112, 113.

5. Jack A. Hirschman, "The Orchestrated Novel: A Study of Poetic Devices in the Novels of Djuna Barnes and Herman Broch and the Influences of the Works of James Joyce upon Them," Ph.D. diss., Indiana University, 1962; cited in Kannenstine, *The Art of Djuna Barnes*, 48, and in Field, *Djuna*, 109. Field also discusses the personal connection between Joyce and Barnes in Paris in the 1920s; *Djuna*, 107–11.

6. See Douglas Messerli, *Djuna Barnes: A Bibliography* (Rhinebeck, NY: David Lewis, 1975), and "A Bibliography of Djuna Barnes, Appendix," xeroxed, for Barnes' written and visual work. Messerli's collection of interviews appeared after this article was completed. *The Book of Repulsive Women* was originally printed in 1915 as one of a series of chapbooks published by Guido Bruno.

7. Kannenstine, *The Art of Djuna Barnes*, 20.

8. *The Bullet* is reproduced in the publication of the Women's Peace Party of New York, *Four Lights: An Adventure in Internationalism* 1 (2 June 1917), n.p., in a clipping in folder B-24, the Barnes Collection. *The Doughboy* exists in the original in the Barnes Collection, unnumbered, University of Maryland.

9. Field, *Djuna*, 58, 59. Information on the Provincetown Players may be found in Helen Deutsch and Stella Hanau, *The Provincetown: A Story of the Theater* (New York: Farrar and Rinehart, 1931); Robert K. Sarlós, *Jig Cook and the Provincetown Players: Theatre in Ferment* (Boston: Univ. of Massachusetts Press, 1982); Max Eastman's two-volume autobiography, *Love and Revolution* and *Enjoyment of Living*; and (for Ida Rauh), Jane Sochen, *The New Woman: Feminism in Greenwich Village, 1910–1920* (New York: Quadrangle/New York Times Book Co., 1972).

10. All three are in folder B-22, the Barnes Collection.

11. Field, *Djuna*, 63.

12. Folder B-29, the Barnes Collection.

13. According to Messerli, the drawing was published in *Vanity Fair*, October 1919, 47, as part of a review, "Helen Westley in 'John Ferguson'" ("Appendix to Bibliography," 130). On the back of the drawing, Barnes gave her address as 220 W. 14 Street, where she lived after she left 86 Greenwich Avenue in early 1919 (Field, *Djuna*, 60).

14. Djuna Barnes, "The Confessions of Helen Westley," New York *Morning Telegraph Sunday Magazine*, 23 September 1917, 5; photograph of Westley in folder B-54, clipping of interview in laminated newspaper articles, the Barnes Collection.

15. Helen Westley was born in Brooklyn and made her first appearance as an actress

in 1897. She was a founding member of both the Washington Square Players and of the Theatre Guild and later went to Hollywood, where she appeared in several movies, among them *Rebecca of Sunnybrook Farm* and *Heidi* (Sarlós, *Jig Cook*, 198). The first play she directed was by Barnes, *An Irish Triangle*, which premiered on 9 January 1920. In March 1920 Westley also directed the next, and last, play by Barnes to be performed by the Provincetown Players, *Kurzy of the Sea* (Sarlós, *Jig Cook*, 111; Deutsch and Hanau, *The Provincetown*, appendix, 239). Douglas Messerli has suggested that Westley and Barnes may have been lovers (personal communication).

 16. The original of the first drawing is not in the Barnes Collection at the University of Maryland; the second is in the same folder as the drawings of Eugene O'Neill and Mary Blair, B-29.

 17. Ida Rauh graduated from law school in 1905; visited Russia in 1907–1908; married Max Eastman in 1911; was a founder, with Westley, both of the Washington Square Players, whom she left after their second bill, and of the Provincetown Players; and was arrested for handing out birth-control information in 1916. She left the Provincetown Players, also hastily, in a disagreement about removing George Cram "Jig" Cook's name from their publicity when he was absent from the group in 1919–20. There were rumors that she was more intimate with Cook than Cook's wife Susan Glaspell would have preferred (Sarlós, *Jig Cook*, 12, 13, 194, 255 n. 62; Sochen, *The New Woman*, 16–18, 66).

 18. Lawrence Langner, *The Magic Curtain*, 111.

 19. Charles Norman, *Poets and People*, (Indianapolis: Bobbs-Merrill, 1972), 18.

 20. A note on the back of the photo (folder Barnes 3, old numbering, the Barnes Collection) identifies Pyne and the two men with her. They are Harry Kemp, to whom she was married (Langner, *Magic Curtain*; Norman, *Poets and People*), and John Pyne. Mary Pyne appeared in four of the Provincetown plays in slightly over a year, from December 1916 to January 1918 (Deutsch and Hanau, *The Provincetown*, appendix, 204, 207, 208, 228). Pyne may also be the friend Barnes mentions in "Vagaries Malicieux:" "Once . . . I had a friend to whom I sent flowers, and now that I may send them no more, flowers have become for me things I shall not think about" (20). She goes on to imagine five frail girl friends or five dying queens to whom she could send birds (alive or baked in pies). The emphasis on frailty and death and on Barnes' desire to give seems to connect this passage with Barnes' feelings for Pyne. Both Langner and Norman group the two together in discussing the beauties of Greenwich Village.

 21. Messerli, "Appendix to Bibliography," 131, 132.

 22. Four images are published in Field, *Djuna*, 113, 114. The Barnes Collection has the following items: a tearsheet from *Gargoyle*, September 1921, with a photograph of a sculpture of a kneeling woman titled "Study" (folder B-4); a composition book of sketches of beer halls and nightclubs, apparently done in Berlin in 1921, inscribed in Wood's hand, "Frances—1922—T.E. Wood," (folder B-41); reproductions of two of the ship-and-ocean-depths silverpoints, one of which is signed "T.E. Wood 1921" (or possibly 1924; folder B-38); a sketch, probably by Wood, found between the two silverpoints, on letterpaper from the "Grand Hôtel des Écoles Coloniale et D'Architecture" (folder B-38); reproduction of a hand spread among plants similar to the hand and foliage reproduced in Field, *Djuna*, 113, signed "T. Wood" (folder B-38); reproduction of three large bovine heads turned towards each other with village houses in the background, not unlike those in Barnes' illustrations (folder B-38).

 23. Pierre Louis Duchartre and René Saulnier, *L'imagerie populaire* (Paris: Librarie de France, 1926).

 24. I would like to thank the artist Natalie Robb for teaching me to see this difference and for pointing out that art may use the process of its own creation as an experiential referent.

 25. Folder B-31, the Barnes Collection.

 26. Duchartre and Saulnier, *L'imagerie populaire*, 12.

27. Duchartre and Saulnier, *L'imagerie populaire*, 26.

28. Duchartre and Saulnier, *L'imagerie populaire*, passim.

29. Folder B-28, the Barnes Collection.

30. Folder B-26, the Barnes Collection.

31. Field, *Djuna*, 26; cf. the photograph following page 98 and Barnes' other drawing of Kate Careless at the foot of the Ryder family tree. Fanny Faulkner is identified from the photograph of her in the Barnes Collection (negative number 15365).

32. Thurn Barnes' journal contains several entries about two women who have dogs, Mrs. S. and Mrs. Gardner. The journal records several visits to Mrs. Gardner, who may have been the source for Molly Dance of the many dogs and children.

33. Douglas Messerli has pointed out that Wendell is the classic picaresque hero, a figure whose goal is not satisfaction but continual movement from one adventure to the next; "Djuna Barnes' *Ryder*," *American Book Review* 3 (March 1981): 17. But one could argue, conversely, that Barnes picked the genre to fit her perception of Wendell's character.

34. Folder B-33, the Barnes Collection.

35. Duchartre and Saulnier, *L'imagerie populaire*, 57.

36. De Pougy also had an affair with Mimi. There is a photograph of her in Liane de Pougy, *My Blue Notebooks*, trans. Diana Athill (New York: Harper & Row, 1979), between pages 128 and 129; cf. Barnes' comment in *Ladies Almanack* on Senorita Fly-About's refusal to shave her head at the death of Dame Musset, "who for no Woman, quick or dead, would alter her Charm" (*LA*, 82). De Pougy had published a thinly disguised account of her own affair with Barney, *Idylle sapphique*, in 1901.

37. Folder B-26, the Barnes Collection.

38. Janet Flanner identifies Natalie Barney as the publisher, as well as Dame Musset, in *Paris Was Yesterday: 1925–1939*, ed. Irving Drutman (New York: Viking, 1972), xvii.

39. See Susan Sniader Lanser, "Speaking in Tongues: *Ladies Almanack* and the Language of Celebration," *Frontiers* 4, no. 3: 40–43, for cautions concerning James Scott's suggested link between Barnes and Scalpel. (See author's revised version in this volume.) Patience Scalpel is identified as Barnes' close friend Mina Loy (Field, *Djuna*, 124). Lanser notes that the figure at the far left of the illustration at the beginning of "January" is Scalpel. The same figure appears in the same position in the illustration at the beginning of "May" (*LA*, 10, 30).

40. Personal communication, Berenice Abbott; personal communication, Sue Perlgut, cofounder of Djunabooks.

41. Frances M. Doughty, "Lesbian Biography, Biography of Lesbians," *Frontiers: A Journal of Women's Studies* 4, no. 3 (Fall 1979): 76–79.

42. For biographies of Barney, see Jean Chalon, *Portrait of a Seductress: The World of Natalie Barney*, trans. Carol Barko (New York: Crown, 1979); and George Wickes, *The Amazon of Letters: The Life and Loves of Natalie Barney* (New York: Putnam's, 1976). On Barnes' relationship with Barney, see Field, *Djuna*.

43. Field, *Djuna*, 102.

44. Solito Solano, "The Hotel Napoleon Bonaparte," *Quarterly Journal of the Library of Congress* 34 (October 1977): 311.

45. Kathryn Hulme, *Undiscovered Country: A Spiritual Adventure* (Boston: Little Brown, 1966), 38–39.

46. Kathryn Hulme to "Jannie, Solita, Lib, Noel, Margaret & Sardine" (Janet Flanner, Solita Solano, Elizabeth Clark, Noel Murphy, Margaret Anderson, Louise Davidson), scrapbook 1–22, Flanner-Solano Papers, Library of Congress, Washington, D.C.

47. Copy of *Ladies Almanack* owned by Alice Rohrer, in the Barnes Collection.

48. See Lanser, "Speaking in Tongues," 39–45; and Doughty, "Lesbian Biography," 77–78.

49. Folder B-18, the Barnes Collection.

50. Negative no. 15380, the Barnes Collection. This description is based on a xerox of the photograph and information supplied by Dr. Blanche Ebeling-Koning, curator of Rare Books and Literary Manuscripts, of the Barnes Collection, University of Maryland–College Park.

51. Notes on Gurdjieff Work, Flanner-Solano Papers. Kathryn Hulme's mother called Rohrer "The 'little Mad Hatter'" (*Undiscovered Country*, 33). This volume offers occasional information on Rohrer, who appears as Wendy; see also the Flanner-Solano Papers in the Library of Congress.

52. "The Barnes among Women," *Time*, 18 January 1943, 55.

53. Peggy Guggenheim, *Out of This Century: Confessions of an Art Addict* (New York: Doubleday, 1980).

9. *Speaking in Tongues:* Ladies Almanack *and the Discourse of Desire*

An earlier version of this essay appeared in *Frontiers: A Journal of Women's Studies* 4, no. 3 (1979), 39–46. The present version was completed in 1984 and would be somewhat different were I writing it now.

1. Louis Kannenstine, *The Art of Djuna Barnes: Duality and Damnation* (New York: New York Univ. Press, 1977), 48.

2. See, for example, Colette, *Le pur et l'impur* [The pure and the impure], chap. 8. It is interesting that in a proposed revision of the foreword to *Ladies Almanack*, Barnes changed the word "neap-tide [to the Proustian chronicle]" to "sister," thus stressing the need for a specifically female counterpart to Proust's text.

3. Robert Burton, *Anatomy of Melancholy* (1621; rpt. New York: Random House, 1977), 69.

4. Monique Wittig, *Les Guérillères*, trans. David Levay (New York: Avon, 1971), 89. All the Barney circle knew the characters' identities, which Barney uncoded in her copy of the text (now in the Bibliothèque Doucet). For example, Cynic Sal is Romaine Brooks, Barney's friend and lover of many years; Janet Flanner and Solita Solano appear as the journalists Nip and Tuck; Radclyffe Hall and her lover Una, Lady Troubridge and the British couple Tilly Tweed-in-Blood and Lady Buck-and-Balk; the heterosexual Patience Scalpel is Mina Loy; Doll Furious is Oscar Wilde's niece Dolly Wilde; Senorita Fly-About is Mimi Franchetti, Bounding Bess is Esther Murphy.

5. She wrote a piece called "Knickerbocker Almanac" in 1931 for *The World* and contributed a monthly "Playgoers Almanack" to *Theatre Guild* during much of 1930 and 1931. These pieces resemble *Ladies Almanack* in language, illustration, and design, though not, of course, in theme. Barnes also contributed with a group of friends to a *Gourmet Almanack* of recipes and lore.

6. A despair expressed most poignantly, I think, in an unpublished letter of 16 October 1963 to Natalie Barney on the occasion of the deaths of Piaf and Cocteau, in which she laments that "our legendary time is being calendared."

7. Readers of *The Well of Loneliness* (New York: Blue Ribbon Books, 1928)—especially 1928 readers, for whom Hall's novel would have been extremely fresh—might well be reminded of its hero, Stephen Gordon, also "meant" to be a boy. Both characters are named with saints in mind; both have fathers who wanted sons; both experience themselves through masculine accoutrements. But the difference is critical, for while everyone seems to concur that "'it do be a pity as [Stephen] isn't a boy'" (40), and while Stephen herself asks her father whether she might become one if she prays hard enough (26), Evangeline celebrates her superiority as much as Stephen laments her lack. From its beginning, then, *Ladies Almanack* is marked by its revision of *The Well of Loneliness* from trivial details such as Stephen's love for a maid with housemaid's knee—turned ribald by Barnes and her Musset—to serious questions of lesbian identity.

8. Adrienne Rich, "Compulsory Heterosexuality and Lesbian Existence," *Signs* 5, no. 4 (Summer 1980): 648.

9. Chapter 49 of *Ryder* is titled "Three Great Moments of History," and one of them, concerning Stonewall Jackson and Barbara Frietchie, parallels the story of Jezebel and Sheba in *Ladies Almanack* down to the "UUUUh HHHHu" (*R*, 305).

10. In *Ryder*, ch. 49, Dr. O'Connor speaks of the man who

being pegged by his mother cannot in after life forget it, and do put much pride by it. . . . Some so magnify its importance to themselves that they leave instructions to have their bodies placed beside it in the grave, as if it were a bride or soul, and some have gone so far as to leave codicils that it be not taped nor swaddled, but left four good round days bared in the coffin, that the breath of life shall not be cut from out it, an it should take it into its head to revive and bespeak itself as still a citizen. (*R*, 302-3)

11. Once again one can see both resonance with and departure from *The Well of Loneliness*, in which the "stigmata" of the "invert" are continually compared to "the wounds of One nailed to the cross" (246) and in which only God really understands; "the Church's blessing was not for them" (405). Indeed, in ending her relationship with Mary Llewellyn so that Mary can lead a "normal" life, Stephen Gordon is renouncing her sexuality, refusing the easy comfort with lesbian life that forms the very premise of *Ladies Almanack*, and taking the painful path of a grimmer martyrdom to fight, with God on her side for the "legions" that will follow her. There are, to be sure, moments of peace and even bliss in *The Well of Loneliness* but the tone is generally tragic and the joy restrained. The same historical personages are presented in both texts, but while Valerie Seymour remains a positive figure—giving "courage" to all the rest—the group is a glum, despairing lot, hanging out in shoddy bars, drinking too much and likely as not to end up dead; indeed, the death and suicide of one couple secures the downward movement of the book.

12. Hélène Cixous, "The Laugh of the Medusa," trans. Keith Cohen and Paula Cohen, *Signs* 1, no. 4 (Summer 1976): 880.

13. James Scott, *Djuna Barnes* (Boston: Twayne, 1976), 79–85.

14. Kannenstine, *The Art of Djuna Barnes*, 47–56.

15. Andrew Field, *Djuna: The Life and Times of Djuna Barnes* (New York: Putnam's, 1983), 124, 127.

16. Bertha Harris, "The More Profound Nationality of Their Lesbianism: Lesbian Society in Paris in the 1920s," in *Amazon Expedition*, ed. Phyllis Birkby et al. (New York: Times Change Press, 1973), 71.

17. Joan Joffee Hall, review of *LA*, 17 December 1972. I have found this review only among the Barnes papers in the McKeldin Library, with the name of the newspaper cut off.

18. Natalie Barney, letter to Djuna Barnes, "day after Easter 1968," in the Barnes Collection, the McKeldin Library, University of Maryland. A French translation of *Ladies Almanack*, *L'almanach des dames*, has recently been published by Flammarion, translated by Michele Causse.

19. Djuna Barnes, letters to Natalie Barney of 16 May 1963 and 3 December 1967, in the Barnes Collection.

20. Field, *Djuna*, 101, 153. My comments on Barnes' relationships with Pyne and Barney are based on research conducted in 1984. I have not had the opportunity to examine papers recently made available.

21. The text gives us no reason to link Barnes, as James Scott does, with *Ladies Almanack*'s lone heterosexual, Patience Scalpel, or even with Maisie Tuck-and-Frill (her name perhaps a salacious spoonerism), who speaks with "the Voice of the Prophet" given "ever to those who go neither Hither nor Thither." Maisie considers lesbianism "a good place," but "a better when seen Indirectly." It is no more plausible to connect Barnes with these characters

than it is to connect her with opposing characters, such as Dame Musset and the British couple.

22. On this phenomenon see, for example, Annis Pratt, "The New Feminist Criticisms," in *Beyond Intellectual Sexism*, ed. Joan I. Roberts (New York: McKay, 1976), 183; and Joan N. Radner and Susan S. Lanser, "The Feminist Voice: Strategies of Coding in Folklore and Literature," *Journal of American Folklore* 100 (1987): 412–25.

23. Harris, "Profound Nationality," 79.

24. Solita Solano, letter to Djuna Barnes, winter 1967, in the Barnes Collection.

25. Natalie Barney, letters of 21 July 1962 and mid-May 1969.

26. The relevant passage in the poem "From Fifth Avenue Up":

> *[We] see you sagging down with bulging*
> *Hair to sip,*
> *The dappled damp from some vague*
> *Under lip.*
> *Your soft saliva, loosed*
> *With orgy, drip.* (BRW, 91)

27. Here Radcylffe Hall provides another point of contrast. *The Well of Loneliness* is as conservative in comparison to Hall's values about lesbianism as *Ladies Almanack* seems to be radical in comparison to Barnes' values. Both texts are thus manifestly "produced" by the ideologies of their intended audiences.

10. *All Women Are Not Women All:* Ladies Almanack *and Feminine Writing*

1. Sandra M. Gilbert and Susan Gubar, eds., *The Norton Anthology of Literature by Women* (New York: Norton, 1985), 1312; Andrew Field, *Djuna: The Life and Times of Djuna Barnes* (New York: Putnam's, 1983), 124; Elizabeth Pochoda, "Style's Hoax: A Reading of Djuna Barnes's *Nightwood*," *Twentieth Century Literature* 22 (1976): 179–91; Ezra Pound, letter 314, *The Letters of Ezra Pound, 1907–1941*, ed. D.D. Paige (New York: Harcourt, 1950), 286.

2. Hélène Cixous, "Sorties," in *New French Feminisms*, ed. Elaine Marks and Isabelle de Courtivron (New York: Schocken Books, 1981), 245–64; Alice Jardine, "Gynesis," *Diacritics* 12, no. 2 (1982): 54–65; Julia Kristeva, "La femme ce n'est jamais ça [Women can never be defined]," in *New French Feminisms*, ed. Marks and de Courtivron, 137–41.

3. On woman's function as the gift, see Gayle Rubin, "The Traffic in Women: Notes on the 'Political Economy' of Sex," in *Toward an Anthropology of Women*, ed. Rayna R. Reiter (New York: Monthly Review Press, 1975), 157–210; Luce Irigaray, "Women on the Market," in *This Sex Which Is Not One*, trans. Catherine Porter (Ithaca, NY: Cornell Univ. Press, 1985), 170–91; Irigaray, "When the 'Goods' Get Together," in *New French Feminisms* ed. Marks and de Courtivron, 107–10; and Jacques Derrida, *Spurs: Nietzsche's Styles*, trans. Barbara Harlow (Chicago: Univ. of Chicago Press, 1978).

In addition, see Hélène Cixous, "Castration or Decapitation?" trans. Annette Kuhn, *Signs: A Journal of Women in Culture and Society* 7, no. 1. (1981): 41–55; Cixous, "The Laugh of the Medusa," in *New French Feminisms,* ed. Marks and de Courtivron, 245–64; Luce Irigaray, *Speculum of the Other Woman*, trans. Gillian C. Gill (Ithaca, NY: Cornell Univ. Press, 1985); Irigaray, "Women's Exile: Interview with Luce Irigaray," *Ideology and Consciousness* 1 (May 1977): 62–76; Julia Kristeva, "Oscillation du 'pouvoir' au 'refus,'" in *New French Feminisms*, ed. Marks and de Courtivron, 165–67; and Kristeva, "Women's Time," trans. Alice Jardine and Harry Blake, *Signs* 7, no. 1 (1981): 13–35.

4. Cixous, "Sorties," 93.

5. Certainly nonlinear, disruptive, fragmentary, experimental texts can be made to support reactionary, patriarchal politics; one would not designate such writing "feminine." In this essay, I am concerned with the ways a woman writer makes formal dislocations emphatically feminine by using them to explore conceptual disruptions.

6. Cixous, "The Laugh of the Medusa," 256; Irigaray, "Women's Exile," 65.

7. Kristeva, "Oscillation," 166; "La femme," 137.

8. Cixous, "The Laugh of the Medusa," 251.

9. Kristeva, "Women's Time," 29. Irigaray writes, "Forgive me, mother, I prefer a woman," suggesting that the mother is part of, rather than a way out of, the masculine economy; *This Sex*, 209.

10. Irigaray, *This Sex*, 76.

11. Mikhail Bakhtin, "Epic and Novel," in *The Dialogic Imagination*, trans. Caryl Emerson and Michael Holquist (Austin: Univ. of Texas Press, 1981), 3–40. One might note Roland Barthes' categories of the text of pleasure and the text of bliss; see *The Pleasure of the Text*, trans. Richard Miller (New York: Hill and Wang, 1975), 19, 21–22.

12. Irigaray, "Women's Exile," 66.

13. Jacques Derrida and Christine V. McDonald, "Choreographies," *Diacritics* 12, no. 2 (1982): 71, 72; see also Jardine, "Gynesis," 64.

14. Roland Barthes, "The Death of the Author," in *Image-Music-Text*, trans. Stephen Heath (New York: Hill and Wang, 1977), 142–48.

15. Cixous, "Sorties," 96, 97.

16. For example, Cixous writes, "Woman must write woman" ("The Laugh of the Medusa," 247); Kristeva comments, "In social, sexual, and symbolic experiences, being a woman has always provided a means to another end, to becoming something else: a subject-in-the-making, a subject on trial" ("Oscillation," 167).

17. Cixous, "Castration or Decapitation?" 52.

18. For example, see Kristeva, "La femme," 138; Cixous, "Sorties," 98; Cixous, "The Laugh of the Medusa," 249n.3, 255–56.

19. Mary Jacobus, "The Question of Language: Men of Maxims and *The Mill on the Floss*," in *Writing and Sexual Difference,* ed. Elizabeth Abel (Chicago: Univ. of Chicago Press, 1982), 39.

20. Sandra M. Gilbert and Susan Gubar, *The Madwoman in the Attic: The Woman Writer and the Nineteenth-Century Literary Imagination* (New Haven: Yale Univ. Press, 1979), 49.

21. Esther Newton, "The Mythic Mannish Lesbian: Radclyffe Hall and the New Woman," in *The Lesbian Issue: Essays from "Signs,"* ed. Estelle B. Freedman, Barbara C. Gelpi, Susan L. Jonson, and Kathleen M. Weston (Chicago: Univ. of Chicago Press, 1985), 16–18.

22. Susan Sniader Lanser, "Speaking in Tongues: *Ladies Almanack* and the Discourse of Desire," in this volume (161).

23. Irigaray, "When the 'Goods' Get Together," 110.

24. Lanser, "Speaking in Tongues," 164. For the attitudes of male critics, see Field, *Djuna* 124; Joseph Frank, "Spatial Form in Modern Literature," in *The Widening Gyre: Crisis and Mastery in Modern Literature* (Bloomington: Indiana Univ. Press, 1963), 26; and Louis F. Kannenstine, *The Art of Djuna Barnes: Duality and Damnation* (New York: New York Univ. Press, 1977), 33.

25. Lanser, "Speaking in Tongues," 163.

26. Irigaray, "When the 'Goods' Get Together," 108.

27. Sigmund Freud, "Some Psychological Consequences of the Anatomical Distinctions between the Sexes," in *The Standard Edition of the Complete Psychological Works of Sigmund Freud*, trans. James Strachey (London: Hogarth Press and the Institute of Psychoanalysis, 1961), 19:253.

28. H.J. Rose, *Religion in Greece and Rome* (New York: Harper, 1959), 272–73.
29. Irigaray, *This Sex*, 78.
30. Lanser, "Speaking in Tongues," 162.
31. Derrida, *Spurs*, 96.
32. Derrida, *Spurs*, 63.
33. Irigaray, "When the 'Goods' Get Together," 101.
34. Irigaray, *Speculum*, 240.
35. The term "hom(m)osexual" was coined by Irigaray. See *Speculum*, esp. 98–104; and *This Sex*, 171.
36. Irigaray, *Speculum*, 101.
37. Derrida, *Spurs,* 101.

11. *The Outsider among the Expatriates: Djuna Barnes' Satire on the Ladies of the* Almanack

Grateful acknowledgment is made to the National Endowment for the Humanities for a Travel to Collections Grant, which enabled me to undertake research in Paris for the essay. I would also like to thank the Scholarly Research Committee and the Summer Research Grant Program of Pace University for their support. Finally, I would like to thank Jean Chalon for permitting me to see Natalie Barney's copy of *Ladies Almanack*.

1. George Wickes, *The Amazon of Letters: The Life and Loves of Natalie Barney* (New York: Putnam's 1976), 15. Natalie Clifford Barney's fortune is usually estimated at between two and one-half and four million dollars, the equivalent of which today would be about a billion dollars; Karla Jay, *The Amazon and the Page: Natalie Clifford Barney and Renée Vivien* (Bloomington: Indiana Univ. Press, 1988), 2.
2. Berthe Cleyrergue and Michèle Causse, interview with Françoise Werner, "France Culture," Radio France, Paris, 2 November 1983.
3. Matthew Josephson, *Life among the Surrealists: A Memoir* (New York: Holt, 1942), 83.
4. Jay, *Amazon*, 33.
5. Natalie Clifford Barney, letter to Djuna Barnes, 17 November 1935, Natalie Clifford Barney Collection, Bibliothèque Jacques Doucet, Paris.
6. Barney, An Impression of Djuna Barnes and Her Book by the Amazon of Remy de Gourmont, MS. NCB 85, 789.10, Bibliothèque Jacques Doucet, Paris.
7. Barney, *Pensées d'une amazone* (Paris: Emile-Paul, 1920), 97.
8. Barney, *Traits et portraits* (1963; New York: Arno, 1975), 166.
9. Liane de Pougy, *My Blue Notebooks* (New York: Harper, 1979), 253.
10. Lillian Faderman, *Scotch Verdict: Miss Pirie and Miss Woods v. Dame Cumming Gordon* (New York: Morrow, 1983), 153–55.
11. Susan Sniader Lanser, "Speaking in Tongues: *Ladies Almanack* and the Language of Celebration," *Frontiers* 3 (1979): 39–45; see also the revision of Lanser's essay which appears in this volume.
12. Esther Murphy had several husbands, among them John Strachy and Chester Arthur, before becoming a lesbian.
13. Quoted in Wickes, *Amazon*, 183.
14. The two Doxies are described as follows: "One (Low-Heel) protesting that women were weak and silly Creatures, but all too dear, the other (High-Head) that they were strong, gallant, twice as hardy as any Man, and several times his equal in Brain, but none so precious" (*LA*, 50).
15. Flanner, *Paris Was Yesterday: 1925–1939* (New York: Penguin, 1981), xviii.

16. Gayle Rubin has presented a slide show on Natalie Barney's life, in which she defines *Ladies Almanack* as a celebration of lesbian sexuality.

17. Louis F. Kannenstine, *The Art of Djuna Barnes: Duality and Damnation* (New York: New York Univ. Press, 1977), 54.

18. Quoted in Andrew Field, *Djuna: The Life and Times of Djuna Barnes* (New York: Putnam's, 1983), 101.

19. Field, *Djuna*, 123.

20. Although the work was partially subsidized by Barney and sold by subscription to members of her circle, it is difficult to imagine that Barney would have asked Barnes to leave herself out of the book, since it was common during the era to portray oneself along with one's coterie, as in several group portraits of the Cénacle.

13. Nightwood: *"The Sweetest Lie"*

1. See especially Ulrich Weisstein, "Beast, Doll, and Woman: Djuna Barnes' Human Bestiary," *Renascence* 15 (1962): 3–11; William Johnsen, "Modern Women Novelists: *Nightwood* and the Novel of Sensibility," *Bucknell Review* 21 (Spring 1973): 29–42; Elizabeth Pochoda, "Style's Hoax: A Reading of Djuna Barnes' *Nightwood*," *Twentieth Century Literature* 22 (1976): 179–91; and Alan Singer, "The Horse Who Knew Too Much: Metaphor and Narrative Discontinuity in *Nightwood*," *Contemporary Literature* 25 (1984): 66–87. Lawrence Schehr studies "the construction and deconstruction of signs" in *Nightwood* to illustrate the significance of the lie from a very different theoretical perspective in "*Nightwood*: Dismantling the Folds," *Style* 19 (Spring 1985): 36–49. Joseph Frank's analysis of the spatial principle of structure in *Nightwood* formed the basis for most later studies; see his "Spatial Form in Modern Literature," in *The Widening Gyre* (Bloomington: Indiana Univ. Press, 1968). Douglas Messerli's *Djuna Barnes: A Bibliography* (Rhinebeck, NY: David Lewis, 1975) provides the most complete list of criticism to 1975; for criticism on *Nightwood*, see Louis Kannenstine, *The Art of Djuna Barnes: Duality and Damnation* (New York: New York Univ. Press, 1977), 86–127, 176–88.

2. Andrew Field, *Djuna* (New York: Putnam's, 1983). Field's unauthorized biography is marred by what are sometimes imprecise interpretations of Barnes' fiction and her motivations, but it does provide evidence for the autobiographical details in *Nightwood*; the parallels that Field notes between specific characters and people whom Barnes knew are particularly enlightening. Field also provides a useful bibliography which places all Barnes' fiction within the context of her social and literary milieus. Kannenstine uses this phrase on page 106. See Kenneth Burke, "Version, Con-, Per-, and In-," *Southern Review* (Spring 1966): 329–46. Although Burke's linguistic analysis becomes a bit farfetched at points, his analysis of *Nightwood*'s rhetorical strategies is brilliant and intriguing. From different perspectives, Kannenstine, Schehr, and Singer provide enlightening discussions of the "rhetoric of the life" in *Nightwood*.

3. Julia Kristeva's analysis of the meaning of the masculine/feminine dichotomy provides an invaluable gloss to this reading of *Nightwood*. See in particular her analysis of language and structure in "The Novel as Polylogue," in *Desire in Language*, ed. Leon S. Roudiez (New York: Columbia Univ. Press, 1980), 159–218, and her essay, "Women's Time," in *Feminist Theory: A Critique of Ideology*, ed. N.O. Keohane et al. (Chicago: Univ. of Chicago Press, 1982), 31–55, where she argues that the correlation between language and gender determines one's relation to power and meaning. For comprehensive reviews of the development and implications of a feminist theory of sexual difference see Stephen Heath, "Difference," *Screen* 19 (Autumn 1978): 51–112, and Gayatri Chakravorty Spivak, "French Feminism in an International Frame," *YES*, 62 (1981): 154–84.

4. Kristeva suggests that the maternal body offers the most accurate figuration of

female identity because it represents the split between subject and object and between semiotic and symbolic, which she theorizes is fundamental to female experience in a patriarchal culture. Her fullest exploration of the meaning of the maternal body is in "Motherhood According to Bellini," in *Desire*, 237–71; and "Place Names," in *Desire*, 271–94. Her concept of abjection is also relevant; see *The Powers of Horror*, trans. Leon S. Roudiez (New York: Columbia Univ. Press, 1982). Adrienne Rich's exploration of the cultural determinants of motherhood in *Of Woman Born* (New York: Norton, 1976) also provides a useful gloss on *Nightwood*.

5. In using the term "narcissistic" and in referring to the problems of difference and separation, I am not relying strictly on psychoanalytic theory, according to which the narcissistic personality is one that has not developed to the Oedipal conflict over sexual identity. In this essay, narcissism and separation are used more loosely to describe, in the first case, a consciousness that acknowledges no difference between what it dreams or imagines and what it experiences and, in the second case, the experience that one is inherently and inevitably different and therefore separate from all other people. For Barnes, all love is based on the desire to recover the narcissistic experience of undifferentiated wholeness, and love always frustrates that desire. In *Nightwood*, she does not consider the reciprocity that can develop from the discovery of difference within a relationship; rather, love only leads to the double bind of desire and estrangement.

6. Julia Kristeva's formulation of "masculine" and "feminine" temporalities in "Women's Time" provides a valuable framework for interpreting the meaning of time in *Nightwood*. Kristeva poses a contrast between those values mythologized in the "masculine" conception of time as history and those mythologized in the "feminine" conception of time as cyclic. To think of time as history, she suggests, is to think of time "as project, teleology . . . departure, progression, and arrival" ("Women's Time," 35). As a conception of time that presumes the logical and comprehensible relationship between events and actions, Kristeva suggests that "this linear time is that of language considered as the enunciation of sentences" ("Women's Time," 35)—that is, of speech in which syntax signifies rational order. The "feminine" experience of a cyclic temporality, in contrast, presumes the inevitability of an eternal renewal: "the eternal recurrence of biological rhythm which conforms to that of nature and imposes a temporality whose . . . regularity and unison . . . is experienced as cosmic time" ("Women's Time," 34). Kristeva proposes that a second experience of temporality may be associated with the feminine: the experience of time as timelessness. She calls this experience "a monumental temporality, without cleavage or escape, which has so little to do with linear time (which passes) that the very word 'temporality' hardly fits" ("Women's Time," 34). This experience of temporality, Kristeva suggests, corresponds to the experience of language as a collection of sound and syllables in which meaning is achieved not by sequence but by intuitive association; it negates, and is not accommodated by a relation to power or a conception of identity that depends upon the logical analysis of causality.

7. Robin represents an experience of temporality very much like that which Kristeva calls "monumental time." See above.

8. In "Motherhood According to Bellini," Kristeva suggests that the Christian Madonna is a hypostatized figure of the split between culture and nature and between Being and nothingness (*Desire*, 238–39). For other discussions of the significance of the Madonna see Mary Daly, *Beyond God the Father* (Boston: Beacon Press, 1973); and Marina Warner, *Alone of All Her Sex* (New York: Vintage, 1976, 1983).

9. See Susan Gubar, "Blessings in Disguise: Cross-Dressing as Re-Dressing for Female Modernists," *Massachusetts Review* 22 (1981): 477–508, for a brilliant analysis of the characterizations of Robin and Matthew. From a different perspective, Alan Williamson suggests that Robin and Matthew provide a "thematic counterpoint" in *Nightwood*; see "The Divided Image: The Quest for Identity in the Works of Djuna Barnes," *Critique* 7

(Spring 1964): 58–74. See also Miriam Fuchs, "Dr. Matthew O'Connor: The Unhealthy Healer of Djuna Barnes' *Nightwood,*" *Literature and Medicine* 2 (1983): 125–34.

10. Kannenstine argues that Barnes was influenced by writings about the unconscious and the afterlife in *transition* (*Art of Djuna Barnes* 107–9).

14. *Laughing at Leviticus:* Nightwood *as Woman's Circus Epic*

This essay, written in 1983–84 for this volume, will also appear in *Cultural Critique* (Fall 1989; unavailable as this book goes to press.). Because it has been widely cited from manuscript, beginning with Shari Benstock's *Women of the Left Bank* (1986), and circulated widely, I resist the urge to revise substantially in reference to subsequent work and hope it will now enter into a dialogue, however belatedly, with others working on Bakhtin's idea of carnival, the revision of modernism, Kristeva's concept of abjection, and Freud on the uncanny. A version of this paper was given at the 1984 MLA American Literature Division meeting in Washington, chaired by Margaret Homans. I am grateful to the panelists (especially Susan Friedman) and the audience for their response. I am also grateful to Shari and Bernard Benstock and their students at Tulsa; to audiences at the University of Wisconsin, CUNY Graduate Center, Northwestern University, University of Utah, Grinnell College, the University of Houston, and the University of Arizona; and to Susan Lanser and the Georgetown Critical Theory Conference, 1987. My thanks to Dean William Livingston and the University of Texas for a research grant that allowed me to work at the Barnes Collection, McKeldin Library, University of Maryland; to Donald Farren and his helpful staff for making the materials needed for this study available to me and for permission to reproduce materials in the collection; and to the Author's League Fund, Herbert Mitgang, holder of the Djuna Barnes copyright. I am also grateful to Beverly Stoeltje for introducing me to Bakhtin's work and discussions of circus from the perspective of folklore, and to the students in my feminist theory seminar at the University of Texas, especially Lee Mellick, Patricia Rezabek, and Ingeborg O'Sickey.

1. Julia Kristeva, *Powers of Horror: An Essay on Abjection* (New York: Columbia Univ. Press, 1982), 100.

2. See Mikhail Bakhtin, *Rabelais and his World,* trans. Hélène Iswolsky (Bloomington: Indiana Univ. Press, 1984). Hereafter cited in text as *Rabelais.*

3. Mary Douglas, *Purity and Danger* (London: Routledge and Kegan Paul, 1966).

4. See Victor Brombert, *Victor Hugo and the Visionary Novel* (Cambridge: Harvard Univ. Press, 1984).

5. Aphra Behn is one of the few precursors to Barnes whose work survives. Most women's bawdy humor available to us is oral, as in Bessie Smith and black women's music; but see Regina Barreca, ed., *Last Laughs: Perspectives on Women and Humor* (London and New York: Gordon and Breach, 1988).

6. Emily Coleman's essay with Djuna Barnes' comments and objections is in the McKeldin Library, University of Maryland, College Park. The Emily Coleman papers are at the University of Delaware.

7. Brombert, *Victor Hugo,* 109.

8. For another analysis of Barnes' excremental imagination, see Louise De Salvo, "'To Make Her Mutton at Sixteen': Rape, Incest and Child Abuse in *The Antiphon,*" in this volume.

9. Bombert, *Victor Hugo,* 116.

10. Michel Thévoz, *The Painted Body* (New York: Rizzoli, 1984).

11. Shari Benstock, *Women of the Left Bank* (Austin: Univ. of Texas Press, 1986).

12. Kenneth Burke, *Language as Symbolic Action* (Berkeley: Univ. of California Press, 1968). Burke notes the God/dog reversal in the last scene of *Nightwood.*

13. Eugène Sue, *The Wandering Jew* (New York: Random House, 1940). A full study of the influence of Eugène Sue on Djuna Barnes remains to be done. It is clear that Sue's career as doctor-sailor-writer is a major source for the character of Matthew O'Connor. The description of Morok the lion-tamer—with his beasts, Judas, Cain, and Death—in chapter 1 of *The Wandering Jew* begins with a three-sided chapbook illustration of his conversion from beast to human, a savage fleeing from wild animals, transformed to their tamer in the last picture. It is not difficult to imagine the young Djuna Barnes' identification with outsiders deriving from the novel after which she was named. Her early journalism produced memorable portraits of misfits and outsiders, and the chapbook or broadsheet is an important motif in her writing and drawing.

14. See Fredric Jameson, *The Political Unconscious* (Ithaca: Cornell Univ. Press, 1981). While I find Jameson's categories valuable for this analysis, one must point out that he does not count feminism as part of the political nor does gender appear in his system. For a good discussion of these issues, see Judith Gardiner's review, *In These Times*, 28 October 1981.

15. Hans Mayer, *Outsiders: A Study in Life and Letters* (Cambridge: MIT Press, 1984). Naomi Schor's essay is in *The Female Body in Western Culture*, ed. Susan Suleiman (Cambridge: Harvard Univ. Press, 1986), 363–72.

16. Jane Marcus, "A Wilderness of One's Own," in *Woman Writers and the City*, ed. Susan Silverman (Cambridge: Harvard Univ. Press, 1986), 363–72.

17. See "Berlin in Person," *TLS*, 28 December 1984, 1507. Heinrich Mann, from whose novel the script of *The Blue Angel* was taken, was surely an influence on Barnes in *Unrath* and *Der Untertak*.

18. For feminist discussions of the importance of transvestism to women artists, see Susan Gubar, "Blessings in Disguise: Cross-Dressing as Re-Dressing for Female Modernists," and Sandra Gilbert, "Costumes of the Mind," both in *No Man's Land* (New Haven: Yale Univ. Press, 1988–89); and Shari Benstock's response to and revision of their arguments in *Women of the Left Bank*. To this debate among feminist critics on the function of transvestism in women's culture, I would add that Barnes' presentation of a male transvestite as hero is a very clever way of privileging the female. Radclyffe Hall's *The Well of Loneliness* (New York: Covici and Friede, 1928) was clearly an influence on *Nightwood*, and I maintain that the structure of *Nightwood* is based on cabaret "acts." *The Well of Loneliness* also gives a guided tour of gay bars in Paris in the 1920s. I believe that the novel's title is a play on the name of a well-known homosexual and lesbian club in London in the 1920s, called the Cave of Harmony after the club in Thackeray's *The Newcomes*, famous for impersonations, improvisations, and dirty songs. Radclyffe Hall's tour includes Monsieur Pujol of the Ideal, who "collected inverts" and entertained his straight clients with photographs of his customers and a sinister locked leather notebook in which he catalogued his "collection" (Hall, *Well*, 441–42). He tells stories like Dr. O'Connor, but their object is not the same. At Le Narcisse the patron is a transvestite who sings both sentimental and lewd songs. At Alec's the whole "miserable army" of inverts is gathered. He sells cocaine to his "fillies" and Stephen is called "Ma Soeur" by a dying young addict of whom she thinks, "It's looking for God who made it" (Hall, *Well*, 449). The contrast between Hall's tragic, despairing vision and Barnes' comic approach is instructive. Barnes never reifies her outcast figure into an "it." Yet Angela Ingram points out that Hall's line repeats the earlier scene where the fox is hounded to death as "scapegoat," and she is referring to all outcasts as hounded beasts, a view she and Barnes might have shared.

19. The figure of the lesbian lover as a fairy-tale prince or page is common in women's writing. In Antonia White's *Frost in May* (1933; rpt. New York: Dial, 1982), the heroine's adored friend in a Catholic girls' school in England, Léonie, is seen as "a young prince, pale and weary from a day's ride, with his lovelocks carelessly tied in a frayed ribbon. . . . Her feeling for Léonie was one of pure admiration, the feeling of page for prince, too cold

and absolute to be called love" (79, 80). Antonia White was part of the Peggy Guggenheim circle at Hayford Hall where Djuna Barnes wrote part of *Nightwood*. For another reading of this novel and of the gender configurations at Hayford Hall, see Broe "Incest as Exile," in *Women's Writing in Exile*.

20. Sigmund Freud, "The Uncanny" (1919), in *On Creativity and the Unconscious* (New York: Harper & Row, 1958), 122–61. Hereafter cited in text as "Uncanny."

21. See Nancy Harrison, "Jean Rhys and the Novel as Women's Text," Ph.D. diss., University of Texas, Austin, 1983.

22. For "The Sand-Man," see *Selected Writings of E. T. A. Hoffmann*, ed. and trans. Leonard J. Kent and Elizabeth C. Knight (Chicago: Univ. of Chicago Press, 1969), vol. 1. Hereafter cited in text as *Tales*.

23. See the review of the Freud-Fleiss letters in the *New York Times Magazine*, 17 March 1985. As Freud repressed physical evidence of father-daughter incest to write his seduction theory, so Marx rejected earlier nonrational socialisms to create Marxism as a science. Consequently, in each ordering and theorizing of self and history an important component is left out and made Other. After Freud, the real incest victims were neglected until quite recently. "Other" socialisms were denied by Marxists. See Barbara Taylor, *Eve and the New Jerusalem* (New York: Pantheon, 1983), for feminist socialisms in pre-Marx English history.

24. I am indebted here to a paper read by Gareth Stedman Jones at Texas in March 1985 on the nonrational origins of socialism in French thought. In a typescript of *Nightwood* in the McKeldin Library, after Robin is called "the infected carrier of the past," the phrase "the *magnetized* beastly" is crossed out; clearly it is a reference to the magnetic theory of somnambulism of Mesmer. Bernard Benstock points out that Marx discusses these thinkers in *Capital*; see "Making Capital Out of Vampires," *Times Higher Education Supplement*, 15 June 1984.

25. As I write, the Barnes family papers at Maryland have been opened to scholars. [The Barnes papers were opened in June, 1985. Ed.] I suspect that both her father, Wald Barnes, and her grandmother, Zadel Barnes, were deeply interested in Fourier, Mesmer, Hugo, and Sue, and that the family experiments in living on their farm owed much to the influence of Fourier's ideas.

26. This information was supplied by Nancy Levine; Wald Barnes' novels and musical compositions are in the possession of Kerron Barnes and Duane Barnes.

27. Freud says that the mother of a girl he had cured regarded psychoanalysis itself as "uncanny." Helplessness causes one to feel "uncanny," he argues, and tells the story of being lost in the streets of a town in Italy on a hot afternoon. Three times, while trying to get out, he returns to the same place, a street where "nothing but painted women were to be seen at the windows" ("Uncanny," 143). This hardly needs a feminist analysis. Though Freud says that he "drifted into this field of research half involuntarily" ("Uncanny," 160), I suggest he was writing the male fear of being castrated by the father as a cover for his own guilt at having mishandled his women patients. For a brilliant analysis of the power of the mesmerized woman and of Freud's relation to hysterical women patients, see Nina Auerbach, *Woman and the Demon: The Life of a Victorian Myth* (Cambridge: Harvard Univ. Press, 1982).

28. Jean Rhys, *Smile Please: The Letters of Jean Rhys*, ed. Francis Wyndham and Diana Melly (New York: Viking, 1984), 20–21.

29. The typescripts of "Bow Down" and *Nightwood* are in the McKeldin Library, University of Maryland, College Park. When it is possible to quote from T.S. Eliot's letters, a full study of his cuts and corrections to *Nightwood* should be made with the aim of restoring and publishing the text as Barnes wanted it. While Eliot did have to think of the censor, many passages could be restored. He corrected her French and German and marked out many passages on Jews, one on King Ludwig, and a scene with the doctor in jail, as well as passages that might be considered obscene. He crossed out, "You can lay a hundred bricks and not be called a bricklayer, but lay one boy and you are a bugger" (202). He told her to think over

whether she wanted to say of Jenny, "when she fell in love it was with a perfect fury of accumulated dishonesty," and he told her to take out Matthew calling himself a faggot, a fairy, and a queen in the scene in the carriage. He crossed out "and the finger of our own right hand placed where it best pleases" and the McClusky passages on a girlish boy in the war. In the description of the "Tuppenny Upright" he crossed out "letting you do it," but she restored it in 1949. He wanted to change "obscene" to "unclean" on the last page and said he couldn't understand why Robin had candles in the chapel at night. Barnes' penciled note says, "Sample of T.S.E.'s 'lack of imagination' (as he said)." Also cut is a homosexual courtroom joke in which the judge asks, "What do I give a man of this sort?" and the clerk replies, "A dollar, a dollar and a half, two dollars." The whole of Matthew's circumcising the regiment scene is cut. The collection also includes Barnes' library. Inside her copy of Eliot's *Collected Poems* she wrote, "He said 'Someday they will say I copied you,'" and in his *On Poetry and Poets* she wrote in 1981, "Mr. E. said of the last act of *The Antiphon* that it was one of the greatest last acts he had ever read. But he did not so write of it."

30. I have discussed this apsect of *Nightwood* in a review of Andrew Field's *Djuna* in *The Women's Review of Books* 1, no. 8 (May 1984). See also Paul Bouissac, *Circus and Culture: A Semiotic Approach* (Bloomington: Indiana Univ. Press, 1976).

31. Note the resemblance of Robin as a beast to the description of Charlotte Brontë's Bertha in chapter 26 of *Jane Eyre*: "What it was, whether beast or human being, one could not, at first sight, tell; it grovelled, seemingly, on all fours; it snatched and growled like some wild animal. . . ."

32. For discussions of carnival, see Barbara A. Babcock, ed. *The Reversible World: Symbolic Inversion in Art and Society* (Ithaca: Cornell Univ. Press, 1978); see in particular David Kunzles, "World Upside Down: The Iconography of a European Broadsheet Type"; and Natalie Zemon Davis, "Women on Top: Symbolic Sexual Inversion and Political Disorder in Early Modern Europe."

33. Marguerite Yourçenar, *Fires* (1935; rpt. New York: Farrar, Strauss, Giroux, 1981); Susan Gubar, "Sapphistries," *Signs* 10, no. 1 (1984). See also Colette, *The Pure and the Impure*, for further connections between woman, circus, cabaret, and lesbianism.

34. For a modern version of Barbette's story see Albert Goldbarth's prose poem, *Different Fleshes* (Geneva, NY: Hobart and William Smith Colleges Press, 1979). Writing of the painter Soutine, Goldbarth says, "No one had ever prayed before in Meat Cathedral," which also recalls Barnes' Rabelaisian use of the butcher motif.

35. Bouissac, *Circus and Culture*, 8.

36. "How It Feels to Be Forcibly Fed," *New York World Magazine*, 6 September 1914, sec. 5, p. 17.

37. Brombert, *Victor Hugo*, 202.

38. Yvonne Mitchell, *Colette: A Taste for Life* (New York: Harcourt, 1975), 177.

39. See Robert H. Abzug, *Inside the Vicious Heart: Americans and the Liberation of Nazi Concentration Camps* (New York: Oxford, 1985), 56, 128–29, 132.

15. *"Woman, Remember You": Djuna Barnes and History*

1. For an account of lesbian experience at this period see Lillian Faderman, *Surpassing the Love of Men: Romantic Friendships and Love between Women from the Sixteenth Century to the Present* (New York: William Morrow, 1981). Jeffrey Weeks describes the significance of the trial of Oscar Wilde and the social context of Radclyffe Hall's work in *Coming Out: Homosexual Politics in Britain from the Nineteenth Century to the Present* (London: Quartet Books, 1979). Dolly Wilde, Oscar Wilde's niece, appeared in the *Ladies Almanack* as Doll Furious, as Andrew Field notes in his discussion of the book in *Djuna: The Life and Times of Djuna Barnes* (New York: G.P. Putnam's Sons, 1983), 124. Barnes also

satirized Radclyffe Hall and her lover, Una, Lady Troubridge, in *Ladies Almanack*, where they appear as Tilly Tweed-In-Blood and Lady Buck-and-Balk (*LA*, 18–26). The Dreyfus affair was inevitably present in the background of her account of both of the Volkbeins, and is suggested particularly by Guido's apprehension in the presence of military men. Dreyfus was crucial to Proust's account of Jews and homosexuals. See my discussion of the Volkbeins and the relation between *Nightwood* and the work of Proust. For a discussion of Radclyffe Hall's *The Well of Loneliness* and the literary choices of lesbian writers, see Catharine Stimpson, "Zero Degree Deviancy: The Lesbian Novel in English," *Critical Inquiry* 8 (Winter 1981): 363–79.

2. For an account of some of the conventions of women's literature, see Nancy K. Miller, *Subject to Change: Reading Feminist Writing* (New York: Columbia Univ. Press, 1988). Although she does not deal with Barnes, Rachel Blau DuPlessis discusses a range of strategies adopted by twentieth-century women writers in order to deal with the limitations imposed by literary conventions; see *Writing beyond the Ending: Narrative Strategies of Twentieth Century Women Writers* (Bloomington: Indiana Univ. Press, 1985).

3. The two most interesting and useful discussions of Barnes as a lesbian writer have been Bertha Harris, "The More Profound Nationality of Their Lesbianism: Lesbian Society in Paris in the 1920's," in *Amazon Expedition*, ed. Phyllis Birkby, Bertha Harris, Jill Johnston, Esther Newton, and Jane O'Wyatt (Albion, CA: Times Change Press, 1973), 77–88; and Susan Sniader Lanser, "Speaking in Tongues: *Ladies Almanack* and the Language of Celebration," *Frontiers* 4, no. 3 (Fall 1979): 39–46. See also Lanser's revision in this volume.

4. Barnes' sense of the limits of the history of the official record was shared by Virginia Woolf. In *A Room of One's Own* (New York: Harcourt, 1929), Woolf described looking for an account of the lives of English women of the past and finding history books that record only "the Cistercians and Sheep-farming . . . The Crusades . . . The University . . . The House of Commons" (77). She went on to imagine the development of the social history of the 1940s and 1950s and specifically the women's history of the 1970s and 1980s. In *A Room* and later in *Three Guineas* (1938), Woolf created a detailed political analysis of the power relations behind the restrictions on the history of the official record.

5. For an account of the Nazi persecution of homosexuals, see Heinz Heger, *The Men with the Pink Triangle*, trans. David Fernbach (Boston: Alyson Publications, 1980); and Richard Plant, *The Pink Triangle: The Nazi War against Homosexuals* (New York: Henry Holt, 1986).

6. J.E. Rivers, *Proust and the Art of Love* (New York: Columbia Univ. Press, 1980).

7. Proust even alludes to the Dreyfus and Wilde cases so as to imply their parallel lessons for Jews and homosexuals. He describes homosexuals: "Their honour precarious, their liberty provisional, lasting only until the discovery of their crime; their position unstable, like that of the poet one day fêted in every drawing-room and applauded in every theatre in London, and the next driven from every lodging, unable to find a pillow upon which to lay his head. . . . excluded even, save on days of general misfortune when the majority rally round the victim as the Jews rallied round Dreyfus." Marcel Proust, *Remembrance of Things Past*, vol. 2, *Cities of the Plain*, trans. C. K. Scott Moncrieff and Terence Kilmartin (New York: Vintage Books, 1982), 623–1169, 638.

8. In her introduction to the 1972 reprint of the *Ladies Almanack* Barnes referred to that work as "neap-tide to the Proustian chronicle" (*LA*, 3). Her library, which has been deposited at the McKeldin Library of the University of Maryland, contains copies of *A la récherche du temps perdu* in French and English. These volumes contain extensive notes made by Barnes, particularly on the first part of *Sodome et Gomorrhe* in which Proust discusses homosexuality most explicitly. Private conversation, Nancy Levine, 8 October 1984. George Wickes, in *The Amazon of Letters: The Life and Loves of Natalie Barney* (New York: Putnam's, 1976), says that Barnes discussed Proust's work in her correspondence with Natalie Barney, "both disapproving of Proust's treatment of lesbianism" (179). The influence of

Proust's account of lesbianism and male homosexuality on the work of other lesbian writers can be seen, for example, in Colette's *Ces plaisirs* (1932; reprinted as *Le pur et l'impur*, 1941).

9. Field, *Djuna*, 183, 165. Elizabeth Pochoda also argues that "the theme of de-evolution or bowing down . . . has implications for the act of writing." But she suggests, "The book moves backward. Beginning with an amusing historical flourish in its famous first sentence it eventually turns its back on history, on faith in coherent expression, and finally on words themselves. The novel bows down before its own impotence to express truth"; "Style's Hoax: A Reading of Djuna Barnes's *Nightwood*," *Twentieth Century Literature* 22, no. 2 (May 1976): 179–91, 180.

10. The story of Felix Volkbein has frequently been viewed as an element added to *Nightwood* primarily for the purposes of obscuring the lesbian aspect of the work. See, for example, Field, *Djuna*, 78, 140.

11. See Faderman, *Surpassing*, and Weeks, *Coming Out*, for histories of the changes in the lives of lesbians and gay men during this period.

12. See Harris, "Profound Nationality," for another discussion of Barnes, lesbian history, and the father.

13. The briefest glance at Barnes' publishing history indicates that publication was usually problematic for her. While *Ryder* was a best seller for its day in the United States, it was also censored. The *Ladies Almanack* was only published and sold privately in Paris in the 1920s before its 1972 second printing. *Nightwood* was rejected by seven publishers, according to Andrew Field (*Djuna*, 20), before it was forced on a reluctant Faber and Faber by T.S. Eliot; all of its editions to date have been burdened by Eliot's prefatory references to "freaks."

16. The Antiphon: "No Audience at All"?

1. I have chosen to quote from the revised text of *The Antiphon* published in *Selected Works of Djuna Barnes*, the last published version approved by Barnes. While there are many small revisions between this text and the first printed version of *The Antiphon* (London: Faber and Faber, 1958), these seem to me mostly tinkerings in search of improved phrasing or rhythm, and I have not been able to find an overall pattern to them. Where I felt a variant was helpful or interesting, I have quoted it within parentheses.

2. Andrew Field, *Djuna: The Life and Times of Djuna Barnes* (New York: Putnam's, 1983), 179–94. Field's view of *The Antiphon* is of a piece with his generally unsympathetic portrayal of Barnes and her work.

3. See, for example, Donna Gerstenberger, "Three Verse Playwrights and the American Fifties," in *Modern American Drama: Essays in Criticism*, ed. William E. Taylor (Deland, FL: Everett/Edwards, 1968).

4. Barnes occasionally wrote little closet dramas, which she called "three-minute plays," for use in her journalistic work; she was familiar with larger closet dramas and would have written one if she had wanted to. Instead, she chose to write *The Antiphon*.

5. She may even have hoped that she, like T.S. Eliot, would be able to reach a more popular audience—and make a little money—by turning to the dramatic form, and the play's successful run in Sweden in 1961, in a translation by Dag Hammarskjöld, gave her great pleasure. Her profound disappointment with the play's first production in New Haven in 1956 did not demonstrate that performance was contrary to her intentions. Rather, it demonstrated that she had quite concrete expectations for the manner of the play's presentation that were not met by the New Haven event—a dramatic reading without decor, by unrehearsed, unprepared, and rather uninspired actors who had not made the effort to understand the motivations of the characters and who did not conform to Barnes' idea of how her characters should look. This last point, which Field adduces as an example of her

eccentricity, points rather to the fact that Barnes conceived of *The Antiphon* as a whole, a carefully integrated visual and auditory production plan, and in this she was wiser than those who had organized the evening in New Haven, which was a dismal failure. See Field, *Djuna*, 220.

6. Some helpful comments on Barnes' decor are provided by Louis Kannenstine, *The Art of Djuna Barnes: Duality and Damnation* (New York: New York Univ. Press, 1977), 148–49.

7. Chosen at random from act 1, *A*, 116–22.

8. Gerstenberger, "Three Verse Playwrights," 120–22.

9. Barnes was involved between 1916 and 1920 first with the experimental Washington Square Players and then with the Provincetown Playhouse in Greenwich Village, which produced three of her early one-act plays (*Three from the Earth*, 1919; *An Irish Triangle*, 1920; *Kurzy of the Sea*, 1920). Later she was involved with the Theatre Guild, in many ways the successor to the Provincetown; she appeared from time to time in productions, including a 1922 appearance as the Madonna in a Theatre Guild production of Claudel's *The Tidings Brought to Mary*; between 1929 and 1931, she wrote features and then a regular column of reviews and theater news for their monthly magazine. We know from this column, and from the evidence of her library, that she was extensively familiar with the history and theory of drama; she was also conversant with the practical life of the theater, with new ideas about set design, direction, character, and interpretation, and with how these ideas were actually realized. As a drama critic for the Guild (and earlier, during her years of journalism), Barnes saw a staggering number of plays and interviewed many theater people, including the eminent actors, writers, producers, and designers of her day.

10. "The Days of Jig Cook: Recollections of Ancient Theatre History But Ten Years Old," *Theatre Guild Magazine*, January 1929, 31–32.

11. One-act plays were particularly amenable to this sort of arrangement, and the people involved in writing and acting them were a diverse bunch, ranging from political radicals like Louise Bryant and Jack Reed to writers who would develop as differently as Edna St. Vincent Millay, Maxwell Bodenheim, Edna Ferber, Wallace Stevens, Barnes, O'Neill. The plan of the Playwright's Theater was that it would allow the writer to give free reign to her or his imagination without considering whether the script was of the "manageable," "saleable" type that would interest a commercial producer.

12. Useful information about the Provincetown and the experimental theater movement generally can be found in Helen Deutsch and Stella Block Hanau, *The Provincetown: A Story of the Theatre* (New York: Russell and Russell, 1931); Jean Gould, *Modern American Playwrights* (New York: Dodd, Mead, 1966); Robert Karoly Sarlós, *Jig Cook and the Provincetown Players: Theatre in Ferment* (Amherst: Univ. of Massachusetts Press, 1982); Julia S. Price, *The Off-Broadway Theater* (New York: Scarecrow Press, 1962); and Walter Prichard Eaton, *The Theatre Guild: The First Ten Years* (New York: Brentano's, 1929).

13. Barnes, "Days of Jig Cook," 32.

14. Barnes, "Why Actors? Brother Sumac Searches for an Answer," *Theatre Guild Magazine*, December 1929, 42–43.

15. Shakespeare of course appears throughout *The Antiphon*. See Louise DeSalvo's essay in this volume.

16. Dolls recur in Barnes' work as images of a fragile but very important trust between human beings which is destroyed or broken. Think of Robin in *Nightwood* giving Nora a doll to symbolize their love and their child, then smashing the doll in a gesture that recalls her uncompleted attempt to murder her biological child, Guido. Another example is Amelia's Aunt Nelly in *Ryder*, who is "like a doll in a holy place," according to Amelia's mother, because she has been seduced and ruined (*R*, 38). Vera in Barnes' one-act play *The Dove* says, "I dreamt I was a Dresden doll and that I had been blown down by the wind and that I broke all to pieces—but that I was surprised to find that my china skirt had become flexible, as if it were made of chiffon and lace" (*AB*).

The destruction of a doll symbolizes not only violation and betrayal but the destruction of personality, the exploitation of an extreme vulnerability. And this is related to the theatrical aspect of the dolls in *The Antiphon*, for dolls acquire their power, become fetishized if you will, by their ability to represent human beings, to "stand in" for people, real or imaginary.

17. "The Dear Dead Days: Love Is Done Differently upon Our Current Stage," *Theatre Guild Magazine*, February 1929, 41–43.

17. *"Tom, Take Mercy": Djuna Barnes' Drafts of* The Antiphon

1. The letters quoted in this article are part of the Barnes Collection at the McKeldin Library, University of Maryland, College Park.

2. The typescripts of *The Antiphon* are also housed in the Barnes Collection at the University of Maryland. The twenty-nine typescripts make up the complete collection of the play from its inception to its publication. I have divided them into five separate draft stages for purposes of study and analysis.

3. In his review of *The Antiphon*, Lionel Abel said: "The characters scarcely talk to each other. Each one is intent on subtilizing and distilling his own thought and feeling into a verse expression adequate to the author's norms of rhetoric, and these are not at all dramatic norms"; "Bad by North and South," *Partisan Review* 25 (Summer 1958): 462; rpt. *Meta-theatre: A New View of Dramatic Form* (New York: Hill and Wang, 1963), 117.

Louis Kannenstine uses Abel's observations to substantiate his argument that *The Antiphon* is a dramatic poem or a closet drama, not meant for staging; *The Art of Djuna Barnes: Duality and Damnation* (New York: New York Univ. Press, 1977), 154.

4. This passage appears in the first four drafts of the play but does not appear at all in the fifth and final draft.

5. Barnes later explained to Karl Gierow, "Miranda does not think herself debased, she was doing her fathers [*sic*] bidding in vindication of her mother and because his 'word' was all she knew—remember the family was 'walled away' from the world."

6. This version is in the second draft, completed in 1955.

7. Here is Augusta's original doll house speech from the earlier drafts; compare with the published version (*A*, 186):

> AUGUSTA (*Bringing both fists down upon the house-top*):
>   Stop it! Stop it! Enough, enough.
>   Whistle off the nightengales
>   That above this house gave song,
>   Let from hence all wings repair,
>   Set the brindled snake to go
>   On his highest hoop away;
>   Let every beast and bird proclaim
>   What this dreadful ark must know!

8. The Cambridge reading took place in May 1956. It was attended by a very select audience: Barnes, Eliot, and the Muirs. The reading proved to be a great disappointment to the author.

18. *"To Make Her Mutton at Sixteen": Rape, Incest, and Child Abuse in* The Antiphon

1. Judith Lewis Herman, with Lisa Hirschman, *Father-Daughter Incest* (Cam-

bridge, MA: Harvard Univ. Press), 21. Virtually all of the insights in this essay about incest are derived from Herman's brilliant book.

I should like to thank Jane Marcus, who insisted that I write this essay, and with whom I discussed many of its ideas. Mary Lynn Broe provided me with the challenge to work through issues that I have discussed in other contexts in relationship to the work of Djuna Barnes, and I would like to thank her for supporting the writing of this essay.

2. As Marie Ponsot has remarked in "Careful Sorrow and Observed Compline," a review of *The Antiphon* that appeared in *Poetry* 95, no. 1 (October 1959): 47–50, "The plot of *The Antiphon* is in the revelation of its characters' history. . . . The action is expository, not fictive. No character develops. Instead, we suspect and slowly see a story" (47–48).

3. See Lynda Curry, "'Tom, Take Mercy': T.S. Eliot and *The Antiphon*," in this volume.

4. Herman, *Father-Daughter Incest*, 12.

5. I should like to thank Jane Marcus for this insight about the misogynist function of sodomy.

6. Herman, *Father-Daughter Incest*, 6.

7. According to Herman, the incidence of mother-son incest is extremely rare. Herman and her associates were able to locate only twenty-two documented cases of mother-son incest; *Father-Daughter Incest*, 18.

8. See Curry, "'Tom, Take Mercy.'"

9. Titus' name is, quite obviously, derived from *Titus Adronicus*. Barnes draws upon the Procne and Philomela story, one of the sources of that Shakespearean play, for many of the images in *The Antiphon*. Worthy of an entire study is the elucidation of the literary allusions in *The Antiphon* and how their use criticizes patriarchal literary forms. Barnes' use of allusion is much like that of Virginia Woolf's. See my "'A View of One's Own': Virginia Woolf and the Making of *Melymbrosia*," in *Virginia Woolf "Melymbrosia": An Early Version of the Voyage Out* (New York: New York Public Library, 1982). The text of *The Tempest* used throughout is G.B. Harrison, ed., *Shakespeare: The Complete Works* (New York: Harcourt, Brace, & World, 1952), 1471–1501.

10. Later in the play, there is a repetition of the image of a male giving birth in the comic scene where Trinculo is pulled out from under Caliban's coat. In this scene, Caliban as male/mother of Trinculo co-opts the maternal function, yet here, as in *The Antiphon*, the act of birth is aligned with the act of defecation, and the mother becomes the monster: Stephano asks Trinculo, "How/camest thou to be the siege [shit] of this mooncalf [monster]?" (2.2.109) It should also be remarked that Prospero has usurped the role of the witch Sycorax and her powers. In fact, *The Tempest* records the loss of power, either through marriage, or through usurpation, of a good number of women.

11. As Marilyn French has observed, Prospero "hypnotizes her into sleep whenever she is in the way. The only will she possesses is totally in line with his, although she does not know that. Her obedience to 'masculine' control is certified"; *Shakespeare's Division of Experience* (New York: Summit, 1981), 322.

Afterword

1. My source is a conversation with the owners of the Three Lives Book Store, in Greenwich Village, New York City, on 21 December 1982.

2. Jacques Derrida, "Force and Signification," *Writing and Difference*, trans. with an introduction by Alan Bass (Chicago: Univ. of Chicago Press, 1978, originally published in France in book form in 1967), 9.

3. Sophia's full name is Sophia Grieve Ryder, i.e., wisdom grieves a rider and grief rides wisdom.

4. Djuna Barnes, *Ryder*, with illustrations by the author (New York: St. Martin's Press, 1956, 1979), 132.

5. Conversation with Fran McCullough, 26 December 1982.

Selected Bibliography

Janice Thom and Kevin Engel

Research and criticism of the life and works of Djuna Barnes have burgeoned in the years since her death in 1982. With the recent reprinting of some of her early publications and the reawakened interest in her unique life and literary presence, this revival should continue to flourish.

The following is a selective bibliography of publications by and about Djuna Barnes. It is intended to give researchers and other interested readers trails into the literature and criticism of the present day and recent past. Writing of a substantive nature has been included in the bibliography without regard to format. Dissertations have been particularly noted as a source of both scholarly writing and the antecedent of future Barnes scholars and publications. This bibliography can serve as a supplement/update to Douglas Messerli's *Djuna Barnes: A Bibliography* published in 1975. Indeed, Messerli's bibliography should be consulted when references are made to certain original Barnes publications.

Allen, Carolyn. "Dressing the Unknowable in the Garments of the Known: The Style of Djuna Barnes' *Nightwood*." In *Women's Language and Style*, ed. Douglas Butturff and Edmund L. Epstein, 106–18. Akron, Ohio: L&S Books, 1978.

———. "Failures of Word, Uses of Silence: Djuna Barnes, Adrienne Rich and Margaret Atwood." *Regionalism and the Female Imagination* 4 (Spring 1978): 1–7.

Bach, Peggy. "Peggy Bach on Djuna Barnes' *Ryder*." In *Rediscoveries II: Important Writers Select Their Favorite Works of Neglected Fiction*, ed. David Madden and Peggy Bach, 315–24. New York: Carroll & Graf, 1988.

Bacon, Peggy. *Off with Their Heads*. New York: McBride & Co., 1934.

Baird, James. "Djuna Barnes and Surrealism: 'Backward Grief'." In *Individual and Community: Variations on a Theme in American Fiction*, ed. Kenneth H. Baldwin and David K. Kirby, 160–81. Durham, North Carolina: Duke University Press, 1975.

Barnes, Djuna. *The Book of Repulsive Women: Eight Rhythms and Five Drawings*. Los Angeles: Sun & Moon Press, 1989.

———. *Creatures in an Alphabet*. New York: Dial, 1982.

———. "Die 'Taube'." *Theater Heute* no. 8 (1989): 34–37.

———. "Drei vom Land." *Theater Heute* no. 8 (1989): 36+.

———. *Greenwich Village as It Is*. Edited by Robert A. Wilson. New York: Phoenix Book Shop, 1978.

———. *I Could Never Be Lonely without a Husband: Interviews*. Edited by Alyce Barry. London: Virago, 1987.

————. *Interviews*. Edited by Alyce Barry. Washington, D.C.: Sun & Moon Press, 1985.

————. *New York*. Edited by Alyce Barry. Los Angeles: Sun & Moon Press, 1989.

————. *Ryder*. New York: St. Martin's Press, 1979.

————. *Ryder*. New York: St. Martin's Press, 1981.

————. *Ryder*. With an Afterword by Paul West. Lisle, Illinois: Dalkey Press, 1990.

————. *Smoke, and Other Early Stories*. Edited by Douglas Messerli. College Park, Maryland: Sun & Moon Press, 1982.

————. *Smoke, and Other Early Stories*. 2d ed. Edited by Douglas Messerli. Los Angeles: Sun & Moon Classics, 1987.

————. "Vagaries Malicieux." *Double Dealer* 3 (May 1922): 249–60.

————. *Vagaries Malicieux: Two Stories*. New York: Frank Hallman, 1974.

————. "Vor die Hunde Gehn." *Theater Heute* no. 8 (1989): 40–42.

Baxter, Charles Morley. "Black Holes in Space: The Figure of the Artist in Nathanael West's *Miss Lonely Hearts*, Djuna Barnes' *Nightwood*, and Malcolm Lowry's *Under the Volcano*." Ph.D. diss., State University of New York at Buffalo, 1974.

————. "A Self-Consuming Light: *Nightwood* and the Crisis of Modernism." *Journal of Modern Literature* 3 (July 1974): 1175–87.

Benstock, Shari. *Women of the Left Bank: Paris, 1900–1940*. Austin, Texas: University of Texas Press, 1986.

Béranger, Elisabeth. "La femme invisible: Introduction a l'ecriture de Djuna Barnes." *Caliban* 17 (1980): 99–110.

————. "*Nightwood* ou du sexe d'une belle indifférence." *Revue Francaise d'Études Américaines* 11 (November 1986): 437–48.

————. "*Nightwood* ou l'anti-millénium." In *Le Facteur religieux en Amerique du Nord, No. 2: Apocalypse et autres travaux*, ed. Jean Béranger, 107–20. Bordeaux: Maison des Sciences de l'Homme d'Aquitaine, Univ. de Bordeaux III, 1981.

Bessière, Jean. "Djuna Barnes nouvelliste et romancière: Du lieu commun a l'imprévisible sens *Spillway* et *Nightwood*." *Revue de Littérature Comparée* 50 (October-December 1976): 455–77.

————. "Dualite de la nouvelle & du roman: Henry James, Djuna Barnes, Thomas Pynchon." *Palinure* 3 (Spring 1987): 28–40.

Blankley, Elyse Marie. "Daughters' Exile: Renee Vivien, Gertrude Stein, and Djuna Barnes in Paris." Ph.D. diss., University of California, Davis, 1984.

Broe, Mary Lynn. "Djuna Barnes." In *The Gender of Modernism*, ed. Bonnie Kime Scott. Bloomington, Indiana: Indiana University Press, 1990.

————. "Gunga Duhl, the Pen Performer." Review of *Interviews*, by Djuna Barnes, edited by Alyce Barry. In *Belles Lettres* 1 (September–October 1985): 2–3.

————. "My Art Belongs to Daddy: Incest as Exile—The Textual Economics of Hayford Hall." In *Women's Writing in Exile*, ed. Mary Lynn Broe and Angela Ingram, 41–86. Chapel Hill, North Carolina: University of North Carolina Press, 1989.

————. "Riotous Anecdotes." Review of *Djuna: The Life and Times of Djuna Barnes*, by Andrew Field. In *Gay Studies Newsletter* 11 (July 1984): 9–11.

Bronfen, Elisabeth. "Wandering in Mind or Body—Death, Narration and Gender in Djuna Barnes' Novel *Nightwood*." *Amerikastudien—American Studies* 33, no. 2 (1988): 167–77.

Broyard, Anatole. "Aged Unconventionally." Review of *Selected Works of Djuna Barnes*, by Djuna Barnes. In *New York Times*, 28 June 1980, 19.

Bruno, Guido, and Djuna Barnes. "An Interview with Djuna Barnes (from 1919)." *Theater Heute* no. 8 (1989): 38.

Burke, Kenneth. "Version, Con-, Per-, and In- (Thoughts on Djuna Barnes' Novel *Nightwood*)." In *Language As Symbolic Action; Essays on Life, Literature, and Method*, 240–53. Berkeley, California: University of California Press, 1968.

————. "Version, Con-, Per-, In-: Thoughts on Djuna Barnes' Novel, *Nightwood*." *Southern Review*, n.s. 2 (Spring 1966): 329–46.

Busch, Alexandra. "Eine Satire fur Fortgeschrittene: Djuna Barnes' *Ladies Almanack*." *Forum Homosexualitat und Literatur* 6 (1989): 41–71.

————. "Rediscovery of the Plays of Djuna Barnes—Some Comments." *Theater Heute* no. 6 (1988): 62.

Cagidemetrio, Alide. *Una Strada nel bosco: Scrittura e coscienza in Djuna Barnes*. Vicenza: Neri Pozza, 1979.

Carpenter, Humphrey. *Geniuses Together: American Writers in Paris in the 1920's*. Boston: Houghton Mifflin Co., 1988.

Catano, Jose Carlos, and Maria Llopis de Aysa, tr. "Retrato de Djuna Barnes." *Quimera: Revista de Literatura* 14 (December 1981): 25–29.

Chell, Cara. "No Myth Is Safely Broken: American Women and the Modernist Period." Ph.D. diss., Indiana University, 1983.

Clark, Susan F. "Misalliance: Djuna Barnes and the American Theatre." Ph.D. diss., Tufts University, 1989.

Cook, Blanche Wiesen. "'Women Alone Stir My Imagination': Lesbianism and the Cultural Tradition." *Signs* 4 (Summer 1979): 718–39.

Core, Deborah Lynn. "'The Atmosphere of the Unasked Question': Women's Relationships in Modern British Fiction." Ph.D. diss., Kent State University, 1981.

Curry, Lynda Catherine. "The Second Metamorphosis: A Study of the Development of *The Antiphon* by Djuna Barnes." Ph.D. diss., Miami University, 1978.

Daley, Suzanne. "Djuna Barnes Dies; Poet and Novelist." *New York Times*, 20 June 1982, sec. 1, 32.

Dalton, Ann. "Book of Repulsive Women: Father-Daughter Incest in the Work of Djuna Barnes," Ph.D. diss., University of California–Davis, 1989.

Davis, Isabel. "The People in Djuna Barnes's *Nightwood*." Ph.D. diss., State University of New York at Stony Brook, 1978.

DeVore, Charles Lynn. "The Works of Djuna Barnes: A Literary Cosmos." Ph.D. diss., University of Tulsa, 1976.

DeVore, Lynn. "The Backgrounds of *Nightwood*: Robin, Felix, and Nora." *Journal of Modern Literature* 10 (March 1983): 71–90.

Dix, Douglas Shields. "The Text as War Machine: Writing to Destroy." Ph.D. diss., University of Washington, 1988.

"Djuna Barnes." In *The Norton Anthology of Literature by Women: The Tradition in English*, ed. Sandra Gilbert and Susan Gubar, 1569–77. New York: Norton, 1985.

Duncan, Erika. "Djuna Barnes and *Nightwood*." Review of *Djuna Barnes: A Bibliography*, by Douglas Messerli. In *Book Forum: An International Transdisciplinary Quarterly* 2, no. 4 (1976): 612–17.

————. *Unless Soul Clap Its Hands: Portraits and Passages*. New York: Schocken, 1984.

Earle, Kathryn. "The Wasteland of *Nightwood*." *The Bulletin of the West Virginia Association of College English Teachers* 9 (Spring 1986): 35–41.

Ebeling-Koning, Blanche T. "Famous, Unknown Djuna Barnes." *New York Times Book Review*, 5 January 1986, 4.

Ecker, Gisela. "Gertrude Stein, Hilda Doolittle (H.D.) und Djuna Barnes: Drei Amerikanerinnen in Europa." In *Weiblichkeit und Avantgarde*, ed. Inge Stephan and Sigrid Weigel, 40–66. Berlin: Argument-Verlag, 1987.

Eliot, Valerie. "Books: Djuna's Sorrow." *Financial Times* (London), 1 August 1987, sec. 29, 12.

Ferguson, Suzanne C. "Djuna Barnes's Short Stories: An Estrangement of the Heart." *Southern Review*, n.s. 5 (Winter 1969): 26–41.

Field, Andrew. *Djuna: The Life and Times of Djuna Barnes*. New York: Putnam's, 1983.

————. *Djuna, the Formidable Miss Barnes*. Austin, Texas: University of Texas Press, 1985.

———. "Djuna Barnes." *New York Times Book Review*, 9 October 1983, 45.

———. "Minor work of a Major Writer." Review of *Creatures in an Alphabet*, by Djuna Barnes and *Smoke, and Other Early Stories*, by Djuna Barnes, edited by Douglas Messerli. In *New York Times Book Review*, 9 January 1983, 9, 30.

Fitch, Noel Riley. *Sylvia Beach and the Lost Generation: A History of Literary Paris in the Twenties and Thirties*. New York: Norton, 1983.

Franci, Giovanna. "'Donna: Mostro o persona?'" *Il Lettore di Provincia* 14 (14 September 1983): 95–97.

Frank, Joseph. "Djuna Barnes: *Nightwood*." In *The Widening Gyre; Crisis and Mastery in Modern Literature*, 25–49. New Brunswick, New Jersey: Rutgers University Press, 1963.

———. "Spatial Form in Modern Literature." *Sewanee Review* 53 (1945): 221–40, 433–56, 643–53.

Fuchs, Miriam. "Djuna Barnes: 'Spillway' into Nightmare." *Hollins Critic* 18 (June 1981): 1–9.

———. "Dr. Matthew O'Connor: The Unhealthy Healer of Djuna Barnes's *Nightwood*." *Literature and Medicine* 2 (1983): 125–34.

Gentile, Kathy Justice. "Speaking the Ineffable Name: The Novels of Emily Bronte, Ivy Compton-Burnett, Djuna Barnes, and Jane Bowles (Lilith)." Ph.D. diss., University of Oregon, 1987.

Gilbert, Sandra M. "Costumes of the Mind: Transvestism as Metaphor in Modern Literature." *Critical Inquiry* 7 (Winter 1980): 391–417.

———. "Costumes of the Mind: Transvestism as Metaphor in Modern Literature." In *Writing and Sexual Difference*, ed. Elizabeth Abel, 193–219. Chicago: University of Chicago Press, 1982.

Gildzen, Alex, ed. *A Festschrift for Djuna Barnes on Her 80th Birthday*. Kent, Ohio: Kent State University Libraries, 1972.

Giroux, Robert. "'The Most Famous Unknown in the World' — Remembering Djuna Barnes." *New York Times Book Review*, 1 December 1985, 3, 30–31.

Green, Zoe. "After Reading Djuna by Andrew Field." *Fiddlehead* no. 146 (1985): 22–24.

Greiner, Donald J. "Djuna Barnes' *Nightwood* and the American Origins of Black Humor." *Critique: Studies in Modern Fiction* 17, no. 1 (1975): 41–54.

Griffin, Barbara J. "Two Experimental Writers: Djuna Barnes and Anaïs Nin." In *American Women Writers: Bibliographical Essays*, ed. Maurice Duke, Jackson R. Bryer, and M. Thomas Inge, 135–66. Westport, Connecticut: Greenwood Press, 1983.

Grogan, Cynthia Alice. "The Damned Heart: Love in Djuna Barnes' *Nightwood*." M.A. thesis, Adelphi University, 1984.

Groves, Robyn Kaye. "Fictions of the Self: Studies in Female Modernism: Jean Rhys, Gertrude Stein and Djuna Barnes." Ph.D. diss., University of British Columbia, 1987.

Gubar, Susan. "Blessings in Disguise: Cross-Dressing as Re-Dressing for Female Modernists." *Massachusetts Review* 22 (Autumn 1981): 477–508.

Gunn, Edward. "Myth and Style in Djuna Barnes's *Nightwood*." *Modern Fiction Studies* 19 (Winter 1973–1974): 545–55.

Hanrahan, Mairéad. "Djuna Barnes' *Nightwood*: Where Man Is with Wo(e)." In *Writing Differences: Readings from the Seminar of Hélène Cixous*, ed. Susan Sellers, 81–94. New York: St. Martin's Press, 1988.

Hanscombe, Gillian E., and Virginia L. Smyers. *Writing for Their Lives: Modernist Women, 1910–1940*. London: The Women's Press, 1987; Boston: Northeastern University Press, 1987.

Hardwick, Elizabeth. "The Fate of the Gifted." Review of *Djuna: The Formidable Miss Barnes*, by Andrew Field and *Smoke, and Other Early Stories*, by Djuna Barnes, edited by Douglas Messerli. In *Times Literary Supplement*, 7 October 1983, 1071–72.

Harper, Phillip Brian. "The Recentered Subject: Marginality in the Development of Post-modern Culture." Ph.D. diss., Cornell University, 1988.

Harris, Bertha. "The More Profound Nationality of Their Lesbianism: Lesbian Society in Paris in the 1920's." In *Amazon Expedition: A Lesbian Feminist Anthology*, ed. Phyllis Birkby, Bertha Harris, Jill Johnston, Esther Newton, and Jane O'Wyatt, 77–88. New York: Times Change Press, 1973.

Hatziconstantinou, Iorgos. "Memory and Kinetic Space in the Metaphor of American Modernism." Ph.D. diss., University of Washington, 1989.

Helle, Anita Plath. "Speculative Subjects: The Uses of Exile to the Imagination of Djuna Barnes, Gertrude Stein, and Mina Loy (Expatriate Women Writers)." Ph.D. diss., University of Oregon, 1986.

Herzig, Carl. "Roots of Night: Emerging Style and Vision in the Early Journalism of Djuna Barnes." *Centennial Review* 31 (Summer 1987): 255–69.

———. "Nightwatch: A Study of Djuna Barnes and 'Nightwood.'" Ph.D. diss., State University of New York at Stony Brook, 1989.

Hirschman, Jack Aaron. "The Orchestrated Novel: A Study of Poetic Devices in Novels of Djuna Barnes and Herman Broch, and the Influences of the Works of James Joyce upon Them." Ph.D. diss., Indiana University, 1961.

Hirsh, Elizabeth Anne. "Modernism Revised: Formalism and the Feminine." Ph.D. diss., University of Wisconsin—Madison, 1989.

Jehle, Volker. *Wolfgang Hildesheimer*. Frankfurt am Main: Suhrkamp, 1989.

Johnsen, William A. "Modern Women Novelists: *Nightwood* and the Novel of Sensibility." *Bucknell Review* 21 (Spring 1973): 29–42.

Kaivola, Karen Lennea. "Writing the Discourse of Desire: The Subversive Lyricism of Virginia Woolf, Djuna Barnes, and Marguerite Duras." Ph.D. diss., University of Washington, 1989.

Kannenstine, Louis F., and Allan Smith. *The Art of Djuna Barnes: Duality and Damnation.* New York: New York University Press, 1977.

Koch, Stephen. "'Nightwood' and the Legend of Djuna Barnes." Review of *Djuna: The Life and Times of Djuna Barnes*, by Andrew Field, *Smoke, and Other Early Stories*, by Djuna Barnes, edited by Douglas Messerli, and *Creatures in an Alphabet*, by Djuna Barnes. In *Washington Post*, 12 June 1983, sec. o, 1.

Koschel, Christine, and Inge von Weidenbaum. "Djuna Barnes." *Theater Heute* no. 8 (1988): 54.

Landes, B. "A Living Legend—Theater Author Djuna Barnes." *Theater Heute* no. 7 (1982): 15–17.

Lanser, Susan Sniader. "Speaking in Tongues: *Ladies Almanack* and the Language of Celebration." *Frontiers* 4, no. 3 (1979): 39–46.

Larabee, Ann E. "First-Wave Feminist Theatre, 1890–1930." Ph.D. diss., State University of New York at Binghamton, 1988.

Latimer, Robin Marcelle. "Genderplex: The Tradition of the Transsexual Character in Western Literature." M.A. thesis, Lamar University, 1987.

Levine, Nancy Joan. "Dreams of Painters, Dreams of Revenge: The Grotesque in Djuna Barnes' *Nightwood*." Ph.D. diss., Columbia University, 1984.

———. "'I've Always Suffered from Sirens': The Cinema Vamp and Djuna Barnes' *Nightwood*." *Women's Studies* 16, no. 3–4 (1989): 271–81.

McCullough, Frances. "Djuna Barnes." *New York Times Book Review*, 17 July 1983, 23.

Mackworth, Cecily. "Djuna Barnes ou l'exploration de la nuit." *Europe—Revue Litteraire Mensuelle* 61 (October 1983): 159–63.

Mandel, Ursula Maria. "Life without Myths: A Comparative Study of Franz Kafka's *The Trial* and Djuna Barnes' *Nightwood*." Ph.D. diss., University of Colorado at Boulder, 1987.

Marcus, Jane. "Carnival of the Animals." Review of *Djuna: The Life and Times of Djuna Barnes*, by Andrew Field. In *Women's Review of Books* 1 (April 1984): 6–7.

Martin, Stephen H. "A Comparative Study of Androgyny in Twentieth-Century Experimental Literature." Ph.D. diss., New York University, 1984.

Messerli, Douglas John. *Djuna Barnes: A Bibliography*. New York: David Lewis, 1975.

———. "Modern Postmodern Fiction: Toward a Formal and Historical Understanding of Postmodern Literature." Ph.D. diss., University of Maryland, 1979.

———. "The Role of Voice in Nonmodernist Fiction." *Contemporary Literature* 25 (Fall 1984): 281–304.

Michel, Frann. "Displacing Castration: *Nightwood, Ladies Almanack*, and Feminine Writing." *Contemporary Literature* 30 (Spring 1989): 33–58.

Mitgang, Herbert. "Book Ends." *New York Times Book Review*, 24 August 1980, 31.

Montague, Gene. "Dylan Thomas and *Nightwood*." *Sewanee Review* 76 (Summer 1968): 420–34.

Morrison, James E. "The Preface as Criticism: T.S. Eliot on *Nightwood*." *Centennial Review* 32 (Fall 1988): 414–27.

Nadeau, Robert L. "*Nightwood* and the Freudian Unconscious." *International Fiction Review* 2 (July 1975): 159–63.

Nelson, Gerald B. *Ten Versions of America*. New York: Knopf, 1972.

Page, Chester. "Djuna Barnes." *New York Times Book Review*, 17 July 1983, 23.

Pais, Sara Via. "Shapes of the Feminine Experience in Art." In *Women, the Arts, and the 1920s in Paris and New York*, ed. Kenneth W. Wheeler and Virginia Lee Lussier, 49–55. New Brunswick, New Jersey: Transaction Books, 1982.

Peternel, Joan. "Doubling the Hero and the Bride: Four Modern Quest Novels." Ph.D. diss., Indiana University, 1981.

Pinckney, Darryl. "Sweet Evening Breeze." *New York Review of Books*, 20 December 1984, 35–43.

Plumb, Cheryl J. *Fancy's Craft: Art and Identity in the Early Works of Djuna Barnes*. Selinsgrove, Pennsylvania: Susquehanna University Press, 1986.

Pochoda, Elizabeth. "Style's Hoax: A Reading of Djuna Barnes's *Nightwood*." *Twentieth Century Literature* 22 (May 1976): 179–91.

Reizbaum, Marilyn. "A 'Modernism of Marginality': The Link between James Joyce and Djuna Barnes." In *New Alliances in Joyce Studies: 'When It's Aped to Foul a Delfian'*, ed. Bonnie Kime Scott, 179–92. Newark, Delaware: University of Delaware Press, 1988.

Riedell, Karyn Lea. "The Struggle toward Androgyny: A Study of Selected American Writers." Ph.D. diss., Arizona State University, 1984.

Rieke, Alison. "Two Women: The Transformations." In *Faith of a (Woman) Writer*, ed. Alice Kessler-Harris and William McBrien, 71–81. New York: Greenwood Press, 1988.

Rose, Phyllis. "Djuna Barnes." In *Writing of Women: Essays in a Renaissance*, 28–34. Middletown, Connecticut: Wesleyan University Press, 1988.

———. "The Stature of an Eccentric." Review of *Djuna: The Life and Times of Djuna Barnes*, by Andrew Field. In *New York Times Book Review*, 26 June 1983, 9, 22–23.

Schehr, Lawrence R. "Djuna Barnes's *Nightwood*: Dismantling the Folds." *Style* 19 (Spring 1985): 36–49.

Schulz, Genia. "Die Rucknahme der Schopfung: Anmerkungen zu Djuna Barnes." *Merkur: Deutsche Zeitschrift fur Europaisches Denken* 40 (April 1986): 331–36.

Scott, James B. *Djuna Barnes*. Boston: Twayne, 1976.

Sharrock, Roger. "Our Health Is the Disease, or the One and the Many." *Agenda* 23 (Spring–Summer 1985): 97–102.

Singer, Alan Stewart. "Discontinuity and Discourse in Modern Fiction." Ph.D. diss., University of Washington, 1980.

———. "The Horse Who Knew Too Much: Metaphor and the Narrative of Discontinuity in *Nightwood*." *Contemporary Literature* 25 (Spring 1984): 66–87.

———. *A Metaphorics of Fiction: Discontinuity and Discourse in the Modern Novel.* Tallahassee, Florida: University Presses of Florida, 1983.

Smith-Rosenberg, Carroll. *Disorderly Conduct: Visions of Gender in Victorian America.* New York: Knopf, 1985.

Stevenson, Sheryl Anne. "The Never-Last Word: Parody, Ideology, and the Open Work." Ph.D. diss., University of Maryland, College Park, 1986.

Stromberg, Kyra. *Djuna Barnes: Leben und Werk einer Extravaganten.* Berlin: Wagenbach, 1989.

Symons, Julian. *Makers of the New: The Revolution in Literature, 1912–1939.* New York: Random House, 1987.

Turchetti, Emanuela. "The Arena of the 'Indecent' Eternal: Immagine corporale e discorso d'amore in *Nightwood* di Djuna Barnes." *Nuova Corrente: Rivista di Letteratura* 29 (January–April 1982): 115–42.

———. "Immagine corporale e discorso d'amore in *Nightwood* di Djuna Barnes." *Nuova Corrente: Rivista di Letteratura* 28 (September–December 1981): 519–48.

Vella, Michael. "Djuna Barnes Gains Despite Critics' Pall." *Lost Generation Journal* 4 (Winter 1976): 6–8.

Wagstaff, Ann Marie. "The Backward-Looking Prophet: An Examination of the Consequences of Childhood Exploitation in the Work of Djuna Barnes." Ph.D. diss., University of California, Davis, 1987.

Weisstein, Ulrich. "Beast, Doll, and Woman: Djuna Barnes' Human Bestiary." *Renascence* 15 (1962): 3–11.

West, Paul. "Djuna Barnes at the Stake: An Imaginary Retort." *Parnassus: Poetry in Review* 15, no. 1 (1989): 71–82.

Williamson, Alan. "The Divided Image: The Quest for Identity in the Works of Djuna Barnes." *Critique: Studies in Modern Fiction* 7 (Spring 1964): 58–74.

Wilson, Deborah Sue. "Lost Boundaries: Kenneth Burke, Nathanael West, Djuna Barnes and the Disorder of Things." Ph.D. diss., University of California—Irvine, 1987.

Wolfe, Judy Louise. "Anti-Patriarchal Strategies in the Major Works of Djuna Barnes." Ph.D. diss., Rice University, 1985.

Zeemann, Dorothea. "Djuna Barnes (1892–1982)." In *Eine Frau Ist Eine Frau Ist Eine Frau . . .*, ed. Elfriede Gerstl, 58–69. Wein: Promedia, 1985.

Notes on Contributors

JULIE L. ABRAHAM is assistant professor of English and Women's Studies at Emory University. Her work on Djuna Barnes is part of a larger study, *"Damned, and Carefully Public": Modern Lesbian Narrative*, forthcoming from Cornell University Press.

CAROLYN ALLEN is associate professor of English at the University of Washington. She has published articles on various modern and contemporary American writers. A previous piece on Djuna Barnes appears in *Women's Language and Style*. She is currently working on the relation of feminist thought to poststructuralist theory; her article "Feminism and Post-modernism" appears in *Tracing Literary Theory* (University of Illinois, 1987).

MERYL ALTMAN, is coordinator of Women's Studies at DePauw University. Her book, *Interlocutions: Men, Women, and Modernisms in American Poetry*, will be published by Northeastern University Press.

MARY LYNN BROE is Louise Rosenfield Noun Professor of Women's Studies and English at Grinnell College. She is author of *Protean Poetic: The Poetry of Sylvia Plath* (University of Missouri, 1980), co-editor with Angela Ingram of *Women's Writing in Exile* (University of North Carolina, 1989), and with Frances McCullough, is completing *Cold Comfort*, a biographical portrait of Djuna Barnes in letters to be published by Random House. She has published essays on contemporary women writers and feminist theory. At present, she is at work on a book about the textual and gender relations of the writers at Peggy Guggenheim's Hayford Hall in the 1930s.

CAROLYN BURKE has published numerous translations and articles on feminist theory in France and the United States and modernist writing by women. She is currently completing a critical biography of Mina Loy to be published by Farrar, Straus & Giroux.

LOUISE A. DESALVO is professor of English at Hunter College. Her most recent work is *Virginia Woolf: The Impact of Childhood Sexual Abuse on Her Life and Work*. She was co-editor of *Vita Sackville-West's Letters to Virginia Woolf* and editor of *Melymbrosia*, an early version of Woolf's novel, *The Voyage Out*, which she reconstructed from the original manuscripts. She is also the author of *Nathaniel Hawthorne* and *Virginia Woolf's First Voyage: A Novel in the Making*, as well as the novel *Casting Off*, and is co-editor of an edition of contemporary stories by Irish women called *Territories of the Voice*. She has recently completed a second novel.

FRANCES M. DOUGHTY's work in feminist theory and lesbian history is currently focused on theory of biography. Her writing includes "Lesbian Biography, Biography of Lesbians," in *Lesbian Studies*, papers on lesbian feminist theory, and book reviews. She has presented her archival research on Djuna Barnes and Margaret Anderson et al. in the illustrated lectures "Gilt on Cardboard" and "Family of Friends" in the United States and Europe. Active in the

414

lesbian and women's movements, she was the first woman co-chair of the National Gay Task Force and founded its Women's Caucus.

KEVIN ENGEL is a native Iowan and has received degrees from Iowa State University and the University of Iowa. He has taught in the Library and Information Science graduate program at the University of Iowa, and he is currently employed providing reference and research assistance in the humanities, sciences, and social sciences at Burling Library at Grinnell College.

ANDREW FIELD is Honorary Professor at Griffith University in Australia. His most recent book is *The Lost Testament of Edward de Vere* (Viking/Penguin), published in England in 1990. He is also the author of biographies of Vladimir Nabokov and Djuna Barnes.

RUTH FORD, an actress and playwright, made her Broadway debut as Jane in *The Shoe-maker's Holiday*—produced by Orson Welles—in 1938. Throughout the years she has performed in productions of *Othello, Cyrano de Bergerac, No Exit, Hamlet, The Skin of Our Teeth*, and *The American Dream*. In 1957 she was nominated by the London drama critics for her portrayal of Temple Drake in *Requiem for a Nun*, which she adapted with William Faulkner.

ALEX GILDZEN is a poet (*The Avalanche of Time: Selected Poems 1964–1984*), scholar ("The Open Theater: A Beginning Bibliography"), librarian ("In the Wind of Wonder: An Exhibition of Selections from the Papers of James Broughton"), and editor (*Dress: The Annual Journal of the Costume Society of America*).

KARLA JAY is professor of English at Pace University in New York City. She has edited, translated, and written seven books, including *The Amazon and the Page: Natalie Clifford Barney and Renée Vivien*. Most recently, she co-edited an anthology entitled *Lesbian Texts and Contexts: Radical Revisions*. She is general editor of a series, The Cutting Edge: Twentieth-Century Lesbian Studies, to be published by New York University Press.

SUSAN SNIADER LANSER has been associate professor of English at Georgetown University and is currently on the faculty of the University of Maryland at College Park. Her work is concerned primarily with feminist literary criticism and with the articulation between feminism and literary form. She has written *The Narrative Act: Point of View in Prose Fiction*, numerous essays, and most recently *Fictions of Authority: Women Writers and Narrative Voice*. Her new project is a study of women critics, 1750–1900.

ANN LARABEE is assistant professor of American Thought and Language at Michigan State University. She has published articles on Eugene O'Neill, Susan Glaspell, Djuna Barnes, and other Provincetown playwrights. Her works in progress include a book-length study of women's drama in the early twentieth century and an analysis of gender myths surrounding the *Titanic* disaster.

JUDITH LEE is an associate professor in the Department of Literature at The American University. She has also taught at Brandeis University and at the University of Colorado, and she was a visiting scholar at the Center for Research on Women at Stanford University. Professor Lee has published articles on Blake, Ariosto, and Isak Dinesen and is the author of *Live Fire, Living Water: Isak Dinesen and the World of Lucifer*.

NANCY J. LEVINE, assistant professor of English at the University of North Florida, received her Ph.D. in twentieth-century literature at Columbia University in 1984. A former Whiting Fellow, she has published on John Hawkes and Djuna Barnes and is now completing a book on Barnes. Other current research includes work on women writers of the grotesque, the hermaphrodite in popular culture, tattooing as a literary theme and cultural phenomenon, the tango craze of the early 1910s, and blues structure in American black literature.

FRANCES MCCULLOUGH, a graduate of Stanford University, is Consulting Editor at Bantam Books in New York City. As well as having been Barnes' editor, Ms. McCullough has edited several poetry anthologies for young people, and was the first recipient of the Roger Klein Award for Creative Editing. She is co-editor, with Ted Hughes, of *The Journals of Slyvia Plath*. With Mary Lynn Broe, she is at work on a biographical portrait of Djuna Barnes through her letters and other documents.

JANE MARCUS is Iris Howard Regents professor of English Literature at the University of Texas-Austin. She has edited three collections of essays on Virginia Woolf, as well as the edition of Rebecca West's early writings, *The Young Rebecca West: 1911–1917*. Her *Virginia Woolf and the Languages of Patriarchy* was published by Indiana University Press in 1987. In 1988, a collection of essays on Wilde, Meredith, Ibsen, Woolf, and feminist theory, *Art and Anger: Reading Like a Woman*, was published by Ohio State University Press.

FRANN MICHEL is assistant professor of English at Willamette University. Her research concerns representations of gender in American novels of the 1920s. She teaches American literature and civilization at the University of Geneva.

HANK O'NEIL first read *Nightwood* while studying under David Owen at Syracuse University in 1961. Six years later O'Neal lived about two hundred yards from Barnes in the Village. He found her books on the remainder tables at Marlboro and began reading once again. In the early seventies, when he was producing *Berenice Abbot: American Photographer* (McGraw-Hill, 1982), the photographer asked O'Neal to look in on her old friend from the teens and twenties, Djuna Barnes. His reminiscence was compiled from notes recorded from memory at the end of long days producing records and managing Hammond Music Studio.

CHESTER PAGE, as a young pianist, was fortunate to have the friendship of Marianne Moore and other literary figures, including Bryher and Elizabeth Bishop.

MARIE PONSOT, poet and professor of English at Queens College, has previously worked as an archivist, translator, and television and radio scriptwriter. Among her poems are *True Minds* and *Admit Impediment*, and *Green Dark*. Her book *Beat Not the Poor Desk* (coauthored by Rosemary Deen) was the winner of the 1983 MLA/M.P. Shaughnessy Medal for the most distinguished research in the teaching of language and literature.

JOAN RETALLACK teaches in the Honors Program at the University of Maryland, College Park, is an Associate of the Bard Institute for Writing and Thinking, and is on the faculty of the summer Language and Thinking Program at Bard. She has won a Pushcart Prize for a literary essay published in *Parnassus*. She has published poetry, criticism, and fiction widely in this country as well as in England. Her volume of poetry is entitled *Circumstantial Evidence*.

JAMES B. SCOTT is a professor of English at the University of Bridgeport, where he has been teaching American literature and modern British and American drama since 1964. He took the B.A. in English and the M.A. in American Literature at the University of Buffalo in 1951 and 1957, respectively, and the Ph.D. at Syracuse University in 1964. Dr. Scott is the author of *Djuna Barnes* (Boston: Twayne, 1976).

SHERYL STEVENSON is assistant professor of English at the University of Akron. Her essays scheduled for publication include a study of intersections between Bakhtin's ideas about language and feminist theories of gender as a social, linguistic construction. The subject of her most recent Bakhtin-inspired essay is Stevie Smith's use of multiple voices, a device which conveys the female poet's concern with problems of articulation and communication.

CATHARINE STIMPSON is University Professor, Dean of the Graduate School, and Vice Provost of Graduate Education at Rutgers University (New Brunswick). The founding editor of *Signs: Journal of Women in Culture and Society*, she now edits a book series on that subject for the

University of Chicago Press. The author of both fiction and nonfiction, she published a selection of her essays, *Where the Meanings Are*, in 1988.

JANICE THOM studied literature and theater at the State University of New York at Binghamton and graduated with a B.A. in Literature and Composition. She received an M.S. in Library Science from the University of North Carolina at Chapel Hill. Ms. Thom currently lives in the Borough of Writers and is Director of Library Services for a Wall Street institutional brokerage firm. In pursuit of truth and beauty, she leaves the canyons of Wall Street to dwell in the Land of Literature.

Index